D1442514

WORLD ERAS

VOLUME 9

INDUSTRIAL REVOLUTION
IN EUROPE
1750 - 1914

WORLD ERAS

VOLUME 9

INDUSTRIAL REVOLUTION IN EUROPE
1750 - 1914

JAMES R. FARR

A MANLY, INC. BOOK

GALE®

THOMSON

GALE

Detroit • New York •   **JACKSON COUNTY LIBRARY SERVICES**   London • Munich
MEDFORD, OREGON 97501

World Eras
Volume 9: Industrial Revolution in Europe, 1750–1914
James R. Farr

Editorial Directors
Matthew J. Bruccoli and Richard Layman

Series Editor
Anthony J. Scotti Jr.

LIBRARY OF CONGRESS CATALOGING-IN-PUBLICATION DATA

World Eras vol. 9: Industrial Revolution in Europe, 1750–1914 / edited by James R. Farr.
  p. cm.—(World eras; v.9)
"A Manly, Inc. book."
      Includes bibliographical references and indexes.
      ISBN 0-7876-6046-9 (alk. paper)
      1. Industrial revolution—Europe—History.
      2. Europe—Economic conditions.
      I. Farr, James R., 1950–. II. Series.

HC240.I5333 2002
330.94′028—dc21   2002015476

Printed in the United States of America
10 9 8 7 6 5 4 3 2 1

ADVISORY BOARD

For Quentin, Mason, Kiran,
Stacia, and Jasmine

CONTENTS

CHAPTER 4: COMMUNICATION, TRANSPORTATION, AND EXPLORATION

CHAPTER 5: SOCIAL CLASS SYSTEM AND THE ECONOMY

CHAPTER 6: POLITICS, LAW, AND THE MILITARY

ABOUT THE SERIES

PROJECT DESCRIPTION

Patterned after the well-received *American Decades* and *American Eras* series, *World Eras* is a cross-disciplinary reference series. It comprises volumes examining major civilizations that have flourished from antiquity to modern times, with a global perspective and a strong emphasis on daily life and social history. Each volume provides in-depth coverage of one era, focusing on a specific cultural group and its interaction with other peoples of the world. The *World Eras* series is geared toward the needs of high-school students studying subjects in the humanities. Its purpose is to provide students—and general reference users as well—a reliable, engaging reference resource that stimulates their interest, encourages research, and prompts comparison of the lives people led in different parts of the world, in different cultures, and at different times.

The goal of *World Eras* volumes is to enrich the traditional historical study of "kings and battles" with a resource that promotes understanding of daily life and the cultural institutions that affect people's beliefs and behavior.

What kind of work did people in a certain culture perform?

What did they eat?

How did they fight their battles?

What laws did they have and how did they punish criminals?

What were their religious practices?

What did they know of science and medicine?

What kind of art, music, and literature did they enjoy?

These are the types of questions *World Eras* volumes seek to answer.

VOLUME DESIGN

World Eras is designed to facilitate comparative study. Thus, volumes employ a consistent ten-chapter structure so that teachers and students can readily access standard topics in various volumes. The chapters in each *World Eras* volume are:

1. World Events
2. Geography
3. The Arts
4. Communication, Transportation, and Exploration
5. Social Class System and the Economy
6. Politics, Law, and the Military
7. Leisure, Recreation, and Daily Life
8. The Family and Social Trends
9. Religion and Philosophy
10. Science, Technology, and Health

World Eras volumes begin with two chapters designed to provide a broad view of the world against which a specific culture can be measured. Chapter 1 provides students today with a means to understand where a certain people stood within our concept of world history. Chapter 2 describes the world from the perspective of the people being studied—what did they know of geography and how did geography and climate affect their lives? The following eight chapters address major aspects of people's lives to provide a sense of what defined their culture. The ten chapters in *World Eras* will remain constant in each volume. Teachers and students seeking to compare religious beliefs in Roman and Greek cultures, for example, can easily locate the information they require by consulting chapter 9 in the appropriate volumes, tapping a rich source for class assignments and research topics. Volume-specific glossaries and a checklist of general references provide students assistance in studying unfamiliar cultures.

CHAPTER CONTENTS

Each chapter in *World Eras* volumes also follows a uniform structure designed to provide users quick access to the information they need. Chapters are arranged into five types of material:

- **Chronology** provides an historical outline of significant events in the subject of the chapter in timeline form.

- **Overview** provides a narrative overview of the chapter topic during the period and discusses the material of the chapter in a global context.

- **Topical Entries** provide focused information in easy-to-read articles about people, places, events, institutions, and matters of general concern to the people of the time. A references rubric includes sources for further study.

- **Biographical Entries** profiles people of enduring significance regarding the subject of the chapter.
- **Documentary Sources** is an annotated checklist of documentary sources from the historical period that are the basis for the information presented in the chapter.

Chapters are supplemented throughout with primary-text sidebars that include interesting short documentary excerpts or anecdotes chosen to illuminate the subject of the chapter: recipes, letters, daily-life accounts, and excerpts from important documents. Each *World Eras* volume includes about 150 illustrations, maps, diagrams, and line drawings linked directly to material discussed in the text. Illustrations are chosen with particular emphasis on daily life.

INDEXING

A general two-level subject index for each volume includes significant terms, subjects, theories, practices, people, organizations, publications, and so forth mentioned in the text. Index citations with many page references are broken down by subtopic. Illustrations are indicated both in the general index, by use of italicized page numbers, and in a separate illustrations index, which provides a description of each item.

EDITORS AND CONTRIBUTORS

An advisory board of history teachers and librarians has provided valuable advice about the rationale for this series. They have reviewed both series plans and individual volume plans. Each *World Eras* volume is edited by a distinguished specialist in the subject of his or her volume. The editor is responsible for enlisting other scholar-specialists to write each of the chapters in the volume and for assuring the quality of their work. The editorial staff at Manly, Inc., rigorously checks factual information, line edits the manuscript, works with the editor to select illustrations, and produces the books in the series, in cooperation with Gale Group editors.

The *World Eras* series is for students of all ages who seek to enrich their study of world history by examining the many aspects of people's lives in different places during different eras. This series continues Gale's tradition of publishing comprehensive, accurate, and stimulating historical reference works that promote the study of history and culture.

The following timeline, included in every volume of *World Eras*, is provided as a convenience to users seeking a ready chronological context.

TIMELINE

This timeline, compiled by editors at Manly, Inc., is provided as a convenience for students seeking a broad global and historical context for the materials in this volume of World Eras. *It is not intended as a self-contained resource. Students who require a comprehensive chronology of world history should consult a source such as Peter N. Stearns, ed.,* The Encyclopedia of World History, *sixth revised edition (Boston & New York: Houghton Mifflin, 2001).*

CIRCA 4 MILLION–1 MILLION B.C.E.
Era of *Australopithecus*, the first hominid

CIRCA 1.5 MILLION–200,000 B.C.E.
Era of *Homo erectus,* "upright-walking human"

CIRCA 1,000,000–10,000 B.C.E.
Paleothic Age: hunters and gatherers make use of stone tools in Eurasia

CIRCA 250,000 B.C.E.
Early evolution of *Homo sapiens,* "consciously thinking humans"

CIRCA 40,000 B.C.E.
Migrations from Siberia to Alaska lead to the first human inhabitation of North and South America

CIRCA 8000 B.C.E.
Neolithic Age: settled agrarian culture begins to develop in Eurasia

5000 B.C.E.
The world population is between 5 million and 20 million

CIRCA 4000–3500 B.C.E.
Earliest Sumerian cities: artificial irrigation leads to increased food supplies and populations in Mesopotamia

CIRCA 3000 B.C.E.
Bronze Age begins in Mesopotamia and Egypt, where bronze is primarily used for making weapons; invention of writing

CIRCA 2900–1150 B.C.E.
Minoan society on Crete: lavish palaces and commercial activity

CIRCA 2700–2200 B.C.E.
Egypt: Old Kingdom and the building of the pyramids

CIRCA 2080–1640 B.C.E.
Egypt: Middle Kingdom plagued by internal strife and invasion by the Hyksos

CIRCA 2000–1200 B.C.E.
Hittites build a powerful empire based in Anatolia (present-day Turkey) by using horse-drawn war chariots

CIRCA 1792–1760 B.C.E.
Old Babylonian Kingdom; one of the oldest extant legal codes is compiled

CIRCA 1766–1122 B.C.E.
Shang Dynasty in China: military expansion, large cities, written language, and introduction of bronze metallurgy

CIRCA 1570–1075 B.C.E.
Egypt: New Kingdom and territorial expansion into Palestine, Lebanon, and Syria

CIRCA 1500 B.C.E.
The Aryans, an Indo-European people from the steppes of present-day Ukraine and southern Russia, expand into northern India

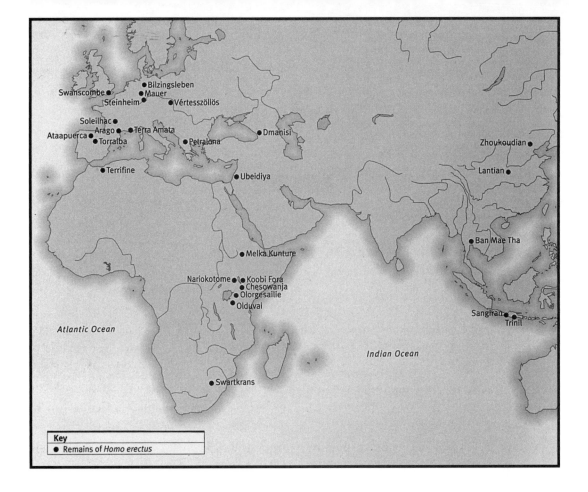

Key
● Remains of *Homo erectus*

CIRCA 1500 B.C.E.
Phoenicians create the first alphabet

CIRCA 1400-1200 B.C.E.
Hittites develop the technology of iron-smelting, improving weaponry and agricultural implements as well as stimulating trade

CIRCA 1200-800 B.C.E.
Phoenicians establish colonies throughout the Mediterranean

CIRCA 1122–221 B.C.E.
Zhou Dynasty in China: military conquests, nomadic invasions, and introduction of iron metallurgy

CIRCA 1100-750 B.C.E.
Greek Dark Ages: foreign invasions, civil disturbances, decrease in agricultural production, and population decline

1020-587 B.C.E.
Israelite monarchies consolidate their power in Palestine

CIRCA 1000-612 B.C.E.
Assyrians create an empire encompassing Mesopotamia, Syria, Palestine, and most of Anatolia

and Egypt; they deport populations to various regions of the realm

1000 B.C.E.
The world population is approximately 50 million

CIRCA 814-146 B.C.E.
The city-state of Carthage is a powerful commercial and military power in the western Mediterranean

753 B.C.E.
Traditional date of the founding of Rome

CIRCA 750-700 B.C.E.
Rise of the polis, or city-state, in Greece

558-330 B.C.E.
Achaemenid Dynasty establishes the Persian Empire (present-day Iran, Turkey, Afghanistan, and Iraq); satraps rule the various provinces

509 B.C.E.
Roman Republic is established

500 B.C.E.
The world population is approximately 100 million

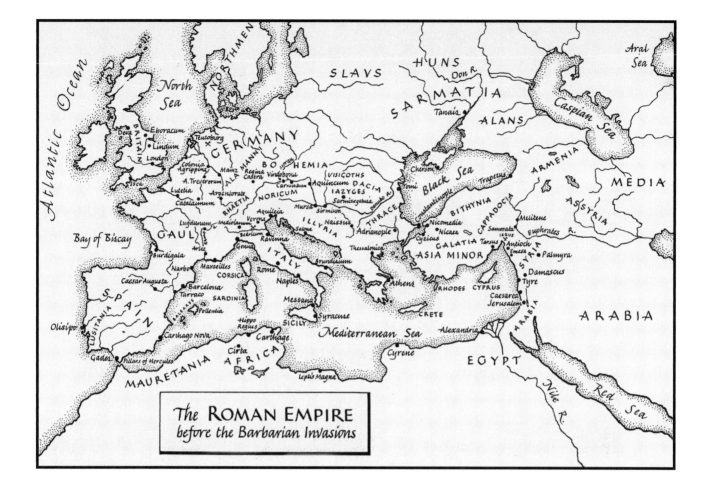

The ROMAN EMPIRE
before the Barbarian Invasions

CIRCA 400 B.C.E.
Spread of Buddhism in India

338-323 B.C.E.
Macedon, a kingdom in the central Balkan Peninsula, conquers the Persian Empire

323-301 B.C.E.
Ptolemaic Kingdom (Egypt), Seleucid Kingdom (Syria), and Antigonid Dynasty (Macedon) are founded

247 B.C.E.-224 C.E.
Parthian Empire (Parthia, Persia, and Babylonia): clan leaders build independent power bases in their satrapies, or provinces

215-168 B.C.E.
Rome establishes hegemony over the Hellenistic world

206 B.C.E.-220 C.E.
Han Dynasty in China: imperial expansion into central Asia, centralized government, economic prosperity, and population growth

CIRCA 100 B.C.E.
Tribesmen on the Asian steppes develop the stirrup, which eventually revolutionizes warfare

1 C.E.
The world population is approximately 200 million

CIRCA 100 C.E.
Invention of paper in China

224-651 C.E.
Sasanid Empire (Parthia, Persia, and Babylonia): improved government system, founding of new cities, increased trade, and the introduction of rice and cotton cultivation

CIRCA 320-550 C.E.
Gupta dynasty in India: Golden Age of Hindu civilization marked by stability and prosperity throughout the subcontinent

340 C.E.
Constantinople becomes the capital of the Eastern Roman, or Byzantine, Empire

395 C.E.
Christianity becomes the official religion of the Roman Empire

CIRCA 400 C.E.
The first unified Japanese state arises and is centered at Yamato on the island of Honshu; Buddhism arrives in Japan by way of Korea

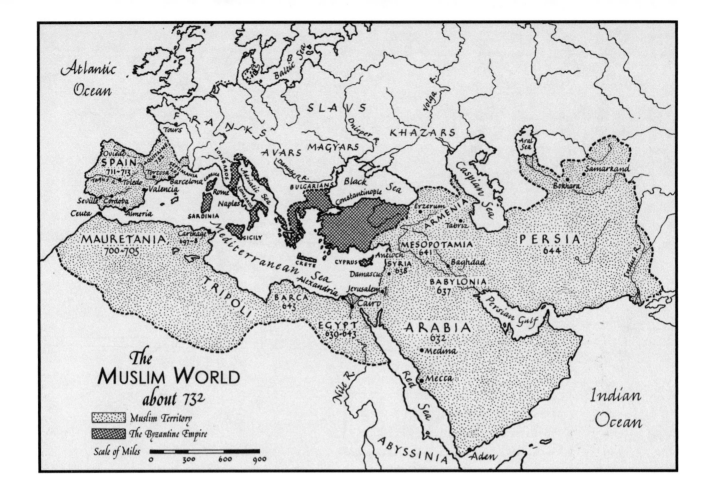

The
MUSLIM WORLD
about 732
- Muslim Territory
- The Byzantine Empire

Scale of Miles
0   300   600   900

CIRCA 400 C.E.
The nomadic Huns begin a westward migration from central Asia, causing disruption in the Roman Empire

CIRCA 400 C.E.
The Mayan Empire in Mesoamerica evolves into city-states

476 C.E.
Rome falls to barbarian hordes, and the Western Roman Empire collapses

CIRCA 500-1500 C.E.
Middle Ages, or medieval period, in Europe: gradual recovery from political disruption and increase in agricultural productivity and population

618-907 C.E.
Tang Dynasty in China: territorial expansion, government bureaucracy, agricultural improvements, and transportation and communication networks

632-733 C.E.
Muslim expansion and conquests in Arabia, Syria, Palestine, Mesopotamia, Egypt, North Africa, Persia, northwestern India, and Iberia

CIRCA 700 C.E.
Origins of feudalism, a political and social organization that dominates Europe until the fifteenth century; based on the relationship between lords and vassals

CIRCA 900 C.E.
Introduction of the horseshoe in Europe and gunpowder in China

960-1279 C.E.
Song Dynasty in China: civil administration, industry, education, and the arts

962-1806 C.E.
Holy Roman Empire of western and central Europe, created in an attempt to revive the old Roman Empire

1000 C.E.
The world population is approximately 300 million

1096-1291 C.E.
Western Christians undertake the Crusades, a series of religiously inspired military campaigns, to recapture the Holy Land from the Muslims

1200-1400 C.E.

The Mali empire in Africa dominates the trans-Saharan trade network of camel caravans

1220-1335 C.E.

The Mongols, nomadic horsemen from the high steppes of eastern central Asia, build an empire that includes China, Persia, and Russia

CIRCA 1250 C.E.

Inca Empire develops in Peru: civil administration, road networks, and sun worshiping

1299-1919 C.E.

Ottoman Empire, created by nomadic Turks and Christian converts to Islam, encompasses Asia Minor, the Balkans, Greece, Egypt, North Africa, and the Middle East

1300 C.E.

The world population is approximately 396 million

1337-1453 C.E.

Hundred Years' War, a series of intermittent military campaigns between England and France over control of continental lands claimed by both countries

1347-1350 C.E.

Black Death, or the bubonic plague, kills one-quarter of the European population

1368-1644 C.E.

Ming Dynasty in China: political, economic, and cultural revival; the Great Wall is built

1375-1527 C.E.

The Renaissance in western Europe, a revival in the arts and learning

1428-1519 C.E.

The Aztecs expand in central Mexico, developing trade routes and a system of tribute payments

1450 C.E.

Invention of the printing press

1453 C.E.

Constantinople falls to the Ottoman Turks, ending the Byzantine Empire

1464-1591 C.E.

Songhay Empire in Africa: military expansion, prosperous cities, and control of the trans-Saharan trade

1492 C.E.

Discovery of America; European exploration and colonization of the Western Hemisphere begins

CIRCA 1500-1867 C.E.

Transatlantic slave trade results in the forced migration of between 12 million and 16 million Africans to the Western Hemisphere

1500 C.E.

The world population is approximately 480 million

1517 C.E.

Beginning of the Protestant Reformation, a religious movement that ends the spiritual unity of Western Christendom

1523-1763 C.E.

Mughal Empire in India: military conquests, productive agricultural economy, and population growth

1600-1867 C.E.

Tokugawa Shogunate in Japan: shoguns (military governors) turn Edo, or Tokyo, into the political, economic, and cultural center of the nation

1618-1648 C.E.

Thirty Years' War in Europe between Catholic and Protestant states

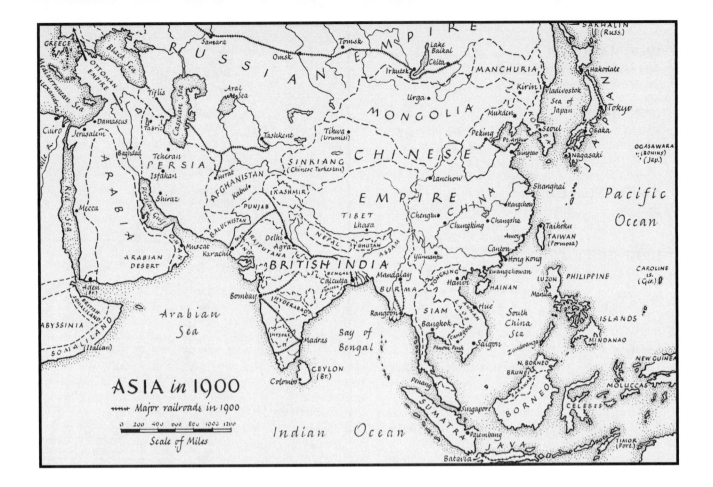

ASIA in 1900

～～～ Major railroads in 1900

0   200   400   600   800   1000   1200

Scale of Miles

1644-1911 C.E.
Qing Dynasty in China: military expansion and scholar-bureaucrats

1700 C.E.
The world population is approximately 640 million

CIRCA 1750 C.E.
Beginning of the Enlightenment, a philosophical movement marked by an emphasis on rationalism and scientific inquiry

1756-1763 C.E.
Seven Years' War: England and Prussia versus Austria, France, Russia, Saxony, Spain, and Sweden

CIRCA 1760-1850 C.E.
Industrial Revolution in Britain is marked by mass production through the division of labor, mechanization, a great increase in the supply of iron, and the use of the steam engine

1775-1783 C.E.
American War of Independence; the United States becomes an independent republic

1789 C.E.
French Revolution topples the monarchy and leads to a period of political unrest followed by a dictatorship

1793-1815 C.E.
Napoleonic Wars: Austria, England, Prussia, and Russia versus France and its satellite states

1794-1824 C.E.
Latin American states conduct wars of independence against Spain

1900 C.E.
The world population is approximately 1.65 billion

1914-1918 C.E.
World War I, or the Great War: the Allies (England, France, Russia, and the United States) versus the Central Powers (Austria-Hungary, Germany, and the Ottoman Empire)

1917-1921 C.E.
Russian Revolution: a group of Communists known as the Bolsheviks seize control of the country following a civil war

1939-1945 C.E.
World War II: the Allies (China, England, France, the Soviet Union, and the United States) versus the Axis (Germany, Italy, and Japan)

1945 C.E.
Successful test of the first atomic weapon; beginning of the Cold War, a period of rivalry, mistrust, and, occasionally, open hostility between the capitalist West and Communist East

1947-1975 C.E.
Decolonization occurs in Africa and Asia as European powers relinquish control of colonies in those regions

1948
Israel becomes the first independent Jewish state in nearly two thousand years

1949
Communists seize control of China

1950-1951
Korean War: the United States attempts to stop Communist expansion in the Korean Peninsula

1957 C.E.
The Soviet Union launches *Sputnik* (fellow traveler of earth), the first man-made satellite; the Space Age begins

1965-1973
Vietnam War: the United States attempts to thwart the spread of Communism in Vietnam

1989 C.E.
East European Communist regimes begin to falter, and multiparty elections are held

1991 C.E.
Soviet Union is dissolved and replaced by the Commonwealth of Independent States

2000 C.E.
The world population is approximately 6 billion

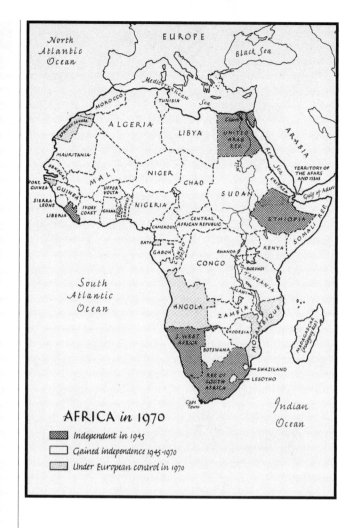

AFRICA in 1970

Independent in 1945
Gained independence 1945-1970
Under European control in 1970

INTRODUCTION

Transition to the Modern Era. Between 1750 and 1914, Europeans experienced revolutionary change in nearly every aspect of their lives, changes that ushered in the modern era. A new system of thought fashioned by the Enlightenment joined a new economy based in industrialism to lay the groundwork for the modern age. Enlightenment thinkers embraced secular reason and drew the conclusion that they could reform and improve the human condition because they could discover the natural laws that controlled the universe. The concept of progress that resulted from this melding of rational optimism with belief in natural laws was nothing short of revolutionary and has informed Western thought to the present day. Industry-driven revolutions occurred as Europeans increasingly employed machines powered by new energy sources to fashion an array of products. The shift to industrialization was so profound that it restructured all of human experience, affecting how Europeans led their daily lives. Altered working and consuming patterns changed the way men and women thought about themselves and the groups they belonged to in society. Economic change in Europe, moreover, was felt throughout the world as Europeans continued their expansion—both in formal empires and informal economic hegemony—across the globe. Occurring at the same time as the Industrial Revolution was a wave of fundamental political revolution and reform. The French Revolution destroyed absolutism and championed the political ideas of freedom and equality. Answers to the questions of what these values meant and to whom they would apply would affect political, social, and intellectual developments well into the twentieth century.

New Economy. In 1750 Europe was on the threshold of fundamental economic change. Already, innovations in agriculture were increasing the food supply, which in turn supported a dramatically growing population. Most Europeans in 1750 lived in the countryside and farmed, but many also were increasingly employed in rural manufacturing. Women would spin thread and men would weave cloth in their homes, while merchants would pay the "cottagers," collect the goods, and sell them in increasingly distant markets. As the population grew and European empires expanded overseas, demand for products increased exponentially, and the sector of the economy that registered it

most dramatically was cotton textiles. Britain was the first nation to take advantage of it. As demand soared, bottlenecks appeared in the production process, first in spinning and later in weaving, and inventors responded with technological innovations to overcome them. Though cotton was king of the British economy well into the nineteenth century, machines appeared in every sector of the economy and forever changed where and how people worked. Steam power from burning coal soon replaced animal and human muscle, and by the end of the century electricity and petroleum had become important energy sources. Factories were built; workforces were increasingly regimented and segmented; cities grew; and European industrialists flooded the world with increasingly standardized, mass-produced goods. By the 1880s the European and world economy had entered a new phase. Most Europeans were now urban dwellers, and as more and more tasks were mechanized, home manufacturing disappeared. Where women and children had been important workers in the early factories, now children went to school, and women found new jobs in business offices and retail stores. Technological innovation contributed to the emergence of this new economy in more ways than one, however, for changes were seen in the nature of warfare as Europeans developed weapons with increased firepower. These weapons were unmatched anywhere else in the world, and Europeans exerted their power by force across the globe. Technology aided imperialism in other ways as well, for innovations in transportation (railroads and steamships) and communication (telegraphs and telephones) both accelerated European expansion and "shrank" the globe. The Industrial Revolution began in England but spread quickly, and by 1914 the economic development of the United States and most of western Europe was generally uniform. Eastern Europe, in contrast, lagged behind, but by the outbreak of World War I it too was industrializing.

Social Changes. Between 1750 and 1914 manufacturing began to rival agriculture as a source of employment and then surpassed it. By the end of the nineteenth century the population of western European countries, which had been growing steadily, was more urban than rural. Cities grew not only in size but also in number. As a result of these sweeping economic and demographic changes, the social structure of Europe was transformed. The traditional aristocracy of landowners lost its dominance, and new classes emerged, the most important being the bourgeoisie and the working class. The bourgeoisie, or the middle class of manufacturers, bankers, lawyers, and store owners, grew in numbers and wealth. As a result, they gained political, economic, and social dominance and fashioned a worldview that reflected their self-consciousness as a distinct and triumphant social class. The new bourgeoisie believed in the privacy of the domestic family and women remaining within the home, values that came to define this class, as did the economic values of thrift, hard work, and sobriety. While this group was forming, so was the working class. The peasant cottagers and urban artisans of the pre-industrial world were gradually absorbed into the new industrial economy and were slowly transformed into factory employees, construction workers, mechanics, and shopkeepers. Those who remained on the farm either acquired more land and joined the middle class, or (more often) became tenant farmers or poor, waged agricultural laborers. Early factories, especially the textile mills, hired more women and children than adult men, and so the earnings of women and children became even more important than ever before to the family economy. Work hours were long; pay was low; machines were dangerous; work-related diseases were common; work was monotonous; and many industries laid off workers seasonally, leaving entire families destitute. Initially, the new workers were poorly organized, but they gradually came to perceive themselves as sharing a place in the new industrial economy, and their collective interests could best be served by concerted action. This working-class consciousness emerged slowly, but by the second half of the nineteenth century many workers measured their interests in opposition to the manufacturers and industrialists. As the economy increasingly mechanized, male skilled workers were in greater demand, and as women and children disappeared from the industrial factory workforce, men began to organize and to demand better working conditions, higher pay, and fewer hours. Economic depressions from the 1870s onward exacerbated worker discontent and spurred further organization, and protests became increasingly directed at individual employers in the form of strikes.

Revolution and Reform in Politics. In 1750 all the major states of Europe except Great Britain were headed by monarchies in which sovereignty theoretically resided exclusively in the person of the king or queen. From the late eighteenth century onward, representative and even republican institutions asserted that sovereignty instead was vested in the people. The great political contest of the industrial era, therefore, focused on the right to vote and was split along class and gender lines. During the French Revolution of 1789 absolutism was destroyed in favor of a series of elected assemblies, most of them following the English model of property qualifications for membership. This development assured that only the well-to-do would rule. Revolutions in France in 1830 and everywhere except

Britain in 1848 challenged the restrictiveness of the franchise; revolutionaries pushed to extend the vote to more, less affluent men. In 1830 in France the upper bourgeoisie triumphed over a restored absolutist government and gained control. Nevertheless, European workingmen generally remained on the outside, and their demand for political participation had much to do with the Revolutions of 1848. Where revolutionary action by the working class generally failed, however, reformist demands were more successful. England is the best example, but nearly everywhere by end of the century the franchise had been extended to include more males. In 1832 in England the middle class won the vote, and for the rest of the century working-class men agitated peacefully (although always wielding the threat of violent revolution) for similar parliamentary reform that would grant them the vote. They were partially successful in 1867 when highly skilled and well-paid workers won the franchise, and in 1884 they were joined by most of their fellows. France followed a similar route, establishing a republic based on universal manhood suffrage in 1870, while a newly unified Germany granted the vote to all men within a constitutional monarchy. The fight for suffrage then shifted gender grounds, as women aggressively began to make similar demands. These efforts did not succeed, however, until the twentieth century.

Nation-States and Nationalism. The nature of electoral politics was a pressing issue across the nineteenth century, and changes occurred within the context of the accelerating formation of the modern nation-state. The two best examples of the continuing propulsion toward state-building in the nineteenth century are the unification of Italy in 1860 and of Germany in 1871. The history of the modern state stretches back before the chronological beginning of this volume, but during the long nineteenth century people and rulers living within increasingly prescribed borders began to identify with their nation. In short, inhabitants of nation-states became increasingly instilled with the sentiment of nationalism, among the most powerful and influential forces in modern history. The imperial expansion of France under Napoleon Bonaparte in the early nineteenth century stirred many peoples to oppose what they took to be foreign influences, and this opposition—especially in Germany and Spain—was cast in the mold of nationalism. From there nationalism left its mark on nearly everything Europeans did. Europeans justified imperial expansion on the grounds of national superiority; they formulated theories, such as social Darwinism, that did the same. National virtues were extolled in art and literature. Moreover, many a soldier marched to war instilled with the desire to perform heroic deeds for the fatherland and to sacrifice his life for its victory.

Politics and Social Reform. For the first time, during the period 1750–1914, politicians and social theorists stressed that parents were not simply raising their children but preparing the future citizens of the nation-state. Governments everywhere, therefore, fashioned policies regulating and protecting family life and childhood. In 1877 Fréderic Le Play summed up the new politics of social reform by succinctly proclaiming that "The family is the foundation of the state." As in so many other areas, the French Revolution was a harbinger of what was to come. Members of the National Assembly in the 1790s enacted laws and regulations designed to guide family life and personal relationships. Property rights were changed; imprisonment of children was abolished; youths reached majority at the age of twenty-one; and women were allowed to divorce their husbands. Napoleon's Civil Code of 1804 might have reinstated many of the older forms of patriarchal dominance, but it continued and extended the role and power of the state in family matters. Moreover, as the middle class came to dominate governments, it brought its own familial values to the state and used the power of law and governance to establish the proper model for *all* families. The domestic ideal of the homemaker wife and innocent child came to inform the protective labor laws, the earliest being the British factory acts of the mid-1830s. These statutes were in part prompted by humanistic concerns about the plight of poor children who worked in textile mills. Bourgeois values saw children as innocents who needed nurture and moral training, neither available in factories; but middle-class politicians also feared that the health of boys would be damaged by factory work, thus rendering them less useful to the army or navy. Concerns arose also that if girls worked in the same environment, they might not be able to bear healthy babies. Similar values inspired educational reform where the state increasingly assumed the role of surrogate parent, especially for the lower classes hit hardest by economic and social transformations of the industrial age. Jules Ferry, premier of the French Third Republic, reminded schoolteachers in 1883 that "You are the auxiliary and, in some respects, the substitute for the father of the family. Speak then to his son as you would wish one to speak to your own."

Welfare Legislation. Whether poor relief was a government responsibility was a much more hotly contested issue than protective legislation. Traditionally, poor relief had been the responsibility of local communities or religious institutions. In the late eighteenth century the French Revolutionaries assumed the responsibility and inaugurated a century-long debate about the advisability of government aid to the poor. Some argued it was a disincentive to work, while others asserted that the government had a moral obligation to adequately house and feed its citizens. For much of the nineteenth century the opponents of government aid won the debate, but in the 1870s the pendulum began to swing toward government assistance. The so-called social question came to the forefront of domestic politics, and the new labor and socialist political parties demanded new legislation. States such as Germany took the lead, creating a welfare system funded by contributions from employers, employees, and the state that provided benefits to workers for illnesses, accidents, and old age. Although initially limited to factory and other industrial workers, the principle that governments should be involved in securing social necessities to its citizens had been established. Similar and broader laws were eventually passed throughout Europe.

Enlightenment, Science, and Technology. The eighteenth century launched industrial and political revolutions, but it was joined by an equally fundamental transformation in thought and attitudes called the Enlightenment. A great many eighteenth-century thinkers embraced the idea that human beings possess a rational faculty that bases the acquisition of knowledge in observation, a premise learned from the preceding Scientific Revolution of the seventeenth century. This way of knowing, called empiricism, had been the tool of scientific analysis in the 1600s, and in the 1700s it was expanded into new areas as the consequences and ramifications of the discoveries of the Scientific Revolution were explored and demonstrated. The Enlightenment brought with it a great sense of optimism about the prospects for humanity's future. Men came to believe that empirical Rationalism was the key to unlocking the secrets of nature. If the forces of nature could be understood by mankind, then those forces could be harnessed and turned toward human improvement. One example of this theory at work was the controlled unleashing of energy from various natural sources, such as steam power from coal-heated water. The Enlightenment therefore not only was an important period in Western intellectual development but also laid the foundations for greater interaction between science, technology, medicine, and health.

Progress, Liberalism, and Socialism. Confidence in human capability spread beyond science and industry and led to a general belief in progress. Through concerted and rationally directed human activity, man could improve his lot on earth. This emphasis on improving the human condition found expression in the language of universal rights such as freedom and equality, and so inspired the profoundly influential nineteenth-century ideologies of liberalism and socialism. Although these systems of ideas differed fundamentally in what these values meant and to whom in society they applied, their foundation was the same—the Enlightenment—and both embraced the belief that politics properly organized could improve, even perfect, the human condition.

Enlightenment and the Arts. Enlightenment thought deeply influenced art. The Enlightenment championed universalism, the idea that the human condition is a collective one and is guided by the same fundamental principles everywhere. Classicism expressed this assumption, and even though Romanticism rejected the cold reasoning of Enlightenment thought, it often embraced ideas such as freedom and individual creativity. To Romantics, empiricism encouraged the notion of the creative genius, the individual whose senses are especially attuned to the world and are blessed with an unusual or even singular ability to express its fundamental meanings through image, word, or sound. The styles in art and especially literature that followed Romanticism and in turn reacted against it, Realism and Naturalism, were deliberately empirical and scientific. Naturalists even went so far as asserting that if art was to be a conveyor of truth, then artists must be like scientists, exact recorders of the phenomena of the world. The influence of the Enlightenment was registered in all aspects of life between 1750 and 1914. Sometimes, however, this influence was expressed in opposition to Enlightenment characteristics. Nationalism and subjective individualism that were so prominent in nineteenth-century and early-twentieth-century art, literature, and music were powerful solvents to universalism. By the end of the nineteenth century, as nation-states solidified and became increasingly bellicose toward one another, artists, writers, and musicians abandoned Realism and Naturalism and embraced Modernism. They increasingly shed their confidence in progress so prominent in Enlightenment thought and replaced it with moods of decadence, pessimism, and nostalgia. Universalism was replaced by discordance and dissonance in music, matched in the visual arts by a sharp drift toward fractured images and abstraction.

Enlightenment and Religion. Enlightenment thinkers championed secular reason and progress, a combined frontal assault against Christianity and its fundamental tenets. Where Christianity taught that God's intentions were ultimately inscrutable and expressed in ways that reason could not completely explain, Enlightenment thinkers and those who subsequently embraced its modes of thought believed that the potential of human reason was unlimited. As confidence in human reason soared, the reliance on divine revelation waned. Joining these intellectual developments hostile to Christianity were political and ideological ones. A group of powerful monarchs known as enlightened despots endeavored to improve the conditions of their subjects by reconstructing their states according to the dictates of reason. These rulers often viewed the Christian church as superstitious and irrational, and thus an obstacle to reform. As liberalism increasingly came to inform government policies in the mid nineteenth century, open hostility to organized religion might not have been formal policy, but one credo liberals usually embraced was the separation of church and state. In this sense socialists were similar to liberals; some, like Karl Marx, expressed open hostility to organized religion. In 1864 Pius IX boldly challenged the liberal and socialist currents of the time with the publication of the "Syllabus of Errors," a list of eighty modern ideas that Catholics were instructed to reject. Catholic popes such as Pius IX tried to reassert the authority of the Church and its leader, but just as fragmentation and particularism marked European culture, it marked religion as well. This situation can be seen clearly by the growth of Protestant "free churches" supported by voluntary contributions and the demise of state-supported established churches. The trend toward the separation of church and

state might have worked against the Catholic Church, but it actually worked to the advantage of many Protestant denominations, particularly the Methodists, Baptists, and other evangelical groups. The intellectual currents of the day accentuated the fragmentation of the Protestant tradition; but whereas some Protestants retreated into the safety of the historic creeds and confessions, others embraced personal religious experiences, while still others sought to defend the faith by accommodating it to the current scientific theories and philosophies of the time. As Protestantism became more diverse, it also enjoyed extraordinary growth. New interdenominational societies were formed to take the Protestant message to all the peoples of the world. Notwithstanding the hostile forces that threatened historic Christianity, during the nineteenth century Protestantism actually grew in vitality and numbers and became more entrenched both in Europe and around the globe.

Acknowledgments. Collaborative ventures such as this one pose many challenges. This venture, in particular, is designed to function both as an encyclopedia full of useful and informative discrete information *and* as a book one could enjoyably read cover to cover and find a narrative held together by overarching themes that penetrate each chapter. The authors, therefore, were asked to write chapters that would cover as comprehensively as possible the particular subject matter of their expertise but would also through their topics, sidebars, and biographies present a thematically cohesive unit. Each chapter, however, is also divided into sections and subsections that are intended to be able to stand alone. First and foremost, then, my thanks go to Mike Aradas, Bruce Bigelow, Terry Billhartz, Chris Corley, Dean Ferguson, Gay Gullickson, and Jeff Horn. They deserve the lion's share of the credit for whatever merits this volume possesses. Each of them hewed closely to the stated editorial designs for the volume and responded willingly to any suggested revisions from me and from the series editors, Anthony Scotti and Karen Rood. Indeed, I offer special thanks to Anthony and Karen for their patient and thorough editing, and to the professional staff at Bruccoli Clark Layman/Manly for bringing this volume to its final, handsome form. My wife, Danielle, has grown accustomed to seeing me perched in front of the computer, writing and editing, and always good-naturedly respects the demands of time and effort that editing volumes such as this one requires. I thank her not only for her patience and understanding but also for the many conversations we have had about the past, conversations that affect the way I understand it, and thus how I write about it.

James R. Farr
Purdue University
West Lafayette, Indiana

ACKNOWLEDGMENTS

This book was produced by Manly, Inc. Karen L. Rood, senior editor, and Anthony J. Scotti Jr., series editor, were the in-house editors.

Production manager is Philip B. Dematteis.

Administrative support was provided by Ann M. Cheschi, Carol A. Cheschi, and Amber L. Coker.

Accountant is Ann-Marie Holland.

Copyediting supervisor is Sally R. Evans. The copyediting staff includes Phyllis A. Avant, Caryl Brown, Melissa D. Hinton, Philip I. Jones, Rebecca Mayo, Nancy E. Smith, and Elizabeth Jo Ann Sumner. Freelance copyeditor is Brenda Cabra.

Editorial associates are Michael S. Allen, Michael S. Martin, Catherine M. Polit, and James F. Tidd Jr.

Permissions editor is Amber L. Coker.

Database manager is Amber L. Coker.

Layout and graphics supervisor is Janet E. Hill. The graphics staff includes Zoe R. Cook and Sydney E. Hammock.

Office manager is Kathy Lawler Merlette.

Photography supervisor is Paul Talbot. Photography editor is Scott Nemzek.

Digital photographic copy work was performed by Joseph M. Bruccoli.

SGML work was done by Linda Dalton Mullinax.

Systems manager is Marie L. Parker.

Typesetting supervisor is Kathleen M. Flanagan. The typesetting staff includes Patricia Marie Flanagan, Mark J. McEwan, and Pamela D. Norton.

Walter W. Ross supervised library research. He was assisted by Jo Cottingham and the following librarians at the Thomas Cooper Library of the University of South Carolina: circulation department head Tucker Taylor; reference department head Virginia W. Weathers; reference department staff Brette Barron, Marilee Birchfield, Paul Cammarata, Gary Geer, Michael Macan, Tom Marcil, Rose Marshall, and Sharon Verba; interlibrary loan department head John Brunswick; and interlibrary loan staff Robert Arndt, Hayden Battle, Alex Byrne, Jo Cottingham, Bill Fetty, Marna Hostetler, and Nelson Rivera.

WORLD ERAS

VOLUME 9

INDUSTRIAL REVOLUTION IN EUROPE
1750 - 1914

WORLD EVENTS:
SELECTED OCCURRENCES OUTSIDE EUROPE

by JAMES R. FARR

1750*		• The Akan tribe breaks away from the large and powerful Asante Empire and founds a new state, the Baoulé kingdom, on the Ivory Coast in western Africa.
1750-1754		• The French and British fight an undeclared war in India.
1752		• The Punjab and Sind provinces are ceded by the weakened Mughul Empire of India to the Afghans.
1753		• Burma is united under the leadership of Alaungpaya, founder of the Konbaung dynasty.
1754	**Spring**	Virginia militia officer George Washington leads colonial troops into the Ohio River valley in order to affirm British claims to the region.
	28 May	Washington defeats a French reconnaissance party near Fort Duquesne, sparking the French and Indian War.
	19 June	Colonial leaders in British North America assemble in Albany to discuss common defense against the French and to enlist the support of the Iroquois Confederacy.
	4 July	A large contingent of French and Native Americans besieges Fort Necessity at Great Meadows and forces Washington to capitulate.
1757		• Mustafa III becomes the Ottoman sultan.
		• Bedouin raiders attack a Damascus caravan journeying to Mecca; thousands of Muslim pilgrims are killed.
	23 June	After seizing Calcutta, the English defeat the French at the Battle of Plassey in India.

***DENOTES CIRCA DATE**

1759

13 September French Canada falls to the British following General James Wolfe's victory at the Plains of Abraham, outside Quebec City. Wolfe is killed in the battle, as is French commander Marquis de Montcalm.

1760

• Ieharu begins a twenty-six-year reign as shogun of Japan.

1761

14 January A Hindu Marathan army is defeated by Muslim forces of Ahmad Shah in the Third Battle of Panipat in northern India.

1762

• Catherine II (the Great) becomes ruler of Russia following the murder of her husband, Peter III.

• The British capture the Spanish possessions of Havana, Cuba, and Manila, the Philippines.

1763

• Senegambia is conquered by the English.

• Ottawa war chief Pontiac leads a failed rebellion against the British in the northern Ohio region.

10 February The Seven Years' War concludes with the Treaty of Paris; Great Britain wins control of Canada, Louisiana (except for New Orleans), and most of India from the French. Spain cedes control of Florida to the British.

1765

7 October British colonists in North America gather at the Stamp Act Congress in New York to protest a new tax on all commercial and legal documents. The British Parliament repeals the tax early the next year but reserves the right to impose taxes on the colonists without their consent (Declaratory Act).

1767

• Parliament approves the Townshend duties (import taxes on glass, lead, paint, paper, and tea) in order to help pay for British rule in North America. The colonists oppose these duties and implement a policy of nonimportation.

1768

• Russian troops advance into the Crimea against Ottoman Turkish forces.

• Egypt, under the rule of Ali Bey al-Kabir, earns greater independence from the Ottomans.

• French ships bombard Tunisian ports in response to the capture of some of its vessels and crews; a peace treaty is signed in 1770.

*Denotes Circa Date

1769
- The Great Famine of Bengal, one of the worst such calamities in recorded history, claims ten million lives.

1770

5 March   In the Boston Massacre, British redcoats fire on a mob, killing five civilians and further inflaming colonial passions against British rule.

1771
- Spain and Great Britain dispute control of the Falkland (Malvinas) Islands off the coast of Argentina.
- A revolt breaks out in Vietnam; the ruling dynasties in the north and south are overthrown; and the country is unified by 1778.

1773
- Emelian Pugachev, claiming he is Peter III, tries to overthrow Russian tsarina Catherine the Great; he fails and is executed in 1775.

16 December   A group of colonists dumps tea from British ships into Boston Harbor. In response to the Boston Tea Party, the following year the British impose a series of acts that allow for the quartering of troops in private homes, close the port, and reduce the legal rights of Bostonians.

1774
- Mustafa III dies and is succeeded on the Ottoman throne by his brother Abdulhamid I.

21 July   The Treaty of Kuchuk Kaynarja ends Russian-Ottoman hostilities. The Crimea is made independent, and Russia gains land along the Dnieper and Bug Rivers.

1775
- Janissaries (Ottoman slave soldiers in service to the sultan) revolt in Aleppo.

19 April   In the Battles of Lexington and Concord in Massachusetts, British regulars and American colonists exchange fire, thereby beginning the American War of Independence.

1776

4 July   Making official their break from Great Britain, representatives of the Thirteen Colonies adopt the Declaration of Independence.

1777

15 November   The Articles of Confederation of the United States are passed.

1780
- Mamluk leader Sulayman Pasha begins governing Baghdad; his reign lasts twenty-two years.
- Portuguese slave traders, exporting their human cargoes primarily to the Western Hemisphere, establish a base of operations in Kilwa in southern Africa.

*DENOTES CIRCA DATE

1780
(CONT'D)

- Tupac Amaru II leads a revolt of native troops against the Spanish in Peru; within two years colonial leaders crush the insurrection.

1781

- The British gain control of the western portions of Sumatra from the Dutch, although the English later give up physical possession in favor of trading rights.

19 October   British general Lord Charles Cornwallis surrenders his troops to a combined American-French army at Yorktown, Virginia.

1782

- Bangkok is made the capital of Siam (Thailand) by Rama I.

1783

- The Treaty of Paris ends the Revolutionary War, and the United States of America is recognized as an independent nation.

- The Treaty of Versailles returns control of Florida to Spain.

- Russia annexes the Muslim-controlled territories in the Crimea.

1787

- Freed British slaves are settled in Freetown, Sierra Leone.

- The Northwest Ordinance is passed by the U.S. Congress to deal with government in the Ohio valley region; the act establishes the manner in which new states are formed and brought into the union, prohibits slavery in the area, and provides for public education.

- Daniel Shays leads a rebellion of debtors and small farmers in western Massachusetts.

17 September   After four months of meetings in Philadelphia, delegates sign the Constitution of the United States.

1788

- Port Jackson, Australia, becomes a British penal colony; by 1800 more than 130,000 convicts are transported there.

- Chinese troops invade Vietnam, but they are defeated by defending forces led by General Nguyen Hue. Nguyen Anh, with the help of the French, captures Saigon and later defeats Hue.

1789

- Abdulhamid dies and is replaced on the Ottoman throne by his nephew, who becomes Selim III. The new ruler reorganizes the army, builds a modern navy, reforms government service, and broadens diplomatic contacts with Europe.

- Mutineers aboard the English ship HMS *Bounty* take control of the vessel after they visit Tahiti.

- Rebels in Minas Gerais, Brazil, attempt to make their region an independent state; they fail in the effort.

*DENOTES CIRCA DATE

1789
(CONT'D)

• A slave rebellion led by Toussaint L'Ouverture, Jean-Jacques Dessalines, and Henri Christophe devastates French rule in Haiti. Toussaint becomes dictator in 1794.

30 April   George Washington is inaugurated as the first U.S. president.

1792

• China invades Nepal.

1793

• Ienari becomes the shogun of Japan and controls the country until 1837.

1794

• King Kamehameha of Hawaii puts his kingdom under British protection.

1795

27 October   American and Spanish representatives sign the Treaty of San Lorenzo (Pinckney's Treaty), establishing the southern boundary of the United States at the thirty-first parallel and allowing for U.S. traffic on the Mississippi River.

1796–1804

• The White Lotus Rebellion flares up in China against the Manchu dynasty. The uprising—led by the White Lotus Society, a Buddhist religious cult that opposes increased taxation and promises the restoration of the Ming dynasty—is suppressed.

1796

• Catherine the Great dies; Paul I becomes the Russian tsar.

• Agha Muhammad Shah establishes the Qajar dynasty in Iran, with their capital in Tehran.

1798

1 July   Napoleon Bonaparte leads French troops into Alexandria and defeats Mamluk defenders at the Battle of the Pyramids (21 July), beginning a three-year occupation of Egypt. An attempt to capture Syria fails after French troops are devastated by disease.

1800

• Gabriel Prosser leads an abortive slave rebellion near Richmond, Virginia.

1801

• The North African state of Tripoli declares war on the United States in an attempt to compel the young nation to pay tribute to Arab pirates who have been raiding American ships along the Barbary Coast. The Americans refuse and respond by building a navy.

• Paul I is assassinated; he is replaced as Russian tsar by his son, Alexander I.

*DENOTES CIRCA DATE

1803

- The Wahhabis, Muslim fundamentalists in Arabia, capture Mecca from Ottoman control.

- Tasmania is settled by the English.

30 April   The United States obtains the Louisiana Purchase from France, which doubles the size of the nation.

1804

- Emperor Gia Long, who came to power in 1802, names his kingdom Vietnam. He rules until 1820, when he is succeeded by his son Ming-Manh.

- Muslim leader Shehu Usuman dan Fodio leads a revolt against the Hausa kings in Sudan; he establishes the Sokoto Caliphate.

1805

- Muhammad Ali, an Albanian officer sent to Egypt by the Ottomans, gains the right to rule the country; he establishes the dynasty that rules until 1953 and begins introducing reforms that set the groundwork for the modern Egyptian state.

1806

- Russian troops invade Moldavia and Walachia, which leads to the capture of much of the Caucuses and Balkans.

1807

- Muhammad Ali repels a British invasion of Alexandria and consolidates power in Egypt.

- Protestant missionary Robert Morrison of Great Britain arrives in China.

29 May   A conservative revolt in Istanbul overthrows Selim III, who is replaced by Mustafa IV; although the revolt is crushed in 1808, Selim dies during the fighting and is replaced on the throne by Mahmud II.

22 December In an effort to avoid entanglement in a British-French war, U.S. president Thomas Jefferson forbids all trade with foreign ports.

1808

- The United States prohibits the transatlantic slave trade.

- Portuguese king John VI transfers his court to Rio de Janeiro in Brazil.

1809

- Russia acquires control of Finland following a war with Sweden.

- Rama I dies, and Rama II takes the Thai throne; he rules until 1824.

- Kamehameha unifies the Hawaiian Islands.

1810

- Simón Bolívar begins a revolution against Spanish rule in South America by taking part in the Venezuelan uprising.

*DENOTES CIRCA DATE

1810
(CONT'D)

- Bahrain and Qatar fall to the Wahhabis.

1811

- Mamluk power in Egypt is destroyed after Muhammad Ali massacres Mamluk leaders at a meeting in Cairo.

- Paraguay declares its independence from Spain.

1812

- The Americans declare war on Britain, triggered by the forced impressment of U.S. sailors into the British navy. The conflict spreads to the western frontier of the United States, where some Native American tribes have allied with the British.

| **28 May** | Facing an imminent French invasion, the Russians sign the Treaty of Bucharest, thereby returning control of Moldavia and Walachia to the Ottomans. |

1813

- Mecca is recaptured by the Ottomans, which leads to the fall in 1818 of the first Wahhabi state.

| **12 October** | Russia annexes Georgia from the Iranians with the Treaty of Gulistan. |

1814

13 May	Great Britain is officially given control of the Cape Colony in South Africa.
September	British troops burn much of Washington, D.C., including the White House and the Library of Congress.
24 December	The Treaty of Ghent ends the War of 1812 between the United States and Great Britain.

1815

8 January	News of the Treaty of Ghent has not yet reached North America, and a British army is defeated by an American force under Andrew Jackson at the Battle of New Orleans.
April	The enormous Tambora volcano erupts in Indonesia and kills ten thousand people. Volcanic ash is so dense that it obscures sunlight and causes crop failures that lead to disease and famine that will take another eighty thousand lives in the region.
22 December	The United States and Algeria sign a peace treaty ending the Barbary Wars, a series of conflicts involving piratical attacks on American shipping in the Mediterranean Sea since 1801.

1816

- Argentina declares its independence from Spain.

*DENOTES CIRCA DATE

1817
- Shaka becomes the ruler of the Zulu kingdom; he rules until he is assassinated by his brothers in 1828.

1818
- Chile declares its independence from Spain after José de San Martin leads revolutionary forces in victorious battle.

1819
- Singapore, in Indonesia, is purchased by the British East India Company.

1820
- Long-staple cotton is discovered in Egypt; cotton production will soon become more than 20 percent of the agricultural output of the nation. This discovery has serious effects on cotton production and prices in the Southern states of the United States.

3 March In an attempt to appease proslavery and antislavery factions, Congress passes the Missouri Compromise: Missouri is admitted as a slave state; Maine becomes a free state; and slavery is prohibited in the northern parts of the Louisiana Purchase.

1821
- Mexico declares its independence from Spain.
- War breaks out between the Ottomans and Persians. At the same time, the Greeks revolt against Ottoman rule; the rebels achieve, with help from France and England, independence in 1830.

1822
- Liberia is founded in West Africa by the American Colonization Society as a haven for freed slaves from the Americas. In 1847 it becomes the first independent republic in Africa.
- Pedro I becomes emperor of Brazil and reigns until 1831.

1823
- A war between Great Britain and the Asante Empire begins in western Africa; the conflict concludes with a peace treaty in 1831.
- An assembly at Guatemala City proclaims the Central American Federation (Guatemala, Honduras, Costa Rica, Nicaragua, and El Salvador). The federation collapses by 1840.

2 December U.S. president James Monroe formulates the Monroe Doctrine, which prohibits further colonization of the Western Hemisphere by European powers.

1824
- The First Burmese War begins when the Burmese attack territories held by the British East India Company. After initial successes the capable Burmese general Bandula dies, and the British are victorious; Burma is forced to grant further territorial concessions to the company in the Treaty of Yandabu (24 February 1826).

* DENOTES CIRCA DATE

1824
(CONT'D)

- Arabian emir Turki ibn Abdallah establishes the Saudi capital at Riyadh.

- Rama III takes control of the Thai kingdom. He rules until 1851.

1825

- Russian tsar Alexander I dies. Despite a military revolt of the Decembrists, Nicholas I succeeds to the throne.

- The Javanese revolt against Dutch rule. The uprising is quelled in 1830, though additional revolts break out in 1849 and 1888.

- Construction of the Erie Canal is completed, opening the western United States to agricultural development.

6 August   Chile declares its independence from Spain.

1826

15 June   The Janissaries are massacred in their barracks in Istanbul, ending their influence on Ottoman politics.

1827

- A revolt, the Anu Rebellion, in Laos is put down by the Thais.

20 October   A British fleet destroys an Egyptian naval force at the Battle of Navarino, blocking Egyptian expansion into the Mediterranean. The Egyptians maintain control of Crete, however, which they had captured in 1823.

1828

- The Dutch annex western New Guinea.

1829

- The treaty of Adrianople gives Russia control of the eastern Black Sea region.

- Perth is founded in western Australia.

1830

13 May   The Republic of Ecuador is formed.

5 July   The French gain control of Algiers. This occupation will be contested by Abd al-Qadir until 1847, when he is captured by the French.

1831

- Samuel Sharp leads a rebellion in Jamaica, forcing slave owners to sign legal documents freeing their slaves; the revolt is suppressed, and British authorities hang Sharp and hundreds of rebellious slaves.

- A slave revolt in Virginia is led by Nat Turner. Scores of whites are murdered before the rebellious slaves, including Turner, are captured or killed.

- The Egyptians begin to occupy Lebanon, Palestine, and Syria.

*DENOTES CIRCA DATE

1832   **24 November**   A South Carolina convention declares null and void the Tariff of 1828 (Tariff of Abominations).

1833
- The British Parliament emancipates slaves in the British colonies but compensates the slave owners.

2 March   U.S. president Andrew Jackson signs a tariff with reduced rates and the Force Act, which authorizes the president to enforce the collection of import duties by use of military force if necessary.

1834
- The Kaffir War erupts in South Africa between Xhosa tribesmen and Dutch Afrikaners. After fierce fighting, the Xhosa are defeated.

- Slavery is abolished in the Cape Colony.

1835
- The Ottomans regain control of Libya.

1836
- The Great Trek of Afrikaners—descendants of Dutch settlers in Capetown in South Africa—begins as they move northward, escaping British rule.

- A rebellion of Texans against Mexico, which had abolished slavery in 1829, results in the declaration of the Republic of Texas. A defending American force is attacked and slaughtered at the Alamo (23 February to 6 March); the Americans revenge this loss by defeating the Mexicans at the Battle of San Jacinto (21 April).

1837
- Ahmad Bey becomes the leader of Tunisia and introduces European reforms to the military and government. He also ends the practice of slavery in the nation.

- Oshio Heihachiro leads a rebellion around Osaka in response to corrupt government and local famine, but the revolt is put down. Ieyoshi becomes the new shogun and rules until 1853.

1838
- The Egyptians defeat the Saudis and remove Emir Faysal ibn Turki, who took over the throne from his father in 1834.

- The United States forces a massive removal of Cherokees from the East to Oklahoma, resulting in the death of nearly 25 percent of these Native Americans.

16 December   A Boer army defeats a Zulu force at the Battle of Blood River, which leads to the establishment by the Boers of Natal.

*DENOTES CIRCA DATE

1839

- The Opium War between China and Britain begins after a Chinese official orders the destruction of twenty thousand chests of opium brought by British merchants to Canton for sale to the Chinese. The Chinese government attempts to prevent the importation of the addictive drug, but the sale of opium is so profitable that the British go to war to keep the market open.

- The British invade Afghanistan in an attempt to overthrow Dost Muhammad, who came to power in 1826. The ruler is temporarily unseated but returns in 1840.

- British troops capture the Arabian port of Aden.

- Sultan Mahmud dies and is replaced on the Ottoman throne by his son Abdulmejid I.

1840

- The Maori tribe in New Zealand cedes sovereignty to Great Britain.

- The last British convicts are transported to Australia.

- The Central American Federation collapses.

- Pedro II comes to the Brazilian throne.

1841

- New Zealand becomes a formal colony of Great Britain.

- The Vietnamese throne is taken by Thieu-Tri, who rules for only six years.

1842

- The Treaty of Nanjing ends the Opium War, further weakening China and opening it to exploitation by the West. China is forced to grant special privileges to Europeans in many ports; Hong Kong is ceded to the British, who do not return it to China until 1997.

- Nasir al-Din Shah, son of Muhammad Shah, becomes the ruler of Iran.

- The French annex the Marquesas Islands and make Tahiti a protectorate.

- Boer and British forces clash in Natal; by 1843 the British have gained control of the region.

9 August   The United States and Canada agree on the northeastern boundary between their countries.

1843

- Faysal escapes from Egypt and returns to rule Arabia. He stays on the throne until 1865.

1845

- Sikhs in India begin a series of revolts against British rule, but they are subdued.

1846

- War breaks out between Mexico and the United States over the southern boundary of Texas.

*DENOTES CIRCA DATE

1846
(CONT'D)

15 June   Great Britain and the United States agree that the 49th parallel will be the northern boundary of Louisiana Purchase lands.

8 August   The Wilmot Proviso declares that slavery should be prohibited in all lands to be captured from Mexico. Although the bill passes in the House of Representatives, it is rejected in the Senate.

1848

• Tu-Duc becomes the emperor of Vietnam and reigns until 1883.

24 January   Gold is discovered in California, sparking a massive migration of Americans and foreigners to the West Coast.

2 February   The Treaty of Guadalupe Hidalgo ends hostilities between the United States and Mexico. Mexico gives up claims to Texas, California, and New Mexico; the Rio Grande is established as the border between the countries; and the United States pays Mexico $15 million.

1849

• Muhammad Ali, who has been senile and unable to personally rule Egypt since 1847, dies. His grandson Abbas Hilmi I had gained control of the state in 1848, but he is murdered in 1854.

21 February   The British defeat Afghan forces at the Battle of Gujat, and India annexes the Punjab and Peshawar provinces.

1850

September   After much debate the U.S. Congress agrees to the Compromise of 1850: California is to be a free state; the residents of New Mexico and Utah are to decide whether or not to have slavery; the slave trade in the District of Columbia is abolished; and a stricter fugitive-slave law is implemented.

1851

• Emperor Wenzong begins a ten-year reign. The Taiping Rebellion against the Manchu dynasty begins in China; Christian rebels are led by the mystic Hung Hsiu-ch'iian, who proclaims himself related to Jesus Christ.

• Rama IV becomes the king of Siam and opens the country to Western influence and ideas. He builds roads, introduces the printing press, creates a currency, and attempts to reform slavery. To educate his children, Rama hires an English governess, who later writes a memoir of her experiences on which the book by Margaret Landon, *Anna and the King of Siam* (1944), and the Rodgers and Hammerstein musical *The King and I* (1951) are based.

12 February   Gold is discovered in Australia.

1852

• The British capture Rangoon.

• New Zealand becomes a self-governing colony of Great Britain.

• Alhaj Umar begins a jihad (holy war) from Upper Guinea in western Africa and founds the Tuculor state on the Middle Niger River.

*DENOTES CIRCA DATE

1853–1868

- The Nian Rebellion supplants the imperial Manchu government in northern China. Only when the emperor fields new armies, equipped with modern weapons, is the rebellion put down.

1854

- The Western-educated Sa'id Pasha takes control of Egypt. He continues modernization reforms in the country.

- Antislavery and proslavery sides begin to battle in Kansas.

13 February   A U.S. fleet commanded by Commodore Matthew C. Perry, which had first visited Japan on 8 July 1853, enters Tokyo Bay; he demands that Japan open its ports to the importation of American goods. Japan concedes its weakness and opens two ports. To slow Western penetration, Japan begins to build a stronger, more modern army.

1855

- Alexander II becomes the Russian tsar upon the death of Nicholas I.

- Tewodros II begins his reign as king of Ethiopia, ushering the country into the modern era by establishing a reformed army and government.

1856

12 July   Natal becomes a British colony.

26 October   The Iranians capture Herat but are forced by the British the following year to give up lands captured in Afghanistan.

1857

- The Sepoy Rebellion breaks out in Bengal, India. The revolt of *sepoys* (Indian soldiers who served in the army of the British East India Company) soon spreads across the subcontinent.

- The Montenegrins revolt against Ottoman rule.

- Slavery is abolished in Libya.

1858

- The British quash the Sepoy Rebellion and begin a period of direct rule of India; British officials replace those of the East India Company.

- Russia and China sign the Treaty of Aigun, establishing borders along the Amur River.

- Iemochi becomes the shogun of Japan.

- The French and Spanish begin colonial expeditions against Vietnam.

1859

- The first railway in the British Cape Colony in South Africa is built.

- Spain sends troops into Morocco and gains some territorial concessions and indemnities.

- Control of Timor is divided between the Dutch and the Portuguese.

*Denotes Circa Date

1859
(CONT'D)

19 October   Abolitionist John Brown leads a group of white and black abolitionists in a raid on the armory at Harpers Ferry (present-day West Virginia) in an attempt to foment a slave uprising. The raid fails, and Brown is later executed.

1860

12 October   British and French troops occupy Beijing.

1861

• Serfdom is officially ended in Russia.

• Abdulmejid dies and is replaced as Ottoman sultan by his brother Abdulaziz.

• Tunisia promulgates the first constitution in an Islamic nation, establishing a limited monarchy, although it is abrogated in 1864.

• Lagos (Nigeria) is made a British Crown colony.

4 March   Abraham Lincoln is inaugurated as the sixteenth president of the United States. In response to his election ten Southern states secede from the Union, form the Confederate States of America, and elect Jefferson Davis as president.

12 April   Confederate forces open fire on Fort Sumter in Charleston (S.C.) harbor, initiating the Civil War.

1862

• Emperor Muzong takes the Chinese throne and rules until 1875.

• The French gain control of three regions of southern Vietnam. By 1867 they expand into western Vietnam.

9 March   Two ironclad warships, the CSS *Merrimac* and the USS *Monitor,* engage in a draw battle in Hampton Roads, Virginia.

17 September   Federal forces repulse a Confederate invasion of Maryland at the Battle of Antietam.

1863

• The French army occupies Mexico City and offers the Mexican throne to Austrian archduke Maximilian, who becomes emperor of Mexico.

• Shir Ali becomes the ruler of Afghanistan after the death of his father, Dost Muhammad, and he stays on the throne until 1879 (although unseated temporarily between 1866 and 1868).

• Sa'id Pasha dies and is replaced on the Egyptian throne by his nephew Khedive Isma'il, who continues rapid modernization. His policies bankrupt the country, which opens the door for foreign occupation.

• An antiforeign rebellion breaks out in Japan; it is put down by an allied European-American force.

1 January   Under the provisions of the Emancipation Proclamation, President Lincoln frees all slaves in territories occupied by Confederate forces.

*DENOTES CIRCA DATE

1863
(CONT'D)

1–3 July   In the turning point of the Civil War, Confederate and Union forces fight a three-day battle at Gettysburg, Pennsylvania. After this engagement the South is placed on the defensive.

4 July   Federal forces capture Vicksburg, Mississippi, effectively dividing the Confederacy in half.

1864

- Aided by Western armies, the Manchu dynasty puts down the Taiping Rebellion.

- Twelve-year-old Kujong, with his father serving as regent, becomes king of Korea and rules until 1919.

1865

- Paraguayan president Francisco Solano Lopez initiates a five-year conflict known as the South American War of the Triple Alliance against Argentina, Brazil, and Uruguay. Much of the Paraguayan army is destroyed, and Lopez is killed. Paraguay loses territory and approximately one-half its male population in the war.

9 April   General Robert E. Lee surrenders his Confederate army to U.S. general Ulysses S. Grant at Appomattox Courthouse, Virginia, effectively ending the Civil War.

14 April   Lincoln is assassinated in Washington by John Wilkes Booth; Andrew Johnson becomes the new president.

18 December   The Thirteenth Amendment is ratified, ending slavery in the United States.

1866

- Russian novelist Fyodor Dostoevsky publishes *Crime and Punishment*.

- Christians on Crete revolt against Muslim rule.

- Iranian mystic Mirza Husayn Ali Nuri founds the Baha'i faith.

- The USS *General Sherman* is attacked and sunk on the Taedong River by the Koreans; all twenty-four American crewmen are killed.

1867

- Mexican emperor Maximilian I surrenders to Benito Juarez's forces. He is condemned to death and is executed by firing squad, ending formal French influence in Mexico.

- Diamonds are discovered in South Africa.

- A British expedition invades Ethiopia in an effort to free some captured British soldiers; Tewodros II commits suicide.

- Russia sells Alaska to the United States.

- Singapore becomes a British Crown colony.

*DENOTES CIRCA DATE

1868

- The Meiji Restoration begins in Japan; Emperor Meiji regains control of national affairs from the shoguns. The new regime limits the power of feudal clans and creates a strong central state dedicated to economic and military modernization.

- Rama IV dies and is replaced on the Thai throne by Rama V, who rules until 1910. Rama V ends slavery, centralizes the government, abolishes feudalism, and modernizes the military.

- Cubans revolt against Spanish rule in a conflict that gains the name the Ten Years' War.

1869

17 November The Suez Canal is officially opened.

1871

- American forces make an aborted attempt to open Korea to American trade.

- Henry M. Stanley searches for and finds the lost explorer David Livingstone near Lake Tanganyika.

1872

- A revolt in Algeria, led by Muhammad al-Muqrani, is put down by the French.

January Yohannes IV takes the Ethiopian throne; he rules until 1889.

1874

- The French gain control of Vietnamese foreign policy.

31 January Despite a victory over British forces the previous year, the Asante suffer a loss at Amoafo, which leads to the decline of their power.

1875

- Muzong dies and is replaced on the Chinese throne by Dezong, who rules until 1908.

1876

- Ottoman sultan Abdulaziz is deposed by his nephew Murad and dies; Murad is quickly replaced by Abdulhamid II. Taking advantage of a weakened Ottoman government in a time of dynastic transition, the Serbs, Montenegrins, and Bulgarians in the Balkans rebel against their Turkish overlords. The Turks quell the uprising but also enact a new constitution that grants more civil and political rights to all subjects of the Ottoman Empire.

- Japan forces Korea to open its ports to Japanese trade.

- The period known as Reconstruction comes to an end in the American South with the disputed election of Rutherford B. Hayes; Democrats soon return to power, eliminating most Republican opposition, and begin establishing laws that gradually restrict the rights of African Americans.

25 June U.S. troops under General George A. Custer are wiped out by Lakota and Cheyenne warriors under Sitting Bull and Crazy Horse at the Battle of Little Big Horn in present-day Montana.

*DENOTES CIRCA DATE

1877
- The traditional samurai warrior class, led by Saigo Takamori, rebels against the Meiji regime in Japan, opposing its modernizing policies. They are defeated by a modern army.

1878
- British and Indian forces invade Afghanistan.

16 January Samoa and the United States sign a treaty of friendship; Pago Pago becomes an American coaling station.

3 March The Russo-Turkish Wars conclude with an Ottoman surrender to the Russians. The Treaty of San Stefano grants independence to Romania, Montenegro, and Serbia, as well as greater autonomy for Bosnia, Herzegovina, and Bulgaria. Russia also gains territorial concessions. The Turkish defeat further signals the decline of the Ottoman Empire. Cyprus is transferred to British control.

1879
- Egyptian emir Khedive Isma'il is deposed and replaced by Khedive Tawfiq.
- Bolivia and Peru declare war on Chile over mining rights. The conflict, known as the War of the Pacific, is won by Chile in 1883.

22 January The Zulus win a stunning victory over the British at the Battle of Isandlwana in South Africa. The British recover and eventually defeat the Zulus; Zululand is then divided into thirteen separate kingdoms.

1880
- Abd al-Rahman Khan becomes the ruler of Afghanistan and remains in power until 1901.
- Great Britain expands its influence in the Middle East, first by gaining control of the foreign policy of Bahrain.
- The British begin to allow a measure of local control in India.
- The United States and Korea establish friendly relations.

1881
- Alexander II dies and is succeeded on the Russian throne by Alexander III.
- Egyptian military officer Ahmad Urabi begins a nationalist revolt, sparking many anti-European riots.
- The French invade Tunisia and establish a protectorate.

1882
- Urabi's army is defeated by the British, who occupy Egypt, and Khedive Tawfiq is returned to power. Jewish immigrants from Europe begin arriving in Palestine in increasing numbers.
- The U.S. Congress passes the Chinese Exclusion Act, blocking Chinese immigration to the United States.

*DENOTES CIRCA DATE

1883

- Tonkin and Cochin China are recognized by European powers as French protectorates. China, however, denounces this imperialistic action. After a series of battles, the French by 1885 gain complete control over Vietnam.

26 August   The volcano Krakatoa explodes in Indonesia. The eruption creates a massive tidal wave that obliterates 163 Indonesian villages and kills more than 36,000 people.

1884

- Germany gains control of several Pacific islands, including the Solomons; the following year it gains the Marshall Islands. Germany also gains a colony in Togo, Africa. Representatives from the European nations interested in colonial expansion in Africa hold a conference in Berlin establishing rules so that they do not begin wars over their colonial possessions.

- Porfirio Diaz establishes a dictatorship in Mexico that lasts until 1911.

1885

- The Sudanese, led by Mahdi Muhammad Ahmad, overthrow Egyptian control of Sudan.

27 December   The first Indian National Congress meets.

1886

- Great Britain annexes Burma to the empire; China recognizes the action in return for tribute payments.

1887

- A massive flood of the Yellow River kills nine hundred thousand Chinese.

- The Yemenis revolt against Ottoman rule, but the rebels are put down by Turkish troops.

- Apache leader Geronimo is captured by U.S. troops.

1888

15 May   Brazil outlaws slavery.

1889

- A constitution in Japan establishes a measure of bicameral government, although the powers of the emperor, such as making war, are carefully delineated.

- Menelik II becomes the king of Ethiopia; he expands Ethiopian territory, establishes Addis Ababa as the capital, and modernizes government functions.

22 April   Land in Oklahoma is opened to settlement, leading to the formation of the territory (it will become a state in 1907). Twelve other western states are brought into the union by 1912, the last of this group being Utah.

16 November   Pedro II is forced into exile, and the first Republic of Brazil is founded.

*Denotes Circa Date

1893
- New Zealand grants female suffrage; women can vote in national elections, a first for any nation.
- France gains control of Laos.

1894
- Nicholas II becomes the tsar of Russia upon the death of Alexander III.

  4 July   The Republic of Hawaii is established after the Hawaiian monarchy, led by Queen Liliuokalani, is overthrown by Sanford Dole and white sugar planters.

1895
- Cubans begin a revolt against the Spanish that will later draw the United States into the conflict.

  17 April   The Sino-Japanese War, begun in 1894, ends with a Japanese victory and a weakening of the Manchu dynasty, setting the stage for a republican revolution in China.

1896
- Nasir al-Din Shah is assassinated by an Islamic activist and is replaced by a weak ruler who gives many oil concessions to the British.
- Mubarak ibn Abdallah gains control of Kuwait from his brother Muhammad ibn Abdallah, who has ruled since 1892. Mubarak obtains support from the British to block Ottoman interests in the state in exchange for a pro-British foreign policy.
- The U.S. Supreme Court upholds the doctrine of "separate but equal" in *Plessy* v. *Ferguson*, which is used by many states and cities, especially in the South, to provide inferior services to African Americans, a policy that will stand until 1954.

  1 March   Italian troops invade Ethiopia, but they are defeated by the Ethiopians at the battle of Adua.

1897
- German troops occupy Jiaozhoa Bay, initiating a surge of European expansion in China.
- The French establish a protectorate over Vietnam.
- Benin is captured by the British. The British also put down a revolt in Uganda.

1898
- The Hawaiian Islands become a protectorate of the United States.
- German kaiser Wilhelm II visits Istanbul and Jerusalem, strengthening relations between Germany and the Ottoman Empire.

  15 February   U.S. battleship *Maine* blows up in Havana harbor, killing 260 American sailors and precipitating the Spanish-American War. The war ends (10 December) in defeat for Spain and the loss of its last colonies in the Americas. Cuba gains its independence, while Puerto Rico, Guam, Wake Island, and the Philippines become American protectorates.

*DENOTES CIRCA DATE

1898-1901

- The Boxer Rebellion breaks out; Chinese nationalists attack foreign diplomats and missionaries, hoping to expel Western influence from China. The United States, Japan, and European nations send troops and put down the uprising.

1898-1908

- Bubonic plague sweeps China and India, killing approximately three million people.

1899

- The Boer War begins in South Africa after Afrikaners deny British advances into the gold-rich Transvaal province.
- Filipino rebels fight against American control of the Philippines.

6 September   U.S. secretary of state John Hay issues the Open Door note, which declares that China must allow free trade to foreign powers.

1900

- Hawaii becomes a territory of the United States (it will become a state in 1959).

1901

- Zionist leader Theodor Herzl proposes to the Ottoman sultan the establishment of an independent Jewish region in Palestine.

1 January   The Commonwealth of Australia is established.

3 March   Filipino rebel leader Emilio Aquinaldo, who has led opposition to both the Spanish and Americans, is captured; formal civil government of the islands is established by the United States under Governor William Howard Taft.

31 May   The British win sovereignty over South Africa with the Treaty of Vereeniging; the Boers win limited local rule and the promise of financial aid to repair war damage.

14 September   President William McKinley is assassinated; Theodore Roosevelt becomes president.

26 September   The Asante kingdom is absorbed into the Gold Coast.

1902

- The British are victorious in the Boer War, but the Afrikaners are granted lands in the Colony of South Africa and are guaranteed legal racial superiority over the African population, thus creating the system of apartheid.
- The foundations of the modern state of Saudi Arabia are established under the rule of Abd al-Aziz ibn Sa'ud, who returns from exile and captures control of Riyadh from the Ottomans.
- The Aswan Dam is built in Upper Egypt.
- Italy takes over colonial control of Libya from the French, leading to an invasion of the country by the Italians in 1911.

*DENOTES CIRCA DATE

1903

- The Social Democratic Party (Marxist) in Russia splits into two factions: the Mensheviks (moderates) and the Bolsheviks (extremists).

- Yemen gains independence.

- The Russo-Japanese War begins. Japanese forces quickly defeat the Russians on land in Manchuria and at sea.

17 December   Orville and Wilbur Wright make the first manned flight at Kitty Hawk, North Carolina, setting a landmark in aviation history.

1904

- The French and English secretly agree to separate spheres of influence in Morocco and Egypt, respectively.

1905

5 September   The Treaty of Portsmouth ends the Russo-Japanese War. The conflict humiliates Russia and prompts a revolutionary uprising by the workers. Korea is later made a Japanese protectorate.

1908

July   Turkish military officers, known as the Young Turks and led by Ahmed Niyazi Bey, rebel in Macedonia and force the reestablishment of the 1876 constitution, which significantly reduces the power of the sultan.

5 October   Bulgaria declares its independence from Turkey.

18 October   Belgium annexes the Congo Free State.

1909

- The Japanese begin a thirty-six-year occupation of Korea, which is formally annexed in 1910.

- Ahmad Shah becomes shah of Iran, the last of the Qajar rulers.

1910

- A revolution begins in Mexico; a new constitution will be enacted in 1917.

- The Manchu emperor abolishes slavery in China.

- Rama VI takes the Thai throne.

- Korea is annexed by Japan.

- The National Association for the Advancement of Colored People (NAACP) is formed to seek civil rights for African Americans.

13 May   The Union of South Africa is formed.

1911

- A revolution ends the 267-year Manchu dynasty and introduces liberal reforms to China. Puyi, the last Chinese emperor, abdicates on 12 February 1912. Nationalist leader Sun Yat-sen, dedicated to the principles of democracy and livelihood for the people, returns from exile and is elected president of the new republic.

*DENOTES CIRCA DATE

1911
(CONT'D)

- Mexican president Diaz is overthrown.

29 September   Italy declares war on the Ottomans and invades Libya.

1912

- U.S. Marines invade Honduras, Cuba, and Nicaragua to protect American business and agricultural interests. American troops will remain in Nicaragua until 1933.

- After years of de facto control of Moroccan affairs, the French establish a protectorate in the country.

- The South African Native National Congress (later the African National Congress) is founded.

30 July   Emperor Meiji dies and is followed on the Japanese throne by Yoshishito.

15 October   The Treaty of Ouchy gives Italy control of Tripoli.

1913

- The British gain exclusive rights to oil exploration in Kuwait.

- Yuan Shikai, provisional president of the Chinese Republic after the resignation of Sun Yat-sen, dissolves the parliament and takes dictatorial powers. When Yuan dies in 1916, political chaos sweeps China and warlordism ensues.

- Ethiopian king Menelik II dies.

4 March   Woodrow Wilson becomes president of the United States.

1914

- Mohandas Gandhi returns to India after twenty-one years living in South Africa; he begins a nonviolent campaign against British rule.

*DENOTES CIRCA DATE

GEOGRAPHY

by BRUCE BIGELOW

CONTENTS

Sidebars and tables are listed in italics.

1756
- The Seven Years' War (known as the French and Indian War in North America) begins in Europe. By 1763 Britain defeats France and her allies and acquires all of Canada, East and West Florida, and the West Indian islands of Grenada, Saint Vincent, Dominica, and Tobago.

1768
- France annexes the island of Corsica.

1772
- Austria, Prussia, and Russia seize nearly one-third of Poland's territory. Another partition occurs in 1793, and by the Third Partition two years later Poland is completely dismembered and divided among the three neighboring states.

1783
- The American Revolutionary War ends. Britain recognizes the independence of the United States and relinquishes control of Louisiana, Florida, and Minorca to Spain; France receives Senegal and Tobago.

1795
- The Netherlands is organized as the Batavian Republic under French control.

1799-1804
- German naturalist Alexander von Humboldt and French botanist Aimé Bonpland engage in a five-year exploration of northern South America, Mexico, and Cuba.

1804
- Humboldt visits President Thomas Jefferson in Washington, D.C., and the two naturalists share information on their research.

1805
- Volume 1 of the *Voyage of Humboldt and Bonpland* is published; twenty-two more volumes are released by 1834.

1806
- French emperor Napoleon I organizes the Netherlands into the Kingdom of Holland; in 1810 he incorporates the area directly into the French empire.
- Napoleon dissolves the Holy Roman Empire and forms the Confederation of the Rhine; all the German states except for Austria, Prussia, Brunswick, and Hesse are now under French control.

1807
- Napoleon creates the Grand Duchy of Warsaw from Polish lands formerly partitioned to Prussia and Austria.

* DENOTES CIRCA DATE

1811
- The first volume of *Political Essays on the Kingdom of New Spain* by Humboldt is published with three more volumes appearing by 1822. This work causes a large outcry with its criticism of Spanish colonial policies.

1815
- At the Congress of Vienna, Poland is once again divided among Austria, Prussia, and Russia. It eventually becomes a semi-autonomous kingdom under Russian control.
- The Netherlands is given sovereignty over present-day Belgium and Luxembourg.

1817
- The first volume of German scholar Karl Ritter's *Geography* is printed; eighteen more volumes are published through 1859.

1819
- The British East India Company establishes a colony in Singapore.

1820
- Ritter assumes the first German university professorship in geography at Berlin and the Prussian Military Academy.

1829
- Greece wins its independence from the Ottoman Empire.

1830
- Gibraltar, a small peninsula in southern Spain on the strategic passage between the Atlantic Ocean and the Mediterranean Sea, becomes a British crown colony. (It had been captured in the early eighteenth century during the War of Spanish Succession.)

1831
- Belgium revolts from the Netherlands and declares its independence; meanwhile, a Polish rebellion against Russia fails.

1842
- The Treaty of Nanking provides for the opening of British trade in the Chinese ports of Hong Kong, Amoy, Ningpo, Foochow, and Shanghai.

1843
- *Central Asia* by Humboldt is published; it is based on his exploration of the Russian empire in 1829.

1845
- Volume 1 of Humboldt's major work *Kosmos* appears in print and is followed over the next seventeen years by four other volumes. Humboldt takes a stance against prevailing opinion and argues that man does not dominate nature.

* DENOTES CIRCA DATE

1848
- The loose union of cantons in Switzerland adopts a constitution and forms the Swiss Confederation.

1860
- All of Italy except for Venetia and a small area around Rome is unified under Victor Emmanuel II, King of Sardinia. Austria relinquishes control of Venetia in 1866.

1863
- After another unsuccessful uprising, Poland officially becomes a Russian province.

1864
- With the backing of French troops, Archduke Maximilian of Austria becomes emperor of Mexico. When the United States reasserts the Monroe Doctrine, French forces withdraw in 1867, and Maximilian is executed.

1871
- Germany is unified under Otto von Bismarck, Chancellor of Prussia.
- Rome becomes the capital of Italy.

1875
- Britain acquires controlling interest in the Suez Canal, linking the Red Sea and the Mediterranean Sea.

1878
- Under the Treaty of San Stefano, the Ottoman Empire recognizes the independence of Serbia, Montenegro, and Romania.

1882
- The first volume of *Anthropogeographie* (Anthropogeography) is written by Frederich Ratzel; the second volume is completed nine years later. Ratzel examines the influence of geography on history.

1884-1885
- The Berlin Conference occurs; Africa is carved up into colonies by the leading European states. Upon annexing territory, each European power is required to notify the other powers in order to avoid disputes.

1887
- English scholar Halford Mackinder receives an appointment as Reader in Geography at Oxford University, and he writes "The Scope and Methods of Geography." This seminal article establishes the framework of study in the field by identifying the close connection between human activity and geography.

* DENOTES CIRCA DATE

1889
- Great Britain, Germany, and the United States sign a tripartite agreement to rule the Pacific island of Samoa. The treaty is renewed ten years later, but Britain cedes its interests to Germany.

1890
- With the accession of Adolph of Nassau as grand duke, Luxembourg breaks its hereditary connections with the Netherlands.
- The German and British governments reach an agreement whereby the African colonies of Uganda, Zanzibar, and Pemba become protectorates of Britain. In exchange, the North Sea island of Heligoland is ceded to Germany.
- Britain and France sign a treaty allowing the British to control northern Nigeria and the French to control Madagascar and the Sahara.

1891
- Portugal agrees to allow British control over Rhodesia (present-day Zimbabwe and Zambia).

1894
- French geographer Paul Vidal de La Blache writes *Histoire et Géographie: Atlas Général* (History and Geography: A General Atlas).

1897
- Ratzel writes *Politische Geographie* (Political Geography).
- Germany acquires trading concessions in the Chinese town of Kiaochow; the next year Kwangchowan becomes a French base.

1898
- Vidal de La Blache becomes chairman of the Department of Geography at the Sorbonne.
- Spain sues for peace following the disastrous Spanish-American War. Control of Cuba, Puerto Rico, the Philippines, Guam, and Wake Island is given to the United States.

1899
- France formally recognizes British claims to Egypt and the Sudan; in exchange, France receives the kingdom of Wadai, which links the French Congo with French possessions in northwestern Africa.

1902
- Ratzel writes *The Earth and Life* in two volumes; meanwhile, Mackinder finishes the regional study *Britain and the British Seas*.

1903
- *Tableau de la Géographie de la France* (Description of the Geography of France) is published by Vidal de La Blache; meanwhile, Mackinder writes the article "The Geographical Pivot of History."

* DENOTES CIRCA DATE

1903
(CONT'D)

- Denmark permits Iceland to have home rule.

1904

- An Anglo-French agreement allows the British to create a protectorate in Egypt and the French to establish one in Morocco. Both Germany and Spain protest the French presence in Morocco.

1905

- Norway declares its independence from Sweden and establishes a monarchy.

1908

- Austria-Hungary annexes Bosnia-Herzegovina.

1914

- By this date the major European countries have colonies in all of Africa except for the independent states of Abyssinia (Ethiopia) and Liberia.

* DENOTES CIRCA DATE

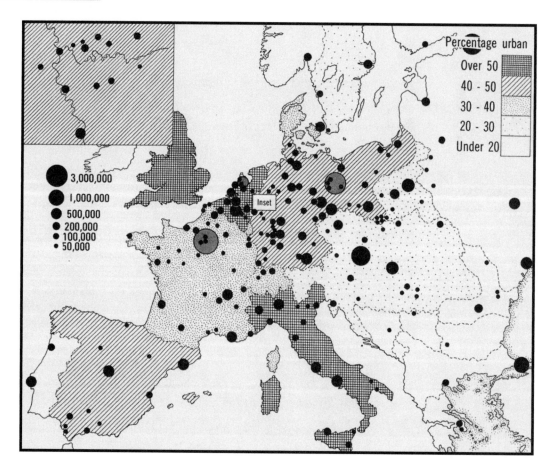

Map of European urban population circa 1910 (from N. J. G. Pounds, *An Historical Geography of Europe*, 1990)

OVERVIEW

Time of Change. The period from 1750 to 1914 was truly revolutionary for Europe. First, the economic base was transformed by industrialism, which caused state societies to become predominantly urban for the first time in world history. Second, state power was based on possession of coal and iron and its production rather than agricultural production; and, therefore, power passed from France to England to Germany sequentially as the strongest European state from the beginning to the end of the era. Third, many European states became so strong militarily relative to non-European peoples that European empires were greatly expanded and large neo-European societies were created abroad. Fourth, the political map of Europe itself was radically transformed in central and eastern Europe (including Russia) from the mid 1700s to 1920 as small states of the same nationality were coalesced, and large antinational empires were broken down into smaller nation-states.

Physical Geography. In order to understand these changes, one has to appreciate the physical and cultural geography of Europe. Possession of coal, iron, water sources, and agricultural lands were all important for economic development. Northwest Europe was the core of the Continent in many ways even before industrialism, and now it was enhanced. Atlantic Europe benefited from a relatively mild climate and a flat plain with rich soils. Also, large rivers and inland seas fostered the development of a market economy in agricultural products as well as the easy flow of industrial goods, the migration of people and the spread of information.

Economic Geography. With rapid industrialization, the European people increased to be about one-quarter of the world's population by 1900 despite massive emigration to the Americas and Australia. England was the cradle, or area of origin, of industrialism in the eighteenth century, and in the nineteenth century industries spread eastward across the northern portion of the Continent. The growth of the railroad network succinctly portrayed this diffusion, as did urbanization, that gave Europe huge new cities that were plagued by pollution and crowding. Urban renewal, best exemplified in Paris, bolstered the rising middle class much more so than the working class.

Political and Cultural Geography. As Europeans industrialized, they reached out for colonies abroad as a source of raw materials, cheap labor, and places to export finished products of European factories. A new surge of imperialism was manifested, and with this competition for empire, European nationalisms flourished. National identity was based on language, so most linguistic groups clamored for their own nation-state. In a few cases religious persuasion was more or equally important than language as a base of national identity (for example, Ireland and Poland, respectively).

Geography as a Discipline. In the nineteenth century, academic geography rose as a distinct discipline in western European universities. The rise of imperialism and nationalism set the context for the founding of geography departments. Also, the production of atlases that displayed the glorious history of European states and empires became popular. Three exemplars of geographic research and publication were the naturalist Alexander Von Humboldt of Prussia, the geopolitician Halford Mackinder of Britain, and the cultural geographer Paul Vidal de La Blache of France.

TOPICS IN GEOGRAPHY

CLIMATES AND LANDFORMS

Bodies of Water. The continent of Europe is flanked by two great bodies of water—the Atlantic Ocean to the west and the Mediterranean Sea to the south. The Mediterranean had been the center of European civilization and trade since antiquity, while the Atlantic became its main highway for international relations after the sixteenth century. Most of Europe was easily connected for commerce by its many navigable rivers that emptied into large inland seas (notably the Baltic Sea to the north and the Black Sea to the southeast). The major rivers of western, central, and eastern Europe, including Russia, tend to flow in a north-to-south axis, thus directing the movement of goods and raw materials between the Mediterranean Sea and the North Atlantic. The great rivers of France are the Garonne in the southwest, the Loire in the northwest, the Rhone in the southeast, and the Seine in the north. Like the Loire and Seine, the Rhine flows northwesterly and drains into the Atlantic. Germany's other great rivers are the Weser and the Elbe, while the mighty Danube bisects eastern Europe, flowing southeasterly through the great cities of Prague, Vienna, and Budapest before emptying into the Black Sea near Odessa. Also, in eastern Europe the Vistula flows through Poland while the Dnieper, the Don, and the Volga course through Ukraine and Russia. Again, these long rivers of eastern Europe created a "river road" linking the Black Sea and the Mediterranean in the south to the Baltic and the Atlantic in the north. During the early industrial age before 1850 and the advent of the railroad, some of these rivers became linked by canals to facilitate further the movement of people and goods.

Climate. Despite much of the continent being situated in northerly latitudes, parts of Europe enjoy a relatively mild climate. Southern Europe flanks the northern shore of the Mediterranean Sea and, like North Africa and the Levant coast of the Middle East, has a mild, wet winter and a long, dry summer. This climate is called Mediterranean Summer-Dry and is similar to the climate of southern California. Europe northwest of the Alps also has a mild winter despite its northerly latitude because of the moderating effect on temperature of the Atlantic Ocean. Through this body of water runs the Gulf Stream, effectively a river within the ocean that originates in the Gulf of Mexico. Warmed by the tropics, its waters run past Florida and across the Atlantic toward western Europe and the British Isles. Warm water meeting cool moist air creates the Marine West Coast climate, which is cool and wet in the summer and relatively warm and wet in the winter. This climate is similar to the coasts of the Pacific Northwest states of Washington and Oregon in the United States, also warmed by an ocean current. Central and eastern Europe, including Russia west of the Urals, are beyond the reach of the warming influence of the Atlantic, and so have much more severe winters. Their climate is classified as Continental. As a rule, the summers become shorter and cooler the further removed the region is from the Atlantic Ocean. The northern reaches of this climate are subclassified as subarctic. Mountainous regions, of course, are cooler than Lowlands and are classified as Highlands. Parts of northern Europe, including Scandinavia, even have Polar climates known as tundra. Here in the southerly parts one finds coniferous forests, or taiga, much like central and northern Canada, although within the Arctic Circle toward the Polar ice cap, snow and ice cover the treeless ground year round, creating the tundra zone.

Landforms. As with its climate, there is considerable variation in Europe's physiography, or landforms. Southern Europe tends to be mountainous as a result of the Alpine System that extends even into North Africa and the Middle East. The massive Alps, which divide southern Europe from northern and western Europe, rise at the highest to nearly sixteen thousand feet. Deep mountain passes (for example, the Brenner and the St. Gothard) have linked Europe for centuries. Other mountains in the system are the Apennines, a spine that divides the Italian Peninsula between East and West, the Pyrenees in the northern reaches of the Iberian Peninsula, and the Carpathians in eastern Europe. Much of the northern portions of western, central and eastern Europe, including European Russia, are covered by the Great European Plain. This area is rich for agriculture because of its flatness, deep fertile soils, and fairly long growing season.

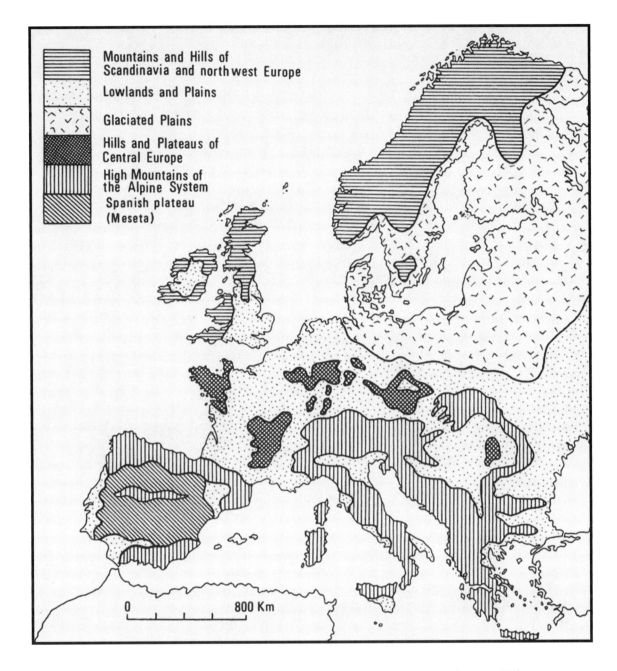

**Mountains and Hills of
Scandinavia and north west Europe**

Lowlands and Plains

Glaciated Plains

**Hills and Plateaus of
Central Europe**

**High Mountains of
the Alpine System**

**Spanish plateau
(Meseta)**

0   800 Km

Map of landforms in Europe (from N. J. G. Pounds, *An Historical Geography of Europe,* 1990)

France was especially blessed with this condition. Two smaller physiographic provinces are the Western Uplands and the Central Uplands. The Western Uplands include the hills of Celtic Britain and Scandinavia and have soils poor for farming. The Central Uplands of southern France, central Germany, and Czechia (Czech Republic) also have poorer soils for agriculture.

Sources:

Atlas of World History (New York: Oxford University Press, 1999).

Fernand Braudel, *A History of Civilizations* (New York: Penguin, 1994).

James R. Penn, *Encyclopedia of Geographical Features in World History: Europe and the Americas* (Santa Barbara, Cal.: ABC-CLIO, 1997).

Lester Rowntree, and others, *Diversity Amid Globalization* (Upper Saddle River, N.J.: Prentice Hall, 2000).

Tim Unwin, ed., *Atlas of World Development* (New York: John Wiley, 1994).

ECONOMIC GEOGRAPHY

Natural Resources. Europe possesses natural resources that were necessary for industrialization, especially navigable rivers and coal basins. In the early phases of industrialization the latent energy in flowing rivers was harnessed to power some of the new machines of the burgeoning textile industry, such as the water-frame. Later, when steam power was employed, the energy from burned coal was tapped to create the steam that powered the all-important railroads and steamships. Coal basins with the mineral close to the surface and thus readily mined were prevalent in Midland England, northeastern England, southern Wales and Lowland Scotland in Great Britain. On the Continent, coal basins were found along the France-Belgium frontier, in

Illustration of the Prussian royal foundry at Gleiwitz, 1841 (Deutsches Museum, Munich)

the Ruhr Valley in western Germany, in southeastern Germany, in Czechia (Czech Republic), and in eastern Ukraine. Europe was also rich in iron ore deposits, many of which were located close to the coal basins. As industrialization shifted from the light industry of textiles to the heavy industry of iron and steel in the middle of the nineteenth century, coal, the lifeblood of industry before the advent of oil in the twentieth century, was now also put to the use of smelting iron in the production of steel.

Demography. In 1650 Europe contained about 18 percent of the world's population; if neo-European North America is added, the percentage is 19. However, by 1900 Europe itself possessed 24 percent of the world's population and 29 percent with neo-European North America and Australia. Europe itself had increased in population from one hundred to four hundred million, thanks mainly to the drop in death rates because of improvements in health care, nutrition, and sanitation. Measures of economic productivity and imperial power from 1650 to 1900 added further to the theme of the revolutionary advance of Europe with industrialism. In the English Midlands, Birmingham emerged as the major heavy industrial center, producing iron and steel. Manchester was the cotton textile center, and Liverpool emerged as the major Atlantic port for the region. All had been small towns before 1800. The

same change occurred in Glasgow in Scotland. On the other hand, London, already huge before industrialism, grew strongly (almost quadrupling) between 1750 and 1850, in part because of the emergence of light industry. The same pattern occurred on the Continent a generation after Britain. By 1850 half of the population of Britain lived in cities, whereas northern continental states like Prussia and France reached that threshold only about 1890 and 1930, respectively. Southern and eastern European states including Russia would be a generation later in achieving this level of urbanization. This situation was a result of large rural-to-urban and small city-to-large city migration. Only by the twentieth century did large cities reproduce themselves through natural increase (greater birth than death rates). As a result, many rural districts and small cities shrank, especially when loss through overseas migration is added. With changes in transportation the urban landscape of Europe, like that of North America, became more sprawling and differentiated in land use and class areas. The railroad encouraged expansion and differentiation between cities from the early nineteenth to the early twentieth century, while first the omnibus and horsecar, then the trolley and subway, moved masses of people within cities. Factories tended to locate near the downtown, although some settled in select suburban areas

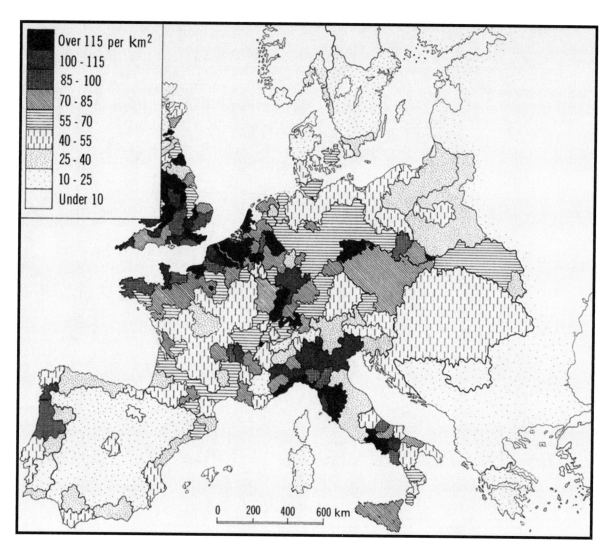

Map of European population density in the early nineteenth century
(from N. J. G. Pounds, *An Historical Geography of Europe*, 1990)

with access to railroads. Social status eventually became correlated with how far one lived from downtown with its unpleasant industrial effluvia, unless one resided on the major avenues.

Industrial Concentration and Railroads. Since the sixteenth century the economic center of gravity in Europe had shifted away from the Mediterranean regions and toward the northwest quadrant. Industrialization after 1780 accelerated this shift, and as railroads were constructed in the second half of the nineteenth century, the economic preponderance of northwestern Europe (northern France, Great Britain, and Germany) became overwhelming. The concentration of rail lines demonstrates this fact vividly. In 1850 Britain was the unquestioned and almost unchallenged industrial leader in Europe, but for the next sixty-five years Germany feverishly closed the gap and eventually surpassed Great Britain in industrial production. The German population soared and, paralleling this growth in human capital, railroad mileage multiplied dramatically as pig iron, steel, and, toward the turn of the century, electrical production skyrocketed. It is no accident that these three

great industrial powers—Germany, Great Britain, and France—were leading combatants in the first industrial war, World War I. Although there were industrializing regions in southern and central Europe, they remained behind the northern and western European nations.

Industrial Cities. According to the great urban historian Lewis Mumford, the Industrial Revolution had two phases—the paleotechnic, or early, and the neotechnic, or later. The paleotechnic period spanned the late eighteenth and nineteenth centuries and was the age of coal, iron, and steam. The neotechnic phase was the age of electricity and the internal combustion engine powered by gasoline derived from oil and occurred during the late nineteenth and twentieth centuries. According to Mumford, the paleotechnic city was "insensate" offensive to the senses because of air and water pollution as well as acrid smells and excessive noise. As he wrote, "from the 1830s on the environment of the mine . . . was universalized by the railroad. Wherever the iron rails went, the mine and its debris went with them. . . . The rushing locomotive brought noise, smoke, grit into the heart of the towns." In these industrial "Coke-

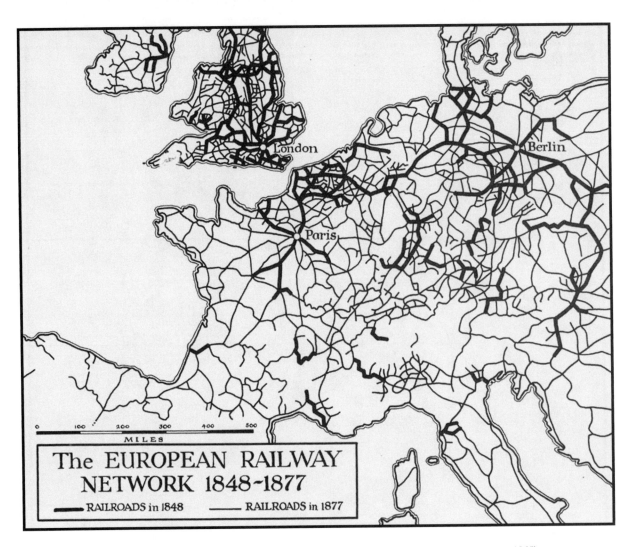

Map of railroad lines during the Industrial Revolution (from Ernest John Knapton, *Europe,* 1965)

towns," as realist author Charles Dickens had named them in his novel *Hard Times* (1854), the permanent insecurity of the working class was a constant characteristic. These men, women, and children were confined to filthy, overcrowded and diseased slums in city centers while the upper middle class escaped, generally upwind, to the suburbs.

Haussmann's Paris. In the nineteenth century several attempts were made to renew older cities that had recently industrialized. A significant case was the transformation of Paris during the Second Empire of Louis Napoleon (1852–1870). The emperor's urban planner was Baron Georges Haussmann. The baron's task was to create wide boulevards through the city to link the many new monuments that were gracing new public squares that were mostly located in middle-class sections of the city. The new boulevards served military as well as aesthetic purposes. In working-class neighborhoods where barricades had been erected in the revolutionary years of 1830 and 1848, the wide boulevards served as efficient highways for the swift movement of troops to quell unrest before it could spread. In addition to building

monuments and boulevards, Haussmann also constructed a new sewer and water supply system to reduce the breeding grounds for disease (cholera epidemics had swept Paris in 1832 and 1849). Water now came from canals hundreds of miles long originating in Champagne in eastern France instead of from the polluted Seine River. In twenty years Haussmann's transformation of Paris converted it from a nearly medieval city of irregular and narrow streets to the modern one of geometrically regular, straight, and wide avenues. During these two decades from 1850 to 1870 the city nearly doubled in population, from about one million to two million people. Natural increase of the population of Paris was negligible. One-half of the increase was from immigration from the provinces of France, while the other one-half was from annexation of predominantly working-class suburbs, most of which were slums.

Impact of Haussmannization. Haussmann's transformation was creatively destructive. Entire neighborhoods were demolished to make way for the ninety miles of boulevards. So vast was this building project that one-fifth of all Parisian workers were employed in construction. As highways cleared territory, many industries were forced to relocate to the suburban ring outside of Paris, leaving the new center of Paris a relatively clean locale for the middle class to enjoy. Luxury apartments, bourgeois homes, and hotels for tourists sprang up, and property values in the city doubled. The working class was not so fortunate. Their neighborhoods of crowded tenements and cottages, if they escaped the wrecking ball, largely remained slums. Overall, the dramatic transformation of Paris from 1850 to 1870 benefited the middle class much more than the working class.

Sources:

David Harvey, *Consciousness and the Urban Experience: Studies in the History and the Theory of Capitalist Urbanization* (Baltimore: Johns Hopkins University Press, 1985).

Paul M. Hohenberg and Lynn Lees, *The Making of Urban Europe, 1000–1950* (Cambridge, Mass.: Harvard University Press, 1985).

David P. Jordan, *Transforming Paris: The Life and Labors of Baron Haussmann* (Chicago: University of Chicago Press, 1995).

David Landes, *The Unbound Prometheus: Technological Change and Industrial Development in Western Europe from 1750 to the Present* (Cambridge: Cambridge University Press, 1969).

John Merriman, *A History of Modern Europe: Volume Two, From the French Revolution to the Present* (New York: Norton, 1996).

Lewis Mumford, *The City in History: Its Origins, Its Transformations, and Its Prospects* (New York: Harcourt, Brace & World, 1961).

Mumford, *The Culture of Cities* (New York: Harcourt, Brace, 1938).

Mumford, *Technics and Civilization* (New York: Harcourt, Brace, 1934).

EMPIRES AND NATION-STATES: POLITICAL GEOGRAPHY

Independence and Imperialism. European overseas empires changed significantly from 1750 to 1914. On the one hand, European states lost colonies to independence movements that swept the late eighteenth and early nineteenth centuries, especially in the British, French, and Spanish dominions. The United States became fully independent of Great Britain in 1783, and Canada, Australia, and New Zealand became self-governing nations within the British Commonwealth by the early twentieth century. Many Spanish and some French colonies on islands in the Caribbean Sea became independent, and in Central and South America Spanish colonies separated from their mother countries as well. The sole Portuguese American colony, Brazil, was also liberated.

New Imperialism. However, in other parts of the globe the pattern was exactly the opposite as the "New Imperialism" took hold in the late nineteenth century. Indeed, Great Britain was expanding its imperial dominion throughout the nineteenth century, especially in southern Asia, adding on average one hundred thousand square miles annually between 1815 and 1905. After Italy became unified in 1860, and Germany became a state in 1871, its leaders were no different than those of other European powers in deciding that international policy must be imperialistic.

Berlin Conference. These designs were clearly expressed at the Berlin Conference in 1884–1885 organized by Chancellor Otto von Bismarck of the German

FRENCH IMPERIALISM

Jules Ferry, twice premier of the French Third Republic between 1880 and 1885, clearly expressed the views of the New Imperialists. He linked French colonial policy with national prosperity and social stability. The lack of an effective policy creating or locating markets for Europe's industrial goods could breed revolution by depressing wages (because of oversupply of products) and creating labor unrest, yet he also saw clearly that imperialism was rooted in international competition, and, despite the necessity for every successful nation to have a colonial policy, portended war.

Colonial policy is the child of the industrial revolution. For wealthy countries where capital abounds and accumulates fast, where industry is expanding steadily, where even agriculture must become mechanized in order to survive, exports are essential for public prosperity. Both demand for labor and scope for capital investment depend on the foreign market. With the arrival of the latest industrial giants, the United States and Germany; of Italy, newly resurrected, not to mention Russia waiting in the wings, Europe has embarked on a competitive course from which she will be unable to turn back. All over the world the raising of high tariffs has resulted in the appearance of fierce competition. The European consumer-goods market is saturated; unless we declare modern society bankrupt and prepare, at the dawn of the twentieth century, for its liquidation by revolution (the consequences of which we can scarcely foresee), new consumer markets will have to be created in other parts of the world. Colonial policy is an international manifestation of the eternal laws of competition.

Source: Jules Ferry, *Le Tonkin et La mere patrie* (Paris: Victor-Harvard, 1890).

Second Reich. The negotiations over the scramble for African colonies by Europeans occurred without African leaders present. In an age of Social Darwinism this slight was justified on the grounds that non-Europeans, including Africans, were biologically inferior beings who could only suffer in the age of the "survival of the fittest."

Markets. The international competition for colonies to serve as markets for home industry exports and as sources for the all-important raw materials for industry (such as rubber, copper, minerals, and, by 1900, oil) escalated in the late 1870s and triggered the New Imperialism. The prime target of European powers was the continent of Africa, so rich in raw materials. By 1900 only Ethiopia and tiny coastal Liberia remained independent of European control. Almost as dramatically, the British, French, and Dutch expanded their empires in South and Southeast Asia. Even the coast of China was carved up into competing European spheres of influences. Russia, too, extended its imperial grasp of non-Europeans in the Caucasus, Central Asia, and the Siberian Pacific. The New Imperialism, especially Ger-

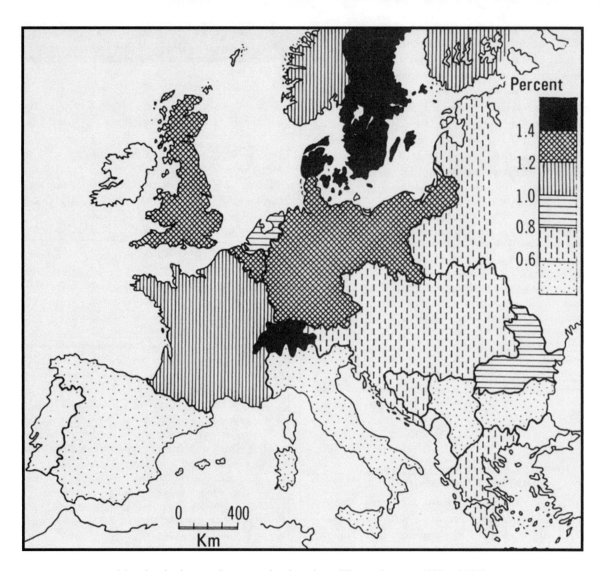

Map showing increase in gross national product of Europe between 1830 and 1910
(from N. J. G. Pounds, *An Historical Geography of Europe,* 1990)

many's aggressive expansionism in Africa and its attempt in southeast Europe, was a prime cause of World War I (1914–1918).

Sojourners vs. Settlers. The expansion of the New Imperialism was staffed by what geographers call "sojourner colonists," or impermanent Europeans abroad who intended to retire to Europe once their service obligations were completed. If one adds to the imperial cultural map former "settler colonies," or sites where Europeans remained permanently, like North America, Australasia (collective name for Australia and New Zealand), and Latin America, then the European influence across the globe becomes truly unrivaled by any other continent.

Nation-States. Historical atlases display the changing map of Europe as the boundaries of some nation-states expanded while others contracted. Amazingly, by 1914 nation-states were found not only in western, central, and northern Europe but also in southern Europe, including the Balkans. The nationalist ide-

ology of the French Revolution could not be contained by conservative forces despite the defeat of Napoleon Bonaparte in 1815. Italy in 1860 and Germany in 1871 appear as unified nations for the first time. Piedmont and Prussia acted as cores for the integration of Italy and Germany, respectively. Expansion of these states from their core regions occurred both by peaceful and violent means. Also, nationalists in the new Italy and Germany, as in later nation-states, demanded further expansion to liberate irredenta or unredeemed brethren outside their national frontiers. For example, Italy claimed Corsica, controlled by France, while Germany wanted Austria. As Europeans expanded their empires abroad under the aegis of the New Imperialism, the sprawling empires within Europe were soon to be dissolved in the name of the sovereignty of the self-determined nation-state. Although the Austrian, Ottoman, and Russian empires would endure to World War I, the peace settlement ending the war in 1919 broke them apart. The Germans were also stripped of their colonies. The victors—principally the British, the French, and the

Americans—understood the war as, in part, the product of imperial competition, and in the name of peace and international stability they announced the directive of national self-determination that theoretically liberated a nation's people from foreign oppressors. As a result, Russia lost its western frontier, including Finland, Estonia, Latvia, and Poland, all which became new nation-states. Also, Austria became a "head without a body" as new nation-states of Hungary, Czechoslovakia, and Yugoslavia split away.

Sources:

Tibor I. Berend and Gyorgy Ranki, *The European Periphery and Industrialization, 1780–1914* (Cambridge & New York: Cambridge University Press, 1982).

Eric J. Hobsbawm, *The Age of Empire, 1875–1914* (New York: Pantheon, 1987).

Roy E. H. Mellor, *Nation, State, and Territory: A Political Geography* (London & New York: Routledge, 1989).

Richard Muir, *Political Geography: A New Introduction* (New York: John Wiley, 1997).

John R. Short, *An Introduction to Political Geography* (London & Boston: Routledge & Kegan Paul, 1982).

LANGUAGE AND RELIGION: CULTURAL GEOGRAPHY

Language. The physical diversity of Europe is reflected by its cultural variety expressed in language. The languages spoken by nine out of ten Europeans in the nineteenth century were Indo-European. The most important subfamilies within this heritage are the Romance, Germanic, and Slavic. Speakers of Romance languages generally inhabit western and southern Europe and include the Spanish, Portuguese, Catalans, French, and Italians. Romanian is also a Romance language. Geographically, the region of Romance dominance reflects the areas where the Roman Empire was most deeply established, and, not surprisingly, Romance languages are in part derived from Latin. Germanic languages dominate in northwestern, central, and northern Europe, all regions never completely integrated into the Roman Empire. By the nineteenth century these languages included English, German, Dutch, and the Scandinavian tongues of Swedish, Norwegian, Danish, and Icelandic. The third major subfamily of the common Indo-European stock is Slavic. Again, beyond Roman influence, the Slavic languages geographically encompass parts of central Europe (Polish, Czech, and Slovak), parts of southern Europe including all of the Balkans (Serbian, Croatian, Slovenian, Macedonian, Montenegrin, and Bulgarian), and all of eastern Europe (Russian, Ukrainian, and Belorussian). Minor Indo-European subfamilies include Celtic (Irish, Scots Gaelic, Welsh, and Breton), Baltic (Latvian and Lithuanian), Greek, and Albanian. Of the 10 percent of Europeans who do not speak an Indo-European tongue, the largest groups are the Uralic Finns of Finland, the Magyars of Hungary, the Altaic Turks in the southeastern Balkans, and the Basques in northwestern Spain.

Mind-Set. The significance of these languages in understanding Europe during the industrial era is how they contributed to the powerful mind-set of nationalism. As Europeans increasingly embraced their nation-states with emotional commitment and loyalty, national pride came to be expressed in terms of national distinction. This development, in turn, was linked to linguistic uniqueness and solidarity. One of the defining characteristics of a nation came to be its national language.

Religion. Another politically and culturally significant aspect of Europe during the period under consideration was religion. Like language, it served to unify regions and nations culturally and distinguish them from others. Europe had three dominant religions between 1750 and 1914: Roman Catholic Christianity, Protestant Christianity, and Orthodox Christianity. The regions that remained within the Church of Rome during the Reformation of the sixteenth century largely encompassed southern Europe (Italy, Spain, and Portugal) and parts of western and central Europe (France and portions of Germany such as Bavaria). Protestantism splintered into countless sects during the Reformation and after, but, in general, the geographic regions of these branches of Christianity that renounced the authority of the Church of Rome were located in northern and central Europe (most of Great Britain, Scandinavia, and northern portions of Germany). Orthodox Christianity dominates in eastern Europe (including Russia) where, unlike Protestantism, it did not emerge as a result of a break with Rome during the Reformation. It had been independent of Rome since the time of the Roman Empire. Its believers stretched southward into the Balkans, and thus Orthodox Christianity was, and is, the dominant faith in Serbia, Macedonia, Romania, and Bulgaria as well as Russia, Belarus, and Ukraine in the former Soviet Union. Islam also found its adherents in Europe, but only in the extreme southeastern section. The Ottoman Turks had controlled Greece and part of the Balkans until well into the nineteenth century (Greece gained its independence in 1829), and so the dominant religion in Bosnia and Albania, as examples, was Islam. Judaism, another of the world's great religions, also counted its adherents within Europe, but nowhere were they in the majority. Centuries of persecution had forced Jews to be mobile (they were often expelled from cities, and sometimes even from entire kingdoms), but during the nineteenth century more were clustered in the cities of central and eastern Europe than anywhere else. Where a religion was dominant, it often served the forces of nationalism. Catholicism in Ireland linked up with nationalism and together led the charge toward home rule (granted in 1922) and eventually independence from the foreign (and Protestant) "oppressor," Great Britain. Religion could, indeed, have political ramifications.

Sources:

Ernest Gellner, *Nations and Nationalism* (Ithaca, N.Y.: Cornell University Press, 1983).

John Merriman, *A History of Modern Europe: Volume Two, From the French Revolution to the Present* (New York: Norton, 1996).

Christopher Moseley and R. E. Asher, eds., *Atlas of the World's Languages* (London & New York: Routledge, 1994).

Lester Rowntree, and others, *Diversity Amid Globalization* (Upper Saddle River, N.J.: Prentice Hall, 2000).

PROFESSIONALIZATION: GEOGRAPHY AS A DISCIPLINE

Second Age of Expansion. The works of geographers and the creation of academic positions for geography were spurred by nationalism and imperialism. Cartographers knew the basic outline of the continents and oceans by the beginning of the industrial era. The period between 1750 and 1914 was known as a "second age of expansion" when surveying the properties of flora, fauna, and the known land was emphasized.

Professional Geographers. The Prussian geographer Alexander von Humboldt was a prime example of this emphasis as he surveyed the Andes and Mexico before returning to Berlin to enjoy political and intellectual influence in the Prussian royal court. It was also during this period that the first university geography professorship was created in the German states at Berlin for Karl Ritter in 1820. After unification, German geography really advanced, and in the 1880s several more university chairs were created in the new empire. One chair went to Friedrich Ratzel at Leipzig in 1886, the father of German geopolitics. He argued that the state was an organism that needed lebensraum (living space). His ideas were enunciated by Karl Haushofer during the Nazi regime in the 1930s.

Atlas. Many atlases stressing national history also proliferated during this era as the new states were portrayed to indicate their wealth and prestige. The Prussian General Staff had created the first atlas for Prussia in 1828. Karl Spruner created the first comprehensive historical atlas of Europe in 1846 that emphasized German history, especially their military victories. August Meitzen created another atlas for Prussia in 1869. However, no truly national atlases were created in Europe before World War I, with the exception of Finland. For Germany the reason given by Alois Mayr, a modern geographer, is that the nation was considered larger than the actual physical state. Only in the 1990s after reunification was the first German national atlas published. In France the first major atlas was published in 1894 by Paul Vidal de la Blache and emphasized the uniqueness of the provinces of the grand nation. He became the father of French geography from his professorship at the Sorbonne (University of Paris) after 1898.

Mackinder. In Britain the first famous geographer was Halford Mackinder, who held the first chair in geography at Oxford in 1887 and created the first geography department there in 1899. Mackinder is known for his depiction in 1904 of the northern Eurasian heartland as the "geographical pivot of history." Mackinder argued that control of eastern Europe is critical for dominating Eurasia, and that a superpower, either Germany or Russia, could emerge there to threaten British hegemony.

Sources:

Jeremy Black, *Maps and History: Constructing Images of the Past* (New Haven: Yale University Press, 1997).

"The First German National Atlas," *Rheinischer Merkor* (11 April 2002): 10.

David Livingstone, *The Geographical Tradition* (Oxford: Blackwell, 1992).

D. W. Meinig, "A Macrogeography of Western Imperialism," in *Settlement and Encounter*, edited by Fay Gale and Graham Lawton (Melbourne: Oxford University Press, 1969).

Mark Monmonier, "The Rise of the National Atlas," *Cartographica* 3 (1994): 1–15.

Hugh Seton-Watson, *Nations and States: An Inquiry into the Origins of Nations and the Politics of Nationalism* (Boulder, Colo.: Westview Press, 1977).

SIGNIFICANT PEOPLE

ALEXANDER VON HUMBOLDT

1769-1859

NATURALIST, TRAVELER AND STATESMAN

Early Life and Career. Alexander von Humboldt was born in Berlin, the son of a Prussian military officer. His older brother Wilhelm became a famous linguist. Alexander attended the University of Gottingen and then studied at the School of Mines in Freiburg. In 1795 he was appointed supervisor in chief in the Prussian Department of Mines in Berlin. Enriched by an inheritance upon his mother's death in 1796, Humboldt resigned his post in the government and prepared for his five-year exploration of Latin America with the French botanist Aimé Bonpland.

Voyages and Books. Humboldt and Bonpland voyaged up the Orinoco River in Venezuela and climbed the Andes of Columbia, Equador and Peru, recording botanical and biological data gathered along the way. Later they explored central Mexico and Cuba. Their voyages gained renown, and on their way back to Europe, Humboldt visited Philadelphia and Washington, D.C. In the American capital he was the guest of President Thomas Jefferson for a week. Upon returning to Europe, Humboldt settled in Paris, remaining there from 1804 until 1827. Here he wrote his multivolume descriptions of his observations, investigations, and experiences in Latin America. These writings had great influence upon young Charles Darwin, but it earned Humboldt little money. Destitute, Humboldt accepted the position of chamberlain at the court of the king of Prussia and returned to Berlin in 1827. Two years later he set out again on a voyage of observation and investigation of nature. This time he headed east, exploring Siberia and Central Asia in the Russian empire. After this journey he retired to the life of a writer, and spent the last thirty years of his life writing his great composite work, *Kosmos* (five volumes, 1845–1862).

Historical Significance. On his travels through Latin America, Humboldt observed more than flora and fauna. He also saw firsthand the human impact of Spanish imperial dominion. As a result, Humboldt became a noteworthy critic of slavery and authoritarianism in the Spanish empire. He published his views during his time in Paris, a four-volume work titled *Political Essays on the Kingdom of New Spain.* The first volume appeared in 1811 and the last in 1822. His critical views of authoritarianism and imperialism earned him the suspicion of political conservatives who were ascendant in Europe after the fall of Napoleon Bonaparte, and his reputation followed him even after he arrived in the Prussian court in Berlin in 1827. Humboldt's scientific reputation, however, was great enough to protect him from retribution.

Methodology. Humboldt embraced the empirical emphasis that positivistic science placed on rigorous observation, but he challenged those who stressed the dominance of nature by man. Instead, as displayed in his major work *Kosmos,* Humboldt argued for an ecological view of man as a part of a larger whole, the natural world. Unlike his fellow Berlin geographer Karl Ritter, Humboldt's vision found no place for God, not even as a creator. In the present age of environmental degradation, the vision of Humboldt is no longer scorned as romantic pseudoscience, but rather as a corrective to the arrogance of earlier inductive positivism which claimed to be objective and progressive. Industrial pollution has become a major by-product of human dedication to controlling nature, and Humboldt's emphasis upon interconnected ecosystems has become a popular alternative. In Humboldt's words, "I have . . . endeavored to comprehend the phenomena of physical objects in their general connection, and to represent nature as on a great whole, moved and animated by internal forces."

Sources:

Margarita Bowen, *Empiricism and Geographical Thought: From Francis Bacon to Alexander von Humboldt* (Cambridge: Cambridge University Press, 1981).

Helmut de Terra, *Humboldt: The Life and Times of Alexander von Humboldt, 1769–1859* (New York: Knopf, 1955).

Richard Hartshorne, *The Nature of Geography: A Critical Survey of Current Thought in the Light of the Past* (Lancaster, Pa.: Association of American Geographers, 1939).

L. Kellner, *Alexander von Humboldt* (London & New York: Oxford University Press, 1963).

HALFORD MACKINDER

1861-1947
GEOPOLITICIAN

Career. Halford Mackinder was born in Gainsborough, in Lincolnshire, England, the eldest son of a doctor. He studied natural science at Oxford University and graduated in 1883; four years later he gained a chair in geography at that university which he held until 1905. In 1899 he created a geography department, contributing to the institutional professionalization of geographical study. This development also illustrates what was occurring throughout the social sciences at the time, the formation of distinct "disciplines." From 1903 to 1908 he served as Director of the London School of Economics. Shortly thereafter he entered politics and was elected to Parliament as a Conservative, where he served from 1910 to 1922.

Scholarship. His first significant publication was the article "The Scope and Methods of Geography." Here he formulated methods of geographical inquiry and helped to lay the foundation of the new discipline. In this article he stated that to properly understand human activity of any kind, one must first place it upon its physical geographic base. Indeed, human activity could not be fully understood apart from its formative geographical context. He exemplified this method in *Britain and the British Seas*, which he published in 1902. This book is a case study of regional geography in which Mackinder deftly and intricately depicts the geographic base of Britain's political power. His most influential work, however, is the article "The Geographical Pivot of History," published in 1904. Mackinder expanded his idea in the book *Democratic Ideals and Reality*, which appeared in 1919. In the article and the book he advanced the following: "Who rules East Europe commands the Heartland: Who rules the Heartland commands the World-Island: Who rules the World Island commands the World." This idea was granted even greater credence in the 1930s and 1940s with the competition between Germany and the Soviet Union and may have influenced Karl Haushofer, the Nazi geopolitician, to urge Adolf Hitler to invade the U.S.S.R. in 1941.

The Discipline. Mackinder also is famous for holding the first university chair in geography and establishing the contours of the new discipline through his influential writings. In doing so he moved geography away from environmental determinism without compromising the environmental perspective of the field (here he was influenced by the writings of the Germans Alexander von Humboldt and Karl Ritter). He envisioned a geopolitical application of his ideas and affirmed that the knowledge gained from geographical study could strengthen and further unify Britain's empire as it faced the rising power of Germany in the late nineteenth and early twentieth centuries. For Mackinder the New Imperialism and the new discipline of Geography mutually reinforced one another.

Sources:
Brian W. Blouet, *Halford Mackinder: A Biography* (College Station: Texas A & M University Press, 1987).

David Livingston, *The Geographical Tradition* (Oxford: Blackwell, 1992).

W. H. Parker, *Mackinder: Geography as an Aid to Statecraft* (Oxford: Clarendon Press, 1982).

PAUL VIDAL DE LA BLACHE

1845-1918
GEOGRAPHER

Academic Positions. Paul Vidal de La Blache was born in a small village in Mediterranean France, the son of a French high-school language teacher. He graduated from the Ecole Normale Supérieure in Paris in 1866 and taught in Athens, Greece, for four years before gaining his doctorate in History at the University of Paris in 1872. That year Vidal de La Blache accepted a post as professor of history and geography at the University of Nancy. While there he traveled frequently in Germany, where academic geography was much better established. In 1877 he accepted the new position in geography at the Ecole Normale Supérieure. While there he was a co-founder of the academic journal *Annales de Géographie* and author of *Histoire et Géographie: Atlas Général* (1894). In 1898 Vidal de La Blache attained a chair in geography at the University of Paris (the Sorbonne). In 1903 his classic *Tableau de la Géographie de la France* was published; *Principles of Human Geography* appeared in print posthumously in 1922.

Annales School. Vidal de La Blache was the founder of academic geography in France. In addition, his students were leaders of the second generation of professional French geographers. These students as well as their teacher were inspirational in starting the Annales school of French historiography, which emerged with the journal *Annales: économies, sociétés, civilisations* in 1929 under the leadership of Lucien Febvre and Marc Bloch. The emphasis upon the foundational importance of geography on historical inquiry received its greatest champion in the Annaliste historian Fernand Braudel. Vidal de La Blache developed the idea of "possibilism" with regard to environmental influence on humans, allowing an escape from environmental determinism. His concept of *genre de vie* emphasized the ecological view of man, similar to Alexander von Humboldt's geographical vision. As Vidal de La Blache wrote in *Tableau*:

> A geographical identity does not result from simple considerations of geology and climate. It is not a thing endowed

in advance by nature. We must abandon the idea that a country is a reservoir of dormant energies created by nature, waiting for man to employ them. It is man who, in bending those resources to his own ends, brings to light the geographic identity of a country. He establishes a connection between unrelated traits; on the incoherent effects of local circumstance, he imposes a systematic order. It is thus that a country comes to be defined and differentiated, and becomes at long last like a medallion engraved with the effigy of a people.

Braudel praised Vidal de La Blache in volume one of *The Identity of France* (1986). In fact, the last one-third of this classic text is called "Was France Invented By Its Geography?", and it is devoted to answering Vidal de La Blache's call for an investigation of the "possible" Frances. Braudel's answer is in accord with Vidal de La Blache's teaching: emphatically no!

Sources:

Fernand Braudel, *The Identity of France. Volume One: History and Environment* (New York: Harper & Row, 1988).

Anne Buttimer, *Society and Milieu in the French Geographic Tradition* (Chicago: Association of American Geographers, 1971).

Paul Vidal de La Blache, *Principles of Human Geography,* translated by Millicent Todd Bingham (New York: Holt, 1926).

DOCUMENTARY SOURCES

Atlas Geografickeskii, Istoricheskii i Chronlogicheskii Rossiiskago (Geographical, Historical, and Chronological Atlas of Russia, 1845)—Analyzes the expansion of Russia without a discussion of the non-Russians within the imperial borders.

C. Colbeck, *The Public Schools Historical Atlas* (1885)—Text that glorifies the British empire.

Charles Dickens, *Hard Times* (1859)—Depicts the environmental pollution, utilitarian education and exploitation of the Industrial Revolution in fictional Coketown based on Preston in northern England.

Johann Gottfried von Herder, *Idea for a Philosophy of History for Mankind,* 4 volumes (1784–1791)—Argues that humans are social beings who need to nurture their national culture rather than a cosmopolitan or universal culture because each linguistic or natural group possesses its own geographical heritage.

Alexander von Humboldt, *Kosmos,* 5 volumes (1845–1862)—A study of the natural world without the invocation of a designer, prime mover, or God; greatly admired and read by Charles Darwin, this work has a holistic or ecological view of man in nature.

Humboldt, *Political Essays on the Kingdom of New Spain,* 4 volumes (1811–1822)—Criticizes the exploitation of slaves and serfs in the Spanish colony of Mexico. Humboldt was disliked by European conservatives for his liberalism.

Lamothe, *Carte des agrandissements successifs de la France sous la monarchie, la république et l'empire* (Atlas of the Successive Additions of France under the Monarchy, the Republic and the Empire, 1873)—Written after the debacle of the Franco-Prussian War of 1870–1871, this atlas asserts the general trend of French expansionism despite the recent setback.

Halford Mackinder, *Britain and the British Seas* (1902)—Regional geography of the British Isles and neighboring seas which minutely depicts the physical base of Britain's geopolitical position and power.

Friedrich Ratzel, *Anthropogeographie,* 2 volumes (Anthropogeography, 1882–1891)—A debate continues about whether this work is a case of environmental determinism (that society is determined by its geography).

Ratzel, *Politische Geographie* (Political Geography, 1897)—Argues that the state is an organism that needs lebensraum, or living space; this work greatly influenced Nazi geopoliticians.

Karl Spruner, *Historical Geographical Hand Atlas of the History of the European States from the Middle Ages to the Present* (1846)—Possibly the first true historical atlas; the Germans are emphasized, especially their military victories.

Paul Vidal de La Blache, *Description of the Geography of France* (1903)—Emphasizes the way of life of various provinces from an ecological perspective.

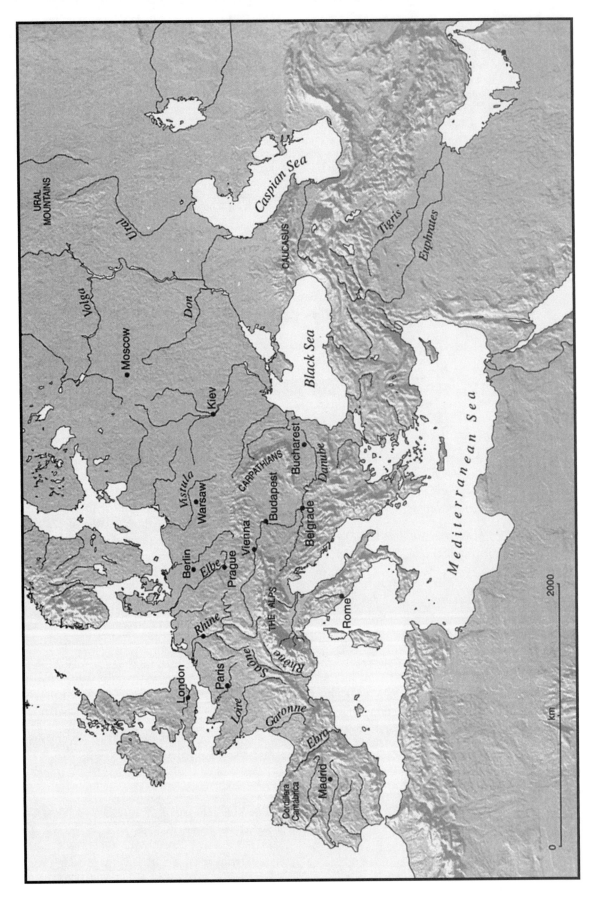

Physical map of Europe (from Brian Graham, ed., *Modern Europe,* 1998)

THE ARTS

by JAMES R. FARR

CONTENTS

Sidebars and tables are listed in italics.

1753
- In his *Essai sur l'architecture* (Essay on Architecture) French architect Marc-Antoine Laugier asserts that the buildings of his contemporaries should be modeled on the architecture of the ancient Greeks and Romans.

1756
- Wolfgang Amadeus Mozart is born.

1759-1767
- Influenced by French satirist François Rabelais and British philosopher John Locke, Laurence Sterne's eccentric novel *Tristram Shandy* is published in installments in England. Later scholars call it a precursor of the twentieth-century stream-of-consciousness novel.

1762
- At six years of age Mozart tours Europe as a child prodigy keyboardist.

1764
- At the age of eight Mozart composes his first symphony.
- Johann Winckelmann publishes *Geschichte der Kunst des Altertums* (The History of Ancient Art), which establishes the artistic principles of the Classical movement.

1767
- Jean-Jacques Rousseau writes his *Dictionnaire de musique* (Dictionary of Music).

1774
- Johann Wolfgang von Goethe publishes *Die Leiden des jungen Werthers* (The Sorrows of Young Werther), an early, best-selling Romantic novel.

1791
- Mozart's first German-language opera, *Die Zauberflöte* (The Magic Flute) is performed in Vienna, illustrating the growing importance of cultural nationalism in music.

1793
- Jacques-Louis David completes his painting *The Murder of Marat*, revealing his sympathies for the Jacobins, who have taken the French Revolution in a radical direction.
- At the age of eleven Niccolò Paganini makes his debut in Genoa as a violin virtuoso.

1800
- Madame Germaine de Staël publishes *De la littérature considérée dans ses rapports avec les institutions sociales* (Of Literature Considered in Relation to Social Institutions), widely considered the first book to discuss the influence of social history and environment on literature.

* DENOTES CIRCA DATE

1804

- Now embarking on the middle phase of his career, Ludwig van Beethoven completes his Third Symphony, the "Eroica," signaling the expansion of the sound, score, and orchestra of Romantic music.

1807

- David completes *The Coronation of Napoleon,* revealing his adaptability to political circumstances in France.

1808-1809

- Beethoven completes three major orchestral works: his Fifth and Sixth Symphonies and his Piano Concerto No. 5.

1810-1814

- Francisco Goya creates *The Horrors of War,* a series of etchings depicting the suppression of Spanish nationalism during the Napoleonic occupation of Spain.

1813

- The founding of the London Philharmonic Society is part of a movement toward the professionalization of orchestras.

1814

- Goya completes two of his greatest paintings, *The Second of May 1808,* and *The Third of May 1808,* depicting the French invasion of Spain and exposing the brutality of war in general.

1818

- The Prado Museum is founded in Madrid, part of the emergence of the museum as a site for the public display of art.

1824

- Romantic poet George Gordon, Lord Byron, is killed in battle at Mussolonghi in the Greek war for independence from Turkey.

- Now entirely deaf, Beethoven completes and conducts his Symphony No. 9, "The Choral Symphony."

1829

- In Great Britain, Sir Charles Wheatstone patents the concertina (a form of accordion), an instrument for playing popular rather than orchestral music.

1830-1848

- Honoré de Balzac publishes *La Comédie humaine* (The Human Comedy), a series of ninety-one novels and stories.

* DENOTES CIRCA DATE

1834
- Composer Hector Berlioz completes his symphony *Harold en Italie* (Harold in Italy), based on Byron's poem *Childe Harold's Pilgrimage* (1812–1818), proclaiming that Romantic literature and music share the same inspiration.

1835
- Gaetano Donizetti's opera *Lucia di Lammermoor,* based on a novel by Walter Scott, has its premiere in Naples.

1836
- British architect A. W. N. Pugin publishes *Contrasts,* praising the Christian virtues of medieval Gothic architecture and asserting that the character of a nation is linked to the quality of its architecture.

1838
- The National Gallery opens in London.

1840
- Swabian merchant Max Schneckenburger writes the poem "Wacht am Rhine" (The Watch on the Rhine). Set to music in 1854, it becomes a popular German patriotic song during the Franco-Prussian War in 1870–1871.

1842
- Ostensibly about the Babylonian captivity of Old Testament Hebrews by the Assyrian king Nebuchadnezzar, Giuseppe Verdi's new opera *Nabucco* is a thinly veiled call for a unified and independent Italy.

1846
- The Paris Opera House is illuminated for the first time by electric-arc lighting.

1848–1876
- Richard Wagner's operatic cycle *Der Ring des Nibelungen* (The Ring of the Nibelungen) proclaims the cultural identity of Germany, which finally achieves political unity in 1871.

1850–1851
- Joseph Paxton designs the Crystal Palace and supervises its construction in London on the site of the Great Exhibition of 1851. Made of iron and glass, it brings together architecture and industrialism.

1853
- Baron Georges Haussmann begins the reconstruction of Paris with wide boulevards and expansive parks such as the Bois de Boulogne, creating the first modern city.

* DENOTES CIRCA DATE

1854-1868
- French architect Eugéne-Emmanuel Viollet-le-Duc publishes *Dictionnaire raisonné de l'architecture française du XIe au XVIe siècle* (Dictionary of French Architecture from the Eleventh to the Sixteenth Century), in which he calls Gothic architecture a perfected structural form.

1857
- Gustave Flaubert publishes *Madame Bovary,* a realistic novel about a middle-class woman who resorts to adultery to relieve the boredom of her stultifying marriage.

1858
- The rebuilding of the Ringstrasse in Vienna accomplishes for the Austrian capital what "Haussmanization" has done for Paris—the creation of a modern city through which masses of people can move efficiently.

1863
- French painter Edouard Manet leads the opening of the "Salon des refusés," a controversial exhibition of paintings that have been rejected by the jury of the official Salon of the French Academy.

1865-1869
- Leo Tolstoy publishes *Voina i mir* (War and Peace), a Realistic novel set just before Napoleon's 1812 invasion of Russia.

1867
- An edition of the first part of Goethe's *Faust* (1808) is the initial publication in the first paperback series, the Reclams Universal Bibliotek of Leipzig, an innovation that is part of the growing commercialization of literature.
- The World's Fair in Paris introduces Japanese art to the West, having a major influence on Manet's style.

1871
- The words of the socialist anthem "L'Internationale" (The International) are written by a French worker, Eugène Pottier. Put to music in 1888 by Adolphe Degeyter, "L'Internationale" is soon adopted by the Socialist International organization and becomes one of the most widely sung songs in the world.

1874
- The first Impressionist exhibition is held in Paris; the name of this new artistic movement comes from *Impression: Sunrise* (1872), one of Claude Monet's paintings in the exhibit.
- Bedrich Smetana completes *Ma Vlast* (My Fatherland), a cycle of symphonic poems illustrating the connection between nationalism and music.

1875-1877
- Leo Tolstoy publishes *Anna Karenina,* a novel about an unhappily married woman who resorts to adultery.

* DENOTES CIRCA DATE

1878
- American expatriate painter James Whistler sues renowned art critic John Ruskin for libel, citing Ruskin's essay on Whistler's work *Nocturne in Black and Gold: A Falling Rocket*, which accuses the painter of "flinging a pot of paint in the public's face."

1882
- The Berlin Philharmonic Orchestra is founded.

1891
- French painter Paul Gauguin emigrates from Europe and settles in Tahiti.
- A posthumous exhibition of paintings by Gauguin's friend Vincent van Gogh (died 1890) opens at the Salon des Independents in Paris.

1900
- Gauguin writes *Noa Noa*, an account of his life and travels in Tahiti.

1902
- Acclaimed operatic tenor Enrico Caruso makes his first recording for a new invention, the phonograph.

1903
- The first "feature" motion picture, *The Great Train Robbery*, is released. At twelve minutes in length, it is the longest movie made to date.
- The first phonographic recording of a complete opera, Verdi's *Ernani*, is released.

1904
- The first radio transmission of music is broadcast in Graz, Austria.

1908
- Architect Peter Behrens designs and constructs the first all steel and glass building, the A.E.G. Turbine Factory in Berlin, Germany.

1914
- Charlie Chaplin appears in his first movie, *Making a Living*.

* Denotes Circa Date

OVERVIEW

The Onset of Change. In 1750 the countries of Europe were poised for radical transformation in all aspects of life, including the arts. Revolutionary changes in economics, politics, and society were about to affect how Europeans expressed themselves and their perceptions of the world in art, architecture, literature, and music. These changes also influenced how people viewed, read, or heard artistic creations and what they expected from them. Even though it is possible to chart a general succession of various artistic "styles" in European art between 1750 and 1914—Classicism, Romanticism, Realism, Impressionism, and Modernism—one must be wary of too rigidly defining the characteristics of any one style. Still, when World War I broke out in 1914, the Classicism that was the dominant mode in 1750 was but a distant memory in a culturally fragmented Western world, where Modernism was establishing itself as the leading artistic style. Like diplomatic missives, declarations of war, or philosophical treatises, artistic images, texts, and sounds can be interpreted as evidence of the shifting beliefs, values, fears, and desires of European artists and their audiences. Historical artifacts—including works of art—must be understood within the context in which they were produced, distributed, and consumed. Why artists chose their subjects and how they decided to portray them were influenced by a variety of intermingled factors, such as spiritual or philosophic concerns, financial reward or necessity, political or social commitment, the desires of an audience (patrons or consumers), and even advertising. Keenly aware of some of these factors while sensing others only vaguely, European artists and their audiences between 1750 and 1914 were caught in a world of dramatic change, and the art of that era reveals some of the deepest meanings of that transformation.

Art in a Court Society. In the middle of the eighteenth century the ruling elite of Europe was organized in what historians have called a court society. The men and women at the apex of the social pyramid, a small minority of the total population, gathered together at various courts. In sumptuous palaces their stylized behavior and luxurious adornment announced to themselves and the rest of society that they possessed a distinction legitimizing their superior position in society as a whole. At the core of this social constellation was a political figure—a king, prince, or duke. Distinction and legitimacy were the twin pillars of this court society, and artists of the time (almost entirely men) were valued deeply because they could produce the beautiful artifacts that symbolized the superiority of this elite. As a result, artists lived largely at the behest of this ruling group.

Aristocratic Patrons. Sometimes churches, cities, or guilds also provided commissions for artists; yet, no artist could survive without a patron. In a world dominated by court society, an artist did not produce his works for an anonymous public to purchase on the open market. The artist was employed by a patron and was commanded to produce artistic works such as paintings, buildings, poems, plays, or symphonies for that patron and a small circle of his or her friends and associates. Thus, art in court society was essentially produced for a narrow audience.

New Wealth, New Publics. The major political, economic, and social changes that struck Europe in the latter half of the eighteenth and the early years of the nineteenth century deeply affected art and artists. By the middle of the eighteenth century, Europe was in the midst of what historians have called a "consumer revolution" stimulated by growing urbanization, population expansion, and a subsequent quickening of demand for everyday consumer goods that resulted in a burgeoning of Continental and Transatlantic trade in them. An Industrial Revolution was in its early stages, supplying vast quantities of cotton textiles for an expanding market. All these developments generated new wealth and opened new markets while enlarging existing ones. A growing mercantile and industrial class rode this wave to prosperity. This consumer and industrial revolution, which brought ever more products into an increasingly complex and diversified market, contributed directly to the commodification of art. Artists (led by painters, playwrights, novelists, and the occasional musician) plunged into a world of growing and anonymous publics that purchased artistic products in the open market. Merchants and industrialists were just as eager as the courtly aristocracy to enlist art and artists in the quest to proclaim distinction, but this new class did so through purchase in the market rather than through private patronage. As a result, artists increasingly severed their ties with patrons and gradually came to depend on sales rather than commissions for survival.

Impact of the Industrial Revolution. As machines moved more and more to the center of production technique and new forms of energy were tapped to power them (first steam and later electricity), the capacity to produce expanded dramatically. These transformations in the economy directly affected society, for good and ill, and artists frequently commented on it. Some, such as British writers William Blake (1757–1827) and Charles Dickens (1812–1870), bemoaned the carnage of the industrial landscape and the dehumanized bodies and souls of factory workers. Others, such as French writer Honoré de Balzac (1799–1850), ridiculed the heartless industrial capitalist who cared more for profit than human dignity. Still others, including German painter Caspar David Friedrich (1774–1840) and British poet William Wordsworth (1770–1850), escaped industrial and urban blight by retreating to nature, where they developed a new appreciation for its mysterious beauty, its stillness and tranquility, and its awesome power.

Political Revolution and Reaction. The Industrial Revolution was not the only revolution affecting artistic representation, for changes in politics were equally important. Beginning in 1789, French revolutionaries challenged the political ideology of absolutism that concentrated political authority in the person of their king. The subsequent dismantling of the absolutist political system (ending with the beheading in 1793 of the deposed king, Louis XVI) was followed by political experiments ranging from constitutional monarchy to representative republic, all in the name of freedom and sometimes equality. (What freedom and equality meant, however, continued to be hotly disputed.) Artists joined the fray with words and images. Some, such as French painter Jacques-Louis David (1748–1825), championed revolution as the march of progress toward the perfect polity that would secure the freedom of the individual, while others, including British poet Samuel Taylor Coleridge (1772–1834), feared the anarchy that freedom and equality seemed to unleash. As Napoleon Bonaparte seized the reins of the French Revolution in 1799 and claimed he was using his power to accomplish its goals, artists everywhere in Europe lined up for or against his designs. Napoleon's fall from power in 1814 ushered in a conservative political reaction throughout Europe, which was led by Austria under the guidance of its chief minister, Klemens von Metternich. Some artists, including French musician Hector Berlioz (1803–1869), considered this reaction a bridling of individual rights and freedom. Throughout the nineteenth century the specter of revolution was never far from European politics. In 1848, for example, revolutions erupted almost everywhere in Europe, in the name of greater political freedom for more people. The revolutionaries were not all in agreement about which members of society should gain such freedom (generally understood as the right to participate in governance). Middle-class men seeking rights for their class alone rubbed shoulders with socialists who championed such rights for all. Some artists, including French socialist painter Gustave Courbet (1819–1877), were active revolutionaries, but many less-radical artists used their medium for carrying political and social commentary to an increasingly wide audience in a market society. Men such as French illustrator Honoré Daumier (1810–1879) were often critical of current political regimes and the social classes that dominated them. In fact, many painters, writers, musicians, and even some architects, were highly politicized.

The Shadow of the Enlightenment: Empiricism. The eighteenth century launched an industrial and political revolution that cast a shadow across the entire period from 1750 to 1914, and this revolution was joined by an equally fundamental transformation in thought and attitudes. The Enlightenment, as this new movement has been called, embraced the epistemological notion that human beings acquire knowledge through reason and sensation. It drew this premise from the Scientific Revolution of the seventeenth century, which affirmed that scientific knowledge of the natural world arrived through observation, experiment, and mathematical measurement, not from the ancient or sacred texts on which so many medieval thinkers had relied. This method is called empiricism, and it revolutionized art for several reasons. First, this kind of rationalism was highly individualistic. The stimuli external to the human organism were infinitely varied and specific to the particular individual receiving them through his or her senses at a specific time and place. Thus, no two individuals could be alike. In art, the application of this new way of knowing was expressed in the notion of the genius, an individual whose senses are especially attuned to the world and who is blessed with an unusual or even singular ability to express its fundamental meanings through image, word, or sound. Empiricism affected art in another way as well. Empiricism was taken to be the true way of acquiring objective knowledge (the legacy of science), and if art were to be a conveyor of truth (a belief many artists firmly embraced), then artists must employ empiricism in their creation of artistic representations. In other words, artists must be like scientists, exact recorders of the phenomena of the world (which by the nineteenth century had come to include not just nature but also society). Such assumptions about the nature and purpose of art gave rise to the "style" of Realism that dominated painting and especially literature for much of the nineteenth century.

Progress and Universalism. The Enlightenment brought with it a great sense of optimism about the prospects for humanity's future. Men came to believe that empirical rationalism was the key to unlocking the secrets of nature. If they could understand nature, they believed, then its forces could be harnessed and turned toward productive uses and human improvement. One illustration of harnessing nature is the capture of energy from various natural sources and the directed, controlled unleashing of it. The best example of this process is steam power from coal-heated water, a release of energy that fueled the Industrial Revolution. This confidence in human capability spread beyond science and industry and came to instill in men a general belief in progress: through concerted and rationally directed human activity, man could improve (some even thought perfect) his lot on earth. This emphasis on improving the human condition found political expression in the language of universal human rights (freedom and sometimes equality). More generally, however, it imbued men with the belief in universalism, the idea that the human condition is a shared, even collective, one and is guided by the same fundamental principles everywhere. Art, once again, represented these values in image, word, and sound, and the style of this expression was called Classicism. Artists such as architect Marc-Antoine Laugier (1713–1769) believed that the Romans and especially the Greeks of antiquity had uncovered the fundamental values of humanity and took the works of these ancients as the authoritative models for the new universalism of the eighteenth century.

Nationalism. No sooner had universalism captured the minds of Enlightenment thinkers and artists than it encountered a profound challenge, the ideal of nationalism. By 1800 Europe had been coalescing into discrete and increasingly sovereign nation-states for several centuries, with each state more and more jealously guarding its territory. Governments became increasingly centralized and bureaucratized. As states became more powerful, the inhabitants of these nations (as these polities came to be called) developed feelings of allegiance to them and acquired national identities. Revolutionaries in France, for example, countered the royalist and absolutist position that the state was embodied in the person of the king with the notion that it comprised its collective citizenry. Nationalism was not just a French phenomenon. In fact, Napoleon's conquests (justified as the proper spreading of the *universal* values of the French Revolution) stirred opposition in Spain and Germany. These opponents rallied around the defense of their own national identities (defined in cultural terms as much as political) that were threatened by French expansion. The value of nationalism thereafter became an unstoppable juggernaut, paralleling the ever-increasing power of the state. By late in the nineteenth century, patriotic citizens were called on to defend the nation militarily, to sacrifice their lives for the fatherland if necessary.

Nationalism was expressed in all media of art as many artists, like their compatriots, embraced and sought to express the deep-rooted values that converted physical topographical formations into particular nations. As folk melodies wafted through nineteenth-century music, and national cultural myths provided the material for operas, many novelists and painters extolled the glories of national heritages, while architects sought to encase the essence of the nation in their buildings.

Cultural Fragmentation and the Coming of War. Nationalism and subjective individualism were powerful solvents to universalism. The artistic style of Classicism collapsed under their combined weight, and Romanticism—rich in nationalist imagery and inspired by individual geniuses—rose to take its place. By the end of the nineteenth century, as nation-states solidified and became increasingly bellicose toward each other, and artists and writers lurched from one expressive style to another, Europe became increasingly fragmented politically and culturally. The outbreak of World War I in 1914 was a result of this political fragmentation, and the artistic style called "Modernism" evolved as its cultural counterpart. The confidence in progress and improvement so prominent in Enlightenment thought and art nearly disappeared as artists and writers came to imbue their works with decadence, pessimism, and nostalgia. Discordance and dissonance in music was matched in the visual arts by a sharp drift toward fractured images and eventually almost complete abstraction. In many pictures artists made no attempt to re-create the visible world. Even when an artist bothered to render a body visibly on canvas, it was extremely peculiar or isolated from other bodies in the picture. As the march of individualism had continued unabated throughout the nineteenth century, extreme subjectivism became the undergirding of Modernism. From the belief in the unique individuality of each person, there ultimately emerged the conviction that absolute knowledge of anything outside one's own consciousness, or psyche, was impossible. As a result, many artists and writers closely focused on the individual consciousness or psyche of the individual. Fragmentation and subjectivism became the essence of the meaning of "modern." Though not entirely undone, the worldview of the Enlightenment—with its emphasis on universalism, optimism, and rationalism—was deeply challenged by Modernism and the devastating war that erupted in 1914.

TOPICS IN THE ARTS

THE AGE OF CLASSICISM: ART AND ARCHITECTURE

Universalism and Consumerism. Inspired by the Enlightenment and guided by the authority of antiquity, eighteenth-century painters embraced the universalist ideal that all individuals share the same human condition and the same fundamental principles. Equally important, painters found themselves working in a new environment, a consumer culture in which artworks increasingly became commercial products. The transition from the old court society to the new market society was gradual, but everywhere signs pointed toward the new. In fact, though it looked to ancient Greece and Rome for models, Classicism as a style owed much of its success to the new conditions of the late eighteenth century. In 1764 Johann Joachim Winckelmann (1717–1768), a German art theorist, laid out the fundamental principles of Classicism in his book *Geschichte der Kunst des Altertums* (The History of Ancient Art). According

to Winckelmann, the ancient Greeks embodied the universal natural laws in their art, and "moderns" could do no better than to imitate them. Winckelmann's book was a major publishing success, spreading the ideas of universalism and natural laws in classicism to readers in an ever-broadening consumer public. Winckelmann's book was influential in another way as well. He introduced the scholarly discipline of aesthetics that centered on the individual's capacity for feeling and sensibility. Winckelmann's ideas were equally influential among elite art theorists and courtly patrons who still used art as a means of displaying distinction and among the growing numbers of artists who merchandised their work and sold it on the consumer market. As the art public became increasingly pluralistic, the width and variety of the market expanded, especially in the large cities of Europe. Classicism became so popular that two snobbish art connoisseurs, Thomas Hope (1769–1831) and Sir William Hamilton (1730–1803), bemoaned "the

Construction of a Road (1774) by Claude-Joseph Vernet (Musée du Louvre, Paris)

fact is that this fad for imitating the ancients caught on, if not with the keenest of minds, at least with those who were most energetic and enterprising. The imitative arts, theatre, literature in general, and everything down to the furniture all manifested the furor to imitate first the Romans, and later the Greeks. . . ." Such imitation, they complained, even applied "to feminine fashions, the decoration of apartments, and the most common utensils." For all the diversity among artists, patrons, and popular consumers they were captive of the empiricism of the Enlightenment, with its trust in the ability of the senses to arrive at truth through observation and employ it in pursuit of progress, and they all judged—and consumed—art accordingly.

Painting and Progress. The Enlightenment values of empiricism and universalism conditioned visual artists to represent the idea of progress. In keeping with contemporary understandings of this idea, artists such as Claude-Joseph Vernet (1714–1789) sought to extol the noble aspiration of public improvement. Through something as commonplace as the building of a road, Vernet hoped to reveal to his viewers the ideal of human betterment through improvements in the public welfare guided by rational principles. Vernet was in fact commissioned by the French state to paint *Construction of a Road* (1774). In the painting one can see what Vernet considered the triumphs of French transport technology. For instance, he included a crane that was invented by the engineer directing the project, Jean-Rodolphe Perronet (1708–1794), who is portrayed as one of the men on horseback in the painting.

Painting and Revolution. As revolution gripped France in the late eighteenth century, painters sought to represent its values in pictures. Universalism was cast in the ideas of the brotherhood of man—the revolutionary slogan "freedom, equality, brotherhood" embraced it as a fundamental human value—and of progress and betterment through revolutionary change. The Classical style served these purposes well. For example, in his *Oath of the Horatii* (1785) Jacques-Louis David (1748–1825) realistically depicted men in Classical garb heroically dedicated to the ideal of brotherhood. Such a value, moreover, was starkly masculine. Viewers did not miss David's commentary, which was shared widely among revolutionaries, that the these new, masculine revolutionaries were capable of toppling the Old Regime, which was aristocratic, decadent, and unnaturally affected (and thus out of step with the true standard of nature). Indeed, its critics often cast it as feminine. An anonymous drawing titled *At the Café Royal d'Alexandre: The Burning of the Coiffures* (circa 1780) uses biting satire to make these points.

Architecture and the Laws of Nature. The empirical method of knowledge acquisition championed by Enlightenment thinkers rested on mathematical science and a new "rationality." These tools, they believed, would permit the discovery of the universal laws of

At the Café Royal d'Alexandre: The Burning of the Coiffures (circa 1780) by an unknown artist (Bibliothèque Nationale, Paris)

nature. In his *Essai sur l'architecture* (Essay on Architecture, 1753) Marc-Antoine Laugier (1713–1769) claimed to have uncovered the fixed and unchanging laws of nature that fundamentally governed the art of building. To discover these structural laws, Laugier asserted, one must examine the primordial constructions of natural man, and the building that hewed the closest to man in his natural state was the hut. Laugier's influence on architectural theory was profound. All Classical architects henceforth assumed that the hut was the primal structure that embodied in its simplicity the pure and fundamental laws of nature.

The Ideal City. With the belief in the idea of progress came an optimism that mankind had the tools not only to improve the human condition but even to perfect it. This confidence in the perfectibility of man rose to a utopianism that influenced almost all aspects of thought. City planning was no exception. Urban architecture and design, true to Classical form, hailed the Greeks and Romans as the ideal models. Enlightenment Classicists therefore believed that progress was linked to a renewal of civic life, specifically that monumental pub-

Unlike painting, architecture, literature, and music, sculpture did not change greatly in form or meaning between the late eighteenth and the early twentieth centuries. And with the exception of Auguste Rodin (1840–1917) late in the nineteenth century, few great artists are associated with sculpture during this period. In the age of Classicism, Antonio Canova (1757–1822) and Bertel Thorvaldsen (1740–1814) were the leading sculptors and became highly influential on young artists. Canova, in good Classical fashion, chose heroic subjects and in that way personified universal values of the Enlightenment. As Napoleon's court sculptor, he carved portraits of his powerful contemporaries, but he invariably presented them in ancient attire and cut his statues from marble, closely imitating ancient Roman technique and making no concessions to the emerging style of Romanticism. Thorvaldsen was equally Classical in his desire to instill his sculptures with universal values such as human dignity and grace, although he departed from the dominant secular mood of the time by combining Christian motifs with ancient ones. Like Canova, he mastered the ancient technique of working with marble.

So great and long-lasting was the influence of Classicism on sculpture that Romanticism never really took hold, and in the few instances where it did (almost entirely in France), it was expressed more in mood than form. The most significant Romantic sculptor was François Rude (1784–1853), and his *Departure of the Volunteers in 1792* (1835–1836), more commonly known as the *Marseillaise*, embodies the Romantic values of emotionalism and political rebellion. This sculpture graces Napoleon's Arc de Triomphe in Paris and, like the Romantic Eugène Delacroix's painting, *Liberty Leading the People*, evokes the French Revolution.

The mid-century trend toward Realism and Naturalism resulted in extraordinary artistic expressions in painting but not sculpture. Under the sway of this style, most sculptors simply produced what critics consider uninteresting, life-like reproductions. An exception was Jean-Baptiste Carpeaux (1827–1875), who sought to convey an enhanced realism through the use of illusionary techniques of texture and shadow, but the real breakthrough in sculpture had to await Rodin. He continued Carpeaux's use of illusion to capture reality but, like the Impressionist painters, explored the play of light on his subject and used it abundantly. As an artist working in a three-dimensional medium, he was also keenly aware of how empty spaces around his forms could contribute to the force, mood, and effect of his sculpture. Rodin combined all these techniques in works of art such as the monumental *Burghers of Calais* (1884–1886), pushing sculpture toward the modern style of Expressionism. The chief objective of his art was to express forcefully the mood of the piece, and he employed sharp contrasts in light, mass, and body poses to gain bold expressive effects. In this sense, Rodin was the last great sculptor of the pre–World War I period. As Modernism took hold after the war, sculpture moved boldly in the direction of abstraction.

Sources: George Heard Hamilton, *Painting and Sculpture in Europe, 1880–1940* (New Haven: Yale University Press, 1993).

Fritz Novotny, *Painting and Sculpture in Europe, 1780–1880* (New Haven: Yale University Press, 1978).

lic buildings and wide-open spaces would be conducive to the nurturing of a public spirit. City planning and urban architecture reflected other influences of the age as well. One of the ideas the Scientific Revolution bequeathed to Enlightenment thought was the concept that the laws of nature were mechanistic and constantly propelling matter into motion. For urban planners and architects such as Pierre Patte (1723–1814) the ideal city would, like a machine, efficiently allow the natural movement of goods, money, people, and ideas. The desire to create a rational, regular, and ordered urban space informed Patte's "Project for an Ideal Street," published in 1769. Patte called for public laws to dictate the proper—that is, rational—mathematical proportion for the relationship between the width of a street and the height of the buildings. The plan of houses and streets would form an interlocking system designed according to regulated ratios. (Symmetry and balance were central to Classical aesthetics.) The result would ensure public health by allowing plentiful circulation of air, sufficient light, and the removal of waste through adequate drainage. Public safety was further guaranteed by spatially separating pedestrians from vehicles.

Sources:
Barry Bergdoll, *European Architecture, 1750–1890* (Oxford: Oxford University Press, 2000).

Albert Boime, *Art in an Age of Revolution, 1750–1800* (Chicago: University of Chicago Press, 1987).

Matthew Craske, *Art in Europe, 1700–1830: A History of the Visual Arts in an Era of Unprecedented Urban Economic Growth* (Oxford: Oxford University Press, 1997).

Arnold Hauser, *The Social History of Art*, volume 2 (New York: Knopf, 1952).

Fritz Novotny, *Painting and Sculpture in Europe, 1780–1880* (New Haven: Yale University Press, 1978).

PROFIL D'UNE RUE

"Project for an Ideal Street" (1769) by Pierre Patte (Royal Institute of British Architects, London)

THE AGE OF CLASSICISM: MUSIC AND LITERATURE

Music: Courts and Patrons. In 1784 a contemporary estimated that there were nearly 350 composers in German-speaking Europe. Most of them were employed in aristocratic houses and considered little more than upper servants. They were expected to write pleasing music according to the accepted standards of classical composition (symmetry and regularity) and perform it for their patrons and guests. Over the course of a career a musician's compositions could—as in the case of Alessandro Scarlatti (1660–1725)—exceed one thousand works. Most of these composers were more craftsmen than artists, but within their ranks were Joseph Haydn (1732–1809) and Wolfgang Amadeus Mozart (1756–1791). Indeed, Mozart wrote twenty-seven symphonies in 1774–1777, while in the employ of the prince-bishop of Salzburg. Powerful patrons could vault their cities to the forefront of the music world, as King Frederick II "The Great" of Prussia (ruled 1740–1786) or Emperor Joseph II of Austria (ruled 1765–1790) did for Berlin and Vienna. Their patronage attracted capable musicians and large audiences. One of Frederick's first acts as king was to have an opera house built in Berlin, while in Vienna in 1791 the imperial court of Joseph and his successor, Leopold II (ruled 1790–1792), was the site of the performance of revolutionary operas such as Mozart's *Die Zauberflöte* (The Magic Flute, 1791), written in the German language rather than the traditional Italian.

The Emergence of Public Concerts. While the great demand for court music continued in the late eighteenth century, the public opera and orchestral concert emerged in European cities, where music was becoming a central component of social life. Outside the courts, music clubs and concert societies with dues-paying members and amateur musicians sprang up to meet the growing demand, which triggered a boom in music publishing as composers scrambled to provide music for the new groups. Late in the century, such clubs and societies were increasingly supplanted by professional musicians who performed before subscription-paying, anonymous audiences. For example, during the "season" when nobles and aristocrats resided in Vienna, they joined army officers, government administrators, and members of the newly wealthy middle class in attending a public concert or opera nearly every night of the week. This transition from private court performance and semiprivate amateur society to the professional, public concert was rooted in two conditions: a growing, diverse class of concertgoers who could afford to pay for the music and a public authority (sometimes imperial or royal, but often municipal) that provided a concert hall or opera house for the performances. In the early nineteenth century the sizes of audiences, orchestras, and concert halls expanded dramatically, and there was a shift in the nature of the music composed and performed. Classicism was giving way to Romanticism.

Literature. Classicism in literature reached its peak before 1750, and thereafter it was challenged and overthrown by Romanticism. While Classicism reigned, the same characteristics that informed painting, architecture, and music held sway: order, regularity, and rationality. Moreover, during this time there emerged a print culture immersed in a broader consumer revolution. Magazines, newspapers, and popular books were consumed by an increasingly public-minded audience of aristocrats and middle-class men, and through printed matter of all kinds they were immersed in Enlightenment ideas. Gradually, with their readers they fashioned what has become known as "public opinion." Some writers, such as the French man of letters Voltaire (1694–1778) or the British poet Alexander Pope (1688–1744), earned fortunes from their pens in this emergent market society while they embodied and widely disseminated Enlightenment ideas and values to this new public. Pope's poetry remained popular among some readers during the second half of the eighteenth century. His poem *An Essay on Man* (1733–1734) provides a clear illustration of the Classical assumption that good poetry starts from a clear idea and gives it form. Samuel Johnson (1709–1784), recognized as an authority on Classicism, added that good poets "must not dwell on the minuter distinctions by which one species differs from another" but should instead always strive for the general and the universal that bind species together.

Sources:

Arnold Hauser, *The Social History of Art,* volume 2 (New York: Knopf, 1952).

Henry Raynor, *A Social History of Music from the Middle Ages to Beethoven* (New York: Schocken Books, 1972).

Ian Watt, *The Rise of the Novel* (Berkeley: University of California Press, 1957).

THE CHALLENGE OF ROMANTICISM: ART AND ARCHITECTURE

Artists and Economic Competition. During the late eighteenth and early nineteenth centuries social and economic forces were at work that eventually transformed the conditions in which artists worked and expressed themselves. The emergence of a consumer-oriented market economy coupled with industrialization created an increasingly pluralistic society with new sources of wealth and an accelerating division of labor. This society included new consumers (more and more of whom were women) with new tastes and money to invest in art, including books, musical concerts, paintings, and buildings. Among artists, most of whom were men, these new conditions brought about growing specialization, increased competition for consumers, and a greater freedom to create original or singular works of art. By the late eighteenth century, European cities—especially Rome, Paris, and London—suffered from a glut of artists, especially painters. Art schools, such as the British Royal Academy, produced more painters than the market could absorb, and many of them had little hope of employment.

The Cult of the Individual Genius. While these competitive conditions left many an artist in economic straits, they also conditioned artists to seek a means to distinguish themselves from others. One way to differentiate oneself from the others was to pose as the isolated, even alienated, eccentric genius—a role still common among artists. An ideology of *self*-expression served the need to differentiate onself, and the desire to give substance to the individual imagination became a hallmark of Romanticism. It had other effects as well. The cult of the individual genius gave rise to an elitism among some artists who believed that

Capuchin Friar by the Sea (1808–1809) by Caspar David Friedrich (Stiftung Preussischer Kulturbesitz, Schloss Charlottenburg, Berlin)

their work must be separated from crass popularism. In a related way, it gave rise to artists such as the English painter James Barry (1741–1806), who spurned commissions for portraits from wealthy consumers because he refused to gratify the vanities of the newly rich. Yet another result of this individualism was the rise of the idea of freedom, both of the individual and of society. The French Revolution initially championed this idea, and many Romantics, including painter Eugène Delacroix (1798–1863) in his *Liberty Leading the People* (1831), expressed it in their art. Some artists, such as William Blake (1757–1827), pursued a personal vision to the point of economic noncompetitiveness and thus to financial ruin. Often, Romantic artists—from the French painter Théodore Géricault (1791–1824) to the German musician Ludwig van Beethoven (1770–1827)—embraced the theme of heroic sacrifice in their works, a notion that paralleled the artist's view of his own activity as a heroic struggle often unappreciated by the ordinary consumer.

Sentiment. The groundwork for the cult of the individual genius was laid during the eighteenth century with the new psychology of sensation—or, as it was called then, "sensibility." The prizing of feeling and emotion over reason emerged from the Enlightenment just as much as the belief in rationality. Both, after all, sprang from nature. By the mid eighteenth century, this psychology increasingly pervaded the new public, and many artists had come to value sentiment more highly than "cold" reason as the mark of true art. During the second half of the eighteenth century the "revolt against reason" became another defining characteristic of Romanticism.

Painting and the Revolt against Reason. The German painter Caspar David Friedrich (1774–1840) signaled the dominant values of Romanticism—individualism and sentiment—when he succinctly announced that "the artist's feeling is law." He encapsulated in his landscape paintings a reality beyond the compass of reason, a boundlessness and immeasurable sense of infinitude set in a scene where stillness and silence hold sway. In this setting, individuals, if there are any in the picture at all, stand isolated and even vulnerable, as in Friedrich's *Capuchin Friar by the Sea* (1808–1809). The world of this painting cannot be known rationally; its meaning can only be felt. The revolt against reason was registered in other ways too, as in the drawings, etchings, and paintings of the Spaniard Francisco Goya (1746–1828). Goya still held out a hope for human progress, but he also perceived a demonic nonrational side of human nature, which he expressed vividly in *Reason Asleep* (1796–1798) and in his series of etchings *The Horrors of War* (1810–1813).

Painting, Nationalism, and National Identity. Enlightenment rationality was challenged by Romantic sentiment. Similarly, Enlightenment universalism, rooted in the authority of antiquity and the style of Classicism, clashed with nationalism, which was also expressed in Romantic style. Writers such as Johann Gottfried von Herder (1744–1803) rejected the timeless authority of the ancients and

Reason Asleep (1796–1798) by Francisco Goya
(Albertina, Vienna)

countered with an argument that cultures were products of specific histories and expressed themselves in a variety of modes. This cultural pluralism became a foundation stone of nationalism, and artists embraced it. Herder's cultural, historical pluralism lent itself to thinking of cultures as organisms; that is, as natural, living entities, they pass through stages of youthfulness, maturity, and decay. A nation's identity was seen to inhere in its artifacts and its people (or "folk"). Artists often seized on the portrayal of ruins as a way to convey a national identity inherited from the past, or sometimes they portrayed it as a yearning for lost vitality, as in *A Veteran Highlander* (1819) by Scottish painter David Wilkie (1785–1841).

Garden Design and Sentiment. The new psychology of sensation was expressed in landscape architecture as well. In the eighteenth century radically new natural-looking garden designs supplanted the geometric and ordered designs of the previous century. In both centuries "gardens" were like parks, sometimes covering hundreds of acres. Seventeenth-century gardens, such as those at the royal palace of Versailles or at Vaux le Vicomte in France, were derided in the next century as contrived and unnatural artifice (and thus disconnected from the primal order of

A Veteran Highlander (1819) by David Wilkie (Paisley Museum and Art Galleries, Renfrewshire, Scotland)

nature). The new "picturesque garden" became popular. Picturesque gardens, which appeared first in England and so became known as "English" gardens, were laid out to give the viewer an impression of a landscape painting, hence the name *picturesque*. These new gardens also were designed so that walking through the park would be an emotive and, in the term invoked at the time, "sensational" experience. The English garden at Stourhead is a fine example of landscape architectural design according to these principles; as one moved through the park, one was confronted with surprising vistas hidden from view until one crested a hill, emerged from a stand of trees, or rounded a bend. Thus, one's senses were continually stimulated by unexpected new landscapes, or "pictures," that evoked a range of moods. Such garden designs were entirely in keeping with the new sensationalist psychology, which held that the natural, human reaction of astonishment heightened the operations of the soul.

The Gothic Revival and Monumental Restoration in Architecture. Architecture, no less than painting, was perceived to bear the stamp of national identity, and—as in painting—nineteenth-century architectural style countered the universalism of Classicism with particularist nationalism. This trend, which associated buildings with the glory of a nation's past, can be seen in the surge in popularity of the Gothic style for new buildings and in the restoration of old ones. The Gothic revival was most visible in England and Germany, nations that increasingly perceived

their character as rooted in a Germanic, or Gothic (as opposed to a Roman and thus Classical), past. New buildings such as the Houses of Parliament in England, which were begun in 1840 after a fire, were designed as a conscious appeal to an organic and unified past. The architect responsible for the decorative elements and furniture in the new buildings, A. W. N. Pugin (1812–1852), intended them to be a vehicle of national unity through which the country, whose social and moral fabric was being torn by industrialization, could heal itself. The Gothic-inspired restoration movement emerged most clearly in France and is associated with the work of Eugéne-Emmanuel Viollet-le-Duc (1814–1879). Sharing the spreading belief that the soul of a nation was embodied in its great architectural monuments from the past, he set about restoring them to their original splendor. His first project was the medieval church of the Madeleine in Vézélay, a small hilltop town in Burgundy. The guiding principle of his enormously influential and widely read ten-volume *Dictionnaire raisonné de l'architecture française du XIe au XVIe siècle* (Dictionary of French Architecture from the Eleventh to the Sixteenth Century, 1854–1868) was Gothicism. As he wrote in his dictionary, he perceived in Gothic architecture a perfected "structural system in which every element contributed to the dynamic equilibrium of the whole, and in which material was reduced to a daring but reasoned minimum."

Sources:

Barry Bergdoll, *European Architecture, 1750–1890* (Oxford: Oxford University Press, 2000).

Matthew Craske, *Art in Europe, 1700–1830: A History of the Visual Arts in an Era of Unprecedented Urban Economic Growth* (Oxford: Oxford University Press, 1997).

Arnold Hauser, *The Social History of Art*, volume 2 (New York: Knopf, 1952).

François Loyer, *Architecture of the Industrial Age, 1789–1914*, translated by R. F. M. Dexter (Geneva: Skira, 1983).

Robin Middleton and David Watkin, *Neoclassical and Nineteenth-Century Architecture* (New York: Abrams, 1981).

Fritz Novotny, *Painting and Sculpture in Europe, 1780–1880* (New Haven: Yale University Press, 1978).

Robert Rosenblum, *Nineteenth-Century Art* (Englewood Cliffs, N.J.: Prentice-Hall / New York: Abrams, 1984).

William Vaughan, *Romantic Art* (New York: Oxford University Press, 1978).

THE CHALLENGE OF ROMANTICISM: LITERATURE AND MUSIC

The New Sentimentalism in Literature. The sensationalist psychology encouraged an intense subjectivism among many writers. Thus, in the literature of the second half of the eighteenth and the first third of the nineteenth century, a common theme in literature is the assertion of personal identity and a sense of the uniqueness of each individual. Often, this theme is cast in a confessional mold, in which authors seek to reveal in their characters (or in themselves) a transparent perception of the characters' inner feelings and thoughts. Jean-Jacques Rousseau (1712–1778) launched this movement with his immensely influential and widely read *Confessions* (1781–1788), written mostly between 1766 and 1770. Rousseau described his most personal and private feelings and experiences, portraying himself as radically different from others and misunderstood. In describing his *Confessions*, Rousseau wrote, "I have resolved on an enterprise which has no precedent, and which, once complete, will have no imitator. My purpose is to display . . . a portrait in every way true to nature, and the man I shall portray will be myself. Simply myself . . . I am made unlike any one I have ever met; I will venture to say that I am like no one in the whole world. I may be no better, but at least I am different." In literature this emphasis on intimacy and subjectivism resulted in a concentration on characterization rather than plot. The Englishman Samuel Richardson (1689–1761) was among the most commercially successful sentimentalist writers. The new reading public and the expanding market for printed matter transformed literary works such as Richardson's into commodities. One reason for this was the subject matter. In Richardson's novels *Pamela* (1740) and *Clarissa* (1747–1748), he was the first novelist to focus on ordinary, middle-class men and women, and—true to the sentimentalist and subjectivist trend—he exposed their most intimate private lives and loves. Written as a series of letters, Richardson's epistolary novels had hardly any plot at all. The purpose of his novels was to analyze emotions and examine the conscience. Like Rousseau's *Confessions*, Richardson's novels struck a responsive chord among his readers and helped to lay the groundwork for Romanticism. Madame Germaine de Staël (1766–1817), a French Romantic novelist, historian, literary critic, and political commentator, followed directly in Rousseau's footsteps, writing that "the soul's elevation is born of self-consciousness." Madame de Staël's recognition of the primacy of individual subjectivity, moreover, meant for her that a woman's vision was just as important as a man's. Her British contemporary Jane Austen (1775–1817) suggested much the same thing in her novels.

The Romantic Hero. The emphasis on character rather than plot in Romantic literature arose from the primacy of sentimentalism, and as a result it created the idea of the Romantic hero. This sort of main character in a novel or a poem always had a distinct, or even unique, personality, which could be expressed in melancholy introspection or in extroverted confidence. Characters of the German writer Johann Wolfgang von Goethe (1749–1832) fall into either category, while those of the Russian poet Aleksandr Pushkin (1799–1837) are melancholy introverts, and the British poet George Gordon, Lord Byron (1788–1824), created confident extroverts, including the title character of his poem *Don Juan* (1819–1824). Introspection and intense examination of the conscience could set a character on a lifelong search for understanding, with no guarantee it would be found. In fact, in Goethe's *Die Leiden des jungen Werthers* (The Sorrows of Young Werther, 1774) the main character becomes obsessed with the primacy of his own, individual feelings and experience. In scrutinizing them he finds only pointlessness and absurdity and ends his life by suicide. Pushkin's novel in verse *Evegeny Onegin* (Eugene

Onegin, 1833–1837), written in 1823–1831, sounds the same note, as the bored title character wanders through a pointless and meaningless existence, yet is moved by an indescribable longing for the unattainable. Goethe's *The Sorrows of Young Werther* was extremely popular among the reading public. It went through sixteen editions between 1776 and 1799 in France alone. It even spawned a fashion fad, as many restless young men sported a yellow waistcoat like the one Werther wore in the novel. Even extroverted and self-confident literary heroes experience a longing for the unattainable, a search that is often expressed in a rootless homelessness. Again, Goethe was an extremely influential force. In his novel *Wilhelm Meisters Lehrjahre* (Wilhelm Meister's Apprenticeship, 1795, 1796) and its continuation, *Wilhelm Meisters Wanderjahre (Wilhelm Meister's Wanderings*, 1821), he introduced and developed the Bildungsroman, or the novel of character building, where the hero gains a growing self-awareness and a deeper understanding of the world in which he moves. Even more clearly expressive of the overconfident Romantic hero is Goethe's title character in *Faust* (1808). Faust barters his soul to the Devil in return for ultimate knowledge of himself and the world. The story is a spiritual journey permeated by the sense of longing for the unattainable, even the infinite. Even though Faust loses the bargain, readers grasped the message that the point of life should be a boundless searching for self-knowledge and self-realization, regardless of the consequences.

Romanticism, Freedom, and the Spirit of Revolt. The Romantic hero and the Romantic artist were most often social outsiders. A preoccupation with subjectivism, difference, and uniqueness bred this sense of isolation, which was often expressed in a renunciation of the prevailing values in the world. Furthermore, Romantic artists' commitment to the primacy of feelings over rule-bound classical rationalism also contributed to an artistic vision that prized creativity spawned by the spontaneous imagination. These ideas were all encompassed in a belief in the supremacy of human freedom. Romantics longed for change that would unshackle human creativity. For some, including British poets William Wordsworth (1770–1850) or Samuel Taylor Coleridge (1772–1834), the French Revolution with its promise of freedom, equality, and brotherhood initially seemed to deliver what they sought. Wordsworth and Coleridge's *Lyrical Ballads* (1798)—which includes Wordsworth's "Tintern Abbey" and Coleridge's "Rime of the Ancient Mariner"—offered a radical challenge to the accepted, Classical style of poetry. In his preface Wordsworth called for a new kind of poetry that would represent the everyday lives and passions of ordinary people in plain, but beautiful, language. He also made the influential statement that poetry should be "the spontaneous overflow of powerful feeling." Perhaps no other Romantic artist exemplified the iconoclastic outsider with a commitment to revolutionary change better than Byron. His advocacy of personal liberty and political revolution led him to fight for the freedom of Greece in its rebellion

The Gardens at Stourhead (circa 1775) by Coplestone Warre Bampfylde (Stourhead House, Warminster, England)

against its Turkish overlords, the war that ended the poet's short life. The critical spirit of Romanticism was also turned against the new industrial world for its denial of freedom for the toiling masses, as in the poem *Jerusalem* (1804–1820) by British poet William Blake (1757–1827). This pessimistic and demonic vision portrays factories and mills as sites of terror and subjugation, where "furnaces howl loud, living, and self-moving." For Blake the new factories were inhuman places where the machines were alive and the workers a living dead who were forced to surrender their dignity and liberty to the hellish "loud sounding hammer of destruction."

Popular Literature, Theater, and Melodrama. Romanticism was a Europe-wide movement, the ideas of which traveled through the established networks of an increasingly integrated market society. Writers lived by their pens, and success reflected shared values between artist and audience. Walter Scott (1771–1832) earned a fortune selling his novels. (He wrote twenty-nine between 1814 and 1831.) In novels such as *Waverley* (1814) and *Ivanhoe* (1819), Scott appealed to the popular mood of national revival that was evident in all the arts of his era. Set in a blend of mythical and historical past, Scott's fiction displayed before his readers the imagined roots of their folk culture in the distant feudal era of the Middle Ages. Scott's novels emphasized plot more than characterization. In this sense they departed from earlier Romantic novels but paralleled contemporary popular theater. The playgoing public in European cities was large and growing in the late eighteenth and early

nineteenth centuries, and many people, especially in the new middle class, liked melodrama. French playwrights Pierre-Augustin Beaumarchais (1732–1799) and Guilbert Pixérecourt (1773–1844), for example, turned out scores of plays that were performed thousands of times before melodrama lost its appeal around 1830. Each play had a clearly defined plot (initial antagonism among characters ultimately overcome in the triumph of virtue over evil) and formulaic characters (such as heroes, villains, and comics). Pixérecourt wrote 120 plays between 1798 and 1814. Judging from the popularity of such plays, the public welcomed stories in which characters are victims of cruel fate and reward and punishment are finally delivered.

Romantic Music. Unlike the Romantic movement in the other arts, which lasted only through the first third of the nineteenth century, Romanticism dominated music for the entire century. The main themes of Romanticism can be found in nineteenth-century music: emotion, the beauty and power of nature, the brotherhood of man, the value of human freedom, the creative genius, and nationalism. It also was a music of the marketplace rather than of the aristocratic court. As patronage gave way to the market as the source of a living for composers and musicians, the music written and performed changed dramatically.

Orchestral Music and Commerce. Concert halls replaced courtly salons as the main venue for nineteenth-century music, and to accommodate the increasing numbers of concertgoers, these halls had to grow in size. Larger spaces, in turn, required more musical instruments to fill them with sound. Composers wrote scores for more, and new, instruments. As the size of orchestras grew, the music became more complex and in some instances difficult to play. When the already legendary Beethoven had his Ninth Symphony performed for the first time in 1824, a young Richard Wagner (1813–1883) was in the audience. The future great composer of German Romantic opera came away baffled by Beethoven's symphony because it seemed a chaos of uncoordinated sound. Wagner's reaction in part can be attributed to the newness and "strangeness" of Beethoven's score, but it also points to a growing problem with performances that were becoming unwieldy. As a result, the conductor began increasingly to exert greater discipline on the orchestra, demanding more and more rehearsals before public performances and a strict adherence to his tempo during them. The increased visibility and authority of the conductor were new developments. Discipline was marked on the business side of musical performances as well, as music directors came to the fore. A good example of this change may be seen in the career of Sir Charles Hallé (1819–1895), born Karl Halle in Germany. He was appointed conductor and director of the Manchester Philharmonic in 1848. During Hallé's tenure he exerted a ruthless discipline over his orchestra, hiring and firing musicians until he had an efficient "workforce," as he called it. He rehearsed them tirelessly through the works of Beethoven, Felix Mendelssohn (1809–1847), Johannes Brahms (1833–1897), and Wagner, seeking perfection but demanding in any case that his orchestra play as well as it possibly could. The precision and professionalism that still marks classical music performances had arrived. While Hallé's orchestra resembled a well-oiled industrial machine with as many as ninety skilled workers contributing to its smooth running, the commercial side of the operation reflected the march of capitalism and the market economy. As music director, Hallé was in charge of marketing tickets, and he insisted that a block of them be made available to the working class. The fact that these tickets inevitably sold out suggests that the taste for this kind of music spanned all classes of society.

The Commercialization of Opera. During the second half of the eighteenth century, opera had an even greater appeal among musicgoers than orchestral concerts. Most operas, even those performed in German-speaking regions, were Italianized in form and libretto. Running with the tide of cultural nationalism, however, operas increasingly adapted to national forms and languages. Mozart's *Die Zauberflöte* (The Magic Flute), written at the encouragement of the Austrian emperor Joseph II (ruled 1765–1790) and performed in 1791, was a landmark in this transition. Opera also adapted itself to the commercialization of music that occurred during the nineteenth century. As audiences expanded, more large opera houses were built and run by commercial-minded managers. Louis Véron (1798–1867), for example, who became the first director of the Paris Opera in 1831, sought to make his operation profitable and to earn himself a fortune. He did both. To accomplish his

goals, he knew he must exploit the tastes of the new middle-class audiences by giving them elaborate stage effects, complete with the new gas lighting. He also offered them a new operatic style, the best examples of which are the operas of Giacomo Meyerbeer (1791–1864). These operas—including *Les Huguenots* (1836) and *Le Prophète* (1849)—were structured to feature gifted tenors and sopranos showcasing appealing melodies. The results were filled houses, virtuoso vocal performers, and new operas written for the ever-more-popular singers.

Romantic Themes in Music. In its various expressions, music in the nineteenth century embodied the main characteristics of the Romantic movement, many of which may be found in the works of Beethoven. Sentimentalist psychology is at the root of the emotional and intense music in the opening bars of Beethoven's Fifth Symphony (1808), the beauty of nature expressed in his Sixth Symphony, the "Pastoral" (1808), and the Faustian soaring toward the infinite in his heaven-storming Ninth Symphony (1824). The Romantic values of individual freedom and the brotherhood of man are central to his opera *Fidelio* (1805, revised 1806 and 1814). Richard Wagner assumed Beethoven's emotionalist mantle, and later in the nineteenth century he adopted the slogan "Drama in Music" to describe what he was trying to accomplish. By the end of the century Gustav Mahler (1860–1911) completed the intensely emotionalist trajectory, creating the last great expression of Romanticism before Modernism took hold. Political radicalism marked much of Romanticism, and some composers joined the other artists in the demand for change. Hector Berlioz (1803–1869), a socialist, wrote in a letter to a friend: "I believe that there is nothing to prevent my uniting my voice and my efforts with those of others for the amelioration of the conditions of the largest and poorest class of people." Wagner supported the radical Revolutions of 1848 but became disillusioned by their failure. He came to the conclusion that music was the supreme unifying force in an age when politics (even revolutionary politics) had become devoid of high principle and had descended to crass expediency. Finally, the concept of the creative genius was just as much a part of Romantic music as any other artistic form, and, as in the other arts, it blended into market society. Franz Liszt (1811–1886), for example, was better known in his time as a pianist than a composer. He expanded technique to the point of wizardry, thrilling audiences (many of whom were women) with his grandiose sold-out performances to packed houses. Ever the showman, Liszt walked through the audience between pieces, greeting guests and engaging them in conversation. He became rich in the process.

Romantic Music and Nationalism. Romanticism often embraced nationalism, and music was no exception. Like the French painter Eugène Delacroix (1798–1863) or the British poet Samuel Taylor Coleridge (1772–1834), the Italian opera composer Gaetano Donizetti (1797–1848) chose subjects from the distant past, and, like the novelist

The Second of May 1808 and *The Third of May 1808*, Goya's 1814 depictions of the Napoleonic invasion of Spain
(Prado Museum, Madrid)

Walter Scott (1771–1832), he blended myth with the actual history of his nation into operas such as *Lucrezia Borgia* (1833). Donizetti's compatriot Giuseppe Verdi (1813–1901) composed operas that made him even more the mouthpiece of Italian nationalism. Before the unification of Italy into a nation-state in 1860, northern Italians (including Verdi) were subjects of the Austrian, German-speaking emperor. Several of Verdi's operas were only thinly veiled calls for freedom and independence. Italian audiences immediately identified with the Hebrew slaves in *Nabucco* (1842), and the haunting melody of their chorus became almost an anthem for Italian independence. Moreover, in *Rigoletto* (1851) and *Un Ballo in Maschera* (A Masked Ball, 1859) Verdi was boldly antimonarchical, writing scenes in which the assassination of a king was laudable. Wagner was no less the voice of nationalism in Germany than Verdi was for Italy. In all Wagner's operas—but above all in the operatic cycle *Der Ring des Nibelungen* (The Ring of the Nibelungen, 1848–1876)—Wagner invoked Germanic history, myth, and gods as the symbols of a national, organic unity, proclaiming that cultural nationalism was deeper than the simple political unification of Germany (which occurred in 1871). In his music he claimed that he was recapturing lost German folk melodies. In fact, many composers in Europe were doing the same thing, also in the name of nationalism. The Czech composer Bedrich Smetana (1824–1884), for example, consciously drew on Bohemian folk tunes, idioms, rhythms, stories, and history for his orchestral music and operas.

Sources:

Gerald Abraham, *The Concise Oxford History of Music* (London & New York: Oxford University Press, 1979).

Philip Gaskell, *Landmarks in European Literature* (Edinburgh: Edinburgh University Press, 1999).

Arnold Hauser, *The Social History of Art,* volume 2 (New York: Knopf, 1952).

Henry Raynor, *Music and Society since 1815* (New York: Schocken Books, 1976).

Martin Travers, *An Introduction to Modern European Literature* (New York: St. Martin's Press, 1998).

THE OBJECTIVITY OF REALISM: ART AND ARCHITECTURE

Public Display. Art in Europe between 1750 and 1914 existed more and more in an urban, industrial, capitalistic market society whose population (especially in cities) was increasing and whose artistic tastes were changing. Art was no longer a luxury item for the elite and became a widely consumed commodity. An expanding public comprising new classes had the means and desire to have access to images and artistic representations, both in their original form and, after the mid nineteenth century, as reproductions. The market was a product of these conditions, and later in the century, so were the exhibition and the public art museum. The art market, the exhibition (which was a form of advertising as well as a source of goods), and the art museum were all forms of public display and remain a fixture of the art world to this day. The initial purpose of public art museums, which were sponsored by governments, was to display the glories of a nation's history to its citizenry. Indeed, museums were organized in such a way that artifacts, the historical products of nations, were displayed to the mobile viewer chronologically, giving a sense of the flow of time from the distant past to the present. These repositories of artifacts culled from a nation's past were, like much of the art itself, products of the rise of nationalism. The Louvre in Paris—which opened in 1793 in the midst of the French Revolution and warfare between the revolutionaries and other states in Europe—was explicitly created to proclaim national greatness and national power. As European nations expanded around the globe over the course of the nineteenth century, both through commerce and imperial conquest and domination, the artifacts of the host nation's past were joined by those gathered from other civilizations.

Realist and Naturalist Painting. Romantic painters often selected landscapes as their subject matter or attempted to portray individuals in such a way as to give the viewer access to the subject's inner self. Realist and Naturalist painters were as committed to these subjects as Romantics, but their style of depiction was decidedly different. Realist painters chose ordinary subjects and depicted them in ways that the viewer could readily imagine seeing in everyday life, while Naturalists were more concerned with an exact depiction of minute details in a given scene. The French Romantic Eugène Delacroix (1798–1863) wrote that painting should be a "feast for the eyes" served up in brilliant colors, and German Romantic Caspar David Friedrich (1774–1840) averred that painting was a leap of the imagination into the world of feeling beyond rationality and the concrete. The Realist painter Gustave Courbet (1819–1877), however, countered the Romantic unreality with its opposite. As he wrote in 1861 in a newspaper called the *Courier du dimanche*, "The art of painting consists only in the representation of objects which the artist can see and touch. . . . I . . . maintain that painting is essentially a *concrete* art and can only consist of the representation of *real* and *existing* things. . . . An *abstract* object, being invisible and non-existent, does not form part of the domain of painting." His attack on Romanticism included its embodiment of nationalism evoked by reference to the past. Courbet believed that "no period should be reproduced except by its own artists. I mean by artists who have lived in it." The German Naturalist Adolf von Menzel (1815–1905), like all painters of this style, rejected Romanticism, employing a style that reveled in detail and exactitude in its rendering of physical reality.

Political and Social Criticism in the Visual Arts. Courbet's realism was driven by a political and social commitment to fundamental change in society. He believed that a romantic retreat to the unreal was escapism and an abdication from the true purpose of art, which was to inform the viewing public of the real nature of the world and so pre-

Room with a Balcony (1845) by Adolf von Menzel (Alte Nationale Galerie, Staatliche Museen, Berlin)

pare people to change it. Courbet was a socialist, and like many other European artists living in the mid nineteenth century, he championed the ultimately unsuccessful Revolutions of 1848. Political and social criticism were expressed by other Realists as well. The French painter and illustrator Honoré Daumier (1808–1879) used biting satire to expose the foibles and corruption of contemporary bourgeois man, or he employed his demonic side to call attention to the deep flaws of politics and society. In *The Dream of the Inventor of the Needle Gun* (1866) he ridicules technological invention and indirectly challenges the connection between industrialism and the idea of progress. Perhaps, instead, it leads to death and destruction. Ever the Realist, Daumier created illustrations that are often set in the everyday world—the teeming, busy, noisy city street—and often depict everyday people, such as *The Blacksmith* (1855–1860).

Photography and Lithography. Photography, invented in 1839 simultaneously in England and France, and lithography represent the industrialization and mass production of the visual media. Photography froze concrete images of reality. In England, William Henry Fox Talbot (1800–1877) perfected what he called calotypes, produced by exposing waxed-paper negatives and sensitized coated-paper positives to sunlight. In France, Louis Jacques-Mandé Daguerre (1789–1851) perfected a technique through which images were projected onto a sensitized silvered metal plate. The shiny daguerreotypes captured such an extraordinary amount of precise detail that they were called "the mirror of nature." The technique of lithography was developed around the turn of the nineteenth century. An image is drawn with an oil-based crayon or a grease-based solution on a smoothly sanded piece of limestone. The resulting image absorbs ink while the stone does not,

The Dream of the Inventor of the Needle Gun by Honoré Daumier (lithograph from *Charivari*, 1866)

and the inked image may be reproduced by pressing a sheet of paper to the stone. This process can be repeated thousands of times, exactly reproducing the original each time. After the invention of photography and lithography, mass-produced representations proliferated among the growing art-consuming public. The impact on the visual art world was enormous. The distribution, and even the idea, of art was transformed. Photography first conquered the market for portrait images created in professional photographers' studios. It then became a medium for amateurs as well, after the portable handheld camera, called a Kodak after the company that made it, became widespread in the 1890s. As photography came to dominate the notion of realistic representation, painters began to abandon Realism, and the new styles of Impressionism and Modernism emerged. Lithographic reproductions of original works aided in the dissemination of affordable art to thousands of people and publicized the works of thousands of artists.

Industrialism in Architecture. By the middle of the nineteenth century, Europe was deeply industrialized, and its market economy was increasingly integrated internally as well as with that the rest of the world. In architecture these developments are vividly represented by the Crystal Palace, designed by Joseph Paxton (1803–1865) and erected in London in 1851. This mammoth building stretched 1,848 feet long and 408 wide, enclosed 19 acres, and, in keeping with the industrial age in which it was built, it was made of more than 6,000 cast-iron columns and 1,245 wrought-iron girders. Within the iron frame thousands of panes of glass were installed, giving the structure its name. Regardless of its aesthetic qualities, which were hotly debated at the time, the place of the Crystal Palace in history is assured because it was the first great building not constructed with masonry, wood, or stone. Erected in only nine months, the Crystal Palace was built to house an exhibition of more than 100,000 objects from Great Britain and the rest of world, showcasing British preemi-

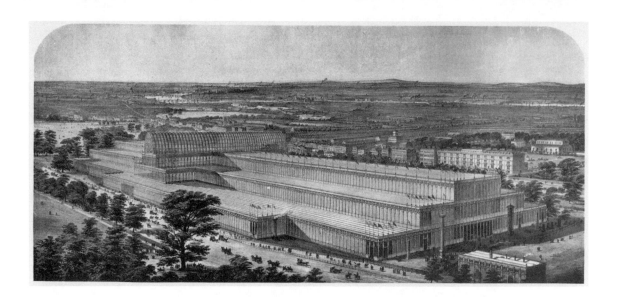

Exterior and interior of the Crystal Palace, designed by Joseph Paxton for the Great Exhibition of 1851 in London
(top: Victoria and Albert Museum, London; bottom: Royal Institute of British Architects, London)

nence in industry and world trade as well as the geographic sweep of the British Empire. After the exhibition, the building was disassembled, moved to Sydenham, and reconstructed there as the focal point of a landscaped park. Inside was a public, architectural museum with huge replicas of different styles of historical architecture. As a landmark representing industrialism and the ever-expanding market economy, the Crystal Palace drew tens of thousands of visitors before it was destroyed by fire in 1936.

Reaction. The Crystal Palace had its critics as well as its champions. John Ruskin (1819–1900), perhaps the greatest art critic of the second half of the nineteenth century, appreciated the Crystal Palace as a feat of engineering but

not as art: "There is assuredly as much ingenuity required to build a screw frigate, or a tubular bridge as a hall of glass. . . . all, in their several ways, deserve our highest admiration; but not admiration of the kind that is rendered to poetry or art." Ruskin, like William Blake (1757–1827) before him, was sounding a common criticism, one condemning industrial capitalism as a system that deprived individuals of their dignity and their freedom. William Morris (1834–1896), a disciple of Ruskin, carried this critique to his Arts and Crafts Movement. Morris sought to renew architecture and society by returning to handicraft production that somehow would stand outside the market economy, thereby defying commercialism and repudiating the profit motive. With Philip Webb he designed and built the Red House, which stands as a monument to the Arts and Crafts Movement. The decorative arts for interior design were coordinated with the architecture of the building, all modeled on the styles of the pre-capitalist and pre-industrial Middle Ages.

Commercial Architecture. The Crystal Palace pioneered the use of iron and glass in construction, and purveyors of the mass-produced consumer items that increasingly came to dominate the market economies of European cities during the last third of the nineteenth century saw a profitable application of this new technology. The use of iron for structural support released more space for glass windows in which merchandise could be displayed. The product of the alliance of architecture and commerce was the department store. The first one, Au Bon Marché, rose on the Left Bank in Paris in the 1850s and underwent major expansion and renovation in 1872. Its architect, Alexandre La Planche, covered load-bearing iron frames with stone facades that were punctuated with large display windows. The outside of the department store thus became a venue for advertising, giving passersby a glimpse of what goods could be purchased within. Once lured inside, shoppers (most of whom were women) were treated to abundant displays of goods amid fantastically ornate interiors, prompting the novelist Emile Zola (1840–1902) to christen the department store "the cathedral of commerce." Stores such as Au Bon Marché or Printemps, which opened in Paris in 1874, were also semipublic spaces for strolling or lingering at refreshment centers. Department stores became a fixture of the urban landscape, and as sites where products were offered at set prices with no obligation to buy, changed shopping from a provisioning task to a leisure activity. The increased purchasing power of the middle classes (with the expansion in the ranks of "white-collar" workers) and the working classes (with emergence of "pink-collar" workers—secretaries and retail workers—and the rise of real wages among factory workers), expanded the ranks of buyers dramatically. Advertising and consumption also affected the places where products were made. More and more factories were designed to advertise what was made inside. Templeton's Carpet Factory (1889–1892) in Glasgow, Scotland, for example, incorporated Assyrian, Persian, and Byzantine architectural motifs in its exterior design as a way of showing the prospective buyer that luxurious, exotic, "oriental" rugs were being made inside.

Domestic Architecture. As the public world for Europeans grew more densely populated, urban, and noisy, the private, domestic world of the family became more secluded and tranquil. In fact, current psychological theory taught that states of mind were directly related to formal surroundings, so architects of domestic buildings and interior designers adopted the canons of privacy and tranquility. The home was to be a soothing and peaceful haven from the bustling and stressful outside world. No longer did domestic interiors announce familial status and history

as Horace Walpole's Strawberry Hill had in the late eighteenth century. Gone were the days when a public figure's dwelling was a semipublic museum as much as a private home. A distinguished essayist and a son of Prime Minister Robert Walpole (1676–1745), Horace Walpole (1717–1797) stocked his home with medieval artifacts and opened its doors to a select group of tourists. Privacy and intimacy had become the prevailing values by the late nineteenth century.

Sources:

Barry Bergdoll, *European Architecture, 1750–1890* (Oxford: Oxford University Press, 2000).

Richard Brettell, *Modern Art, 1851–1929: Capitalism and Representation* (Oxford: Oxford University Press, 1999).

Arnold Hauser, *The Social History of Art,* volume 2 (New York: Knopf, 1952).

François Loyer, *Architecture of the Industrial Age, 1789–1914,* translated by R. F. M. Dexter (Geneva: Skira, 1983).

Robin Middleton and David Watkin, *Neoclassical and Nineteenth-Century Architecture* (New York: Abrams, 1981).

Fritz Novotny, *Painting and Sculpture in Europe, 1780–1880* (New Haven: Yale University Press, 1978).

Robert Rosenblum, *Nineteenth-Century Art* (Englewood Cliffs, N.J.: Prentice-Hall / New York: Abrams, 1984).

THE OBJECTIVITY OF REALISM: LITERATURE

Laissez-Faire Capitalism and Realism in Literature. While Romanticism continued to hold sway in music until the rise of Modernism in the twentieth century, European writers, like their contemporaries in the visual arts, turned to Realism and Naturalism to depict the life of their times. Composers of music believed their medium to be a purer form of expression than painting or writing, and thus, almost by definition, no "realist" music could be written. During the 1830s and 1840s various European nations (notably England and France) established political regimes whose economic policies encouraged the development of free-market capitalism. A market economy had already been coming into existence for decades, but during the 1830s and 1840s its development was hastened by experiments with laissez-faire capitalism. In such an economic system the prices goods could command in an unregulated market were the sole guiding principle for establishing value, and supporters of this kind of capitalism believed that the market would regulate itself toward equilibrium. In such an environment, competition dominated. Success or failure could hinge on close attention to detail and was measured in the accumulation of wealth. The production and consumption of literature operated within this context. Authors such as Charles Dickens (1812–1870) and Honoré de Balzac (1799–1850) wrote novels that were either published serially in affordable periodicals or in inexpensive paper-covered monthly installments that the reader could later have bound together as a book if he or she so desired. These methods of publication gave writers access to an ever-growing reading public. Balzac supplied the periodical *La Presse* with a serialized novel annually from 1837 to 1847. The value of a novel was determined by demand (how well it would sell), and the author's pay was propor-

Exterior and interior of the Paris department store Au Bon Marché in 1872, with a new façade and steel infrastructure by
Alexandre La Planche and interior design by Louis-Charles Boileau (from Barry Bergdoll,
European Architecture, 1750–1890, 2000)

Templeton's Carpet Factory in Glasgow as it appeared in 1889–1892 (National Monuments Record, Scotland)

tional. Dickens's first full-length serial novel, *The Pickwick Papers* (1836–1837), sold forty thousand copies in cheap monthly installments. Since Dickens met with immediate success, largely with a new class of readers who had never read novels before, the demand for his works was enormous. Not only did the publication format of Realist novels fit their economic context, but so did their style, philosophy, mood, and subject matter. In France during the 1830s and 1840s preoccupation with money dominated public and private life, and Balzac portrayed the power of money and the workings of finances in minute detail, conveying his characters' insecurity about their precarious money-linked social status. Money is a despotic master, and for Balzac the capitalistic world was one in which his characters are constantly surrounded by enemies and rivals. Success is measured through the property, social position, and political influence that only money can obtain. Balzac's novels, and some of Dickens's, are realistic representations of the social world in which free-market capitalism operated. They are also social commentary. In *Hard Times* (1854) Dickens exposed the negative social effects of capitalistic industrialization, while Balzac portrayed capitalism as a destructive force unleashing egoistic human ambition, which breaks down traditional institutions (such as the church and the family) that held society together in the past. The messages of these novels are all the more compelling because of their unremitting Realistic style. By a sober and extraordinarily detailed examination of the facts of social and economic life, Balzac, Dickens, and other Realist writers broke with the dream and fantasy of Romanticism and focused on the material factors of life, against which their characters struggle and often fail.

Positivism and Realist and Naturalist Literature. Between 1830 and 1842 Auguste Comte (1798–1857) published *Cours de philosophie positive* (Course in Positivist Philosophy). At the core of this philosophy is the assertion that true, "positive" knowledge can be based only on observable facts, which in turn illustrate the operation of immutable natural laws. This assumption had guided scientific endeavor for more than a hundred years before Comte, but Comte extended the principles of scientific analysis to the examination of society. Realist literature embraced this philosophy. In *La Comédie humaine* (The Human Comedy), a series of novels and stories published between 1830 and 1848, Balzac created more than two thousand characters and made them subjects of his minute analysis and classification. Balzac described his approach: "There is but one Animal since the creator used a single pattern for all organized beings. This basic animal takes its variations in form from the environment in which it is obliged to develop. . . . Society is seen as resembling nature, producing social species comparable to zoological species." Through a positivistic presentation of these "human animals" in his novels, where they are arrayed and displayed against their material world, Balzac exposes the general laws that bring "social effects" into being and then govern the characters. For Balzac the one general law that underlies all the rest is "the great law of Self for Self." The novels of Naturalist Gustave Flaubert (1821–1880) are equally positivistic; yet, he believed that to arrive at objective truth the author must not only allow the material data of life to dictate causality, but he must also remove himself as much as possible from his creation. As he said in 1866, "great art is scientific and impersonal." For this reason, Naturalist writers such as Flaubert employed third-person narrators and withdrew to a position of ubiquitous observer. As Flaubert wrote in an 1852 letter to his friend Louise Colet, "I am in a . . . world . . . of attentive observation of the dullest details. My eyes are fixed on the spores of mildew growing on the soul. . . . In my book I do not want there to be a *single* movement, or a *single* reflection of the author. . . . Let us be magnifying mirrors of external truth." The Russian Realist Leo Tolstoy (1828–1910) echoed these same principles in his novels, including *Voina i mir* (War and Peace, 1865–1869). Like Balzac and Dickens, Tolstoy was an unerring observer of social reality and a critic of capitalism, and, like the Naturalists Flaubert and Emile Zola (1840–1902), he claimed that facts spoke for themselves. About *War and Peace,* for example, he wrote, "everywhere in my novel that historical personages speak and act, I have invented nothing, but have made use of the materials which I have found and which in the course of my labors have amounted to a whole library." The well-known French literary critic E. M. de Vogüé (1848–1910) summed up Realism in 1886 as "an art of observation rather than of imagination, one which boasts that it observes life as it is in its wholeness and complexity with the least possible prejudice on the part of the artist. It takes men under ordinary conditions, shows characters in the course of their everyday existence, average and changing."

Women and Realist Literature. Realist writers often showed how the conditions of life affected women. Frequently, female characters in Realist literature are portrayed as victims trapped in tragic lives by male ignorance and arrogance, legal and moral restraints, and unhappy marriages. In Flaubert's *Madame Bovary* (1857) Emma Bovary escapes from a deadening, monotonous, provincial marriage through sexual fantasy, adultery, and suicide. Tolstoy's main character in *Anna Karenina* (1875–1877) follows the same tragic yet inevitable trajectory. Her escape also leads to adultery and, with the shame that accompanies it, inexorably to suicide. Not all women in Realist literature, however, were hapless victims. George Sand (Armantine-Aurore-Lucile Dupin, 1804–1876) wrote in the preface to her novel *Indiana* (1832) that she was motivated by "a powerful instinct of protest" against patriarchal power, which led her to cast her heroine against "the injustice and barbarity of those laws which still govern women in marriage, in the family, and in society." In his play *Et dukkehjem* (A Doll's House, 1879) Norwegian playwright Henrik Ibsen (1828–1906) sounds the same note of protest against patriarchy. His female protagonist, Nora, a bourgeois housewife, attacks and ultimately rejects the social convention that she must unquestioningly and totally submit herself to her husband.

Sources:

George J. Becker, *Master European Realists of the Nineteenth Century* (New York: Ungar, 1982).

Henry Raynor, *Music and Society since 1815* (New York: Schocken Books, 1976).

Martin Travers, *An Introduction to Modern European Literature* (New York: St. Martin's Press, 1998).

THE TURN TO MODERNISM: ART AND ARCHITECTURE

Cultural Fragmentation, Subjectivism, and Nonrepresentation. During the nineteenth century, the political map of Europe became increasingly defined by territorial, sovereign nation-states. The leaders and the people of these states, moreover, came to embrace nationalism, which often opposed the glories of one nation against the inferiority of others. By the last third of the century these European states had also entered into a global competition for colonies and trade, and they came to view warfare as a rational and logical way for states to settle their competitive differences. As a result, Europe became increasingly fragmented politically and culturally. The outbreak of World War I in 1914 was a thunderous result of political fragmentation, and the artistic style called Modernism was a consequence of growing cultural differences. Long gone from the artistic scene was the confidence in progress, improvement, and universalism that marked Classicism. The subjectivism of Romanticism remained, but Modernist artists and writers expressed it in moods of decadence, pessimism, and nostalgia. Cultural fragmentation in music resulted in discordance and dissonance, while in painting, fractured images led eventually to almost complete abstraction. Since the Renaissance, artists had assumed that art was fundamentally a representation of the real, visible world, but no such assumption guided the Modernists. Fragmentation and subjectivism had become the essence of the meaning of the term *modern.*

Impressionist Painting. Impressionism represents a fundamental transition in art, bringing to a close the era in which artists assumed that art was the study and representation of the external appearance of nature. This guiding idea had held sway since the Renaissance and the invention of three-point perspective, which creates the illusion of depth in a picture. Of course, movements such as Romanticism explicitly filtered representation through the imagination of the creative genius, but the images produced were still visibly identifiable as the world that humans directly perceive. Realism, as Gustave Courbet (1819–1877) stated, was the most extreme expression of objective representation. In one sense Impressionism was a reaction to and a rejection of such literalism, but as an imitation of natural objects (landscapes or people) it remained within the Renaissance objectivist tradition, as demonstrated by the paintings of the great Impressionists—Camille Pissarro (1830–1903), Edouard Manet (1832–1883), Edgar Degas (1834–1917), Claude Monet (1840–

Lane near a Small Town (1864–1865) by Alfred Sisley (Kunsthalle, Bremen)

Impression: Sunrise (1872) by Claude Monet, the painting from which the Impressionist movement got its name
(Musée Marmottan, Paris)

Playwright Henrik Ibsen sympathized with the individual's struggle against predominant social values and mores. Although he was never a feminist, his portrayal of Nora in *A Doll's House* was received with praise by feminists and with disdain by traditionalists. Set in the middle of a nineteenth-century Norwegian winter, the play shows the limitations married women faced with regard to control over property, children, and even their individualism. The following excerpt is from the last scene, where Nora decides to let her husband, Torvald Helmer, know what she has felt about the eight years of their marriage.

Nora. In all these eight years—longer than that—from the very beginning of our acquaintance, we have never exchanged a word on any serious subject.

Helmer. Was it likely that I would be continually and for ever telling you about worries that you could not help me to bear?

Nora. I am not speaking about business matters. I say that we have never sat down in earnest together to try and get at the bottom of anything.

Helmer. But, dearest Nora, would it have been any good to you?

Nora. That is just it; you have never understood me. I have been greatly wronged, Torvald, first by papa and then by you.

Helmer. What! By us two—by us two, who have loved you better than anyone else in the world?

Nora (*shaking her head*). You have never loved me. You have only thought it pleasant to be in love with me.

Helmer. Nora, what do I hear you saying?

Nora. It is perfectly true, Torvald. When I was at home with papa, he told me of his opinion about everything, and so I had the same opinions; and if I differed from him I concealed the fact, because he would not have liked it. He called me his doll-child, and he played with me just as I used to play with my dolls. And when I came to live with you. . . .

Helmer. What sort of an expression is that to use about our marriage?

Nora (*undisturbed*). I mean that I was simply transferred from papa's hands into yours. You arranged everything according to your own taste, and so I got the same tastes as you—or else I pretended to, I am really not quite sure which—I think sometimes the one and sometimes the other. When I look back on it, it seems to me as if I had been living here like a poor woman—just from hand to mouth. I have existed merely to perform tricks for you, Torvald. But you would have it so. You and papa have committed a great sin against me. It is your fault that I have made nothing of my life.

Helmer. How unreasonable and how ungrateful you are, Nora! Have you not been happy here?

Nora. No, I have never been happy. I thought I was, but it has never really been so.

Helmer. Not—not happy!

Nora. No, only merry. And you have always been so kind to me. But our home has been nothing but a playroom. I have been your doll-wife, just as at home I was papa's doll-child; and here the children have been my dolls. I thought it great fun when you played with me, just as they thought it great fun when I played with them. That is what our marriage has been, Torvald.

Helmer. There is some truth in what you say—exaggerated and strained as your view of it is. But for the future it shall be different. Playtime shall be over, and lesson-time shall begin.

Nora. Whose lessons? Mine, or the children's?

Helmer. Both yours and the children's, my darling Nora.

Nora. Alas, Torvald, you are not the man to educate me into being a proper wife for you. . . . Didn't you say so yourself a little while ago—that you dare not trust me to bring them up?

Helmer. In a moment of anger! Why do you pay any heed to that?

Nora. Indeed, you were perfectly right. I am not fit for the task. There is another task I must undertake first. I must try and educate myself—you are not the man to help me in that. I must do that for myself. And that is why I am going to leave you now.

Helmer (*springing up*). What do you say?

Nora. I must stand quite alone, if I am to understand myself and everything about me. It is for that reason that I cannot remain with you any longer.

Source: Henrik Ibsen, *A Doll's House* (New York: Washington Square Press, 1968), pp. 108–111.

1926), Pierre-Auguste Renoir (1841–1919), and Mary Cassatt (1844–1926). *Lane near a Small Town,* painted by Alfred Sisley (1839–1899) in 1864–1865, is a typical example of how Impressionists rejected literal realism without foregoing objective representation.

Toward Modernism. Impressionism, however, was a leap toward Modernism. Like Romantic painters, Impressionists recognized the subjectivity of the act of representa- tion, but many of them carried this awareness to a new level by asserting that painting was consciously about the *act* of representation more than the subject matter of the painting. They recognized that painting was more a record of the artist's experience than an account of perceived natural objects. Impressionists did not totally invent the images they represented in paint, but they often reduced the significance of the subject to complete banality or even utter meaninglessness and therefore directed the viewer's attention to *how* the artist represented the world rather than *what* he represented. Renoir forcefully drove this point home in *The Luncheon of the Boating Party* (1881). Although individuals are clearly depicted, the overwhelming impression upon the viewer is the play of light and the effect of texture one gets from the artist's application of paint to canvas. Not all Impressionist painters stripped their pictures of meaning, however. Manet or Degas, for example, used their subject matter to comment on the social fragmentation that was emerging in modern life. According to some social critics, industrialism had led to a class society and driven a wedge between social groups while creating a sense of isolation and anomie among individuals. Manet captured this disconnectedness between people in *The Bar of the Folies Bergère* (1881–1882), in which a dispirited and disinterested barmaid gazes blankly toward the viewer. On closer inspection, the viewer observes in a mirror behind her a bourgeois man (who is from a different social class than the barmaid) intently returning her gaze. The viewer is initially struck by the disjuncture between the seeming isolation of the woman and the physical proximity of the man. Moreover, the mirrored reflection does not faithfully represent reality. The man in the mirror is impossibly close, and the woman's back is reflected at an angle that logically suggests it cannot belong to the woman facing the viewer. Degas also sometimes commented on the isolation of modern life. In *L'Absinthe* (1876) he portrays a modern, working-class couple who attempt to obliterate their meaningless existence by drinking an addictive and sense-deadening alcoholic beverage.

Symbolism and Expressionism. More than their Impressionist precursor, Symbolist and Expressionist painting were a conscious reaction against Realism. Where an empiricist scientism had come to guide Realism, Symbolists and Expressionists returned to the Romantic notion that a higher spiritual existence was attainable not through rationalism but rather through feeling. Like Romantics, Symbolists and Expressionists sometimes sought to explore the psyche and investigate the meaning of identity. In their explorations of the imagination, however, they continued the Impressionist departure from faithfully representing visual reality. Symbolism, as the name suggests, conveys meaning through the use of representational images, while Expressionism seeks an unmediated "expression" of the artist's inner, and individualistic, vision. Paul Gauguin (1848–1903), Vincent van Gogh (1853–1890), the Norwegian Edvard Munch (1863–1944), and Paul Cézanne (1839–1906) are among the best-known painters working in these styles.

Gauguin. Disgusted by the bourgeois culture of his homeland, Gauguin emigrated in 1891 from his native France to the French colony of Tahiti, where he painted a series of works that illustrate a blending of cultures in an age of imperialism and colonialism. His paintings also raise the related question about the formation and meaning of an individual's identity. While many of his Tahiti paintings depict nearly nude natives, *Ancestors of Tehamana* (1893), a portrait of his Polynesian wife, shows a native woman wearing European dress and adopting a traditional European pose. Contrasted to this Western representation, however, is a background that displays Polynesian linguistic and religious ancestral images. Gauguin therefore suggests that identity is a malleable construct, the product of blended cultures. Making the same statement about the cultural construction of identity and more clearly Symbolist in style is Gauguin's painting *Where Do We Come From? What Are We? Where Are We Going?* (1897), which again combines European and non-Western motifs. On the one hand, it is a symbolic representation of the Christian story of the fall of man and a lost paradise. On the other hand, it embraces non-Western images of nearly nude women representing the life cycle from birth to death, and Polynesian icons (such as the fruit picker) preside over this paradise.

Van Gogh. Van Gogh's paintings also probed the psyche and were all the more poignant than Gauguin's in that they often powerfully expressed van Gogh's own mental state. In paintings such as *The Church at Auvers* (1890) van Gogh visually warped reality, forcing the viewer to see the world from his own tormented perspective and so pressing further the subjectivist trajectory of much of nineteenth-century art.

Munch. An equally disturbing Expressionist painting is Edvard Munch's *The Scream* (1893). Often interpreted as a desperate and frantic cry from the archetypal isolated individual in modern society, this painting also represents a culture that—through fragmentation and disorientation—has lost its bearings and its moorings and is careening catastrophically into a frightening future.

Cézanne. Like van Gogh and Gauguin, the French painter Paul Cézanne also abandoned Impressionism to accomplish something less limited. He shared the Impressionists' proclivity to avoid representational meaning in his paintings, but through short, almost blunt brush strokes (stabs of color, at times in shapes of rough rectangles and squares) he pushed painting to near abstraction. By breaking down an object into what would seem on close inspection to be disconnected shapes, Cézanne profoundly influenced the young artists (some of whom became Cubists) who flocked to view a retrospective and posthumous exhibition of his works in 1907.

Cubism. In 1909 in Paris, Georges Braque (1882–1963) and Pablo Picasso (1881–1973) exhibited paintings that signaled to the public a decisive break with representation. Often heralded as nonobjective representations (that is, works of art that do not appear visually as the objects for which they stand), Braque's and Picasso's "Cubist" paintings are often considered the first abstract works of the twentieth century. Viewers must certainly have thought so. Although the paintings were still recognizably pictures of things or persons, such as Picasso's *Portrait of Ambroise Vollard* (1910), they appeared decidedly unreal. By constructing their works with scores of short brush strokes and breaking up or breaking down the objects they depicted, Braque and Picasso reached yet another stage in the march of subjectivism and Modernism. Like so much art at the turn of

The Luncheon of the Boating Party (1881) by Pierre-Auguste Renoir (The Phillips Collection, Washington, D.C.)

The Bar of the Folies Bergère (1881–1882) by Edouard Manet (Courtauld Institute Gallery, London)

In his 17 January 1889 letter to his brother Theo, an art dealer on whom he was financially dependent, Vincent van Gogh wrote of his poverty and his estrangement from Paul Gauguin, who for a time in 1888 had painted with van Gogh in the south of France. (Though van Gogh's paintings are now valued at millions of dollars, during his lifetime they earned him little.) As this letter reveals, van Gogh could not clearly understand why Gauguin had ended their friendship and returned to the north. Written just after van Gogh had returned to Arles from being hospitalized for psychological disorders and less than a year before his death by suicide, this letter is filled with evidence of the painter's emotional instability.

. . . It is unfortunately complicated in various ways, my pictures are valueless, it is true they cost me an extraordinary amount, perhaps even in blood and brains at times. I won't harp on it, and what am I to say about it?

. . .

. . . I have started work again, and I already have three finished studies in the studio, besides the portrait of Dr. Rey, which I gave him as a keepsake. So there is no worse harm done this time than a little more suffering and its attendant wretchedness. And I keep on hoping. But I feel weak and rather uneasy and frightened. That will pass, I hope, as I get back my strength.

Rey told me that being very impressionable was enough to account for the attack that I had. . . . I took the liberty of [asking] M. Rey . . . whether he had seen many madmen in similar circumstances fairly quiet and able to work; if not, would he then be good enough to remember occasionally that for the moment I am not yet mad.

. . .

If Gauguin stayed in Paris for a while to examine himself thoroughly, or have himself examined by a specialist, I don't honestly know what the result might be.

On various occasions I have seen him do things which you and I would not let ourselves to, because we have consciences that feel differently about things. I have heard one or two things said of him, but having seen him at very, very close quarters, I think that he is carried away by his imagination, perhaps by pride, but . . . practically irresponsible.

. . .

. . . Lord, let him do anything he wants, let him have his independence?? (whatever he means by that) and his opinions, and let him go his own way as soon as he thinks he knows it better than we do.

. . .

Whatever happens, I shall see my strength come back little by little if I can stick it out here. I do so dread a change or move just because of the fresh expense. I have been unable to get a breathing spell for a long time now. I am not giving up work, because there are moments when it is really getting on, and I believe that with patience the goal will at last be reached, that the pictures will pay back the money invested in making them.

. . .

Although this letter is already very long, since I have tried to analyze the month's expenses and complained a bit of the queer phenomenon of Gauguin's behavior in choosing not to speak to me again and clearing out, there are still some things that I must add in praise of him.

One good quality he has is the marvelous way he can apportion expenses from day to day.

While I am often absent-minded, preoccupied with aiming at the goal, he has far more money sense for each separate day than I have. But his weakness is that by a sudden freak or animal impulse he upsets everything he has arranged.

. . .

As for me, I have ceased to be able to follow his actions, and I give it up in silence, but with a questioning note all the same.

From time to time he and I have exchanged ideas about French art, and impressionism. . . .

It seems to me impossible, or at least pretty improbable, that impressionism will organize and steady itself now.

. . .

. . . Gauguin has a fine, free and absolutely complete imaginary conception of the South, and with that imagination he is going to work in the North! My word, we may see some queer results yet.

And now, dissecting the situation in all boldness, there is nothing to prevent our seeing him as the little Bonaparte tiger of impressionism as far as . . . I don't quite know how to say it, his vanishing, say, from Arles would be comparable or analogous to the return from Egypt of the aforesaid Little Corporal, who also presented himself in Paris afterward and who always left the armies in the lurch. Fortunately Gauguin and I and other painters are not yet armed with machine guns and other very destructive implements of war. I for one am quite decided to go on being armed with nothing but my brush and my pen.

Source: Letter 9, *Vincent van Gogh 1853–1890* <http://www.van-gogh-art.co.uk/artist/letter9.htm>.

Ancestors of Tehamana (1893) by Paul Gauguin (The
Art Institute of Chicago)

Way, 1913) by Marcel Proust (1871–1922) is the first part of
the tellingly titled family saga *A la recherche du temps perdu* (In
Search of Lost Time, 1913–1927), first translated into
English as *Remembrance of Things Past* (1922–1932). In
Swann's Way, the only novel in the series published before the
war, readers could not miss the nostalgia of Proust, who
through his narrator recalls a childhood lost in the mists of
time. Through that memory emerges a longing for a unity of
life that, on the eve of World War I, seems irretrievably lost
and so at odds with the dislocated world around him. Pessimism often joins nostalgia in early Modernist literature. The
British literary critic, essayist, and poet Matthew Arnold
(1822–1888), who may be seen as a transitional figure
between Victorian and Modernist sensibilities, wrote in *Culture and Anarchy* (1869) that industrial society had departed
from the laudable trajectory toward perfection that the
Enlightenment had charted. The ship of progress and harmony (embodied in an organic "culture") had, he believed,
foundered on the shoals of the disunity engendered by capitalist industrialism. This result, the "anarchy" of Arnold's title, is
reflected in a class society marked by extremes of wealth and
comfort at one end and of poverty and suffering at the other.
Although many of Matthew Arnold's essays seem to hold out
hope that a new world could be salvaged from the wreckage of
the nineteenth century, his poem "Dover Beach" (1867) is
filled with pessimism and horror at destruction bred of ignorance. As the speaker looks out over the English Channel at
night, he listens to

> the grating roar
> Of pebbles which the waves draw back, and fling,
> At their return, up the high strand[.]

In them he hears "The eternal note of sadness" that long ago
reminded Sophocles of "the turbid ebb and flow / Of human
misery." The speaker's thoughts then turn to the contemporary loss of conviction about the Enlightenment sense of perfectibility:

> The Sea of Faith
> Was once, too, at the full, and round earth's shore
> Lay like the folds of a bright girdle furl'd.
> But now I can only hear
> Its melancholy, long, withdrawing roar,
> Retreating, to the breath
> Of the night-wind, down the vast edges drear
>   And naked shingles of the world.

Then he turns to the woman who is with him and expresses
the sort of disillusionment and pessimism that underlies the
writings of the great Modernists:

> Ah, love, let us be true
> To one another! For the world, which seems
> To lie before us like a land of dreams,
> So various, so beautiful, so new,
> Hath really neither joy, nor love, nor help for pain;
> And we are here as on a darkling plain
> Swept with confused alarms of struggle and flight,
>   Where ignorant armies clash by night.

the twentieth century, the deliberate fragmentation of Cubist
paintings can also be understood as a symbolic representation
of a fragmented culture.

Sources:

Richard Brettell, *Modern Art, 1851–1929: Capitalism and Representation*
(Oxford: Oxford University Press, 1999).

Timothy J. Clark, *The Painter of Modern Life: Paris in the Age of Manet and His
Followers* (New York: Knopf, 1984).

George Heard Hamilton, *Painting and Sculpture in Europe, 1880–1940* (New
Haven: Yale University Press, 1993).

Anne McCauley, *Industrial Madness: Commercial Photography in Paris, 1848–
1871* (New Haven: Yale University Press, 1994).

THE TURN TO MODERNISM: LITERATURE AND MUSIC

Modernist Literature. Modernist literature came to maturity in the 1920s, but its dominant themes and concerns were
already becoming evident in novels, poems, and plays of the
late nineteenth and early twentieth century. Growing social
unrest, which was signaled by unprecedented strikes among
industrial workers and the spread of political anarchism,
evoked moods of decadence, pessimism, and nostalgia for a
more unified and meaningful past. Moreover, in the literature
of the 1890s and the first decade of the twentieth century, one
can sense an apocalyptic tone and a foreboding that civilization is coming to an end. *Du Côté de chez Swann* (Swann's

THE WHITE MAN'S BURDEN

The idea that Europeans had a moral duty to impose their civilization, religion, and value system on people of other cultures, often with no consideration for their own religious and moral beliefs, is perhaps best expressed in "The White Man's Burden" (1899), a popular poem by Rudyard Kipling:

Take up the White Man's burden—
  Send forth the best ye breed—
Go, bind your sons to exile
  To serve your captives' need;
To wait, in heavy harness,
  On fluttered folk and wild—
Your new-caught sullen peoples,
  Half devil and half child.

Take up the White Man's burden—
  In patience to abide,
To veil the threat of terror
  And check the show of pride;
By open speech and simple,
  An hundred times made plain,
To seek another's profit
  And work another's gain.

Take up the White Man's burden—
  The savage wars of peace—
Fill full the mouth of Famine,
  And bid the sickness cease;
And when your goal is nearest
  (The end for others sought)
Watch sloth and heathen folly
  Bring all your hope to nought.

Take up the White Man's burden—
  No iron rule of kings,
But toil of serf and sweeper—
  The tale of common things.
The ports ye shall not enter,
  The roads ye shall not tread,
Go, make them with your living
  And mark them with your dead.

Take up the White Man's burden,
  And reap his old reward—
The blame of those ye better
  The hate of those ye guard—
The cry of hosts ye humour
  (Ah, slowly!) toward the light:—
"Why brought ye us from bondage,
  Our loved Egyptian night?"

Take up the White Man's burden—
  Ye dare not stoop to less—
Nor call too loud on Freedom
  To cloak your weariness.
By all ye will or whisper,
  By all ye leave or do,
The silent sullen peoples
  Shall weigh your God and you.

Take up the White Man's burden!
  Have done with childish days—
The lightly-proffered laurel,
  The easy ungrudged praise:
Comes now, to search your manhood
  Through all the thankless years,
Cold, edged with dear-bought wisdom,
  The judgment of your peers.

Source: *McClure's Magazine* (February 1899).

The same moods of pessimism and pointlessness—so common to Modernist literature—may also be found in the plays of the Russian writer Anton Chekhov (1860–1904). In *Tri sestry* (Three Sisters, 1901) and *Vishnevyi sad* (The Cherry Orchard, 1904) Chekhov portrays families dominated by their memories of an unrecoverable glorious past and mired in the present, the forces of which they only dimly understand. The title characters in *Three Sisters* exist in a "rot of boredom" and see no hope in the future, while the aristocratic family of *The Cherry Orchard* feel only an "oppressive sense of emptiness" and fatalism as they lose the family estate to a businessman embodying the new capitalistic spirit of economic development.

Subjectivism and Consciousness. Ever since Romanticism, artists and writers had probed the inner self in search of inspiration, beauty, and truth. This subjectivism became a hallmark of nearly all nineteenth- and early-twentieth-century art. Toward the end of this period, subjectivism received two powerful added stimuli from the philosophy of Friedrich Nietzsche (1844–1900) and the early psychoanalytic theories of Sigmund Freud (1856–1939). Both of these thinkers pointed toward the existence of an inner self that was stirred by nonrational urges toward chaos and pleasure. These psychic forces could drive the individual toward a pleasure-seeking hedonism that might carry with it the seeds of evil and destruction. Freud called these forces the *id* and posited that in the mature individual the *ego*, or sense of self, is compelled by the urge for self-preservation, to mediate between the id and the *superego*, or sense of morality and ethics. The Irish poet, essayist, and novelist Oscar Wilde (1854–1900) illustrated such destructive hedonism metaphorically in *The Picture of Dorian Gray*

The Church at Auvers (1890) by Vincent van Gogh (Musée d'Orsay, Paris)

(1891). Although Wilde, like the French poet Arthur Rimbaud (1854–1891), elsewhere seems to extol the "new hedonism" of the latter part of the nineteenth century, which gloried in the youthful human body as a temple of pleasure, in *The Picture of Dorian Gray* he pessimistically conveyed the notion that youth is lost forever. Like the title character, the individual cannot arrest, even with the help of magic, the inevitable decay that awaits everyone in the future. Equally popular at the time was *The Strange Case of Doctor Jekyll and Mr. Hyde* (1886) by Robert Louis Stevenson (1850–1894). Within the psyche of the rational and orderly Dr. Jekyll lurks the evil, irrational, and chaotic Mr. Hyde. These characters are excellent literary examples of the Freudian conflict between the superego (Jekyll) and the id (the murderous Mr. Hyde), which Freud described in his *Neue Folge der Vorlesungen zur Einführung in die Psychoanalyse* (New Introductory Lectures on Psychoanalysis, 1933) as "that cauldron full of seething excitations . . . filled with energy reaching it from the instincts." Joseph Conrad (1857–1924) situated the Freudian conflict of superego and id in the Belgian Congo in his well-known story "Heart of Darkness" (1902), in which he linked this psychic battle to a withering critique of European imperialism, whose proponents argued that they were extending progress and morality to uncivilized peoples. Instead of carrying this "white man's burden" to people supposedly in need of Europeanizing and progress, Conrad's Kurtz, the station manager for a European company of ivory traders, has become overwhelmed by the wilderness into which he has been thrust, and to assert his power over the natives, he has surrounded his house with posts bearing human heads. Kurtz has abandoned European notions of decency and civility (the Freudian superego) and surrendered himself to "brutal instincts . . . and monstrous passions." The story is simultaneously about the fragility of the superego in comparison to the id and the moral bankruptcy, and ultimate futility, of the civilizing mission of European imperialism.

 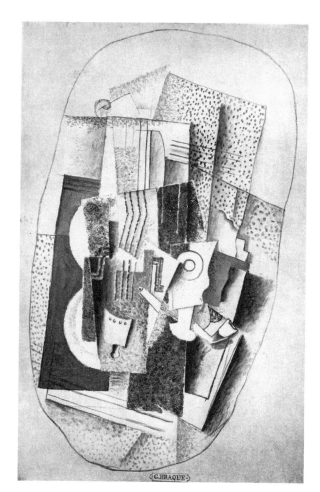

Two Cubist paintings: *Portrait of Ambroise Vollard* (1910) by Pablo Picasso (Pushkin State Museum of Fine Arts, Moscow) and *Music* (1914) by Georges Braque (The Phillips Collection, Washington, D.C.)

Modern Music: Discordance and Dissonance. More than in any other field of art, Romanticism held sway in music to the end of the nineteenth century. As late as 1906 Richard Strauss (1864–1949) composed an opera that was fully within the Wagnerian tradition and its enormous orchestral scale. Indeed, even the Modernist composers' spirit of innovation follows a logical trajectory from nineteenth-century music, which focused on the creative genius. Whereas much Romantic music had been written for the virtuoso performer, much modern music can be thought of as the work of a virtuoso composer. Much as the Impressionist painters became more concerned with showing the act of representation than with depicting a subject, so too in music composers began to focus more on the act of composition than on conveying a theme. Still, the forces of fundamental change and fragmentation can be glimpsed in the works of several turn-of-the-century composers, who were on the threshold of change as revolutionary as that which occurred in painting with Impressionism, Symbolism, Expressionism, and Cubism. The Expressionist composer Arnold Schoenberg (1874–1951), for example, introduced atonality (the twelve-tone scale), a fundamental challenge to the definition of Western music that had stood for centuries. Notes in his compositions were deliberately dissociated from melodic harmonies and, moreover, were completely meaningless. Sometimes he radically reduced the length of a composition. For example, three of his *Sechs kleine klavierstücke* (Six Little Piano Pieces, 1911) are only nine bars each. Schoenberg's scores were also written for a sharply reduced orchestra, marking an abrupt departure from the enormous ensemble of musicians that was typically required to play a Romantic symphony. For his first Chamber Symphony (1906), for example, Schoenberg remarked that he had written his composition for "fifteen solo instruments," clear testimony to the individualism and sense of disunity that had become a cultural trait. Igor Stravinsky (1882–1971) echoed these notions in his work *L'Histoire du soldat* (The Soldier's Tale, 1918), which called for a much smaller orchestra than required for nineteenth-century Romantic music and even his own score for the ballet *Rite of Spring* (1913).

Serious versus Light Music. The dissonance, discord, and atonality that marked much of the emergent Modernist music did not appeal to mass audiences. Indeed, when Stravinsky's *Rite of Spring* was first performed, the audience was so upset that it bombarded the musicians with catcalls and jeers so intense that they were forced to interrupt the performance and quit the stage. The seeds of such popular dissatisfaction had been planted many years before. Giuseppe Verdi (1813–1901) was upset that audiences preferred his operas *Il Trovatore* (1853) or *La Traviatta* (1853), which treated them to simple cascades of melodies, to his more musically complex and demanding works, such as *Simon Boccanegra* (1857). As orchestras grew in the nineteenth century and compositions became more complex, audiences began to separate into groups who, on the one hand, were "sophisticated" enough to appreciate the demanding music and, on the other, were mainly interested in being entertained. The "Great Schism" that still exists in music had arrived. There were enough music consumers in this "Age of the Masses" to make both serious and popular music commercially profitable. Late in the nineteenth century many great, elaborate concert halls were constructed for performances of "serious" music by the increasingly pro-fessional and prestigious orchestras. At the same time, many working-class neighborhoods had music halls for the performance of "popular" music. This growing separation correlated to the class divisions that had taken hold in nineteenth-century industrial society. Increasingly, the educated upper classes embraced "serious" opera and orchestral music, while the middle and working classes preferred the light operas of William Gilbert (1836–1911) and Arthur Sullivan (1842–1900), the Viennese waltzes of Johann Strauss (1825–1899), or the ragtime and vaudeville of the music halls.

Sources:

Henry Raynor, *Music and Society since 1815* (New York: Schocken Books, 1976).

Martin Travers, *An Introduction to Modern European Literature* (New York: St. Martin's Press, 1998).

SIGNIFICANT PEOPLE

JANE AUSTEN

1775-1817
NOVELIST

Early Years. Jane Austen was born in 1775 in Steventon, Hampshire, England, where her father, George Austen, was a rector in the local parish church. As an Anglican clergyman, he earned a modest income. The rectory was home not only to George Austen, his wife, Cassandra, and their eight children, but also to pupils George Austen tutored to earn extra money. Jane Austen's education was informal, relatively brief, and no more rigorous than the schooling given to most girls of her time and social class. In 1782 she accompanied her older sister, Cassandra, and a cousin to study in the home of an aunt named Mrs. Ann Cawley, first in Oxford and then in Southampton. They remained with Mrs. Cawley until autumn 1783. In 1784 the sisters were sent to a girls' boarding school in Reading, which was similar to Mrs. Goddard's casual school in Austen's novel *Emma* (1815), and remained there until December 1786. The rest of Austen's education occurred at home, where she learned to play the piano and to draw. Neither Jane nor Cassandra Austen ever married.

Reading. Above all, Jane Austen was an active reader of nonfiction as well as a less-respectable and relatively new form, the novel. Apparently, her entire family delved into the books in her father's substantial library, for she later wrote that everyone in her family were "great novel readers, and not ashamed of being so." She read the epistolary novels of seduction and betrayal by Samuel Richardson (1689–1761), the often bawdy books of Henry Fielding (1707–1754), and the fiction of the most popular female writer of her time, Fanny Burney (1752–1840). Indeed, Austen had great respect for women writers, and in her "Defense of the Novel," which was included in *Northanger Abbey* (1818), all three of the novels she explicitly praised were by women: *Cecilia* (1782) and *Camilla* (1796) by Burney and *Belinda* (1801) by Maria Edgeworth (1768–1849).

The Classics. While her family was living in Bath in 1803, Jane Austen sold her first novel, *Northanger Abbey,* for only £10 to a publisher who later decided not to publish it. Several decades would pass before writers such as Honoré de Balzac (1799–1850), Charles Dickens (1812–1870), and Emile Zola (1840–1902) were able to earn comfortable incomes just from writing. Though Austen never achieved financial independence, she continued to write novels and sell them. In 1805 her father died, leaving his wife and unmarried daughters with only a meager income and largely dependent on the Austen brothers. The three women lived for a time with brother Frank Austen in Southampton, and in 1809 they moved to Chawton in Hampshire (not far from Steventon), where they were provided a small house on the estate of brother Edward, who had been adopted by a wealthy cousin. Jane Austen wrote little in Bath and not at all in Southampton, but once back in Hampshire she wrote ceaselessly. She revised a 1795–1796 manuscript as *Sense and Sensibility* (1811) and a 1797 work as *Pride and Prejudice* and began *Mansfield Park* (1814). In 1810 a publisher accepted *Sense and Sensibility* but agreed to print it only if Austen agreed to pay printing costs if the book did not break even. It eventually earned her the modest sum of £140. The novel appeared anonymously, with "By a Lady" on the title page, and during her lifetime her subsequent novels were attributed to "the author of" one or two of her previous works. She then sold *Pride and Prejudice*—which she called her "own darling child"—in November 1812, and it was published two months later. At first only her family knew of her authorship, but the secret could not be kept for long. On hearing a group of Scottish ladies praise *Pride and Prejudice,* Jane's brother Henry revealed that his sister was the author. She had sold *Pride and Prejudice* for the flat fee of £110 and so earned no royalties from it, even when a second edition was published in autumn 1813, along with a second edition of *Sense and Sensibility.* By this time Austen's books were attracting attention, and when *Mansfield Park* was published in 1814, the first edition sold out in six months. She then started to write *Emma*, which some literary critics have praised more highly than *Pride and Prejudice,* and saw it published in 1815, the same year she started *Persuasion* (1818).

Death. Austen's writing career came to an end when she became seriously ill with what was probably Addison's disease, a tubercular disease of the kidneys. Sister Cassandra was at her side when she died in 1817. She was buried in Winchester Cathedral. *Persuasion* and *Northanger Abbey* were published posthumously the following year.

Between Classicism and Realism. Writing in domestic tranquility in rural Hampshire, Jane Austen honed her skills as a keen observer of middle-class provincial society. She was the first novelist to focus on the trivial comedy of provincial family life, through which she examined the perplexities of emotion and conduct. She followed Richardson in the minute presentation of daily life but avoided his weeping emotionalism. Like Fielding, she treated subjects with a comic-ironic detached attitude; and, like Daniel Defoe (1660–1731) as well as Fielding, she retained a psychological closeness to the inner world of her characters. Characterization was becoming more important than plot in some Romantic novels, and Jane Austen was the first great novelist to combine harmoniously in her narrative the internal and external formation of character. In this sense her fiction is both a climax of the eighteenth-century novels of Richardson, Fielding, and Defoe and a harbinger of the Realists of the nineteenth century, Honoré de Balzac and Emile Zola. Novelist Walter Scott (1771–1832) said of Austen well after her death, "That young lady had a talent

for describing the involvements, feelings and characters of ordinary life which is to me the most wonderful I have ever met with. The big bow-wow I can do myself like any one going; but the exquisite touch which renders commonplace things and characters interesting from the truth of the description and the sentiment is denied to me." Later in the century, Henry James (1843–1916) made a comment about women writers in general that applies to Austen in particular, as James intended: "women are delicate and patient observers; they hold their noses close, as it were, to the texture of life. They feel and perceive the real with a kind of personal tact, and their observations are recorded in a thousand delightful volumes."

Sources:
Roger Gard, *Jane Austen's Novels: The Art of Clarity* (New Haven: Yale University Press, 1992).

Park Honan, *Jane Austen: Her Life* (New York: St. Martin's Press, 1988).

Oliver MacDonagh, *Jane Austen: Real and Imagined Worlds* (New Haven: Yale University Press, 1991).

Carol Shields, *Jane Austen* (New York: Viking, 2001).

Ian Watt, *The Rise of the Novel* (Berkeley: University of California Press, 1957).

LUDWIG VAN BEETHOVEN

1770-1827
COMPOSER

Early Life and Career. Ludwig van Beethoven was born in Bonn, where his father, Johann (1740–1792), was a musician at the court of the archbishop elector of Cologne. Ludwig's mother, Maria Magdalena Keverich (1746–1787), was the daughter of a kitchen overseer in the palace of Ehrenbreitstein. During the future composer's early childhood he showed no inclination for music, but at the age of eleven he began to demonstrate extraordinary talent as a keyboard player and soon thereafter as a composer. At twelve he composed and published three complete piano sonatas of three movements each, which won acclaim for their sophistication and are still highly praised. By the age of thirteen he showed signs that composing music was becoming a compulsion for him, and for the rest of his life he wrote music prolifically. Beethoven remained in Bonn until 1792, when he moved to Vienna, the musical capital of Europe and a city of two hundred thousand souls, where he came under the influence of one of the most successful composers in Europe, Joseph Haydn (1732–1809). Beethoven's physical appearance always made a striking impression on contemporaries. One colleague described him thus: "Short in stature, broad in the shoulders, short neck, large head, round nose, dark brown complexion; he always bent forward slightly when he walked." By 1795 Beethoven had become quite popular as a composer and pianist in Vienna, and his subscription concerts were so financially successful that he contemplated a concert tour of other cities in Europe. A serious illness in 1797 (perhaps typhus) cut short these plans and may have been the cause of his subsequent encroaching deafness.

Composing for Money. Until 1800 Beethoven continued to perform piano concerts in Vienna for money, but he also began selling his compositions to eager publishers, who competed to buy the works. The published scores were sold to music clubs, concert societies, and the many new professional orchestras that desired new music to play at their increasingly frequent and popular concerts. Beethoven was a successful entrepreneur in marketing his music, selling pieces to any publisher who would pay well for it. As he wrote in a letter to a friend in 1801, "My compositions bring in a good deal; and I may say that I am offered more commissions than it is possible for me to carry out. Moreover, for every composition I can count on six or seven publishers, or even more if I want them; people no longer come to an arrangement with me. I state my price and they pay."

A Passion. Financial success was not Beethoven's only motivation to compose. He was also driven by a kind of creative compulsion, feverishly composing piece after piece. As he wrote in one of his many letters to friends, "I often produce three or four works at the same time." His absorption in his music became total: "I live entirely in my music; and hardly have I completed one composition when I have already begun another." Mixed with Beethoven's obsession with his music was an almost overpowering sense of despair and impending death, likely triggered by his chronic ill health and growing deafness. (He drew up a last will and testament in 1803.) Shortly after recovering from an illness in 1802, he wrote, "I am not very well satisfied with the work I have thus far done. From this day on I shall take a new way." The first giant step he took on this new path was his astonishingly original and deeply personal Third Symphony, the "Eroica," or "Heroic," symphony, completed in 1804 and first performed in February 1805. Its length and grandeur were unprecedented, and its thunderous, triumphant sounds set a course that continued through nearly all Beethoven's orchestral compositions, most notably his Violin Concerto in D (1806), his Fifth Piano Concerto (1809), and his last symphony, the Ninth (1824). Initially, the "Eroica" was dedicated to Napoleon Bonaparte, whom Beethoven viewed as the champion of the universal rights of liberty and justice. In May 1804, on hearing that Napoleon had declared himself emperor, however, Beethoven flew into a rage and tore the dedication from the manuscript for the recently completed symphony and threw the page on the floor. When he heard the news of Napoleon's coronation, Beethoven reportedly shouted to a friend: "Now he will trample all human rights underfoot, and only pander to his own ambition; he will place himself above everyone else and become a tyrant!"

Immortal Beloved. Beethoven never married, largely because he never felt financially secure enough to establish a household and support a family. He did, however, fall passionately in love and wrote letters expressing his ardent love for his "immortal beloved." He never explicitly identified this woman, giving rise to controversy among historians trying to discern her identity. Most likely she was Antonie von Birkenstock Brentano, the wife of Franz Brentano. Beethoven met Brentano and his wife in 1810 and became friends with the couple, even spending considerable time as their houseguest.

Becoming Deaf. Beethoven lived with chronic ill health, constantly complaining of severe gastrointestinal discomfort, respiratory disorders, headaches, and rheumatism. His most distressing physical affliction was his growing deafness. As his deafness grew worse, normal conversation with him became impossible, and people had to shout to be heard. Around 1813 Beethoven began to employ mechanical hearing aids, ear trumpets that were largely ineffective. In 1819, desperate for some cure, he tried a remedy suggested to him by a friend: inserting pieces of cotton saturated with horseradish juice into his ears as frequently as possible. By the time he conducted the premiere of his Ninth Symphony in 1824, he was totally deaf. A member of the audience reported: "At the close of the performance an incident occurred which must have brought tears to many an eye in that room. The master, though placed in the midst of this confluence of music, heard nothing of it at all and was not even sensible of the applause of the audience at the end of his great work, but continued standing with his back to the audience, and beating the time, till Fräulein Ungher, who had sung the contralto part, turned him . . . round to face the people, who were still clapping their hands, and giving way to the greatest demonstrations of pleasure. His turning round . . . acted like an electric shock on all present, and a volcanic explosion of sympathy and admiration followed, which was repeated again and again, and seemed as if it would never end."

Death. In December 1826 Beethoven fell seriously ill, probably with liver disease. The visible sign of his illness being a distended abdomen, four operations were performed in the next three months to relieve the swelling. None was successful, and Beethoven lapsed into a coma on 24 March 1827. Forty-eight hours later, during a violent thunderstorm, a loud peal of thunder shook the room and a flash of lightning illuminated it. According to an eyewitness, "Beethoven opened his eyes, raised his right hand, and gazed fixedly upwards for some seconds, with clenched fist, and a solemn threatening expression. . . . His hand dropped . . . and his eyes were half-closed. . . . The spirit of the great master had passed from this false world to the kingdom of truth."

Sources:

Emily Anderson, ed. and trans., *The Letters of Beethoven*, 3 volumes (New York: St. Martin's Press, 1961).

Barry Cooper, *Beethoven* (Oxford: Oxford University Press, 2000).

Cooper, ed., *The Beethoven Compendium: A Guide to Beethoven's Life and Music* (London: Thames & Hudson, 1991).

Peter J. Davies, *Beethoven in Person: His Deafness, Illnesses, and Death* (Westport, Conn.: Greenwood Press, 2001).

William Kinderman, *Beethoven* (Oxford: Oxford University Press, 1995).

FRANCISCO GOYA

1746-1828
ARTIST

Birth and Early Career. Born in Fuendetodos, Spain, Francisco Goya was a son of a small land-owner who could provide only a rudimentary education for his son. As a boy, Francisco showed a keen interest in and talent for drawing and painting, first developing his craft in copying works by masters such as Rembrandt (1606–1669) and Spanish court painter Diego Velásquez (1599–1660). At the age of fourteen Goya painted a series of frescoes for the local church in Fuendetodos. The next year he entered the San Louis Academy in Zaragoza. At the age of seventeen he went to Madrid, where he was influenced by the great Venetian Rococo artist Giovanni Tiepolo (1696–1770). Goya also met the Neoclassical painter Anton Raphael Mengs (1728–1779). In 1770 Goya ventured to Italy, reportedly working his way to Rome as a bullfighter. Once in Rome he apparently painted little, but he did complete a full-length portrait of Pope Benedict XIV, painted in a single sitting that lasted only a few hours. After Goya's return to Spain in 1771, he was asked to design a fresco for the basilica of Nuestra Señora del Pilar in Zaragoza. His first important commission, the work was completed in 1772. The following year he married Josefa Bayeu, a sister of Francisco Bayeu (1734–1795), personal painter to King Charles III. Goya and his wife had twenty children, only one of whom survived their father. In 1775 Mengs commissioned Goya to make sketches for tapestries destined for the Spanish royal palaces, the Prado and Escorial, introducing the twenty-nine-year-old artist to a world in which he was surrounded by the princely and most aristocratic society of Spain. Continuing to draw designs for tapestries, Goya finished fourteen in 1778 alone.

A Master of Portraiture. After the death of Charles III in 1788, Goya was appointed official painter to the court of Charles IV. A series of genre paintings and portraits quickly established him as the leading Spanish painter of his day. As a portrait painter, he became known as one of the finest Romantic artists of Europe. A hallmark of Romanticism was individualism, and in so many of his portraits—including one of himself painted in 1790—he captured the elusive quality of individual personalities. This accomplishment is all the more remarkable because Goya worked rapidly. As his son later recalled, "he paints only in one sitting which sometimes lasts up to 10 hours, but never in the evening; and in order to heighten the effect of a portrait, he adds the final touches at night under artificial light." Hundreds of luminaries posed for Goya, and above all he deftly captured on canvas all the great ladies of the court. A serious illness in 1792 left Goya deaf, prompting a disaffection with the world that changed and deepened his art. He ceased to be interested in pleasing his subjects with flattering portraits. Instead, he revealed their innermost characteristics—both strengths and weaknesses. Perhaps the best example is his portrait of Doña Antonia Zárate (1810?), which depicts a slightly coquettish woman who is also proud and faintly melancholy. Contrast and contradiction (another Romantic characteristic) marked the portrait of La Condesa de Chinchón (1800), a tender woman who looks at the viewer from the face almost of a child. The frail frame of her upper body contrasts starkly with the full dress that dominates the bottom and foreground of the portrait. Goya also explored etching as a medium, and in 1799 he published a series of them called *Los Caprichos* (Caprices). Daringly dedicated to the king, these etchings use corrosive and bitter humor to mock society's vices, frivolities, and absurdities.

In The Deaf Man's House. After becoming deaf, Goya withdrew from court and retired to La Quinta del sordo (The Deaf Man's House). By the turn of the century he had turned inward, but he continued to comment with increasing ruthlessness on the frightful horrors that beset humankind in that supposed age of Enlightenment. Napoleon's invasion and conquest of Spain in 1808 instilled in Goya a deep hatred for what he considered a brutal and reactionary political regime that—far from championing the rights of man and citizen espoused by the French Revolution—was crushing them underfoot. Between 1810 and 1814 the Napoleonic regime's violent suppression of Spanish nationalistic opposition became the subject of Goya's best-known series of etchings, *The Horrors of War,* and two of his greatest paintings, *The Second of May, 1808* and *The Third of May, 1808,* both completed in 1814. The paintings expose the pointless brutality of war, depicting no heroes, just dispassionate killers and hapless victims. When Ferdinand VII was restored to the throne of Spain in 1814, he invited Goya to his court. Unhappy, totally deaf, and growing blind, he declined the offer. Isolated and melancholy in The Deaf Man's House, Goya produced his nightmarish and visionary *Black Paintings* (1820–1822) and covered his walls with them. Exploration of the demonic was a characteristic of Romantic art, and Goya confirmed his fascination with it in his depictions of witches' sabbaths. Paintings such as *Saturn Devouring One of His Children* (1821–1823) also announce a Romantic departure from the past through the inversion of Classicism. A mythological subject (typical of Classicism) is rendered in a dramatically different way. While the form of Classicism was symmetrical and regular in its proportions, in his painting Goya grotesquely distorted his figures. In 1824 he left Madrid for Bordeaux, France, where he produced his acclaimed series of bullfighting lithographs. He died in Bordeaux in 1828.

Transitional Figure. Like many Romantics, Goya was influenced by the Enlightenment but also reacted against it. Like Voltaire and other Enlightenment figures, he despised irrationality—including the superstition, obscurantism and intolerance of the Christian Church that was exposed most visibly in the Spanish Inquisition, which began in 1478 and continued, with some interruptions, until 1834. He was a lifelong defender of individual freedom and the fundamental rights of individuals, a sharp-eyed caricaturist who mercilessly used his art to expose the absurdities and vileness of the world around him. Yet, he also gave rein to an unbridled imagination, conforming to the Romantic model of the inspired genius. In effect, Goya was a man of his time and a keen and clear-sighted commentator on it. Like Wolfgang Amadeus Mozart (1756–1791) or Ludwig van Beethoven (1770–1827), he was a transitional figure between the Enlightenment and the Romantic age, and he revealed in his art the deep contradictions of Spain, and indeed of Europe, during the late eighteenth and early nineteenth centuries.

Sources:
Pierre Gassier and Juliet Wilson, *The Life and Complete Work of Francisco Goya* (New York: Reynal, 1971).

Fred Licht, *Goya in Perspective* (Englewood Cliffs, N.J.: Prentice-Hall, 1973).

CLAUDE MONET

1840-1926
PAINTER

Early Life and Career. Claude Monet was born in Paris, the eldest son of a grocer. When Claude was five, the family moved to Le Havre, a port city on the English Channel, where he spent his childhood. The coastline and tempestuous skies of Normandy appear frequently in his later paintings, suggesting that the environment had a formative influence on him. As a teenager he was an accomplished caricaturist. In 1858 a meeting with the painter Eugène Boudin (1824–1898) directed Monet's artistic efforts toward landscape painting in the out-of-doors. As Monet recalled, "All of a sudden, it was like a veil torn from my eyes and I understood at last, I realized what painting could be; thanks to the example of this painter. . . . My own destiny as a painter opened up before me." Within a year he was in Paris studying at the Académie Suisse, and he met Camille Pissarro (1830–1903), another future Impressionist. After serving with the French military in Algeria during 1861 and 1862, Monet returned to Paris, where he became friends with three more future Impressionists: Pierre-Auguste Renoir (1841–1919), Alfred Sisley (1839–1899), and Frédéric Bazille (1841–1870). In 1865, while sharing a studio with Bazille, Monet publicly exhibited two seascapes, and then a year later he won the praise of Emile Zola for *Woman in a Green Dress*, a portrait of Monet's mistress, Camille Doncieux, who gave birth to their first child in 1867. Despite such critical acclaim, however, Monet was nearly destitute.

The Birth of a Movement. In 1870, the year in which his friend Bazille was killed in action in the Franco-Prussian War, Monet married Camille and began a decade of prolific painting. While working with Edouard Manet (1832–1883) and Renoir in Argenteuil on the Seine River, the still penurious Monet needed financial assistance from the successful Manet. In 1873 the French Salon rejected paintings submitted by Monet, Pissarro, Renoir, Paul Cézanne (1839–1906), and Sisley for their annual exhibition, prompting Monet and his friends to start their own exhibitions, holding eight between 1874 and 1886. The group called themselves the Anonymous Society of Artists and did not restrict their shows to group members, but an unimpressed reviewer of their first show derisively called them "Impressionists" after Monet's painting *Impression: Sunrise* (1872), and the name stuck. In fact, despite their differing styles, the artists themselves accepted the label as indicative of at least one of their common aims. At this point Monet began to receive popular and critical acclaim. Some of Monet's best work dates from the 1870s, including his series of Gare Saint-Lazare paintings (1876–1878). One year after the death of Camille Monet in 1879, Monet had a one-man exhibit of eighteen paintings, followed three years later by another solo exhibit in which he presented fifty-six more pictures. He also displayed paintings at the seventh (1882) and the eighth (1886) Impressionist Exhibitions. In 1883 he settled at Giverny in Normandy, renting a house that he eventually bought in 1890, and resided there until his death in 1926. In 1892 he married Alice Hoschedé, who died in 1911.

Monet at Giverny. In the year he purchased the house in Giverny, Monet began two series of paintings, *Poplars* and *Haystacks*. In these paintings he took an approach that he employed often in later works as well: representing the play of light on the same subjects at different times of the day and year (an approach also evident in his *Rouen Cathedral* series of 1892). Forever an open-air painter, at Giverny, Monet constructed a water garden that was the inspiration for and subject of some of his best-known paintings. In fact, painting the water lilies in his pond occupied him off and on for the rest of his life. In 1899, 1904, and again in 1906 he completed water-lily paintings, spending all 1906 on a single painting, which was exhibited in 1909 to great popular success. In 1910 he painted a new series of them, and in 1916 he began a series of large decorative water-lily panels that were commissioned by Premier Georges Clemenceau. As evidenced by this state commission, the seventy-six-year-old Monet was at the peak of his popularity and influence. By the 1920s Monet was the last surviving Impressionist. (Edgar Degas had died in 1917, Renoir in 1919.) Since 1908 Monet had suffered from impaired vision, and in 1923 an operation for the removal of a double cataract restored enough of his sight for him to complete the panels, his final work. On 5 December 1926, Claude Monet died at Giverny, and the panels were shortly thereafter installed at the Musée de l'Orangerie in Paris in a room especially designed for them.

Sources:

Kathleen Adler, *Impressionism* (London: National Gallery Publications, 1999).

Denis Rouart, *Claude Monet* (Paris: Editions d'Art Albert Skira, 1958).

Paul Hayes Tucker, *Claude Monet: Life and Art* (New Haven: Yale University Press, 1995).

NICCOLÒ PAGANINI

1782–1840
VIOLINIST

Early Years. Niccolò Paganini was born in Genoa, Italy. His father was a minor artisan who may also have been a simple porter at the harbor of Genoa, but he was also an accomplished enough player of the mandolin to recognize that his young son had a special talent for music. By the time Paganini was twelve, his violin playing had surpassed that of his teachers in Genoa, and he was sent to Parma to study with the renowned violin teacher and composer Alessandro Rolla (1757–1841). By the time Paganini reached the age of twenty, his reputation for adroit violin technique had become widespread. In fact, Paganini played the violin like no one before him. As he performed more and more public concerts, he gained financial independence from his parents, and for three years Paganini, by his own admission, led a dissolute life. His health suffered badly, and he never fully recovered. During this period he is thought to have contracted syphilis, for which there was then no completely effective treatment. Despite his ailments, Paganini embarked on a life of playing concerts that became the sole source of his income. In this sense, Paganini is an example of an early Romantic musician, who—unlike his Classical predecessors—depended on the public marketplace, not on the largesse of aristocrats.

The Image. Paganini consciously cultivated an eccentric image, which combined with his almost "demonic" ability to play the violin to make him famous. As his renown spread, box-office receipts from his concerts grew. He wore his wavy black hair long and invariably performed in a black coat, long trousers, and a colored waistcoat. Emaciated and gangly with long, spidery fingers and a playing posture that seemed almost contorted, he looked like some kind of black puppet. He kept his audiences waiting for his appearance, and as the curtains slowly parted, he emerged from the wings onto the stage to the accompaniment of a dramatic drum roll. As the virtuoso pianist and composer Franz Liszt (1811–1886) later observed, "The excitement he created was so unusual, the magic that he practiced upon the imagination of his hearers so powerful, that they would not be satisfied with a natural explanation. Old tales of witches and ghost stories came into their minds; they attempted to explain the miracle of his playing by delving into his past, to interpret the wonder of his genius in a supernatural way; they even hinted that he had devoted his spirit to the Evil One, and that the fourth string of his violin was made from his wife's intestines, which he himself had cut out." Paganini's sinister reputation was further secured in 1816, when he was accused of impregnating a woman half his age and then trying to convince her to abort the fetus. Paganini claimed he was innocent and being framed because he was rich and famous, but nonetheless he was fined and sentenced to a brief term in prison.

Technique. Paganini's virtuoso technique enthralled not only mass audiences but connoisseurs as well. As the great German violinist Louis Spohr (1784–1859) wrote later, "No instrumental player has ever captivated the Italians as he. . . . one hears on all sides from unmusical people, that he is the true master in the art of witchcraft, and that he draws sounds out of the violin never heard before. The connoisseurs, on the contrary, say that his enormous facility with his left hand, his double-stops, and his excellence in all kinds of difficult passages is undeniable; but they add that the qualities which captivate the masses are spoiled by charlatanism. . . ." Paganini did sometimes amaze his untutored audiences with an array of variations on one string, the G string, and for effect he removed the other three. Or he would play, as Spohr put it, "a peculiar kind of pizzicato for the left hand, without the help of the right hand or the bow." Sometimes he would thrill his audiences with playing that imitated the voices of old women, the crowing of a rooster, the chirping of a cricket, the howling of a dog, or the braying of a donkey.

Fame, Fortune, and an International Tour. In the early 1820s Paganini played scores of concerts in various cities in northern Italy. He also contemplated a tour north of the Alps, but it was delayed by his ill health. In 1822 he contracted tuberculosis, which, combined with his syphilis, endangered his life. Though he never fully recovered, Paganini felt fit enough by 1828 to accept an invitation from Prince Klemens von Metternich to come to Vienna. Paganini's performances spellbound Austrian audiences just as they had in Italy. He started a consumer craze. Women wore their hair "à la Paganini," while men donned Paganini hats. Some bakeries sold loaves of bread shaped like violins. His tour also took him to Berlin, where a similar reception awaited him. A newspaper critic wrote that "never in my life have I heard such weeping [from a violin]. It was as if the torn heart of this suffering human being were bursting with its sorrow. . . . I never knew that music possessed such sounds. . . . When the final trill came, there was an explosion of joy. . . . The ladies leaned over the balustrade of the balcony to show they were applauding; the men stood on the chairs so as to see him better and call to him; I have never seen a Berlin audience like this." Such popularity brought financial success. Paganini made so much money from his concerts in Vienna, Berlin, and then Warsaw that he had no need to play ever again. Yet, he continued to perform, touring France, England, and Ireland during the 1830s. During three months in early 1832 he gave sixty-five concerts in thirty cities, keeping up a feverish pace that was far from unusual on his tours.

Later Years. Such a pace could hardly be sustained. In 1833 he returned to Italy, and in 1836—suffering from ill health and exhaustion—he ceased performing altogether. He then embarked on an entertainment business venture in Paris, the Casino Paganini, where he and his partners hoped to combine gambling, musical performances, and dancing in one venue. It failed miserably, and Paganini's partners sued him for breach of contract, arguing that he had agreed to play there and had not. The French courts ruled against Paganini, levying a large fine on him. He refused to pay and moved to the South of France, his further passage to Italy delayed by his illnesses. Frail and suffering from tuberculosis of the larynx, he was unable to speak. Hounded by French legal officials, he died in May 1840. Paganini's sinister reputation dogged him even after death. Claiming there was no evidence that Paganini had any religious beliefs at all, the bishop of Nice would not allow his body to be buried in consecrated ground. His embalmed body was stored in the cellar of the house where he had died, and then taken two months later to a leper hospital in Villefranche. Its voyage was not yet over; from there it was moved to an olive-oil factory, and five years after his death, it was moved yet again to the Villa Gaione in Italy after the duchess of Parma gave permission for the legendary virtuoso to be buried there. Thirty years later Paganini's remains were finally moved to consecrated ground.

Sources:

Alan Kendall, *Paganini: A Biography* (London: Chappell, 1982).

Henry Raynor, *Music and Society since 1815* (New York: Schocken Books, 1976).

EMILE ZOLA

1840-1902
NOVELIST

Early Years. Born in Paris, Emile Zola was the only child of Francesco and Emilie Aubert Zola. His twenty-one-year-old mother was from a working-class family, while his father (twenty-three years his wife's senior) was a Venetian civil engineer who had immigrated to France. When Emile was not yet seven years old, his father died. For the next eleven years Emile lived with his mother in Aix-en-Provence, the town where his father had worked and died, and formed a lifelong friendship with the future Impressionist painter Paul Cézanne (1839–1906). Zola and his mother returned to Paris in 1858. The following year, after repeatedly failing the oral component of the *baccalauréat* examination, which students had to pass for admission to all university studies, Zola was forced to seek employment. In early 1860 a friend of the family found him employment as a copy clerk. This job lasted scarcely two months, after which Emile Zola decided to earn his living as a writer. He threw himself into his new vocation, telling a friend "My dream is to publish within two years from now two volumes, one of prose and one of verse. As for the future, who knows? If I definitely embark on a literary career, I shall be true to my motto: All or nothing." Zola struggled for several years to make ends meet, living in squalor in the slums of Paris, taking a room for a time in a building that also housed pimps and prostitutes. In 1862 he found work with the publishing house Hachette, eventually working in the publicity department. In 1866 he left Hachette and began a career as a journalist, working first for the periodical *L'Evénement.*

An Art Critic and Serial Novelist. Zola began his journalism career writing literary and art criticism, and this endeavor brought him into contact with the emerging Impressionist movement, which included his friend Cézanne. Zola knew many of the Impressionists well and socialized with them at their favorite Parisian haunts. He was one of the early champions of the paintings of Edouard Manet (1832–1883), a controversial artist whose paintings outraged much of the public and were excluded from juried exhibitions. Zola was impressed by the objectivity of Manet's paintings, especially figures such as the prostitute in *Olympia* (1863), who were portrayed as pure objects divulging nothing of their inner selves. Zola captured this visual effect in his first novel, *Thérèse Raquin,* published in 1867. Manet and Zola became friends, and each man influenced the other. While continuing to work as a journalist, he wrote, for example, a stark and lurid account of the aftermath of the slaughter of the Communards in Paris for *La Sémaphore* in 1870. Zola embarked in 1868 on a project of writing a connected series of novels, which—like the fiction of Honoré de Balzac (1799–1850) and Charles Dickens (1812–1870) before him—were published in installments. *La Fortune des Rougon* (The Fortune of the Rougons) the first volume of the *Rougon-Macquart* novels, was serialized in *Le Siècle* in 1870–1871 and published in book form later in 1871. Seven more novels—including the explosive and shocking *L'Assommoir* (serialized in 1876–1877)—followed over the next decade, and the final, twentieth volume in the series, *Le Docteur Pascal* (Doctor Pascal), was serialized in 1893. These novels track the generations of two branches of a fictional family and express what Zola called "the vast democratic upheaval of our time." In his literary art Zola emerged as the greatest Realist of his generation and defined what it meant to be a literary Naturalist.

The Science of Literature. Zola held an unshakable belief in the powers of reason and objective observation—that is, science—as tools for the betterment of mankind, and he shaped his art to accomplish this task. He expressed his doctrine in *Le Roman expérimental* (The Experimental Novel, 1880), where he explained that his fiction was "a simple piece of analysis of the world as it is. I merely state facts. It is a study of man placed in a milieu without sermonizing. If my novel has a result, it will be this: to tell the human truth, to exhibit our mechanism, showing the hidden springs of heredity and the influence of environment." His novels are filled with cold, emotionless, detailed depictions of the external world and the almost soulless figures that move within it. The actions of human beings, good and evil, are portrayed as products of heredity and environment. In his novels squalor and poverty gave rise to promiscuity, delinquency, alcoholism, workers' riots, and violence. As he wrote in the preface to an early novel, *Thérèse Raquin* (1867), "people [are] completely dominated by their nerves and blood, [and are] without free will, drawn into each action of their lives by the inexorable laws of their physical nature." Perhaps Zola's most controversial, and most popular, novel was *Nana*. This story of an actress/prostitute who ultimately dies in the gutter, "a heap of matter and blood," met with great success. The periodical *Le Voltaire* serialized it in 1879–1880, publicizing it so aggressively that Zola told a friend the "insane advertising" was "humiliating." When it appeared in book form in 1880, the first printing of 55,000 sold out so quickly that ninety more printings were required before the end of the year to meet public demand. Zola continued to write at a furious rate, failing to produce a novel in only six of the thirty-one years between 1871 and 1902.

Artistic Method. Zola's writing methods closely followed those of science. For every novel in the Rougon-Macquart series, he first roughed out a story line and then began gathering "documentation." As he wrote, he said, "I concern myself with documents; I seek them out with care. . . . my work is 'settled' only when I have all my documents and I have discovered the reflexive effect of subject on documents and of documents on subject." This method included close scrutiny of Catholic ritual and liturgy. Intending to open the novel *La Faute de l'abbé Mouret* (Abbé Mouret's Transgression, 1875) with a priest celebrating the Eucharist, Zola made sure every detail was accurately presented. He studied glossaries of workers' slang to make the dialogue of his working-class characters in *L'Assommoir* completely true to life. For his novel *Le Ventre de Paris* (The Belly of Paris, 1874), set in the central markets of the French capital, Zola researched his subject scrupulously, repeatedly visiting the markets at different times of the day, and in all manner of weather, to gauge the various rhythms. He even spent the night there so he could observe the arrival of provisioning carts before dawn and record the bustle in his notebooks. After such research excursions, he returned to his study with mounds of notes and composed his novels with vivid depictions of real, often sordid, worlds.

The Dreyfus Affair. In his novels Zola criticized the social and political conditions of the world in which he lived, but true to his "objectivist" stance, he refused to become politicized. His position changed in 1898, however, when he became involved in the deepest political scandal of the Third Republic, the Dreyfus Affair. Captain Alfred Dreyfus was a French army officer who was accused in 1894 of transmitting military secrets to the Germans. The prosecutors in his military trial had only flimsy circumstantial evidence, but Dreyfus was Jewish and was thus assumed to be more likely than a Christian to commit an unpatriotic act against France. Dreyfus was con-victed and sentenced to the penal colony on Devil's Island. After compelling evidence pointing to the guilt of another soldier, Major Ferdinand Walsin-Esterhazy, came to light, the army refused to give Dreyfus a new trial. Convinced of Dreyfus's innocence, Zola had already written a few articles and pamphlets on his behalf, when—in January 1898—a military court found Esterhazy innocent. Fearing that Dreyfus would be completely forgotten, Zola wrote perhaps his best-known journalistic work, "Open Letter to the President of the Republic," which was published in the 13 January 1898 issue of *L'Aurore*, as "J'Accuse!" (I Accuse!). In this public letter he championed the principle that evil means do not justify laudable ends. He gave the names of the generals who had been accused of allowing irregularities in Dreyfus's trial and accused the entire war ministry of complicity. He then challenged the French government to put the generals on trial. Zola knew that, according to the press law of 1881, his article was libelous. In fact, he quoted passages from that law to demonstrate that point. He clearly was trying to provoke authorities to arrest him so he could use his trial as a venue from which to expose the corruption of the military. Zola was duly tried and convicted in 1898, sentenced to a year's imprisonment, and fined 3,000 francs. He appealed his conviction and lost. As anti-Semitic French nationalists screamed in the right-wing press "Down with Zola! Down with the Jews!" Zola left for England to avoid personal harm and imprisonment and to await a shift in political circumstances in France. In 1899 Dreyfus was given a new trial and once again found guilty, even though Esterhazy had fled the country and confessed, and another conspirator had killed himself to avoid prosecution. The French president pardoned Dreyfus later that year, but he was not exonerated until 1906.

Death under Suspicious Circumstances. In 1902 Zola returned to France, and on 29 September was found dead on the bedroom floor of his home in Paris. Cause of death was soon determined to be carbon-monoxide poisoning from inhaling toxic fumes from the coal-burning fireplace. A coroner's inquest found no blockage of the flue and so ruled the death accidental but inexplicable. Fifty years later a man reported that twenty-five years previously a friend of his had told him that he and his mates, all anti-Semites who hated Dreyfus and Zola, had deliberately sealed up the chimney one evening and then returned in the morning to clear away the evidence. This hearsay evidence has never been confirmed, but it does point to the controversial reputation Zola had acquired in his lifetime.

Sources:

William J. Berg, *The Visual Novel: Emile Zola and the Art of His Times* (University Park: Pennsylvania State University Press, 1992).

F. W. J. Hemmings, *The Life and Times of Emile Zola* (New York: Scribners, 1977).

Alan Schom, *Emile Zola: A Biography* (New York: Holt, 1987).

Documentary Sources

Jane Austen (1775–1817), Letters—Glimpses of novelist's intimate life, especially in her letters to her sister, Cassandra, that shed light on the inspirations for her novels; modern edition: Deirdre Le Faye, ed., *Jane Austen's Letters* (Oxford: Oxford University Press, 1995).

Ludwig van Beethoven (1770–1827), Letters—Documents offering unusual access into Beethoven's life and personality in letters to business associates, friends, and loved ones; modern edition: Emily Anderson, ed. and trans., *The Letters of Beethoven*, 3 volumes (New York: St. Martin's Press, 1961).

Hector Berlioz (1803–1869), *Memoires de Hector Berlioz* (Paris: Michel Lévy frères, 1870)—Autobiographical writings by a Frenchman who was well acquainted with many other Romantic composers and recorded valuable information about the personal and political sides of his contemporaries; modern edition: David Cairns, ed. and trans., *The Memoirs of Hector Berlioz* (New York: Norton, 1975).

Vincent van Gogh (1853–1890), Letters—Revelations about a disturbed, tormented, yet brilliant, painter and his relationships with other artists, especially in his letters to his brother Theo; modern edition: *The Complete Letters of Vincent van Gogh* (Boston: New York Graphic Society, 1978).

Jean-Jacques Rousseau (1712–1778), *Les Confessions*, 3 volumes (Geneva, 1781–1788)—An introspective psychological autobiography noted for the subjective individualism that became a hallmark of Romanticism; modern edition: Angela Scholar, trans., *Confessions*, edited by Patrick Coleman (Oxford: Oxford University Press, 2000).

John Ruskin (1819–1900), *Modern Painters*, 5 volumes (London: Smith, Elder, 1843–1860); *The Seven Lamps of Architecture* (London: Smith, Elder, 1849); *The Stones of Venice*, 3 volumes (London: Smith, Elder, 1851–1853); *The Opening of the Crystal Palace, Considered in Some of its Relations to the Prospects of Art* (London: Smith, Elder, 1854)—Writings on art and architecture by the most influential critic of the second half of the nineteenth century; modern editions: Robert L. Herbert, ed., *The Art Criticism of John Ruskin* (Garden City, N.Y.: Doubleday, 1964); Philip Davis, ed., *Selected Writings: Modern Painters, The Stones of Venice, The Seven Lamps of Architecture, Praeterita* (London: Everyman, 1995).

Richard Wagner (1813–1883), *Mein Leben* [My Life], 2 volumes (Munich: Bruckmann, 1911)—An autobiography of the leading Romantic opera composer during the second half of the nineteenth century; modern edition: Andrew Gray, trans., *My Life*, edited by Mary Whittall (Cambridge: Cambridge University Press, 1983).

Oscar Wilde (1854–1900), *Art and Morality: A Defense of "The Picture of Dorian Gray,"* edited by Stuart Mason (London: Jacobs, 1907)—A defense of the independence of art from moral constraints by a writer who deliberately outraged bourgeois moralists with his unconventional lifestyle.

Johann Joachim Winckelmann (1717–1768), *Geschichte der Kunst des Altertums* [The History of Ancient Art] (Dresden, 1764)—The most influential and widely read eighteenth-century theoretical work on art, which established classical forms of ancient Greece and Rome as the models for contemporary art; modern edition: G. Henry Lodge, trans., *The History of Ancient Art*, 2 volumes (New York: Ungar, 1969).

Emile Zola (1840–1902), *Le Roman expérimental* [The Experimental Novel] (Paris: Charpentier, 1880)—A didactic explanation of Zola's scientific method of novel writing and his objective to create true representations of the real world; the work that defined the standards by which all writers of Naturalist fiction are assessed; modern edition: Belle M. Sherman, trans., *The Experimental Novel* (New York: Haskell House, 1964).

COMMUNICATION, TRANSPORTATION, AND EXPLORATION

by TONY BALLANTYNE

CONTENTS

Sidebars and tables are listed in italics.

1752
- England and its colonies adopt the Gregorian or New Style Calendar, which adds ten days to the Julian or Old Style Calendar. Sweden follows suit the next year.

1766
- Louis-Antoine de Bougainville commands the first French expedition around the world, visiting Tuamotu, Tahiti, Samoa, New Hebrides, and the Louisiade and New Britain Archipelagoes before returning home in 1769.

1768

26 August — James Cook leaves Plymouth in the *Endeavour* in order to explore the southern Pacific Ocean. He discovers and charts the coasts of New Zealand, Australia, and New Guinea before returning to England in 1771. This expedition initiates an age of European exploration, commerce, and conquest in the region.

1770
- Scotsman James Bruce searches for the source of the Nile River but instead finds the headwaters of one of its tributaries, the Blue Nile. His *Travels to Discover the Source of the Nile* appears in print in 1790 and sparks much interest in the Dark Continent.

1772
- Cook embarks on his second voyage of discovery to the Pacific with two ships, the *Resolution* and the *Adventure*. He conducts a three-year expedition in search of the great southern continent then believed to exist. Cook encounters the Antarctica ice fields, stops at Tahiti and New Hebrides, and discovers New Caledonia.
- French navigator Yves-Joseph de Kerguelen-Tremarec discovers the subantarctic Kerguelen, or Desolation Island, in the southern Indian Ocean.

1773
- British naval captain Constantine John Phipps attempts to sail across the North Pole; he reaches Spitsbergen before turning back.

1776
- Cook begins his third and final voyage to the Pacific. With the *Resolution* and the *Discovery*, he attempts to find the Northwest Passage, an Arctic waterway connecting the Atlantic and Pacific Oceans. He charts the North American Pacific coast as far as the Bering Strait before being killed in Hawaii in 1779.

1789
- Scotsman Alexander Mackenzie explores western Canada and reaches the Pacific coast in 1793.

1794

August — Claude Chappe presides over the first optical telegraph line (semaphore visual telegraph), a series of signal posts running 180 miles from Paris to Lille.

* Denotes Circa Date

1796
- In Munich, Aloys Senefelder invents lithography, a process of printing from a plane surface (such as smooth stone or metal) on which the image is ink-receptive and the blank area ink-repellent.

1798
- Friedrich Hornemann joins a caravan and becomes the first European in modern times to cross the Sahara Desert.

1801
- Matthew Flinders, an English mariner and hydrographer, begins to survey the Australian coast; he completes the first circumnavigation of the continent in 1803.

1820
- Russian, English, and American ship captains all claim the first sighting of Antarctica.

1824
- The Russian explorer Baron Ferdinand von Wrangel maps the northeastern coast of Siberia.

1826

18 August Alexander Gordon Laing becomes the first European to reach Timbuktu.
- The Menai Strait Bridge, the longest suspension bridge to date, is constructed in Wales; it is rebuilt in 1940.

1829
- British engineer George Stephenson builds the steam locomotive Rocket. With a top speed of thirty-six miles per hour, the Rocket marks the birth of the railway era.

1830

15 September The Liverpool and Manchester Railway, the first commercial railway that uses only steam locomotives, opens.

1831
- Richard and John Lander finish tracing the course of the Lower Niger River to its delta.

1838
- The *Sirius* and the *Great Western* become the first ships to cross the Atlantic Ocean entirely under steam power.

1840

January French navigator Jules-Sebastien-Cesar Dumont D'Urville leads an expedition that comes close to the South Magnetic Pole.
- Britain adopts a new system of simplified and standardized postal charges, triggering a massive boom in the public's use of postal communication.

* DENOTES CIRCA DATE

1841

- The first European overland journey across Australia is completed by Edward John Eyre; the account of his experiences, *Discoveries in Central Australia,* is published four years later.

1842

- The first newspaper photograph is printed in the *Illustrated London News.*

1844

- Over the course of the next two years, Parliament approves the construction of four hundred new rail lines in Great Britain.

1845

- The *Great Britain,* designed and built by Isambard Kingdom Brunel, becomes the first propeller-driven steamship to cross the Atlantic; propellers soon replace the paddle wheels.

- English explorer Sir John Franklin sets out on a two-year Arctic expedition to discover the Northwest Passage. His ship is caught in the ice, and the entire crew perishes. Fourteen years later a search mission finds skeletons and a written account of the expedition near Lancaster Sound. It is debatable whether some of the crew ever found the Passage.

1850

- The first underwater telegraph cable is laid, linking France and England.

- German geographer and historian Heinrich Barth begins a five-year odyssey through North and Central Africa; he travels a total of ten thousand miles and later writes a popular account of his experiences.

1851

1 May   Queen Victoria opens The Great Exhibition of the Works of Industry of All Nations. Held in London's Hyde Park, the exhibition celebrates Britain's strength as an industrial producer and imperial power.

- Scottish missionary and explorer David Livingstone discovers the Zambezi River; four year later he discovers Victoria Falls.

1852

- W. H. Fox Talbot patents photoengraving, a process for making linecuts and halftone cuts by photographing an image on a metal plate and then etching.

1858

30 January   Brunel launches the *Great Eastern,* the largest steamship to date; it is 689 feet long and can carry 1,500 passengers.

- John Speke discovers Lake Victoria, but not until 1862 is he able to confirm it as a major source of the Nile.

* DENOTES CIRCA DATE

1859 7 September The clock known as Big Ben is fully functional in the tower of Westminster Palace in London; designed by Edmund Beckett Denison, it has a thirteen-ton bell.

1865 • International Telegraphic Union is established to supervise and police international telegraphic communication.

1866 • The first transatlantic telegraph cable becomes operational.

• Livingstone begins an expedition to explore the watershed of Central Africa and the sources of the Nile.

1869 17 November The Suez Canal, connecting the Mediterranean and Red Seas, opens for navigation.

1870 • Over the course of the next eighteen years, the Russian Nikolay Przhevalsky explores Central Asia, especially eastern Tibet, the Gobi Desert, and the watershed between the Hwang Ho and Yangzi (Yangtze) Rivers.

1874 • A telegraph code later used in teletypewriters is invented by the Frenchman Jean-Maurice-Emile Baudot.

1875 • Verney Cameron becomes the first European to cross equatorial Africa from coast to coast.

1879 • Swedish geologist and explorer Adolf Nordenskjold is the first to locate the Northwest Passage.

1880 • The Statutes (Definition of Time) Act sets Greenwich Mean Time as the standard for the United Kingdom.

1883 • The Orient Express, developed by Belgian businessman Georges Nagelmackers, makes its inaugural run. The first European transcontinental express railroad, it is 1,700 miles long and connects Paris to Constantinople.

* DENOTES CIRCA DATE

1884

- The International Meridian Conference held in Washington, D.C., sets Greenwich in London as the international meridian and creates twenty-four time zones worldwide.

1890

4 March   An 8,248-foot-long cantilever railway bridge is completed across the Firth of Forth in Scotland after seven years of construction.

1891

- Construction begins on the Trans-Siberian Railroad. Completed in 1904, it is 5,778 miles long, connecting Moscow with the eastern port of Vladivostok.

1894

- Italian physicist Guglielmo Marconi develops a prototype wireless telegraph; several years later he makes a successful demonstration by sending and receiving signals over a distance of twelve miles.

1895

- The Sixth International Geophysical Conference in London formally declares a need for further Antarctic exploration.

1900

- Members of the Italian polar expedition under Luigi Amedeo, Duke of Abruzzi, reach the northern record of 86 degrees 34 minutes North.

1901

December   The first successful transatlantic wireless transmission is achieved by Marconi when he sends signals between Cornwall, England, and St. John's, Newfoundland.

- Englishman Robert Falcon Scott leads a three-year expedition to Antarctica; he surveys South Victoria Land, takes soundings of the Ross Sea, and discovers King Edward VII Land.

1902

- The Italian railroad system completes electrification of its main line.

1909

- An expedition commanded by the Irishman Ernest Henry Shackleton reaches a point approximately ninety-seven miles from the South Pole. Upon his return to Britain, he publishes an account of his adventures titled *Heart of the Antarctic.*

1910

- There are approximately 125,000 telephones in use in Great Britain.

* DENOTES CIRCA DATE

1911

14 December   Norwegian explorer Roald Amundsen successfully reaches the South Pole ahead of rival German, Australian, British, and Japanese expeditions.

1912

17 January   Scott and four companions reach the South Pole a month after Amundsen; all of them perish on the return trip.

• *Selandia,* a Danish vessel and the first diesel-powered steamship, is launched. It demonstrates its superior fuel conservation by completing a nonstop twenty-six-thousand-mile voyage from Bangkok to London.

1913

• The first use of diesel-electric railway engines occurs in Sweden.

1914

• Shackleton undertakes the first trans-Antarctic expedition, but he fails when his ship *Endurance* is later crushed in pack ice; the crew is eventually rescued.

* Denotes Circa Date

Dredging equipment on the Suez Canal, circa 1860

OVERVIEW

Growing Interdependence. During the nineteenth century a series of technological innovations and political transformations dramatically reshaped communications at a global level. As a result of industrialization and imperialism, fundamentally entwined processes, European nations extended their sovereignty over non-European communities. They explored Africa, Asia, and the Pacific, exploited the natural resources of colonized regions, and exported manufactured goods to colonial markets that had been opened up by exploration, conquest, and missionary activity. Communities previously separated by both physical and cultural distance were brought into sustained and close contact by both the technologies of the Industrial Revolution (including the electric telegraph, the steamship, and the railway) and a new and aggressive age of European imperialism.

Shrinking and Accelerating World. These new forms of communication and transport connected communities in ways that were unimaginable in the middle of the eighteenth century, when both transport and communication were relatively slow and inefficient, as they remained tied to the pace of a human on foot, a fast horse, or a ship under sail. The new networks fashioned by railroads, steamship routes, and electric telegraph wires in the nineteenth century were more extensive than the communication systems of the mid eighteenth century, as they encompassed more and more space. They reached into the hinterlands of Europe and connected the major commercial and political centers of European empires. They allowed communication to occur at far greater speeds. Whereas in 1780 news would only travel as fast as a messenger on horseback, by 1880 news could be transmitted at the speed of an electrical current traveling through the long-distance underwater cables used by telegraph companies. In the realm of transportation the development of steam locomotives and steamships not only accelerated the velocity of transport but also significantly increased its capacity. This development meant that larger cargoes (including mail and newspapers) could be carried, speeding up commerce, facilitating further gains in industrial production, and making the distribution of manufactured goods more efficient.

Communication and Imperialism. Communication and transport technologies were central to the global economic and cultural systems fashioned by international trade and European imperialism. Indeed, in the context of colonialism these technologies played a central role in the creation, maintenance, and projection of European hegemony. In those cases where Europeans encountered literate communities that possessed sophisticated communication networks of their own, as in India, Southeast Asia, and parts of the Middle East, they devoted a great deal of effort to infiltrating these indigenous systems and tried to "turn" them to their own advantage. It was only after Europeans had clearly established a permanent commercial and political presence that they attempted to fashion their own independent communication systems and to introduce new forms of transport, such as the railway. The Pacific Islands and Africa present a different case, as Europeans encountered nonliterate communities where social communication was based on the power of oratory and the authority of oral tradition. In such cases the creation of written languages and the construction of institutions to teach reading and writing were fundamental to the civilizing mission and the introduction of Christianity, commerce, and European culture.

Symbolic Power of Technology. Within this framework of global imperialism, communication and transport technologies came to be important symbols of modernity and European hegemony. European merchants, missionaries, and colonial officials frequently justified the inequities of imperialism by emphasizing their role as civilizers and modernizers who dispensed the gift of new technology to "backward" subject populations. At a material level the ability of Europeans to finance the development of new technologies and to deploy scientific knowledge in the construction of machinery was a telling reminder to many colonized peoples of the growing economic divergence between Europe and the rest of the world.

Disputing Technology. Not surprisingly, technology came to occupy a central place in the writings and campaigns of indigenous reformers and nationalists. In some cases, such as Japan, new technologies such as the steam locomotive were rapidly embraced in the face of Western intrusion by indigenous elites eager to prove the modernity, or at least the capacity for modernity, of their own community. In other cases, however, colonized peoples launched withering attacks on the effects of these new technologies. Mohandas Karamchand Gandhi, for example, argued that the introduction of railways to India promoted the spread of disease and, as agents of capitalism, also created enormous disparities of wealth within India. Questions of communication and transport thus assumed great significance in colonized societies and were often at the heart of the most important debates over imperialism.

Transport and Communication in Europe. These new methods of communication and transport were also of vital economic, social, and cultural significance within Europe. The extension of railways, the growth of telegraph networks, and the development of a streamlined and affordable postal system linked the great commercial and political centers, such as London and Paris, more firmly to their ever expanding hinterlands. These technologies also played a central role in the growth of industry and commerce, allowing raw materials to be transported cheaply, finished goods to be distributed more efficiently, and news to be disseminated more quickly. While they were pivotal in generating the great wealth enjoyed by industrialists and financiers, these technologies also transformed working-class life. Not only did factory workers encounter steam-powered machinery in their workplace, but they also increasingly traveled to work from the fringes of industrial cities on steam trains. Affordable postage and the extension of literacy also meant that letter writing was not the preserve of the elite but an almost universal feature of nineteenth-century life.

Exhibiting Progress. The great exhibitions that proved so popular in late-nineteenth-century Europe were also targeted at working-class audiences. These state-sponsored events were believed to be effective tools for public education, and they demonstrated the latest technologies, confirmed the seemingly relentless advances of science and industry, and affirmed the value of progress to mass audiences. London's Great Exhibition of 1851 in the Crystal Palace served this purpose, but it was also an important instrument for educating the population as a whole about European colonies, for disseminating information about potential destinations for migrants, and for celebrating the advance of empire.

Technology, Empire, and Interconnectedness. These displays were the most striking manifestation of a growing sense of interconnectedness that is discernible in nineteenth-century culture, whether in Europe or its colonies. The development and dissemination of these new transportation and communication technologies played a central role in creating the networks that increasingly wove previous disparate communities into shared spaces of economic, social, and cultural exchange. In a real way the steamship, the steam locomotive, and the electric telegraph transformed time and space. Not only did railway companies take the lead in creating time zones within countries, but the speed of the telegraph and the steamship also necessitated the creation of Greenwich Mean Time and the implementation of a regimented international system of time zones. Most important, the acceleration of communication and transportation intensified cultural exchanges across national boundaries, allowing the rapid movement of capital, commodities, people, and ideas and, as a result, creating a profound awareness of global connectedness. Yet, these connections also exacerbated existing inequalities and created new disparities of wealth and power, both within and between nations. Thus, these communication and transport technologies played a pivotal role in the creation of the modern world, a global order marked by both growing interdependence and the painful political and cultural scars of imperialism.

TOPICS IN COMMUNICATION, TRANSPORTATION, AND EXPLORATION

EXHIBITIONS: EMPIRE AND INDUSTRY

Public Displays. The late nineteenth century has been identified as an "age of exhibitions" as European, North American, and various colonial governments sponsored public displays that celebrated imperial power and the march of industry. These events emerged out of older European traditions of the collection and display of curiosities, ethnological artifacts, and technological wonders. Yet, where eighteenth-century collectors were from elite backgrounds and their collections were either private or attached to exclusive institutions, the late nineteenth century witnessed a democratization of display as states invested heavily in the Imperial Exhibitions, Expositions Universelles, and, later, World's Fairs that were aimed at the masses. Although an important French tradition of public exhibitions emerged at the close of the eighteenth century (beginning with the large exhibition organized by the Marquis d'Aveze at the Maison d'Orsay in 1798), the age of exhibitions was truly inaugurated by "The Great Exhibition of the Works of Industry of All Nations" held in 1851. Opened by Queen Victoria on 1 May, the exhibition was held in the Crystal Palace, designed by Sir Joseph Paxton and erected in London's Hyde Park. This immense facility housed more than fifteen thousand exhibitors (drawn from all over the British Empire, Europe, and the United States) who demonstrated a huge range of art, artisanal skills, and industrial technologies, including a steam-powered Jacquard loom, an envelope machine, and a reaping machine from the United States. Taken together, these displays celebrated the value of technology, the rise of industrial production, and the British Empire's wealth.

Powerful Model. The Great Exhibition of 1851 proved a powerful model for the many exhibitions that proliferated in the later nineteenth century, as European nations and the United States celebrated their industrial power, colonies demonstrated their economic significance and social progress, and noncolonized nations, such as Japan, attempted to proclaim their "modern" status. Between 1852 and the outbreak of World War I in 1914, major international and imperial exhibitions were held in London

The Crystal Palace, built for the Great Exhibition in London in 1851 (Victoria and Albert Museum, London)

Interior of the Crystal Palace in Munich during the Industrial
Exhibition of 1854 (Deutsches Museum, Munich)

Gallery of machines from the Exposition Universelle in Paris, 1900

(1862, 1871–1874, 1886, 1899, and 1911), Dublin (1865), Sydney (1870 and 1879–1880), Paris (1855, 1867, 1878, 1889, and 1900), Melbourne (1861, 1866–1867, 1875, 1884–1885, and 1888), Calcutta (1883–1884), Vienna (1873), Philadelphia (1876), Amsterdam (1883), New Orleans (1884–1885), Chicago (1893), Delhi (1903), and St. Louis (1904). Although many contemporaries believed that these exhibitions were popular spectacles of only fleeting significance, they did have profound and, in many cases, permanent social, cultural, and political outcomes. Not only did these exhibitions introduce new technologies and consumer goods to mass audiences, but they also underpinned the emergence of new institutions such as public museums and art galleries (the Great Exhibition, for example, formed the basis for the later establishment of Royal Albert Hall, the Science Museum, the National History Museum, and the Victoria and Albert Museum) and produced dense bodies of official and popular literature.

Culture of Empires. Exhibitions and expositions were an integral component of the culture of empires. By displaying the commodities and goods produced in the colonies and by exhibiting the new industrial and communication technologies, imperial exhibitions downplayed the violence of imperialism, instead celebrating the "progress" and "modernity" produced by colonialism. Exhibition organizers also identified exhibitions as crucial forums for inculcating the ideas that held empires together: ideologies of social and moral progress, the inherent value of technology and industrial innovation, and notions of imperial citizenship and unity. This faith in the cultural

THE CRYSTAL PALACE

The centerpiece of the Great Exhibition of 1851, the Crystal Palace was a potent symbol of the technological and social innovations of the Victorian age. Designed in just ten days by the renowned architect Sir Joseph Paxton, the innovative Palace featured interchangeable glass and steel components that greatly reduced construction cost of the huge greenhouse-like building. In response to widespread concern that Paxton's design would not stand up to the weight and motion of huge crowds, a model was constructed and extensively tested, including stress testing under the regimented marching of a battalion of soldiers. The building, which included 4,000 tons of iron and 900,000 square feet of glass, was 1,848 feet long and 408 wide, enclosed some 772,784 square feet (19 acres), and this space, an area four times that of St. Peter's Cathedral in Rome or six times that of St. Paul's Cathedral in London, provided the central display for the exhibition as a whole.

Widely celebrated as a marvel of industrial engineering, the Crystal Palace was moved to Sydenham Hill in South London after the Great Exhibition closed. This new 200-acre Crystal Palace Park was opened by Queen Victoria in June 1854 and quickly became a crucial site in the world of Victorian sporting culture. It served as the premier athletics venue in Britain well into the twentieth century. Starting in 1857, cricket was played in the park, and in 1861 the first Crystal Palace football team was formed. Twenty finals of the Football Association Cup—the premier trophy in football—were played at Crystal Palace between 1895 and 1914, drawing crowds in excess of 100,000. In 1911 the Crystal Palace temporarily reverted to its original function, hosting the Festival of Empire. After World War I, John Logie Baird selected it as the site for his television company. Based in the south tower, the Baird Television Company had four fully equipped studios at Crystal Palace from June 1934. In 1936 a fire devastated the building, and although the Park remained an important sporting and cultural center, the gutting of the Palace itself marked the destruction of one of the most important architectural achievements and cultural landmarks of the industrial age.

Sources: Peter H. Hoffenberg, *An Empire on Display: English, Indian, and Australian Exhibitions from the Crystal Palace to the Great War* (Berkeley: University of California Press, 2001).

John Tallis, *Tallis's History and Description of the Crystal Palace, and the Exhibition of the World's Industry in 1851*, 3 volumes (London & New York: J. Tallis, 1852).

observers were critical of exhibition commissioners and the representation of work and industry, urban laborers and their families were a prominent component of the exhibitions' audiences. Special transport arrangements and reduced ticket prices for laborers helped swell the massive attendance at these displays. Some five million visitors, for example, attended the Colonial and Indian Exhibition held in South Kensington in 1886. Exhibitions in the colonies proved equally popular, with, for example, more than one million attendees at the Calcutta International Exhibition in 1883–1884. These numbers are a clear testament to the power and popularity of these great imperial spectacles.

Sources:
Paul Greenhalgh, *Ephemeral Vistas: The Expositions Universelles, Great Exhibitions and World's Fairs, 1851-1939* (Manchester: Manchester University Press, 1988).

Peter H. Hoffenberg, *An Empire on Display: English, Indian, and Australian Exhibitions from the Crystal Palace to the Great War* (Berkeley: University of California Press, 2001).

Louise Purbrick, ed., *The Great Exhibition of 1851: New Interdisciplinary Essays* (Manchester: Manchester University Press, 2001).

Robert W. Rydell, *World of Fairs: The Century-of-Progress Expositions* (Chicago: University of Chicago Press, 1993).

Rydell, John E. Findling, and Kimberly D. Pelle, *Fair America: World's Fairs in the United States* (Washington, D.C.: Smithsonian Institution Press, 2000).

EXPLORATION

Growth of Geographical Knowledge. Between 1750 and 1914 there was a rapid transformation in the scope and detail of geographical knowledge, largely as a result of European empire building and colonization. Imperial governments, trading companies (such as the East India Company), learned and missionary societies, colonial scientists, and solitary adventurers invested large amounts of capital and effort into exploration and cartography. These processes were central to the making of the modern industrialized world as they fixed the location of valuable natural resources (from whale-breeding grounds to mineral deposits), facilitated the creation of new trade routes and posts, and laid the foundations for military conquest, colonial expansion, and colonization by white settlers.

Pacific Ocean. In this period there were two major forms of exploration: oceanic exploration and the exploration of continental interiors. Oceanic exploration largely focused on the Pacific during the eighteenth and nineteenth centuries. By this time the Atlantic and Indian Oceans were well known and accurately charted as a result of their incorporation into European trading networks and empires from the late fifteenth century. Europeans first entered the Pacific Ocean in the sixteenth century, and Ferdinand Magellan was the first European to cross the vast ocean in 1520. During the remainder of the sixteenth century and throughout the seventeenth century, Spanish, Portuguese, and Dutch explorers tentatively probed the region, but they assembled only a partial and frequently unreliable image of its geography. In the first half of the eighteenth century, British and French navigators explored the central Pacific, but the resulting additions to the map of the Pacific were

significance of imperial and colonial exhibitions rested upon an insistence that these events were effective media of education. Mass participation was a fundamental element of these Victorian exhibitions in both Europe and its various colonies. Although some radical and working-class

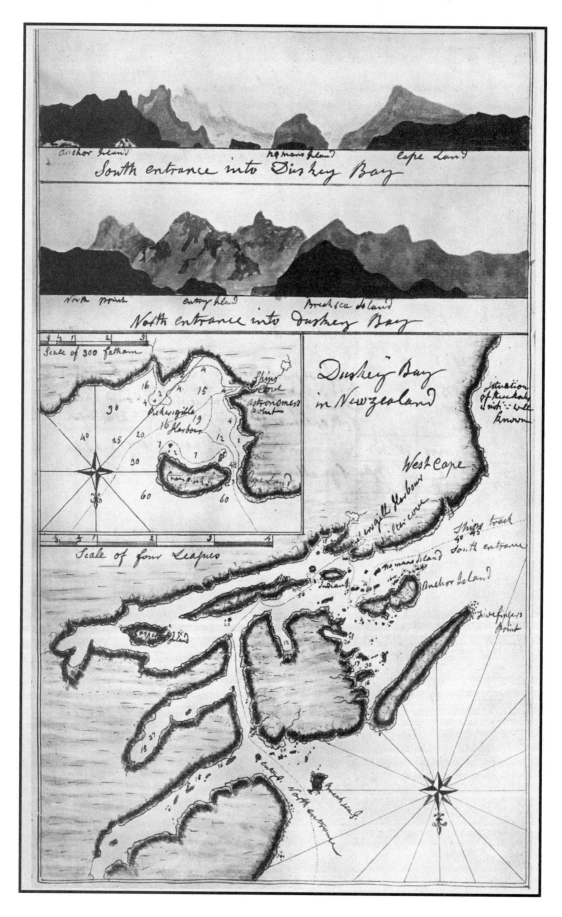

Map of part of the New Zealand coastline from the journal of Captain James Cook
(Public Record Office, London)

English captain Robert Falcon Scott (far left) with companions at the South Pole, January 1912

fragmentary, and most of the southern Pacific remained a mystery. The limitations of European knowledge of the Pacific are best seen in the notion of *Terra Australis Incognita*, "The Unknown Southern Land," the great continent that supposedly dominated the South Pacific. This belief was widely supported by European geographers until the mid eighteenth century. The three Pacific voyages of British captain James Cook vanquished this myth. Between 1768 and 1779 Cook mapped much of the Pacific, constructing detailed maps of Australia, New Zealand, Hawaii, and the northwest coast of North America. His third voyage also disproved the notion that an easily navigable Northwest Passage linked the Pacific to the Atlantic (in 1906 the Norwegian explorer Roald Amundsen did complete a three-year journey from the Atlantic to the Pacific through Canada's Arctic islands and iceberg fields, but this dangerous route has never been commercially viable). Cook's voyages were truly revolutionary, as they fixed the location of the major landmasses of the Pacific and opened up the region to European commercial and imperial activity. Most important, Cook opened the way for exploration of two of the three continental interiors that were extensively mapped for the first time in the nineteenth century: Australia and Antarctica.

Australia. From their arrival in Australia in 1788, European colonists rarely ventured far inland, preferring the rich resources of the coast and easily explored coastal plains. The rugged mountain chains and arid deserts that lay inland were a daunting barrier that slowed the spread of European settlement and protected the Aboriginal communities of Australia's interior from immediate contact with the colonists. Not until 1813 did Gregory Blaxland, William C. Wentworth, and William Lawson first cross the Blue Mountains, which lie some fifty miles to the west of modern-day Sydney. This initial foray into the interior was not extended until 1829–1830, when Charles Sturt traversed the Great Dividing Range (of which the Blue Mountains are part), exploring the Murrumbidgee, Darling, and Murray Rivers before ending his journey at the confluence of the Murray at Encounter Bay on the southern coast. This journey confirmed that Australia's interior was arid, disproving the popular theory that it contained a vast inland sea, and was pivotal in the selection of South Australia as a site for British colonization. In the 1840s, as a result of the epic journeys of Edward John Eyre and George Grey in southern Australia and the long journey of Robert Burke and William John Wills from Melbourne in the southeast to the Gulf of Carpentaria in the North, much of Australia's interior was mapped and its land was opened up for pastoralism, mining, and white settlement.

Antarctica. The first tentative explorations of Antarctica occurred in the 1840s. James Ross, in command of the British navy's *Erebus* and *Terror,* explored the coast of Antarctica's Victoria Land. The body of knowledge he gathered as a result of his venture was not extended until the 1890s, when the Norwegian whaler Leonard Chris-

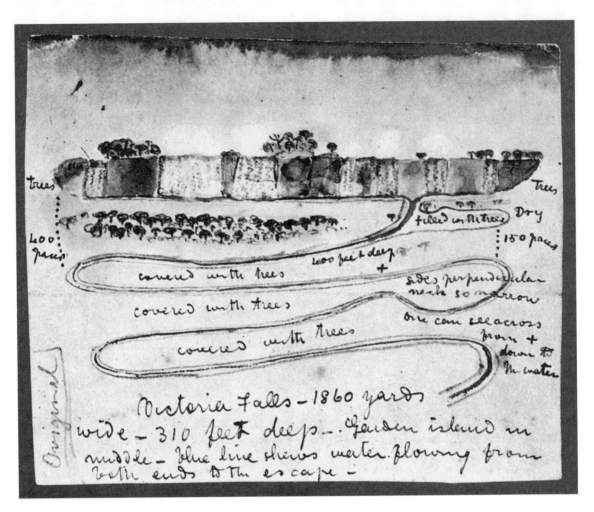

In the sketch, handwritten annotations read:

trees · trees · Dry · 400 paces · filled in th trees · 150 paces · 400 feet deep · covered with trees · sides perpendicular neck so narrow · covered with trees · one can see across from + down to th water · covered with trees · Original · Victoria Falls – 1860 yards wide – 310 feet deep – Garden island in middle – blue line shews water flowing from both ends to th escape –

Sketch of Victoria Falls from David Livingstone's notebook (Royal Geographical Society, London)

tensen landed at Cape Adare. When he disembarked in 1894, he became the first human to set foot on the Antarctic continent. News of Christensen's landing sparked great interest in Antarctica's resources. In the first decade of the twentieth century British, German, and French explorers began mapping the continent's coastline and interior. The quest for the South Pole became an intense battle for personal and national glory. The British explorer Robert Falcon Scott and his party reached the pole on 17 January 1912, only to find that the Norwegian Roald Amundsen had already reached the pole on 14 December 1911. Tragically, Scott's entire party perished in a blizzard on their return journey.

Africa. While the exploration of Australia and Antarctica completed the cartographic revolution in the Pacific initiated by Cook, the prime focus of European continental exploration in the nineteenth century was Africa. Although there was a long history of contact between Europe and Africa, European knowledge of the continent in the late eighteenth century was largely restricted to its coastline: Europeans had only a sketchy understanding of the huge river systems that shaped the continent. Moreover, early attempts to push into the interior were hampered by exceptionally high rates of morbidity and mortality. Malaria remained the chief barrier to the fulfillment of the Euro-

pean desire to open up the interior of Africa in the early nineteenth century. Europeans in tropical Africa experienced mortality rates up to forty times higher than those who remained at home in London, Paris, or Berlin. Although it was not until 1897 that European scientists identified the *Anopheles* mosquito that spread malaria, white settlers in Africa started in the 1820s to experiment with quinine as a deterrent to the disease. Quinine is an alkaloid produced from the bark of the cinchona tree. David Livingstone, who took quinine daily during his great African expeditions, was convinced of the efficacy of this remedy, and his faith was borne out by a rapid decline in the rate of European mortality in Africa in the final decades of the nineteenth century.

Probes in the Interior. Europeans attempted to map the interior of Africa and open up the continent to European commerce. Mungo Park, a young Scottish surgeon, was the first European to explore the interior of West Africa in the late 1790s, compiling the initial maps of the river Niger. The Englishman Richard Lander, who followed the river down to its mouth in 1830, extended Park's pioneering work. Further south, the Zambezi, the great river of southern central Africa, remained unknown to Europeans until the epic journey undertaken by David Livingstone between 1853 and 1856. His last expedition, from 1865 to 1871, initiated at the behest of the president of Britain's Royal Geographical Society, explored the complex drainage system between Lake Nyasa and Lake Tanganyika and charted the Congo's headwaters.

Nile River. Livingstone had hoped to discover the ultimate source of the Nile River, a quest that had enchanted Europeans and the people of North Africa for centuries, but he ultimately failed in this mission. In fact, the first step toward confirming the basic structure of the Nile was undertaken under the direction of the Ottoman Viceroy in Egypt, Muhammad 'Ali, who dispatched three expeditions up the Nile between 1839 and 1842. They ultimately reached Juba, only 250 miles from the Nile's source. The exact nature and location of that source remained uncertain. The explorations of three German missionaries in the 1840s, Johann Ludwig Krapf, Johannes Rebmann, and Jacob Erhardt, located the mountains of Kilimanjaro and Kenya, which they believed were potential sources of the river. In light of this intelligence the British explorers Richard Burton and John Speke followed the long-established Arab trade routes into the interior of East Africa, discovering Lake Tanganyika in 1857. From there, Speke pushed north to a lake that he believed was the Nile's source, which he named Victoria Nyanza (Lake Victoria). In a subsequent expedition in 1862 Speke collected more evidence to support his contention, that it drained into and began the Nile, but it fell to Henry Morton Stanley to finally confirm this theory. In 1875 Stanley circumnavigated Lake Victoria, mapping the course of the Lualaba River to the Congo River. He then followed the Congo to its mouth. The journey produced a detailed image of the structure of the key African river systems and paved the way for a new age of European imperialism in the continent. This situation culminated in the partition of Africa among the European powers in the final two decades of the nineteenth century.

Sources:

J.C. Beaglehole, *The Exploration of the Pacific* (London: Black, 1934).

Anne Hugon, *The Exploration of Africa: From Cairo to the Cape* (New York: Abrams, 1993).

John Parker, ed., *Merchants and Scholars: Essays in the History of Exploration and Trade* (Minneapolis: University of Minnesota Press, 1965).

A. L. Rice, *Voyages of Discovery: Three Centuries of Natural History Exploration* (New York: C. Potter, 1999).

Donald Simpson, *Dark Companions: The African Contribution to the European Exploration of East Africa* (New York: Barnes & Noble, 1975).

Peter Whitfield, *New Found Lands: Maps in the History of Exploration* (New York: Routledge, 1998).

Lynne Withey, *Voyages of Discovery: Captain Cook and the Exploration of the Pacific* (New York: Morrow, 1987).

Richard Worth, *Stanley and Livingstone and the Exploration of Africa in World History* (Berkeley Heights, N.J.: Enslow, 2000).

LETTER WRITING

Colonized Peoples. Letter writing was a central feature of life in Europe and its empires during the nineteenth century. Long-established as a feature of familial, commercial, and diplomatic communication in Europe, letter writing took on even greater significance within the context of empire building, and it remained absolutely foundational to imperial politics and colonial cultures into the twentieth century. Within modern imperial systems and colonial societies letter writing fulfilled four essential functions. First, it played a crucial role in imperial diplomacy and international relations. In Asia, European merchants and colonial administrators encountered local populations that possessed vibrant literary cultures and sophisticated diplomatic conventions. This development meant that Europeans had to work within these traditions in order to win trade concessions, to negotiate political relationships, and to fix commercial arrangements. In the eighteenth and early nineteenth centuries, leading Dutch, French, and British traders and colonial officials spent many years mastering these traditions and using their letter-writing skills to protect the interests of their companies and nations. In India the British East India Company initially relied heavily upon local *munshis,* expert writers and diplomats, who guided the British in the conventions that structured their social and political relationships with the Mughals and regional kingdoms. As time passed, the British tried to break free of their reliance on "native informants," and company officials published textbooks (such as Francis Gladwin's *The Persian Moonshee*) that distilled the knowledge of local experts for use in the classrooms of the company's training colleges in Calcutta, Bombay, and Madras. In colonial contexts (such as in southern Africa or Australasia) where Europeans encountered nonliterate peoples, letter writing became an extremely important form of communication after the introduction of literacy by missionaries and by colonial schools. Literate members of indigenous communities seized upon the power of letter writing, using it to communicate with other leaders, to request medical aid or doctrinal clarification from missionaries, or to explain their aspirations and grievances to colonial administrators. Thus, letter writing was an essential medium for the negotiation of cross-cultural differences and conflicts in the colonial world.

Imperial Administration. A second essential function of letter writing was its role in imperial administration. Handwritten correspondence was of vital importance in the machinery of imperial government as European officials in the colonies wrote to their masters in Europe, providing the latest news and seeking advice on important policy matters. In the eighteenth and early nineteenth centuries such correspondence was slow, and frequently officials in the colony had to make decisions before they received advice in the return post from Europe. Communications between colonial and metropolitan governments were revolutionized with the advent of the electric telegraph, which allowed rapid and efficient communication between colony and metropolis. By the 1870s letter writing was of greatly reduced significance in colonial administration as crucial news and policy decisions were transmitted by the telegraph rather than through the exchange of letters.

Private Correspondence. A third function of letter writing was its role throughout the eighteenth, nineteenth, and twentieth centuries in the general dissemination of information among private individuals. People corresponded with one another for a range of reasons: shared political and intellectual interests, common economic concerns, or most commonly, familial bonds. In light of the divergent forces that underpinned correspondence, letters dealt with a range of topics. For example, they might describe changing political circumstances, emergent economic opportunities, or conflict within a community or a family. Such correspondence often played a key role in the shaping of cross-cultural understandings, policy making, the establishment of new commercial ventures, or an individual's decision to migrate. Letters allowed correspondents not only to share news but also to provide sustained analysis or commentary on recent developments and to communicate their feelings and emotions. Thus, letter writing tended to be more discursive and personal than other forms of communication, especially in comparison to the abbreviated and elliptical style of telegraphic communication or the often dispassionate voice of newspaper reports.

Traditional Bonds. A fourth important function of the exchange of letters was to maintain and affirm bonds of connection amid the upheavals and disruptions that characterized the new industrial and imperial world. Movement to urban centers by masses of people in search of work, men engaged in overseas service in the military or in merchant fleets, and waves of migrants to distant colonies stretched family structures and potentially undercut the ties of affection and affiliation that linked individuals to their traditional communities. Letter writing was one way to maintain these connections. With the growth of literacy throughout the world in the nineteenth century it became an increasingly important way of creating and sustaining social relationships. Letter writing took on particular importance for Europeans living or serving in distant colonies, as it provided a vital link with home. These imperial networks of personal correspondence were important in the social life of the colonies, as the latest gossip, news, books, fashions, and even seeds were disseminated along these lines of communications. Letter writing might not have been an adequate substitute for the intimacies of face-to-face contact, but it was one of the most important forms of social communication within a world where "traditional" social relationships were disrupted by migration, industrialization, and colonialism.

Sources:

C. A. Bayly, *Empire and Information: Intelligence Gathering and Social Communication in India, 1780-1870* (Cambridge & New York: Cambridge University Press, 1996).

Roger Chartier, Alain Boureau, and Cécile Dauphin, eds., *Correspondence: Models of Letter-writing from the Middle Ages to the Nineteenth Century*, translated by Christopher Woodall (Princeton: Princeton University Press, 1997).

David Fitzpatrick, *Oceans of Consolation: Personal Accounts of Irish Migration to Australia* (Ithaca, N.Y.: Cornell University Press, 1994).

Frances Porter and Charlotte MacDonald, eds., *My Hand Will Write What My Heart Dictates: The Unsettled Lives of Women in Nineteenth-century New Zealand as Revealed to Sisters, Family, and Friends* (Auckland: Auckland University Press, 1996).

POSTAL SYSTEMS

Preindustrial Period. Postal systems—networks of transportation dedicated to the dissemination of letters and written messages—have a long history. The ancient Greek, Roman, Persian, and Chinese empires each developed complex systems of runners and routes for the conveyance of messages. These complex systems atrophied in Europe and the Mediterranean during the medieval period, where the most important communication networks were run not by the state but rather by universities (such as the University of Paris), monastic orders (such as the Benedictines), and commercial communities (such as the Hanseatic League). In the early modern period, royal courts again assumed responsibility for the key networks of messengers, frequently opening them up to public use while at the same time keeping them under strict surveillance. In the late eighteenth century, postal networks within Europe expanded as increasingly complex road systems reached further into the countryside, and states were increasingly aware of the commercial and revenue benefits that resulted from postal communication. By the mid 1760s most towns in Britain received mail every day, and France had a similarly dense network of postal delivery (although in France every letter had to go through Paris, where it might be vetted). In the final two decades of the eighteenth century these road networks were extended, especially by Napoleon Bonaparte in Europe, and the surfaces of roads were greatly improved. These innovations allowed for the use of horse-drawn mail coaches instead of a solitary postboy, increasing both the volume of mail that was able to be carried and the speed with which it was transported: in 1780 postboys would travel at around three or four miles an hour, but by 1800 mail coaches were traveling at ten miles an hour, cutting long-distance postal times in half.

Railroads and Steamships. During the nineteenth century two major transformations further reshaped postal services. The first of these developments was steam power. In the mid 1830s the major cities in both Britain and France were beginning to be connected by fast and reliable rail and postal communications. By the 1850s significant market towns, military garrisons, and regional political centers enjoyed swift and regular rail-based postal service, and as a result horse-drawn mail coaches disappeared. While the steam locomotive greatly reduced the time it took to deliver a letter within any particular European nation, the steamship revolutionized international postal communications. Early transatlantic steamer services were devoted to mail in the 1830s, and by 1870 most major cities, whether in Europe, Asia, Africa, Australia, or the Americas, were connected to international mail networks serviced by steamships. This situation greatly reduced communication times, increasing the speed with which news and information traveled. Where a letter from London to New York would take almost a month to arrive in 1830, it took little more than a week by 1870. A letter from London to Bombay would take

Postal cart in Cornwall, England, circa 1890 (British Post Office, London)

just under a month to arrive in 1870 rather than the six months that was common in 1830.

Reduced Charges. The second major transformation that reshaped postal services in the nineteenth century was the simplification and reduction of postal charges. In the eighteenth century, European states prized postal communications because of the large amount of revenue generated by the taxes levied on letters. In the 1830s, however, a new generation of reformers argued that postal communications could be streamlined by introducing a standard basic charge and by reducing the bureaucratic machinery that registered every letter and used complex equations to calculate the charge for each piece of mail. Rowland Hill argued that any letter that was less than half an ounce in weight should cost one penny to send anywhere in the United Kingdom. Hill's proposal was greeted with skepticism within the government and postal bureaucracy but won tremendous popular support. In 1839 this simplified system became law in Britain, and it soon became the model for the British colonies and other European nations. It made postal communications simple and affordable. The post was increasingly used by a large cross section of society, and the volume of mail rapidly increased. Between 1839 and 1840 the number of letters sent in Britain doubled, by 1850 the volume of post was four times greater than it had been in 1839, and by 1870 it was ten times greater.

Colonies. European authorities also attempted to transplant this new standardized postal model to their colonies. In India, for example, the British encountered a society that had an elaborate preexisting messenger system, the *dak*. Under the emperor Akbar in the early seventeenth century, India had more than two thousand miles of post roads. The political instability that undercut Mughal authority in the eighteenth century weakened this system, and in the 1760s and 1770s the East India Company first infiltrated and then reformed the *dak*. Still heavily reliant on structures and personnel inherited from the *dak*, the East India Company opened its new postal service for public use in 1774. By the 1830s there were deep concerns about the efficiency and security of this system, and in response the Imperial Post was established in 1837. The Imperial Post exercised a monopoly over postal communications between Calcutta and principal provincial towns, while a variety of local services connected these provincial centers to their hinterlands. In 1850 these parallel systems were merged under a director general and, following the metropolitan example, a uniform postage rate was also introduced.

International Networks. A drive to streamline and regularize postal communications between nations also occurred in the mid nineteenth century. International postage became increasingly efficient and popular in the 1870s as a result of two important changes. First, improvements in transport, especially the establishment of long-distance steamer routes and the construction of the Suez Canal, drastically reduced transportation times. Second, the formation of the Universal Postal Union in 1875 established a standard framework for international postage. Its members, who included almost all nation-states, agreed that the charges for items posted would not be shared, as the country in which the item was posted would collect the revenue while the nation where the mail was delivered received no payment. The foundation of the Universal Postal Union allowed the smooth and equitable administration of international postal communications, a vitally important innovation given the centrality of letter writing and postal communication in nineteenth-century commerce and culture.

Sources:

C. A. Bayly, *Empire and Information: Intelligence Gathering and Social Communication in India, 1780-1870* (Cambridge & New York: Cambridge University Press, 1996).

M. J. Daunton, *Royal Mail: The Post Office since 1840* (London & Dover, N.H.: Athlone, 1985).

Daniel R. Headrick, *When Information Came of Age: Technologies of Knowledge in the Age of Reason and Revolution, 1700–1850* (Oxford & New York: Oxford University Press, 2000).

Richard R. John, *Spreading the News: The American Postal System from Franklin to Morse* (Cambridge, Mass.: Harvard University Press, 1995).

Mohini Lal Majumdar, *Early History and Growth of Postal System in India* (Calcutta: Rddhi-India, 1995).

Howard Robinson, *The British Post Office: A History* (Westport, Conn.: Greenwood Press, 1970).

RAILWAYS

Emergence. The development of railway systems during the nineteenth century had profound cultural and political consequences at a global level as railroads played a key role in industrial production, the development of high-speed mechanized travel, and the creation of colonial economic networks and political structures. The emergence of this new transportation technology relied on two technological innovations: metal rails and the steam-powered locomotive. Primitive railroads emerged in Europe during the sixteenth century, as flanged-wheel carts, propelled by human or animal power along wooden tracks, were used to transport coal from the mine face to storage yards and shipping depots. These wooden tracks imposed limits on the weight and speed of carriages and were prone to warping, resulting in high maintenance costs. In 1789 the English engineer William Jessop developed the first cast-iron rails, which were a great improvement on the capacity and durability of wooden rails. By the early nineteenth century, wrought iron had displaced cast iron, and as the century progressed steel rails became almost universal. Constructing safe and efficient steam locomotives was an even more daunting task. British experiments with steam-powered locomotives in the early nineteenth century culminated in George Stephenson's construction of the Rocket in 1829. Capable of reaching thirty-six miles per hour, the Rocket was the first steam locomotive that was both powerful and reliable enough to be commercially viable. The Rocket's success ensured that the Liverpool and Manchester Railway, the thirty-mile line that linked the port of Liverpool with the industrial hinterland of Lancashire, was the first railway service that relied entirely on steam-powered locomotives when it opened in 1830.

Sinews of Empire. The opening of the Liverpool and Manchester line is generally identified as marking the birth of the "Railway Age," which saw the rapid dissemination of railway technology in continental Europe, North America, and in European colonies in Africa, Asia, South America, and Australia. Railroads formed the steel "sinews of empire," the vital lines of communication and transport that allowed European empires to move commodities, people, and troops with a speed and efficiency that was unimaginable in the eighteenth century. In accelerating the pace of transport and reducing the cost of shipping large consignments of cargo, railways were essential in the intensification of the Industrial Revolution in the nineteenth century and in integrating much of the world into a powerful, if

GANDHI ON THE RAILWAYS

The following discussion of the impact of rail travel comes from Mohandas Gandhi's *Hind Swaraj, or, Indian Home Rule* (1909). Written in the form of a dialogue between a newspaper editor (representing Gandhi) and a reader (representative of the Indian public at large), *Hind Swaraj* explored the key political and cultural questions that concerned Indian nationalists, offering a distinctive and trenchant critique of modern civilization, including industrial technologies such as railways:

READER: I shall hear you on the railways.

EDITOR: It must be manifest to you, but for the railways, the British would not have such a hold on India as they have. The railways, too, have spread the bubonic plague. Without them, masses could not move from place to place. They are the carriers of plague germs. . . . Railways have also increased the frequency of famines, because, owing to facility of means of locomotion, people sell out their grain, and it is sent to the dearest markets. . . . They accentuate the evil nature of man. Bad men fulfil their evil designs with greater rapidity. The holy places of India have become unholy. Formerly, people went to these places with very great difficulty. Generally, therefore, only real devotees visited such places. Nowadays, rogues visit them in order to practise their roguery. . . . So the railways can become a distributing agency for evil. . . . It may be a debatable matter whether railways spread famines, but it is beyond dispute that they propagate evil.

Source: Mahatma Gandhi, *Hind Swaraj, or, Indian Home Rule* (Ahmedabad, India: Navajivan / Weare, N.H.: Greenleaf, 1982).

Modern reconstruction of George Stephenson's Rocket (Royal Scottish Museum, Edinburgh)

uneven, system of industrial production, distribution, and consumption.

British India. British India was the first colony where large-scale railway construction was undertaken, and railways quickly came to play a central place in that nation's development. Railways were a key element of the modernizing public-works programs initiated by James Ramsay, Lord Dalhousie, the Governor-General between 1847 and 1856. The East India Company was alive to both the commercial and strategic significance of the railways, realizing that the new technology would both allow goods from rural India to be transported to major cities and ports much more effectively, while also allowing the Company to redistribute its troops and resources at greater speed. In April 1853 the first steam locomotive in South Asia traveled over the newly completed track linking Bombay to Thana. By 1860 some one thousand miles of tracks had been laid. Ten years later more than five thousand miles were in operation, linking Bombay with Delhi and Calcutta and Madras with Bombay, effectively connecting the crucial military and commercial centers of British India. These routes, which opened up the interior of India, were crucial in the reconstruction of British authority after the rebellions of 1857–1858, and they also cemented India's position in the imperial economy as a producer of raw materials (especially cotton) and as a con-

sumer of manufactured British goods (especially textiles). By 1900 India had the most extensive rail system of any colony in the world, with twenty-four thousand miles of track connecting regional market towns and pilgrimage sites to the main trunk lines of the national network. Despite the fears of conservative religious leaders and the critiques of nationalists (including Gandhi), rail travel quickly became part of South Asian life, and the rail network played a central role in the development of national religious reform movements, stimulated a renaissance in pilgrimage, and underpinned growing political and cultural bonds between regions and communities.

Political Unification. Locally based British contractors and Indian capitalists played a central role in the development of South Asia's railroads, a pattern that was repeated throughout European empires. In Canada and Australia, local interests rather than administrators and capitalists in distant London dictated the development and location of new rail routes. In the hinterlands of Australia, South Africa, and Canada, railways opened up new land for white settlement and enabled the exploitation of important natural resources, but they also accelerated the transmission of diseases to indigenous communities and created increased conflict between encroaching white settlers and indigenous tribes. These railroads also played a key role in uniting far-flung

Photograph of a train on the first public railway in Wales, circa 1850 (Gernsheim Collection, Harry Ransom Humanities Research Center, University of Texas at Austin)

regions into a unified political system. The Confederation of Canada in 1867, for example, was enabled by the construction of railroads that linked the maritime areas to Ontario. The completion of the Canadian Pacific Railway in 1885 tightened the bonds between British Columbia (which had joined Canada in 1871) and the eastern provinces. In Australia, the promise to construct a railway linking Perth to cities in the east ensured that Western Australia became part of the federal Commonwealth of Australia in 1901 (the transcontinental railway connecting Perth and Kalgoorlie with Adelaide was not completed until 1917).

Symbols of Power. While railways played a key role in the political development of colonies, the intensification of the Industrial Revolution, and the acceleration of global trade, they were also central symbols of European power and colonial domination. Cecil Rhodes was the most ardent advocate of the cultural and political power of the railroad in an imperial context. Perhaps the leading advocate of "railway imperialism," Rhodes envisaged the construction of a complex railroad network that would ultimately link the northern and southern tips of Africa, running from Cape Town in the south to Cairo in the north. Rhodes believed that such a network would demonstrate the superiority of Europe to the natives of Africa while sealing Britain's imperial paramountcy. Rhodes's South Africa Company pushed railway lines

ahead of the imperial frontier, extending his own private empire of mining interests into central Africa, and in its wake opening up new opportunities for British settlement and commerce. Although Rhodes's elaborate dream of knitting northern and southern Africa together with British-controlled railways was never fully realized, his career is a powerful testament to the symbolic importance of the railroad in Victorian imperialism and the crucial role it played in Europe's exploitation of precious commodities found in the non-European world. No technology dramatizes the intersection between industrialization and imperialism so clearly as the railroad.

Sources:

Clarence B. Davis and Kenneth E. Wilburn Jr., eds., *Railway Imperialism* (New York: Greenwood Press, 1991).

Michael Freeman and Derek Aldcroft, *The Atlas of British Railway History* (London & Dover, N.H.: Croom Helm, 1985).

Daniel R. Headrick, *The Tentacles of Progress: Technology Transfer in the Age of Imperialism, 1850-1940* (Oxford & New York: Oxford University Press, 1988).

Headrick, *The Tools of Empire: Technology and European Imperialism in the Nineteenth Century* (Oxford & New York: Oxford University Press, 1981).

Ian J. Kerr, *Building the Railways of the Raj, 1850-1900* (Delhi: Oxford University Press, 1995).

Wolfgang Schivelbusch, *The Railway Journey: Trains and Travel in the 19th Century* (New York: Urizen, 1979).

David Norman Smith, *The Railway and Its Passengers: A Social History* (North Pomfret, Vt.: David & Charles, 1988).

The United Kingdom was the first country to impose a standard time system. With the growth of rail travel, there was a greater need to organize time measure to ensure the coordination of the movements of different trains and to guarantee the accuracy of timetables. The first railway to adopt London time as standard was the Great Western Railway in November 1840, and other railways quickly followed suit. In 1847 the Railway Clearing House, an industry-standards body, recommended that London's time be adopted at all stations as soon as possible, and by 1855 most public clocks in Britain were set to London's Greenwich Mean Time. In the 1880s, however, the legal system caught up with popular practice when the Statutes (Definition of Time) Act received the Royal Assent on 2 August 1880.

Larger nations where there was a significant divergence between the "solar time" in different regions, such as the United States, faced even more serious problems than the United Kingdom. In 1883 American railways implemented a system of standardized time zones, breaking away from the "local reckoning" that had been previously dominant. Many cities, however, resisted this change; not until August 1918, when Congress passed the Standard Time Act, were the standard time zones used by the railroads ratified.

In 1884, long before the United States government adopted a standard national time, forty-one delegates from twenty-five nations met in Washington, D.C., for the International Meridian Conference. The speed of telegraphic communication and steamships had made it clear that international standards for the measurement of time and space were needed, and the conference fixed an international meridian and international time zones. The conference delegates agreed that Greenwich, which already functioned as Britain's standard-setter, would serve as a global meridian and that all longitude would be calculated both east and west from this meridian. Thereafter, Greenwich Mean Time functioned as a global baseline from which international time zones were established, creating a unified system that has become the international standard.

Source: Michael Freeman and Derek Aldcroft, *The Atlas of British Railway History* (London & Dover, N.H.: Croom Helm, 1985).

STEAMSHIPS

Emergence. The Scottish engineer and inventor James Watt was the chief pioneer of steam power, and his experiments between the 1770s and the 1790s produced increasingly efficient steam engines that had a variety of potential uses. Not until the first decade of the nineteenth century, however, did pioneer steamboats such as the *Charlotte Dundas* in Scotland and the *Clermont* in Upstate New York demonstrate the practicality of steam-driven shipping. Despite these initial successes, however, steam power was introduced to ship construction in a piecemeal fashion, especially for ships traveling longer distances than those required on the canals of Scotland and New York. In the 1810s steam engines were added to some transatlantic sailing ships, but on these hybrid vessels steam power was only an auxiliary to sail power. The large amounts of fuel required to feed a steam engine and difficulties in adapting steam engines to operate in saltwater environments limited the use of this new technology in transatlantic shipping until the late 1830s. In 1838 the *Sirius* and the *Great Western* became the first ships to cross the Atlantic entirely under steam power, and in 1840 the first regular transatlantic steamship service began.

India. Both the British and French governments established steam routes serving their interests in the Mediterranean. British East India Company officials in India also began experimenting with steam-powered shipping, believing that it would cut the long journey times between Britain and India. Initially anxious about the high cost of providing the large amounts of coal required to fuel steamships, by the early 1830s company officials were convinced that the greater speed of steamships offered significant commercial and strategic benefits. By 1837, when the British government established a Select Committee to inquire into maritime communication with India, it was clear that steam power had made the overland routes to India (through Egypt and the Red Sea or from Syria down to the Persian Gulf) more efficient than the old sea route to Asia around the Cape of Good Hope. The ascendancy of the route through the Red Sea was confirmed in 1839 when the East India Company succeeded in annexing Aden to provide a shipping way station at the western edge of the Indian Ocean. Although the conquest of Aden was initially the subject of outcry in Britain, it soon became a crucial strategic key for British interests in the East.

Private Passenger Service. In the 1840s popularization of steam travel occurred, as private interests soon began running steamship services that linked distant parts of the empire together in increasingly fast and efficient travel networks. The most important of these was the Peninsular and Oriental Steam Navigation Company, popularly known as P&O, which became the dominant passenger service in both the British Empire and the world by the 1860s. P&O's origins lay in the Dublin and London Steam Packet Company, which established a route to Vigo in Galacia and then to Malta and Alexandria. By 1842 it was renamed P&O, and it began operations in the Red Sea and the Indian Ocean. Within three years it was serving Penang, Singapore, and Hong Kong, and by the 1860s it also provided a regular steamer service to Australia.

Technology. This steam boom was underpinned by three important technological shifts. First and most important, the rise of efficient and reliable steamships

Painting of the *Great Western,* circa 1838 (Bristol Museum and Art Gallery, United Kingdom)

depended upon a shift from ships constructed from wood to iron. Because of the greater strength of iron, these new ships could be much larger than the old wooden ships and carry a higher percentage of cargo. In fact, cargo made up less than half of the total weight of most wooden ships, but it could comprise around two-thirds of the total weight of iron ships. Moreover, a ship constructed in iron was faster, more durable, and safer than wooden ships. The iron steamers of the 1850s not only dwarfed all previous ships, but they were also much less likely to sink or catch fire than either the hybrid steam-sail ships of the 1810s or the pioneering wooden steamers of the 1820s. Second, new engine technology pioneered by Samuel Hall in the 1830s (and subsequently refined during the 1840s) allowed engineers to avoid the salt deposits that had previously plagued oceangoing steamships. Third, in 1838 the screw propeller was used as a method of propulsion for the first time, and it was quickly adopted as the new standard form of propulsion for seaworthy steamers. It replaced the older paddle wheel that was better suited to river travel than the rigors of the open sea.

Size, Speed, and Efficiency. These technological refinements allowed the rapid expansion of steam shipping in the Victorian age, a new technology that brought distant parts of the empire into closer connection. In the 1820s it could take up to eight months for an East India Company official to reach India from London. By 1858 it was possible to travel by steamer from London to Bombay in a month. Travel not only

became quicker and easier but also allowed increasing numbers of individuals to travel at speed. In 1839 less than three hundred people traveled to India via the Red Sea, but by 1850 this number exceeded five thousand. The size, speed, and efficiency of steamships meant that they played a key role in moving millions of migrants from Europe to North America, southern Africa, and Australasia from the 1860s through to 1914. Their increased capacity and greater speed made migration not only more comfortable but also more profitable. Equally important, steam travel made imperial postal systems more efficient, delivering large volumes of letters and printed material at a speed that was unimaginable in even the 1820s. By the second half of the nineteenth century, steam travel became commonplace, and steamer routes provided the crucial filaments that knitted the empire together. Along these routes the ideas, commodities, and personnel of empire flowed.

Sources:
Boyd Cable, *A Hundred Year History of the P. & O., Peninsular and Oriental Steam Navigation Company, 1837–1937* (London: I. Nicholson & Watson, 1937).

Henry Fry, *The History of North Atlantic Steam Navigation with Some Account of Early Ships and Shipowners* (New York: Scribners, 1896).

Daniel R. Headrick, *The Tentacles of Progress: Technology Transfer in the Age of Imperialism, 1850-1940* (Oxford & New York: Oxford University Press, 1988).

Headrick, *The Tools of Empire: Technology and European Imperialism in the Nineteenth Century* (Oxford & New York: Oxford University Press, 1981).

K. T. Rowland, *Steam at Sea: A History of Steam Navigation* (New York: Praeger, 1970).

A SHRINKING WORLD: SHIPPING TIMES, 1830-1870

The following table demonstrates the quickening pace of maritime transport during the nineteenth century as the result of the introduction of steam power. The numbers represent days of travel.

To London from	1830	1840	1850	1860	1870
Gibraltar	18	11	8	8	6
New York	26	21	12	13	9
Istanbul	30	25	17	10	10
Quebec	35	32	14	12	13
Cape Town	69	66	66	39	35
Buenos Aires	76	74	72	40	33
Bombay	129	47	30	27	23
Sydney	142	137	109	54	54
Singapore	176	115	unknown	52	36

Source: Yrjö Kaukianen, "The Improvement of Communication in International Freight Markets," in *Information, Media and Power Through the Ages*, edited by Hiram Morgan (Dublin: University College Dublin Press, 2001), p. 141.

THE SUEZ CANAL

Linking Two Seas. A 101-mile waterway, the Suez Canal separates Africa from Asia, runs north-south across the Isthmus of Suez in Egypt, connects the Mediterranean and the Red Seas, and provides the shortest maritime route between Europe and the Indian Ocean. Running from Port Said in the north to Suez in the south, the canal is a lockless open cut with major bends, which makes use of an intricate series of lakes to both the north and south of the main canal. Over the long sweep of history, imperial powers have been sensitive to the value of a canal linking the Mediterranean and the Red Sea. It seems that the Egyptians around 1850 B.C.E. constructed the first canal, and the Romans later extended it. After the collapse of Rome the canal came under Byzantine control and fell into disrepair, but it was reopened during the Arab conquest of North Africa before being finally filled in by the Abbasid caliphs in 775 C.E. More than one thousand years later, following his invasion of Egypt in 1798, Napoleon Bonaparte conducted a survey with the aim of reconstructing a canal across the isthmus. His plan was abandoned when his engineers argued that the Red Sea was more than thirty feet higher than the Mediterranean. This assessment proved untrue in the 1830s, and interest in the canal was quickly reignited. The French took the lead, hoping that a canal would solidify their commercial interests in the Mediterranean, boost the commercial power of Marseilles, and tip the balance of power in the region away from Britain. Fearing the commercial and strategic advantages that might accrue to its rivals by the canal's construction, the British vehemently opposed the scheme and continued work on a railway that they had begun in 1851 across the isthmus.

Construction. The French diplomat and entrepreneur Ferdinand de Lesseps drafted the initial plans for the formation of a company to undertake the construction of the canal, gaining the support of Muhammad Said Pasha, the Ottoman khedive (viceroy) of Egypt. In November 1854 the Compagnie Universelle du Canal Maritime de Suez was established. In the face of intense international pressure Muhammad Said Pasha granted a concession in January 1856 to the company to run the canal for ninety-nine years, after which time it would return to Egyptian control. With a 60-million-franc subscription from Said Pasha, de Lesseps toured Europe to raise the remaining capital. Construction began in 1859. The bulk of the laborers were Egyptian, while the overseers and technical experts were French. Construction took a decade rather than the planned six years as a result of ongoing labor problems, difficulties supplying the workforce with fresh water, and a cholera epidemic in 1865.

Tightening Imperial Ties. Finally completed in November 1869, the canal was celebrated internationally as European governments, navies, companies, and settlers cheered the rapid reduction of travel time that followed its construction. Although the canal did not generate a profit until 1875, it breathed new life into the port cities of the eastern Mediterranean as ships traveling to and from India and East Asia now could take the canal in preference to the long journey around southern Africa. In effect, the canal tightened the ties of empire, bringing India closer to Britain, solidifying the connections between the Dutch East Indies and the Netherlands, and strengthening France's grip over its Asian holdings. Given its strategic and commercial importance, it is hardly surprising that the canal was also sub-

Procession of ships during the opening ceremony of the Suez Canal in 1869

ject to intense dispute. This controversy focused on the canal's international status. Britain, which purchased the khedive of Egypt's shares in the canal in 1875, was at the center of these debates. Although it effectively controlled the canal by the time the Convention of Constantinople discussed international use of the Suez Canal in 1888, Britain refused to attend the convention. It was only in 1904 that Britain affirmed the convention's recommendations that the canal was truly international and that it should be open to all ships in times of both peace and war. Nevertheless, Britain continued to exercise its power over the canal. It blocked the passage of the Spanish navy in 1898 while Spain was at war with the United States (thereby helping the Americans oust the Spanish from the Philippines), and it prevented the transit of German ships through the canal during both world wars. By the middle of the twentieth century the Suez had become the most strategically important waterway in the world, and the subsequent conflicts over the control of the canal in 1956 and the 1970s underlined the ongoing importance of the canal in international trade and diplomacy.

Sources:

Ferdinand de Lesseps, *The History of the Suez Canal: A Personal Narrative,* translated by Sir Henry Drummond Wolff (Edinburgh & London: Blackwood, 1876).

D. A. Farnie, *East and West of Suez: The Suez Canal in History, 1854–1956* (Oxford: Clarendon Press, 1969).

Charles W. Hallberg, *The Suez Canal: Its History and Diplomatic Importance* (New York: Columbia University Press, 1931).

Hugh J. Schonfield, *The Suez Canal in Peace and War, 1869-1969* (London: Vallentine & Mitchell, 1969).

TELEGRAPHS

Optical Telegraph. The rise of the electric telegraph is frequently identified as marking a revolutionary shift in the history of communications. Information could, for the first time, travel faster than the fastest horse-borne rider or ship, covering considerable distance nearly instantaneously. Early experiments with telegraphy, however, predated electricity. The French in particular constructed an elaborate and efficient telegraph system before the advent of electricity. In the late eighteenth century Claude Chappe developed a new system of long-distance communication, an optical telegraph that used T-shaped transmission posts that were located at the top of steeples, towers, or hills. By placing the *régulateurs,* the horizontal boards that topped the "T", and the *indicateurs,* the smaller boards fastened at each of the *régulateurs,* in different positions, the operators of these transmission posts could relay encoded information at surprising speed. In 1794, under the direction of the Ministry of War, Chappe presided over the first telegraph line, a series of posts running from Paris to Lille. Although signaling required both good visibility and the

Charles Wheatstone's ABC telegraph, patented in 1858 (British Post Office, London)

use of complex codebooks that deciphered the various combinations in which the *régulateurs* and *indicateurs* were placed, it was a remarkably swift and efficient system. In good conditions a simple message could be conveyed the 180 miles between Paris and Lille in less than three minutes. With the assistance of his brothers, Chappe was responsible for the rapid expansion of the French optical telegraph system: by 1800, lines connected Paris to Dunkirk in the North, Marseilles in the South, and Brest in the West. These French networks soon encompassed other important European political and commercial centers, including Brussels, Milan, Venice, and Antwerp.

Electric Telegraph. Although France both pioneered and dominated optical telegraphy before the 1840s, Britain and the United States championed the electric telegraph. The emergence of this new communication technology was enabled by progress in physics and in the development of the first reliable electric batteries. In 1837 Sir William Fothergill Cooke and Sir Charles Wheatstone patented an electric telegraph in Britain that employed six wires and five needle pointers that responded to various electric transmissions by pointing to specific letters and numbers on their mounting plate. A simpler and more cost-effective system was developed by the American Samuel Morse, who devised a system of dots and dashes to represent letters and numbers. This "Morse code" was used in the electromagnetic telegraph he patented in 1837. In 1843 Morse obtained support from the U.S. government to build a demonstration telegraph system between Washington, D.C., and Baltimore. Telegraph operators valued the simplicity of the Morse system, and a modified form (that allowed for the use of diacritic marks) known as International Morse Code was adopted as standard in 1851. In Britain and the United States, electric telegraph networks proliferated from the early 1840s. Typically, telegraph lines were constructed alongside railway tracks, and rail companies were the first to adopt the new technology, using fast and efficient transmissions to regulate the movements of rail traffic. By the late 1840s dense telegraphic networks had been constructed in both Britain and the United States, while the French government, which had remained wedded to optical telegraphy, finally adopted the technology in 1850.

Commerce and Empire. The speed and capacity of the electric telegraph—which was at least six times faster than optical telegraphy and could operate at night and under any weather conditions—was seen as a particularly important tool in an age of international commerce and

The *Great Eastern* leaving England in 1866 on the voyage to lay the Atlantic cable (Gernsheim Collection, Harry Ransom Humanities Research Center, University of Texas at Austin)

EASTERN TELEGRAPH COMPANY

The Eastern Telegraph Company, established in 1872, oversaw the telegraphic networks that connected Britain to the Middle East, Africa, Asia, and the Pacific. By the 1890s Britain controlled more than 65 percent of the world's telegraphic networks through the Eastern Telegraph Company: the only region that was not under company domination was the Atlantic, where several companies laid cables linking Europe and the United States. Formed out of four companies that operated telegraph networks between India and Britain, Eastern Telegraph extended these networks out into East Asia and the Pacific. The company connected Australia and New Zealand in 1876, and from 1879 to 1889 it laid the key submarine cables along the coasts of Africa, including the line running from the company's base of operations in Aden (in present-day Yemen) to Durban in South Africa. The British government subsidized the company's global reach as it emphasized the importance of "all-British" cable routes as a foundation of imperial strategy. The vast networks created and run by Eastern Telegraph were thus seen as fundamental to the empire, allowing the speedy movement of armed forces, ensuring the swift implementation of imperial policy, and enabling the rapid transmission of political and commercial intelligence. Moreover, as they connected distant parts of the empire into a shared web of communication, they were extolled by Parliamentarians and colonial officials as powerful instruments of imperial unity.

Source: Brian Winston, *Media, Technology and Society: A History from the Telegraph to the Internet* (London & New York: Routledge, 1998).

imperial expansion. Colonial administrators, migration agents, capitalists, and journalists were keen supporters of the construction of international telegraphic networks to promote the speedy transmission of news, prices, and military intelligence. This international interest in the application of the telegraph resulted in the formation of the International Telegraphic Union in 1865 to supervise and police international telegraphic communication. The foundation of the International Telegraphic Union came at a moment when international telegraphic networks were proliferating. After several failures, the first successful transatlantic underwater cables were laid in 1866, connecting Britain to Canada and the United States. Three years earlier, in 1863, the government of India sponsored the laying of a submarine cable from Karachi to Fao in the Persian Gulf, greatly reducing communication times between India and Europe. From 1865 Britain established its dominance over international telegraphic communication, sponsoring the construction of lines that were deemed of commercial or strategic importance. In the 1870s key submarine cables connected Bombay to Obok (in present-day Djibouti) and Aden (1870), Penang and Singapore to Madras (1875), Broome and Darwin (both in Australia) to Singapore (1875), Hong Kong and Jakarta to Singapore (1875), and Nelson (in New Zealand) to Sydney (1879). By 1890 Britain controlled more than two-thirds of the world's submarine cables, reflecting the high value placed on using "all-British" cable networks by both the Colonial Office and various colonial governments. Telegraphic communication had revolutionized imperial communications in little more than two decades. Where a message sent from Singapore, Sydney, or Suva (in Fiji) would have taken weeks or months to reach London even in an age of steamships, the complex grid of electric telegraph routes spanning the

The following table demonstrates the acceleration of communications during the nineteenth century as a result of improved maritime technology and the spread of telegraphic technology. The numbers represent days of travel.

To London from	1830	1860	1870
New York	26	13	2
Barbados	37	21	4
Cape Town	69	39	4
Buenos Aires	76	41	3
Bombay	129	26	3
Hong Kong	141	54	3
Sydney	142	53	4

Source: Yrjö Kaukianen, "The Improvement of Communication in International Freight Markets," in *Information, Media and Power Through the Ages,* edited by Hiram Morgan (Dublin: University College Dublin Press, 2001), p. 148.

globe in the 1880s ensured that such a message would reach London in a few days, or more frequently, just hours. The rapid dissemination of this technology made the world seem a much smaller place.

Sources:

Lewis Coe, *The Telegraph: A History of Morse's Invention and its Predecessors in the United States* (Jefferson, N.C.: McFarland, 1993).

Daniel R. Headrick, *When Information Came of Age: Technologies of Knowledge in the Age of Reason and Revolution, 1700–1850* (Oxford & New York: Oxford University Press, 2000).

Gerald J. Holzmann and Bjorn Pehrson, *The Early History of Data Networks* (Los Alamitos, Cal.: IEEE Computer Society, 1995).

Brian Winston, *Media, Technology and Society: A History from the Telegraph to the Internet* (London & New York: Routledge, 1998).

SIGNIFICANT PEOPLE

THOMAS BRASSEY

1805-1870
RAILWAY CONTRACTOR

Early Years. Thomas Brassey was perhaps the most important civil-engineering contractor in the world in the nineteenth century. He was born into a respectable rural family in northern England in 1805. His father worked a small family farm in addition to cultivating a large farm owned by the Marquess of Westminster. Thanks to these resources, Thomas received a solid education in Chester, where he studied commercial subjects until the age of sixteen. After his sixteenth birthday in 1821 he was apprenticed to a surveyor, and on the completion of his apprenticeship he soon became the partner of his master. The local surveys he conducted throughout the north of England provided the foundations of his career as a railway surveyor and contractor. Well-respected and financially secure, Brassey began undertaking contract work in the fledgling British rail system in the 1830s. His first building design project was a railway viaduct at Bromborough. Soon afterward, Brassey won a contract to build the Grand Junction Railway, marking his emergence as the most important individual in Britain's railway boom.

France. Brassey's ambitions were not confined to Britain alone, however, as his interests expanded into mainland Europe. From 1841 to 1843 he built the Paris-Rouen Railway (together with William Mackenzie), and over the coming decades he was responsible for the construction of more than one-half of the French rail network. Brassey returned to England in 1843 to build the Lancaster & Carlisle Railway, initiating a string of important contracts including the Caledonian Railway, the Tilbury & Southend Railway, the Shrewsbury & Hereford Railway, and the Great Northern Railway (built between 1847 and 1851, this line connected London to the coalfields and industrial centers of Yorkshire and Lancashire). By the early 1850s Brassey had overseen the construction of almost seven thousand miles of railroad in the United Kingdom. His British interests were not restricted to the rail system, as he played an active role in the development of Britain's industrial north and was also pivotal in the construction of the Victoria Docks in London.

Colonies. The experience, wealth, and authority that Brassey accumulated in Europe positioned him well to exploit colonial rail booms. In partnership with Sir Samuel Morton Peto and E. L. Betts, he won the prized contract to construct Canada's major rail artery: the 1,100 miles of the Grand Trunk was built between 1853 and 1859. Brassey also oversaw the erection of the lengthy bridge over the St. Lawrence River. These Canadian projects marked the beginning of Brassey's sustained period of rail construction in the colonies. He executed contracts in India (1858–1865), Australia (1859–1863), and Argentina (1864), providing the capital and technical expertise that facilitated the opening up of distant frontier zones and the modernization of colonial societies.

Manager of Money and Men. Brassey's successful juggling of multiple contracts in far-flung parts of the empire rested not only on shrewd financial management (enabling him to survive the financial crashes in the rail industry during the 1840s and 1860s) but also on his ability to raise and run a huge labor force. More than ten thousand workers were routinely employed by Brassey and, according to legend, at one point this number exceeded seventy-five thousand. His workers generally respected Brassey because he believed well-fed and well-rested workers were more efficient and produced better results than laborers who were poorly paid and fed. While the scope of Brassey's contract work carried high risk, it also generated tremendous wealth, and by the 1860s he was renowned as one of the richest men in the British Empire. Brassey's success certainly owed much to his ability to capitalize fully on the global boom in railway construction, but it was also the result of his renowned diplomacy, which allowed him to negotiate effectively with foreign governments, and his insistence on the swift completion of any contract, qualities that secured him a reputation as the most honest and reliable contractor in a high-risk business. As a result, Brassey was showered with honors: in Britain, he was awarded the cross of the Legion of Honour, while he received the cross of the Order of St. Maurice and St. Lazarus from King Victor Emmanuel of Italy, and the emperor of Austria presented Brassey with the Iron Crown (an honor that had not been previously conferred on any foreigner) for his distinguished service in the construction of European railways. At the time of his death on 8 December 1870 in Sussex, his estate was valued at £3.2 million and he was widely celebrated as a "great builder" of the empire. In 1872 the prolific Victorian historian Arthur Helps produced a popular history of Brassey's life titled *The Life and Labours of Mr. Brassey*, which reached its seventh edition by 1888 and secured Brassey's reputation as one of Britain's leading industrialists in the age of empire.

Sources:

Arthur Helps, *The Life and Labours of Mr. Brassey* (London: Bell & Daldy, 1872).

Keith Middlemas, *The Master Builders: Thomas Brassey, Sir John Aird, Lord Cowdray, Sir John Norton-Griffiths* (London: Hutchinson, 1963).

Charles Walker, *Thomas Brassey: Railway Builder* (London: Muller, 1969).

JAMES COOK

1728-1779

NAVIGATOR AND CARTOGRAPHER

Love of the Sea. The renowned navigator James Cook was born in Marton-in-Cleveland in Yorkshire on 27 October 1728. He was the second of the seven children of James Cook, an agricultural laborer, and his wife, Grace Pace. The Cooks were not able to afford to pay for an extended education for their children, but their employer funded young James Cook's basic education at Postgate school in Great Ayton, Yorkshire. After completing school, James Cook was apprenticed to a haberdasher in the small north Yorkshire fishing port of Staithes. Cook disliked shop work, finding his only pleasure watching the sea and fishing boats that plied Yorkshire's coastal waters. In July 1746, at the age of seventeen, Cook left Staithes for a new apprenticeship with the Walker family, shipowners, at the port of Whitby. Cook served his apprenticeship on colliers—large, slow-moving ships of three hundred to four hundred tons—in the North Sea, the type of ship that he would later use on his Pacific voyages. Cook quickly became a skilled sailor and devoted his spare time to the study of mathematics and cartography. By 1749 he was an able seaman. In 1752 he was promoted to mate, and in 1755 he was offered command of a Whitby-based collier. Despite this rapid advancement, Cook turned his back on private shipping when he volunteered for the Royal Navy in 1755, serving initially on the sixty-gun ship *Eagle* in the English Channel. Within two years he had risen to the position of master, and in 1757 he was shifted to the *Pembroke*, a sixty-four-gun ship, which was sent to support the war effort against the French in North America. During his service off the Atlantic coast of North America, Cook refined his navigational skills and learned the techniques of trigonometrical surveying under the supervision of Samuel Holland, a well-respected military surveyor. Cook's fine draftsmanship and the accuracy of his maps resulted in his appointment by the navy to the newly created position of the Surveyor of Newfoundland in 1763. For five years he commanded the schooner *Grenville*, producing detailed charts of Canada's Atlantic coasts and navigable waterways. This work won him influential patrons, including Sir Hugh Palliser, the governor of Newfoundland, and also attracted the attention of Britain's leading learned body, the Royal Society of London.

First Pacific Voyage. These connections bore immediate fruit. In February 1768, while Cook was still in Newfoundland, the Royal Society petitioned the British government to send observers to the Southern Hemisphere to view the passage of the planet Venus across the disc of the sun, in the hope it would help astronomers fix the exact distance of the Earth from the Sun. The government backed this proposal, and in April 1768 they appointed Cook, whose skills as a naval officer, astronomer, and cartographer were ideally suited to this mission, to lead this scientific expedition. Cook was to command the *Endeavour,* a renovated collier, on a voyage to the Pacific Ocean, where he would observe the transit of Venus in Tahiti, and to search for evidence of *Terra Australis Incognita,* the fabled southern continent. After rounding Cape Horn, the *Endeavour* spent four months in Tahiti before sailing south. He sighted New Zealand in October 1769. After a circumnavigation of New Zealand, Cook headed for the east coast of Australia in April 1770. He charted its coastline as the *Endeavour* made its way north to Jakarta. He eventually reached Britain in July 1771.

Second Pacific Voyage. Exactly one year later, Cook again set out for *Terra Australis Incognita.* This time he commanded the *Resolution,* while Tobias Furneaux commanded the *Adventure.* Cook crisscrossed the Pacific, pushing deeply toward Antarctica and refining his survey of New Zealand in addition to producing detailed maps of the central Pacific. On his return to Britain, Cook published *Journal of the* Resolution's *Voyage, in 1772, 1773, 1774, and 1775* (1775), a detailed summation of the second voyage, which established him as a careful naturalist and important ethnographic observer.

Third Pacific Voyage. Cook's third and final voyage was a search for another geographical phantom, an easily navigable Northwest Passage that supposedly linked the Atlantic and the Pacific. Cook left Plymouth in July 1776 with two ships under his command, the *Resolution* and the *Discovery*. After sailing via the Cape of Good Hope at the southern tip of Africa, Cook again visited New Zealand before heading to the Pacific coast of North America via Tahiti and Hawaii. In December 1778 Cook returned to a warm reception in Hawaii, arriving at the time of the *Makahiki* (New Year) festival when Hawaiians believed that the god Lono returned and regenerated the natural order. Cook was initially received with great enthusiasm on this second visit, seemingly because many Hawaiians identified Cook as the god Lono himself. Relations between Cook and the Hawaiians deteriorated quickly, and amid considerable confusion Cook was killed at Kealakekua Bay on 14 February 1779. There is strong evidence to suggest that Cook's death was the result of the Hawaiian identification of him with Lono, and as the *Makahiki* festival traditionally ended with the "killing" of a symbolic representation of Lono, Cook died as Lono's proxy. Cook's death devastated the morale of the *Resolution* and the *Discovery* crews, and the two ships headed home for Britain under the command of Charles Clerke. Captain Clerke died of tuberculosis at Kamchatka in 1779, and John Gore assumed command of the final leg of the voyage from Kamchatka to Britain. Once news of Cook's death reached home, the British public celebrated him as a national hero, but his real significance lies in his navigational and cartographic achievements in the Pacific. In extending and refining European knowledge of the Pacific, he laid the foundations for a new age of imperialism in the region.

Opening the Final Frontier. Prior to Cook's voyages, European knowledge of the Pacific was patchy, and navigating a path through the vast ocean was a difficult and dangerous task. Improvements in navigational technology, especially the use of John Harrison's fourth chronometer (which allowed Cook to accurately calculate longitude) and the assistance of Polynesian experts such as Tupaia (who traveled with Cook from Tahiti to New Zealand, Australia, and on to Batavia, or modern Jakarta in the Dutch East Indies), enabled Cook to explore and chart the coastlines of the Pacific with a new confidence. The accuracy of his charts and their rapid dissemination in Europe created a reliable navigational and cartographic framework for Europeans entering the Pacific. This shift in European knowledge of the Pacific had profound consequences. Where less than 450 ships crossed the Pacific from Ferdinand Magellan's entry into the Pacific in 1521 until 1769, in the wake of Cook's voyages large numbers of ships entered the Pacific with confidence. Armed with accurate maps, they searched for valuable natural resources, including whales, seals, timber, flax, sandalwood, and even sea slugs and sea cucumbers. Missionaries and colonists soon followed, and the islands of the Pacific were integrated into a complex mesh of commercial, religious, and political networks that linked them to Asia, the Americas, and, increasingly, Europe. Thus, Cook broke the barrier of the Pacific's vastness, and Europe's final frontier was opened. This important turning point in global history initiated a series of profound and painful transformations as the peoples of the Pacific struggled to deal with new diseases, depopulation, and the alienation of their land, resources, and sovereignty.

Given the persistence of these issues, Cook's place in contemporary Pacific culture remains hotly contested.

Sources:

J. C. Beaglehole, *The Life of Captain James Cook* (London: A. & C. Black, 1974).

Marshall Sahlins, *Islands of History* (Chicago: University of Chicago Press, 1985).

Alan Villiers, *Captain Cook, the Seaman's Seaman: A Study of the Great Discoverer* (London: Hodder & Stoughton, 1967).

Lynne Withey, *Voyages of Discovery: Captain Cook and the Exploration of the Pacific* (New York: Morrow, 1987).

DAVID LIVINGSTONE

1813-1873
MISSIONARY AND EXPLORER

Youthful Ambitions. The most renowned explorer of the nineteenth century, David Livingstone was born in Blantyre, Lanarkshire, in 1813. He was raised in a pious family that strictly abided by the Calvinist tenets of the Scottish-established church. While working in a textile factory as a youth, he began studying Greek and Latin. An 1834 public appeal for medical missionaries in China caught Livingstone's imagination, and he prepared himself for the mission field by studying medicine and theology at the University of Glasgow. The Opium War (1839–1842) prevented Livingstone from going to China, but after meeting Robert Moffat (a notable Scottish missionary stationed in South Africa), he shifted his ambitions to Africa.

Africa. In November 1840 he was ordained as a medical missionary by the London Missionary Society and left for the Society's South African mission the following month. In July 1841 he reached the Kuruman station, which was run by Moffat. From this base Livingstone traveled widely, pushing into the Kalahari to take the gospel and medicine to indigenous populations beyond the frontier. These efforts in the Kalahari won few converts, aroused the ire of white settlers, and placed Livingstone in great danger. When he was working to establish a mission station at Mabotsa in 1844, he was badly mauled by a lion, permanently damaging his left arm. However, this incident did not curb Livingstone's commitment to his mission or his growing love of exploration. Throughout the remainder of the 1840s he journeyed extensively, often accompanied by his wife, Mary (Robert Moffat's daughter, whom he married in 1845). As a result of his discovery of Lake Ngami in August 1849, he gained considerable fame as a scientist and surveyor, and he received a gold medal and monetary prize from Britain's Royal Geographical Society.

Journey into the Interior. This achievement marked the beginning rather than the culmination of Livingstone's career as an explorer, and after the return of his wife and children to Scotland, Livingstone dedicated himself to pushing northward into the heart of Africa. He charted lands unknown to Europeans and sowed the seeds of "Christianity, Civilization and Commerce." His first great expedition was to cross southern Africa, from the Zambezi River to the Congo River, and then on to Luanda, the capital of Angola on the Atlantic coast. This journey, which lasted from January 1853 to May 1854, was undertaken with the hope that it would open up new legitimate commercial routes, thereby undercutting the vestiges of the African slave trade. In September 1854 he left Luanda for his return across the continent, reaching the Indian Ocean in May 1856. En route he was the first European to lay eyes on the enormous, thundering waterfalls on the Zambezi that he named Victoria Falls after Queen Victoria of Great Britain. After completing this arduous expedition, Livingstone returned to England in December 1856, and in the following year he published his *Travels and Researches in South Africa*. This work, which was a publishing sensation, not only secured Livingstone's status as a national hero but also disseminated the immense store of geographical and ethnological knowledge he had accumulated during this eleven-thousand-mile journey.

Zambezi Expedition. *Travels and Researches in South Africa* and the many speeches he delivered during 1857 generated immense public interest in Africa. Indeed, his lectures at the University of Cambridge Senate (which were published as *Dr. Livingstone's Cambridge Lectures* in 1858) were the spur for the foundation of the University's Mission to Central Africa in 1860. Meanwhile, Livingstone returned to Africa in 1858 as the newly appointed British Consul at Quelimane, where he was to be responsible for "the promotion of Commerce and Civilization with a view to the extinction of the slave-trade." With a paddle steamer and a well-supplied entourage (including his wife), Livingstone began to explore the Zambezi river network. Livingstone's high hopes for the expedition soon were dashed by administrative decisions in Britain and by personal tragedy. Although his party comprised the first Europeans to explore Lake Nyasa and its environs (in modern Malawi), this disease-plagued and rather chaotic expedition was recalled before completion by the British government, and Mary, Livingstone's wife, died on the Zambezi. It was only in the long term, after the creation of the British Central Africa Protectorate in 1893 (which became Nyasaland in 1907), that the true fruits of this voyage were seen.

Source of the Nile. On the completion of the Zambezi expedition Livingstone crossed the Indian Ocean to Bombay, where he sold his steamer and briefly returned to Britain, publishing his *Narrative of an Expedition to the Zambezi and Its Tributaries* (1865). He returned to Africa as British Consul-at-Large, with the aim of exploring the river networks of central Africa and with the hope that he might discover the ultimate source of the Nile. Almost from the outset difficulties plagued this expedition, and it was surrounded by drama as a number of his retinue abandoned the expedition in September 1866, announcing to European journalists that Livingstone was dead. With a depleted entourage Livingstone pushed north from Lake Nyasa, discovering Lake Mweru in November 1867 and Lake Bangweulu in July 1868, before reaching Lake Tanganyika in February 1869. Battling fatigue and illness, Livingstone pressed further west than any previous European, reaching Nyangwe, on the Lualaba River leading into the Congo River. Returning to Lake Tanganyika in October 1871, Livingstone encountered Henry Morton Stanley, a correspondent for the *New York Herald*, who replenished Livingstone's rations and medical supplies before returning to Britain. After Stanley's departure, Livingstone pushed south again, but his desperate search for the source of the Nile was halted by illness. In May 1873, at Chitambo in modern Zambia, he was found dead kneeling beside his bed as if in prayer. Livingstone's heart was buried in Africa, but his body was embalmed, and it finally reached the coast after a nine-month journey. The corpse was shipped back to London, and amid national mourning he was buried in Westminster Abbey on 18 April 1874.

Sources:

David Livingstone and the Victorian Encounter with Africa (London: National Portrait Gallery, 1996).

Denis Judd, *Livingstone in Africa* (London: Wayland, 1973).

Andrew Ross, *David Livingstone: Mission and Empire* (London: Hambledon & London, 2002).

Richard Worth, *Stanley and Livingstone and the Exploration of Africa in World History* (Berkeley Heights, N.J.: Enslow, 2000).

HENRY MORTON STANLEY

1841-1904
JOURNALIST AND EXPLORER

Welsh Workhouse. Originally known as John Rowlands, Henry Morton Stanley was born on 28 January 1841 in Denbigh, Wales. An illegitimate child, Stanley's early life was unhappy, as he was fostered by reluctant relatives and spent some time in the St. Asaph Workhouse. Although Stanley would construct elaborate tales of persecution in the workhouse and narrate a tale of daring escape from its confines, it seems that his time in St. Asaph was both considerably less dramatic and more productive for Stanley, as he left the workhouse at the age of fifteen with a good education. Finding limited opportunities in Britain, Stanley set off in 1859 for the United States, serving as a cabin boy on an Atlantic crossing from Liverpool to New Orleans. A prominent Louisiana merchant, Henry Hope Stanley, befriended the young Welshman, and in recognition of this debt and with a desire for a new start, John Rowlands adopted his benefactor's first and last names ("Morton" was added only later in life). After this act of reinvention, however, Stanley soon moved on from New Orleans and began a prolonged period of wandering, during which he served in the American Civil War and in the U.S. Navy, traveled to Turkey, and worked as a journalist on the American frontier. He discovered that he was a better writer than sailor or soldier, and as a result of his gift of self-promotion Stanley soon secured a series of important assignments as a foreign correspondent with a variety of newspapers.

Encounter with Livingstone. In 1867 James Gordon Bennett of the *New York Herald* appointed Stanley as a special correspondent with the British expeditionary force in Ethiopia. As a result, Stanley gained some renown as the first journalist to report the fall of Magdala in 1868. He was then commissioned as the *New York Herald's* roving reporter in the Middle East and Africa in 1869. One of Stanley's main priorities in this new position was to locate David Livingstone, whose fate was shrouded in uncertainty after departure for Africa in 1866 to search for the source of the Nile. In March 1871 Stanley set off from his base in Zanzibar, leading an expedition that was well funded and outfitted by American sponsors. After a difficult period of travel through the conflict-and-disease-ridden lands east of Lake Tanganyika, Stanley reached Ujiji, Livingstone's last known port of call. Stanley soon located Livingstone, who was ill and struggling with limited supplies. The Welsh-American journalist greeted the explorer with the words Stanley later made famous in his own writings: "Dr. Livingstone, I presume?" After a short interlude exploring the terrain around Lake Tanganyika's northern shores, Stanley returned to the coast, dispatching fresh supplies to Livingstone with the hope that the great Victorian hero might finally discover the source of the Nile. Stanley returned to London, where he completed his best-selling travel narrative *How I Found Livingstone* (1872). Amid much controversy over his nationality and qualifications, the Royal Geographical Society awarded him their Patron's Gold Medal.

Dark Continent. In 1873, around the time of Livingstone's death, Stanley returned to Africa to serve as a war correspondent in Asante, but by then his primary goal was to extend Livingstone's pioneering exploration of central Africa. With funding from the *New York Herald* and London's *Daily Telegraph*, Stanley assembled a caravan in Zanzibar, leaving in November 1874 for Lake Victoria. En route, Stanley visited King Mutesa of Buganda, laying the foundations for the establishment of a British missionary presence and the eventual creation of a British protectorate in Uganda. After reaching Lake Victoria, Stanley's entourage was drawn into several skirmishes with local tribes, and Stanley's use of force aroused considerable outcry in Britain, where there was growing skepticism of his credentials and methods. Meanwhile, Stanley pushed on from Lake Victoria to Lake Tanganyika, establishing that Tanganyika had no connection with the Nile system. His expedition then headed west to the Lualaba River, which they followed downstream to the sea on 12 August 1877, an epic journey memorialized in Stanley's *Through the Dark Continent* (1878).

The Congo. Stanley hoped that the British would capitalize on the knowledge he had gathered by developing the Congo. These hopes were misplaced, and Stanley became disillusioned with Britain. He therefore took service with the King of Belgium, Leopold II, who aimed to annex the region for himself. From August 1879 to June 1884 Stanley was in the Congo basin, where he built roads from the lower Congo into the interior and established steamer routes on the upper Congo. Stanley's work was to pave the way for the creation of the Congo Free State, under the sovereignty of King Leopold. Stanley returned to Britain in 1885. His role in "opening up" the Congo is described in *The Congo and the Founding of Its Free State* (1885).

Final Expedition. His final African expedition was to relieve Mehmed Emin Pasha, governor of the Equatorial Province of Egypt, who had been cut off by the Mahdist revolt of 1882. Stanley left England in January 1887, arriving at the mouth of the Congo in March. His expedition reached the navigable head of the river in June 1887. After problems coordinating the two columns of his expedition, Stanley eventually reached Emin. In April 1889 Stanley's relief party, Emin, and his supporters left for the coast, arriving at Bagamoyo on 4 December 1889. Along the way Stanley identified the Ruwenzori Range (Ptolemy's "Mountains of the Moon") and completed the final gaps in European knowledge of the Nile system. Stanley's immensely popular *In Darkest Africa* was published in 1890, and in that year he married Dorothy Tennant. He represented North Lambeth in Parliament from 1895 to 1900 and became Sir Henry Morton Stanley in 1899. His death in 1904 marked the passing of one of the most popular and most controversial heroes of the imperial age.

Sources:

John Bierman, *Dark Safari: The Life Behind the Legend of Henry Morton Stanley* (New York: Knopf, 1990).

Charles P. Graves, *A World Explorer: Henry Morton Stanley* (Champaign, Ill.: Garrard, 1967).

Dorothy Stanley, ed., *The Autobiography of Sir Henry Morton Stanley* (Boston: Houghton Mifflin, 1909).

Richard Worth, *Stanley and Livingstone and the Exploration of Africa in World History* (Berkeley Heights, N.J.: Enslow, 2000).

DOCUMENTARY SOURCES

D. K. Clark, *Railway Locomotives: Their Progress, Mechanical Construction and Performance: With the Recent Practice in England and America* (1860)—An illustrated contemporary history of the development of steam locomotives and rail systems.

James Cook, *A Compendious History of Captain Cook's Last Voyage* (1784)—Edited version of Cook's journal of his third Pacific voyage, published posthumously.

Cook, *Journal of the* Resolution's *Voyage, in 1772, 1773, 1774, and 1775* (1775)—Published account of Cook's second voyage, when he explored the central and southern Pacific.

Great Exhibition of the Works of Industry of All Nations, 1851. Official Descriptive and Illustrated Catalogue (1851)— Official guide to the 1851 exhibition.

John Hawkesworth, *An Account of the Voyages Undertaken by the Order of His Present Majesty for Making Discoveries in the Southern Hemisphere: And Successively Performed by Commodore Byron, Captain Wallis, Captain Carteret, and Captain Cook* (1773)—Popular and influential compilation of accounts of Pacific explorers.

Rowland Hill, *Post Office Reform: Its Importance and Practicability* (1837)—Influential reformist tract that argued for the simplification and standardization of postal charges.

David Livingstone, *Missionary Travels and Researches in South Africa* (1857)—An important and popular account of Livingstone's travels and the peoples he encountered in southern Africa.

The M. P. Atlas: A Collection of Maps Showing the Commercial and Political Interests of the British Isles and Empire Throughout the World (1907)—Typical atlas of the era depicting the triumph of European empires.

Official Programme, Festival of Empire Exhibition (1911)— Guide to the imperial exhibition held in London in 1911.

Robert Sabine, *The History and Progress of the Electric Telegraph, with Descriptions of Some of the Apparatus* (1872)— Contemporary history of the development of the telegraph.

Henry Morton Stanley, *How I Found Livingstone: Travels, Adventures and Discoveries in Central Africa: Including an Account of Four Months' Residence with Dr. Livingstone* (1872)—Immensely popular account of Stanley's expedition to locate the famed Scottish missionary and explorer.

Stanley, *In Darkest Africa, or the Quest, Rescue and Retreat of Emin, Govenor of Equatoria* (1890)—An account of Stanley's last African expedition.

CHAPTER FIVE

SOCIAL CLASS SYSTEM AND THE ECONOMY

by GAY L. GULLICKSON

CONTENTS

Sidebars and tables are listed in italics.

1764*
- Englishman James Hargreaves invents the spinning jenny, a multiple-spindle machine for spinning wool or cotton. He patents the device in 1770.

1765
- Charles III of Spain abolishes the monopolies enjoyed by Seville and Cádiz and allows other Spanish cities to trade with colonies in the Americas.

1769
- Scottish engineer James Watt patents the first efficient steam engine; he is financed by the English manufacturer Matthew Boulton.
- English inventor Sir Richard Arkwright patents the water-powered spinning frame, moving the spinning process away from the home and into factories and mills.

1775
- Boulton and Watt establish a plant for manufacturing steam engines.

1776
- Scottish economist Adam Smith publishes *Inquiry into the Nature and Causes of the Wealth of Nations*. The book is a powerful statement of the science of economics, or political economy. Smith supports noninterference of business by government, and this economic doctrine, known in France as *laissez-faire*, appeals to the new capitalists of the Industrial Revolution.
- Watt's steam engine finds its first commercial application pumping water from mines in Cornwall.

1779
- English inventor Samuel Crompton develops the spinning mule, which hastens the end of cottage spinning by permitting the mass manufacture of high-quality thread and yarn.

1785–1787
- Edmund Cartwright patents the power loom for machine weaving.

1789
- Paris has a population of five hundred thousand people.

1790
- Boulton patents a steam-powered coin press.

1791
- The Le Chapelier Law and the Allarde Law in France abolish guilds and labor organizations, or unions.

* DENOTES CIRCA DATE

1794

- Warsaw has a population of 120,000 people.

1798

- English economist Thomas Malthus writes *An Essay on the Principle of Population* in which he asserts that any improvement in the plight of the poor would be offset by a rise in population because population usually increases to the limit of the means of subsistence. He concludes that poverty, starvation, disease, and war are the lot of humankind. In a second edition of this book written in 1803 Malthus states that the only conceivable alternative is "moral restraint" as a preventive check to this situation.

1799–1800

- The British Combination Acts forbid strikes and labor organizations, or unions.

1800

- The population of Europe is approximately 190 million. Nine percent of Europeans (excluding Russians and Hungarians) live in urban areas. The region has 363 cities with 10,000 or more inhabitants; 17 of them have populations with more than 100,000 residents. The city of London alone has nearly 1 million people.

- British manufacturers are producing one million tons of iron annually.

- By this time the enclosure movement in Britain has greatly improved agricultural efficiency by combining farmland and commons with large estates. Many small farmers are deprived of their livelihoods, and they migrate to the cities to find employment.

1803

- St. Petersburg has a population of 250,000.

1805*

- French social reformer Comte de Saint-Simon begins to preach a type of socialism combining the teachings of Jesus with ideas of science and industrialism. His system, known as Saint-Simonianism, soon spreads throughout Europe.

1806

- The first gaslighting of cotton mills occurs in Manchester, England; this invention allows employees to work longer hours during the winter months.

1808

- French social theorist Charles Fourier writes *Théorie des quatre mouvements et des destinées générales,* advocating a society formed into phalanxes, each one providing for the industrial and social needs of the group. Cooperative communities based on his ideas are started in France and the United States.

1810s

- Luddite riots break out in England; led by anti-machine-skilled workers who fear losing their jobs to mechanization, the rioters attack and destroy machines in the textile mills.

* DENOTES CIRCA DATE

1814
- Welsh socialist and philanthropist Robert Owen creates a successful cooperative community of workers at New Lanark mills in Manchester. He stops the employment of children, establishes sickness and old-age insurance, and opens educational and recreational facilities. Nevertheless, attempts to establish similar Owenite communities elsewhere in Britain and in the United States fail.

1815
- The Corn Law in Britain bans the importation of cheap grains.

1817
- English economist David Ricardo writes *Principles of Political Economy and Taxation*, developing his theory on the "iron law of wages." According to Ricardo, wages inevitably accumulate to an amount just capable of maintaining life.

1818
- Agricultural prices begin to fall in Italy and continue to do so for the next eight years. The declining prices are caused by an influx of Russian wheat and foreign agricultural advancements.

1819
16 August A crowd listening to anti–Corn Law speeches at a rally in St. Peter's Fields, Manchester, England, is attacked by royal troops and local militia, resulting in the Peterloo Massacre, in which eleven people are killed and more than four hundred injured.

1820s
- The Industrial Revolution spreads to Belgium and France.
- Railroads begin to transform the transportation of people, manufactured goods, and farm products. By mid century, Britain has 6,074 miles of track; Germany has 3,630 miles; and France has 1,807 miles.

1821
- The Bank of Lisbon is established.

1824
- The British Combination Acts are repealed.

1825
- The Spanish government introduces a tariff to protect agriculture and industry as well as establishes a stock exchange in Madrid.

1829
- Railway construction begins in Spain with the passage of a special law.

* DENOTES CIRCA DATE

1830s
- Anti-worker rules spark several strikes of silk workers in Lyon, France.

1832
- The British Parliamentary Reform Act enfranchises much of the middle class.

1833

23 August   Parliament abolishes slavery in the British colonies over a five-year period and provides for £20 million in compensation to slave owners.

29 August   The first effective Factory Act is passed in Britain; it establishes age restrictions for workers, sets work standards, and provides for inspectors.

1834
- In Germany the *Zollverein* (Customs Union) establishes a protective tariff.

14 August   A new Poor Law is passed in England; it forces healthy individuals who are unemployed and seeking assistance to go to workhouses, in which the conditions have been purposely made harsh to discourage malingering.

1836
- Chartism, a utopian working-class radical movement, emerges in Britain as workers, especially those in the declining textile industries, struggle with changing economic conditions. They seek universal suffrage, secret ballots, and an end to unequal political districts.

1837
- A protective tariff is passed in Portugal.

1840
- French journalist and socialist-anarchist Pierre-Joseph Proudhon publishes *Qu'est-ce que la propriété?* (What Is Property?). He believes that reliance should be placed upon small producers and workers and that there should be neither private property nor authoritarian government. Proudhon emphasizes education over violence in creating the anarchist state. He also opposes equal opportunities for women.
- In Spain the government creates the Ministerio de Fomento (Ministry of Development), sells uncultivated and Crown lands, and abolishes guilds. Meanwhile, the Barcelona Commission of Factories demands state protection for its industries but declines to provide protection for workers.

1847
- The Ten-Hour Bill (Fielden's Factory Bill), establishing maximum work hours for women and children, is passed by the British Parliament.

1848
- Revolutions break out on the European continent, including upheavals in France, Germany, Prussia, Austria, Italy, Moldavia, Walachia, Switzerland, Denmark, Spain, and Belgium.

* Denotes Circa Date

1848
(CONT'D)

- Serfdom is abolished in Austria.

- German political philosopher Karl Marx and German socialist Friedrich Engels publish *The Communist Manifesto*. This book maintains that the proletariat (laboring class) will eventually rise up and establish the communist state.

- The Swiss canton of Glarus restricts men to a thirteen-hour workday or a ten-hour night shift.

1850

- The Second Industrial Revolution begins. While the First Industrial Revolution was marked by advancements in textiles, steam, and iron, the Second Industrial Revolution is associated with the production of steel, chemical fertilizers, synthetic dyes, electricity, and oil. In addition, a marked increase in the use of semiskilled factory workers occurs.

- The European population is approximately 266 million. Fifty percent of the population of England and Wales and 25 percent of the population of France and Germany reside in towns. Meanwhile, eastern Europe remains a rural region with limited industrial manufacturing.

- The British fix the workday for factory employees at 6 A.M. to 6 P.M. with 1½ hours for meals—a ten-and-a-half-hour day.

1851

- The Melun Act in France allows medical authorities and building inspectors to enter homes and other edifices in the name of public health. They are allowed to condemn private property for posing health hazards and to excavate it for the construction of sewers and water mains. Britain passed a similar law three years earlier.

1852

- Railways in Switzerland become privately owned.

1856

- English engineer Sir Henry Bessemer begins his process for manufacturing steel cheaply and in large quantities (he decarbonizes melted pig iron by means of a blast of air). At this time Great Britain, Belgium, France, and Germany are producing 125,000 tons of steel annually; by 1913 this figure rises to 32,020,000 tons.

1858

- A single silver currency—the guilder—is introduced in Austria-Hungary.

1861

- Serfdom is abolished in Russia.

- Mikhail Aleksandrovich Bakunin emerges as the leading anarchist in Europe. An associate of Marx and Proudhon, Bakunin advocates the use of violence and establishes many secret revolutionary groups among the Slavs.

* DENOTES CIRCA DATE

1864
- The International Workingmen's Association (later called the First International) is founded in London through the efforts of Marx. The organization falls apart by 1876 because of a lack of capital and internal dissension between socialists and anarchists.

1867
- Marx publishes the first volume of *Das Kapital*, an analysis of the economics of capitalism.
- Skilled male workers in Britain get the right to vote.

1871
- Unions are legalized in England.
- The Paris Commune (a ten-week revolution) passes laws favored by workers; the uprising is violently put down by troops from Versailles.

1873
- The use of electricity to power machinery is first employed in Vienna.

1873-1896
- A major economic depression, largely caused by agricultural competition from North America, South America, and Asia, ravages Europe.

1880s
- Industrialism results in a rise of white-collar jobs.
- Chemical fertilizers are introduced.

1882
- The Married Women's Property Act is passed in Britain. It gives married women the right to own property separately from their husbands.

1883-1889
- The Prussian Reichstag passes social insurance laws (illness, accident, and old age pensions for industrial workers); other nations follow suit.

1884
- The Combination Laws in France are repealed, and workers can legally organize unions.

1885
- A British statute lowers the interest rates for the construction of cheap housing; Germany and France soon follow suit.
- German engineer Gottlieb Daimler patents the four-stroke internal-combustion engine, trying it first on a motorcycle and then in 1886 on a horse carriage.

* DENOTES CIRCA DATE

1887
- In Switzerland new legislation limits the workday to eleven hours and Sundays off, forbids children under the age of fourteen from factory employment, and regulates women's work.

1893
- German steel production surpasses that of Britain; by 1914 the figure is almost doubled.
- The Bank of Italy is created. Meanwhile, state banks in Italy are prohibited from making real estate loans.

1895
- The diesel engine and wireless telegraphy are invented.

1896
- A census in France maintains that of 575,000 establishments, 534,500 have less than ten employees; most workers continue to be employed in small workshops.

1897
- In Russia a new law limits the workday in factories with more than twenty employees.

1900
- The European population is 401 million.

1904
- French workers strike for the eight-hour day in France, but their effort fails.

1906
- The first general strike occurs in France.

1910
- The population of Europe is an estimated 447 million people.

1911
- Britain passes the first state-run unemployment insurance system.
- Forty-four percent of the French population and 60 percent of the German population reside in urban centers.

* DENOTES CIRCA DATE

OVERVIEW

New Era. In 1750 the British Isles and the European continent were on the verge of enormous change. Innovations in farming would increase the food supply; more children would survive childhood; the population would grow dramatically; machines would change where and how people worked; and canals, improved roads, and railroads would move people, food, and manufactured goods with unprecedented speed and ease. Factories would be built; cities would grow; and new economic classes would appear. All of these changes began in England, but they spread to the Continent, and by 1914 the economic development of western Europe was generally uniform. Eastern Europe lagged behind, but it too was industrializing by the eve of World War I (1914–1918). Of course, change is always easier to see in retrospect than it is in advance, and no one knew in 1750 that the world as they knew it would not last much longer.

Industrialization or Industrial Revolution? Historians are divided as to whether it is more accurate to refer to the changes that occurred in manufacturing as "industrialization" or "the industrial revolution." *Industrialization* emphasizes the drawn-out nature of the changes that occurred. Factories were a startling new innovation, but for many decades they existed only in textile-producing areas; most people continued to live and work as their parents and grandparents had. *Industrial revolution* emphasizes the enormity of the changes that occurred. People who lived in 1750 would not have recognized the world of 1914 and vice versa. Industrialization profoundly changed the world.

Preindustrial Agriculture and Manufacturing. In the mid eighteenth century, society was arranged hierarchically. A person's status was based on his or her ancestry (nobility, for instance, was inherited), economic resources, and occupation. The vast majority of people lived on farms and in small villages; there they produced food, clothing, shoes, plows, and other necessary items. Manufacturing was done in homes or small workshops. In many areas peasants alternated farming with spinning and weaving or with the manufacture of small metal objects such as nails. Trained artisans and merchants produced everything from shoes to bricks to bread, and everyone—carpenters, shoemakers, and blacksmiths as well as peasants—worked on the harvest. At the top of the hierarchy, a small nobility dominated politics, society, and the economy.

Transformations. In the nineteenth century, manufacturing began to rival agriculture as a source of employment; by the end of the century the population of western European countries was more urban than rural. Cities grew in size and number; gaslights, and then electricity freed people from the darkness of night; farms produced more food; roads, canals, and railroads cut across the land; and the population grew. In the process of these changes the aristocracy lost its dominance. A new class, alternately called the bourgeoisie, or middle class (for example, manufacturers, bankers, lawyers, store owners), gained political, economic, and social dominance, but members of this class still ranked lower in the social scale than the nobility in many places, no matter how much money they had. Peasant manufacturers and artisans of the preindustrial world were slowly transformed into factory workers, transport workers, construction workers, and employees of small urban putting-out industries. New agricultural classes appeared, too. Some farmers acquired more land and became wealthy, forming a kind of rural middle class, while others lost their land. The owners of large farms, factories, banks, and transportation companies entered an upward economic spiral. Men in these bourgeois and large landowning families worked long hours, increased the size of their operations, and lived newly lavish lifestyles. Women in these families became leisured, at least in the technical sense of not working for pay or producing goods for sale. They became mistresses of large homes and families, and their children received more education.

The Rich and the Poor. While the rich became richer, many of the poor initially became poorer. Early factories, all of which produced textiles, hired more women and children than adult men. Older male workers, many of them highly skilled, often found themselves unable to make the transition. In many families the earnings of women and children became even more important than they had been in the preindustrial world. Machines that were replacing skilled workers became the target of protestors. As more and more machines were invented and factories began to hire men, the targets of protest changed. Workers and reformers abandoned their attacks on machines and directed their attention to working conditions, pay, and hours.

Poor Conditions. Work hours were long; pay was low; machines were dangerous; work-related diseases were common (as factories aged, they became dirtier and more unhealthy for workers); tasks were monotonous; and many industries laid off workers seasonally, leaving them unemployed and destitute. As cities grew larger, living conditions grew worse for many people. Urban tenements where workers lived were crowded and dirty, water had to be carried up from the street and was likely to be contaminated, contagious diseases swept up and down the hallways, and women who worked had little time or energy to prepare family meals.

Discontent. Economic depressions in the 1840s, and again in the 1870s to 1890s, made matters worse. In 1848 political revolutions involving both the middle classes and working classes engulfed the capital cities of Europe. The sole exception was in Britain, where the extension of the franchise in 1832 to include many in the middle class split the interests of them and the working class. The revolutions produced few changes for workers, and protest continued. Now, however, protests were directed at individual employers in the form of walkouts, or strikes, and national legislatures began to pass legislation protecting those who were regarded as the most vulnerable workers—women and children.

Transitions to Modernity. In the 1880s the economy entered a new phase. A majority of the population of western Europe lived in towns and cities. More tasks were mechanized; home manufacturing disappeared; and electricity and steam engines transformed workplaces. Artificial light enabled employers to standardize work hours regardless of the season. Machines powered by electricity and steam could work faster and produce more. Agriculture also was mechanized, as was office work. Everything grew bigger—factories, banks, stores, offices, and apartment buildings. White-collar jobs in offices, stores, banks, post offices, and shipping companies expanded steadily and rapidly. Child and female labor in factories decreased at the same time that women found new jobs in offices and shops.

Organizations. In the 1880s labor leaders organized workers into large national and international organizations that matched their strength against that of employers. Socialist and Labour Parties also appeared, and members began to win seats in legislatures and parliaments. The strike became the way workers expressed grievances and attempted to negotiate with employers. Governments also began to respond to the grievances and demands of workers with the passage of legislation that regulated work conditions, pay, and hours. The success of these efforts gradually resulted in shorter work hours, higher pay, overtime pay, vacation pay, and (later in the twentieth century) improved safety conditions.

Modern Era. By 1914 the modern world had come into existence. There were no computers or televisions, but electricity, automobiles, airplanes, typewriters, and telephones had made their appearance. Most of society was divided into classes—including the middle class and the working class. In western Europe more people lived in urban areas than on farms. Class conflict and struggle had not ended, but they took the form of strikes and debates rather than revolution. Wages and living standards rose, and the middle class began to respond to the worst conditions created by industrialization. In the West the era of revolution was almost over. In eastern Europe, industrialization lagged behind the West, and the Russian Revolution (1917) was yet to come, but serfdom had ended and some strides were made in modernizing agriculture. Even war had been transformed by industrialization. Machine guns, tanks, and airplanes began to replace hand-to-hand combat, bayonets, and horse brigades. Trains and trucks moved troops; battleships and submarines replaced sailing ships. During World War I more-deadly weapons would be invented. The modern era had begun.

TOPICS IN SOCIAL CLASS SYSTEM AND THE ECONOMY

AGRICULTURAL GROUPS AND CLASSES

The Aristocracy. The aristocracy (or nobility) occupied the apex of the social hierarchy in preindustrial and industrializing Europe. It was the privileged class. Nobles had considerable economic and political power; in many places they paid no taxes. They considered themselves superior to other people by blood (noble status was inherited) and by training and education. While the nobility is sometimes referred to as a class, it is more accurate to speak of the nobles as constituting a rank or an order. Class terminology came into use later. The other traditional orders were the clergy and the commoners. In France these groups were referred to as estates. The clergy were members of the first estate, and the nobility constituted the second estate. High-church officials were the younger sons of the nobility, which means these two groups largely overlapped. Everyone else, regardless of occupation or wealth, was a member of the third estate. Compared with the rest of the population, aristocrats were a small group. In the eighteenth century they constituted about 1 percent of the population in France and Germany, slightly more in Britain, and 4.6 percent in Spain. In western Europe the eighteenth-century nobility divided its time between country estates, where the land was worked by tenant farmers, and city houses or royal palaces such as Versailles. In eastern Europe the nobility was larger in numbers, less mobile, and more likely to stay on their large rural estates.

Roles and Social Rank. The social ranks were distinguished by their roles in society. Aristocrats were responsible for defense and governance; the clergy prayed; and the commoners met economic needs. Inherent in the noble/non-noble division was a distinction between those who worked with their hands (commoners) and those who did not (aristocrats). The aristocracy owned much of the land, but the commoners farmed it. Nobles, at least in theory, could not earn money from commerce, manufacturing, or mining.

Social Mobility. The nobility of Europe was neither closed to entry nor uniform in status. The older and

wealthier a noble family was, the higher its status. But even old and wealthy families needed to husband their family wealth carefully and could find themselves in need of an infusion of cash or land. They found new incomes in three ways: they improved farming techniques on their land and, hence, crop yields; they circumvented the rules about what they could not do and engaged in mining (on their land) or commerce (especially the transportation of goods to foreign markets); and they sought advantageous marriage partners for their children. Confronted with economic decline, an established noble family might marry a son or a daughter to a newly ennobled family with great wealth or even to a wealthy commoner. In most cases, only one son (usually the eldest) would inherit the family's land. This system kept the family's land and wealth intact, but it placed younger sons and daughters at a distinct disadvantage. Only the eldest son and one daughter were likely to marry. Indeed, the provision of a dowry for a daughter was likely to be the single greatest drain on the family's resources. Younger sons were expected to enter the priesthood or the military (all officers were of noble birth) or to leave home to engage in commerce. Unmarried daughters either entered a convent or remained in their parents' or another sibling's home. Wealthy common families thus could enter the nobility through marriage; through the purchase of a landed estate and the adoption of a noble lifestyle; or, in France, through the purchase of a government office such as that of tax collector. The status conveyed by land ownership was so great that many wealthy merchant families, even after the beginning of industrialization, took money out of their businesses and purchased country estates. Some nobles resisted industrialization, but the intermarriage of noble and wealthy merchant families, the nobility's circumvention of the cultural notion that they should not engage in commerce or manufacturing, and the entry of younger sons into the commercial world positioned many aristocratic families to take advantage of industrialization as it occurred.

Nineteenth-Century Aristocracy. The decline of nobility began toward the end of the eighteenth century.

Spanish rural workers on a lunch break in 1894

In France the revolution that began in 1789 eliminated the legal privileges that nobles had enjoyed and declared everyone to be equal before the law. In other countries the nobles retained privileges for a longer time. In monarchies they retained considerable control of politics. In Britain, for instance, the upper house of the two-chamber Parliament was the House of Lords; in France the relatively short-lived nineteenth-century monarchs and emperors appointed new nobles to influential government positions and gave them considerable power. But the age of manufacturing brought the rise of the bourgeoisie in wealth and political power and started the decline of the nobility, who remained tied to the land and agriculture. Nobles who invested in manufacturing, commerce, and the railroads could and sometimes did acquire considerable additional wealth, but in general the noble lifestyle was becoming more expensive to maintain and the sources of income less lucrative. To make matters even more confusing, wealthy bourgeois families such as the French Rothschilds were often given noble titles.

Peasants and Farmers. In the eighteenth century the overwhelming majority of the European population engaged in farming. Nothing was more important or consumed more labor than the production of food. On the Continent those people who earned their living from agriculture were called peasants; in England they were farmers. Peasants and farmers either owned a few fields, rented fields for a cash amount, or worked as sharecroppers on land owned by the nobility or church. In some areas wealthy peasants also owned large fields and employed other peasants to work for them. In many areas, however, the majority of peasants were poor.

Enclosure. During the eighteenth century many peasants lost their scattered fields as wealthy farmers with an eye for the capitalistic marketplace consolidated their holdings, enclosed them with fences and hedges, and introduced new crops. These dispossessed peasants also lost access to the village common lands. Traditionally this area had been where everyone grazed animals; now it too was divided and sold. Small farmers who lost their land had few choices. They could live in small cottages on the larger farms and work for the new landowners, hire themselves out by the day, labor on agricultural gangs, or migrate to towns and cities to work in the factories. Wealthy farmers and peasants, in contrast, now grew wealthier. They hired more and more laborers to do the work of the farm. Women, who had run the dairy part of the farm, now supervised hired milkmaids. Men oversaw planting, weeding, harvesting, and the construction of new fences and hedges. Children, or at least boys, were sent to school, and girls learned social graces such as fancy sewing and piano playing.

Servants and Day Laborers. Farm servants lived with and worked for relatively large landowners. Traditionally these servants had shared bedrooms and meals with the family, but during the late eighteenth and nineteenth centuries they increasingly were relegated to separate quarters. They were usually young, single men and women who worked on one-year contracts. While they received room and board from the family for which they worked,

Russian landowner and his family at Sunday lunch with the local priest and his wife, circa 1880

they were paid wages only once a year; if the harvest failed or was small, they might not be paid at all. Day laborers, in contrast to servants, did not live on the farm where they were employed. They stayed in small peasant villages and walked to and from the fields and farms. Day laborers were often older than the farm servants. Their work was seasonal and their lives precarious.

Sexual Division of Labor. All members of farming families worked on the farm. Except during the harvest, when everyone went into the fields to gather crops, farmwork was divided along spatial, age, and gender lines. Men were responsible for work in the fields. They plowed, decided when to plant, thinned growing crops, and organized the harvest. Women were responsible for work in the farmyard and tended fruit trees and bushes, the house, and the children. They milked cows, churned butter, and made cheese. Many regarded dairy work as the most physically arduous part of farming. Women also fed chickens, gathered eggs, collected feathers, and sold these three items at markets. They cared for young farm animals and produced any nongrain or grape crops on the farm. Children of both sexes worked with their mothers until they were adolescents. Then boys learned to do their fathers' work while girls continued to do their mothers' work. Everyone worked on the harvest, but even then work was divided by gender. Women used sickles to cut the crops while men used scythes, and women were responsible for gathering and binding the cut grain into bundles and for gleaning the fields for fallen grain.

Cottage Industry. It is a mistake to think of peasants and farmers as engaging purely in agricultural work. Instead, they regularly combined farming with cottage manufacturing, especially the carding, combing, and spinning of yarn and the weaving of cloth. In some areas peasants and farmers used the wool from their own sheep; in others they raised flax plants whose fibers could be turned into linen thread and fabric. By the middle of the eighteenth century many also were working with imported cotton. During planting and harvesting, when everyone might be needed in the fields, cottage industry was put aside. At other times, especially during the winter, spinning and weaving were major occupations for poor peasants whose agricultural earnings often were not enough for them to survive.

Serfs. In eastern Europe, including Russia, peasants were not free. Neither they nor their children could leave one noble and go to work on the land of another. Called *serfs,* they belonged either to the land (owned by a noble) or to the landlord himself. In many ways their position was quite comparable to that of American slaves. They could be sold by their landlord to another noble. They had to obtain permission, which was rarely given, to marry outside of the noble's estate. They engaged both in agriculture (their most typical work), which many combined with cottage industry, and in various merchant occupations. Unlike American slaves and their owners, however, serfs and their landlords were members of the same racial group. Serfs could sue their owners for mistreatment, which slaves could not. Nobles could be tried if they killed their serfs. During the reign of Catherine the Great (1762–1796), about twenty landlords were tried for causing the deaths of their serfs. Seven of them received harsh sentences.

Causes of Serfdom. In eastern Europe, landowning nobles constituted only 1 percent of the population. Their serfs numbered around three million at the beginning of the nineteenth century. Farms in eastern Europe were large, and hundreds of serfs typically worked on the estate belonging to a single noble landowner. Serfs lived in villages, called communes, on the land of the noble who owned their labor. In eastern Europe the enserfment of peasants began in the sixteenth century, the impetus of which was economic. Nobles desired an inexpensive labor force so they could sell their crops cheaply in western Europe, and they worried that free peasants might leave their farms and seek better conditions or work elsewhere, including in cities.

End of Serfdom. By the nineteenth century many Europeans no longer regarded serfdom as an acceptable economic and social situation. Nevertheless, many landlords were loath to emancipate their serfs, regarding them as a sign of their social status. Nobles were on the losing side of this view, however. Europeans increasingly considered serfdom as a moral evil and a hindrance to economic development. Reformers' critiques—and economic, social, and political developments—finally led to its abolition. In 1807 Prussian and Polish serfs were freed; in 1816 and 1819 the same was true for the serfs of the Baltic States. The revolution of 1848 freed the serfs of the Austrian Empire, and the tsar emancipated Russian serfs in 1861. Finally, the last European serfs, those in Romania, were freed in 1864. In Russia the freed serfs were entitled to half of the land (all of which had previously belonged to the nobles) but had to pay a redemption fee in order to obtain it. The redeemed land belonged to peasant villages rather than to individual peasants.

Sources:

Jerome Blum, *Lord and Peasant in Russia from the Ninth to the Nineteenth Century* (Princeton: Princeton University Press, 1961).

M. L. Bush, *Rich Noble, Poor Noble* (Manchester & New York: Manchester University Press, 1988).

Jonathan Dewald, *The European Nobility: 1400–1800* (New York: Cambridge University Press, 1996).

Robert Forster, *The Nobility of Toulouse in the Eighteenth Century: A Social and Economic Study* (Baltimore: Johns Hopkins University Press, 1960).

Peter Kolchin, *Unfree Labor: American Slavery and Russian Serfdom* (Cambridge, Mass.: Belknap Press of Harvard University, 1987).

Ivy Pinchbeck, *Women Workers and the Industrial Revolution, 1750–1850* (London: Routledge, 1930).

K. D. M. Snell, *Annals of the Labouring Poor: Social Change and Agrarian England, 1660–1900* (Cambridge & New York: Cambridge University Press, 1985).

Lawrence Stone and Jeanne C. Fawtier Stone, *An Open Elite?: England, 1540–1880* (Oxford: Clarendon Press / New York: Oxford University Press, 1984).

THE COUNTRYSIDE: ECONOMIC CONTINUITY AND CHANGE

Importance of Agriculture. Even during the era of industrialization, the production of food was of primary importance. In fact, as cities grew and housed burgeoning, non-food-producing populations, the countryside was called upon to produce ever greater surpluses of food products to be shipped to urban markets. Before the coming of the railroad and steamboat, transporting grain and dairy goods was slow, expensive, and risky. In times of bad harvests, for example, wagons and barges filled with food for urban areas were often attacked and emptied by starving villagers and peasants.

Fallow Farming. Until well into the nineteenth century various factors limited the amount of food Europeans could produce. In the absence of artificial fertilizers and knowledge about crop rotation, fields were fertilized by grazing cows and other animals while the land lay fallow. In most areas fields lay fallow one out of every three years, but in some places, it was one out of every two years. Peasants rotated fields in and out of fallow in blocks. They owned or rented land in at least three blocks so they would always have fields to plant. Only wealthy peasants and farmers owned farm animals, but everyone needed fertilizer. Thus, until enclosure changed this arrangement, fields were unfenced and animals were allowed to roam freely on the unplanted fields.

Agricultural Improvement. During the eighteenth century, agricultural production increased in western Europe.

THE SUCCESSFUL FARM FAMILY

A satirical ditty pokes fun at the transformation of the farm family in the nineteenth century. In other early-nineteenth-century agricultural families, women and children worked on labor gangs while men tried to get work as day laborers on large farms.

1743

Man, to the Plough,

Wife, to the Cow,

Girl, to the Yarn,

Boy, to the Barn,

And your Rent will be netted.

1843

Man, Tally-ho

Miss, Piano,

Wife, Silk and Satin,

Boy, Greek and Latin,

And you'll all be Gazetted.

Source: Ivy Pinchbeck, *Women Workers and the Industrial Revolution, 1750–1850* (London: Routledge, 1930), p. 37.

The key to improved crop yield was the introduction of new crops and the adoption of crop rotation. If farmers alternated grain crops with other crops—such as turnips, clover, and legumes—they could eliminate the rotation into fallow fields. The new crops replaced nutrients removed by grain, improved crop yields, and provided fodder for animals, thus allowing for more dairy and plow animals. Improvement occurred piecemeal. Not all farmers could afford seeds to plant the new crops. Those who could bought and sold land to group their fields together and enclosed them behind fences and hedges to keep out their neighbors' grazing animals. Those who could not afford new seeds, fences, and hedges, or who were suspicious of the new crops, often lost out in this process, becoming landless laborers with seriously reduced incomes and diets. By the late nineteenth century, machines began to appear in farmers' fields. Steam-powered plows appeared in 1858, and the gasoline-powered tractor came into use in 1892. In the 1880s some farmers began to use chemical fertilizers to increase crop yields. In eastern Europe, in contrast, the existence of serfdom well into the nineteenth century retarded the adoption of new farming techniques. The grouping and enclosing of fields, and mechanical and chemical changes in farming, did not take place there until after World War I (1914–1918).

Agriculture and Industrialization. Agricultural improvement was directly tied to the industrial, transportation, commercial, and population revolutions. The production of more food allowed the population to increase. This advance in turn provided workers for factories and more consumers for the increased food supply. Improved transportation made it possible for food to be transported to these new consumers, ending starvation that local harvest failures had caused before and encouraging regional specialization in agriculture. This step forward then led to a yet greater increase in the production of foodstuffs. Finally, a growing commercial sector organized the transportation and sale of agricultural goods to city dwellers and manufactured goods to rural farmworkers. By the middle of the nineteenth century, in western Europe at least, urban and rural worlds had become much more distinct than ever before. Rural dwellers engaged in any occupation but farming, and gone from the workers' yards in small towns and cities were the chickens and pigs.

Family Economy. In the preindustrial world no individual stood alone. For the vast majority of the population, no one could earn enough to survive on his or her own. Survival depended on the family, which depended upon the work of everyone. Children, beginning at the age of five, worked alongside adults, and women labored alongside men. Households always contained a biological family group (perhaps with additional nonkin workers). Much rarer were households of unrelated individuals who had banded together to survive. Men were always paid more than women regardless of the kind of work, but even so, men were not paid enough to support even two adults without assistance. A husband and wife working

Russian peasant woman at her loom, circa 1885

together could support themselves and perhaps one or two young children. In the simplest form of the family economy, members of the household contributed to the whole by producing either farm goods or manufactured items. This production invariably involved a sexual division of labor where the primary occupations of the men and women were distinct. If manufacturing were involved, for example, the man might be a blacksmith or brickmaker and the woman a spinner or seamstress. In practice, during slow periods in their own occupation, men might help with the women's work, tasks they would have learned as boys in any case, as all children were expected to assist their mothers. The family economy held sway in both urban and rural settings of traditional, preindustrial Europe. Industrialization, however, gradually destroyed it over the course of the nineteenth century. Wages rose for both men and women, and this increase made it possible for many nonfarm women to exit the paid labor force for at least a part of their adult lives.

Cottage Industry. Cottage industries were ubiquitous in rural, preindustrial Europe. The difficulty and expense of transporting manufactured goods and agricultural produce meant villages or clusters of villages tried to produce everything they needed. Fabric, shoes, clothing, ropes, furniture, farm implements, building materials, and a full range of crops were produced everywhere, although many peasants engaged especially in spinning thread from wool or flax and

Samuel Bamford was born into a successful weaving family. Both of his parents, as well as other relatives, were cotton weavers. This passage from his memoir paints a happy picture of cottage manufacturing but also reveals how hard this work was. The scene must have occurred in the 1790s; spinning had moved into factories, and women, who previously had been cottage spinners, as well as men were working at handlooms.

Some two or three weeks before Christmas, it was the custom in families to apportion to each boy or girl weaver a certain quantity of work which was to be done ere his or her holidays commenced. An extra quantity was generally undertaken to be performed, and the conditions of the performance were such indulgences and gratuities as were agreeable to the working parties. In most families, a peck or a strike of malt would be brewed; spiced bread and potato custard would be made, and probably an extra piece of beef, and some good old cheese would be laid in store, not to be touched until the work was done. The work then went on merrily. Play hours were nearly given up, and whole nights would be spent at the loom, the weavers occasionally striking up a hymn or Christmas carol in chorus. A few hours of the late morning would perhaps be given to rest; work would be then resumed, and the singing and rattle of shuttles would be almost incessant during the day. In my uncle's family we were all singers, and seldom a day passed

on which several hymns were not sung; before Christmas we frequently sung to keep ourselves from sleep, and we chorussed "Christians awake," when we ourselves were almost gone in sleep.

Christmas holidays always commenced at Middleton on the first Monday after new-year's day. By that day every one was expected to have his work finished. That being done, the cuts were next carefully picked, and plated, and made up for the warehouse, and they having been dispatched, the loom house was swept and put in order; the house was cleaned, the furniture rubbed, and the holidays then commenced. The ale was tapped, the currant-loaf was sliced out, and lad and lass went to play as each liked best; the boys generally at foot-ball, and both boys and girls at sliding, when there was ice on the ground. In wet weather we should have a swinging rope in the loom-house, or should spend the day in going from house to house amongst our playmates, and finishing at night by assembling in parties of a dozen or a score, boys and girls, where on some warm, comfortable hearth, we sat singing carols and hymns, playing at [the game of] "forfeits," proposing riddles, and telling "fyerin tales" [scary stories] until our hair began to stiffen, and, when we broke up, we scampered homeward, not venturing to look behind lest the "old one" himself [the Devil] should be seen at our heels.

Source: Samuel Bamford, *Early Days* (London: Simpkin, Marshall, 1849), pp. 131–135.

---

weaving this thread into cloth. Many of these items were used by the family that made them, or they were sold locally. Peasants alternated the tasks of cottage industry with agricultural demands, both seasonally and by time of day. In the winter, manufacturing occupied most of the days, while in summer or fall, while crops needed tending, manufacturing might be abandoned or done in the evening hours.

Location of Cottage Industries. Cottage production depended on the terrain, the type of farming common to the area, and the proximity of a city or town with a merchant population. In many areas large numbers of women spun thread, and men wove cloth for nearby city merchants who provided workers with raw materials and paid them for the finished products. This method was called "the putting-out system of manufacturing." In mountainous Switzerland, women spun for urban merchants, but the terrain was too steep for the transportation of heavy warps of cloth and finished fabrics. Thus, no weaving was done there. Men joined the women in spinning thread. In mining areas, nails and other small metal objects were made in the cottages. With industrialization, cottage manufacturing gradually disappeared. Peasant families that had depended upon it for part of their income gradually found themselves, or at least their children, forced to join the new industrial labor force.

Protoindustrialization. In the eighteenth century an intensification of rural manufacturing production occurred. Urban merchants sought more and more cottage workers to produce goods for national and international markets that were growing significantly. Historians call this process protoindustrialization. With accelerating demand for manufactured products, protoindustries employed far more people than the traditional cottage industries. Traveling merchants transported raw materials to villagers and carried finished items back to the cities for sale. In some rural areas a majority of the population worked for the urban putting-out merchants. People worked in their own homes, as they always had, and used traditional tools—spinning wheels, hand looms, anvils, and hammers. The difference was in the scale of production. In some areas the protoindustrial merchants acquired substantial resources that they later invested in building new machines and factories. What made rural workers desirable from the urban merchants' point of view were their availability, the low wages for which they would work, and the absence of guilds that controlled production and quality in the cities. What made the work attractive to peasants and farmers was their sheer poverty. Areas with poor soil, hilly terrain, or the concentration of land in a few hands (which meant the majority of peasants were landless) forced the local peasantry to accept work eagerly from the putting-out merchants. Cottage manufacturing in both its small traditional form and as protoindustrialization was eventually replaced by factory production, but this transformation was a protracted process. Even as some manufacturing moved into factories, outwork or cottage work expanded as manufacturers sent work home to be done by the families. This arrangement was particularly the case in the garment industry where women did fine needlework and finishing in their homes.

Sources:

Maxine Berg, ed., *Markets and Manufacture in Early Industrial Europe* (London & New York: Routledge, 1991).

Jerome Blum, *The End of the Old Order in Rural Europe* (Princeton: Princeton University Press, 1978).

J. D. Chambers and G. E. Mingay, *The Agricultural Revolution 1750–1880* (London: Batsford, 1966).

Gay L. Gullickson, *Spinners and Weavers of Auffay: Rural Industry and the Sexual Division of Labor in a French Village, 1750–1850* (Cambridge & New York: Cambridge University Press, 1986).

Pat Hudson and W. R. Lee, eds., *Women's Work and the Family Economy in Historical Perspective* (Manchester & New York: Manchester University Press, 1990).

Olwen Hufton, "Women and the Family Economy of Eighteenth-Century France," *French Historical Studies*, 9 (Spring 1975): 1–22.

Ivy Pinchbeck, *Women Workers and the Industrial Revolution, 1750–1850* (London: Routledge, 1930).

K. D. M. Snell, *Annals of the Labouring Poor: Social Change and Agrarian England, 1660–1900* (Cambridge & New York: Cambridge University Press, 1985).

Louise A. Tilly and Joan W. Scott, *Women, Work and Family* (New York: Holt, Rinehart & Winston, 1978).

Two maids from a middle-class Kent household, circa 1880

INDUSTRIAL AND URBAN CLASSES

Bourgeoisie or Middle Class. Prior to the Industrial Revolution there were people of the middling sort, as historians are now inclined to say, but there was not yet a bourgeoisie. The bourgeoisie, or middle class, was created by the Industrial Revolution. The size, wealth, and political dominance of this group grew steadily from the late eighteenth century to the beginning of World War I (1914–1918). It also encompassed a wide range of occupations and wealth, leading to the common use of terms such as lower middle class, middle class, and upper middle class (or petite bourgeoisie, moyenne bourgeoisie, and haute bourgeoisie). In English some of these people are referred to as being "petty bourgeois." The phrase is an anglicization of the French petit bourgeois and refers not to the attitudes of the person but identifies him or her as lower middle class. The bourgeoisie distinguished itself from the classes above and below it by its values, wealth, and lifestyle as well as by its occupations or source of wealth. Some bourgeois families were amazingly successful. The Rothschilds, for instance, became the wealthiest financial family in all of Europe. They founded banks and funded kings and governments in Frankfurt, Vienna, Manchester, London, Naples, and Paris. In Germany the Krupp family turned a small armaments factory into one of the world's largest munitions plants, the Krupp Works of Essen. In Britain, the birthplace of industrialization, no one amassed the kind of wealth from manufacturing, commerce, or finance that continental or American families such as the Rockefellers,

Carnegies, or Vanderbilts did. The great fortunes in Britain were still largely invested in landed estates.

Occupations. In classic terms, the bourgeoisie constructed, owned, and operated the new factories, mines, and railroads; built and ran commercial enterprises—shipping lines and stores, for instance; and owned banks. As the nineteenth century progressed, the liberal professions—the ministry, law, medicine, and university teaching—also attracted sons of the bourgeoisie. These occupations too were products of the industrial era, acquiring relatively high status and specific educational requirements for entry. Technically, of course, people who built the early factories, such as English inventor Richard Arkwright, were merchants and tinkerers, not bourgeois. If their inventions and factories were successful, again like Arkwright, they became members of the new class. Below the richest level of the bourgeoisie was a large and growing number of people who managed factories, banks, shops, and shipyards; who owned and ran their own small enterprises (the proverbial butcher, baker, and candlestick maker); and who simply worked in these businesses. Indeed, more than three rungs are necessary on the bourgeois ladder to encompass the variety of occupations and wealth that provided one membership.

Bourgeois Family. As the scale of manufacturing increased, the bourgeois home and workplace became sepa-

In 1861 twenty-four-year-old Isabella Beeton and her husband published an enormously popular book of advice for middle-class women. The book (1,112 pages) instructed women how to cook, treat their servants, and rear their children. Writing the book, of course, fell outside of the role she advised women to play. She died before her thirtieth birthday.

Preface.

I must frankly own, that if I had known, beforehand, that this book would have cost me the labour which it has, I should never have been courageous enough to commence it. What moved me, in the first instance, to attempt a work like this, was the discomfort and suffering which I had seen brought upon men and women by household mismanagement. I have always thought that there is no more fruitful source of family discontent than a housewife's badly-cooked dinners and untidy ways. Men are now so well served out of doors,—at their clubs, well-ordered taverns, and dining-houses, that in order to compete with the attractions of these places, a mistress must be thoroughly acquainted with the theory and practice of cookery, as well as be perfectly conversant with all the other arts of making and keeping a comfortable home....

Chapter I.

The Mistress

1. As with the commander of an army, or the leader of any enterprise, so is it with the mistress of a house. Her spirit will be seen through the whole establishment; and just in proportion as she performs her duties intelligently and thoroughly, so will her domestics follow in her path. Of all these acquirements, which more particularly belong to the feminine character, there are none which take a higher rank, in our estimation, than such as enter into a knowledge of household duties; for on these are perpetually dependent the happiness, comfort, and well-being of a family. In this opinion we are borne out by the author of "The Vicar of Wakefield," who says: "The modest virgin, the prudent wife, and the careful matron, are much more serviceable in life than petticoated philosophers, blustering heroines, or virago queens. She who makes her husband and her children happy, who reclaims the one from vice and trains up the other to virtue, is a much greater character than ladies described in romances, whose whole occupation is to murder mankind with shafts from their quiver, or their eyes."

The mistress of a house ... ought always to remember that she is the first and the last, the Alpha and the Omega in the government of her establishment; and that it is by her conduct that its whole internal policy is regulated. She is, therefore, a person of far more importance in a community than she usually thinks she is. On her pattern her daughters model themselves; by her counsels they are directed; through her virtues all are honoured;—"her children rise up and call her blessed; her husband also, and he praiseth her." Therefore, let each mistress always remember her responsible position, never approving a mean action, nor speaking an unrefined word....

Cherishing, then, in her breast the respected utterances of the good and the great, let the mistress of every house rise to the responsibility of its management; so that, in doing her duty to all around her, she may receive the genuine reward of respect, love, and affection!

Source: Isabella Beeton, *The Book of Household Management* (London: S. O. Beeton, 1861), pp. iii, 1, 18–19.

---

rated by greater distances, making it difficult for women to integrate the tasks of work and child care. In the course of a generation bourgeois women thus withdrew from the family business and devoted themselves to domesticity and child care. This new sexual division of labor gave these women responsibility for everything in the domestic sphere, while men took responsibility for the family's economic or public concerns. A leisured, or at least nonworking, wife and the nurturing of children by their mother became hallmarks of the bourgeoisie and set members of the class apart from the other classes. Working-class women continued to labor for many decades, although, like bourgeois women, working-class mothers preferred not to work for pay if at all possible. An emphasis on the nurturing of children distinguished the bourgeoisie from both the aristocracy, which the former regarded as unfeelingly giving their children over to servants to rear, and the working class, where many children remained in the paid labor force. The nurturing of children also involved the provision of education and this value, too, became associated with the bourgeoisie.

Bourgeois Values. Hard work and frugality are also associated with the bourgeoisie. They tended to invest profits back into their businesses. In 1860 Scottish author Samuel Smiles wrote *Self-Help*, neatly summing up what by then was the bourgeois business ethic. "Youth must work in order to enjoy," he concluded. "Nothing credible can be accomplished without application and diligence." Moreover, the ideal man should be self-reliant. "Heaven helps those who help themselves," he quoted. "The spirit of self-help is the root of all genuine growth in the individual. ... Help from without is often enfeebling in its effects, but help from within invariably invigorates."

Consuming Class. Contradictorily, the frugal bourgeoisie became a consuming class, desiring more-spacious, elegant, homes; fancier clothing; and better food. In many countries secularism became associated with bourgeois men who, among other things, saw some of the messages of the Christian churches as antithetical to their capitalistic desires. Bourgeois women, in contrast, often became more

St. Petersburg soup kitchen for unemployed Russian workers, circa 1905 (State Archive of Film and Photographic Documents, St. Petersburg)

religious. They placed high value on love and morality, and both men and women engaged in charitable giving and assistance to the poor.

Artisans and Merchants. The artisan usually was an independent craftsman who made and sold a particular product. Sometimes these people were called merchant artisans. Merchants who were not artisans primarily produced and sold foodstuffs or ran establishments such as cafés, taverns, and small hotels. Some artisans and merchants became wealthy producers, but most remained lower on the economic scale, working hard to just make a living. Manufacturing and marketing existed everywhere in preindustrial Europe. A multitude of artisans produced everything people needed, and countless merchants brought goods to market: fabric, shoes, stockings, clothing, needles, thread, sheets, blankets, bricks, boards, ropes, barrels, plows, furniture, baskets, horseshoes, pots, pans, and nails. Artisans milled grain into flour, baked bread, tanned hides, brewed beer, and made wine. Artisans and petty merchants in small towns and villages put down their tools and helped with the harvest, but otherwise they did not engage in agriculture.

City Artisans. While merchants and artisans existed everywhere, their crafts dominated employment in towns and cities. Until the nineteenth century, artisan manufac-turers were organized into guilds that controlled the teaching of skills, the quality of products, the number of people working in the trade, and sometimes even the amount charged for goods or paid in wages. Children were apprenticed to a particular trade at young ages. They then lived with and assisted a craftsman or craftswoman, sometimes for as long as seven years. When they reached the end of their apprenticeship, they became journeymen who, at least formally, traveled around the country, assisting and learning even more skills from master craftsmen. When young men (and much less often women) completed both stages of learning, they could establish a shop of their own and become masters. If anything interrupted the journeyman stage, such as a decision to marry (journeymen were often forbidden to marry), he would never become a master craftsman. For one reason or another, a great many young men and women never completed the journeyman stage and remained in that subordinate position for life. Most artisans were the children of artisans. They learned the craft from their fathers and, if they were old enough, sometimes took over the family shop when the father died.

Family Businesses and Division of Labor. During the eighteenth century husbands and wives in prosperous artisan and merchant families usually worked together to keep the family business solvent and growing. The workshop or

London street sweeper in the late 1870s (Local
History Library, London Borough
of Greenwich)

guild system. Guilds also came under attack during the late
eighteenth and early nineteenth centuries by the new
free-trade ideology of liberalism. In country after country,
legislation was passed abolishing guilds. What legislation
failed to do, industrialization finished. Artisans had been a
self-conscious social group aware and proud of their independent status, but over the course of the nineteenth century they fragmented into subclasses of mechanics, waged
factory workers, and shopkeepers. By 1914 the traditional
artisan had ceased to exist.

White-Collar Workers. Clerical work in offices, stores,
banks, government offices, post offices, shipping companies, and other areas were traditionally held by men,
many of whom were learning the ropes and climbing the
company ladder. In the 1880s these jobs underwent significant change. The number of people employed in
what were now called white-collar jobs rose precipi-
tously; machines such as the typewriter and telephone
were introduced; and employers began to seek out
women as well as men to work in their offices and shops.
Initially, as employment expanded, far more men than
women were hired in these fields, but over time there
was a gradual shift to an all-female labor force in offices
and shops. As the labor force became feminized, upward
mobility was severely restricted, as were the variety of
tasks each man had previously performed. Women were
hired to do one task; they did it all day long and for the
entire time they were employed. They were typists (originally called typewriters in English), stenographers,
receptionists, and file clerks. In shops women worked as
salesclerks, cashiers, stock girls, and cash girls. White-
collar jobs did not pay well, and their work was as routinized as that of factory workers. Nevertheless, the jobs
were highly desired. Workers wore white shirts and
shirtwaists—the distinctive uniform that gave the jobs
their descriptive title. They were required to have the
equivalent of a high-school education and were paid a
weekly salary. White-collar workers perceived themselves, and were perceived by others, as having higher
employment status than factory and other manual workers. The daughters and (for a long time) the sons of
working-class families who took these jobs became
members of the lower middle class, or the petite bourgeoisie. White-collar women had much shorter careers
than men. Only young, single women were hired to be
office help, salesclerks, and telephone operators. When
they ceased to be young or when they married, they were
let go from their jobs.

Domestic Servants. In the eighteenth century youths
and adults who lived with and worked for families other
than their own were categorized as domestic servants.
The age at which youths usually entered domestic service was between thirteen and fourteen, although poverty forced some children to enter service at younger
ages. The vast majority of servants worked for families
whose economic resources were slim but whose productive work required more help than members of their own

salesroom might occupy the ground floor of the home or a
building adjacent to or across the backyard from the house.
This arrangement made it possible for women to participate fully in the business and to engage in minimal child
care, which was culturally assumed to be a woman's
responsibility. Women who were married to artisans often
kept the books, dealt with customers and suppliers, performed preparatory or finishing tasks, and knew how to do
all of the artisan's work. Indeed, if an artisan or merchant
died without a grown son, his widow often carried on the
work. Most artisans were men, although some were
women, and here again one finds a distinct sexual division
of labor. In France skilled female artisans made lace,
embroidery, lingerie, and verdigris; spun fine yarns; and
worked alongside their artisan husbands in crafts such as
brocade weaving, although technically only their husbands
were master weavers. Everywhere, female seamstresses
sewed women's and children's clothing, and male tailors
sewed men's clothing.

End of the Artisan. In the eighteenth century, textile
merchants who imported raw cotton from the United
States and Asia began to circumvent the guilds' control of
urban work. Hiring wagoners and traveling merchants,
they sought out rural dwellers to produce yarn and fabric.
The low pay for which peasants would work offset the
transportation costs and led merchants to hire more and
more of them. This competition undermined the urban

A medical doctor, journalist, and railroad official, Samuel Smiles exemplified middle-class liberal attitudes that justified the position of that group in society. In books such as *Self-Help* (1860), liberals such as Smiles claimed that the poverty and oppression of the working classes were their own fault. Here Smiles explains that the work ethic was a fundamental basis of English success during the age of industrialization.

Indeed, all experience serves to prove that the worth and strength of a State depend far less upon the form of its institutions than upon the character of its men. For the nation is only an aggregate of individual conditions, and civilization itself is but a question of personal improvement of the men, women, and children upon whom society is composed.

National progress is the sum of individual industry, energy, and uprightness, as national decay is of individual idleness, selfishness, and vice. What we are accustomed to decry as great social evils, will for the most part be found to be but the outgrowth of man's own perverted life; and though we may endeavor to cut them down and extirpate them by means of Law, they will only spring up again with fresh luxuriance in some other form, unless the conditions of personal life and character are radically improved. If this view be correct, then it follows that the highest patriotism and philanthropy consist, not so much in altering laws and modifying institutions, as in helping and stimulating men to elevate and improve themselves by their own free and independent individual action.

One of the most strongly marked features of the English people is their spirit of industry, standing out prominent and distinct in their past history, and as strikingly characteristic of them now as at any former period. It is this spirit, displayed by the commons of England, which has laid the foundations and built up the industrial greatness of the empire. The vigorous growth of the nation has been mainly the result of the free energy of individuals, and it has been contingent upon the number of hands and minds from time to time actively employed within it, whether as cultivators of the soil, producers of articles of utility, contrivers of tools and machines, writers of books, or creators of works of art. And while this spirit of active industry has been the vital principle of the nation, it has also been its saving and remedial one, counteracting from time to time the effects of errors in our laws and imperfections in our constitutions.

Source: Samuel Smiles, *Self-Help* (Chicago: Belford, Clarke, 1881), pp. 48–49.

family could provide. This kind of domestic service was one of the largest employers of labor through the end of the nineteenth century.

Marriage among Servants. Having worked as a farm servant or a cotton, wool, or linen spinner, a woman had the skills she would need if she were to marry a farmer or weaver—two of the most common male occupations. In addition, of course, she had to have acquired the minimal goods required to set up housekeeping—a pot or two, a mattress, sheets, her own clothing, and a chest in which to store extra linens and clothing. Owning a few pillows also was nice. The acquisition of these items in most cases took a decade or more, making the marriage age high for women. Men were supposed to bring land to farm or an occupation to pursue (weaving was a possibility, although many weavers also farmed), and land usually had to be inherited. So younger sons who worked as farm and textile servants, and who would never inherit land, were less likely than female servants to leave service and marry, although they could try to survive as day laborers, living on their own, possibly marrying, and performing the same type of work as when they were servants. Many men and women never acquired the necessary economic foundations of marriage and worked as servants for life. Servants were almost always unmarried; one could not aspire to marry a fellow or sister servant and remain in service. To marry was to set up a household of one's own.

Household Servants, Chamber Maids, and Janitors. The middle class hired servants in increasingly large numbers during the nineteenth century. In these urban families, servants performed household tasks (for example, cleaning, laundry, cooking, silver polishing, and waiting on table) and similarly were unable to remain in service if they married. In the nineteenth century another occupation, often labeled domestic service, emerged. As factories, shops, banks, and hotels grew in size, they hired increasing numbers of women and men as janitors and chambermaids. This work was akin to that which many servants performed for individual families—hence the name domestic service. Unlike other forms of service, men and women who worked in these jobs lived on their own and were able to marry.

The Proletariat. People have always worked, but they have not always identified themselves as workers. Before industrialization, occupational identities were specific. One was a shoemaker, silk winder, blacksmith, seamstress, and so on. With industrialization a new category was created—waged factory work. Men who labored in factories were identified as simply "workers." Female factory workers constituted a kind of anomaly, even though the majority of early factory workers were women, and they tended to be identified as "women workers" in England. In France the two groups were distinguished by endings on the word *oeuvre* (work). Male factory workers were *ouvriers* and female factory workers were *ouvrières*.

Japanische Tändeleien nach Nappo, oder wie die Lasten des Staates gleichmäßig vertheilt sind, um die Krone balanciren zu können.

Der Proletarier vom Bürger gequetscht, der Bürger vom Adel belästigt,
So wird die Pyramide des Staats gepfropft und schlau befestigt,
So zeigt ein Jeder auf Höhern Befehl der Kraft und Balance Proben,
Getreu dem alten Naturgesetz: der Druck kommt stets von Oben!

Verantwortlicher Redakteur: E. Dohm — Verlag von A. Hofmann & Comp. in Berlin, Unterwasserstraße 1. — Druck von F. Draeger in Berlin.

Mid-nineteenth-century caricature from the satirical magazine *Kladderadatsch,* showing the king of Prussia standing with the help of the nobility, who in turn are being supported by the bourgeoise. Proletarians are at the bottom (British Library, London).

Before the twentieth century, factory workers worked for piece rates. They were paid for the amount they produced just as workers in cottage industry and the putting-out industries were. They worked long hours—as many as fourteen hours a day—for wages that were differentiated by age and sex. Children earned the least, men the most, with women falling in between. In the earliest textile mills, primarily women and children were employed, but as spinning machines grew larger the nature of the work changed and with it the gender classification of jobs. Men and women rarely competed for the same jobs despite women's willingness to work for lower wages. Nevertheless, men often perceived women as a threat and preferred to have no women working in factories, a desire that was almost met except in the textile and garment industries.

Standard of Living of the Working Class. Whether factories, and the towns and cities that grew up around them, worsened or improved people's standard of living has been a source of great debate among historians. No broad generalizations are possible, but, in the short run, living standards deteriorated for many people. This downturn included those people whose cottage jobs were being taken away by mechanization and many who worked in the new cotton mills. For some factory workers, however, life was better than it had been on the farm. This improvement was especially true for children who had worked on agricultural "gangs." By the second half of the nineteenth century, mechanization had led to rising wages for everyone (men, women, and children) and the withdrawal of married women and young children from the labor force. Work might be monotonous, fast paced, and dangerous, but it paid better, and people ultimately lived better lives.

Working-Class Consciousness. Men and women who worked in factories had much more contact with their fellow workers than farmers, cottage workers, and putting-out workers. By the 1830s many of them were organizing themselves into unions so they could put pressure on their employers. Early protests were often about control of the workplace and were led by skilled workers who had formerly been independent artisans. Later issues included increased pay, reduced hours, and the end of a whole set of practices that workers found insulting and demeaning. The creation of working-class organizations led to a second great debate among historians about the formation of class identity and class consciousness. The most persuasive of these historians was E. P. Thompson. In *The Making of the English Working Class* (1963) he argued that "class happens when some men, as a result of common experiences (inherited or shared), feel and articulate the identity of their interests as between themselves, and as against other men whose interests are different from (and usually opposed to) theirs. The class experience is largely determined by the productive relations into which men are born—or enter involuntarily. Class-consciousness is the way in which these experiences are handled in cultural terms: embodied in traditions, value-systems, ideas, and institutional forms." The great advantage of Thompson's formulation of class identity is that he regarded it as arising from something people did. They discovered their shared interests through common actions. For Thompson, workers were not simply passive victims crushed by the overwhelming and abstract forces of industrialism, but rather were effective actors who adjusted themselves as best they could to new and often hostile circumstances and thereby went about making rational decisions about their lives. As convincing as Thompson may be in this regard, he tended to ignore women's experiences in the workplace. He also disregarded the role of families in which members worked at different kinds of jobs. A wife might work in an office (a lower-middle-class occupation) and a husband in a factory (a working-class occupation). How these two occupations in the same family affected class identity is difficult to determine, and this situation cautions one from too easily simplifying such a complex issue as class consciousness.

Sources:

Geoffrey Crossick, ed., *The Lower Middle Class in Britain, 1870–1914* (New York: St. Martin's Press, 1977).

Leonore Davidoff and Catherine Hall, *Family Fortunes: Men and Women of the English Middle Class, 1780–1850* (Chicago: Chicago University Press, 1987).

James R. Farr, *Artisans in Europe, 1350–1914* (Cambridge & New York: Cambridge University Press, 2000).

Colin Heywood, *Childhood in Nineteenth-Century France: Work, Health, and Education among the "Classes Populaires"* (Cambridge & New York: Cambridge University Press, 1988).

E. J. Hobsbawm, *Labouring Men: Studies in the History of Labour* (London: Weidenfeld & Nicolson, 1964).

Olwen Hufton, "Women and the Family Economy in Eighteenth-Century France," *French Historical Studies*, 9 (Spring 1975): 1–22.

Jurgen Kocka and Allen Mitchell, eds., *Bourgeois Society in Nineteenth-Century Europe* (Oxford & Providence, R.I.: Berg, 1993).

R. J. Morris, *Class and Class Consciousness in the Industrial Revolution, 1780–1850* (London: Macmillan, 1979).

William M. Reddy, *The Rise of Market Culture: The Textile Trade and French Society, 1750–1900* (Cambridge & New York: Cambridge University Press, 1984).

Samuel Smiles, *Self-Help: With Illustrations of Character and Conduct* (London: Murray, 1860).

Bonnie G. Smith, *Ladies of the Leisure Class: The Bourgeoises of Northern France in the Nineteenth Century* (Princeton: Princeton University Press, 1981).

E. P. Thompson, *The Making of the English Working Class* (London: Gollancz, 1963).

Louise A. Tilly and Joan W. Scott, *Women, Work and Family* (New York: Holt, Rinehart & Winston, 1978).

INDUSTRY: ECONOMIC TRANSFORMATIONS

Factories. Before the Industrial Revolution, people worked at home or in small workshops. Factories as concentrated sites of production where multiple tasks were performed under one roof were rare. The increasingly widespread appearance of factories was a clear sign that the process of manufacturing was changing. Indeed, they became a fundamental image in the European artist's eye, appearing on canvasses with regularity. French Impressionists in the 1870s and 1880s often included them as a matter of course in their landscapes.

Beginnings. Factories were initially small and spread around the countryside. Hardly more than large workrooms, women working with spinning jennies (a system by which eight threads could be spun rather than just a single thread) powered the machines by hand. As the machines grew larger and needed external sources of power, factory building was concentrated along streams, especially those with falling water, where waterwheels could be constructed to generate power. The next stage of development came with the introduction of the steam engine to power factory machinery. In the early years of factory work, people walked from their homes to the mills and back again. These treks could be several miles. As the size of the mills increased, urbanization around the factories followed. More and more housing was built nearby for workers and their families, and people began to abandon farming for factory work.

Routines and Dangers. Factories routinized work in a way that had not been the case before. Work began and ended daily at prescribed times, unless the factories ran overtime, and then workers were expected to stay on the job. The pace of work was determined by the machines and varied only when employers decided to increase the machines' speed. The introduction of gaslight in 1806 made night work possible, and owners began to standardize work into shifts. In the 1880s electric-power plants and electric light were introduced, furthering the standardiza-

British workers building the Whitby-to-Loftus railroad line, early 1880s (Greater London Council, Photographic Unit, Department of Architecture and Civic Design)

tion of labor. Initially factories had no protective coverings over the machines, and it was easy for workers to be pulled into the machines and seriously injured. Machines were especially hazardous for women, whose long hair could be tangled in a whirring gear. The result was what workers referred to as "scalping." In textile mills the prevalence of lint in the air damaged workers' lungs and led to the aptly named "brown lung" disease. The passage of protective laws in the mid to late nineteenth century and workers' use of the strike began to shorten the workday and to improve working conditions.

Light Industry. Textile production in cottage industry occupied almost as many people as agriculture did in the preindustrial world. By 1750 virtually every rural woman possessed a spinning wheel and spent at least part of her work time using it. In fact, spinning was so associated with women that the terms *spinster* (a female spinner) and *distaff* (the stick on which one stuck the raw fibers to be spun) became synonymous with *woman* and *female* in English.

Fabric was made from four fibers—wool, flax, silk, and cotton. Wool-producing sheep and flax plants existed throughout Europe. Mulberry trees and silk worms existed only in the region of Lyon, France. Silk weavers in other places had to import silk from there or from Asia. Cotton, too, was an imported fiber. It was not grown anywhere in Europe, but it was becoming popular because it was lightweight (compared with linen and wool), easily washed, and much less expensive than silk. The earliest machines associated with the Industrial Revolution were constructed for the spinning of cotton.

Bottlenecks. Spinning was a bottleneck in the production process. It employed far more people than weaving, but the spinners still did not produce enough thread to supply weavers with the necessary material to meet demand. The problem was made even more severe by John Kay's invention of the flying shuttle in the 1730s, which speeded up weaving, and a carding machine, invented in 1748, which increased the speed with which raw fibers could be prepared for spinning. By 1750 it took anywhere from six to ten spinners working full-time to keep one weaver fully supplied with thread for an entire workday. In the 1760s inventors began to tinker with ideas and materials to eliminate the spinning bottleneck. James Hargreaves invented the first spinning machine around 1764. He called it a spinning jenny. By employing multiple distaffs of raw fiber and bobbins around which to spool the thread, a woman could produce up to twenty times more thread than she could have with a spinning wheel. The jenny produced fine, but not particularly strong, yarn and was immediately successful. The first machines were built and used in England, but the technology spread rapidly to the Continent. Though larger than the spinning wheel, the jenny was small enough to be set up in women's homes. In 1769 Richard Arkwright patented a second spinning machine—the spinning frame, or water frame. It operated on a different principle from the jenny and made stronger, but not very fine, yarn. Threads from the water frame were used for the warp threads on the loom while the threads from the jenny were wound onto bobbins and used for the weft threads. The water frame needed a nonhuman source of power—coursing water—and had to be set up in mills or factories. With the jenny, mass production of cotton fabric became possible for the first time in Europe. A third invention, Samuel Crompton's spinning mule, was patented in 1779. It spun stronger yarn than the jenny and finer yarn than the water frame. Its name derived from the fact that it was a hybrid of two processes, just as the animal of the same name is a cross between a donkey and a horse. The mule worked on the same principle as the jenny but was powered by water (and later by steam). Like the water frame, it was too large to be set up in people's homes, and spinning moved rapidly into mills. Because the mule produced a better product, it was worthwhile for factory owners to invest in ever larger machines. By the turn of the nineteenth century, technology was adjusted so wool and linen spinning could also be done by these machines. Women and children were initially hired to operate the new machines. Later, factory spinning became men's work.

Weaving Machines. Weaving was the last stage of the textile manufacturing process to be mechanized. Carding, scutching, and roving machines were introduced; bleaching and dyeing were improved; steam engines replaced waterwheels as a power source; and the invention of the cotton gin in the United States (1793) increased the supply and reduced the cost of raw cotton. Even after a power loom had been invented by Edmund Cartwright in 1787, its use spread slowly. Hand-loom weavers were intensely hostile to its introduction, and many early weaving factories were invaded, the machines broken, and the pieces burned. The power loom was an inevitable development, however, and its adoption in the early nineteenth century spelled the end of hand-loom weaving. As weaving moved into factories, it became women's work.

Railroads and Heavy Industry. In the early nineteenth century, railroads (called railways in Britain) seemed even more emblematic of the Industrial Revolution than factories. They made it possible to transport raw materials, manufactured goods, agricultural products, and people faster and in larger quantities than ever before. Traveling at up to 30 mph, the early trains moved faster than coaches pulled by horses (maximum speeds of 10 mph). People felt as if they were flying through the countryside, a feeling enhanced by the fact that in the beginning they were sitting in the open air. Like factory production, railroad building began in Britain, starting slowly in the late 1820s. Ten years later railroads were being constructed on the European continent. In 1830 in Britain there were only 100 miles of track, but then a building frenzy set in and by 1852 there were 6,600 miles. By 1901, 19,000 miles of rails crisscrossed Great Britain.

Railroad Constructing. Railroads were huge construction projects. Laws allowed the railroad owners to purchase property for their tracks, regardless of the social standing, wealth, or opposition of local landowners. Bridges were built, tunnels dug, viaducts erected, railroad stations constructed, land smoothed out, and track laid. In major cities the stations were massive and ornate as befitted what the railroad entrepreneurs thought of as the grandeur of their undertaking. As Michael Freeman, in *Railways and the Victorian Imagination* (1999), has observed, "Directors did not call their railway companies 'Great' for nothing." The railroad introduced more people to industrialization than factories. They were marvels of engineering and construction. They brought steam engines and manufactured goods to far-flung villages. The future had arrived, but it came on the backs of men and boys working at a furious pace with preindustrial tools—shovels, pickaxes, horses, wagons, and gunpowder. Disabling accidents and death were common among the workforce. Local residents and bourgeois observers were appalled at the workers' lawlessness, squalid living conditions, heavy drinking, and lack of religion.

Financing the Railroads. Building a railroad required large amounts of capital investment. In Britain, where no expense was spared, the capital outlay was £34,000 per mile in the 1840s. Initially the new British manufacturing elite (largely cotton-mill owners) financed the building of railroads with its accumulated wealth. Landed aristocrats wanted nothing to do with the railroads; they fought the appropriation of their land and the invasion of their estates by the noisy, smoke-belching machines. When public stock was offered as a means to attract investment capital and returns promised handsome profits, however, landed aristocrats as well as the wealthy bourgeoisie invested in the construction projects. The risks and rewards could be great. Some investors made millions; many others lost everything. In Belgium, France, and Germany the governments were heavily involved in the financing and building of railroads.

Class Distinctions. Trains both reinforced and disturbed class distinctions. In the beginning everyone sat on benches in the open air. Those who purchased first-class tickets could ride in trains that made fewer stops and reached their destinations faster. Quickly, first-, second-, and third-class cars were created. First- and second-class passengers entered com-

Drawing of the great Silesian ironworks at Konigshutte, circa 1830 (from T. C. W. Blanning, *The Oxford Illustrated History of Modern Europe*, 1996)

partments with comfortable seats and glass windows. As one might expect, first-class cabins had more comfortable seats and larger windows. In Britain third-class passengers continued to ride in open cars until the British Parliamentary Railway Regulation Act of 1844 required that all passengers be protected from the weather (and concomitantly from the danger of falling out). Then, having little consideration for their working-class and poor rural passengers who traveled on inexpensive tickets, railroad companies herded third-class travelers into windowless boxcars for their journeys. On the Continent, class was even enforced in railroad stations, where passengers were required to wait in first-, second-, and third-class waiting rooms.

Working-Class Riders. While the wealthy were traveling in comfort, workers were using the trains to commute to and from work and for holiday excursions. By 1913 one-quarter of all train trips in Britain were made by working men and women. Cheap special-excursion train trips were created, and the working class rode trains to the beach and resort towns for weekend and summer vacations. Affronted by the invasion of "their" towns by the lower classes, wealthy residents and vacationers complained fruitlessly about their lack of manners, poor clothing, excessive drinking, and generally indecorous behavior.

Sources:

Phyllis Deane, *The First Industrial Revolution* (Cambridge: Cambridge University Press, 1965).

Michael Freeman, *Railways and the Victorian Imagination* (New Haven, Conn.: Yale University Press, 1999).

David S. Landes, *The Unbound Prometheus: Technological Change and Industrial Development in Western Europe from 1750 to the Present* (London: Cambridge University Press, 1969).

Ivy Pinchbeck, *Women Workers and the Industrial Revolution, 1750–1850* (London: Routledge, 1930).

William M. Reddy, *The Rise of Market Culture: The Textile Trade and French Society, 1750–1900* (Cambridge & New York: Cambridge University Press, 1984).

Wolfgang Schivelbusch, *Geschichte der Eisenbahnreise* (New York: Urizen Books, 1979); translated by Angela Davies as *The Railway Journey: The Industrialization of Time and Space in the Nineteenth Century* (Berkeley: University of California Press, 1986).

E. P. Thompson, *The Making of the English Working Class* (London: Gollancz, 1963).

LABOR AND LABORING CONDITIONS

Sweated Work. The garment industry was one of the major employers of female labor throughout the nineteenth century. As spinning machines and power looms increased the production of fabric, demand for seamstresses multiplied. Sewing was one job virtually every woman knew how to do. In the preindustrial economy women had been assigned the sewing of women's and children's clothing, while male tailors made men's clothing. The first major change of the industrial era in the garment industry occurred with the introduction of machine-cut pieces. In a continuation of the putting-out process, women picked up these precut pieces and took them back to their urban apartments to sew together with needle and thread. These women then returned the finished articles of clothing to their employers. The labor of seamstresses who worked in putting-out industries was extremely easy for employers to exploit. These women worked for piece rates and paid their own overhead costs. Initially these expenses included light, heat, rent, needles, and thread. Later they rented sewing machines from their employers. Working at home, and thus isolated from fellow workers, they had no way to orga-

Russian laborers pulling a barge loaded with timber on a tributary of the Volga River in the late nineteenth century

nize for higher wages. Moreover, the number of seam-stresses looking for work undercut any bargaining position those employed may have sought. Consequently, employers were able to pay extremely low rates and force them to work long hours. Hunched over their work in poorly lit conditions, these women worked in what, for good reason, came to be called the "sweated trades." The second major change in sewing occurred in 1851 when Isaac Singer invented a foot-treadle sewing machine, which, like spinning machines and mechanical looms, increased the number of garments a woman could produce in a day. Sewing remained a home industry until the end of the century. When Singer introduced an electric sewing machine in 1889, the sewing industry moved into small factories. These factories became known as "sweatshops."

Rural Child Labor. In the nineteenth century, child labor became a subject of debate and concern, but children's work was nothing new. It simply became more visible. In the countryside, children's work was crucial to the economic survival of most families. Most children worked for their own families, although some were sent to work for others or were apprenticed in a trade. Beginning perhaps as early as age five, children were assigned productive tasks. They helped with the washing, carding, and combing of wool for their mothers to spin. They gathered eggs, chased

birds from the fields, carried water, and looked after farm animals such as sheep and pigs. As they approached the age of ten, they helped care for younger children, thus freeing their mothers for productive work. They also began to cook and do laundry. At harvesttime they helped gather and bind sheaves of grain, gleaned fields for grain that had dropped to the ground during the first cutting, and carried food to adult workers. Around the age of twelve, children's work became gender specific. Girls continued to help their mothers, as all younger children had, but boys began to help their fathers in the fields or at tasks such as weaving, smithing, or brickmaking. Many children remained part of the family work unit until they married, although staying at home to work probably reduced the possibility of marriage for all but the eldest son, who would inherit the family farm or small business. Not all children remained at home until marriage, however. Many left in their early teenage years to work as servants or apprentices.

Child Labor. The early cotton mills primarily employed women and children. Even later, mill owners who employed men to operate heavy machinery continued to hire children to perform a variety of tasks on the factory floor. Children crawled under machinery to repair broken threads with their fingers, carried bobbins to spinners, pulled heavy cords for weavers, and wound silk on bobbins.

A Mrs. Burrows recalls her labor in the fields when she was a young girl:

In the very short schooling that I obtained, I learnt neither grammar nor writing. On the day that I was eight years of age, I left school, and began to work fourteen hours a day in the fields, with from forty to fifty other children of whom, even at that early age, I was the eldest. We were followed all day long by an old man carrying a whip in his hand which he did not forget to use. A great many of the children were only five years of age. You will think that I am exaggerating, but I am *not*; it is as true as the Gospel. Thirty-five years ago is the time I speak of, and the place, Croyland in Lincolnshire, nine miles from Peterborough. I could even now name several of the children who began at the age of five to work in the gangs, and also the name of the ganger.

We always left the town, summer and winter, the moment the old Abbey clock struck six. . . . We had to walk a very long way to our work, never much less than two miles each way, and very often five miles each way. The large farms all lay a good distance from the town, and it was on those farms that we worked. In the winter, by the time we reached our work, it was light enough to begin, and of course we worked until it was dark and then had our long walk home. I never remember to have reached home sooner than six and more often seven, even in winter. In the summer, we did not leave the fields in the evening until the clock had struck six, and then of course we must walk home, and this walk was no easy task for us children who had worked hard all day on the ploughed fields.

In all the four years I worked in the fields, I never worked one hour under cover of a barn, and only once did we have a meal in a house. And I shall never forget that one meal or the woman who gave us it. It was a most terrible day. The cold east wind (I suppose it was an east wind, for surely no wind ever blew colder), the sleet and snow which came every now and then in showers seemed almost to cut us to pieces. . . . I have been out in all sorts of weather but never remember a colder day. Well, the morning passed along somehow. . . . Dinner-time came, and we were preparing to sit down under a hedge and eat our cold dinner and drink our cold tea, when we saw the shepherd's wife coming towards us, and she said to our ganger, "Bring these children into my house and let them eat their dinner there." We went into that very small two-roomed cottage, and when we got into the largest room there was not standing room for us all, but this woman's heart was large, even if her house was small, and so she put her few chairs and table out into the garden, and then we all sat down in a ring upon the floor. She then placed in our midst a very large sauce-pan of hot boiled potatoes, and bade us help ourselves. Truly, although I have attended scores of grand parties and banquets since that time, not one of them has seemed half as good to me as that meal did. I well remember that woman. . . .

For four years, summer and winter, I worked in these gangs—no holidays of any sort, with the exception of very wet days and Sundays—and at the end of that time it felt like Heaven to me when I was taken to the town of Leeds, and put to work in the factory. Talk about White Slaves, the Fen districts at that time was the place to look for them.

Source: Mrs. Burrows, "A Childhood in the Fens About 1850–60," in *Life as We Have Known It by Co-Operative Working Women*, edited by Margaret Llewelyn Davies (London: Wolff, 1931), pp. 109–112.

As young adolescents, they began tending mechanical looms by themselves. Most disturbing of all, perhaps, children also worked in mines. They led donkeys on underground rails, worked ventilation doors, and when they were strong enough, dug for coal. The sight of thin, poorly clothed children trudging to and from work in a mill or mine disturbed many a bourgeois. This new middle class came to embrace a domestic ethic that viewed children as young people who should be nurtured and cherished in the home, not sent out to work. As long as adult wages were too low to support a family, however, working-class families had little choice but to send their children to the factories and mines.

Work Hours. The workday of preindustrial workers could be as long as it was for early factory workers, up to fourteen hours. The difference was the regularity of factory work. In cottage industry, men and women worked in bursts of activity demanded by the merchants' commercial delivery schedule. Now men, women, and children remained on task in factories day in and day out, dictated by the manufacturers' incentive to meet a seemingly limitless demand for cotton fabric and to keep his expensive machinery in as full use as possible. Greater production justified the investment in the physical plant and raised profits. Undoubtedly, unscheduled breaks from work occurred regularly as machinery broke down, power failed, or threads snapped. During such stoppages all workers remained in the factory, but children could sleep or play and adults could relax. If such stoppages had not occurred, children as young as six years of age simply would not have been able to remain awake during the working day.

End of Child Labor. So great was the need for a child's contribution to the family budget that mill and mine owners knew they could hire youngsters for extremely low pay. Not surprisingly, these owners feared that eliminating child labor from their establishments would increase labor costs. The end to child labor would only come from government action. The earliest factory acts were targeted directly at

Berlin weaver and his wife with a loom in their bedroom, circa 1890

factories using machines and employing at least twenty workers—the textile mills. Provisions of these laws were weak, although they probably got the youngest children (under age eight or nine) out of the mills. Later legislation raised the minimum age for work, forbade the work of girls underground in mines, and eventually applied rules to more workplaces. Despite this legislation, however, throughout the nineteenth century many children continued to work in unregulated and unrestricted occupations. More effective than protective legislation in ending child labor were increases in men's wages and the passage of compulsory education laws. By the end of the century almost no children in the paid labor force were under thirteen years of age.

Shortening the Workday. Attempts to shorten the work day to ten hours were made repeatedly from the 1840s until the end of the century. Gradually national legislatures passed laws establishing maximum hours for certain workplaces (usually mines and factories using machinery) and for specific groups of workers. Called "protective legislation" or "factory acts," these laws at first applied to children and women. In factories that also employed men, the shortened hours sometimes were extended to them as well.

The greatest progress toward a shortened working day for men came as a result of union organization and socialist political party agitation. Arguing that some of the benefits of increased production that resulted from mechanization should be passed on to workers, socialist parties and unionized workers demanded a day divided equally between work, leisure, and sleep. Employers viewed such proposals as attacks on productivity and profit, and so remained adamantly opposed to them until after World War I (1914–1918). It was only then that the demands of laborers resulted in the adoption of the eight-hour workday in most of industrialized Europe.

Lighting the Workplace. The emergence of the factory provided an incentive for the creation of a new source of light. People working alone in their own homes, or a few people working in a small workshop, could use traditional candles and oil lamps for illumination before sunrise and after sunset. Lighting a factory by hundreds of candles, however, was prohibitively expensive. At the beginning of the nineteenth century, British engineer William Murdoch installed the first set of pipes to convey gas from a gas plant, where it was produced by baking coal, to a cotton factory in Manchester where it was burned for light. The first gasworks and gas delivery system had been created. The same principles and procedures were later used to light streets, public buildings, and bourgeois homes in cities. The lighting of factories made it possible to standardize the workday year-round. No longer could workers expect to work fewer hours in the winter and more hours in the summer. Gas lighting was not problem free, however. There remained the constant danger of explosion, gruesomely demonstrated on several occasions by spectacular explosions that killed many people. Gas also polluted the ground around gasworks and the air in homes and factories. Rooms had to be well-ventilated, otherwise headaches or even asphyxiation might occur if the flame went out and the gas continued to flow. Toward the end of the nineteenth century, Thomas Edison, an American inventor, improved upon the inventions and work of others and produced an incandescent electric lightbulb. This invention revolutionized lighting. Electric light had none of the drawbacks of gas light. It was clean, did not burn up oxygen, and presented no danger of poisoning or asphyxiation. Now, more than ever, factories could be illuminated by artificial light. Electricity became ubiquitous in the twentieth century, altered life and work in innumerable ways, and provided power for a multitude of machines as well as light.

Sources:

Duncan Blythell, *The Sweated Trades: Outwork in Nineteenth-Century Britain* (New York: St. Martin's Press, 1978).

Judith Coffin, *The Politics of Women's Work: The Paris Garment Trades, 1750–1915* (Princeton: Princeton University Press, 1996).

Gary Cross, *A Quest for Time: The Reduction of Work in Britain and France, 1840–1940* (Berkeley: University of California Press, 1989).

Hugh Cunningham, *Children and Childhood in Western Society since 1500* (London & New York: Longman, 1995).

Colin Heywood, *Childhood in Nineteenth-Century France: Work, Health, and Education among the "Classes Populaires"* (Cambridge & New York: Cambridge University Press, 1988).

Eric Hopkins, *Childhood Transformed: Working-Class Children in Nineteenth-Century England* (Manchester & New York: Manchester University Press, 1994).

William M. Reddy, *The Rise of Market Culture: The Textile Trade and French Society, 1750–1900* (Cambridge & New York: Cambridge University Press, 1984).

Wolfgang Schivelbusch, *Disenchanted Night: The Industrialization of Light in the Nineteenth Century,* translated by Angela Davies (Berkeley: University of California Press, 1988).

James A. Schmiechen, *Sweated Industries and Sweated Labor: The London Clothing Trades, 1860–1914* (Urbana: University of Illinois Press, 1984).

E. P. Thompson, "Time, Work-Discipline, and Industrial Capitalism," *Past and Present,* 38 (1967): 56–97.

RESPONSES TO INDUSTRIALIZATION: BIG BUSINESS, UNIONS, AND STRIKES

Big Business. In the second half of the nineteenth century the scale of many businesses increased dramatically. Some of this expansion was driven by the cost of the newest machines in heavy industry, such as steel; only the largest and wealthiest companies could afford them. Many of those who could not afford to invest in new technologies were driven out of business. In some industries, such as electrical equipment, production was con-

Meeting of anarchists and workers in Barcelona before a strike in 1909

trolled by two or three manufacturers. Banks increased in size as well, and in some countries manufacturers banded together into cartels to set prices and production quotas. This situation was particularly the case in Germany, where there were three hundred cartels by 1900. Big businesses increased pressure on workers as well as on competitors. They increased discipline on the job, sped up the pace of work by increasing the speed at which the machines worked, and assigned workers to cover more machines than in the past.

Labor Unions. The response to heavy industrialization on the part of many workers was to join labor organizations known as unions. Until the 1890s most unions were small and organized on the basis of particular crafts. Many workers in many industries remained completely unorganized in the late nineteenth and early twentieth centuries. In the 1890s large industrial unions broke from the tradition of craft unions and organized all workers in a variety of industries regardless of the kind of labor they performed. These general unions had names such as the *Confédération générale du travail* in France and the *Confederazione generale del lavoro* in Italy. Membership in unions increased rapidly in the 1890s. By 1900 there

Flag of the German Workers' Society (Deutsches Historisches Museum, Berlin)

were about three million union members in Britain and two million in Germany. France, with a smaller population, had one million union members. The economic depression and inflation of the late nineteenth century, as well as the increasingly impersonal workplace, lay behind the increase in union membership. In many industries, workers' wages declined relative to the cost of goods (real wages). In other cases, real wages rose but not as rapidly as they had in the pre-1870 era. Workers often agreed about general goals such as the decreased workday and thus increased leisure time, but disagreed about specific objectives. Some wanted an eight-hour workday; others wanted a full day of rest (not two half days); and still others wanted a half day on Saturday, as well as Sunday off (these demands reflect practices already in place in different countries and industries).

Strike. The primary tactic of unions was the strike. By 1900, hundreds of thousands of workers went on strike every year. In some countries, workers tried to organize general strikes in which all workers refused to work until some demand was met. A general strike in Russia in 1905 led to an attempted revolution. In some cases where the national union was quite large, the mere threat of a strike could induce owners to negotiate settlements. In eastern Europe, where industrialization was much newer, strike rates were higher than they were in the west. In the east, workers also made political demands such as gaining the right to vote and granting of civil liberties. In the west, where workers had acquired many of these political rights before unionization, their grievances were more purely economic. A high percentage of strikes everywhere involved violence, in some cases initiated by workers. More often, however, the violence was initiated by owners who paid thugs and local police to beat up the striking workers.

Sources:

Mary Ann Clawson, *Constructing Brotherhood: Class, Gender, and Fraternalism* (Princeton: Princeton University Press, 1989).

Gary Cross, *A Quest for Time: The Reduction of Work in Britain and France, 1840–1940* (Berkeley: University of California Press, 1989).

Laura L. Frader and Sonya O. Rose, eds., *Gender and Class in Modern Europe* (Ithaca, N.Y.: Cornell University Press, 1996).

Dick Geary, *European Labour Protest, 1848–1939* (New York: St. Martin's Press, 1981).

Peter N. Stearns, *Lives of Labor: Work in a Maturing Industrial Society* (New York: Holmes & Meier, 1975).

Charles Tilly, Louise Tilly, and Richard Tilly, *The Rebellious Century, 1830–1930* (Cambridge, Mass.: Harvard University Press, 1975).

RESPONSES TO INDUSTRIALIZATION: INFORMAL AND VIOLENT CONFRONTATION

Unemployment. To many Europeans of the late eighteenth century, industrialization appeared neither inevitable nor desirable. Cottage workers and artisans were especially concerned about its effect on their employment. Small spinning jennies that could be set up in people's homes increased a spinner's productivity without throwing other people out of work, but larger jennies, Arkwright's water frame, and Crompton's mule did more than increase productivity. They moved workers into factories and threw hand spinners out of work. Unemployment likewise resulted for shearmen, who hand cut the nap from woolen cloth, when a shearing machine was invented; for weavers, when mechanical looms began to spread; and for stocking knitters, when a new flat knitting frame was invented.

Luddism. Unemployed workers and their sympathizers, as well as men who worked with machines and who wanted to put pressure on their employers to improve conditions or pay, periodically took matters into their own hands and smashed the new machines. A wave of machine breaking swept the Midlands of England in 1811, and these demonstrators claimed they were led by a Captain or General Ludd. Soon his name appeared at the bottom of threatening letters sent to mill owners. Whether or not Ludd was a real person (and he probably was not), the name was used by machine-breakers in England, France, and Germany, and the demonstrators were referred to as Luddites. Attacks on machines continued periodically until the end of the 1840s. The major issue was not really the machines but social justice. Unemployment or low wages were no fault of the workers, and they undermined the rural family economy and threatened the survival of the family. For workers, saving their livelihood and their family was more important than the increased profits that machines produced for mill owners.

Chartism. In the late 1830s Britain suffered a series of bad harvests, which raised the price of food. A simultaneous downturn in the industrial economy led to a series of business failures that depressed wages and threw people out of work. By the summer of 1837 in the textile city of Manchester fifty thousand workers were either unemployed or working shortened hours. Adding to the frustration of the poor was the deeply resented English Poor Law (1834) that forced able-bodied men and women into workhouses if they were to qualify for government aid. As the plight of agricultural and manufacturing workers worsened, middle-class reformers and working-class radicals sought to alter the political system. Their unifying belief was that the House of Commons in Parliament should become the People's House and thereby pass legislation aiding workers and the poor. For this change to happen, workers needed something they did not currently have: the right to vote. A loose coalition of farmworkers, factory workers, hand-loom weavers, cottage manufacturers, and skilled artisans from England, Scotland, and Wales rallied around the People's Charter. Drawn up by William Lovett, a former cabinet maker and head of the London Workingmen's Association,

Nineteenth-century engraving of the Peterloo Massacre (1819) in which the British military dispersed a crowd of workers advocating economic reform (from T. C. W. Blanning, *The Oxford Illustrated History of Modern Europe*, 1996)

Karl Marx and Friedrich Engels wrote *The Communist Manifesto* in 1848. The following selection describes the struggle between classes.

The history of all hitherto existing society is the history of class struggles. Freeman and slave, patrician and plebeian, lord and serf, guildmaster and journeyman, in a word, oppressor and oppressed, stood in constant opposition to one another, carried on an uninterrupted, now hidden, now open fight, a fight that each time ended, either in a revolutionary reconstitution of society at large, or in the common ruin of the contending classes. . . .

The modern bourgeois society that has sprouted from the ruins of feudal society, has not done away with class antagonisms. It has but established new classes, new conditions of oppression, new forms of struggle in place of the old ones.

Our epoch, the epoch of the bourgeoisie, possesses, however, this distinctive feature: it has simplified the class antagonisms. Society as a whole is more and more splitting up into two great hostile camps, into two great classes directly facing each other—bourgeoisie and proletariat. . . .

The bourgeoisie has played a most revolutionary role in history. . . . [W]herever it has got the upper hand, [it] has put an end to all feudal, patriarchal, idyllic relations. It has pitilessly torn asunder the motley feudal ties that bound man to his "natural superiors," and has left no other bond between man and man than naked self-interest, than callous "cash payment." . . .

It has been the first to show what man's activity can bring about. It has accomplished wonders far surpassing Egyptian pyramids, Roman aqueducts, and Gothic cathedrals; it has conducted expeditions that put in the shade all former migrations of nations and crusades. . . .

In place of the old local and national seclusion and self-sufficiency, we have intercourse in every direction, universal inter-dependence of nations. . . . National one-sidedness and narrow-mindedness become more and more impossible, and from the numerous national and local literatures there arises a world literature. . . .

It has created enormous cities, has greatly increased the urban population as compared with the rural, and has thus rescued a considerable part of the population from the idiocy of rural life. . . .

Of all the classes that stand face to face with the bourgeoisie today, the proletariat alone is a really revolutionary class. The other classes decay and finally disappear in the face of modern industry; the proletariat is its special and essential product.

The essential condition for the existence and sway of the bourgeois class, is the formation and augmentation of capital; the condition for capital is wage-labor. . . . What the bourgeoisie therefore produces, above all, are its own grave-diggers. Its fall and the victory of the proletariat are equally inevitable. . . .

The proletarians have nothing to lose but their chains. They have a world to win.

Workingmen of all countries, unite!

Source: Karl Marx and Friedrich Engels, *The Communist Manifesto* (New York: International Publishers, 1976), pp. 1–2, 5–9, 20, 24, 62.

the Charter made six demands: universal manhood suffrage, annual elections for Parliament, voting by secret ballot, equal electoral districts, abolition of property qualifications for members of Parliament, and salaries for members of Parliament. The last point was of particular importance because working-class men, who lived on their wages, could serve in political office only if it were a paid occupation. A few Chartists (as supporters of the Charter were called) also supported female suffrage, but the majority of members believed women should be represented by men. Activism and support for the Charter waxed and waned as the economy careened in and out of depression during the late 1830s and 1840s. Chartists held torch-lit parades, convened meetings throughout the country, and presented three petitions with millions of signatures to the Parliament. Despite the Chartists' large numbers, the aristocratic- and bourgeois-dominated House of Commons voted repeatedly to reject their suggestions. Chartists shared a distrust of capitalism and capitalists, but they disagreed about tactics. Some proposed the use of force to bring Parliament to their position; others believed in moral persuasion. This disagreement, as well as the difficulty in organizing a mass movement from diverse occupations and with diverse needs led to the movement's collapse in 1848. Chartism was both behind and ahead of its time. Its emphasis on political reform and its appeal to a wide spectrum of the poor, rather than just to industrial workers, made it the last of the early reactions to industrialization. But its attempt at mass mobilization foreshadowed the future, when workers would organize into national and international trade unions and political parties to pressure employers as well as governments for change. By 1918, of the six Chartist demands, all but the demand for annual elections had been accepted by Parliament.

Revolutions. In 1848 a revolution that began in France spread across Europe. Only Britain seemed untouched. At the beginning of the revolutions segments of the working class and the middle class joined forces and agreed upon goals. Revolutionaries everywhere wanted the franchise broadened to include all male citizens and democratically elected legislatures or parliaments. Many also wanted an end to the monarchy ruling their particular country. In the case of the Austrian Empire, this demand meant an end to Habsburg rule over at least a dozen different nationality and language groups. Socially, the revolutionaries' goals were more diverse. Some wanted the abolition of serfdom. Others desired the establishment of a socialist republic in which workers, rather than the bourgeoisie, would own the means of production and where much greater economic equality could be attained. Some, but not all, of these goals would be accomplished.

Example of Success. France was the first country to experience revolution, and it was the only nation in which the revolution was successful, if only for a short time. The uprising in Paris began on the night of 21 February when King Louis-Philippe forbade a political banquet that had been planned for the next day. Barricades were hastily erected in working-class neighborhoods. The government called out the National Guard, but it failed to respond. The king promised electoral reform, but it was too late. A demonstration outside the house of the prime minister resulted in the deaths of twenty demonstrators. The crowd, now turned revolutionary, marched through the streets carrying their dead comrades. On 24 February, Louis-Philippe abdicated the throne and left Paris. The revolution had succeeded. A republic was established; universal manhood suffrage was instituted; and the new government established National Workshops to ensure employment for all workers. The workshops were less than the workers had desired and were a sign that the bourgeois men who had gained control of the new government were not entirely allied with their working-class supporters. Louis Blanc, leader of the working class, wanted a Ministry of Progress that would organize a network of social workshops or worker-owned factories. By May the conflict between the bourgeoisie and the socialist workers had grown acute. In June street fighting began again. This time the new bourgeois republican government called out the army against the Parisian working class. Ten thousand people were killed or wounded, and another eleven thousand were arrested and deported to the colonies. To everyone, the June conflict appeared to be class warfare. Coincidentally, German political theorists Karl Marx and Friedrich Engels had predicted just such a struggle only a few months earlier in *The Communist Manifesto*.

Example of Failure. Meanwhile the Austrian Empire had begun to break apart. Hungary declared itself constitutionally separate from the empire; Vienna declared itself a republic; the Czechs who lived in Bohemia called for a pan-Slav congress; and the German states prepared to unite and called a pan-German congress to meet at Frankfurt. A handful of new states with constitutions and elected legislatures seemed about to emerge. Then it all collapsed. Different nationality groups within Hungary fought with each other. The Austrian monarch mobilized his army and all of the areas of the Habsburg Empire, including most of Italy, were brought back under control. The movement to unify Germany similarly collapsed. Thus the protests and revolutions that began with a coalition of interests between the bourgeoisie and the working class collapsed. In many

WHEREAS,
Several **EVIL-MINDED PERSONS** have assembled together in a riotous Manner, and **DESTROYED** a **NUMBER** of

FRAMES,

In different Parts of the Country:

THIS IS

TO GIVE NOTICE,

That any Person who will give Information of any **Person or Persons** thus wickedly

BREAKING THE FRAMES,

Shall, upon **CONVICTION**, receive

50 GUINEAS

REWARD.

And any Person who was actively engaged in **RIOTING**, who will impeach his Accomplices, shall, upon **CONVICTION**, receive the same Reward, and every Effort made to procure his Pardon.

☞ Information to be given to Messrs. **COLDHAM** and **ENFIELD**.

Nottingham, March 26, 1811.

Early-nineteenth-century poster encouraging the apprehension of Luddites (Nottingham County Library)

places the monarchs whose power had been seriously threatened regained control. Only in France did the king remain in exile and the bourgeoisie retain control of the government. The republican government was toppled by a coup in 1851 by the man who had been elected to lead it— Louis-Napoleon Bonaparte. Like his uncle Napoleon Bonaparte, Louis-Napoleon would become an emperor, crowned Napoleon III. The classes produced by industrialization had discovered the limits of their combined interests and had broken apart into opposing groups once again.

Sources:
Craig Calhoun, *The Question of Class Struggle: Social Foundations of Popular Radicalism during the Industrial Revolution* (Chicago: University of Chicago Press, 1982).

E. J. Hobsbawm, *The Age of Revolution, 1789–1848* (Cleveland: World, 1962).

Hobsbawm, *Labouring Men: Studies in the History of Labour* (London: Weidenfeld & Nicolson, 1964).

Gareth Stedman Jones, *Languages of Class: Studies in English Working Class History, 1832–1982* (Cambridge & New York: Cambridge University Press, 1983).

John M. Merriman, *The Agony of the Republic: The Repression of the Left in Revolutionary France, 1848–1851* (New Haven: Yale University Press, 1978).

Kirkpatrick Sale, *Rebels against the Future: The Luddites and Their War on the Industrial Revolution: Lessons for the Computer Age* (Reading, Mass.: Addison-Wesley, 1995).

Malcolm I. Thomis, *The Luddites: Machine-Breaking in Regency England* (Newton Abbot, U.K.: David & Charles / Hamden, Conn.: Archon, 1970).

RESPONSES TO INDUSTRIALIZATION: LEGAL AND POLITICAL

Protective Legislation. The earliest protective labor laws were passed in Britain. By the mid 1830s, five laws, known as factory acts because they applied only to factories (all other workplaces were exempt), had been passed. They were largely prompted by humanistic concerns about the plight of poor children who worked in textile mills. Child labor existed before the mills, but when children began to work in these factories, they became publicly visible in a way they had not been before. Simultaneously, the bourgeoisie, whose political influence was increasing, was coming to see children as innocents who needed nurture and moral training, neither of which seemed to be available in factories. Middle-class reformers wrote eyewitness accounts of working-class life and urged the passage of legislation, limiting or eliminating the work of women and children and increasing the wages of men to compensate for the loss of their earnings. The motivations of reformers were mixed. Some of their concern was genuinely humanitarian, but they also worried about the damage factory work did to children's health, fearing boys would not be strong enough to serve in the army or navy and girls would not be able to bear healthy babies in the future. In addition, they feared women's factory work was undermining the working-class family. The dilemma for factory owners and bourgeois legislators was that their ideas about the proper way to treat children and their belief that women's natural role was homemaker conflicted with their desire to hire the cheapest possible workers—women and children. If women and children were to be eliminated from the paid labor force, men would have to be paid more, and that, too, was undesirable from the employers' perspective.

Provisions of the Laws. In the 1830s and 1840s, France and Prussia followed Britain's lead and passed laws dividing childhood into two phases and limiting the working hours children could work in each phase. Children under the age of eight or nine were forbidden to work in the factories. The laws also required schooling of children and forbade night work for children under the age of thirteen, sixteen, or eighteen, depending upon the country. Later laws gradually raised the minimum work age, forbade the work of women and girls underground in mines, and extended the ages of compulsory education. These laws, however, never came fully to grip with the needs and desires of working-class families, much less

Workers' demonstration in Moscow in 1905

the values of the bourgeoisie. Gradually, middle-class manufacturers came to identify manhood with the performance of paid work and womanhood with motherhood. Jules Simon, a liberal French writer and politician, put it succinctly in 1860: "The woman who becomes a factory worker (ouvrière) is no longer a woman."

Welfare Legislation. Traditionally charity, or poor relief, was the responsibility of local communities, religious institutions, and the wealthy. They dispensed aid to the poor on a regular basis and especially in times of poor harvests, when entire communities found themselves on the verge of starvation. In the late eighteenth century French revolutionaries confiscated church property and decreed that the state assume responsibility for aiding the poor. The intention may have been admirable, but the national government was never able to care adequately for the poor during the revolution. Europe-wide debates about the advisability of government aid to the poor followed the French Revolution and accompanied the process of industrialization. Some argued that aiding the poor simply encouraged them to avoid work. Others argued that the government had an obligation to make certain its citizens were adequately housed and fed. For much of the nineteenth century, the opponents of government aid won the debate. Cities and states reduced aid they provided to the poor and made it increasingly difficult and demeaning to acquire. The English Poor Law of 1834, sponsored by the bourgeoisie that had just won the franchise two years previously, abolished what was called outdoor relief for the able-bodied (and their families). Henceforth the unemployed could not receive charitable assistance unless they and their families moved into workhouses. Before the 1834 law the poor had been able to stay in their own homes and receive aid while they looked for work or improved wages. In Russia, public assistance virtually disappeared with the abolition of serfdom in 1861.

Rise of Government Assistance. In the 1870s the pendulum began to swing back toward government assistance. The inadequacy of private and religious charity and the inhumanity of governments refusing to help the poor became obvious to everyone. In addition, events such as the revolutions of 1848 and other urban riots of the poor now worried the bourgeoisie. They began to speak of the "social question" and to consider new legislation. Workers' organizations and liberal, labor, and socialist political parties provided considerable support for the legislation. Prussia took the lead. Between 1883 and 1889 the Reichstag passed a series of laws that provided benefits to workers for illnesses (up to thirteen weeks in 1883, extended to twenty-six weeks in 1903), workplace accidents, and old age (a small pension for workers seventy and older). This welfare system differed from earlier systems by requiring workers and employers to contribute to the funds (accident insurance was paid for entirely by employers). It also was limited to factory and other industrial workers who were a minority of the population. Despite the large number of people left unaided by this legislation, the pattern of social insurance based on employment and employee contributions (such as the current social security system in the United States) had been established. Similar, and eventually broader, laws were passed throughout Europe. In France, laws provided for prenatal care, gave allowances to needy families with more than three children, and granted childbirth leaves of absence for working mothers (the French government wanted badly to increase the population). In Britain the National Insurance Act of 1911 provided health insurance for workers in a wide range of occupations, including servants, and introduced unemployment insurance for well-paid occupations that suffered from periodic unemployment such as construction and shipbuilding. Employers as well as employees contributed to the plans. Even so, most workers remained uncovered by social insurance legislation until after World War I (1914–1918).

Utopian Socialism. In the early nineteenth century, reform movements now known as utopian socialism sought new ways of organizing work and family life. The most famous of these movements were led by Henri de Saint-Simon, Charles Fourier, Etienne Cabet, and Robert Owen. The first three were French; the fourth was British. The term *utopian socialism* was applied to their ideas by German political philosopher Karl Marx, who thought of them as impractical dreamers. In contrast, he regarded himself as a scientific socialist. The utopians rejected the label, preferring to think of themselves also as scientific thinkers, but the label *utopian* is apt in several ways. The utopians believed they could reform society by creating model communities that would serve as examples of the best way to organize community and gender relations. Their goal was social harmony and, unlike the French revolutionaries, they believed in peaceful change rather than revolution. Like all socialists, they believed in collective rather than private ownership of property. All of the utopian socialists were reacting to industrialization. They were not necessarily opposed to machines and factories (Owen was a mill owner), but they opposed the poverty and dislocation factories and urbanization had caused. They perceived the bourgeoisie as the major beneficiary of industrialization; English journalist Henry Mayhew and French writer Flora Tristan believed radical reform was necessary to spread its benefits.

Utopian Objectives and Experiments. Many utopian socialists criticized the patriarchal family and the position of women in modern society: Fourier, for example, believed social progress was to be measured by the degree of women's freedom from oppression. The St. Simonians searched for a female messiah and pronounced the emancipation of women. Some of Owen's followers believed women as well as working-class men should have the same political rights (for example, the vote) as

Rosa Luxemburg, a Polish Jew, addressing a meeting of the German Social Democratic Party in 1907

middle-class men. (In 1832 most middle-class men in Britain were enfranchised.) Followers of Fourier, Saint-Simon, Owen, and Cabet formed model communities in Europe and North America (including Brook Farm in Massachusetts and New Harmony in Indiana). These experiments tended to be bucolic and did not fare well economically. Owen, a textile mill owner, also created a model community and factory for his own employees. He paid higher wages; reduced work hours; built schools, housing, and company stores where goods were sold at cheap prices; and tried to correct drunkenness and vice. This experiment worked far better than the one he led at New Harmony, where there was no industry. The utopian socialists are known for some of their quirky ideas as well as for their dedication to improving society. Fourier believed, for instance, that the ideal community should contain exactly 1,620 persons, each working at tasks to which he or she was naturally inclined. Cabet wanted to eliminate all forms and signs of inequality including differences in clothing. The St. Simonians believed their community should be led by a male pope and a female pope. Utopian socialists also founded the first trade unions, developed producer and consumer cooperatives in working-class communities, and raised social and economic questions that helped to create a climate for revolution in 1848. Governments reacted harshly to the writings and activities of the utopian socialists, arresting them, forcing them into exile, and sometimes executing them.

Socialist Political Parties. The concept of socialism existed throughout the nineteenth century. Marx and Friedrich Engels, the utopian socialists in France and England, Louis Blanc and Pierre-Joseph Proudhon in France, the Fabian socialists in Britain, and many others espoused various socialist critiques of industrialization and called for reform. Almost none of these socialists were from the working class. Instead they were middle- and upper-class men and women who believed profoundly that the poverty they saw had been caused by capitalism and was immoral. In the 1880s socialist and labor political parties appeared with membership that was primarily working class. They grew rapidly. By 1913 France had more than one hundred socialist deputies in its National Assembly, while the German socialist party received four million votes in the same year. Socialist parties thrived elsewhere as well. The British Labour Party was created in the 1890s. Austria, Italy, the Netherlands, Denmark, and the Scandinavian countries also had thriving socialist parties. While some socialists continued to believe economic equality and worker ownership of the means of production could be achieved only through political revolution, others were willing to work for change through the existing political system. The nonrevolutionary moderates or revisionists gradually gained the upper hand in their parties and devoted their attention to electing their members to office and enacting legislation. In general, the parties sought passage of welfare legislation, improvements in schools, and municipal services in working-class neighborhoods. The most sweeping experiment with socialist government would not begin until near the end of World War I (1914–1918) when revolution transformed Russia (1917) and the surrounding countries into the Soviet Union.

Sources:

Peter Baldwin, *The Politics of Social Solidarity: Class Bases of the European Welfare State, 1875–1975* (Cambridge & New York: Cambridge University Press, 1990).

James E. Cronin and Carmen Siranni, *Work, Community, and Power: The Experience of Labor in Europe and America, 1900–1925* (Philadelphia: Temple University Press, 1983).

Gay Gullickson, "Womanhood and Motherhood: The Rouen Manufacturing Community, Women Workers, and the French Factory Acts," in *The European Peasant Family and Society: Historical Studies,* edited by

Richard L. Rudolph (Liverpool: Liverpool University Press, 1995), pp. 206–232.

B. L. Hutchins and A. Harrison, *A History of Factory Legislation* (Westminster, U.K., 1907).

Mary Lynn Stewart, *Women, Work and the French State: Labor Protection & Social Patriarchy, 1879–1919* (Montreal: McGill-Queen's University Press, 1989).

Michael Sullivan, *The Development of the British Welfare State* (New York: Prentice Hall, 1996).

Barbara Taylor, *Eve and the New Jerusalem: Socialism and Feminism in the Nineteenth Century* (London: Virago, 1983).

Pat Thane, *Foundations of the Welfare State* (London & New York: Longman, 1982).

Lee Shai Weissbach, *Child Labor Reform in Nineteenth-Century France: Assuring the Future Harvest* (Baton Rouge: Louisiana State University Press, 1989).

SIGNIFICANT PEOPLE

RICHARD ARKWRIGHT

1732-1792

INVENTOR AND ENTREPRENEUR

Poor Beginnings. Richard Arkwright was born into a poor family and was reportedly the youngest of thirteen children. Unlike most boys of his economic circumstances, he learned to read, being taught by one of his uncles. He was apprenticed as a barber and worked for years making and selling wigs. When the market for wigs declined in the 1760s, he found himself looking for a new source of income. Textile merchants had been trying to invent a practical spinning machine since the early 1700s. James Hargreaves had recently invented the spinning jenny with which a spinner could produce fine (and delicate) yarn much more quickly. Arkwright's idea was quite different. Using an idea similar to a machine invented by Lewis Paul and John Wyatt in the 1730s, Arkwright imagined a machine that would use rollers to draw out and twist raw cotton into yarn. He enlisted the aid of two friends to help him make the necessary parts, rented a secluded cottage, and constructed what he called the spinning frame in 1767. The extent to which this invention was new and to which Arkwright, rather

than his friends, was responsible for it was argued at the time and has been debated by historians ever since. What is not debatable is the success of Arkwright's machine. The spinning frame made strong cotton fibers that could be used for warp threads. Combined with yarn from the spinning jenny, it made 100 percent cotton fabric possible for the first time in Europe.

Entrepreneur. Arkwright now turned to building spinning mills. His first mill used horses walking on a treadmill to turn the rollers of his machine, but horses were expensive (they had to be fed); so he turned to water power. His invention henceforth came to be called the water frame. Later, when the rollers were turned by steam power, the machine was renamed the throstle. By 1775 Arkwright had combined all of the steps in the production of yarn (carding, drawing, spinning rovings, and spinning yarn) under one roof. Arkwright's path to entrepreneurial success was not smooth, however. His desire for privacy while he built his first machine was almost his undoing. Suspicious neighbors were alarmed by the coming and going of so many men and by a strange humming sound coming from his cottage. Some were convinced that the men were practicing witchcraft and that the humming noise was the devil tuning his bagpipes. (The humming presumably came from the turning rollers.) Other mill owners and inventors challenged his patents; cottage workers who saw their livelihood threatened by machines destroyed one of his mills; and his workers resisted working at the steady pace of the spinning machines. He had a talent for entrepreneurship, however, and his factories made him one of the richest men in England. In 1786 he was knighted by George III, making him Sir Richard Arkwright.

Sources:

W. English, *The Textile Industry: An Account of the Early Inventions of Spinning, Weaving, and Knitting Machines* (London: Longman, 1969).

Karen Fisk, "Richard Arkwright: Cotton King or Spin Doctor?" *History Today,* 48 (March 1998): 25–30.

Eric Kerridge, *Textile Manufactures in Early Modern England* (Manchester, U.K. & Dover, N.H.: Manchester University Press, 1985).

ROSA LUXEMBURG

1871–1919

REVOLUTIONARY

Brilliant Youth. Born in the Russian part of Poland, Rozalia (Rosa) Luxemburg grew up in an anti-Semitic world. She spent her earliest years in a village where her father owned a timber business. In 1873, with the business in decline, the family moved to Warsaw, where her parents believed their children could receive a better education than in the village. The Luxemburgs were more secular than religious and desired integration into the non-Jewish Polish population. Integration was impossible to achieve in a Poland that still considered Jews to be the killers of Christ and whose population periodically engaged in attacks on Jews that resulted in suffering and death. Luxemburg was further isolated by a childhood illness that left her with a permanent limp. A brilliant child, she was one of few Jewish children to be admitted to a Russian Gymnasium for Girls. By 1888, when she graduated from secondary school, she was fluent in four languages—Polish, Yiddish, German, and Russian. She also had been introduced to the radical political philosophies of Marxism and socialism. Aware of the hardships and discrimination to which Jews and workers were subjected, she was on her way to becoming the most famous female revolutionary of the early twentieth century. Aided by the intellectual leaders of the socialist movement in Poland, desirous of more education than was available there, and already wanted by the police for her political activities on behalf of striking workers, Luxemburg left Warsaw when she was eighteen and enrolled at the University of Zurich. The Polish Marxists' judgment of her intelligence was well founded. She became one of the most authoritative spokespersons of German political philosopher Karl Marx's ideas in the late nineteenth and early twentieth centuries and an outspoken critic of Vladimir Lenin's ideas immediately after the Russian Revolution in 1917 and 1918.

Radical. Luxemburg loved animals and the study of botany, geography, and geology. In another time, she might have been a scientist, but the late nineteenth century was a time of revolution, and she lent her physical and intellectual efforts to the socialist/communist cause. In Zurich a group of radical students formed around her, listening to her ideas and debating them. In 1892 she and her lover, Lithuanian radical Leo Jogiches, founded the Social Democratic Party of Poland. In 1897 she received a doctorate of laws from the University of Zurich for a dissertation titled *The Industrial Development of Poland.* She then moved to Germany, where she worked in the German Social Democratic Party and the communist Second International. To provide her greater personal security and citizenship in Imperial Germany (a conservative state not sympathetic to socialism), she and her friends decided she should marry Gustav Lubeck, the son of Prussian radicals, Karl and Olympia Lubeck, although she was in love with Jogiches. Luxemburg and Lubeck parted immediately after the wedding (1895), and she obtained a divorce from him five years later. Her relationship with Jogiches continued until her death.

The Spartacus League. During World War I (1914–1918) Luxemburg was arrested for her left-wing organizing and writing, and she consequently spent most of the years of the war in prison. Released briefly in 1916, she and Karl Liebknecht, Clara Zetkin, and Jogiches concluded that the leaders of the Social Democratic Party had begun to act in their own interests rather than in those of the masses. They broke with the party and founded their own organization, the Spartakusbund (Spartacus League). When German liberals and socialists attempted to organize a new government to replace the defeated German Empire in 1919 some members of the Spartakusbund tried to push the leaders of the new government in a more radical direction by attempting to seize power in Berlin. Luxemburg and Liebknecht believed the attempt was misguided but supported the revolutionaries as they believed they should. Opting for solidarity had fatal consequences.

Execution. On 11 January 1919 the attempt failed, and four days later Luxemburg and Liebknecht were arrested. They were held briefly in police custody, and then taken separately into the streets where they were beaten ruthlessly by German soldiers. Liebknecht was then told to walk and was shot in the back "trying to escape." Luxemburg was shot in a police car and her body dumped into a river. At the time of her death Rosa Luxemburg was a small, forty-eight-year-old, Jewish woman who walked with a limp. She also was an intellectual powerhouse. She had spent her adult life working for a better world for workers. She believed they were the revolutionary class, and she hoped for international revolution. Socialism, she believed, would bring true equality of people and nations and usher in a new peaceful era with no pogroms, no wars, and no prejudice.

Sources:

Richard Abraham, *Rosa Luxemburg: A Life for the International* (Oxford & New York: Berg, 1989).

Mathilde Jacob, *Rosa Luxemburg: An Intimate Portrait,* translated by Hans Fernbach (London: Lawrence & Wishart, 2000).

Donald E. Shepardson, *Rosa Luxemburg and the Noble Dream* (New York: Peter Lang, 1996).

LADY CONSTANCE GEORGINA LYTTON

1869-1923
SUFFRAGETTE

Aristocratic Background. Lady Constance Georgina Lytton's father was the first earl of Lytton and the queen's viceroy, or ruling representative, of India. She spent most of her childhood in India and then returned to England with her parents. After her father's death, her mother was appointed a lady-in-waiting to Queen Victoria. Her brother, the second earl of Lytton, was a Conservative member of the House of Lords and, like his sister, a supporter of the women's suffrage movement. In 1908 Lytton met Emmeline Pethick-Lawrence and Annie Kenney, two of the leaders of the Women's Social and Political Union (WSPU), a militant suffrage organization. The meeting changed her life. The suffrage movement already appealed to Lytton because of its cross-class alliances. Through the WSPU she found a way to channel that interest and to escape from a life of domestic and charitable caretaking. In her devotion to the militant suffrage movement, she followed, perhaps, in the footsteps of her paternal great-grandmother Anna Wheeler, an early-nineteenth-century feminist and a supporter of the working class.

Demanding the Vote. On 14 January 1910 Lytton disguised herself as a working-class seamstress, assumed the name Jane Warton, and led a suffrage demonstration demanding the vote for women. During the demonstration she hurled a rock wrapped in brown paper at the house of the governor of Walton Gaol. For this act, she was arrested, tried, and sentenced to fourteen days in jail. Like many suffragettes, she refused to eat while in custody and was forcibly fed, which involved forcing the mouth open, running a tube down the throat or through the nose, and pouring liquid into it. The procedure was both painful and dangerous. Lytton's decision to conceal her upper-class identity was a deliberately calculated act. She was devoted to the cause of female suffrage and was appalled at the class-differentiated treatment women (regardless of their offence) received in jail. In February 1909 she had engaged in a suffrage demonstration without, however, disguising her identity as a member of the nobility. She was arrested and incarcerated, but knowing who she was and that she had a heart condition, the prison officials treated her gently. She was placed in the prison's hospital ward and given extra food. Opposed to such favorable treatment while her colleagues of other social classes were treated more harshly, she demanded repeatedly to be allowed to join the other prisoners in their cells. The officials refused, and when Lytton engaged in a hunger strike the prison officials simply released her from jail rather than forcibly feeding her. Later that year she was again arrested and released when she went on a hunger strike. Lytton knew she had been given preferential treatment because of her high social standing and was determined to prove it. Thus disguised as Warton, her weak heart was not discovered, and she was forcibly fed eight times before her failing health and reports of her true identity prompted the officials to release her.

A Stroke and Victory. Lytton continued her suffrage activities until 1912, when she suffered a stroke from which she never fully recovered. She taught herself to write with her left hand and wrote a gripping account of her prison experiences in *Prisons and Prisoners: Some Personal Experiences by Constance Lytton and Jane Warton, Spinster* (1914). Her personal commitment to universal political rights and her book made her a revered and charismatic figure in the British women's suffrage movement. Women over the age of thirty in Great Britain ultimately gained the right to vote in 1918, and ten years later the age was lowered to what it had been for men, twenty-one. British women's right to vote was won largely as a result of the actions by suffragettes such as Lytton.

Sources:

Betty Balfour, ed., *Selected Letters of Constance Lytton* (London: Heinemann, 1925).

Elizabeth Crawford, *The Women's Suffrage Movement: A Reference Guide, 1866–1928* (London: UCL Press, 1999).

Constance Lytton, *Prisons and Prisoners: Some Personal Experiences by Constance Lytton and Jane Warton, Spinster* (London: Heinemann, 1914).

Marie Mulvey-Roberts, "Militancy, Masochism or Martyrdom? The Public and Private Prisons of Constance Lytton," in *Votes for Women*, edited by June Purvis and Sandra Stanley Holton (London & New York: Routledge, 2000), pp. 159–180.

HENRY MAYHEW

1812-1887
JOURNALIST

Early Years. Henry Mayhew was born in London. His father was an attorney, but Mayhew had no desire to follow suit. Indeed, his rejection of a bourgeois lifestyle and values was in large part a rejection of his father, who punished him for running away from school when he was fifteen by sending him to sea for a year. When he was in his twenties and thirties he participated in a literate and intellectual bohemian culture—writing plays, biographies, novels, and travel books. He was one of the founding members and joint editor of the satirical magazine *Punch* and in 1849 joined the staff of the left-leaning *Morning Chronicle*. What drew Mayhew to the lower classes is unclear, but by 1849 he had developed a flair for social investigation and vivid writing and began work on the book that made him famous.

Tales of the Down-and-Out. Mayhew traveled the streets and alleys of London in the 1840s, recording the tales of the down-and-out and the myriad ways they found to earn money. Children and adults, men and women, the able-bodied and the crippled sold everything from nutmeg graters and funnels to dogs, bird's nests, pea soup, and cooked eels. They swept streets and sang songs, hoping for a few pennies from passersby. They worked on the docks, loading and unloading ships, collecting old clothing, and catching rats.

Queen's Rat Catcher. It is not known if Mayhew took notes, but he had a knack for recounting people's stories in what appear to be their own words. In one memorable interview, Mr. "Jack" Black, who advertised himself as the queen's rat catcher, took Mayhew home with him, showed him the tools of his trade, and told him the dangers of rat catching. "I've been bitten nearly everywhere," Black reported, "even where I can't name to you, sir, and right through my thumb nail too, which, as you can see, always has a split in it though it's years since I was wounded. I suffered as much from that bite on my thumb as anything. It went right up to my ear. I felt the pain in both places at once . . . but the worst of it was, I had a job at Camden town one afternoon . . . and I got another bite lower down on the same thumb, and that flung me down on my bed, and there I stopped, I should think, six weeks."

London Labour & the London Poor. Mayhew's purpose in writing *London Labour & the London Poor* (1851) was not simply to tell stories, although he was good at that. His goal was reform, which he hoped to achieve by making the truly desperate, as well as the merely poor, visible to the reading public. Crowded into the alleys of London, his subjects lived lives that were virtually unaffected by industrialization. Far from working with machines, they swept up after horses, sang songs on the street, and hoped the middle class would give them a few pennies for their efforts. Believing the city needed to employ more street cleaners, Mayhew even included information on the amount of food horses consumed and the amount they excreted in a twenty-four-hour period. Published in two volumes, his personal account of what he saw and heard has made gripping reading for a century and a half. Just how many people read *London Labour & the London Poor* is not known, but the book was popular enough to be reissued in 1861, 1862, 1864, and 1865 with additional material and supplementary volumes. In the twentieth century additional editions appeared. In *The Unknown Mayhew: Selections from the Morning Chronicle, 1849–1850* (1971), E. P. Thompson, the foremost British labor historian of the twentieth century, considered Mayhew's study to be "the most impressive survey of labour and of poverty at the mid-[nineteenth-]century which exists."

Sources:
Henry Mayhew, *London Labour & the London Poor: A Cyclopaedia of the Condition and Earnings of Those That Will Work, Those That Cannot Work, and Those That Will Not Work* (London: Griffin, Bohn, 1851).

Mayhew, *Mayhew's London: Being Selections from "London Labour & the London Poor,"* edited by P. Quennell (London: Spring Books, 1949).

E. P. Thompson and Eileen Yeo, eds., *The Unknown Mayhew: Selections from the Morning Chronicle, 1849–1850* (London: Merlin, 1971).

FLORA TRISTAN

1803-1844
REFORMER AND FEMINIST

Difficult Beginnings. Flora Tristan (the pen name of Flore-Celestine-Therèse-Henriette Tristan-Moscoso) was born in France to a French mother and a Spanish Peruvian father. As a child she knew the young Simón Bolívar, who became a leader of the Peruvian independence movement. When Tristan's father died in 1807, France was at war with Spain. He left no will; the marriage documents had been left in Spain and were never found; and his family refused to recognize the marriage and inheritance rights of Tristan and her mother. Now impoverished, Madame Tristan, Flora, and Flora's brother lived a life far removed from the one Flora had known. Her attempt to escape poverty by marriage failed, and she set out to try to recover her inheritance by traveling to Peru to meet her father's family. She failed to win her inheritance, but she recorded her travels in a two-volume autobiography called *Peregrinations of a Pariah* (1838). Tristan's social attitudes and activities reflected her sense of personal loss (her secure childhood) and her immersion in the social critiques of capitalism that were occurring during her era. Part of her quest was personal—she believed women as well as men should have personal freedom—and part was political. She observed the workers' daily struggles to survive and honed an individual critique of the class struggle and capitalism.

Reformer. Pursuing a career as a writer, Tristan proposed prison reform and equal treatment of women and men, analyzed the origins of prostitution, criticized the lives of bourgeois married women, and proposed an international organization of workers that would improve working and living conditions and ward off more violent revolution. She also became interested in the utopian socialists for their social critique and their feminism.

Remarkable Life. Tristan lived a short but remarkable life. She traveled extensively, alone, including a trip across the Atlantic Ocean on a ship on which she was the only woman, a rather remarkable feat. She was a feminist, an advocate of the poor, and an early labor organizer. She married disastrously, had three children, and then left her husband (divorce was not allowed in France at this time). He stalked and pursued her, attempted to win custody of the children, and finally shot her in 1838. She survived, despite a bullet lodged in her chest, and continued her traveling and writing. Tristan referred to herself as a pariah. One might be more likely to call her a rebel. She was a woman who tried to earn her own living; who acted independently despite the legal and social barriers to female independence; who abandoned her husband; and who thought intelligently about social and political affairs. On a tour of France to promote her ideas about the ideal society, she fell ill (probably with typhoid fever) and died. She was only forty-one years old. The hearse that took her to her grave was followed by a procession of literary figures and workers.

Sources:

Doris Beik and Paul Beik, eds. and trans., *Flora Tristan, Utopian Feminist: Her Travel Diaries and Personal Crusade* (Bloomington: Indiana University Press, 1993).

Maire Cross and Tim Gray, *The Feminism of Flora Tristan* (Oxford & Providence, R.I.: Berg, 1992).

Dominique Desanti, *A Woman in Revolt: A Biography of Flora Tristan*, translated by Elizabeth Zelvin (New York: Crown, 1976).

DOCUMENTARY SOURCES

Isabella Beeton, *The Book of Household Management* (1861)—Includes sections on how to be a good house mistress and how to manage servants.

Edwin Chadwick, *Report on an Enquiry into the Sanitary Condition of the Labouring Population of Great Britain* (1842)—A groundbreaking investigation into health conditions in the factories and cities.

Friedrich Engels, *The Condition of the Working Class in England* (1845)—Written during the German socialist's stay in the manufacturing center of Manchester. It examines the social consequences of industrial capitalism.

James Kay-Shuttleworth, *The Moral and Physical Condition of the Working Classes of Manchester* (1832)—An influential exposé of conditions in British factories by a progressive medical doctor, which led to sanitation improvements in this industrial city.

Rosa Luxemburg, *The Mass Strike, the Political Party, and the Trade Unions* (1906)—The author argued for a general strike of workers to initiate a socialist revolution.

Constance Lytton, *Prisons and Prisoners: Some Personal Experiences by Constance Lytton and Jane Warton, Spinster* (1914)—An autobiographical account of the author's experiences during the fight for female suffrage in England.

Karl Marx and Engels, *The Communist Manifesto* (1848)—A call for socialist revolution.

Henry Mayhew, *London Labour & the London Poor: A Cyclopaedia of the Condition and Earnings of Those That Will Work, Those That Cannot Work, and Those That Will Not Work* (1851)—An investigative masterpiece delving into the daily lives of the poor who lived in the streets of London.

Robert Owen, *A New View of Society* (1813)—A utopian socialist's concept of how life should be lived, based on his concept that environment played an important role.

Report of the Commissioners on the Employment of Children in Factories (1833)—An official government inquiry into child labor in British factories.

David Ricardo, *Principles of Political Economy and Taxation* (1817)—A comprehensive exposition of this English economist's views on economic policies, including his "iron law of wages," which argues that a larger pool of workers lowers wages.

Samuel Smiles, *Self-Help: With Illustrations of Character and Conduct* (1860)—A work promoting industry, thrift, and self-improvement written by a medical doctor, who had supported Chartism and parliamentary reform but was disillusioned.

Adam Smith, *Inquiry into the Nature and Causes of the Wealth of Nations* (1776)—Advocated economic individualism, less government participation in economic affairs, a self-regulating economy, and an end to mercantilism.

Robert Southey, *Letters from England* (1807)—An autobiographical work by the English poet, which included his observations of child labor in the factories.

CHAPTER SIX

POLITICS, LAW, AND THE MILITARY

by MICHAEL ARADAS

CONTENTS

Sidebars and tables are listed in italics.

1756

- The Seven Years' War breaks out between Prussia and Austria, France, Sweden, Russia, and several small German principalities. The conflict quickly escalates into a colonial war between Great Britain and France in North America, India, and the Caribbean.

1757

- Robert-François Damiens is tortured and executed for the attempted assassination of Louis XV.

- A British force defeats a French army in India at the Battle of Plassey, opening the way for the eventual control of all of the region by the East India Company.

1759

- The city of Quebec falls to the British.

1761

- François-Marie Arouet (more popularly known as Voltaire) becomes the defense attorney of Jean Calas, a French Protestant accused of murdering his son in order to prevent his marriage to a Catholic woman. Although Calas is found guilty and executed, Voltaire uncovers enough evidence to overturn the conviction in 1764.

1762

- Tsarina Elizabeth of Russia dies. The new tsar, Peter III, is an ardent admirer of Frederick II and disengages Russia from the Austro-French coalition before he is deposed by his wife, Catherine II (the Great). The Russian defection forces France and Austria to the peace table by the end of the year.

- The British capture Havana, Cuba, and Manila, the Philippines, from the Spanish.

1763

- The Treaty of Hubertusburg ends the Seven Years' War in Europe without any significant changes in prewar boundaries on the Continent. Meanwhile, the Treaty of Paris ends the fighting between Britain and France, and the British obtain Canada, Senegal, Florida, and the West Indian island of Grenada; France cedes Louisiana to Spain.

1768

- The Russo-Turkish War begins; it ends in 1774 with Russia gaining a foothold on the coast of the Black Sea.

1772

- Austria, Prussia, and Russia conduct the First Partition of Poland. In 1793 the Second Partition occurs, and by the Third Partition in 1795, Poland ceases to exist as a state.

1775

- The American War of Independence begins; efforts on behalf of the American colonists, especially their naval building program, eventually bankrupt the French state.

* Denotes Circa Date

1780
- Russia, Denmark, and Sweden form the League of Armed Neutrality to thwart British aggression on the high seas.

1781
- French minister of finance Jacques Necker publishes *Compte Rendu,* a record of governmental accounts.

1787
- The French Assembly of Notables refuses to accept taxation reform.

1788
- Whig politicians begin to challenge the "rotten borough" (an election district that has fewer inhabitants than other election districts with the same voting power) system in the British Parliament.
- The British establish a penal colony at Port Jackson in New South Wales (present-day Sydney, Australia).

1789
- A French mob storms the Bastille, and the French Revolution begins.

1790
- British statesman Edmund Burke writes *Reflections on the Revolution in France,* a conservative denunciation of the French Revolution.

1791
- Louis XVI attempts to flee France rather than participate in a constitutional monarchy.

1792
- French Revolutionary forces defeat an invading Austrian-Prussian army at Valmy.

1793
- The Reign of Terror under the dictatorship of the Committee of Public Safety begins in France. Louis XVI is executed, and by the next year approximately twenty-eight thousand people are killed by the guillotine for alleged treason.

1795
- The five-person Directory becomes the executive body of the French government.

1799
- General Napoleon Bonaparte, a Corsican by birth, takes control of the French government by becoming First Consul.

* DENOTES CIRCA DATE

1800
- The Bank of France is created in Paris.

1802
- France and Britain sign the Peace of Amiens; warfare starts again the next year.

1804
- Napoleon crowns himself emperor. He also begins reforming and codifying French law (Code Napoleon).

1805
- The Royal Navy defeats a combined Franco-Spanish fleet at Trafalgar, marking the beginning of 140 years of British naval dominance.
- Napoleon wins the Battle of Austerlitz, and the Russians and Austrians sue for peace.

1806
- The Prussians are defeated by Napoleon at the battles of Jena and Auerstadt.
- Napoleon establishes the Continental System, prohibiting all trade with Britain.

1807
- Napoleon and Tsar Alexander I sign the Treaty of Tilsit, and Russia joins the Continental System.

1810
- Russia withdraws from the Continental System and resumes relations with Britain.

1812
- The French invade Russia. Although Napoleon captures Moscow, he is forced to retreat by the severe Russian winter.

1813
- Napoleon is defeated by a combined army of Austrians, Prussians, Russians, and British at Leipzig; the next year he abdicates and goes into exile on the small Mediterranean island of Elba.

1815
- Napoleon returns from Elba, but he is defeated at Waterloo, and the Napoleonic Wars end. He is exiled again, but this time to the remote South Atlantic island of St. Helena. The Congress of Vienna provides a flexible means of ensuring peace in Europe for the next ninety-nine years.

1821
- Greece begins a revolt against the Ottoman Empire.

* DENOTES CIRCA DATE

1825
- The Decembrist Uprising, led by reformers dedicated to constitutional monarchy and the abolition of serfdom, is brutally suppressed in Russia.

1827
- Britain, France, and Russia sign the Treaty of London, pledging to aid Greece. A combined fleet then destroys a Turkish-Egyptian navy at Navarino Bay.

1829
- The Treaty of Adrianople is signed, and Greece officially wins its independence the next year.

1830
- French king Charles X issues four reactionary ordinances restricting freedom of the press, dissolving the Chamber of Deputies, calling for new elections, and limiting the franchise to the wealthiest people. These decrees provoke the July Revolution in which Charles X abdicates and Louis Philippe, Duke of Orleans, is crowned king.

1831
- Belgium declares its independence from the Netherlands.

1832
- The Reform Bill in Great Britain is the first recognition in British political life of the changes wrought on society by the Industrial Revolution. This statute extends suffrage and redistributes seats in Parliament to conform with the growth of population in the new industrial centers.

1834
- Prussian-sponsored *Zollverein* (customs unions) are introduced across Germany.

1836
- Johann Nikolaus von Dreyse invents the breech-loading Needle Gun, so named because of its long, sharp firing pin; it is adapted by the Prussian army in 1841.

1838
- The Chartist Movement (named for the "People's Charter") begins in Great Britain, calling for universal manhood suffrage, vote by secret ballot, annual Parliaments, equal electoral districts, removal of property qualifications for elected officials, and salary payment of members of Parliament.
- Attempts begin in Britain to repeal the Corn Laws. These statutes, passed in 1815 and 1828, are meant to help farmers by imposing a sliding tariff on imported wheat. The Corn Laws are finally repealed in 1846.

* DENOTES CIRCA DATE

1848
- A series of liberal and nationalistic revolutions occur throughout Europe. In France the February Revolution ousts Louis Philippe and the Second Republic is founded; Louis Napoleon, a nephew of Napoleon I, is elected president. Meanwhile, in Germany the Frankfurt Parliament offers the German crown to Frederick William IV of Prussia. He rejects the offer, as he is opposed to constitutionalism and a limited monarchy.

1851
- Louis Napoleon gains the support of the army and populace to revise the Constitution in order to save the French Republic. He lengthens the presidential term to ten years.

1852
- Louis Napoleon becomes Napoleon III, Emperor of France, "by the grace of God and the will of the nation."
- The French government begins deporting convicts to the penal colony of Devil's Island, off the northern coast of French Guiana. By the time the colony is abolished in 1938, more than seventy thousand criminals had been imprisoned there.

1853
- The Crimean War begins when Russia seizes two provinces (Moldavia and Walachia) belonging to the Ottoman Empire. Fearing Russian expansion in the eastern Mediterranean, Britain and France enter the conflict on the side of the Ottoman Turks. The war ends three years later with the Russians relinquishing control of the contested areas. The image of Russian strength, in place since the end of the Napoleonic Wars, is now shattered.

1859
- The Austro-Sardinian War occurs. The Sardinians receive French military assistance and defeat the Austrians at Magenta and Solferino.

1860
- Otto von Bismarck is appointed chief minister in Prussia.
- The northern Italian states of Tuscany, Parma, and Modena overthrow Austrian rule and ally themselves with Sardinia.
- Meanwhile, Giuseppe Garibaldi leads an expedition to the Kingdom of the Two Sicilies and gains control of the island after three months.

1861
- Victor Emmanuel II of Sardinia-Piedmont becomes king of Italy; all of the Italian peninsula except for Venetia (still under Austria) and Rome (the last remnant of the Papal States) is united.
- The serfs are emancipated in Russia.
- The French begin a six-year military intervention in Mexico.

* DENOTES CIRCA DATE

1866
- The Seven Weeks' War, or the Austro-Prussian War, occurs and results in a Prussian victory. Prussia is now the dominant force among the German states.
- Italy annexes Venetia.
- Swedish manufacturer and philanthropist Alfred Nobel invents dynamite.

1870
- The Franco-Prussian War begins. By the next year Prussia is victorious, and the German Empire is created.

1871
- Rome is annexed to the Kingdom of Italy.

1872
- The first penal codes are published in Germany.

1873
- The League of the Three Emperors is established by Bismarck; Germany, Austria-Hungary, and Russia pledge strict mutual neutrality in time of war.

1875
- Britain acquires control of the Suez Canal in the Near East.

1877
- Another Russo-Turkish war begins. In the Treaty of San Stefano signed the next year, the Slavic states in the Balkans are freed of Ottoman rule, and Russia receives territory and a large monetary indemnity.

1878
- Because the British and Austrians fear Russian supremacy in the Near East, the Congress of Berlin is held to revise the Treaty of San Stefano. Russia obtains Bessarabia and parts of Armenia; Austria-Hungary acquires Bosnia-Herzegovina; and Britain occupies Cyprus. The independence of Serbia, Montenegro, and Romania is recognized.

1881
- Tsar Alexander II of Russia is assassinated by the People's Will, a group of revolutionaries and terrorists.

1882
- The Triple Alliance is formed by Germany, Austria-Hungary, and Italy.

1884
- The machine gun is perfected by Hiram Maxim, an American inventor living in England.

* DENOTES CIRCA DATE

1890

- Bismarck is dismissed from office by the new German emperor Wilhelm II. In the same year Wilhelm II allows German membership in the League of the Three Emperors to lapse.

1898

- The Spanish-American War results in a defeat for Spain, which is forced to relinquish control of Cuba and the Philippines.

1899

- The Boer War begins; by 1902 the British crush the rebellion of South African farmers.

- Representatives of twenty-six countries meet at The Hague in the Netherlands to discuss the curtailment of armaments. Although no agreement is reached on this issue, the First Hague Conference does establish an international tribunal for the arbitration of disputes and the codification of the laws of war. A second conference (attended by delegates from forty-four nations) in 1907 adopts humane restrictions on war practices.

1904

- The Entente Cordiale is formed between France and Britain.

- The Russo-Japanese War begins; within one year Russia is defeated and withdraws from the Liao-tung Peninsula and Manchuria.

1905

- Confronting mounting political discontent and labor unrest, Russian tsar Nicholas II issues a manifesto guaranteeing individual rights and providing for the election of a duma, or representative assembly.

- In order to test the bounds of the new Entente Cordiale, German emperor Wilhelm II makes a speech supporting the independence of Morocco (a French colony).

1906

- The Conference of Algeciras ends the First Moroccan Crisis by confirming French control of the North African colony.

- The HMS *Dreadnought*, the first turbine-powered, big-gun warship, is launched. This type of war vessel dominates the world's navies for the next thirty-five years and accelerates a naval arms race between Great Britain and Germany.

1907

- An Anglo-German naval arms race and British concern over German ambitions in the Near East provoke the British to form the Triple Entente with the French and the Russians.

1908

- Austria-Hungary officially annexes Bosnia-Herzegovina.

1914

* DENOTES CIRCA DATE

- Archduke Franz Ferdinand, heir to the throne of Austria-Hungary, is assassinated by a Bosnian nationalist in Sarajevo; World War I begins.

OVERVIEW

Monarchies. In 1750 all the major states of Europe except Great Britain were headed by monarchies in which one man theoretically held absolute authority. Over the course of the eighteenth, nineteenth, and early twentieth centuries all of these monarchies would face serious challenges to their power. Ultimately, most of these challenges were the result of the Industrial Revolution's impact upon European society. Despite the presence of royal families at the head of the governments of the most powerful states of Europe, there was considerable variation among European monarchies.

Absolutism. France is the classic example of royal absolutism in theory and practice. Here the king theoretically held all the political power in the kingdom. He promulgated laws and conducted foreign policy by the grace of God and without the consent of his subjects. His administration and officials existed merely to carry out his will. In practice the king's power was limited—to rule he needed many large, loyal government institutions. Kings purchased the loyalty of their wealthy subjects through the sale of offices and titles of nobility that the elite coveted. The king was frequently forced to negotiate deals with local magnates when royal and local interests came at loggerheads. The Bourbon regime in France remained remarkably stable through the seventeenth and well into the eighteenth century; however, the cumulative effect in the 1780s on the French economy of over one hundred years of French military aggression in Europe was bankruptcy. In the ensuing crisis the French monarchy was destroyed by a rising wave of increasingly radical republicanism. Monarchy returned to France after the defeat and exile of Napoleon I in 1815. The restoration Bourbons and the July Monarch Louis Philippe were, however, painfully aware of the fate of their predecessor Louis XVI, who was executed during the French Revolution. This awareness provoked a bitterly antirepublican reaction from the early-nineteenth-century French kings Louis XVIII and Charles X. Such aggressive royalism only polarized French politics and led directly to revolutions in 1830 and 1848, the last of which swept monarchy from France for good.

Constitutional Monarchy. In a constitutional monarchy the king's power was shared with a representative institution. In Great Britain, the best example of a constitutional monarchy, the crown and Parliament ruled together, though by the mid eighteenth century much of the crown's authority in matters of domestic and foreign policy had eroded. By the late eighteenth and early nineteenth centuries British kings and queens, such as the mentally unstable George III, were essentially figureheads. Great Britain acquired a huge world empire during the eighteenth and nineteenth centuries. By 1900 it included the British Isles (Scotland, Ireland, England, and Wales), India, Burma, Australia, South Africa, Canada, the Bahamas, the Falklands, Egypt, Hong Kong, Singapore, Gibraltar, and Guiana. The struggle against Napoleon I spurred the Industrial Revolution in England. The social repercussions of this revolution bred challenges to the traditional parliamentary election process from newly wealthy industrialists.

Enlightened Despotism. The kingdom of Prussia grew slowly from the 1750s until German unification in 1871. Eighteenth-century, Enlightenment-influenced autocrats, such as Frederick II (Frederick the Great), exercised judicious leadership in government and developed a highly centralized and efficient administration. After the Franco-Prussian War in 1870 the independent states of Germany—Wurtemburg, Bavaria, and Saxony, for example—voluntarily joined an imperial German union under Prussian aegis. In Russia autocratic despotism remained the norm in government until the Revolution of 1917.

Administration. Government administration through the eighteenth and nineteenth centuries was marked by a considerable rise in professionalism. Virtually all government officials were literate and, especially during the later nineteenth century, were university educated. The bulk of these men were still drawn from the aristocracy, the traditional leaders in society. Nonaristocrats, however, were occasionally appointed to important positions (for example, Jacques Necker, the finance minister of France in the 1780s). Large, bureaucratic institutions became the governmental norm across Europe. As the nineteenth century progressed, the officials who staffed these bureaucracies increasingly drew their livelihood from their government stipends rather than from their personal wealth.

Government Institutions. The growth of republican or representative institutions was a key characteristic of European government through the eighteenth and nineteenth centuries. Great Britain's Parliament had existed since the Middle Ages, but during the eighteenth and nineteenth centuries it gradually expanded to reflect new sources of political power and wealth. In France representative institutions were underdeveloped (before 1788 the Estates General had not been called since 1614). During the French Revolution, France was governed by a series of rather chaotic, if patriotic, assemblies. In both Great Britain and France property qualifications determined one's eligibility to serve in these assemblies and to vote for those who did. Russian government was divided into colleges (for example, war and foreign affairs), which were staffed by boyars (nobles). Prussian kings utilized the talents and loyalty of their nobles (called junkers) and wealthy burgers to create a series of efficient bureaucracies across the state.

Changes in Warfare. From 1750 to 1850 artillery and musket-armed infantry dominated the battlefields of Europe. The development of the *levée en masse,* large numbers of militarily conscripted foot soldiers, during the French Revolution dramatically increased the size of European armies. Increased government spending on military infrastructure, barracks, ports, and supply depots, for example, created a permanency in the military that had not existed previously. Starting in the 1850s new technologies that were developed during the Industrial Revolution transformed warfare profoundly. The mass-produced repeating rifle, which first made its presence felt during the American Civil War (1861–1865), became the standard infantry weapon. Its effective range far exceeded that of the musket, and, perhaps more important, it could be loaded and fired rapidly from a prone or kneeling position. The use of premade cartridges, in which gunpowder, wadding, and shot were all encased in a single shell, further sped up the firing process. Perhaps no weapon better typified these huge increases in infantry firepower than the machine gun. Capable of spewing hundreds of rounds per minute over a large area, the machine gun quickly became the infantry's weapon of choice. The development of stable chemical explosives in the 1860s such as TNT and cordite allowed artillery to pack far more punch then the cannons of the early nineteenth century. As infantry and artillery weapons increased in power and railroads provided dramatically improved mobility for troop supply and deployment, the military usefulness of cavalry declined until, by 1870, it served principally a scouting role. Fortresses also became less important—it was nearly impossible to build a fort, even out of concrete, that could withstand the new artillery.

Naval Warfare. New Industrial Revolution technologies also changed the nature of war at sea. Until the 1850s wooden-hulled, square-rigged ships with smoothbore, bronze cannons patrolled the seas. No country produced a better navy than Great Britain. The Royal Navy's destruction of the Franco-Spanish fleet at Trafalgar (1805) inaugurated 140 years of British naval dominance. The development of steel-hulled, steam-powered ships (such as the American "ironclads" CSS *Virginia* and the USS *Monitor* that appeared during the Civil War), however, made the frigates and ships of the line of the days of Trafalgar obsolete. To puncture the new steel hulls, warships had to be equipped with rifled artillery that fired shells filled with chemical explosives. Again, Great Britain led the European states in naval development: the first modern battleship, the HMS *Dreadnought* was launched by Britain in 1906. It was the first ocean-going, all-steel, steam-powered, propeller-driven warship. Furthermore, for firepower it relied solely on eight mammoth eleven-inch guns. The guns were situated in four rotating armored turrets that protected the gun crews and allowed the ship to fire in a wider variety of directions. German construction of ships based on the *Dreadnought* design contributed significantly to Great Britain's decision to join France and Russia in a defensive pact against Germany in 1913.

Crime and Punishment. Criminal-law codes in Europe through the nineteenth century were generally written to protect the elite and their property. Laws in Great Britain, for example, forbade poaching and trespassing. These laws could be quite harsh—violation of any of the laws of the Black Act (1723–1823), which covered poaching, for example, brought a death sentence. Secular courts, such as the assizes in Great Britain and the *parlements* in France, determined the guilt or innocence of accused criminals. Trials made increasing use of witnesses and evidence. Police forces emerged as the principle tools by which the state apprehended criminals. As these forces grew in size and capability, the number of criminals they caught also increased. By the mid nineteenth century the success of the police forces in France and Great Britain virtually eliminated the need for public executions, which prior to this time had served as frightful deterrents to crime. Further, hangings and decapitations gradually gave way to imprisonment and reform under the influence of the Enlightenment and nineteenth-century social liberalism.

TOPICS IN POLITICS, LAW, AND THE MILITARY

ADMINISTRATION: FORMS OF GOVERNMENT

Kings and Queens. Monarchy, in which a single person possesses complete authority over a state and claims that authority by the grace of God, was the accepted form of government in most nations of Europe in the mid eighteenth century. On the monarch's death the crown was passed to an anointed heir, usually the eldest son. In some states, such as Great Britain and Russia, the sex of the heir was not a great issue; queens could rule as well as kings. In other states, France for instance, women were not allowed to reign as queens in their own right. Because all state power was technically vested in the hands of a single person, the personality, intelligence, mental stability, and character of a monarch were of paramount importance. Strong monarchs gave their administrations a sense of confidence and direction while weak monarchs did not.

France and the Old Regime. During the early modern period French absolutism worked reasonably efficiently because strong kings such as Henry IV (1589–1610) and Louis XIV (1643–1715) governed France with attentive leadership. This was not the case, however, in the later eighteenth and nineteenth centuries. Neither Louis XV (1715–1774) nor Louis XVI (1774–1792) was particularly interested in nor adept at solving the problems the French state faced and left the actual governing of France to an increasingly professional corps of ministers. Louis XV rev-

The King is Dead, a popular late-eighteenth-century print by an unknown artist of Louis XVI's execution (Bibliothèque Nationale, Paris)

WHAT IS THE THIRD ESTATE?

In the Abbé Emmanuel-Joseph Sieyès's famous declaration one can see something of the fascination the French patriots had with English representative government, and how those ideas guided the initial phases of the French Revolution.

What is a nation? A body of associates, living under a common law, and represented by the same legislature, etc.

Is it not evident that the noble order has privileges and expenditures which it dares to call its rights, but which are apart from the rights of the great body of citizens? It departs there from the common law. So its civil rights make of it an isolated people in the midst of the great nation. This is truly *imperium in imperia*. In regard to its political rights, these also it exercises apart. It has its special representatives, which are not charged with securing the interests of the people. The body of its deputies sit apart; and when it is assembled in the same hall with the deputies of simple citizens, it is none the less true that its representation is essentially distinct and separate: it is a stranger to the nation, in the first place, by its origin, since its commission is not derived from the people; then by its object, which consists of defending not the general, but the particular interest. The Third Estate embraces then all that which belongs to the nation; and all that which is not the Third Estate, cannot be regarded as being of the nation.

What is the Third Estate?

It is the whole.

Source: William H. Sewell, *A Rhetoric of Bourgeois Revolution: The Abbé Sieyès and What Is the Third Estate?* (Durham, N.C.: Duke University Press, 1994).

eled in hunting and all-night drinking parties, and Louis XVI was fascinated by the inner workings of clocks, but neither man paid much attention to governing France. This weak leadership eroded obedience to the crown across French society but most especially among the nobles and the leaders of the French *parlements* (law courts) on whom the king depended for help in governing France. French prestige fell with defeat at the hands of the English in the Seven Years' War (1756–1763). Especially galling was the loss of Canada and several sugar-producing islands in the Caribbean. By its victory Great Britain supplanted France as the preeminent power in Europe. Yet, France's victory over Great Britain in the American War of Independence (1775–1783) revived French prestige but so crippled the state economically that it was forced to default on many of its loans and eventually declare bankruptcy. Economic crises wracked the French government through the 1760s, 1770s, and 1780s, making it difficult to find a lender who did not view the crown as a bad credit risk. Several government officials, Chancellor Réne-Nicolas de Maupeou, for example, attempted to raise taxes or create permanent taxes on the nobility, who paid little if anything in taxes. These

policies were as unpopular with the peasantry, who had little money anyway, as they were with the nobility, who usually had money but did not want to spend it on taxes. Maupeou himself was dismissed in 1775. In 1781 the minister of finance, Jacques Necker, published a record of the government's accounts, titled the *Compte Rendu*, in an Enlightenment-influenced attempt to demonstrate the rationality of the crown's economic policy. The plan backfired, however. Instead of solid economic policy the *Compte Rendu*'s readers perceived a government that spent far more than it brought in. This serious financial crisis and lack of royal leadership provoked many French nobles and wealthy lawyers to demand that a constitutional monarchy be set up in France. In exchange they agreed to pay taxes.

French Revolution of 1789. The revolutionary assemblies that ruled France after 1789 were not any better at governing France then the Bourbon kings had been. The National Assembly (1789–1792) was France's first attempt at a constitutional monarchy. Its leaders, the Abbé Emmanuel-Joseph Sieyès and the marquis de Lafayette, for example, uprooted much of the governmental infrastructure of the Old Regime in an effort to create a truly new state. Privileges, such as tax exemption and separate legal status, were abolished, as was much of the Old Regime's administration. Louis XVI did not react well to the offer of constitutional monarchy. The National Assembly's constitution gave the king veto power over legislation created by the Assembly, but the veto could only suspend laws, not defeat them. Further, while the king still retained some control over foreign policy, the Assembly had to approve all of his measures. Troubled by the revolution's violence and deeply ambivalent about surrendering royal power to the masses, Louis XVI and his family attempted to flee France in June of 1791. Had his flight succeeded, Louis probably would have tried to rally support from the other monarchies of Europe for a counterrevolutionary invasion of France. Louis and his family were, however, recognized and apprehended outside the town of Varennes and were returned to Paris under armed guard. Any popular support for the king or the constitutional monarchy was dashed after his attempted flight. Louis XVI lived as a virtual prisoner in Paris until his execution in 1793.

French Revolutions of 1830 and 1848. Monarchy returned to France after the fall of Napoleon I in 1814. However, the kings of the Bourbon Restoration (Louis XVIII and Charles X) seemed to have learned little from the fate of their predecessors. Both kings had to deal with a representative bicameral legislature (a holdover from the revolution), but neither was able to reach an accord with it. Louis XVIII (1814–1824) understood that the liberal gains of 1789 could not be erased at once but failed to realize the popularity of Napoleon I's legacy. The execution of Napoleon I's former marshals provoked waves of unrest that culminated in the assassination of the archroyalist Duke de Berry (1820). Charles X (1824–1830), Berry's father, succeeded Louis XVIII as king and was even more reactionary then Louis. Arrests, executions of

Coronation of Wilhelm I as emperor of Germany; painting by Anton von Werner,
late nineteenth century (Bismarck Museum, Schonhausen)

suspected republicans, and the suppression of the press led to a great deal of antiroyalist sentiment in France. Charles responded by dissolving the legislature and abolishing the voting rights of the bourgeoisie. Charles abdicated in 1830, just before his government was overthrown by antiroyalist mobs. The July Revolution of 1830 brought Charles X's cousin Louis Philippe to the throne. The new king worked closely with his ministers to spur industrialization in France. In the process he helped make many bankers, entrepreneurs, and industrialists wealthy. High property requirements for voting rights alienated the monarchy from elements of the bourgeoisie and from the working class. The July Monarchy collapsed in February 1848 amid a series of riots orchestrated by republican-inspired tradesmen and workers in Paris. Surrounded by rioters in his Paris apartments, a frightened Louis Philippe abdicated his throne, perhaps hoping that one of his grandsons might be proclaimed king in his place. A coterie of liberal democrat and republican tradesmen and bankers in the nearby Chamber of Deputies, however, proclaimed instead the Second Republic (1848–1852).

Military Dictatorships. The revolutionary republican governments of 1793–1799 and 1848–1852 were neither centralized nor powerful enough to offer France clear and well-directed government. As a result of these chaotic situations, dictators who promised to rule fairly and justly in the name of the people could easily sway the French people. The Corsican Napoleon I rose through the ranks of the French republican army during the 1790s and saved the republican Directory in Paris from a royalist uprising in 1795. Military success in Italy against the Austrians made Napoleon a hero in France and allowed him to conduct foreign and military policy virtually without opposition. In 1799 he, his brother Lucien, and the Abbé Sieyès overthrew the Directory and established a dictatorship. In 1804 he had himself crowned emperor. His inspired leadership and military expertise allowed him to bring much of Europe under his rule; only his disastrous Russian campaign (1812) toppled him. After a brief exile on the Isle of Elba he returned to France in 1815 to a joyous welcome. Defeat at Waterloo (1815) brought him permanent exile on the island of St. Helena. Napoleon's military skill, leadership, and instincts toward sound government inspired among the French people a reverence for him that few, if any, historical characters could match. He not only won battles but also published a unified law code (the *Code Napoleon*), established the Bank of Paris, and fostered meritocracy in his administration and army. His almost mythic legacy was powerful and helped his nephew Louis Napoleon Bonaparte to become elected president of the second republic in 1848. Following in his uncle's footsteps, Louis Napoleon declared himself emperor (Napoleon III, 1852–1870) and ended the Second French Republic. Napoleon III, however, did not possess the martial skills of his uncle and was defeated in a disastrous war with Prussia. His capture at the Battle of Sedan (1870) effectively ended his reign and empire.

Nicholas I (1825–1855) directed an aggressive foreign policy that ultimately aimed at securing Russian control of the Turkish-held Dardanelles and the Bosporus. With this geostrategically important set of straits in his hands, Nicholas could send Russian warships and merchantmen into the Mediterranean Sea without opposition. To this end, in 1853, against the advice of most of his cabinet members, the tsar called for the Slavs and Orthodox Christians of the Balkans to rise up against the Turks. He also pledged to protect them if war came. The cabinet generally felt that these actions would provoke a war with Great Britain or France, who feared Russian power in the Mediterranean. Nicholas disagreed. When Wallachia and Moldavia revolted against the Turks, Nicholas sent Russian troops to aid them. Nicholas, however, underestimated the amount of furor his invasion would cause. Eager to protect its interest in India and the Mediterranean, Great Britain vigorously opposed Russia's Balkan advances by promising military aid to the Turks. Napoleon III, looking for a military victory to cement his regime's power, joined Great Britain. The allies selected the port city of Sevastopol on the Crimean Peninsula as the target of their military campaign. Nicholas I, realizing that he had overplayed his hand, withdrew from the Balkans and made offers of a negotiated peace. The allies ignored him and began an ill-planned and disastrously conducted war. The Anglo-French commanders assumed, for example, that the land bridge connecting the Crimea to southern Russia could be easily interdicted with naval gunfire. At its narrowest the strip of land is barely five miles wide. The allies, however, neglected to consult a sounding chart for the Black Sea. The water around the land bridge is extremely shallow for several miles into the Black Sea; it would not accommodate the allies' deep-draught ships. The allies only discovered this when their ships began to run aground in the littoral. By the war's end nearly six hundred thousand men would die on the Crimean Peninsula, though more than 80 percent of those deaths were due to disease. Nicholas's aggression cost Russia dearly at the peace table: the Black Sea became neutral; Wallachia and Moldavia became the independent country of Romania; and France and Britain guaranteed Turkey's independence. Nicholas I did not live to see the fruits of his work, however, as he died in 1855.

Sources: Florence Nightingale, *Letters from the Crimea, 1854–1856*, edited by Sue Goldie (New York: St. Martin's Press, 1997).

Trevor Royle, *Crimea: The Great Crimean War, 1854–1856* (New York: St. Martin's Press, 2000).

Absolutism in Spain. Spanish power collapsed after its defeat in the Thirty Years' War (1618–1648). The Spanish Empire that survived the war (and the loss of many parts of its world empire to the predations of English and Dutch privateers) was weak and decentralized. Only Castile was directly ruled by the crown; the principalities of Aragon, Catalonia, and Valencia, for example, had centuries-old constitutions that granted them a great deal of autonomy, especially over legal issues and tax collection. At the head of each of these regions was a *cortes* (court), which was run by the local nobility. The power of the Spanish nobility was too great and too entrenched for the economically and militarily exhausted crown to overcome in the sixteenth and seventeenth centuries. In the late seventeenth century, generations of Hapsburg inbreeding produced the succession of the sexually sterile and mentally deficient Charles II to the Spanish throne. Charles II was himself incapable of administering the government—in the power vacuum that followed his accession, political leadership fell to a series of noble-dominated royal councils that oversaw virtually all aspects of Spanish government. After the childless Charles II's death a general European war (the War of the Spanish Succession, 1701–1713) broke out to decide who would rule Spain. The Peace of Utrecht (1713) ended the war and placed the mentally unstable Phillip V, Louis XIV of France's grandson, on the Spanish throne.

Bourbon Monarchy. Though the Peace of Utrecht specified that the crowns of France and Spain were supposed to remain separate, the French government used its close relations with Philip V and Philip's own mental deficiencies to virtually control Spanish foreign policy through the eighteenth century. The ruthless predations of British privateers in Spain's New World colonies spurred a series of secret alliances between Spain and France, which were designed to protect Spain's empire. In this arrangement (known collectively as the Bourbon Family Compact), however, Spain was never so much France's ally as a useful instrument to be used against England. Disputes with England over trade, smuggling, and piracy in the New World led in 1739 to the short, but costly, War of Jenkins' Ear (1739–1740). With Philip V's death in 1740 and the ascension of Ferdinand VI some stability returned to the Spanish throne. Though Ferdinand VI himself was also subject to fits of insanity, he also realized that Spain needed peace if it were to rebuild its institutions and regenerate its economy. Ferdinand IV's tranquil reign ended in 1759 when he died without issue. His mentally stable half brother Charles III became king and continued the economic and political reforms Ferdinand had sponsored. By the 1770s the power of the Spanish grandees and their family councils was broken, and uniform tax and legal codes were in place across Spain. Despite the relatively rapid pace of royal reform it took at least a decade before these uniform codes truly became functioning parts of Spanish society. The Spanish monarchy worried that the chaos of the Revolution of 1789 in France might spill over into Spain and disrupt the fragile economic and social regeneration that had been taking place there since the reign of Ferdinand VI.

Tsar Nicholas II opening the first session of the First State Duma in the Winter Palace on 27 April 1906

Spain and the French Revolution. Charles IV, son and heir of Charles III, was genuinely terrified by the harsh treatment the French royal family had received from their own countrymen through 1793. The executions of Louis XIV and Marie Antoinette sent the king into fits of paranoia and rage. Charles IV and his ministers attempted to seal Spain off from all revolutionary ideas by imposing a statewide ban on the importation of all literature and newspapers from France. This isolation functioned well until Napoleon's coup d'état—Napoleon threatened invasion unless Spain consented to an alliance with France against Great Britain. Napoleon's callous use of Spain as a tool of French foreign policy, especially against British-allied Portugal, caused a great deal of enmity between France and Spain. To counter a British army, which had landed in Lisbon in 1808, Napoleon invaded Spain with one hundred thousand troops and headed for Portugal. Spanish protestations prompted him to overthrow the Spanish monarchy and install his brother Joseph as the new king. By 1808 anger at the harshness and brutality of the French occupation boiled over into a general Spanish uprising that succeeded in driving the French from Madrid. For the next five years the people of Spain worked together and kept up a damaging guerrilla war against the French army. Out of this grass-roots uprising grew modern Spanish nationalism; the effort against Napoleon required cooperation across class boundaries and fostered a palpable sense of national unity. With Napoleon's defeat and exile, Ferdinand VII, Charles IV's heir, was placed on the Spanish throne by the British army. The war against Napoleon, however, had changed the political complexion of Spain. In the absence of a king, the Spanish people had formed themselves into regionally elective juntas through which they ran the government. They would not accept an absolute monarch again without, at the least, constitutional guarantees against royal corruption. In 1812 a collective Grand Junta in Madrid promulgated a liberal constitution, which allowed for an elected unicameral assembly, freedom of the press, and a tightly controlled monarch. Ferdinand VII, however, declared the constitution illegal and systematically persecuted those responsible for it. In 1820 an uprising among disgruntled soldiers in Madrid spread quickly to the merchant class, and toppled Ferdinand. The newly restored French monarchy, nervous about the political instability in Spain, invaded and placed Ferdinand back on the throne. His restored government was even more repressive than his earlier one, and he faced two new problems: the Monroe Doctrine seriously eroded Spanish involvement in the Americas, and Ferdinand himself, married four times, was gravely ill and had no son to succeed him. Ferdinand's death in 1833 provoked a civil war between the rival claimants to his throne. Ferdinand's fourth wife Maria Cristina stood as regent for their infant daughter, Isabella II (reigned 1833–1838) against Ferdinand's brother Don Carlos. Don Carlos's insurgency was put down, but the regency's heavy-handed rule was marked by widespread corruption. Further, petty squabbles with regional administrations produced political paralysis in Madrid that rapidly became endemic and led to a serious loss of public confidence in the government. The locus of Spanish power began to migrate from the crown to the army, the only state institution not generally perceived as corrupt or failing.

Repressive Government. For the next ninety-eight years (1833–1931) Spain was ruled by a series of repressive army generals who themselves held political power largely as regents for young Spanish monarchs. Generals such as Baldomero Espartero, Leopoldo O'Donnell, Juan Prim y Prats, and Francisco Serrano y Dominguez generally removed the concept of popular sovereignty from government and eliminated such liberal reforms as freedom of the press, civil marriages, and jury trials. The generals did not offer much in the way of constructive domestic policy, and, abroad, wasted Spain's resources on desperate attempts to hold onto the shrinking world empire. The brutal repression of the 1896 uprising in Cuba by Spanish troops serves as an example of this type of policy, but it also underscored the problems Spain encountered in pursuing such a policy. The violent excesses of the Spanish troops concerned the United States, which immediately sent troops and ships to Cuba. The destruction of the battleship USS *Maine* in Havana harbor provoked a short, but bitter war between Spain and the United States in 1898. The Spanish-American War went badly for Spain, which was far outclassed militarily. In the ensuing peace Spain lost Cuba, Puerto Rico, and the Philippines, thus ending its four-hundred-year reign as a world power.

Constitutional Monarchy in Great Britain. By the mid to late 1700s government in Great Britain consisted of a king, whose power had decreased significantly since the sixteenth century, and Parliament. The king still appointed the prime minister, the leader of Parliament, and other cabinet ministers and could declare war or peace; however, he could only do these things with Parliament's cooperation and consent. Parliament was a bicameral legislature that oversaw virtually all aspects of British political life. Government was conducted by the prime minister in Parliament. Throughout the 1700s and the first half of the 1800s Parliament was dominated by a small clique of landowning nobles in Parliament's upper house, the House of Lords. Under their leadership Great Britain had defeated France twice (in 1763 and in 1815) but had been defeated by the French-supported American colonists in their bid for independence (1775–1783). Since the late eighteenth century, profiting from the Industrial Revolution, many wealthy industrialists and entrepreneurs sought entry into the government. They were consistently opposed by the aristocratic Parliament and the king. The 1830 Revolution in France alarmed many conservatives in England. Frightened that something similar could happen in Great Britain, Parliament passed a series of reforms under the guidance of Lord John Russell that became known as the First Reform Bill (1832). The bill apportioned 143 of the 200 "rotten borough" seats in Parliament to underrepresented urban districts and extended the voting franchise to men paying a certain annual rent. This event enlarged the voting populace by 50 percent. Seeing an ever more expanding voting franchise, the cabinet-maker William Lovett founded the London working men's association in 1836. Lovett referenced the Magna Carta of 1215 as the inspiration for his People's Charter, a petition to Parliament that demanded annual elections and universal manhood suffrage. The Chartist program was rejected by Parliament in 1838, and the Chartist movement fragmented into increasingly violent radical cells that the government crushed by force. The Chartists held their last meeting in 1848.

Enlightened Despotism in Prussia. Monarchs, such as Frederick II (the Great), led the Prussian government through the eighteenth century. They were ably assisted by a multitude of loyal officials who generally placed efficiency above personal ambition. Though it was able to seize Silesia from Austria in the 1740s, Prussia was a small, resource-poor state that depended upon alliances with larger powers, Great Britain for example, for its survival. Napoleon I crushed Prussia in the battles of Jena and Auerstadt in 1806; these disastrous events

so discredited enlightened despotism in Prussia that King Frederick William III (1770–1840) was forced to abolish serfdom and remove class barriers to the military in order to regain the throne after Napoleon I's demise. The Revolutions of 1830 and 1848 in France touched off waves of unrest among students and workers across Germany, including Prussia. However, as Germany (unlike France and Britain) had no tradition of political liberty, it was difficult for republicanism to take root. When the Frankfurt Assembly, a motley collection of German statesman, professors, and political liberals, attempted to hand the Prussian king Frederick William IV (1795–1861) the crown of a united Germany in 1848, he rebuffed them with the comment that he would not accept "a crown offered up from the gutter." It was not until the chancellorship of Otto von Bismarck (1815–1898) that serious interest in a unified Germany entered the minds of the rulers of Prussia. Bismarck, one of the most astute political minds of the nineteenth century, understood that Prussia would have to embrace the rest of Germany if it were to survive as a power in central Europe. In geopolitical terms Russia and France were far too close and far too powerful for Prussia to ignore. French bellicosity, which led directly to the Franco-Prussian War (1870), instilled a fear in the German states, especially those on the Rhine, that they could not withstand French aggression. France's past record of war-like behavior, especially under Napoleon I, and Napoleon III's demand of German territory as compensation for French neutrality in the Austro-Prussian War of 1866, convinced the majority of the German states to voluntarily join a Prussian-led Confederation of German States. This union was initially only a loose confederation. However, after the victory over the French in 1870, it became a Prussian-led empire. Emperor Wilhelm I, under Bismarck's guidance, established a pan-German, elected diet in Berlin. To the outside it appeared as a constitutional complement to the Emperor, but in fact it held no power at all. Bismarck himself considered the diet's judgments and either acted on them or ignored them as he saw fit. He was under no compulsion to obey the decisions of the diet. For Bismarck the diet was useful as a sounding board for his policies across Germany and as a foil against any claims of Prussian hegemony in Germany.

Enlightened Despotism in Russia. Russian government remained remarkably stable, if unimaginative and reactionary, through the eighteenth and nineteenth centuries. The government was headed by the tsar, a hereditary autocrat. In 1801 Tsar Alexander I (1801–1825) succeeded his father, who had been assassinated earlier that year. Russia was a vast, sparsely populated land in which the serfs, more than 80 percent of the population, were legally tied to land owned by either the tsar himself or by the boyars (nobles). Alexander asked the Russian nobles to voluntarily free their serfs as a preliminary step toward social and economic liberalism. The boyars, however, were cool to his request. Alexander also attempted to reorganize the Russian government along the lines of Prussian cameralism in an effort to increase its efficiency. By 1815, however, Alexander had become increasingly paranoid, and his regime followed his character. Censorship was violent and

Nineteenth-century painting of Giuseppe Garibaldi leading the Red Shirts to victory over a Neapolitan army at the Battle of Calatafimi, an event that hastened Italian unification (Museo del Risorgimento, Milan)

brutal. The police burned or smashed presses that did not conform to Alexander's vision of Russia. The repression spawned some clandestine opposition, especially among educated boyars and military officers, but they did not act until after Alexander's death in December 1825. A cabal of nobles, army officers, and soldiers occupied St. Petersburg Square and stood outside the palace shouting the name *Constantine.* Their chant referred to their favorite candidate in the then–brewing succession dispute. Constantine, Alexander's eldest son, eventually declined the throne, demurring to his younger brother Nicholas. The new ruler ordered the elements of the army that were loyal to him to attack the soldiers in the Square. All the leaders of the uprising were executed.

Reactionary Government. The humiliation of defeat in the Crimean War weighed heavily on the new tsar Alexander II (1855–1881). It was clear that Russia would have to modernize its military if it were going to compete as a Great Power. To accomplish this, Russia needed factories, and Alexander began efforts at industrialization. However, Russia was by no means socially or economically capable of rapid change.

Further, Alexander was as politically reactionary as his father had been and had no intention of reforming the Russian government along liberal lines. Instead, the tsar's secret police, the notorious Third Section, arrested, tortured, tried, and executed anyone suspected of republican leanings. Waves of uncoordinated anarchist attacks swept across Russia; Alexander II himself was killed by a bomb attack in 1881. His son, Alexander III (1881–1894), succeeded him, and vowed to avenge his father. The Third Section was unleashed with unprecedented brutality upon the liberals, intellectuals, and republicans of Russia.

Sources:
T. C. W. Blanning, *The Origins of the French Revolutionary Wars* (New York: Longman, 1986).

John Brewer, *The Sinews of Power: War, Money, and the English State, 1688–1783* (New York: Knopf, 1991).

Clive Church, *1830 in Europe: Revolution and Political Change* (New York: Oxford University Press, 1983).

William Doyle, *Origins of the French Revolution* (Oxford: Oxford University Press, 1988).

Norman Gash, *Aristocracy and People: Britain, 1815–1865* (Cambridge, Mass.: Harvard University Press, 1979).

Theodore Hamerow, *Restoration, Revolution, and Reaction: Economics and Politics in Germany, 1815–1871* (Princeton: Princeton University Press, 1958).

James F. McMillan, *Napoleon III* (New York: Longman, 1991).

Derek Offord, *Nineteenth-Century Russia: Opposition to Autocracy* (London: Longman, 1999).

R. R. Palmer, *The Age of Democratic Revolution: A Political History of Europe and America, 1760–1800*, 2 volumes (Princeton: Princeton University Press, 1959–1964).

Otto Pflanze, *Bismarck and the Development of Germany: The Period of Unification* (Princeton: Princeton University Press, 1963).

Isser Woloch, *The New Regime: Transformations of the French Civic Order, 1789–1820s* (Princeton: Princeton University Press, 1994).

ADMINISTRATION: OFFICES AND INSTITUTIONS

Professionalism. From 1750 to 1914 government officials across Europe became increasingly professional. During the eighteenth century most officials held their government posts either because they purchased them or because they received them as part of a favorable political negotiation with the crown. Few men were career bureaucrats with any formal training. By the nineteenth century, however, this situation was changing, especially in Britain.

French Republican Assemblies. Venal officeholding existed in France until the Revolution of 1789, when electoral politics and radical republicanism replaced the administrative infrastructure of the Old Regime. France's republican assemblies relied on elected officials who, initially, had no experience in government at all. High property requirements for officeholding and voting helped to restrict the membership of the assemblies to the wealthy elite. Two-thirds of the National Assembly in 1789, for example, were relatively well-off lawyers. During the Terror (1793–1794) the property requirements for voting and sitting on the assembly (known by this time as the National Convention) were lowered such that the number of representatives quadrupled. The Convention, however, had no real power—Maximilien Robespierre and his twelve-member Committee for Public Safety instead wielded near dictatorial powers from behind the scenes. The Committee for Public Safety rooted out, arrested, tried, and executed anyone suspected of antirepublicanism. Under the Directory the property requirements for both the franchise and officeholding were more than doubled. This development effectively returned government to the landed rich. French government benefited from an increasingly stable financial situation, which was itself the product of an increasingly professional government. The establishment of the Bank of France by Napoleon in 1800 gave the French state its first efficient and unified fiscal system. Under the Second Republic (1848–1852) the voting franchise and candidacy for public office were again determined by property requirements, but they were kept quite high (ownership of a minimum of 400 acres of land) so that only the wealthiest Frenchmen could vote or hold office. The policies of the assemblies of the Second Republic essentially supported a French plutocracy. The situation persisted under Napoleon III's Second Empire (1852–1870), except that the assemblies themselves had virtually no power and were merely sounding boards for the emperor.

Engraving calling for an independent Bulgarian state, 1878 (National Library, Sofia)

British Crown and Parliament. British government through the eighteenth and mid nineteenth centuries was in essence a series of negotiated compromises between the crown and Parliament. The crown still retained the power to make war and peace, as well as the power to appoint anyone to any position in government, the church, or the military. These powers, however, did not exist in a vacuum. Parliament not only had to be informed when they were used but frequently had to be consulted as well. Clashes between George III and Parliament over many of his early appointments, especially that of the hated Earl of Bute, raised the question of ministerial responsibility. The concept of a "loyal opposition" in Parliament emerged from these clashes. This opposition was most vocal among the Whig country gentlemen in the House of Commons. Few if any Whigs, except perhaps the radical John Wilkes who was stripped of his Parliamentary seat for advocating universal manhood suffrage, would have gone beyond the principle of ministerial responsibility. The revolutions in France in 1789, 1830, and 1848, however, frightened many in Britain's government. Fear of a French-style revolution in England encouraged a gradually increasing number of parliamentarians to back reform legislation. William Gladstone gradually emerged as the Liberal ("Whig" became "Liberal" in the 1850s) Party leader; he served as Prime Minister 1868–1874, 1880–1885, 1886, and 1892–1894. Though initially a conservative on voting franchise and free trade issues, in 1866 Gladstone began proposing amendments to the 1832 Reform Act that had extended the franchise to the wealthy

Caricature of King Leopold II gazing down upon the Belgian populace demanding
enfranchisement, 1884 (Staatsbibliothek, Berlin)

bourgeoisie. Although no conservative members of Parliament were ready in 1866 to create a larger, less controllable electorate, the widespread violence of the 1848 revolutions in Europe convinced many of them of the wisdom of defusing social tensions by broadening the voting franchise. The result was the Reform Bill of 1867, which granted the right to vote to the better-off men of the working class. By 1874 Gladstone and his cabinet had made considerable progress in reforming voting qualifications, the justice system, the government bureaucracy, and the military. A conservative backlash, however, swept him from office. Benjamin Disraeli became the Conservative ("Tory") Party prime minister and held the post until 1880. Queen Victoria (1837–1901) was ambivalent about Gladstone, though she respected him; on the other hand, she adored Disraeli. By Victoria's time the monarch's powers were largely symbolic, though as a symbol Victoria herself could wield enormous influence. She was insulated from her subjects, however, and was quite ignorant of their lives—she spoke against factory reforms, increased education for the working class, and an expanded voting franchise. She nonetheless endured as the quintessential symbol of respectability in Britain. Her popularity remained high in Britain, even among liberals.

Property Requirements. The Reform Acts of 1832, 1867, and 1884 extended voting rights to previously disenfranchised citizens. The 1832 act eliminated the most notorious

of the "rotten boroughs," such as Old Sarum, which had no inhabitants at all but sent two members to Parliament. Large urban centers, such as Manchester and Liverpool, received some representation. Reapportionment altered the makeup of Parliament. Gradually, it came more accurately to represent the British people. The 1832 act also gave the power to vote to any man owning a household worth £10. This development added 217,000 new votes to an electorate of 435,000, so that now about 20 percent of British men could vote. The 1867 act extended the franchise even further down the class ladder. Over 900,000 new voters were added, many of whom were working class. Conservatives railed against the act in Parliamentary speeches that detailed the dangers that such a democratic shift would create in Britain, but to no avail. "High culture," one speech stated, "would recede into oblivion." The 1884 Act tripled the electorate; most of the new voters were agricultural laborers. By the 1880s voting was coming to be regarded as a citizen's right, not simply as a privilege of a select few.

Prussia and Germany. Following Napoleon's defeat in 1815, virtually all of the German states returned to some form of conservative monarchy. Elected assemblies were limited by the establishment of high property requirements for voting, and revolutionary constitutions were either weakened by amendment or simply eliminated. The Revolution of 1830 in France and the Polish revolt of 1831 against Russia, however, spurred popular disturbances across Germany. In Prussia the uprisings were quickly quashed by armed force. Many German states were not, however, powerful enough to suppress the disturbance. The rulers of Hesse-Kassel, Hanover, and Saxony all had to enact liberal constitutions or risk their government's collapse. Eventually, most of these constitutions were suspended as the revolutionary threat abated. Unlike Great Britain and France, which had complex traditions of individual liberty and freedom, Prussia and the German states had no real heritage of political liberty. A respect for traditional monarchist ideology was deeply rooted in the German people. Liberal change of the type that occurred in Gladstone's Britain, therefore, was virtually unthinkable in Germany. Instead, liberalism in Germany became increasingly tied to the German unification movement.

Austria-Hungary. Revolts also wracked the Austro-Hungarian Empire in 1848. At issue there, however, were the basic legal rights of ethnic groups within the empire, especially the Czechs and the Hungarians. In addition, many Austrians in Vienna demanded a representative assembly and voting rights. During the initial wave of revolts the Emperor Ferdinand (ruled 1835–1848) and his government panicked. The unpopular foreign minister Count Klemens von Metternich (1773–1859; one of the principle architects of the Congress of Vienna of 1815) was forced to resign, and the emperor agreed to a constitution, freedom of the press, and the creation of a small electorate for the diet. The revolutionaries were not, however, united and could not agree to accept the emperor's offer. As more violence flared around Vienna, Ferdinand withdrew his promises and unleashed the army on the revolutionaries. By the end of the year the insurgent movements were crushed. Ethnic nationalism and political liberty were, for the moment, silenced. In 1850–1913 the leadership of Austria carefully excluded non-Germanic folk from the government and the military. Only the Hungarians were allowed to participate in the administration. This privilege was only extended to them because of the loyalty the Magyar (Hungarian) nobility had demonstrated during the 1848 revolts. Archduke Franz Ferdinand's proposal that the Serbs of Bosnia-Herzegovina (annexed to Austria-Hungary in 1908) be granted similar privileges in the empire in order to defuse tensions in the Balkans provoked jealous outrage among the Hungarian nobility.

Sources:

Derek Beales, *From Castlereagh to Gladstone, 1815–1885* (London: Nelson, 1969).

Georges Duveau, *1848: The Making of a Revolution*, translated by Anne Carter (New York: Pantheon, 1967).

Hajo Holborn, *History of Modern Germany*, 3 volumes (New York: Knopf, 1968).

Colin Lucas, ed., *The Political Culture of the French Revolution* (New York: Oxford University Press, 1989).

R. R. Palmer, *The Twelve Who Ruled: The Year of Terror in the French Revolution* (Princeton: Princeton University Press, 1989).

Alan Sked, *The Decline and Fall of the Habsburg Empire* (New York: Longman, 1989).

E. L. Woodward, *The Age of Reform, 1815–1870* (Oxford: Oxford University Press, 1962).

Theodore Zeldin, *The Political System of Napoleon III* (New York: St. Martin's Press, 1971).

INTERNATIONAL RELATIONS

Diplomats. European governments through the eighteenth century conducted international diplomacy with each other largely by means of amateur diplomats. Diplomats were usually, but not exclusively, from the nobility, and foreign language skills, not bloodlines, determined one's fitness for the job. A multilingual ambassador could converse with foreign dignitaries, eavesdrop on court conversations, and intercept and read people's mail. Information gleaned by spying frequently proved critical when negotiating treaties. Some diplomats such as France's Charles Maurice de Talleyrand or Austria's Count Klemens von Metternich were incredibly charismatic and possessed exceptional diplomatic skills. By the nineteenth century, diplomats (and diplomacy) were becoming increasingly professional. European states formally exchanged ambassadors and established a permanent infrastructure of diplomacy (for example, telegraph machines, typewriters, mail and messenger services, permanent embassy buildings, and honor guards) in each others' countries.

Alliances and Neutrality Pacts. The wars against Napoleon I had been conducted largely through a series of fragile coalitions. Initially, Napoleon had been able to divide the allies from one another by making a quick peace with some of the countries in the coalitions and then ruthlessly attacking the others. By 1813 Great Britain, Russia, Austria, and Prussia had become wise to this strategy. As a result the last coalition against Napoleon

Mid-nineteenth-century caricature of Prince Metternich surveying the chaos of Europe after his resignation as Austrian foreign minister (from Alan Palmer, *Metternich*, 1972)

Nineteenth-century painting of the Congress of Vienna by Jean Baptiste Isabey (National Library, Vienna)

did not fall apart but agreed to fight until France was defeated and Napoleon was deposed. The coalitions of the Napoleonic Wars (1793–1815) were essentially defensive alliances in which the signatories pledged to defend each other if attacked. This form of diplomatic agreement was effective, but it limited the freedom of the individual states within the coalition by tying their foreign policies together. By the 1860s coalition alliances were being mixed with far more flexible agreements, such as the neutrality pact. In a neutrality pact the states involved simply pledged not to interfere with each other's foreign or domestic affairs. Otto von Bismarck utilized a series of complex and flexible neutrality pacts to diplomatically isolate his enemies (especially France). The Austro-Prussian War (1866) and the Franco-Prussian War (1870–1871) were both preceded by months of feverish diplomacy in which Bismarck skillfully and ruthlessly deprived his enemies of any possible allies. In this way, Bismarck's opponents were always forced to fight Prussia alone.

Three Emperors League. Perhaps the zenith of Bismarck's diplomatic achievements was a renewable series of neutrality pacts between Austria, Germany, and Russia known as the Three Emperors League (1873–1878, 1881–1890). Bismarck recognized that after the Franco-Prussian War France would be looking for an opportunity for revenge against Germany. To Bismarck the most dangerous political alignment was one in which France and Russia became allies. In this situation Germany would face a potentially disastrous two-front war. To head off this possibility, Bismarck bound both Russia and Austria to Germany with generous neutrality pacts. Russia was accorded a free hand in the Caucasus and in the Balkans against the Turks, while Austria was given a similar guarantee in the Balkans. Germany agreed to mediate disputes in case Russian and Austrian aims collided. In this way Bismarck restricted France's potential pool of allies and thereby reduced the possibility that France would attack Germany. Bismarck himself, however, sowed the seeds of the collapse of the Three Emperors League in 1879 when he penned a secret defensive treaty with Austria that specifically stated that German arms would support any Austrian claims in the Balkans. In 1882 Italy joined the pact, making it the Triple Alliance. When Russian diplomats learned of this secret treaty, they began to worry that their Balkan interests were being compromised.

Triple Entente. French diplomats recognized the fragility of the German/Russian neutrality pact and worked hard to undo it. French investment in Russia increased dramatically in the 1880s and 1890s, especially in the development of railways, mines, and foundries. By 1914 25 percent of all foreign investment in Russia was French. Kaiser Wilhelm I of Germany died in 1890. His son and heir, Wilhelm II (ruled 1890–1918), was young, arrogant, and headstrong. Wilhelm II forced Bismarck

DIPLOMACY AT WORK

Otto von Bismarck's neutrality treaties were master-strokes of diplomacy. The Three Emperors League treaty was arguably one of his finest creations. Note how the treaty carefully balanced the interests of Germany, Russia, and Austria, especially in the case of conflicting Austro-Russian claims in the Balkans.

18 June, 1881

The Three Emperors League

The Courts of Austria-Hungary, of Germany, and of Russia, animated by an equal desire to consolidate the general peace by an understanding intended to assure the defensive position of their respective States, have come into agreement on certain questions. . . .

With this purpose the three Courts . . . have agreed on the following Articles:

ARTICLE 1. In case one of the High Contracting Parties should find itself at war with a fourth Great Power, the two others shall maintain towards it a benevolent neutrality and shall devote their efforts to the localization of the conflict.

This stipulation shall apply likewise to a war between one of the three Powers and Turkey, but only in the case where a previous agreement shall have been reached between the three Courts as to the results of this war.

In the special case where one of them shall obtain a more positive support from one of its two Allies, the obligatory value of the present Article shall remain in all its force for the third.

ARTICLE 2. Russia, in agreement with Germany, declares her firm resolution to respect the interests arising from the new position assured to Austria-Hungary by the Treaty of Berlin.

The three Courts, desirous of avoiding all discord between them, engage to take account of their respective interests in the Balkan Peninsula. They further promise one another that any new modifications in the territorial status quo of Turkey in Europe can be accomplished only in virtue of a common agreement between them.

Source: Petr Aleksandrovich Saburov, *Memoirs* (Cambridge: Cambridge University Press, 1929).

---

alliance blocks. Perhaps the most important aspect of the situation was that for the first time in more than forty years France was not diplomatically isolated. Instead, Germany faced the real (and soon to be realized) threat of a two-front war.

Sources:

James Joll, *The Origins of the First World War* (New York: Longman, 1984).

Lawrence Lafore, *The Long Fuse* (New York: Praeger, 1965).

George F. Kennan, *The Fateful Alliance: France, Russia, and the Coming of the First War* (New York: Pantheon, 1984).

Augustus Oakes, *The Great European Treaties of the Nineteenth Century* (Oxford: Clarendon Press, 1918).

J. L. Richardson, *Crisis Diplomacy: The Great Powers Since the Mid-Nineteenth Century* (Cambridge: Cambridge University Press, 1994).

George H. Rupp, *A Wavering Friendship: Russia and Austria, 1876–1878* (Cambridge, Mass.: Harvard University Press, 1941).

Petr A. Saburov, *The Saburov Memoirs, or Bismarck and Russia: Being Fresh Light on the League of the Three Emperors, 1881* (Cambridge, U.K.: Cambridge University Press, 1929).

THE MILITARY

Linear Warfare. By the eighteenth century all of the European great powers maintained permanent standing armies. These armies were led by aristocratic officers who used a variety of forms of brutal corporal punishment to instill discipline among the troops. The soldiers of these armies came from a variety of backgrounds and included unemployed tradesmen, indebted poor, criminals, and unfortunate folk who got caught in military conscription dragnets. The standard infantry weapon in Great Britain was the .75-caliber smoothbore Brown Bess musket, a cumbersome firearm with a slow and complex reloading process (a fully trained soldier could fire three times per minute). The Brown Bess had to be loaded and fired from a standing position and was only accurate out to about 100 yards. It discharged a lead ball with a muzzle velocity of 800–950 feet per second. All European armies used similar muskets. To minimize the weapon's disadvantages, most armies adopted linear warfare tactics. Opposing troops would be arrayed in three ranks and would fire by sections. Not only could such a drill keep up a steady rate of fire, but the sheer mass of lead that volley fire could put into the air also insured at least some of the shots would hit a target. A tremendous expansion of military infrastructure across Europe also occurred in the eighteenth century. Hundreds of barracks, depots, roads, ports, parade grounds, and prisons were erected all over Europe as armies and navies became increasingly permanent institutions. Because of relatively rudimentary supply and provisioning systems, however, it was difficult for an army to operate far from home. Most military struggles such as the Seven Years' War (1756–1763) turned into wars of attrition in which the side with the largest bankroll and manpower reserves prevailed.

French Reforms. In order to meet the threat of foreign invasion, the French Revolutionary Republic instituted a variety of military drafts, which became systematized in 1793 as the *levée en masse*. The *levée en masse* enabled the French military to draft huge numbers of able-bodied

---

to resign in 1890 over a nasty incident in which Wilhelm overheard Bismarck refer to him as an "impudent whelp." After 1890 Bismarck's firm hand no longer guided German diplomacy. Wilhelm II allowed the Three Emperors League to lapse in 1891, and by 1892 Russia and France had signed a mutual-defense treaty against the Triple Alliance. The Anglo-German rivalry, especially over the presence of a sizable German war fleet in the Baltic, eventually pushed Great Britain into the Franco-Russian pact, creating the Triple Entente. Thus, in 1913 Europe stood divided into two powerful

HMS *Warrior,* the first ironclad warship in the Royal Navy, May 1859 (National Maritime Museum, London)

Frenchmen into the army and navy. In 1799, for example, the French republic had nearly 2 million men under arms. French generals such as Charles-François du Périer Dumouriez and Napoleon Bonaparte successfully harnessed their troops' revolutionary patriotism as a motivation in battle. Of France's 6,000 prerevolution army officers (over 90 percent of whom were noble) more than 4,500 emigrated from France in 1789. As a result the French Republican Army had to create new officers. In fine republican spirit it created a system based on merit—the skilled advanced, regardless of lineage. This open system allowed highly skilled yet common men to rise quite high in rank. Napoleon, for example, started as a corporal in the republican army in 1790, rose to the rank of lieutenant colonel by 1796, and was promoted to general in 1797. Under Napoleon the French Army was initially provisioned by an expanded storehouse system. However, after the conquest of Italy and central Europe this system proved inadequate and was eventually superseded by semiorganized acts of plunder. Freed from the long supply lines common to mid-eighteenth-century warfare, Napoleon's armies could strike quickly and forcefully and had much greater mobility then their predecessors. Since they provisioned themselves by living off of the land they conquered, the French armies quickly became unpopular. In battle Napoleon typically massed his artillery and opened with a bombardment of his opponent. The barrage served to break up the enemy's formations. In the ensuing chaos Napoleon attacked with deep columns of infantry, which broke through and overwhelmed the enemy's army.

Naval Warfare. From the eighteenth century to the mid nineteenth century, war at sea was conducted with wooden, sail-powered vessels. One of the largest of these, the HMS *Victory,* was Admiral Nelson's flagship at Trafalgar (1805). *Victory* stretched to 151 feet in length and displaced 2,162 tons. It was armed with one hundred cannons, which fired a variety of types and weights of shot. Twelve-pound deck guns were packed with grapeshot, a burlap sack filled with iron balls and nails. Grapeshot was useless against a ship itself, but against the crew exposed on the top gun deck it could be murderous. Other cannons fired twenty-four-pound iron cannonballs that shattered the timbers of the opponent's hull or shredded its rigging. *Victory* also had thirty-two-pound hull-crackers and a swivel-mounted fifty-pound carronade nicknamed *Smasher.* *Victory,* launched in 1765, was an old ship by the time of Trafalgar. It had, however, been refitted extensively on three occasions and was still one of Britain's top fighting ships until the 1830s when sailing ships began to be replaced by steam-powered vessels. The ships' officers were usually noblemen or persons of some wealth or quality, while the crew was composed of volunteers, criminals, homeless poor, and abductees rounded up in naval press gangs. Service as a crewman usually involved a twenty-year tour of duty, followed by a government pension (assuming one survived).

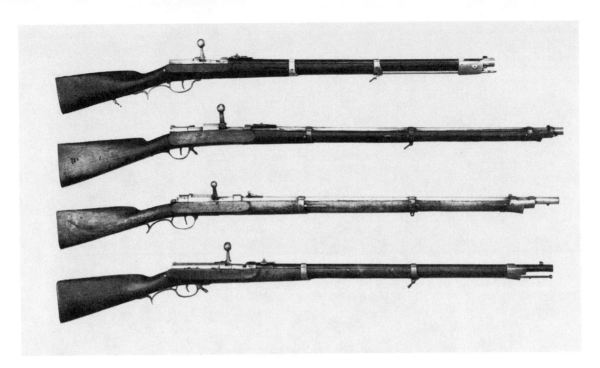

Different models of the Prussian breech-loading needle gun (Mansell Collection, London)

Royal Navy Supremacy. The British Royal Navy was, arguably, the best navy in the world during the eighteenth and nineteenth centuries. Since the invasion of the Spanish Armada in 1588 the British government had been keenly aware of the Royal Navy's crucial role in defending Britain itself from invasion. Its leaders also knew that equally essential was keeping open the long and highly profitable commercial trade routes to India, the Caribbean, China, and Egypt. To this end the crown and Parliament spent a great deal of money maintaining and expanding the Royal Navy. The Battle of Trafalgar stands as the fruit of these labors. At the time Napoleon Bonaparte needed only to conquer England to complete his mastery of western and central Europe. The ships and crews of Britain's Royal Navy, however, so badly outclassed those of France, and France's erstwhile ally Spain, that the French navy had simply conceded control of the seas to Britain and put to port. The lone example of French maritime aggression occurred in 1798, and it was a disaster. Napoleon invaded Egypt and captured Suez and Cairo (key points along Britain's trade route to India). In the ensuing sea battle, however, he lost most of the French Mediterranean fleet and allowed the British to trap some thirty thousand French troops in the North African desert.

Railroads. Many industrial technologies that had been developed for commercial use during the mid 1800s also found military applications. Armies across Europe quickly adopted railroads, for example, once the steam engine's commercial efficiency was proven. In 1870 Otto von Bismarck and the Prussian general staff established an army mobilization plan that relied upon railroads for nearly all of its large-scale military movements. Everything from bringing recruits to training centers to taking them to the front lines was conducted by rail. It was the speed and precision of this plan that allowed Prussia to defeat France so swiftly in 1870 in the Franco-Prussian War.

Breechloading Weapons. European armies adopted breechloading small arms in the mid 1800s. In 1836 the Thuringian gunsmith Johann Nikolaus von Dreyse first adapted the breechloading system (in use in hunting weapons since the 1700s) to a military weapon; it was formally accepted by the Prussian army five years later. His weapon, known as the "Needle Gun" because of its long, sharp firing pin, significantly altered military tactics and strategy. Breechloading weapons utilized ammunition (called the "shell") in which the shot (bullet), gunpowder, and wadding was encased in a single brass cartridge. The shell was loaded in a smooth, quick motion into a receiver on the breech above and behind the trigger. The gun could literally be fired as fast as one could shove shells into the receiver. Unlike the muzzleloaded musket, this weapon could be loaded while lying down, thus affording the soldier the option of firing from cover in a prone position. Further, most breechloading weapons also employed a rifled barrel (corkscrew grooves inside the bore), which helped them shoot farther and straighter. When the gun was fired, its bullet would catch slightly in the rifled corkscrew track and spin. The spinning motion helped it maintain its trajectory and increased a weapon's effective range up to twenty times that of a musket. Rifles allowed European armies to break from the traditional volley-fire formations of the eighteenth century. No longer did armies have to stand face to face, barely three hundred feet apart, in order to hit each other. Military formations after the introduction of breechloading, rifled small arms

In 1805 Napoleon decided to attack the Royal Navy itself as a preparatory move in an invasion of Britain. He amassed an impressive fleet: 33 ships with a total of 2,640 guns. The vessels were, however, undermanned, and the crews poorly fed, poorly trained, and poorly led. The Royal Navy, on the other hand, was led by a highly professional officer corps who punished the slightest act of disobedience among the crew with brutal corporal justice. The cat-o'-nine-tails, a nine-tailed whip studded with knots, was a favorite flogging tool. The crews were generally well fed and displayed a spirit of professionalism similar to that of their officers, even though some of them shared criminal backgrounds. The Franco-Spanish Navy aggressively sought the Royal Navy for battle by sailing to the British naval base at Gibraltar. At first sight of the Royal Navy the Franco-Spanish fleet formed a long battle line and prepared to fire its broadsides at the British. Traditionally, the Royal Navy might have formed a line of ships parallel to the Franco-Spanish line and swapped broadsides until one side was defeated. The fleet's commander, Admiral Horatio Nelson, however, broke with tradition. He divided his 27 ships into three groups and attacked the French line head-on and along two perpendicular courses. The Royal Navy broke through the French line and enveloped it. In the ensuing fighting at close range the gunnery and sailing skills of the British sailors were superior. The British sank 5 ships and captured 15 others; they lost none of their own. Despite this success, Nelson was mortally wounded by a French sharpshooter. With the victory at Trafalgar and the destruction or capture of the Franco-Spanish fleet, the Royal Navy inaugurated a period of naval dominance that would last until World War II.

Source: René Maine, *Trafalgar: Napoleon's Naval Waterloo,* translated by R. Eldon and B. W. Robinson (New York: Scribners, 1975).

became more open and fluid. They allowed individual soldiers to take advantage of any cover the battlefield's geography afforded them.

Repeating Weapons. The first repeating rifles were produced during the American Civil War (1861–1865). These weapons did not have to be reloaded after each shot but could typically hold up to five shells. The apex of repeating weapon technology, however, was the Maxim machine gun. First developed by the American-born Hiram Maxim in 1884, the Maxim gun was a belt-fed, .30-caliber weapon that fired upward of five hundred rounds per minute. A single Maxim and a crew of six men could easily hold off a much larger enemy force. The British army adopted the Maxim gun in 1889. It was first employed in battle in 1893 in the Matabele War in South Africa. In one fight 50 British soldiers armed with four Maxim guns held off more than 5,000 Matabele warriors. More than 1,500 Matabele were killed in three days of fighting, while the British lost not one man. In this battle the British army employed a tactic that placed machine guns in a line at one-hundred-yard intervals. The firing arcs of the guns could intersect and thereby create murderous killing zones. The Battle of Omdurman in 1898 was even more illustrative of the increased firepower of the Maxim and the repeating rifle. In under four hours 500 Maxim-armed British soldiers killed some 11,000 Dervishes in the Sudanese desert at the cost of only 48 of their own. By the end of the nineteenth century the machine gun had demonstrated its value as an infantry weapon. All of Europe's major armies had adopted variations of Maxim's weapon. During World War I (1914–1918) machine guns would ultimately prove to be the linchpins that held the trench networks together. Any assault on a trench line whose machine guns had not been first silenced (usually only possible with snipers or artillery barrages) was suicidal.

Artillery, Land Mines, and Poison Gas. The German arms manufacturer Friedrich Alfred Krupp developed in the 1840s many of the steel-casting techniques necessary for the production of large, modern artillery pieces. He exhibited several of his new guns, a pair of mammoth ten-inch cannons, at the Great Exhibition of 1851 in London. By the 1860s his designs were so successful that they could be found in every major European army. The new artillery pieces could throw much larger projectiles than those of the Napoleonic Wars (1793–1815). Napoleon's largest cannon was a mortar that fired a 50-pound ball. In contrast, Krupp produced a forty-two-centimeter mortar that fired a 250-pound exploding shell. By the 1860s European chemists had developed stable chemical explosive compounds, such as thermite and cordite, which packed more than one hundred times the explosive force of traditional gunpowder. By the late nineteenth and early twentieth centuries these chemicals gave artillery shells far more destructive power than ever before. At the same time, European armies also experimented with a variety of different delivery systems for the new explosives. The chief results of these labors were land mines (buried explosive shells that were triggered by hidden trip wires) and poison gas shells. Poison gas shells were launched by cannon and carried a payload of compressed mustard or chlorine gas instead of explosives. When fired, the poison gas canister was preset to explode in the air above enemy lines, releasing a fog of toxic gas that descended upon enemy soldiers. Mustard and chlorine gases were designed to burn the lung's tissues when inhaled. During World War I tens of thousands of soldiers in the trenches of the Western Front died horrible, slow deaths when they were caught in gas attacks without their gas masks.

Steel-Hulled and Steam-Powered Warships. By the 1850s the sailing ships had been replaced by steam-powered

The Battle of Borodino, painted by Baron Louis-Francois Lejeune in the early nineteenth century (from Curtis Cate, *The War of the Two Emperors,* 1985)

vessels. Early steamships used the power their boilers generated to turn enormous side- or rear-mounted paddle wheels. By the 1860s the paddle wheel had given way to the far more efficient (and seaworthy) stern-mounted propeller. Steam-driven ships were much faster than their sail-powered predecessors. Early-nineteenth-century sailing ships took about five weeks to cross the Atlantic, while the slowest steamships managed it in a mere nineteen days. Steel hulls also first appeared in the mid nineteenth century. The notion of a cast-steel hull derived from early experiments at armoring wooden ships by riveting steel plates to their hulls. In the early 1860s shipwrights in the Confederate States of America built the CSS *Virginia* (also known as the *Merrimac*), the first all-steel, steam-powered warship. Its success against the wooden steamships of the Northern states prompted the building of the USS *Monitor,* a low-slung, all-steel steamship that protected its guns in a rotating turret. The two ships met in a heated battle off the coast of Virginia, near Hampton Roads on 8–9 March 1862. During the engagement the two ships hammered away at each other for almost fourteen hours. Their cannonballs simply bounced off one another's armor plating, and neither ship was seriously damaged. In the 1880s, when improvements in land-based artillery and shells were incorporated into naval gunnery, steel-armored steamships now became vulnerable. As disputes between Germany and Great Britain in the 1890s over the sizes of their respective

war fleets escalated into the world's first modern arms race, the first modern battleship was launched. Frightened that Germany might outstrip Britain in seapower, the British Admiralty (the naval general staff) developed the radically new HMS *Dreadnought* (1906), the first modern battleship. The cost of navies was never small, but outfitting fleets with battleships swelled the naval budget considerably in the late nineteenth and early twentieth centuries. By 1912, for example, the British government was spending approximately 70 percent of its revenues on the maintenance and expansion of the Royal Navy.

General Staff System. As European armies increased in size and became far more mobile over the course of the mid to late nineteenth century, it became impossible for a commander in chief to lead an army as Napoleon had. Instead of living with one's soldiers and conducting the course of a battle personally from horseback, the generals of the late nineteenth century plotted and executed their battle plans from behind desks in map-filled war rooms far from the actual combat. Communication with officers in the field was effected by telegraph. These new generals created an overall battle strategy and delegated much of the tactical control of a battle to their field officers. Commanding generals became battle planners and coordinators and were far less involved in the actual fighting. The Prussian Helmuth von Moltke, the general who put together the Prussian army's blueprint for success against France in 1870, was the

The Prince of Wales (later King Edward VII) test firing a Maxim machine gun at Wimbledon in August 1888 (Gernsheim Collection, Harry Ransom Humanities Research Center, University of Texas, Austin)

first European general to fully embrace this approach. The Schlieffen Plan (1905), brainchild of General Alfred von Schlieffen and Germany's de facto war plan in 1914, stands as a model example of this new type of impersonal, strategic leadership. The document encompasses nearly ten thousand printed pages and describes in minute detail the duties each German officer would be responsible for once the plan was put into effect. Almost half of the Schlieffen plan is dedicated to railroad timetables, which were designed to coordinate precisely the rapid mustering and movement into France of the German army (approximately four million soldiers in 1914). While the general staff system certainly improved military efficiency, it also robbed armies of flexibility. It was, for example, difficult for armies using general-staff systems and plans such as the Schlieffen Plan to respond quickly to changes in the tactical or strategic situation. The Schlieffen Plan itself presumed (not without reason) that France would eventually attack Germany in an effort to avenge the humiliation of 1870. General von Schlieffen and his staff felt that the best way to parry a determined French attack was to preempt it with a massive German strike into France. The plan did not, however, take into account the possibility of war in the East or in the Balkans. When World War I erupted in the Balkans between Austria-Hungary and Serbia, Germany's only operational recourse was to attack France, even though France was not a belligerent and had little if anything to do

with the situation. The German generals in 1914 were trapped by their own efficient but highly inflexible plan.

Aircraft. Since the Middle Ages military reconnaissance had been conducted by lightly armed horsemen who scouted ahead of their army for signs of the enemy. During the American Civil War the Union army attempted to use hot-air balloons for reconnaissance, as they could float above an enemy position and see it in its entirety. Unfortunately, the balloonists themselves were easy targets for enemy snipers, and European armies did not widely adopt the American practice. The appearance of the first reliable aircraft, specifically the one in which Louis Blériot crossed the English Channel in 1909, however, gave European armies a new and highly effective scouting platform. Aircraft had far more freedom of movement than either horses or balloons—they could scout over and behind enemy positions and could even carry cameramen who could photograph enemy positions. Within one year of Blériot's historic channel crossing, all major European armies had assembled aircraft-reconnaissance squadrons. By 1913 the airplane was recognized as a first-rate reconnaissance vehicle, but it would not be until World War II (1939–1945) that it would begin to emerge as the arbiter of battle that it is today.

Sources:
Fred Anderson, *The Crucible of War: The Seven Years' War and the Fate of Empire in British North America* (New York: Knopf, 2000).

Alan Forrest, *Conscripts and Deserters: The Army and French Society During the Revolution and Empire* (New York: Oxford University Press, 1989).

James George, *History of Warships: From Ancient Times to the Twenty-first Century* (Annapolis: Naval Institute Press, 1998).

Brayton Harris, *The Age of the Battleship, 1890–1922* (New York: Watts, 1965).

J. Hittle, *The Military Staff* (Harrisburg: University of Pennsylvania Press, 1961).

John Keegan, *The Mask of Command* (New York: Viking, 1987).

Cecil King, *H.M.S.; His Majesty's ships and their forbears* (London: Studio Publications, 1940).

René Maine, *Trafalgar: Napoleon's Naval Waterloo,* translated by R. Eldon and B. W. Robinson (New York: Scribners, 1975).

Robert Massie, *Dreadnought: Britain, Germany, and the Coming of the Great War* (New York: Random House, 1991).

Gunther Rothenberg, *The Art of Warfare in the Age of Napoleon* (Bloomington: Indiana University Press, 1978).

SYSTEMS OF LAW, CRIME, AND PUNISHMENT

Legislation and Institutions. Law in eighteenth- and nineteenth-century Europe was a vast system of social controls by which the propertied elite maintained a rigid stranglehold on society and social development. These laws could be quite harsh—violation of any one of the more than one hundred antipoaching laws comprising the Black Act (1723–1823) in Great Britain, for example, could bring a death sentence. Secular courts, such as the assizes in Britain and the *parlements* in France, determined the guilt or innocence of accused criminals in trials that made increasing use of witnesses and evidence. The Prussian judiciary was the best-educated in Europe. The crown selected judges on the basis of competence, not social rank. Thus, besides being highly competent, the Prussian judiciary was also the most socially mixed in Europe. More then two-thirds of Berlin's judges, for example, were from the middle class. In Russia justice was largely meted out by local boyars, who had nearly autocratic powers on their own lands. These boyar-judges generally were not formally educated and usually just bent the law to serve their own interest.

Enlightenment Thought. During the mid to late eighteenth century French philosophes such as Charles-Louis de Secondat, baron de Montesquieu, and François-Marie Arouet (Voltaire) argued that the social and political institutions of France (and Europe in general) were constraining progress and did not reflect humanity's capacity for achievement. Most philosophes argued that justice should be secularized, that a crime's punishment should not be linked to whether or not an act was a sin in the church. Further, virtually all philosophes were concerned over the enormous advantage the privilege elite possessed in the courtroom. Not only did wealth and prestige allow for a covert manipulation of the judicial system (for example, by bribing judges), but French laws were usually written with separate punishments for the privileged and the common masses. Men such as Montesquieu reasoned that this could only be dealt with through a standardized judicial process in which the law was applied equally to everyone. The philosophes communicated their ideas largely through literary works, books, pamphlets, dictionaries, and legal briefs, for example, not through violence.

A CERTAIN SUBORDINATION

In Adam Smith's famous economic treatise *An Inquiry into the Nature and Causes of the Wealth of Nations* (1776), one finds some interesting and cogent theoretical arguments concerning the funding and functioning of the judicial system. Note his argument that if the judges and lawyers of a country are not well paid, they will not execute their offices fairly or efficiently.

Book V, Chapter 1 "Of the Expenses of the Sovereign or Commonwealth"

Part 2 "Of the Expense of Justice"

The second duty of the sovereign, that of protecting, as far as possible, every member of the society from the injustice or oppression of every other member of it, or the duty of establishing an exact administration of justice, requires, too, very different degrees of expense in the different periods of society. . . .

Civil government supposes a certain subordination. But as the necessity of civil government gradually grows up with the acquisition of valuable property, so the principal causes which naturally introduce subordination gradually grow up with the growth of that valuable property. The causes or circumstances which naturally introduce subordination, or which naturally, and antecedent to any civil institution, give some men some superiority over the greater part of their brethren, seem to be four in number. . . .

Justice, however, never was in reality administered gratis in any country. Lawyers and attorneys, at least, must always be paid by the parties; and, if they were not, they would perform their duty still worse than they actually perform it. The fees annually paid to lawyers and attorneys amount, in every court, to a much greater sum than the salaries of the judges. The circumstance of those salaries being paid by the crown can no-where much diminish the necessary expense of a law-suit. But it was not so much to diminish the expense, as to prevent the corruption of justice, that the judges were prohibited from receiving any present or fee from the parties. . . .

The office of judge is in itself so very honorable that men are willing to accept of it, though accompanied with very small emoluments. The inferior office of justice of peace, though attended with a good deal of trouble, and in most cases with no emoluments at all, is an object of ambition to the greater part of our country gentlemen. The salaries of all the different judges, high and low, together with the whole expense of the administration and execution of justice, even where it is not managed with very good economy, makes, in any civilized country, but a very inconsiderable part of the whole expense of government.

Source: Adam Smith, *Inquiry into the Nature and Causes of the Wealth of Nations,* edited by Robert Reich (New York: Modern Library, 2000).

Montesquieu. Two major works highlighting Enlightenment thought and jurisprudence were written by Montesquieu. In *The Spirit of the Laws* (1748), a critical historical study of European legal institutions, he argued that laws and justice systems were subject to the historical process and developed over time. In *The Persian Letters* (1721) Montesquieu stated that nature itself revealed a universal standard of justice which was applicable to all people regardless of lineage at all times. Montesquieu became convinced that only a strong, noble-dominated representative government could balance the potentially autocratic power of the king. His ideal in this regard was Britain's Parliament.

Voltaire. The views of Arouet (he took the name Voltaire for unknown reasons) diverged from those of Montesquieu in that Voltaire did not trust kings or the nobility to vouchsafe the rights of their subjects. To Voltaire the House of Commons in Britain's Parliament constituted the best possibility of protection of one's rights. Voltaire's writings tended to be more acerbic then Montesquieu's. In *Candide* (1759), for example, Voltaire indicted superstition and fanaticism and confronted the contradictory nature of a good, loving God and an evil world. In Voltaire's view religion's utility lay in its potential to induce good behavior in society. Unfortunately, Voltaire reasoned, deeply held religious beliefs too easily led to fanaticism and intolerance. Religious zealotry became his bête noire, and he attacked it in the courtroom. In 1761 Voltaire undertook the legal defense of the Protestant Calas family in Toulouse. The father, Jean Calas, was accused of murdering his son to prevent his elopement with a Catholic girl. The father was convicted by the royal court of Toulouse and tortured to death. Voltaire investigated the case and highlighted both the lack of real evidence linking the father to the son's death and the barbaric torture the father endured before his death. In 1764 the royal court of Toulouse reversed its decision.

Beccaria. Cesare Bonesana, Marquis of Beccaria, exercised, perhaps, more influence on European jurisprudence than any single person. Beccaria was a professor of political philosophy and a royal adviser to the Habsburg monarchy. However, he is best known as the author of *Crimes and Punishment* (1764), a widely read and highly regarded text on the practical application of Enlightenment notions of jurisprudence. Beccaria states, for example, that standardized trial procedures are essential to ensure that the guilty are punished. He rejected capital punishment and torture because he felt that these practices actually encouraged disrespect for the law. As evidence for this argument he cited a series of public executions in Vienna and in Italy during which the observing crowds became so rambunctious that they began looting and vandalizing property. The element of Beccaria's work that most influenced judicial procedure in Europe was his notion that the accused should be considered innocent until proven guilty. Beccaria's text was popular and influential: Duke Leopold II of Tuscany, Gustavus III of Sweden, and Frederick II of Prussia all banned torture in their countries after reasoned consideration of the book. The "Enlightened Despot" Joseph II, Beccaria's own monarch, resisted the ideas in *Crimes and Punishment* at first, and only redressed torture in the Austrian penal system when the book came to earn wide respect throughout Europe.

French Parlements. In France *parlements* (regional royal courts) were headed by a group of judges who were all appointed to their posts by the crown, though most of the judges in fact achieved their appointments by purchasing their offices. In a trial the panel of judges heard evidence and witnesses and rendered both verdict and sentence. In the eighteenth century the king depended upon the *parlements* to cement his power in regions beyond central France. Besides hearing cases in civil and criminal law, the *parlements* also reviewed and usually registered royal edicts and decrees in their jurisdiction. *Parlements* could impede the crown by refusing to register a law, but the king could counter this refusal by appearing in person at the *parlement* (known as a *lit de justice*) and forcing the *parlement* to register the edict forthwith. The political and economic crisis in France in the late eighteenth century frequently set the crown and the *parlements* against

British policemen, circa 1890

one another, and because of these situations the *parlements* became popularly associated with the defense of the nation's rights against the monarch. The *parlement* of Paris, the most important of the French courts, took issue with Louis XV over Jansenism (a dissident Catholic movement banned by the Pope in 1713) in the 1750s. Louis expected obedience and angrily denounced the *parlement* of Paris for flouting his will. His open and vitriolic recriminations of the Paris *parlement,* however, only served to put the *parlement* in the position of defending the liberties and independence of the Gallican church against royal absolutism and papal control. Taken together, these perceptions contributed significantly to an erosion of the monarchy's prestige. During the economic crisis of the 1770s and 1780s the *parlements* and the crown again locked horns over the issue of taxation. Royal chancellors attempted to solve the crown's revenue problems by raising taxes. The *parlements* opposed these measures as it was generally felt among the nobles that any rise in taxes would be followed by waves of peasant unrest. Louis XV rewarded the *parlements* for their resistance by abolishing them in 1773 and replacing them with new, docile law courts that owed their allegiance solely to the king. Lawyers across France turned their courtrooms into forums for political opposition and generally debated whether actual sovereignty in the French state lay with the people (represented by the *parlements*) or with the crown in the person of the king. Even after the *parlements* were restored in 1774, it was clear that they were not strong enough to prevent royal despotism. Many lawyers came to the conclusion that only a British-style parliament could do that. The crown could also take the law into its own hands through an instrument known as a lettre de cachet. These documents were issued in the king's name and allowed the arrest and indefinite detention (frequently in the Bastille) of anyone for anything, thus bypassing any semblance of due legal process. Traditionally, the crown used the lettres to silence opposition to royal policy, and because of this they became a byword for despotism. A *cahier de doléance* (list of grievances) from 1788 demanded, for example, that "no citizen lose his liberty, except according to law; that consequently no one be arrested by virtue of special orders, or . . . that the prisoner be handed over to the regular courts of justice within forty-eight hours." Ironically, the *parlements* went the way of royal lettres de cachet, abolished by the Revolution that they helped to start.

English Assizes. The assizes were permanent, regional courts in Britain that developed from sixteenth-century itinerant courts. English constitutional law was founded on documents such as the Magna Carta (1215), the Petition of Right (1628), and the Bill of Rights (1689), and on the country's traditional ("common") legal institutions and practices (for example, the jury system). In Britain, unlike France, Prussia, or Russia, one's trial was conducted in the courtroom by a single judge and a prosecuting attorney. A defense attorney attempted to demonstrate the accused's innocence. After the prosecution "rested" its case, determination of guilt was left to a jury of twelve of the accused's peers. The jury system was unique in Europe and exercised a considerable subsequent influence on the judicial systems of continental Europe. In addition, since the Habeas Corpus Act of 1679, defendants were guaranteed a speedy trial at which the prosecution had to present physical evidence, not merely hearsay, linking the accused to the crime. Lawyers studied law either on the continent at a law school, such as the University of Bologna, or at the increasingly prestigious Cambridge and Oxford law schools.

Law Codes. Civil law codes across Europe during the eighteenth and nineteenth centuries were promulgated by landowners who wished to protect their property. Law codes of the early to mid eighteenth century reflected the stranglehold that the aristocracy held over the rest of society. By the nineteenth century, however, that hold was slipping, and the legislation reflected this. As law codes came to protect and represent larger proportions of society, they also strongly reaffirmed the legal subordination of women to men.

Black Act. Since the sixteenth century, English landowners had been steadily expanding and enclosing their property, including their "deer parks" (fenced-in hunting preserves), into lands which had once been commonly held. English peasants continued to use these lands anyway as they had done traditionally, partly to protect the erosion of their customary hunting, fishing, and gleaning (collecting firewood) rights. Initially, the English propertied elites defended their newly emparked lands by setting vicious mantraps and snares in them to snag poachers. The peasantry, however, continued to hunt. In 1723 the Black Act was enacted by Parliament to stop illegal hunting (poaching), and as a result over fifty new capital offences were voted into law. Among the new offences were such things as blackening one's face with charcoal or grease (hence the act's name), carrying weapons, poaching game, illegal fishing, tree felling, and gleaning. In *The Adventures of Joseph Andrews* (1775) by Henry Fielding one catches a glimpse of this sanguinary law code in action: "Jesu!' said the squire, 'would you commit two persons to Bridewell (prison) for a twig?' 'Yes,' said the lawyer, 'and with great leniency too; for if we had called it a young tree they would have been both hanged.'" The British peasantry responded with clandestine, uncoordinated agrarian violence, burning barns, killing cattle, and breaking windows. This violence only subsided when the British elites stopped encroaching on common lands in the early nineteenth century, but by that time there was precious little of it left. The Black Act was repealed in 1823 on the grounds that it was no longer necessary to keep peace in the countryside.

Code Napoleon. Most of the *cahiers de doléances* submitted to Louis XVI on the eve of the French Revolution complained that French laws were neither uniform nor systematically implemented. A codification actually started under the National Convention during the Revolution but was interrupted by the Terror and was not finished. Napoleon, who desired to be known to history as the French Justinian (author of an imperial Roman law code), took up the task in 1804 and finished it in 1807. In France there were literally hundreds of different regional law codes, each a product of the historical development of a particular area. In the south written Roman law predominated, while customary

French coin with a portrait of the famous political philosopher (from Albert Sorel, *Montesquieu*, 1887)

parental blessing. Of course, only the groom could actually ask the parents for permission to wed. The Code was a monument to simplicity, accomplishing the goal of the council to create a complete, logical guide to French law that any citizen could understand. Concrete details and matters of enforcement were frequently omitted in favor of brevity. Article 146, governing marriage validity, for example, reads simply, "There is no marriage when there is no consent." In addition to codifying the law, the Code also altered French juridical practice. The jury, for example, was adopted from the British legal system. The Code Napoleon proved quite influential across Europe. Wherever Napoleon's armies went in conquest, the Code followed. Even after Napoleon's fall and exile in 1815 the transplanted law codes remained in force. Even countries that had despised Napoleon and his armies, such as Spain, had great respect for his law code. In western Germany, northern Italy, and the Netherlands the Code was enormously popular. In Prussia, where Napoleon was generally hated, the Code was abolished in 1815 but was reinstated in 1838 when a council of Prussian jurists who had attempted to create their own standardized law code could produce nothing better.

Corn Laws. The laws collectively known as the Corn Laws were passed by the British Parliament in 1815 and 1828. They imposed a sliding tariff on imported wheat (then called "corn" in Europe), which kept cheap foreign grain out when the price of British grain was high and allowed expensive foreign grain in when the price of British grain was low. The laws were designed to protect landowners but were unfavorable to merchants who imported grain and to British consumers, who had no choice but to pay the high prices for bread. As the population of Britain grew, the demand for grain increased commensurately. A series of bad harvests (1839–1841) were followed by the Potato Famine in Ireland (1845–1846) when approximately one million died of starvation and another one million immigrated to the United States. The specter of a revolution brought on by the "Great Hunger" spurred many liberal politicians to ally with economically liberal businessmen and form the Anti-Corn Law League in 1839. The League enjoyed enormous support from the working class, who were feeling the most dire effects of the famine, but it was ultimately the fear of a Britain-wide workers' rebellion that convinced the conservative prime minister Robert Peel (1788–1850) that the Corn Laws had to be repealed. By 1846, after a hard-fought struggle with the propertied elites, the Corn Laws were undone. However, the effort won Peel many powerful conservative enemies; in the same year Peel's government collapsed and he was swept from office.

Urban Police Forces. Through the eighteenth century catching criminals in Europe was left either to very small, barely trained protopolice groups, elements of the military, the local nobility, or to no one. Most criminals were not caught, and most crimes went unpunished. The French Revolution of 1789–1799, however, especially the "Great Fear" in which thousands of French peasants destroyed the feudal documents that bound them to the nobility, provoked a great deal of fear in Britain and across continental Europe. The

law, based upon local traditions, was common in the north. Napoleon hand-selected the members of a council of lawyers to codify the French legal morass, personally observed its work, and weighed in on critical decisions. Of the 2,287 articles ensconced in the Code, 1,851 dealt with the rights of property owners. The three sections of the Code were titled: *Of Persons; Of Property and Different Modifications of Property;* and *Of the Different Modes of Acquiring Property.* After property the next largest subject in the Code was the family. While Napoleon certainly did not author the entire Code, his hand is visible at certain points. Napoleon personally disliked the feminine influence he perceived in society, and the laws in the section *Of Persons* reflects this prejudice. Though the Code permitted divorce, the divorce process was made quite difficult (only an option after two years of marriage, and women could not apply for it by themselves). Under the Code, wives owed obedience to their husbands and were forbidden from buying, selling, mortgaging, or giving away property. Parental authority, especially that of the father, was recognized as the glue that held the modern state together. To this end, for example, no marriages could occur without

European middle and upper classes were terrified at the thought of a successful popular insurgency. To reassure them, many European countries created increasingly professional urban police forces that wore special paramilitary uniforms, patrolled the streets, and arrested lawbreakers. In Britain, Home Secretary and future prime minister Robert Peel created an unarmed municipal police force, nicknamed "bobbies" in his honor, which rigorously combed the avenues of British cities for criminal activity. France and Prussia followed Britain's lead. The new French gendarmerie was four times larger than Britain's police force, but because it was not well organized nor centrally controlled, it was not as effective at fighting crime. Prussia's police force, on the other hand, was quite small (only four hundred officers watched more than four hundred thousand Berliners), but it was effective. This efficiency was due partly to aggressive patrolling and the use of new methods of criminal investigation (including criminal profiling and fingerprint gathering) and partly to a willingness on the part of the Prussian police force to savagely beat their suspects. This reputation for brutality made the Prussian police unpopular with liberals but also made them feared by criminals.

Censorship. Virtually all eighteenth- and nineteenth-century European governments relied on some form of censorship to control their citizens. In places such as Great Britain, where constitutional liberalism had made inroads, the press had a fair amount of freedom to print its opinions. In places such as Russia, where autocrats ruled, the press was kept on a short leash—visits from the secret police ensured the cooperation of the print shops. Across Europe, government punished those presses whose publications contained ideas that were deemed subversive or seditious. Criticism of the government could result in nocturnal beatings, secret arrests, the closure of the shop and confiscation of the printing presses themselves, or, at worst, the destruction of the shop itself (usually by fire). In France the iron grip that the early Bourbon monarchs had exercised on the French presses had slipped quite a bit, but monarchs such as Louis XV could still control the print shops when the need arose. His favorite tactic was to arrest a publisher in the middle of the night with a lettre de cachet and imprison him for a few years. Voltaire, for example, was arrested twice and imprisoned in the Bastille for a time. By the late nineteenth and early twentieth centuries the press had become a powerful political tool. Court cases such as that of Henrietta Caillaux, the wife of Joseph Caillaux, the former president of France, were virtually tried in the newspapers. Reporters hung like vultures outside of the courtrooms and published each day's events, which the French populace eagerly devoured. The frenzied excitement that the press built up around such cases (Henrietta Caillaux had murdered a newspaper editor in 1913 after he attempted to blackmail her) transformed them into national scandals and directly affected the careers of those involved. Joseph Caillaux, who as president had sought political accommodation with Germany rather than military confrontation, was vigorously accused of weak-kneed pacifism in the press. The evidence for his weakness was, according to *Le Figaro*, a popular French tabloid, the fact that Joseph did not himself murder the editor in order to defend his wife's honor. An editorial stated that if Caillaux could not defend his own wife, he could not defend France. Caillaux's political career was badly damaged, and he disappeared from public life until 1924. The editor whom Henrietta murdered worked for *Le Figaro*. In Great Britain the presses were under the watchful eye of the government until the liberal political reforms of the mid-to-late nineteenth century transformed them into the mouthpieces of British political opinion. In Prussia, Russia, and Austria the press existed on the whim of the ruler.

Imprisonment. Generally, anyone who was arrested in Europe was held in a prison until his or her trial. A convicted criminal could also be remanded to a prison for incarceration as part of a sentencing, though this was not common before the 1820s. Prior to the reforms of Beccaria and the Code Napoleon, prisons such as Bridewell in Britain and the Bastille in France were essentially holding areas where corporal punishment was administered to criminals. The most common form of corporal punishment was flogging with a knotted-rope lash. Bridewell (built in 1618 and expanded in 1834) had cells for 800 inmates. Sanitary conditions were generally poor, but until the mid nineteenth century the prison population was not generally very large. After the introduction of professional urban police forces, the percentage of criminals who were actually caught rose considerably and overwhelmed the existing European prison system. European judicial systems struggled under the weight of so many new inmates; many adopted a variety of creative, if cruel and brutal, solutions to the problem. Workhouses, well-policed sweatshops in which convicts were put to work making a variety of products, were quite common across Europe. The underlying principle behind workshops was in essence that very hard work and enforced prayer could reform rogues and allow them to return to society. Beggars and vagrants, who were frequent targets of police roundups, often found themselves incarcerated in workshops—the judicial systems of Europe generally accepted the notions that all beggars were essentially lazy and that hard work was the only way to cure them of this. For the more dangerous criminals (which the justice system deemed unreformable) exile was a common punishment. From 1787 to 1875, for example, Britain exiled some 135,000 criminals to Australia. A further solution was to expand the actual prison system. However, this was expensive and took some time. As a temporary solution, many states resorted to confining prisoners in old ships, which were anchored in rivers or harbors. Food and water were occasionally ferried out to them, and the conditions onboard were uniformly nightmarish. It was also expected that the families of the prisoners would pay the costs of the inmates' food and lodging. In Russia a vast system of prisons, known as the gulags, was being built in western Siberia. The gulags were labor camps where convicts broke rocks in quarries all day in subzero temperatures.

Capital Punishment. Through the eighteenth and mid nineteenth centuries, death sentences were carried out in public as huge judicial spectacles. Thousands of onlookers would crowd around the executioner and his victim. The crowd

The Dreyfus Affair represented both a judicial scandal and a military scandal of epic proportions. France's humiliating defeat at the hands of Prussia in 1870 spurred a great deal of right-wing nationalist rhetoric and action, all of which was obsessed with avenging the French defeat. A variety of political and military scandals, such as General Georges Boulanger's suicide and the sale of Legion of Honor medals, shook the Third Republic through the 1880s and 1890s. To the French these scandals seemed to reveal a government and a military that were unprepared for France's future wars, especially against Germany. As paranoia over France's perceived inability to meet the German military threat mounted, anti-Semitism rose to a fever pitch. Though there were not more than ten thousand Jews in France (out of a population of forty million), the belief that the Jews were partly responsible for the 1870 debacle against Prussia had gained much credence among French politicians of all stripes. French anti-Semitism and France's deep-seated fears over its own military inadequacy came to a head in an epic scandal known as the Dreyfus Affair. Captain Alfred Dreyfus, an Alsatian Jew who left his homeland after it was ceded to Germany in 1870, was accused of passing secret documents to the Germans in 1894. The evidence against him was circumstantial, but, given the paranoid and anti-Semitic tenor of the French government and the fact that Dreyfus was Jewish, he was arrested and court-martialed. Dreyfus maintained his innocence. Never allowed to see the evidence against him and with few supporters, he was stripped of his rank and sent to the infamous penal colony of Devil's Island. However, his arrest did not stop the flow of documents to Germany. In 1896 the new chief of army intelligence, Lieutenant Colonel Georges Picquart (himself a confirmed anti-Semite) became convinced that the true culprit was one Major Walsin Esterhazy, not Dreyfus. The French army, however, was not willing to tarnish its image by admitting its error and freeing an innocent Jew. Picquart was sent to a post in Tunisia, and Esterhazy was acquitted. The novelist Emile Zola wrote newspaper articles on Dreyfus's behalf that attacked the army and government for falsifying and covering up evidence. The result was a firestorm of nationalist and anti-Semitic rhetoric, which generally charged Zola and Dreyfus with purposely undermining the prestige and effectiveness of the French army. Other attempts to pin the loss of other documents on Dreyfus failed. He was finally given a presidential pardon in 1899; his military rank was not restored until 1906.

Zola's spirited defense of Dreyfus was crucial to his eventual release. In this letter we see not only Zola's zeal but also the depth of his investigation—he knows, and points out, the guilty parties in no uncertain terms.

L'Aurore, January 13, 1898

Monsieur le Président:

Will you allow me, out of my gratitude for the gracious welcome with which you once received me, to convey my concern for your well-earned reputation, and to tell you that the good fortune of your glory is now threatened by the most shameful and indelible of stains? . . .

I accuse Lt-Col du Paty de Clam of having been the fiendish agent of a miscarriage of justice, unwittingly, I would like to believe, and then of having defended this nefarious enterprise for the past three years through the most absurd and guilty machinations.

I accuse General Mercier of having been at the least the weak witted accomplice of one of the greatest iniquities of this century.

I accuse General Billot of having had in his hands proof positive that Dreyfus was innocent, of having suppressed it, and of having committed this crime against justice and against humanity with the political objective of saving a compromised General Staff.

I accuse Generals de Boisdeffre and Gonse of having been the accomplices of this same crime, the first out of clerical conviction, no doubt, and the second perhaps acting out of the esprit de corps which considers the War Department the impregnable ark of the covenant. . . .

In making these accusations, I am not unaware that I open myself to charges under Articles 30 and 31 of the law on the press of July 29, 1881, which punish libellous acts. I deliberately expose myself to that law.

As for those I accuse here, I do not know them; I have never seen them; I bear them neither rancor nor hatred. They are for me no more than mere entities, the representatives of social malfeasance. And my action here is but the revolutionary means to hasten the explosion of truth and justice.

I have but one passion: that light be shed, in the name of a humanity which has suffered so much and has the right to happiness. My burning protest cries out from the depths of my soul. Let them dare to summon me before a court of law! Let the inquiry be held in broad daylight!

I am waiting.

Source: James F. Brennan, *The Reflection of the Dreyfus Affair in the European Press, 1897–1899* (New York: Peter Lang, 1998).

Front-page newspaper coverage of the Dreyfus Affair, 1898 (Yale University, New Haven, Connecticut [left]; Musée Carnvalet, Paris [right])

jeered at the convict and cheered his death. Until the invention of the guillotine in the 1780s, common criminals were hanged, and nobles were decapitated with either an ax or a sword. Sympathetic family members frequently slipped money to the executioner to make the death as quick and easy as possible. If this precaution were not undertaken, the criminal might endure great pain while he waited to die. Accounts of English executions abound with stories of beheadings in which it took the executioner as many as fifteen (and sometimes more) blows to sever the neck. The belief was that a gruesome execution would deter criminal activity by providing a horrifying example of justice. A terrifying example of this kind of spectacle can be seen in the 1 March 1757 execution of Robert-François Damiens, a man who attempted to kill Louis XV of France. He was "taken and conveyed in a cart, wearing nothing but a shirt, holding a torch of burning wax weighing two pounds"; then, "in the said cart, to the Place de Grève, where, on a scaffold that will be erected there, the flesh will be torn from his breasts, arms, thighs and calves with red-hot pincers, his right hand, holding the knife with which he committed the said parricide, burnt with sulphur, and, on those places where the flesh will be torn away, poured molten lead, boiling oil, burning resin, wax and sulphur melted together and then his body drawn and quartered by four horses and his limbs and body consumed by fire, reduced to ashes and his ashes thrown to the winds." Influenced by Enlightenment calls for more humane forms of punishment, Dr. Joseph-Ignace Guillotin pushed the National Assembly in 1789 to approve a bill that guaranteed criminals a quick execution. Though he did not invent the "guillotine" execution machine, his name became associated with it because of the legislation he proposed in the assembly. The guillotine's weighted blade could easily cut through a victim's neck in a single, quick blow, without any torture. Capital punishment in France also became more egalitarian in that criminals with death sentences from all social classes ended up in the same place: on the guillotine.

Sources:

Daniel Balmuth, *Censorship in Russia, 1865–1905* (Washington, D.C.: University Press of America, 1979).

Edward Berenson, *The Trial of Madame Caillaux* (Berkeley: University of California Press, 1992).

Michael Burns, *Dreyfus: A Family Affair, 1789–1945* (New York: Harper-Collins, 1991).

John Davis, *Conflict and Control: Law and Order in Nineteenth-Century Italy* (Atlantic Highlands, N.J.: Humanities Press International, 1988).

E. J. Hobsbawm and George Rudé, *Captain Swing* (New York: Norton, 1975).

Marie-Christine Leps, *Apprehending the Criminal: The Production of Deviance in Nineteenth-Century Discourse* (Durham, N.C.: Duke University Press, 1992).

George Rudé, *Criminal and Victim: Crime and Society in Early Nineteenth-Century England* (Oxford: Oxford University Press, 1985).

Bernard Schwartz, *The Code Napoleon and the Common-Law World* (New York: New York University Press, 1956).

Robert M. Schwarz, *Policing the Poor in Eighteenth-Century France* (Chapel Hill: University of North Carolina, 1988).

E. P. Thompson, *Whigs and Hunters: The Origin of the Black Act* (New York: Pantheon, 1975).

SIGNIFICANT PEOPLE

COUNT OTTO EDWARD LEOPOLD VON BISMARCK

1815-1898

FIRST CHANCELLOR OF GERMANY

Early Years. Otto von Bismarck, or Otto Edward Leopold, Prince von Bismarck, Count von Bismarck-Schönhausen, Duke von Lauenburg, was a powerful Prussian statesman who helped found the German Empire in 1871 and served as its first chancellor for nineteen years. Bismarck was born on 1 April 1815 at Schönhausen, northwest of Berlin. He studied law and entered government service in 1836. Unhappy in his post, he resigned a year later and took over the management of his family's estate. Driven by a strong sense of personal ambition, Bismarck entered politics in 1847. He emerged as a rigid conservative and delegate to Prussia's first diet. At the outbreak of the Revolution of 1848 he rushed to Berlin and urged King Frederick William IV to suppress the uprising. His loyalty earned him the appointment as Prussia's representative to the German Confederation in 1851.

Domestic Policy. From the 1850s until 1878 Bismarck allied himself primarily with the National Liberals, who sought a republican government in Germany. Together they created a civil and criminal code for the new empire, placed the deutsch mark on the gold standard, and moved the country toward free trade. Liberals, who had written off Bismarck as an archconservative, now viewed him as a comrade—a man who had rejected his conservative roots. Many conservative leaders agreed with this assessment: his policies had promoted rapid industrialization and concurrent social change. Their fears were further enhanced when he joined liberals in the *Kulturkampf* (a campaign against political Catholicism) in 1873. These views, however, ignored Bismarck's essential and deep-seated conservativism—embracing liberal political groups did not in any way mean that he would suffer republicanism in Germany.

Enemies of the Empire. Bismarck was surprised by the emergence of new political parties such as the Catholic Center, the Liberal Progressives, and the Social Democrats, all of which began participating in imperial and Prussian elections in the early 1870s. He labeled them enemies of the empire as each, in its own way, rejected his vision of a united Germany. To the Progressives the empire was too conservative, while the socialists worried over its capitalist nature. The Catholic Center was concerned that Protestant voices counted far more than Catholic ones. Bismarck despised the Catholic Center—he (and the liberals) feared the appeal of a clerical political party to the one-third of Germans who professed Roman Catholicism.

Falk. In Prussia the minister of public worship and education, Adalbert Falk, with Bismarck's blessing, introduced a series of bills establishing civil marriage, limiting the movement of the clergy, and dissolving religious orders. All church appointments were to be approved by the state. He purged clerical civil servants from the administration. The *Kulturkampf*, however, failed and actually convinced the Catholic minority that their fear of persecution was real. Bismarck gradually relaxed his campaign, especially after the death of Pope Pius IX in 1878. Pius IX had worked openly for Catholic rights in Germany. Nevertheless, Bismarck continued his anticlerical tirades until his fall in 1890.

Crude Attacks. By 1878 Bismarck's failure to establish an empowered representative government in Germany signified to many liberals that he was not truly one of them. Liberal ministers such as Falk and Rudolph Delbrück resigned and were replaced by conservatives. Beginning in 1879 the landed nobility, major industrialists, the military, and higher civil servants formed an alliance to prevent the emergence of republican government in Germany. Ever since the Commune of Paris (1871) Bismarck had developed a hatred for socialists and anarchists. He expressed this hatred quite crudely. On one occasion he wrote, "They are this country's rats and should be exterminated." In fact, the number of socialists in the Reichstag never exceeded 10 percent of the diet. Bismarck attempted to outlaw socialist political parties on several occasions, but his crudely formulated attacks merely invoked sympathy for the socialists. After two assassination attempts against Wilhelm I, Bismarck prorogued the diet and blamed the socialists (unjustly as it turned out) for the attacks. In this atmosphere Bismarck was easily able to ban socialist political parties from the Reichstag. Bismarck was also aware of the appeal republicanism had to the working class in Europe, especially France, and enacted legislation designed to lure workers away from political radicalism. During the 1880s the government introduced accident insurance, workers' pensions, and a type of socialized medicine. Nevertheless, Bismarck was never able to successfully connect with the working class, who increasingly supported the Social Democrats. The election of 1890 was a disaster for Bismarck in that the Catholic Center, the Social Democrats, and the Progressives gained more than half of the seats in the Reichstag. The new young emperor William II (reigned 1888–1918) did not want to begin his reign with a bloodbath or a coup d'état. In 1890, at age seventy-five, Bismarck resigned.

Blood and Iron. In 1861 Bismarck was named minister-president of Prussia and immediately began to expand the Prussian army. He warned those who quarreled over the added expenses that "the great questions of the day [meaning German unification] will not be settled by speeches and majority decisions . . . but by blood and iron." Public opinion began shifting to his side in 1864, when he used the expanded Prussian army to wrest the provinces of Schleswig and Holstein from Denmark in a lightning-fast military campaign. In 1866 Prussia declared war on Austria after a quarrel over hegemony in Germany. The resulting Austro-Prussian War lasted barely seven weeks before Vienna capitulated and surrendered its claim to power in Germany. Bismarck was deftly able to unite all of the northern and central German states under Prussian leadership in the North German Confederation. Faced with these achievements, the Prussian Reichstag bowed to him (he also browbeat his political enemies into obedience with accusations of treason). In 1870 Bismarck trapped France into a war with Prussia. Fear of French aggression prompted the reluctant southern German states to join a united Germany. In another fast-moving military campaign France was crushed and its government collapsed. In 1871 the German Empire, which included southern Germany, superseded the North German Confederation, and Wilhelm I, King of Prussia, became the German emperor, called the kaiser. Once the empire was established, Bismarck adroitly pursued a peaceful foreign policy that succeeded in preserving general European order until his dismissal in 1890. As imperial chancellor, Bismarck consolidated the newly united state. Externally, he sought to strengthen the empire by a network of defensive alliances with Russia and Austria-Hungary while at home he fought all who questioned his policies. When Wilhelm I died in 1888, his son, Wilhelm II, ascended the German throne. Wilhelm II disliked Bismarck's cautious foreign policy and reactionary domestic schemes and dismissed Bismarck in 1890. Bismarck retired to his estate, Friedrichsruh, where

he died on 30 July 1898. Bismarck must be reckoned as one of the preeminent statesmen of the nineteenth century.

Sources:

Lothar Gall, *Bismarck: The White Revolutionary*, 2 volumes, translated by J. A. Underwood (Boston: Allen & Unwin, 1986).

Bascom B. Hayes, *Bismarck and Mitteleuropa* (Rutherford, N.J.: Fairleigh Dickinson University Press, 1994).

Matthew Seligmann, *Germany from Reich to Republic, 1871–1918: Politics, Hierarchy and Elites* (New York: St. Martin's Press, 2000).

A. J. P. Taylor, *Bismarck, the Man and Statesman* (London: Hamilton, 1955).

David Wetzel, *A Duel of Giants: Bismarck, Napoleon III, and the Origins of the Franco-Prussian War* (Madison: University of Wisconsin Press, 2001).

CATHERINE II (THE GREAT)

1729-1796

TSARINA OF RUSSIA

Prussian Princess. Originally named Sophie Fredericke Auguste von Anhalt-Zerbst, Catherine was born in Stettin, Prussia. The daughter of a minor German prince, she moved to Russia in 1744 and married Grand Duke Peter of Holstein, a grandson of Peter the Great and heir to the Russian throne, in 1745. Catherine's father was one of many German nobles who aided the Russian tsars with their attempts at Westernization; he had many important connections at the Russian court and managed to parlay these into a royal marriage for his daughter. While the marriage was fraught with difficulties, the precocious, intelligent, and extremely ambitious grand duchess managed to learn a great deal in her adopted country. She learned Russian, survived court intrigues (as well as successfully engaging in some), and by all accounts adapted quickly to Russia. She was required to convert from Lutheranism to Russian Orthodoxy before marrying Peter. While this might have dismayed some, Catherine displayed great devotion to both her new religion and nation. With the death of Empress Elizabeth I (1762) Peter became Emperor Peter III of Russia. His reign, however, lasted only a few months. Peter was mentally unstable and quite paranoid: he immediately antagonized the court, the Orthodox Church, and the leading elements in the army. He also planned to rid himself of Catherine. In July 1762 Catherine and the imperial guard led by her lover Count Grigory Orlov overthrew Peter in a palace coup, and Catherine was declared empress as Catherine II. Orlov's brother Alexey murdered the deposed tsar in prison several days later.

Enlightened Reforms. Catherine fancied herself an accomplished intellectual and political liberal; she quoted from Montesquieu's *The Spirit of Laws* (1748) and exchanged letters with Voltaire and Diderot. Her first attempt at political reform in Russia, however, ended in failure. Catherine convened a legislative commission in 1767 to codify Russian laws. The commission consisted of 564 deputies, 28 appointed from state institutions and 536 elected by the boyars and the wealthy merchants. Of the elected deputies 161 came from the landed gentry, 208 from the merchants, 79 from the peasants, and 88 from the Cossacks and national minorities. The serfs (agricultural laborers bound to an estate and its owner) and clergy were not allowed to vote. Catherine wrote out a series of instructions for the commission. Though they seemed rather liberal, the instructions actually preserved the tsarina's autocracy and the boyars' agrarian power. The commission met for a year and a half, held 203 sessions, and was predictably dominated by the boyars, who refused even to recognize the peasant and Cossack representatives. Issues such as the abolition of serfdom were not even discussed. It is likely that Catherine herself expected and desired this result: the commission gave her reign the appearance of liberalism, while maintaining autocracy. The outbreak of war against the Ottoman Empire in 1768 provided a good excuse for Catherine to disband the commission.

Pugachev Rebellion. From 1773 to 1774 much of central and southeastern European Russia convulsed with violence in the great Pugachev rebellion. The illiterate Don Cossack Yemeleyan Pugachev exploited grievances among Cossacks of the Ural Mountains toward their Russian rulers (and toward the Russian army, which was fighting the Ottomans) to urge the Cossacks to revolt. Pugachev proclaimed himself tsar and quickly united all of the Cossacks under his banner. Serfs, miners, Old Believers (a dissident religious group), Bashkirs, Tatars, and other minority peoples flocked to Pugachev and swelled his Cossack army's ranks. At its height the rebellion encompassed a vast area in eastern European Russia. Important cities such as Kazan were seized, and Moscow itself was briefly in danger. Pugachev promised to execute all royal officials and boyar landlords, free the serfs, and end taxation and compulsory military service. The rebels displayed little organization; however, their efforts ultimately failed. Pugachev's motley troops could not compete with the regular army once it arrived in considerable numbers. Defeated in battle, the rebellion dissolved as quickly as it had arisen. Pugachev's own men handed him over to the Russian army. In Moscow he was tried and executed by drawing and quartering. After his execution his body was burned, and his bones were loaded into a cannon and fired in the direction of the Urals. After Pugachev's rebellion Catherine's flirtation with liberalism ended. The tsarina allied herself closely with the boyars and delegated much local power to them. Individual boyars were given free reign on their lands as long as they remained revolt free. She reorganized Russia's administrative units to allow the military to work hand in glove with the boyars to maintain peace. Catherine did this without impairing her ultimate control from St. Petersburg. The result of this was an even stronger, more-entrenched serfdom than before as boyars cemented their control of their lands. The French Revolution also increased Catherine's hostility toward liberal ideas. Several outspoken critics of serfdom, such as Nikolay Novikov, were imprisoned. Catherine might have been planning to join a European coalition against France when she died on 17 November 1796 in St. Petersburg. An important characteristic of Catherine's reign was the role played by her lovers or favorites. Ten men occupied this semiofficial position; at least two, Grigory Orlov and Grigory Potemkin, were important in formulating foreign and domestic policy.

Expansive Foreign Policy. Catherine II's main successes lay in her expansive foreign policy and her continuation of the process of Westernization, especially of the military. Her armies were victorious in two major wars against the Ottoman Empire (1768–1774 and 1787–1792), which extended Russia to the shores of the Black Sea. The Ottoman Turks by the 1770s had fallen far behind the European powers in military technology. Russia's armies were able to push the Turks out of the Crimea and the Caucasus region; the Sea of Azov became Russian and the port of Sevastopol was established. Treaties with Prussia and Austria led to three partitions of Poland (1772, 1793, and 1795), which effectively removed Poland from the map and extended Russia's territory into central Europe. In the short run the dismemberment of Poland satiated the desires of those states for territory; however, in the long run it destroyed a weak country that had formed an effective buffer between the three Eastern European rivals. After 1795 Russia, Prussia, and Austria could expand in eastern Europe only at each other's expense. Catherine's support for the Westernization of Russia included the invitation of French philosophes to St. Petersburg, the patronage of court poetry that glorified Peter the Great (the progenitor of Westernization in Russia) and Catherine II herself, and the improvement of the Russian army. On her death in 1796 Catherine II's son Paul I succeeded her on the Russian throne.

Sources:
John Alexander, *Emperor of the Cossacks; Pugachev and the Frontier Jacquerie of 1773–1775* (Lawrence, Kans.: Coronado Press, 1973).

Vincent Cronin, *Catherine, Empress of all Russias* (New York: Morrow, 1978).

Joan Haslip, *Catherine the Great* (London: Weidenfeld & Nicolson, 1977).

Isabel de Madariaga, *Russia in the Age of Catherine the Great* (New Haven: Yale University Press, 1981).

GIUSEPPE GARIBALDI

1807-1882
ITALIAN NATIONALIST

Wanted Man. Garibaldi was born in Nice, France, into a family of fishermen; he was largely self-educated and spent much of his youth as a sailor on Mediterranean merchant ships. Sometime before 1833 he joined the navy of Sardinia-Piedmont and gained his first military experiences. In 1833 he joined Giuseppe Mazzini's Young Italy movement, which was dedicated to freeing the Italian people from foreign rule and to unifying the country as a self-governing republic. In 1834 Garibaldi participated in a mutiny aboard a Piedmontese warship in a plot designed to spark a republican revolution in Piedmont, but the plot was discovered and foiled by the local police. Garibaldi was condemned to death in absentia by a Genoese court, but he escaped to France and then to South America. In 1836–1848 he lived as an exile in South America. He volunteered for the navy of the republic of Rio Grande do Sul, which was attempting to break away from Brazil, and quickly displayed unusual qualities of military leadership. Despite his best efforts, the Brazilian military was too large for the tiny breakaway republic to defeat; Garibaldi left the service of the Rio Grande with his lover, a married woman named Anna Maria Ribeiro da Silva (known affectionately to Garibaldi as Anita). In 1842 he, Anita, and their son entered Uruguay, which was fighting for independence from Argentina. He volunteered for the Uruguayan navy and within a few months became its head. In 1848 he commanded a group of Italian expatriates in the defense of the Uruguayan capital, Montevideo; these men became the core of his famous "Red Shirts" brigade. After a series of victories Garibaldi, his family, and sixty of his Red Shirts returned to Italy in the hopes of fomenting a republican rebellion there.

Italian Unification. He joined the movement for Italian freedom and unification, thereafter known as the *Risorgimento* (revival). He offered his services to Pope Pius IX and King Charles Albert of Sardinia-Piedmont, but he was rebuffed in both cases. The army of Sardinia-Piedmont scoffed at his self-taught martial skills and advised the king to turn him away. Garibaldi went next to Milan, where he was warmly welcomed. Despite some successes against the Austrians, who held much of Lombardy, the Milanese were heavily outnumbered, and Garibaldi was forced to flee across the border to Switzerland. In 1849 Pope Pius IX fled Rome in the face of a republican uprising; Garibaldi led his volunteers to Rome to support the fledgling Roman Republic. Garibaldi heroically defended the city against attacks by superior French and Neapolitan forces but was finally compelled to withdraw. Although he was allowed to depart with about five thousand of his followers, their line of retreat lay through Austrian-controlled territory; most of his force was killed (including his beloved Anita), captured, or dispersed, and Garibaldi had to flee Italy to save his life. The defense of Rome and his spirited retreat across Italy made him a heroic figure to the people of Italy. He fled first to Tangiers, then to Staten Island, New York, where he worked as a candlemaker, and then to Peru.

Red Shirts. In 1854 Count Camillo di Cavour, the chief minister of Sardinia-Piedmont, invited Garibaldi to return to Italy, with the proviso that he eschew Mazzini's radicalism. Garibaldi returned and bought a home on the island of Caprera, northeast of Sardinia. Garibaldi became convinced that the road to freedom and unity for Italy lay in alliance with the liberal ruler Victor Emmanuel II, king of Sardinia-Piedmont. Cavour enjoined Garibaldi to lead a volunteer force against the Austrians in Lombardy, and by mid 1859 Garibaldi and his men had captured Varese, Como, and much of the southern Tyrol. Thousands of other Italian patriots and revolutionaries were influenced by Garibaldi's position, a fact that did much to enhance the fortunes of the Sardinian monarch and influence the course of Italian history. Garibaldi became deeply involved in the complicated military and political struggles that took place from 1860 to 1870. King Victor Emmanuel II of Sardinia-Piedmont and Cavour recognized Garibaldi's value as a leader but were frightened that any further moves toward Italian unification would cause an Austro-French invasion. Garibaldi himself became frustrated with the king's vacillation, especially after his hometown of Nice was returned to France (1860). Garibaldi set out on his own in 1860 on a campaign that would ultimately result in the unification of Italy. He sailed from Genoa on 6 May with approximately one thousand men clad in red shirts (their only uniform) and reached Marsala, Sicily, on 11 May. The people of Sicily, especially the peasants and tradesmen, swarmed to his banner and swelled his army's ranks. He and his Red Shirts seized Palermo from the King of Naples and by 19 August had crossed the Straits of Messina into southern Italy. By September, Garibaldi and his men had deposed the King of Naples and had seized Naples itself. A tremendous victory on the Volturno River against the last remnants of the Neapolitan army delivered the Kingdom of the Two Sicilies into Garibaldi's hands—he promptly surrendered the conquered state to King Victor Emmanuel II.

Jealousies. Despite Garibaldi's unparalleled success, Victor Emmanuel II still feared him, perhaps even more after the conquest of southern Italy. Garibaldi had become popular and had spoken vigorously on his desire for a united Italian republic. Jealous and humiliated, the generals of the army of Sardinia-Piedmont convinced Victor Emmanuel II to refuse Garibaldi a role in the governing of the territories he had just conquered. Garibaldi criticized the king's mismanagement of these areas and complained that his volunteers, who had risked their lives for the king, had gone unrewarded. His arguments were ignored. However, Garibaldi was held in high esteem abroad—Abraham Lincoln offered him a command in the Union Army, and during a visit to Britain he was feted wherever he went.

On to Rome. In 1862 Victor Emmanuel II and his advisers developed a plan to capture Venice from the Austrians and convinced Garibaldi to lead a volunteer force in the campaign. They planned to preoccupy the Austrians by attacking them in the Balkans and then to invade Venice. Garibaldi, however, led his forces toward Rome, which was garrisoned by French troops. To Garibaldi, Rome was the natural capital of a united Italy. Victor Emmanuel II was frightened of French intervention and sent an army to stop him; Garibaldi was wounded in the resulting clash at Aspromonte and was taken prisoner. Victor Emmanuel II, however, fully realized Garibaldi's value—he was freed and in 1866 was given another independent command when war broke out in the Tyrol against Austria. The war ended when Victor Emmanuel II's forces, including Garibaldi, captured Venice. Though the Italians fought well, they were victorious mainly because the Austrians were also engaged in a war with Prussia (the Austro-Prussian War of 1866) and could not deploy their full might in the Tyrol. Garibaldi attempted to seize Rome on his own again in 1867, but the attack was poorly coordinated and resulted in defeat. For the next two years Garibaldi lived the life of a farmer on Caprera. In 1870 he offered his services to the French government and fought in the Franco-Prussian War. Again he distinguished himself as an excellent leader with an amazing grasp of battlefield tactics. Even so, France lost the war, and Garibaldi returned to Italy. Rome was annexed to Italy in October 1870, and Garibaldi was elected a member of the Italian parliament in 1874. In his last years he sympathized with the developing socialist movement in Italy and other countries.

Sources:

Autobiography of Giuseppe Garibaldi (London: W. Smith & Innes, 1889).

Christopher Hibbert, *Garibaldi and His Enemies: The Clash of Arms and Personalities in the Making of Italy* (London: Longmans, 1965).

Peter de Polnay, *Garibaldi: The Legend and the Man* (London: Hollis & Carter, 1960).

Denis Mack Smith, *Cavour and Garibaldi, 1860: A Study of Political Conflict* (New York: Oxford University Press, 1985).

Andrea Viotti, *Garibaldi: The Revolutionary and His Men* (Poole, U.K.: Blandford, 1979).

WILLIAM EWART GLADSTONE

1809-1898
BRITISH PRIME MINISTER

Religious Upbringing. William Ewart Gladstone was born in Liverpool to John Gladstone, a prosperous merchant of Scottish origin. His devoutly evangelical upbringing profoundly influenced his life. Gladstone distinguished himself at Christ Church, University of Oxford, but after much soul-searching he chose politics rather than a career in the church. Nevertheless, his religious convictions remained strong throughout his life. In 1839 he married Catherine Glynne; they had eight children.

Political Development. Gladstone was first elected to Parliament in 1832 with the Conservative Party. Throughout the 1830s the young Gladstone opposed almost all reform; his first speeches defended slavery in the West Indies and the Church of England. In 1843 he became president of the Board of Trade in the Conservative cabinet of Sir Robert Peel. Gladstone supported Peel's movement toward free trade, but in 1846, when Peel repealed the Corn Laws to help stave off starvation in Ireland and England, the Conservative Party lost the support of the landed elites, and Peel's government collapsed. Between 1846 and 1859 Gladstone was politically isolated. During this isolation his views changed from conservative to liberal because of the horrific famine in Ireland and the general fear that it could lead to an 1848-style revolution as had occurred in France. Religious intolerance in Great Britain, especially the exclusion of Jews and Catholics from government, had long irritated Gladstone's powerful religious convictions: his political isolation facilitated the transformation of this irritation into political action. He also supported the cause of Italian nationalism and unity. In 1859 he joined the Liberals and served as chancellor of the exchequer under Lord Palmerston. He gradually accepted the idea of an expanded voting franchise as a means of defusing the dangerous tensions that were building in British society; this made him a champion of the lower classes. In 1866 Gladstone proposed an amendment to the Reform Acts, which would further enfranchise the working class by using monetary amounts paid to landlords as qualifiers. This act, in effect, would allow people without land the right to vote. The proposal failed, however. Benjamin Disraeli, Gladstone's great rival, presented an amendment that was more palatable to the British social and political elites: financial qualifications for voting rights were lowered, and householders, including many urban workers, were included in the franchise. Disraeli's bill passed in 1867.

First Ministry. In his first ministry (1868–1874) Gladstone's reform record was impressive. One of his most significant acts was to create a national elementary education program for all British children (1870). His government made major reforms in the justice system, making the central courts more efficient; in the civil service, basing employment on merit; and in the military, abolishing the purchase of army commissions. Perhaps Gladstone's most difficult policy project was his effort to resolve the festering conflict in Ireland. The Irish had long demanded independence from Britain. However, the Potato Famine and the British government's unwillingness to alleviate the situation had radicalized many formerly moderate Irish people and had led to considerable violence. The British government, which had traditionally been unwilling to grant Ireland any autonomy, was even more opposed to Irish independence after the waves of violence began. The majority of the Irish population was Roman Catholic. However, several hundred years under the yoke of British imperialism had brought many Anglican and Presbyterian settlers from Great Britain to Ireland, most of whom became powerful landlords. Gladstone removed support for the Anglican Church in Ireland: Irish Catholics were no longer forced to pay taxes to support it. Irish tenant farmers had long been vulnerable to surprise evictions by their British landlords; Gladstone ameliorated this situation by requiring that the landlords pay compensation to any evicted tenants. The wealthy and propertied of Britain, however, grew worried that the changing voting franchise would upset their traditional political power—in 1874 the Conservatives were voted into office with Disraeli as Prime Minister.

Second Ministry. Gladstone was sharply critical of the practices of the Disraeli government in Britain's overseas empire. During the election of 1880 Gladstone's cogent opposition to the British annexation of the South African Republic, the Afrikaner (or Boer) state in the Transvaal region of what is now northern South Africa, won him many supporters. Gladstone felt that the annexation of South Africa was morally wrong but also worried about Great Britain's ability to protect such a distant and unstable place. His critiques were well taken by the voters; he won the election of 1880 and resumed his place as prime minister. The Reform Act of 1884 was the most important piece of legislation in Gladstone's second ministry. This act further lowered financial qualifications for voters and extended the vote to many rural citizens. He ushered in the Land Act of 1881, which gave Irish tenant farmers greater control over the land they farmed, through Parliament, but peace remained elusive. In 1884, for example, the chief secretary and the undersecretary for Ireland were assassinated by Irish radicals. While Gladstone had come to believe that Irish home rule was necessary if further violence were to be prevented, his views were not popular in Parliament. In foreign affairs he was criticized for abandoning the Transvaal to the Afrikaners in 1881; for bombarding Alexandria during an Egyptian revolt; and for failing to get relief troops to the Sudan in time to prevent the death of Charles "Chinese" Gordon, a popular British general, in 1885. Gladstone and his cabinet were slow to react to problems in the empire—he argued that continued imperial expansion was morally unjustifiable and amounted to slavery.

Third and Fourth Ministries. Gladstone's third (1886) and fourth (1892–1894) ministries were dominated by his pursuit of home rule for Ireland. His first Irish home-rule bill (1886) split the Liberal Party: many Liberals saw the Irish as little more than rabid animals and refused to support any reduction in British power over Ireland. In 1893 a second home-rule bill passed the House of Commons but was rejected by the House of Lords. Gladstone wanted to continue to struggle for Irish home rule, but his cabinet, many of whom worried about the effect the fight would have on their careers, refused. He therefore resigned as prime minister in 1894 and retired.

Impact. He died of cancer at the age of eighty-eight and was buried in Westminster Abbey. Gladstone mobilized an idealistic liberalism in the British public; he believed that government reform could improve life for all British citizens. His efforts to increase the voting franchise to include urban workers and farm laborers defused dangerous social tensions and probably prevented a revolution in Britain. His sponsorship of public education also allowed the children of these same laborers the hope of upward mobility. The Liberal Party grew strong under Gladstone, and his governments provided political stability in England for almost three decades. He was guided by firm religious beliefs, he distrusted imperialism, and he decried mistreatment of people throughout the world.

Sources:
D. A. Hamer, *Liberal Politics in the Age of Gladstone and Rosebery: A Study in Leadership and Policy* (Oxford: Clarendon Press, 1972).

Roy Jenkins, *Gladstone, a Biography* (New York: Random House, 1997).

H. C. Matthew, *Gladstone, 1809–1874* (Oxford: Clarendon Press, 1986).

Richard Shannon, *Gladstone* (Chapel Hill: University of North Carolina Press, 1984).

MARIE-JOSEPH-PAUL-YVES-ROCH-GILBERT DU MOTIER, MARQUIS DE LAFAYETTE

1757-1834
FRENCH STATESMAN AND MILITARY OFFICER

Noble Birth. Marie-Joseph-Paul-Yves-Roch-Gilbert du Motier, marquis de Lafayette, was born on 6 September 1757 into a prestigious noble family: he was the son of Michel Roche Gilbert du Motier, marquis de Lafayette, colonel of the grenadiers, and Marie Louise, daughter of Joseph Yves Hyacinthe, marquis de la Riviere. In 1768 he attended the College of Louis-le-Grand, and in 1770 he inherited an immense fortune when both his mother and grandfather died. He became a page to the queen, Marie Leczinska, in 1771. Through her influence he received a lieutenant's commission to the Royal Musketeers. On 11 April 1774 he married Anastasie Adrienne de Noailles, second daughter of the duke d'Ayen. He joined the circle of courtiers around King Louis XVI but soon became consumed with the desire to win military glory. An enthusiastic devotion to liberty and the rights of man was then emerging among Frenchmen from all social classes. Many young officers were eager to go to America, some because of a well-reasoned interest in the cause at stake there and others from a love of romantic adventure or a desire to strike a blow at the English in revenge for the disasters of the Seven Years' War (1756–1763).

American Revolution. In July 1777 Lafayette left France for America to seek glory in the fledgling American Revolution. The charming and charismatic Lafayette struck up a lasting friendship with the American commander in chief, General George Washington, who gave him the rank of major general. Lafayette fought with distinction at the Battle of Brandywine in Pennsylvania (September 1777) and conducted a masterly rearguard action during the retreat following the Battle of Barren Hill (May 1778). In 1779 Lafayette returned to France to help persuade the government of Louis XVI to send an expeditionary force to aid the colonists against England. By the next year Lafayette's efforts had succeeded; he returned to the colonies and was immediately put in command of an army in Virginia. He aggressively pursued the English commander Lord Charles Cornwallis, outflanked him, and forced the British general to retreat to the Virginia coast, where he became trapped at Yorktown in the summer of 1781. A sizable French fleet cut off Cornwallis's seaborne supplies, and the timely arrival of several more colonial armies sealed Cornwallis's doom. He surrendered on 19 October. Lafayette returned to France a hero in 1782 and was promoted to the rank of brigadier general. His return to America in 1784 was widely celebrated; several states in the newly formed United States of America made him an honorary citizen.

French Revolution. From 1784 to 1789 Lafayette, powerfully influenced by his experiences in America, became a leader of the liberal aristocrats. He advocated religious tolerance and the abolition of slavery and was elected as a representative of the nobility to the Estates General (May 1789). Lafayette supported the bourgeois deputies in their bid for increased representation at the Estates and in their creation of the National Assembly. He helped pen the Declaration of the Rights of Man and was elected commander of the newly formed National Guard. Lafayette, however, was no radical: he believed that a constitutional monarchy on the English model was the most appropriate government for France. When a crowd of radical revolutionaries stormed Versailles on 6 October 1789, Lafayette ordered his troops to rescue the king and queen. Lafayette's popularity was at its apex through 1790—he supported the National Assembly's policies, especially the transference of political power from the aristocracy to the bourgeoisie, but worried that too broad a franchise would encourage the lower classes to attack property rights (the Great Fear only added to his misgivings). On 17 July 1791 a mob gathered on the Champ de Mars in Paris and demanded the abdication of the king—Lafayette, fearing for the monarch's safety, ordered the National Guard to open fire. The resulting bloodshed wrecked Lafayette's high standing with the revolutionaries, who were becoming increasingly radical, and forced him to resign his command. At the outset of the war against Austria in 1792 Lafayette was given the command of an army. From his camp he wrote to the National Assembly and denounced the dangerously radical policies of the Jacobins. Lafayette plotted to march on Paris with his army and suppress the radical democrats who were rapidly moving France away from a constitutional government. Before the plan was completed, news arrived of the imprisonment of the king. Lafayette refused to obey the orders of the assembly and arrested the commissioners it sent to his camp. The assembly removed him from command and appointed Charles-François du Périer Dumouriez in his place (19 August). Since Lafayette's soldiers were in sympathy with the radicals, he fled to Belgium. He was taken prisoner by the Austrians and spent nearly four years in the dungeon at Ohnutz, where he was starved and tortured. In the United States many felt sympathy for him. Washington appealed to Emperor Francis I that Lafayette be allowed to come to the United States on parole. He was finally set free on 23 September 1797 after Napoleon's victorious campaign against Austria. After a sojourn in Holland he returned to France (March 1800) and retired to his castle of La Grange. Napoleon sought his loyalty by offering him positions in the government, including the position of minister to the United States, but Lafayette declined these offers. He also declined President Jefferson's offer of the governorship of Louisiana. During Napo-

leon's rule Lafayette remained at La Grange. His wife died there on 24 December 1807.

Later Years. After years of seclusion he was elected to the chamber of deputies (1818–1824) where he espoused moderately liberal policies: he opposed censorship of the press and restrictions on private property. In 1824 Lafayette was invited by Congress and President James Monroe to visit the United States. He arrived 15 August 1824 in New York and visited each of the twenty-four states. Everywhere he went he received tokens of enthusiastic reverence and affection. In consideration of his services in the Revolutionary War, Congress voted him a grant of $200,000 and twenty-four thousand acres of land. In the July Revolution of 1830 in France he became commander of the National Guard and was instrumental in overthrowing the conservative King Charles X and in placing Louis Philippe on the throne: Lafayette still hoped to give France a constitutional monarchy. He remained a member of the chamber of deputies until his death. He left one son, George Washington, and two daughters, Anastasie and Virginie. Among all the eminent Frenchmen of the revolutionary period he was perhaps the only one with nothing to be ashamed of in his career. His character was so thoroughly imbued with American ideas of constitutional liberty that he found it difficult to identify with any of the violent movements originating in the French Revolution of 1789.

Sources:

Peter Buckman, *Lafayette: A Biography* (New York: Paddington, 1977).

Lloyd Kramer, *Lafayette in Two Worlds: Public Cultures and Personal Identities in an Age of Revolutions* (Chapel Hill: University of North Carolina Press, 1996).

Sylvia Neely, *Lafayette and the Liberal Ideal, 1814–1824: Politics and Conspiracy in an Age of Reaction* (Carbondale: Southern Illinois University Press, 1991).

PRINCE KLEMENS WENZEL NEPOMUK LOTHAR VON METTERNICH

1773-1859
AUSTRIAN STATESMAN AND DIPLOMAT

Early Powerful Connections. Prince Klemens Wenzel Nepomuk Lothar von Metternich was born in Coblenz on 15 May 1773 to Count Georg, Austrian envoy of the court of Vienna at Coblenz, and Maria Beatrix, née Countess von Kageneck. He studied philosophy at the University of Strasburg (1788–1790) and law and diplomacy at Mainz (1790–1793). In 1795 he married Countess Eleonore Kaunitz, heiress and granddaughter of the former Austrian state chancellor Wenzel Anton, Graf von Kaunitz. The marriage connected him to the highest of the Austrian nobility and gave him access to positions of power that would have been otherwise unobtainable. Metternich began his public career in 1801 as Austrian ambassador to the court of Dresden. Though he had studied for a diplomatic career, he was fortunate in receiving an ambassadorial appointment as his first assignment. It is likely that his father, the envoy to the Rhenish principalities of the Holy Roman Empire, interceded on his behalf. Only two years later he was made ambassador to Berlin. The Austrian emperor considered it very important to have a minister at Berlin who could gain the favor of the Prussian Court.

War with Napoleon. Napoleon I's star had risen high in France and Europe, and his empire was at its zenith. Emperor Francis needed his ablest ambassador at Napoleon's Court, and in May 1806 he sent Metternich to Paris. Metternich found himself in the difficult position of representing Austria to Napoleon. Though he could count no real diplomatic successes in Paris, Metternich's efforts allowed him to form important contacts with members of Napoleon's inner circle, such as his sister Caroline Murat and the foreign minister Charles Talleyrand. Through these contacts Metternich gained insight into Napoleon's mind and character. His overestimation of the impact of the Spanish uprising (1808) upon France led Metternich to advise Emperor Francis I to go to war with France in 1809. Though victorious at Aspern, the Austrians could not follow up their good fortune and were crushed at Wagram. Despite the defeat, Metternich was able to play upon Napoleon's vanity by offering him a diplomatic marriage to Archduchess Maria-Louise, Francis I's daughter. The marriage allowed Metternich some diplomatic maneuvering room—Austria was not required to join Napoleon's Confederation of the Rhine, nor become a client state with a French ruler. The war left Austria economically and militarily broken. However, by 1810 Napoleon had lost interest in Austria and was busily preparing for the 1812 campaign in Russia. Metternich took advantage of this breathing space to attempt a reform of the Austrian government along Prussian cameralist lines, but Francis I resisted allowing nonnobles and non-Germans into the government. In 1812 Austria was obliged to send troops to aid the French army during the invasion of Russia. The French military disaster in Russia caught Metternich off guard, but by 30 January 1813 he had concluded an armistice with Russia and withdrawn all Austrian forces from Russian soil. As France reeled from the debacle in Russia, Napoleon desperately formed a new French army. The 1813 Russo-Prussian offensive into French-held central Europe proved premature—Napoleon was wounded but not yet ready to give up. Metternich mediated the peace among the three powers in 1813 and determined that the complete collapse of French power would allow Russia virtually uninhibited influence in Europe. Napoleon obstinately refused to honor the agreement, and Austria, Russia, and Prussia went to war against France in late 1813. At the Battle of Leipzig (October 1813) Napoleon was decisively defeated and lost control of central Europe—Metternich was awarded the hereditary title of prince by Francis I for his work in assembling the victorious coalition. Though allied to Prussia and Russia, Metternich carefully preserved the independence of the south German states and worked to prevent Russian and Prussian expansion into central Europe. Clearly, he did not want to swap Napoleon I's dictatorship for that of a Prussian king or Russian tsar.

Congress of Vienna. The Congress of Vienna (September 1814–June 1815) constituted the apex of Metternich's diplomatic career. Metternich worked to gain territories in Italy and Germany for Austria and strove to include defeated France at the conference table, especially as a counterweight to Russia. For the settlement of future difficulties several congresses were held: Aix-la-Chapelle, 1818; Karlsbad, 1819; Vienna, 1820; Troppau, 1820; Laibach, 1821; and Verona, 1822. When the Russian councillor Kotzebue was assassinated by a student at the Karlsbad Congress, Metternich took measures to put an end to the political troubles in Germany. All publications of less than twenty folios were subjected to censorship; government officers were placed at the universities to supervise them; and representative constitutions were suppressed. Despite England's and Russia's resistance, Metternich intervened in the Italian states, which were threatened by internal unrest. This measure made Austria very unpopular in Italy. Austria and Russia also split on the question of freeing Greece from the Turkish yoke. Austria feared Russian domination of the Balkans and supported the Turks. The Russians were incensed and gained English support for the Greek insurgents. The result was a blow to Metternich's policy—his influence was waning as that of Russia and Prussia waxed. The moderation and skill that Metternich displayed through the negotiations produced a very successful balance of the European powers—it was not seriously upset until World War I.

Later Years. The reconstruction of Austria, however, did not proceed along such positive lines. Francis I refused to establish departmental ministries (which Metternich had demanded) and rejected the creation of a series of provincial diets which would represent the empire's various nationalities. Though Metternich was certainly no fan of political liberalism, he realized that there was a growing voice in the empire for nationalist representation and did not want that voice transformed into rebellion. Further, Metternich was unable to prevent the creation of liberal representative governments across central and southern Germany in 1817–1820. Dismayed, he threw Austrian support behind the increasingly reactionary and conservative German nobility (the junkers). Despite his flagging prestige, Metternich was made Austrian state chancellor in 1821. Under Emperor Ferdinand I (ruled 1835–1848) the direction of state affairs was in the hands of a regency-like council, which consisted of Arch Duke Ludwig (the emperor's uncle), State Chancellor Metternich, and Court Chancellor Franz Anton, Graf von Kolowrat. Kolowrat outmaneuvered Metternich on the council by gaining Ludwig's ear and thus ensured that Metternich's influence over Austria's internal affairs was marginal at best. After 1826

Count Kolowrat's influence was decisive. Many Austrians envied Metternich his preeminence; his fall from power was not mourned. When the July Revolution of 1830 in France spawned insurrections in Belgium, Poland, and Germany, Metternich, despite his declining influence, was generally viewed by political liberals as a dark, reactionary force of repression and became the object of nationalist hatred. The orders for the violent excesses of the Austrian generals Alfred Windischgrätz and Joseph Radetzky in their brutal suppression of the 1848 Revolution were widely believed to have come from Metternich himself. Actually, he had precious little influence over Austrian affairs by that time. In 1848 Metternich, hounded by scaling liberal criticism, resigned his position a defeated man. He went in exile to England and returned to Vienna in 1851. He died eight years later in his palace at the age of eighty-six.

Sources:

Robert Billinger, *Metternich and the German Question: States' Rights and Federal Duties, 1820–1834* (Newark: University of Delaware Press, 1991).

Charles S. Buckland, *Metternich and the British Government from 1809 to 1813* (London: Macmillan, 1932).

Arthur J. May, *The Age of Metternich, 1814–1848* (New York: Holt, Rinehart & Winston, 1962).

WILLIAM PITT THE ELDER

1709-1778

BRITISH PRIME MINISTER

Great Commoner. William Pitt was born on 15 November 1708 to Robert Pitt and his wife, Lady Harriet Villers. Though the Pitt family was not aristocratic, they had, through their own initiative and strength of will, succeeded in a variety of enterprises, and had amassed some land and a small fortune. William's grandfather, Thomas "Diamond" Pitt, had been the governor of Madras in India, for example. While there, "Diamond" Pitt amassed a tidy fortune through lucrative black market deals. When he returned to England, he purchased several rotten boroughs, including the infamous Old Sarum that William Pitt himself represented when he became a Member of Parliament (MP). As an MP and as Prime Minister (PM) Pitt successfully played upon his nonaristocratic origins to create a powerful popular base of political support. Pitt graduated from Eton (attended 1719–1726) with honors, and attended Trinity College, Oxford (1726–1727), and the University of Utrecht (1728). Though he received high marks from virtually all of his professors, he particularly excelled at oratory, forensics, and debate. Pitt was in many ways a born actor: from his college days he learned to study his gestures and expressions in a mirror before going out in public in order to maximize the effects of his statements. His opponents accused him of vanity, superciliousness, and egotism but also conceded that he was a fiery patriot. His oratory skills soon pointed him in the direction of a political career, though without an aristocratic pedigree he was forced to tread a more populist path to political power. This approach occasionally got him into trouble. In 1736 he was, for example, expelled from the Royal Army (in which his parents had purchased him a commission in 1731) for reading a speech that was critical of the influence Hanover (King George II's ancestral land) had on Britain's foreign policy. The speech raised the ire of George II, who took Pitt's remarks as a personal affront. For the next twenty-four years the king worked energetically to exclude Pitt from government, especially from any office with cabinet rank. Being the object of royal enmity was certainly politically disadvantageous to Pitt; however, his forthright stature through the ordeal earned him a great deal of respect among the English common folk and Whigs and Tories alike. When he entered Parliament, Pitt played up his plebeian origins and adopted the sobriquet *Great Commoner.* In 1737 he received the appointment of Groom of the Bedchamber of the Prince of Wales, a position that kept him well out of London.

Parliament. British politics in the 1730s centered on the creation of a policy that would both expand domestic industry and keep the European peace. The PM was Sir Robert Walpole, a hard-drinking man with a reputation for having the finest head for figures in England; he steered British foreign policy away from military confrontations in Europe by making peace with both France and Spain (Britain's traditional economic and colonial rivals). This strategy, as well as Walpole's relentless purging from his cabinet of anyone with policy ideas differing from his own, successfully alienated many of Walpole's own Whig party members from him and effectively created a sizable opposition to him in Parliament. Walpole excluded Pitt from his administration largely to placate George II, who still held a grudge against Pitt. Nevertheless, Pitt still sat as an MP. He used his seat to savagely attack Walpole's foreign policy; he openly questioned whether Britain's foreign policy had been subordinated to that of Hanover, especially with regard to the hated Spanish. His speeches in Parliament and in public helped whip England into a bellicose furor over the general mistreatment of British sailors at the hands of Spain. The grisly tale of Captain Robert Jenkins, who claimed that his ear had been cut off by Spanish sailors in 1731 while his vessel was being searched, created an angry and war-like mood in England and eventually forced Walpole to declare war on Spain in 1739 (the War of Jenkins' Ear). George II's worries over the fate of Hanover, however, meant a cautious war strategy, even when the War of the Austrian Succession (1740–1748) exploded across Europe and threatened to absorb Britain's tiff with Spain into its maelstrom. The British public, which generally wanted revenge for what was perceived as predatory Spanish behavior, was infuriated by Britain's neutrality at the war's outset, especially since this was effected largely to preserve Hanover's integrity. Scandalous broadsides questioned the competence of the king's ministers, especially Walpole, and presented the public with images that questioned royal authority (in one image Britain is represented as a large, dull-witted dog whose leash is held by a fat, beer-drinking German with "Hanover" printed on his hat). By 1742 a battered Walpole resigned. Despite Walpole's fall, the Whig dominance of the House of Commons ensured that they would maintain control of the government. In 1744 Henry Pelham ousted the new PM, John Carteret, Earl Granville, and then himself became PM. Pelham brought many young Whigs into his cabinet, except Pitt, whom George II still despised. Pelham was a savvy politician but did not have a wide political base. For this he relied on his brother, the duke of Newcastle, who, through bribes and patronage, held more pocket boroughs then any person in England. Though they balanced one another well, Pelham and Newcastle merely continued Walpole's neutralist foreign policy. Pitt was isolated from cabinet or ministerial office but still sat as an MP. He again used this position as a bully pulpit and spoke vigorously and persuasively against any peace with Spain. Pitt suspected, and stated as much in his speeches, that the Bourbon monarchs of Spain and France had signed some sort of secret pact between themselves against Britain. In fact this had occurred, but few outside Paris and Madrid were yet aware of it. In such a situation, Pitt reasoned, peace with either country was dangerous to Britain, regardless of Hanover. Pitt called for war and spelled out his plan for a successful military venture against Spain. By the late 1740s Pitt had developed a reputation for having the keenest understanding of British foreign policy, especially its military aspects, of anyone in England. In 1746 Pelham suggested the addition of Pitt to the cabinet on the basis of his considerable foreign policy expertise; George II, who nursed grudges against many of Pelham's allies (including Newcastle), flew into a rage and refused to allow it. Disgusted with the king's lack of objectivity, Pelham and his cabinet resigned en masse as a protest. George II, however, could find no one able or willing to form a majority in Parliament and was forced to accept Pelham's demands. Pitt was allowed into the cabinet, but only at a junior level. This relatively stable political arrangement was cut short by Pelham's death in 1754. Newcastle succeeded Pelham as PM, but, despite the fact that he controlled many pocket boroughs and held a majority in Parliament, Newcastle was not a savvy politician and found it difficult to formulate workable policies. Newcastle, for example, ignored the ominous clashes between French and British forces in North America and India through the early 1750s. He argued before Parliament that these disturbances were unimportant and would not lead to war. Newcastle apparently believed his own rhetoric; he did little, if anything, to prepare the military for what many already knew was going to be a long, tough fight.

Empire. When the Seven Years' War (1756–1763) broke out in Europe, the conflict spilled quickly into the colonies. Great Britain was caught unprepared and by mid 1757 was in danger of losing its commercial entrepots in India and its colonies in America. For his part, Pitt stepped up his verbal assault on the government and charged Newcastle with incompetence. Military defeats piled up, and public criticism against Newcastle mounted; he was forced to resign in 1758. George II surprisingly yielded to parliamentary and public pressures: he allowed Pitt into the cabinet as the secretary of state and gave him virtually dictatorial control of England's war effort. Pitt buried what differences he had with Newcastle and invited him into the new cabinet. In the cabinet of 1758 Newcastle served as a figurehead PM and used his influence in the House of Commons to ensure the passage of legislation; Pitt, on the other hand, actually crafted the government's policies. Pitt proved himself to be one of England's best wartime ministers. In 1757 he enthusiastically began a complete new reorganization of the British military. Incompetent field commanders were retired or recalled, and young talented officers, such as George Augustus Howe and James Wolfe, were promoted. The troops themselves were outfitted with new equipment, uniforms, and weapons, received regular supply shipments, and had their overall level of manpower increased. Pitt also planned Britain's overarching war strategy and individual military campaigns himself. His primary aim was to break France's colonial empire in North America and India. In India, Pitt allowed the brilliant new British commander Robert Clive to pursue an aggressive, and ultimately successful, strategy against the French. In Europe and North America, however, Pitt carefully managed each phase of the war. Realizing that France's armies must be tied down in Europe if Britain were to have success in the colonies, Pitt secured huge cash loans from Parliament to Frederick II of Prussia. These subsidies proved to be crucial to Prussia's survival. With French troops effectively bogged down in Europe, Pitt's reorganized military was able to successfully seize and hold Canada. In 1758 British and colonial forces captured the key forts of Louisbourg, Duquesne, and Oswego. In 1759, after a daring nighttime amphibious assault, Wolfe took Quebec and effectively choked off the rest of Canada from any French resupply efforts. With the capitulation of Montreal in 1760 French rule in Canada effectively ceased. These victories were followed by English military successes in India, where the outnumbered British used treachery and guile to drive the French from Bengal. Spain, now anxious to avoid a war with Britain, ceded Florida as the price of peace. England's victories in the Seven Years' War and consequent gains at the Peace of Paris (Canada, Cape Breton, Senegal, and Florida) constitute the greatest military achievement in English history, and established the foundations of the British Empire—Pitt himself, through his deft handling of the military and diplomatic situation, could claim a great deal of the credit for the victory. For Prussia, however, the war had not gone as well: British subsidies had achieved Frederick II's survival; however, much Prussian territory was still occupied by Austrian, Russian, and French armies. Redressing the situation diplomatically at the peace table would likely have entailed Britain surrendering some of the territory it won at France's expense. Pitt was unwilling to give back Canada or India and advocated continuing the war. The new king, George III, and his advisers, especially the king's personal friend John Stuart, Earl of Bute, were reluctant to continue the war, as its economic cost had nearly bankrupted the state. Pitt's arguments for the continuation of the war made his position in the cabinet untenable, and he was forced to resign in 1761. By mid 1761, however, considerable evidence had surfaced that not only demonstrated Spain's war-like intentions but also proved the existence of a secret pact between the Bourbon courts in Paris and Madrid. Bute, now PM, had to declare war despite his earlier protestations. Many English people felt that the gains at the Peace of Paris (1763) did not adequately reflect the magnitude of Britain's victory. Parts of Bengal, for example, were returned to France, but no compensation was exacted for Britain elsewhere. Bute and George III, who had chaperoned the treaty through Parliament together, were greeted with a chorus of popular disapproval. Worse followed for Bute as George III was mentally unstable from 1765–1766. His government crippled, Bute resigned in early 1766.

Illness. After the king had recovered, he offered the PM position to Pitt in an effort to stabilize the government. Pitt accepted; however, his disgust with the party system in Parliament, which he saw as perpetuating corruption, made him bitter and irascible. Instead of knitting together the politically fissured government, Pitt's domineering tenor merely exacerbated existing divisions. Pitt's biggest mistake, however, was in accepting the title of Earl of Chatham as a reward from George III for his war record in 1766. As a member of the peerage, Pitt was now excluded from the House of Commons, where his oratory had been the key to his success. Further, Pitt and George III locked horns over Britain's policy toward the American colonies: Pitt favored a conciliatory approach that would not drive the colonist into revolt, while the king preferred to browbeat the colonists and force their obedience. Pitt led an attack on George Grenville's Stamp Act (1765), for example, but his failing health prevented him from fully addressing the issue. Exhausted and gaunt, Pitt retired to his estate to rest. Despite his illness he wrote hundreds of letters to various MPs urging or deploring various policies. On 1 April 1778 he attended the House of Lords for a debate on the situation in the colonies with the intention of opposing the duke of Richmond's motion to give the colonies their independence (which Pitt felt was a mistake). Pitt collapsed during an argument and was carried from the House of Lords to his estate, where he died on 11 May at the age of 68.

Significance. Pitt's historical importance rests mainly on his early achievements as war minister. His successful prosecution of the Seven Years' War, made especially difficult by royal attempts to undercut him, gained England the most territory of any modern war England has fought in, and established it as the dominant world power through the eighteenth and nineteenth centuries.

Sources:

Jeremy Black, *Pitt the Elder* (Cambridge & New York: Cambridge University Press, 1992).

Peter D. Brown, *William Pitt, Earl of Chatham, the Great Commoner* (London: Allen & Unwin, 1978).

Kate Hotblack, *Chatham's Colonial Policy: A Study in the Fiscal and Economic Implications of the Colonial Policy of the Elder Pitt* (London: Routledge, 1917).

Marie Peters, *The Elder Pitt* (London & New York: Longman, 1998).

DOCUMENTARY SOURCES

Laure Junot Abrantès, *Memoirs of Napoleon, his Court, and Family* (1836)—Abrantès's memoir does for Napoleon I what Suetonius did for the Roman Caesars: rather than concentrate on Napoleon's political or military machinations, Abrantès focuses on the steamy and seamy side of Bonaparte's rule.

Cesare Beccaria, *On Crimes and Punishments* (1764)—This influential corpus contains a wealth of information on crime, courts, police forces, and punishment in the eighteenth century.

Bismarck, the Man and the Statesman, 2 volumes (1899)— An autobiography of the first chancellor of Germany, written after his retirement from public office.

Carl von Clausewitz, *On War* (1833)—A military textbook that has influenced martial doctrines and behaviors around the world since it was first published. The work is coldly brutal in its advocacy of a form of total war, in which the cities and peoples of an enemy country are considered military targets.

The Correspondence of Prince Talleyrand and King Louis XVIII during the Congress of Vienna (1881)—French documents dealing with issues raised during the 1814–1815 international meeting. Statesmen representing countries that had defeated Napoleon (primarily Austria, Russia, Prussia, and Great Britain) redrew the map of Europe and restored conservative political order.

The Dispatches and Letters of Vice Admiral Lord Viscount Nelson, 7 volumes (1845–1846)—Not as elegant as Lafayette's nor as salacious as Metternich's memoirs; however, they do include a wealth of information on life at sea in the eighteenth and nineteenth centuries. Especially interesting are his descriptions of the many foreign ports and peoples he dealt with over his long career.

William Ewart Gladstone, *A Chapter of Autobiography* (1868)—Offers some insight into Gladstone's considerable abilities as a statesman.

Memoirs, Correspondence, and Manuscripts of General Lafayette (1837)—An intriguing collection of documents compiled by the family of the marquis.

Memoirs of Prince Metternich (1773–1815)—Metternich recorded not only his political insights and strategies but also such things as which women he fancied at court and how he planned to seduce them.

Florence Nightingale, *Notes on Nursing: What It Is, and What It Is Not* (1860)—A British nurse who served with distinction in the Crimean War, Nightingale spurred positive changes in the British army's medical corps.

Abbé Emmanuel-Joseph Sieyès, *What is the Third Estate?* (1789)—This pamphlet raised the author to prominence at the beginning of the French Revolution.

Napoleon in his coronation robe; painting by François Gerard, 1805 (Musée du Chateau de Versailes)

LEISURE, RECREATION, AND DAILY LIFE

by DEAN FERGUSON

CONTENTS

Sidebars and tables are listed in italics.

1752
- Now about 11 days behind the solar year, England changes from the old, Julian calendar to the modern, Gregorian calendar, which has been used in western Europe since 1582. Unlike the Julian calendar, which has 365 days, the Gregorian calendar accounts for the fact that the earth takes 365¼ days to orbit the sun by adding a day to February every four years.

1766
- Mathurin Roze de Chantoiseau opens the first Parisian restaurant.

1783
- François Ami Argand invents a home oil lamp that burns more brightly than earlier lamps.

1793
- The Revolutionary government of France abolishes sumptuary regulations, which have forbidden the lower classes to dress like their social superiors or to wear clothing that might encourage immorality.

1796
- Nicolas Appert, a chef in the French Revolutionary army, devises a method of preserving perishable foods in glass bottles.

1810
- Appert begins preserving food in tin cans instead of glass containers, an innovation that paved the way for the modern canned-food industry.

1811
- Eleven Surrey women play eleven Hampshire women in cricket.

1816
- Friedrich Ludwig Jahn publishes his *German Gymnastics.*

1824
- Pierre Parissot opens a Paris shop to sell inexpensive, fixed-price work clothes.

1842
- Edwin Chadwick writes his *Report on the Sanitary Condition of the Labouring Population of Great Britain* for the Poor Law Board, calling attention to the squalid, overcrowded conditions in which most workers live.

1843
- Lea & Perrins Worcestershire Sauce is bottled and sold.
- The Rochdale Pioneers' first cooperative grocery store opens in England.

* DENOTES CIRCA DATE

1846
- The Rugby School publishes the rules for rugby football.

1848
- The British Public Health Act sets in motion efforts to improve working-class housing.

1850
- Scotsman James Harrison invents the first ice-making machine.

1851
- The Crystal Palace Exhibition in London displays technological innovations and new consumer goods.

1859
- Frenchman Ferdinand Carré unveils a device to make ice cubes.

1863
- The English Football Association is established.

1867
- Henri Nestlé begins marketing infant formula.

1869
- Aristide Boucicaut lays the cornerstone for a new, large building for his Au Bon Marché store, which becomes the first modern department store in Paris.

1872
- Thomas Lipton opens the first of his Lipton's Markets groceries in Glasgow.
- The Wanderers beat the Royal Engineers 1–0 in the first Football Association Cup championship game.

1877
- The All-England Croquet and Lawn Tennis Club sponsors the first Wimbledon tennis tournament.

1878
- Cadbury's chocolate manufacturers build a rural factory, in part to allow workers to work and exercise in the countryside.

1880
- The first international cricket competition is held between England and Australia.
- Bastille Day (14 July) becomes the official commemoration of the French Revolution.
- The first British electric power plant is built.

* Denotes Circa Date

1895
- Willibald Gebhardt and Carl Peters found the Deutschen Bund für Sport, Spiel, und Turnen (German League for Sports, Games, and Gymnastics).

1896
- The first modern Olympics competition is held in Athens, Greece.

1904
- The British ministry of education publishes a *Syllabus of Physical Exercises*, prescribing gymnastics and military-drill exercises for youths of both sexes.

* **DENOTES CIRCA DATE**

Surrey County Cricket Club playing Australia at the Oval, in South Croydon, England, 1888 (Public Record Office, London)

OVERVIEW

Between Two Wars. Two world wars serve to frame the historical era between 1750 and 1914: the Seven Years' War (1756–1763), whose American component was the French and Indian War (1754–1763), and the "Great War," now known as World War I (1914–1918). In the Seven Years' War, the dynastic aims of eighteenth-century European monarchs intertwined with their ambitions for colonial and maritime dominance to spark a conflict that occupied Europeans worldwide. That war, however, had specific territorial objects and did not target civilian populations. Furthermore, it was fought with weapons lacking the lethal power of those used in World War I. This conflict among industrialized states was fought on land by huge armies outfitted with machine guns, tanks, large artillery pieces, biplanes, and mustard gas, and at sea by submarines and fleets of steel-clad, coal- and oil-powered battleships. It was a total war with significant numbers of civilian casualties. Eighteenth-century soldiers had limited contact with their families at home. At the height of the Great War, soldiers in the trenches frequently commented on the surprising intrusions of daily life. "England," one soldier wrote home, "is so absurdly near." In fact, the mails rapidly transported many of the comforts of home to the front: including newspapers, magazines, record players, new boots, home-cooked pastries, cheeses, wines, canned foods, chocolates, and even fresh flowers. Some department stores put together special gift assortments for the troops. The new sensibility of leisure also extended into the inhospitable world of the trenches. Before the modern era, war had been the "sport of kings" and likened to hunting, jousting, swordplay, or chess. The games had changed by 1917. In an act of bravado, Captain W. P. Nevill distributed four footballs to each of his company platoons and offered a prize to the men who first advanced its ball to the German front line. The signal for the advance was a long kick toward the German lines. By 1917, loyal troops intimately associated national identity with practices of consumerism and leisure that had been integral to routines of daily life since the turn of the twentieth century. That English troops ate preserves from Harrods or that German soldiers wallpapered their bunkers and installed electric lights may appear inconsequential next to the horrors of modern industrialized combat. In fact, such intrusive consumerism reveals the degree to which daily life and leisure had been transformed during the nineteenth century.

A Pre-Industrial Consumer Revolution. The development of a consumer society in nineteenth-century Europe resulted from a variety of interrelated changes with roots extending back into the pre-industrial period. Fashion had long been set by the royal courts of Europe. Beginning in England in the eighteenth century, however, the commercial marketplace became the arbiter of taste, and styles of dress and household furnishings came in and out of fashion on an annual or even seasonal basis. As Samuel Johnson commented in 1759, "The trade of advertising is now so near perfection that it is not easy to propose any improvement." By 1800, the fear of falling out of fashion motivated consumers across Europe. New advertising techniques fueled such anxieties. Fashion magazines broadcast the latest styles from London or Paris. Testimonials in daily news sheets hawked everything from fine porcelain to razors.

Advertising Tactics. The eighteenth-century commercial revolution rested at least in part on new merchandising techniques: the testimonial and the newsprint advertisement. Josiah Wedgwood, well known for his fine porcelains, employed what today would be called "niche marketing" to target aristocratic consumers and to solicit endorsements from them that he could use in future marketing schemes. For example, in offering a new product line to regular customer Sir Robert Murray Keith, Wedgwood mentioned in a 1 March 1786 letter, "They have not yet been made public in this Kingdom, His Royal Highness the Prince of Wales only being in possession of a set of them." Wedgwood then appealed to Sir Robert's patriotism: "If these little things should appear to your Excellency likely to place the ingenuity of the manufacturers of this Kingdom in a favourable point of view to Foreigners, I shall not doubt your Excellency will do me the honor to take them under your patronage in the circle of your friends." Once his porcelain wares became prestige items, Wedgwood was able to sell them to well-heeled members of the middle class through his showrooms and catalogues. Another sucessful businessman, George Packwood, devoted his promotional talents to peddling razor strops for sharpening straight-edge razors, creating the advertising jingle that had become commonplace a century later. The

10 March 1796 issue of *The True Briton* included "A LESSON FOR LOVERS: OR THE VIRTUE OF THE RAZOR STROP":

> To Packwood, my agent, for comfort repair,
> "He'll give you a face that shall soften your fair,
> "His strop shall those bristles that fright me remove,
> "And the maid shall exchange all her hatred to love."
> The youth bo'd obedience, to Gracechurch-street went,
> And told Packwood the errand on which he was sent.
> Packwood smil'd, and display'd the best goods in his shop,
> His most fav'rite Paste—his most excellent Strop.
> The youth purchas'd both, since he each much approv'd,
> And obtain'd what he wanted the maid that he lov'd.
> Thus Venus with kind and ineffable grace,
> Has giv'n Packwood the means to improve on the face.

Bourgeois Consumption. Merchandising through mail-order catalogues and showroom displays exposed wider and wider audiences to new products and styles. Intensified fashion anxiety reflected status competition between social groups. Merchants, artisans, and servants tried to emulate the fashions of their social superiors, while the higher ranks used fashion to maintain a visible distinction between themselves and their social inferiors and so to proclaim their elevated status. Through the nineteenth century the old ruling classes—court society and the aristocracy—continued to influence tastes, but their dominant cultural position no longer went unchallenged. The first phase of the Industrial Revolution, which lasted from the mid eighteenth century until the middle of the next century, enriched and politically empowered entrepreneurs, financiers, manufacturers, and industrialists. Aristocratic tastes faced challenges from this middle class, which was still uncertain of its place in society. On the one hand, the bourgeoisie was increasingly wedded to the values of self-discipline, hard work, and thrift, so they loathed aristocratic luxury as wasteful. The classic symbol of the new middle-class man became the black three-piece suit. On the other hand, however, many members of the bourgeoisie spent lavishly on home decor, adopting styles of feudal lords of centuries past. They thereby sought to legitimize their recent accession to political leadership with rich, ornamental, luxurious furnishings that evoked the leisured existence, discriminating tastes, and hierarchical social relations of the old ruling elites.

Mass Consumption. While factories began to appear during the "First Industrial Revolution," bourgeois consumption still rested on the work of skilled craftsmen in their shops rather than on factory labor. By the end of the late 1870s, however, a new phase of industrial productivity extended the technological and marketing innovations of the industrial era to a mass market. The effects of this "Second Industrial Revolution" on daily life and leisure can be seen clearly in the mass consumption of food and sport. Mass-produced "processed foods" rapidly standardized food consumption in most national markets, with certain name brands available in the grocery stores that sprang up in urban centers. By 1880, a grocer in an English small town, for example, stocked his shelves with Wotherspoon's corn flour, Symington's pea flour, Nestlé's condensed milk, Cross & Blackwell jams, and Cadbury's chocolates. A decade later, a shopper in the United States could purchase from his grocer Heinz pickles, National Biscuit Company (Nabisco) soda crackers, and Kellogg's cereals. Systems of mass distribution were connected by an integrated network of railway lines. The same British railroads also hauled thousands of supporters of working-class football (soccer) clubs to games, where the athletes kicked a standardized ball consisting of a bladder (made of rubber imported from English colonies) inside a mass-produced leather shell. After the game, fans visited neighborhood pubs, frequently franchises of national breweries, and relived the match while downing a pint or two, perhaps of Guinness, brewed at Saint James Brewery, the largest brewery in the world during the late nineteenth century.

Politics and Everyday Life. As at other times of important social change, the nineteenth-century transformation of daily life had political dimensions. The French Revolution of 1789, for example, had as immediate an impact on the practices of daily life as it did on the "rights of man." To ensure the freedom of artisans to enter and practice any trade they chose, the Allarde Law of 1791 abolished the guild system, which limited competition by restricting the number of craftsmen who could enter each trade and by requiring that each member have a single, different specialty. From 1791 to 1866 legislation inspired by liberal, "free-trade" ideology gradually eliminated guild control over artisan production, first in England, France, and the Low Countries, and later in central and southern Europe. Freed from guild restrictions, many merchants and entrepreneurial artisans established new merchandising venues—restaurants, grocery stores, and, later, department stores. Another result was the increasing standardization of production techniques and products, such as ready-to-wear clothing and shoes.

Freedom of Dress. In 1793 French revolutionary lawmakers also overturned centuries of sumptuary legislation with the decree that "No person of either sex can force any citizen, male or female, to dress in a particular way. . . . Everyone is free to wear the garment or garb suitable to his or her sex that he or she pleases." By this time pressures of consumerism, particularly in England, had already done much to undermine such restrictions, which had originally been established to create distinctions among social classes and to discourage immoral behavior by banning suggestive clothing. The end of the Old Regime of fashion was marked by a legislated "freedom of dress." As the Revolution in France spread to Europe by Napoleonic conquest at the beginning of the nineteenth century, it unleashed a spirit of nationalism across Europe, which frequently found expression in dress, cuisine, entertainments, and celebrations. Nationalist antiquarians in search of traditional identities seized on regional peasant garb as authentic symbols of cultural nationalism.

Public Utilities. Political reform movements of the nineteenth century also focused attention on everyday life. The threat posed to bourgeois political leadership by the restive laboring classes of the early industrial era encouraged unprecedented efforts by all the major European governments to take control of urban environments. The urban poor did not always welcome these efforts. Street lamps, for example, were often the first targets of urban rioters, not just to cover criminal behavior with the protection of darkness but as a politically symbolic attack on the forces of order. Despite such resistance, an entire infrastructure of public utilities—street lighting, public sewage systems, and municipal water supplies—was developed to bring order to the city. While these urban reforms were inspired by anxieties about the working class and public health, this vast public investment galvanized the emerging middle-class preoccupation with privacy. The private home became a protected space shielded from the disease and crime the bourgeoisie associated with the dangerous classes beyond their front doors.

TOPICS IN LEISURE, RECREATION, AND DAILY LIFE

CHANGES IN TIME

Pre-Industrial Rural Time. Modern societies schedule work routines, household management, sleep, and entertainment according to demarcations of time. This temporal allocation is a product of an abstract reckoning generally based on a twenty-four-hour day and a seven-day week. This way of thinking had much to do with the increasing importance of efficiency and profit in business or industrial enterprises. Pre-industrial life, in contrast, took place in a different temporal system. For peasants across Europe, time was calculated by seasonal and agricultural rhythms and by the social routines of the village. The year was not primarily conceived in terms of months, but rather as *veillées*, times for sowing, haying, and harvesting in rural France. These events were social occasions at which villagers gathered to repair farm implements, shell nuts, spin thread, embroider, or prepare jams or wine. They began sometime after All Saints' Day (1 November) and concluded in the spring just before planting. These gatherings were not just times for work. They also featured music, dancing, storytelling, courtship, and rough athletic competitions. They served the important function of securing cultural coherence within and among generations.

Pre-Industrial Urban Time. In early modern cities, as in the countryside, time was not yet divided into fixed mathematical units. At the beginning of the nineteenth century most urban craftsmen had little need for a precise daily schedule. Fewer than half of all Parisians, for example, owned watches. Instead, city residents structured time around religious services, patron saints' feast days, or the liturgical calendar. The workday, rather than being a fixed amount of time, as became common for factory workers, contracted or expanded with the demands of particular jobs. Leisure was every bit as important as work, probably more so. For example, the late eighteenth-century Parisian glazier Jacques-Louis Ménétra frequently accompanied comrades to a tavern in the middle of the workday, and, like other artisans, he observed "Saint Monday," a time for drinking and reveling with his fellow craftsmen or recovering from weekend excesses.

Industrial Time. The temporally rigid factory regime had no place for Saint Monday, leading to its extinction. For both peasants and urban workers, nineteenth-century mechanization and industrialization eventually changed earlier agrarian or artisanal pursuits. By 1914 the farmer and the factory worker had acquired a new sense of time. Factory work required the worker's rigid subordination to the repetitive, mechanical, and regularized discipline of clock time. Everything operated according to the regular demands of spinning machines, lathes, presses, or other mechanized "labor-saving devices." Railroad schedules, school bells, factory whistles, and pocket watches marked the rhythm of industrial time. By the time the punch clock was patented in 1888, workers had long been subordinated to the continuous, regular, mechanical activity of the factory floor. With the demarcation of "productive" time, measured by worker output against time increments, leisure time increasingly came to mean time free from workplace demands, time devoted to family pursuits, entertainment, and consumption.

Bourgeois Time. For a nineteenth-century bourgeois man, the use of one's time had social implications. One mark of elevated social distinction for the elites of the Old

A PEEP AT THE GAS LIGHTS IN PALL-MALL.

Cartoon about public reaction to the installation of the first gas streetlights in London, 1807–1808 (by G. M. Woodward; from Dean Chandler and A. Douglas Lacey, *The Rise of the Gas Industry in Britain*, 1949)

Regime had been an ostentatious keeping of late hours. Similarly, during the nineteenth century the middle classes sought to distinguish themselves from artisans, shopkeepers, and workers by filling their evenings with social activities. Work dictated that artisans and workers must rise early, so the "better sort" rose later, arriving at the office well after laborers and working into the evening after laborers had gone. The middle class dined late and retired even later. Middle-class men divided their time according to a cycle of social engagements, which could be observed in their changes of clothing over the course of the day: a dressing gown for a morning at home, a black suit for business or calling on others, and formal wear for evening socializing. A bourgeois woman's time was also marked by a schedule of clothing changes. According to Frenchman Henri Despaigne's 1866 behavior manual:

> A society woman who wants to be well dressed for all occasions at all times needs at least seven or eight toilettes per day: a morning dressing gown, a riding outfit, an elegant simple gown for lunch, a day dress if walking, an afternoon dress for visiting by carriage, a smart outfit to drive through the Bois de Boulogne, a gown for dinner, and a gala dress for evening or the theater. There is nothing exaggerated about this, and it could be more complicated still at the beach, in summer, with bathing costumes, and in autumn and winter, with hunting and skating costumes, if she shares these wholesome activities with men.

Such manuals outlined a rigorous schedule for the bourgeois housewife. She was the first to rise in the morning (to avoid being seen in disarray by her husband) and began to oversee a complex domestic routine. She spent her morning supervising servants, seeing children off to school, and planning the daily round of family meals, evening outings, and social visits or receptions. Well-bred women supervised the errands of their servants to purchase coal, wood, or food. Seldom did a middle-class woman do such errands herself, for to be seen performing such tasks told the world that she had an insufficient staff and thus was not of the social status she claimed. Her afternoons were consumed with the social obligations of receiving visitors, paying calls to others, and strolling in the park or riding in the carriage, yet another form of social display. She devoted her evening hours to overseeing the preparation and service of family or formal dinners, and then she accompanied her husband to musical performances, social visits, or other entertainments.

Darkness and Light. Historians have often noted the "tyranny of darkness" as a characteristic of pre-industrial life. Before the widespread availability of artificial light, nightfall had a sinister significance. Every evening pre-industrial urban communities prepared for darkness by locking city gates, proscribing night work (for fear of fire from an unattended candle), enforcing curfews, and patrolling streets in search of malefactors. Household security was no less important. As night fell, householders barred their doors, fastened their shutters, and kept sticks, stones, bed staves, cudgels, swords, and sometimes firearms within easy reach. One of the consequences of nineteenth-century artificial lighting—fueled by oil, kerosene, gas, or later, electricity—was a trans-

Nineteenth-century entrepreneurs and factory managers attempted to increase efficiency and profits by regularizing laborers' work hours. In particular, they attempted to eliminate "Saint Monday," a day that workers regularly took off either to recover from a drunken Sunday or to carouse with friends and co-workers. In England, Saint Monday was also a common day for wedding celebrations among the working classes. The following verses commemorate this bygone unofficial holiday:

Half-Past Nine, or My Wedding Day
I'm longing for next Monday 'cos I'm going to tie the knot
With little Georgie Puddingy-Pie, a nice young man I've got
And when the parson says the word that makes two into one,
I want you all to just come round and join us in the fun.
Chorus:
For next Monday morning is my wedding day;
When the supper's over if the company wants to stay,
Me and Georgie we shall resign,
We're going to blow the candles out at half-past nine.

The Jovial Cutlers
How upon a good Saint Monday,
Sitting by the smithy fire,
Telling what's been done o't Sunday,
And in cheerful mirth conspire,
Soon I hear the trap-door rise up,
On the ladder stands my wife:
    "Damn thee, Jack, I'll dust thy eyes up,
    Thou leads a plaguy drunken life;
    Here thou sits instead of working,
    Wi' thy pitcher on thy knee;
    Curse thee, thou'd be always lurking.
    And I may slave myself for thee."

Fuddling Day or Saint Monday
Saint Monday brings more ills about,
    For when the money's spent,
The children's clothes go up the spout,
    Which causes discontent;
And when he staggers home,
    He knows not what to say,
A fool is more a man than he
    Upon a fuddling day.

Sources: Douglas Reid, "The Decline of Saint Monday, 1766–1876," *Past and Present*, 71 (1976): 76–101.
Reid, "Weddings, Weekdays, Work, and Leisure in Urban England 1791–1911: The Decline of Saint Monday Revisited," *Past and Present*, 153 (November 1996): 135–163.
E. P. Thompson, "Time, Work-Discipline, and Industrial Capitalism," *Past and Present*, 38 (1967): 56–97.

berers then regularly rose from this "first sleep" sometime after midnight, remaining awake for up to two hours before returning to bed. These regular nocturnal interruptions may have provided opportunity for sexual intimacy, which was not easily arranged in the cramped dwellings of the poor, where many people crowded into a single room and even the same bed. With the spread of artificial light sources, this interrupted sleep pattern gradually disappeared. Another result of the advent of artificial, and increasingly inexpensive, lighting was the extension of business or entertainment activity well into the night for more people. For the urban, bourgeois elite, an evening out with wives and friends at the theater, opera, or restaurant might be followed by strictly male visits to a gambling house or a brothel, often lasting until three in the morning. Gaslight and later electric street lamps illuminated the way home for these men as it did for factory workers off to their jobs just before dawn. Public lighting also made possible strolls along city boulevards, window shopping at the illuminated storefronts of new, late-nineteenth-century department stores, or visits to a neighborhood café, tavern, or pub. By the turn of the twentieth century, the tyranny of darkness had largely been overcome nearly everywhere. Evening was transformed into a time for family and leisure activities.

Rituals and Celebrations. Daily routines in all cultures are punctuated by festive events that attach meaning to the utilitarian experiences of life. In traditional societies, R. Caillois has said, "a man lives in remembrance of one festival and in expectation of the next." In pre-industrial Europe many of these events were religious in nature, and the growing secularization of European life during the eighteenth century did not reduce the importance of ritually significant times. In nineteenth-century Spain, as in other Mediterranean countries, traditional religious commemorations associated with Christmas, Easter, saints' days, and the Corpus Christi cycle united the liturgical calendar with civic and family celebrations. In these countries the passion and social significance of religious ritual did not much diminish during the nineteenth century. Alongside religious events came national days of patriotic remembrance. School holidays, which also became family vacations, broke up the academic year. The summer season became a time for the bourgeois to rent country cottages, vacation in hotels, or visit the seashore. These annual migrations of the urban middle class clearly identified its members as leisured, despite the contradictory moral strictures of the middle-class work ethic. Sunday also acquired a new, secular importance as a day for family gatherings and visits to the country or the park, promenading alongside other city folk.

Patriotic Festivals. The American people, like citizens of most modern nations, maintain a calendar of events designed to unify diverse communities by celebrating the glorious past of the United States: Fourth of July parades, Thanksgiving Day feasts, and Memorial Day fireworks. Traditions such as these arose and flourished everywhere in Europe during 1750–1914. In the eighteenth century Jean-Jacques Rous-

formation of European sleep routines. Pre-industrial sleep patterns were "segmented" into two major intervals of sleep interrupted by an hour or more of wakefulness. Most Europeans retired to their beds around nine or ten o'clock. Slum-

The Festival of the Supreme Being, held on the Champs-de-Mars in Paris on 8 June 1794 as part of the attempt by the French Revolutionary government to replace Christianity with a state religion based on reason (Musée Carnavalet, Paris)

seau, for example, encouraged the Polish government to adopt the ancient Greek tradition of staging festivals that featured public games and sports, advising that such activities would uplift the people and infuse the nation with patriotic emotion. In the 1790s the French revolutionary governments established a full calendar of patriotic commemorations. Other nations followed suit. Aspiring German nationalists commemorated heroic and mythic events from their past in many early-nineteenth-century festivals. Perhaps the most influential of these early rites, the Hambach festival of 1832, attracted more than 30,000 German celebrants, who watched formations of workers parading in archaic regional costumes. Other German patriotic festivals, before and after unification in 1871, featured torch-light processionals, political speeches, folk dancing, and gymnastic exhibitions. After the 1870s, with the emergence of mass politics, new public ceremonies and national holidays joined with older, now regularized patriotic rites and secured the multiple associations of sport, family time, leisure activity, and patriotic enthusiasm. Bastille Day (14 July), whose official celebration dates only from 1880, annually commemorates the French Revolution with festivities, fireworks, street dances, and military parades. After the Prussian defeat of France in the Franco-Prussian War in 1870, commemorations of the pivotal Battle of Sedan combined similar festivity and patriotic speeches. In 1883, at a Sedanfest in Oldenburg, Germany, more than 1,500 inhabitants marched in a torchlight procession, sang patriotic songs, and listened to patriotic speeches until 1:30 in the morning. The revelers then danced until 5:00 A.M. After the unification of Italy in 1860, nationalist Massimo Taparelli, Marchese d'Azeglio, described the function of such celebrations: "We have made Italy: now we must make Italians." Indeed, these recurring events became linked to consumer strategies, family rituals, and public entertainment in the nineteenth-century development of nationalism in Europe.

Carnival. In addition to patriotic, family, and religious holidays, people in many parts of nineteenth-century Europe celebrated ancient festivitals such as Carnival. During the carnival season in late-eighteenth-century Rome, city streets decorated with flowers and tapestries became the settings for improvised dramas and puppet shows, as well as raucous partying and wanton behavior by masked celebrants. Though the government made a small monetary contribution and provided minimal crowd control, the Roman people staged Carnival themselves. Carnival was a time of social inversion, which was usually absent in most nineteenth-century domestic or patriotic festivals. On the Corso, the main street of Rome, noblemen, soldiers, beautiful courtesans, and local dignitaries gathered for chaotic carriage parades that attracted thousands of viewers. Participants staged mock battles with sugar-coated almonds and comfits, and at nightfall they endeavored to blow out each others' candles or lanterns. Johann Wolfgang von Goethe described one such battle:

No matter whether the person next to you is an acquaintance or a stranger, you equally try to blow out his light, and on his rekindling it to blow it out again. . . . "Sia ammazzato!" (Be murdered!) is heard from all ends and corners. "Sia ammazzato chi non porta moccolo!" (Murder to him who does not carry a taper!). . . . All ages and classes contend furiously with each other. They jump on the steps of each other's coaches. No pendant light, hardly a lantern is safe. The boy blows out his father's flame and never ceases crying, "Sia ammazzato il Signore Padre!" All in vain for the father to scold him for his impudence; the boy asserts the freedom of the evening and only the more savagely murders his father.

Sacred Family Time, The Battle for Christmas.
Patriotic and secular festivals did not supplant the religious calendar. For Europeans of all classes, the cycle of sacred commemoration still retained its vitality. However, the meaning of religious holidays changed significantly during the nineteenth century. The "battle for Christmas" illustrates the transformation of a religious holiday from a public event to a family ritual. In preindustrial Europe, Christmas, like Carnival, was a time of excess and social inversion. During the Christmas season the poor, who normally owed deference to their betters, inverted the social order by demanding gifts and respect from their social superiors. Marching through a village, bands of poor boys and young men "went a-wassailing," claiming the right to receive gifts, food, drink, and entertainment from their wealthier neighbors. Wassailing carried a veiled threat, as one wassail song makes clear:

> We've come here to claim our right . . .
> And if you don't open up your door,
> We will lay you flat upon the floor.

Instead of seeing this apparent aggression as a threat to the social order, the rural gentry may in fact have viewed it as an enhancement of their social position, taking this opportunity to demonstrate their generosity while allowing the rural poor to vent their pent-up frustrations. With industrialization and the spread of wage labor, however, many employers bent on efficiency no longer wished to tolerate the seasonal interruption of business. Furthermore, the wassail tradition exposed the entrepreneurial classes to more strident forms of social protest and antagonism. To protect themselves from the intrusion of the lower classes, bourgeois families began to isolate themselves from such carnivalesque Christmas practices and to insulate themselves in family rituals. The Christmas tree, a Scandinavian tradition, and the manger (or crèche) gradually made their way into European homes, with trees arriving after 1840 in England and France and somewhat earlier in Germany. Placed next to the family hearth, these seasonal shrines became symbolic of the family and turned the focus of Christmas revelry away from street scenes to the home. European families began to give presents to their children, replacing the obligation to the poor that had been part of the wassailing tradition. Whether children put slippers before the fireplace or hung stockings on the chimney and received their gifts from the baby Jesus, Père Noël, Santa Claus, or St. Nicholas, the gift giving reinforced intergenerational family bonds. The battle for Christmas was won by the nuclear family, and Christmas no longer united the poor with their betters.

Sources:

Alexander Falassi, ed., *Time out of Time: Essays on the Festival* (Albuquerque: University of New Mexico Press, 1987).

ADVICE TO THE YOUNG LADIES

The following suggestions for young ladies appeared in *Manuel de la bonne companie; ou, guide de la politesse et de la bienséance* (Manual of Good Company; or, Guide to Manners and Decorum, 1834) by Elisabeth-Felicité Bayle-Mouillard, otherwise known as Madame Celnart. Such etiquette books were important guides to proper middle-class behavior throughout Europe.

Everyone knows that no matter how much a young lady's dowry is, her manner of dress must always . . . be elegant and less brilliant than that of married women. Expensive cashmeres, very rich furs, diamonds are forbidden her, as well as much other showy attire. . . .

Until the age of about thirty, a young lady can never go out without being accompanied. For her errands in the city, to shops, to visit intimate friends, to church, she may go with a maid; but when it is a question of ceremonial visits, of *promenades,* of parties, of balls, she may appear only with her mother, or with a lady of her acquaintance who will take her mother's place. . . .

[When visiting] one does not leave the table before the end of the meal except for an unexpected call of nature. If this unpleasantness should happen to a lady, she asks a friend to accompany her; a young lady withdraws with her mother. . . .

The gait of a woman should be neither too fast nor too slow. . . . Her expression must be sweet and modest.

It is not in good taste for a woman to speak with too much animation or too loudly. When she is seated, she should never cross her legs. . . .

But what is especially insufferable in a woman is a restless, bold, domineering manner, for this manner goes against nature. . . . No matter what her worth, no matter that she never forgets that she could be a man by virtue of her superiority of mind and the force of her will, on the outside she must be a woman! She must present herself as that creature made to please, to love, to seek support, that being who is inferior to man and who approaches the angels.

Source: Erna Olafson Hellerstein, Leslie Parker Hume, and Karen M. Offen, eds., *Victorian Women: A Documentary Account of Women's Lives in Nineteenth-Century England, France, and the United States* (Stanford: Stanford University Press, 1981), pp. 96–97.

Eric Hobsbawm and Terence Ranger, eds., *The Invention of Tradition* (Cambridge: Cambridge University Press, 1983).

George L. Mosse, *The Nationalization of the Masses: Political Symbolism and Mass Movements in Germany from the Napoleonic Wars through the Third Reich* (New York: Fertig, 1975).

Stephen Nissenbaum, *The Battle for Christmas: A Cultural History of America's Most Cherished Holiday* (New York: Knopf, 1997).

Michelle Perrot, ed., *From the Fires of Revolution to the Great War,* translated by Arthur Goldhammer, volume 4 of *A History of Private Life,* general editors Philippe Ariès and Georges Duby (Cambridge, Mass.: Harvard University Press, 1990).

CLOTHING AND APPEARANCE

Pre-Industrial Clothing. Clothing has always served as a richly revealing expression of differences in social status, age, wealth, and sexuality. During the period between 1750 and 1914 there was a revolution in clothing production and distribution patterns, in styles and materials, and in the meanings of fashion. Nothing like the modern retail-clothing business existed before the nineteenth century. Before standard-sized ready-to-wear clothes could be bought off the rack, Europeans purchased apparel to order. To have a suit of clothes made, one visited a draper to purchase cloth by the yard, a mercer for ornaments, fasteners, and other accessories, and a tailor, who assembled the outfit to the buyer's specifications. Such a decentralized system of production was reflected in a wide division of labor in the garment industry. There were underwear makers, dressmakers, tailors for men's clothes, tailors for women's and children's clothes, seamstresses, glove makers, hatters, hosiers, and many other artisans, with their own customs and clientele. Great couturiers satisfied the demands of court and "high society" while respectable but less expensive tailors fashioned the clothing of middle-class consumers. The lower classes and the poor had to make do with previously owned clothing discarded by (or perhaps stolen from) their betters. Sometimes little better than rags, these items filtered into the inventories of street vendors from the servants of prosperous folk. Until the nineteenth century, used-clothes dealers, known as fripperers, were suspected of carrying disease and fencing stolen clothing. Most of them maintained small shops, either adjacent to open-air markets or—as in Lyon—on a few city streets that became known as centers for the used-clothing trade. In Paris during the first decade of the nineteenth century, four sheds covering more than ten thousand square meters were constructed to house this flourishing trade. In each shed an array of items could be found, ranging from well-worn rags piled in bins and sifted through by the truly destitute, to work clothes and housewares, or even a rare still-stylish outfit discarded by its well-to-do first owner.

Paying for Clothes. Compared to food allowances, money for clothing was typically a much smaller part of the household budget, at least for those on both extremes of income, with expenses for women's clothes consuming a greater proportion of the family budget than those for men's garments. A worker earning £78 annually in the 1890s might spend only £5 for clothes, as compared to £21 for food. This man had a meager wardrobe, much of which was purchased second- or thirdhand. At the same time, a single working woman earned less but spent more on clothes—perhaps as much as £10 a year, which would buy a

Upper- and middle-class men's clothing in the early and late nineteenth century
(left: from *Le Beau Monde,* 1806; right: from *The Gazette of Fashion,* 1881)

new dress, a pair of shoes, underwear, and some accessories. Clerks, cashiers, and salesmen were expected to spend higher proportions of their earnings on clothes, and their employers frowned on their wearing used or tattered attire. The cost of social emulation would be even higher for the bourgeoisie, with more than 10 percent of the family income devoted to the purchase of fashionable apparel. The wealthiest people in absolute terms spent more on clothing than anyone else, but a relatively small portion of their annual income, about 6 percent.

Ready-to-Wear. As the European population grew during the nineteenth century—especially in cities, where people almost never made their own clothes—the need to purchase clothing increased as well. To meet the demand, manufacturers and merchants began producing and selling ready-to-wear clothing at prices affordable to the swelling working class and lesser bourgeoisie. New retail shops displaying such items began to appear after 1800. In 1824 Pierre Parissot opened the doors of his Paris shop and sold inexpensive work clothes tagged with fixed, clearly visible prices. Parissot's success led to an explosion in the making and selling of ready-made clothing. Legions of tailors, seamstresses, cloth cutters, and other garment workers were enlisted to work in an increasingly standardized industry. By mid century the sewing machine was replacing hand stitching and increasing the efficiency of clothing manufacture. As ready-to-wear clothing flooded the market, the used-clothing vendor and the independent tailor nearly disappeared. By mid century, off-the-rack dresses for bourgeois and working-class women were increasingly common, but the ready-to-wear industry found it difficult to meet the demands of female fashion. Men preferred staid, loose-fitting, durable, and predictable daily attire and were thus fairly easy to fit with ready-to-wear clothing. Women, however, demanded a precise, individualized fit, which limited the degree to which feminine dress could be mass-produced.

The Department Store. The revolution in ready-made clothing coincided closely with the beginnings of the department store. Eighteenth-century London shopkeepers and even provincial merchants had already begun to use innovative window displays and store decor to attract shoppers, and ready-to-wear merchants had already experimented with fixed pricing that eliminated haggling when the stores that became modern department stores opened in the late 1830s. They began as dry-goods stores—or what the French called *magasins de nouveautés* (novelty stores)—selling a diverse array of clothing accessories, ready-made outfits, dressmaking fabrics, furs, umbrellas, gloves, hosiery, and other goods, transforming retail commerce by selling in volume at low prices to turn over their wares quickly. These vendors advertised broadly and encouraged browsing (a departure from the tradition by which shoppers were expected to buy if they looked), and they offered fixed-price merchandise in well-lit and attractive displays. As this formula proved profitable, the novelty store increased in size and expanded the range of merchandise it offered, rapidly taking on the dimensions and organization of modern department stores. In Paris, Au Bon Marché, the Louvre, and the Bazar de l'Hôtel de Ville all opened in the 1850s, and another precursor of a department store, Printemps, was founded in 1865. The arrival of the first true department store in France is generally dated 1869, the year in which Aristide Boucicaut began construction on a new building for Au Bon Marché that featured the kind of organization and display areas that have become common in modern department stores. In England, mass-produced footwear and men's clothing, generally for working-class consumers, were marketed through networks of stores. British department stores on the Parisian model, such as Harrods, Whiteley's, and Swan and Edgar's, opened during the 1880s. The department store was an entertainment attraction in its own right, thus encouraging consumption.

Fashion. In the eighteenth century, aristocrats of both sexes dressed in vivid colors and richly textured fabrics. By the middle of the nineteenth century, however, colorful, elaborate dress and the "folly" of fashion belonged to women alone. Perhaps at no other time in European history had fashion served so effectively to differentiate the genders or had stylistic conformity been so widely observed. Victorian women's fashions contrasted distinctly with the styles of female dress during the decades on either side of the period. Dresses in the Empire style of 1800–1815, inspired by Roman and Greek clothing, were cut with a high waist and made of light-colored linens or flimsy silks contoured to flow with the body. Around 1900 light, clinging fabrics and dainty colors were again the rage. During the middle decades of the nineteenth century, however, wire hoops and later an entire cage made of whalebone, steel, or watch-spring wire widened the base of the skirt and kept crinoline petticoats away from the legs. Padded shoulders, wide sleeves, V-shaped corsets, and bodices combined with these full skirts to produce the coveted hourglass figure. During the middle decades of the century, skirts and petticoats expanded to near-comic proportions. By the end of the 1860s, however, styles that hid the figure had been replaced by a new, fitted dress that accentuated the bust and the buttocks while also attracting attention to the thighs. To achieve this fashion statement, a woman wore a "Grecian bend" corset that thrust the bust forward and accentuated the buttocks with a bustle and padding as well as flounces and bows on the backs of her gowns. By the 1890s, attention had shifted from the skirt, with its exaggerated bustle and folds of cloth, to the bodice. This new fashion made a woman seem more statuesque, erect, and voluptuous than the wasp-waisted female of the mid nineteenth century. After the turn of the twentieth century, the fashionable silhouette became increasingly vertical, no longer molded by bustles and corsets but by brassieres and girdles designed to flatten and shape. This look, which was the basis for fashion during the entire twentieth century, carried connotations of sexual liberation, relaxed femininity, and elegant good taste.

Trendsetters. Ironically, the women who set fashion trends for the middle and upper classes were the women of the demimonde (on the fringes of polite society): divorcées, mistresses of the famous and well-to-do, or actresses. At balls, races, promenades, seaside resorts, theaters, or onstage these demimondaines inaugurated new styles and attracted the attention of fashion journalists, couturiers, and, of course, the wives and daughters of respectable bourgeois businessmen. Because they were closely associated with scandal, fashion innovations drew the ire of moralists. Nonetheless, new styles drew the attention of middle- and upper-class women, who wanted to distinguish themselves from less affluent women wearing cheaper, ready-to-wear imitations of the previous year's styles. Mass production and effective publicity ensured that fashion trends established in Paris or London rapidly spread to cities across the Continent. Middle- and upper-class women from Moscow to Madrid took their clothing cues from couturiers in Paris and London, even in the face of protests by prominent clergymen that, as the Austrian Bishop of Lainbach contended in 1913, "The newest fashions in clothes are designed to serve the cause of lust."

Dress for Every Occasion. A woman's wardrobe provided a means by which she could dress to indicate her mood swings, moral qualities, wealth, and social rank. She also dressed to suit the time of day and the season. As one anonymous wit put it in 1857, women had:

Dresses for breakfasts and dinners and balls;
Dresses to sit in and stand in and walk in;
Dresses to dance in and flirt in and talk in;
Dresses in which to do nothing at all.

Morning apparel, either a dressing gown or peignoir, was for the home and suggested domestic warmth as well as luxury. Beneath the morning robe, a woman wore a full-length day shift and corset. Completing the ensemble were slippers, a bonnet, or hair curlers hidden under a lace head covering. Neither the heat of the season or the relative privacy of the domestic setting was adequate excuse to dress more lightly. Strangers were not to see a woman in her morning wear, so a change of clothes was required for afternoon public excursions. Calling on others required a careful evaluation of the status of the host and the purpose of the visit. Consoling the bereaved or visiting the poor necessitated somber dress. A trip to the homes of good friends might allow for more casual dress, while visiting those of higher social status demanded appropriately respectful attire. Seated in the family carriage and parading with the carriages of other reputable women in an afternoon procession—during which women scrutinized each other's apparel, judging taste, income, and social status accordingly—women could dress somewhat more extravagantly, tastefully yet bordering on the provocative. In the evening a bourgeois woman could display her sexuality and her husband's material wealth. Plunging necklines suggested erotic potential and revealed the milk-white skin that distinguished these elite women from the suntanned inferior classes. Necklaces or strings of pearls ornamented bare shoulders and boasted the wealth of the wearer. Fans, calling cards, or bouquets of flowers were held in gloved hands, their movements suggestive and graceful. Long trains, shimmering fabrics, gold brocade, and delicate laces exhibited the wealth and taste of the fashionable woman. The revolutionary "bloomers," introduced by Amelia Bloomer in 1851, shocked the public because the long pantaloons displayed beneath a knee-length tunic suggested masculinity as well as immodesty. Despite their practicality, as the journal *Le Sport* editorialized in 1873, "*Le pantalon*, in a word, is a man's article of clothing . . . and because of that, women who have the true intuition of elegance of their sex will always abstain from it."

Middle-Class Men's Clothing. In the late eighteenth century an ideology of masculine modesty emerged, and elite men renounced the finery that had characterized aristocratic dress for most of the early modern period. This "great masculine renunciation" had its roots in the English aristocracy's assertion of sturdy, grave, and decidedly manly simplicity as the mark of political legitimacy following the Glorious Revolution of 1688. Contrasting their clothing with the excesses of dress across the English Channel in France, English gentlemen disparaged any evidence of luxury, effeminacy, and foppishness. Middle-class reformers in the late eighteenth and early nineteenth centuries seized this language of manly public virtue and also renounced finery, bright colors, or ostentatious display in their dress. By the 1830s an ideal of "inconspicuous consumption" characterized men's fashions, visually proclaiming their commitment to the values of thrift, industry, and individual success. On the Continent, the French Revolution and the spread of revolutionary ideas contributed to a similar simplification of masculine attire. Arnould Frémy applauded this development, contrasting the "showy rags, the embroideries, the jewels, and lace, the ceremonial swords, the taffeta suits, and all the smart and ruinous accessories of the aristocratic costume" with the "basically egalitarian . . . simple, plain, and unpretentious" fashions of men in a republic. The simplicity and uniformity of middle-class men's wear nonetheless indicated social status just as clearly as aristocratic powdered wigs had in the past, and so distinguished the middle-class wearer from the lesser sort.

Three Changes of Clothing. Just as a middle- or upper-class woman required outfits to fit the time of day and the season, so too did their male counterparts, who typically changed their clothing three times a day. At home during the day, an elaborate and colorful dressing gown was worn, sometimes even when guests were present. In the evening men wore formal dress, a black suit with a tail coat, a white or black satin vest, a white cravat, and white gloves. Formal dress might also be worn to call on a social superior. Dressing for work or business, however, demanded sobriety—a black waistcoat, a starched shirt, pinstriped or fine checked trousers, and a vest. By 1850 the pants and vest were cut of the same cloth as the jacket. This three-piece suit, the daily uniform of the middle-class male, allowed little room for style change. Where once knee breeches had accentuated manly calves, pants were now ankle length, and the cut of the legs varied only slightly over the course of the nineteenth century. The suit jacket cut served as an important social sign, the length of the coattails indicating age, importance, and position. An overcoat, again black, completed the basic ensemble. Jewelry, which had once so effectively displayed the wealth and status of the aristocracy, was reduced to a timepiece, a pince-nez, or perhaps a snuffbox, each inconspicuously displayed or kept in a pocket. A silk, satin, or velvet cravat, knotted around the bourgeois gentleman's neck, might offer a dash of color and served as a useful means of distinguishing those with impeccable taste. With each season, the width, the particular knot of the tie, and the time and art associated with properly tying it all served to distinguish the wearer. Glove wearing also followed a prescribed regimen: dark-colored gloves in the morning, lighter shades for afternoon visits, and white gloves in the evening. The final piece of a man's wardrobe, the top hat, served little functional purpose, as it neither protected its wearer from the elements nor provided any appreciable warmth. It did, however, emphasize the upright, sober bearing of its middle-class wearer. Other hats, such as the bowler or the straw boater, could be worn in informal settings. Masculine vanity in the nineteenth century was perhaps most evident in beards, moustaches, or mutton-chop sideburns, and barbers offered more than twenty styles from which to choose. Overt masculinity was expressed through well-groomed facial hair. The clean-shaven look—which one author characterized as "unnatural, irrational, unmanly, [and] ungodly"—suggested effeminacy.

Undergarments. Nineteenth-century Europeans developed an obsession for undergarments. The private became a subject of a good deal of public comment. "Lingerie," as Mrs. Eric Pritchard wrote in the magazine *The Lady's Realm* (April 1903), "is an enthralling subject." Undergarments have not always been so closely associated with the erotic imagination. Medieval undergarments more often suggested chastity and sexual restraint. Nevertheless, with the exception of a shift, a long shirt, worn beneath one's outer garments, most people before 1820 did not wear underdrawers. Though they were first considered immoral for women because pants of any sort were thought of as men's garments, women of the working and middle classes began to wear them beneath their day shifts. Physicians began to recommend them as protection from the cold and infection. With the introduction of elastics after 1876 and the decreasing expense of cotton fabrics, lighter, more easily washed, and more affordable undergarments became available to a mass market. As wearing underdrawers became commonplace, elite women, once again following the lead of the demimondaine (including can-can dancers), adopted silk or satin drawers trimmed with lace, as well as lace petticoats and colored lingerie. René Mazeroy described their appeal in his novel *L'Adorée* (1887): "So light, so brief, with cascades of Valenciennes lace and frills of ribbons, these *pantaloons* which do not descend beyond the lace garters . . . drive a lover crazy better than the immodest state of nudity." Such elegant underclothes combined comfort with elements of seduction and eroticism, and ultimately—despite being hidden behind skirts—the potential for display so important to bourgeois consumerism. In contrast to women's undergarments, nineteenth-century male underwear was not suggestive. Men's underpants, which were introduced at the same time as trousers, covered the legs and lower body in a shell of cotton, linen, or flannel cloth. Like the simple, ubiquitous black suit, men's underwear testified to bourgeois society's attribution of sensuality and eroticism to the female, while the male represented the values of self-control, discipline, and hard work.

The Corset. Victorian obsessions with the moral and hygienic implications of undergarments led to an ongoing controversy about the character-building and body-forming qualities of the corset. As an anonymous writer commented in a February 1871 letter to the *Englishwoman's Domestic Magazine,* "The corset is an ever-present monitor, indirectly bidding its wearer to exercise self-restraint. The

Upper- and middle-class women's clothing in the nineteenth century (top left: from *The Lady's Magazine*, 1808; top right: from *La Belle Assemblée*, 1828; bottom left: an 1886 fashion plate; bottom right: from *The West End*, 1899)

restraint of the corset may be said to be insensibly imitated by the mental faculties over the moral character. . . . If you want a girl to grow up gentle and womanly in her ways and her feelings, lace her up tight." Yet, another anonymous letter writer rejoiced in their ability to create "fascinating undulations of outline that art in this respect affords to nature" (*Englishwoman's Domestic Magazine,* June 1867). As Eugene Chapus wrote in his *Manuel de l'homme et de la femme comme-il-faut* (Manual for the Proper Man and Woman, 1862), "A woman in a corset is a lie, a falsehood, a fiction, but for us this fiction is better than the reality." Doctors were quick to notice the health hazards created by tight corsets. As the French physician A. Debay wrote in his *Hygiène vestimentaire* (Clothing Hygiene, 1857):

Of 100 young girls wearing a corset:
25 succumbed to diseases of the chest;
 5 died after their first delivery;
15 remained infirm after delivery;
15 became deformed;
30 alone resisted, but sooner or later were afflicted with serious indispositions.

In his *Considerations on Five Plagues: The Abuse of the Corset, the Use of Tobacco, the Passion for Gambling, the Abuse of Strong Drink, and Speculation* (1857), Charles Dubois reported on a young wife who died from "intestinal inflammation" because, doctors concluded, "her corset was from eight to ten centimeters too tight."

Working-Class Attire. The French Revolution expressly politicized workers' dress, with the uniform of the radical sansculottes, (a red cap, wide-legged pants, wooden shoes, and a jacket). This attire briefly served as the symbol of proper revolutionary fervor. After the Revolution, differences in clothing materials and style continued to distinguish working men from the middle class. Shirts with soft collars contrasted with the starched collar of the bourgeois man, while working men wore caps instead of top hats, and coveralls or smocks rather than three-piece suits. Durable corduroy was a favored working-class fabric, as was sturdy fustian, a twill fabric woven from cotton or a blend of cotton and linen. Friedrich Engels noted a change around the middle of the nineteenth century, as woolens and linens were replaced by much-inferior cheap cotton shirts and print dresses. These fabrics, Engels argued in *The Condition of the Working Class in England* (1845), "afford much less protection against cold and wet, remain damp much longer . . . and have none of the compact density of fulled woolen clothes."

Rural Dress. While in industrial cities fashion distinguished members of the bourgeoisie from the working classes, in rural communities clothing frequently differed according to age, ethnicity, or regional origin. Yet, even in the countryside, mail-order sales and peddlers of second-hand clothing belatedly introduced villagers to new fashions, so rural dress was frequently out-of-date city clothing. During the Romantic era of the early nineteenth century, however, the middle and upper classes throughout Europe discovered—or more often invented—the "traditional folk

NANA

Nana, Emile Zola's 1880 novel about an actress-courtesan, describes the influence of the demimondaine on the dress of middle- and upper-class women:

Her success was sudden and decisive, a swift rise to fame in the garish light of lunatic extravagance and the wasteful follies of beauty. She at once became queen among the most expensive of her kind. . . . When she drove along the boulevards in her carriage, people would turn around and tell one another who she was with all the emotion of a nation saluting its sovereign, while she lolled back in her flimsy dresses, smiling gaily under the rain of little golden curls which fell around the blue of her made-up eyes and the red of her painted lips. And the remarkable thing was that that buxom young woman, who was so awkward on the stage, so comical when she tried to play the respectable woman, was able to play the enchantress in town without the slightest effort. There she had the lithe grace of a serpent, a studied yet seemingly involuntary carelessness of dress which was exquisitely elegant, the nervous distinction of a pedigreed cat, an aristocratic refinement. . . . She set the fashion, and great ladies imitated her.

Source: Frederick Brown, *Emile Zola: A Life* (New York: Farrar Straus Giroux, 1995), p. 425.

dress" of rural society, wearing it as an expression of regional or national identity and as a critique of modernization. For example, the "traditional" clan-tartan kilt of Highland Scotland was not the day-to-day wear of Scots in the eighteenth or nineteenth century, and the identification of a clan with a specific tartan did not occur until the Romantic literary movement began its rehabilitation of folk culture and rural traditions. In a similar transformation, Greek-Albanian peasant dress became identified as the "traditional" national dress of the entire newly independent nation of Greece. During the Greek war for independence, this dress was adopted by Greek nationalists in the cities, and in 1833 Otto, the Bavarian prince who became king of Greece, made it official court dress. Even though Greek men and women were wearing modern dress by the end of the nineteenth century, the peasant man's *foustanella,* with its short full skirt, is as linked in the modern mind to Greece as the kilt is to Scotland. Likewise, *lederhosen* became an important symbol of the regional cultures of Alpine Germany, Switzerland, and Austria. Yet, their common usage dated only to the early eighteenth century, and during the nineteenth century they were worn mostly during festivals and folkloric celebrations. Elsewhere in Europe, the idealization of rural life in the aftermath of the Industrial Revolution combined with efforts to forge national identities from heterogeneous populations to foster the establishment of distinctive national and regional costumes. In fact, the availability of inexpensive, mass-produced cloth and the introduction of sewing machines to rural villages actually promoted the development of distinctive regional dress that bourgeois tourists then imagined to be the timeless folk dress of rustic villagers.

Sources:

Dorothy Davis, *Fairs, Shops, and Supermarkets: A History of English Shopping* (Toronto: University of Toronto Press, 1966).

Victoria De Grazia and Ellen Furlough, eds., *The Sex of Things: Gender and Consumption in Historical Perspective* (Berkeley: University of California Press, 1996).

Joanne B. Eicher, ed. *Dress and Ethnicity: Change Across Space and Time* (Oxford: Berg, 1995).

Neil McKendrick, John Brewer, and J. H. Plumb, *The Birth of a Consumer Society: The Commercialization of Eighteenth-Century England* (Bloomington: Indiana University Press, 1982).

Michael B. Miller, *The Bon Marché: Bourgeois Culture and the Department Store, 1869–1920* (Princeton: Princeton University Press, 1981).

Philippe Perrot, *Fashioning the Bourgeoisie: A History of Clothing in the Nineteenth Century*, translated by Richard Bienvenu (Princeton: Princeton University Press, 1994).

Aileen Ribeiro, *Dress and Morality* (New York: Holmes & Meier, 1986).

Daniel Roche, *The Culture of Clothing* (Cambridge: Cambridge University Press, 1994).

Valerie Steele, *Fashion and Eroticism: Ideals of Feminine Beauty from the Victorian Era to the Jazz Age* (New York: Oxford University Press, 1985).

DOMICILES: THE HOUSING OF EUROPEANS

Peasant and Urban Working-Class Housing. The great preoccupation of pre-industrial Europeans was avoiding hunger. During the second half of the eighteenth century, subsistence continued to be a problem for the poor and a potential source of rebellion. By the middle of the nineteenth century, however, concerns about housing had shifted to the fore—a change that was probably less an indication of an improved diet for the poor than a symptom of the growing bourgeois preoccupation with domestic accommodations. For the middle class, residential dwellings had implications for morality, gender relations, authority, social status, and wealth. To such observers, peasant huts in France, for example, seemed barely habitable for humans, "dug in the ground and deprived of every comfort" and "destined rather as a retreat for wild beasts." In fact, peasants frequently shared their homes with livestock and had done so for centuries. Such intermingling of animals and humans disturbed the middle-class sense of propriety. Urban slums also troubled middle-class reformers. Friedrich Engels observed in *The Condition of the Working Class in England* (1845) that "in the workingmen's dwellings of Manchester, no cleanliness, no convenience, and consequently no comfortable family life is possible; . . . only a physically degenerate race, robbed of all humanity, degraded, reduced morally and physically to bestiality, could feel comfortable and at home." Above all, middle-class commentators called the crowding of slum housing unforgivable. Poor families were packed into single rooms, often sharing one bed. Or, they shared an apartment with other families. Sometimes they also took boarders into their already crowded dwellings. Such overcrowding obliterated the boundaries that bourgeois families had constructed around themselves as essential to the entire notion of private domesticity. In an 1891 survey of

A backyard of a working-class residence in Leeds, England (1887), with a doghouse and a privy on the right (Public Record Office, London)

Parisians, 14 percent of those surveyed lived in overcrowded conditions, which were defined as homes where the number of residents was more than double the number of rooms. As attuned to the significance of consumer items as to cleanliness and privacy, bourgeois observers also found household furnishings in poor residences to be wretched. In the typical home of an urban worker, middle-class observers were appalled by the unruly mix of work implements, tools, and crockery; the few tattered furnishings and filthy garments; and, above all, the unkempt bed upon which the whole family lay amid the odor of poverty.

Improvements in Housing. Despite social reformers' gloomy portrayals of working-class housing, several important changes took place during the nineteenth century in the accommodations of the agrarian classes and the urban working poor. Despite regional variations, European peasant housing before the middle of the nineteenth century shared several characteristics. A peasant's house was usually a single-storied building with a single chimney and often only one room. In addition, rural houses were built with few doors and windows to restrict the intrusion of cold drafts, to avoid the extra cost of latches, bolts, or other fasteners, and—in France—to avoid a "door-and-window" tax that was not abolished until 1917. By the last quarter of the nineteenth century, however, roofs were more likely to be covered with slate or tiles instead of thatch or wooden shingles, and they were built with a steeper pitch to create more space for storage. Second stories were added, and increased numbers of windows and doors let in more light. These changes came

A drawing room in Stuttgart, Germany, circa 1860 (Stadtarchiv, Stuttgart)

about as costs for manufactured construction materials decreased, and more-prosperous farmers copied building styles they observed in bourgeois homes. Urban working-class housing also improved. Some of the changes can be traced to the reports of reformers intent on ameliorating tenement conditions. In Paris, for example, a corporation established in 1849 to construct apartment complexes (*cités*) throughout the city attracted substantial investment. One such low-rent housing complex still stands today. At its opening in 1851 the Cité Napoléon included two-hundred, one-bedroom apartments and offered amenities lacking in most tenements. Each floor had its own toilet and sink instead of the privy that stood in the courtyard of a tenement, and residents had access to a laundry room and baths. Childcare, janitorial services, and even free consultations with a resident physician were offered to tenants. Philanthropic ventures encouraged similar housing experiments in provincial French cities, though the demand for subsidized housing far outstripped supply. In England, Edwin Chadwick prepared *Report on the Sanitary Condition of the Labouring Population of Great Britain* (1842), encouraging legislative and philanthropic efforts to improve working-class housing. Though the results of these efforts may be seen in housing projects throughout England, the experiments were most effective in London, particularly after

1862, as urban authorities endeavored to clear slums and regulate new construction. In Petticoat Square in London, for example, apartments built in 1885 included shop space on the ground floor with living accommodations in the rear and four floors of living space above, divided into apartments of up to three rooms. On each floor, four apartments shared two water closets and a scullery, or washroom. By the early twentieth century, though horrible slums still existed, private philanthropic and speculative building combined with governmental regulation to establish greatly improved housing for the poor and working classes in many European cities.

Middle-Class Housing. Unfavorable descriptions of working class and peasant homes tell modern scholars a good deal about the housing of the poor, but they also reveal what kinds of housing the middle classes valued. Urban apartment buildings segregated their inhabitants along a vertical axis, with the bourgeois residing on the lower floors and the poor occupying the upstairs and garret apartments. In the Ringstrasse apartments of Vienna, for example, the ground floor was rented to retailers while the second floor, known as the *Nobelstock,* contained spacious flats affordable only to wealthy families. In some buildings the third story repeated the spacious floor plans of the second, but just as often the third floor was subdivided into smaller apartments. "Imperial" stairways modeled on palace or monumental architecture led visitors to second- and occasionally third-floor residences. Beyond the third story, simple staircases mounted to the upper reaches of the building. The exterior façade of the building also signaled this vertical segregation, with pillars, window heights, and ornamentation announcing the distinction of second story apartments. Industrial cities also began to establish horizontal segregation, as working-class neighborhoods became cut off from those of the middle classes. In 1873, for example, German industrialist Alfred Krupp, who had earlier built a family residence on the grounds of his factory in Essen, moved to the outskirts of the city, where he built a palatial new family residence on a hill overlooking the city. Middle-class housing separated work from domestic life. It established spaces specific to each gender, separated intimate spaces from areas in which guests were welcome, and, as much as possible, kept the servants—of rural or working-class origin—apart from the family. To create these divisions, the number of rooms in middle-class residences increased significantly during the nineteenth century.

Porches and Anterooms. Entry into a middle-class house or apartment was typically gained through an anteroom, or foyer, that served as a waiting room for visitors and as a cloakroom where coats, umbrellas, and other outdoor clothing was stored. In rural or small-town residences (especially in the United States) an external porch served as an additional buffer between the outside world and the home.

The Parlor. From the porch or the anteroom, a guest was led into a "grand salon," or parlor, a visiting space where the family accorded hospitality to other members of their social class and displayed consumer items that demonstrated their middle-class taste and status. For those with social aspirations, furnishing the parlor required careful attention to changing fashions and an income adequate to making periodic changes in decor. Middle-class consumers acquired information about new home-furnishing trends from friends, family, and the many nineteenth-century advice books on home decorating. Consumers' choices were also guided by furniture makers, who in the 1870s began to display model rooms in their showrooms. Sometimes the bourgeoisie gathered ideas from the commercial parlors of hotels, restaurants, and even steamboats or railroad cars. According to "New Furniture," an article published in an 1850 issue of the widely read magazine *Godey's Lady's Book,* the up-to-date parlor included a collection of stuffed "sofas and ordinary chairs, covered with satin damask, crimson and black, deeply tufted or knotted," as well as "lounging or arm-chairs," pianos, sofa tables, leather-bound books, and a long list of other accoutrements.

The Dining Room and Kitchen. Unlike modern houses, the nineteenth-century middle-class home established distance between the kitchen and the dining room. The kitchen, after all, was a work space for household servants and was filled with the odors of cooking and cleaning, which were considered unwelcome impositions on guests. Planners of nineteenth-century middle-class homes were little concerned with the appearance or efficiency of the kitchen. As the set-

ting for family meals and dinners with guests, the dining room received somewhat more attention. An example of how these two rooms might have been furnished by a middle-class householder is the inventory made after the death of Nicolas Antoine Gruyer in 1829. His estate included a well-stocked wine collection and a kitchen well supplied with copper pots, kettles, frying pans, and many less-expensive articles of cookware. His dishes were kept in a marble-topped oak buffet in the dining room, which also held a walnut dining table, two walnut chairs, lamps, vases, platters, and a liquor cabinet. Though they usually spent more on the dining room than the kitchen, middle-class householders frequently allocated less than 6 percent of the value of all their possessions for furnishing the dining room. They spent far more on outfitting bedrooms and parlors. Unlike those rooms, dining rooms rarely had stoves or fireplaces for heat. Furthermore, they often faced the rear of the house and had fewer windows than other rooms. Along with typically dark-stained, heavy wood dining furniture, a lack of direct sunlight made the dining room a decidedly dark and "masculine" space, which contrasted with the "feminine" parlor.

The Private Bedroom. In the nineteenth century the middle class increasingly aspired to have "privacy" and a room of one's own. In part this desire was motivated by medical preoccupations. With the development of germ theory, and particularly after the French cholera epidemic of the 1830s, middle-class dwellings began to include private bedrooms. Among the furnishings of such a bedroom was a bedside cupboard that concealed the chamber pot and held other articles of personal hygiene. In addition to hygienic considerations, segmenting the home into individualized spaces was also motivated by sexual concerns. The master bedroom then became a sanctuary where sexual relations could be carried out in privacy. As such it became a symbol of the permanence and solidity of the marital union, and—though it was no longer socially permissible to receive visitors in the bedroom as had once been the custom—the master bedroom was still furnished in a manner befitting the family's social status. Adding to the husband and wife's privacy, servants and children also had separate bedrooms, so that the household was separated by age, class, and gender.

The Bed. By the end of the nineteenth century even most rural peasants slept in raised, wood-framed beds with pillows, sheets, blankets, and comforters instead of straw pallets on bare floors. Generally the first possession of newlyweds, the bed was enclosed by a curtain and set apart in an alcove, affording a degree of conjugal privacy. A bed was a costly item. At the beginning of the eighteenth century, it represented a quarter of the value of a typical wage earner's furniture, and nearly 40 percent of the value of a servant's. Over the course of the nineteenth century, urban professionals and shopkeepers purchased beds of superior craftsmanship that were designed for more comfort. A sturdy piece of furniture, the conjugal bed was constructed from solid wood, frequently mahogany, with a high headboard and footboard and wide sideboards. In the prosperous nineteenth-century home, it was covered with rich draperies that matched the bedroom

Edwin Chadwick's *Report on the Sanitary Condition of the Labouring Population of Great Britain* (1842) included witnesses' testimony about the miserable housing conditions of the British working poor throughout England and Scotland. Many connected poor hygiene and overcrowded housing to disease and immorality.

Dr. Scott Alison

"In many houses in and around Tranent, fowls roost on the rafters and on the tops of bedsteads. The effluvia in these houses are offensive, and must prove very unwholesome. It is scarcely necessary to say that these houses are very filthy. They swarm likewise with fleas. Dogs live in the interior of the lowest houses and must, of course be opposed to cleanliness. I have seen horses in two houses. . . . Several of the family were ill of typhus fever, and I remember the horse stood at the back of the bed."

Mr. Riddall Wood

"In a cellar in Pendleton, I recollect there were three beds in the two apartments of which the habitation consisted, but having no door between them, in one of which a man and his wife slept; in another a man, his wife and child; and in a third two unmarried females. . . . In a cellar in Liverpool, I found a mother and her grown-up daughters sleeping on a bed of chaff on the ground in one corner of the cellar, and in the other corner three sailors had their bed. In Manchester . . . a man, his wife and child sleeping in one bed; in another bed, two grown-up females; and in the same room two young men, unmarried. I have met with instances of a man, his wife, and his wife's sister in the same bed together.

". . . I have frequently met with instances in which the parties themselves have traced their own depravity to these circumstances. As, for example, . . . a prostitute . . . . stated that she had lodged with a married sister, and slept in the same bed with her and her husband; that hence improper intercourse had taken place. . . . In the case which I have mentioned of the two daughters and the woman where I found the sailors, I learned, from the mother's admission, that they were common to the lodgers. In all of these cases the sense of decency was obliterated."

Mr. Baker

"In the houses of the working classes, brothers and sisters, and lodgers of both sexes, are found occupying the same sleeping-room with the parents, and consequences occur which humanity shudders to contemplate."

Chadwick also described cases in which unclean living conditions adversely affected personal hygiene, quoting a woman's report on a servant who had been attentive to neatness and cleanliness:

"Her attention to personal neatness . . . was very great; her face seemed always as if it were just washed, and with her bright hair neatly combed underneath her snow-white cap, a smooth white apron, and her gown and handkerchief carefully put on, she used to look very comely. After a year or two, she married the serving man, who . . . [took her to live in a "wretched" neighborhood]. After they had been married about two years, I happened to be walking past one of these miserable cottages. . . . I found it was the home of the servant I have been describing. But what a change had come over her! Her face was dirty, and her tangled hair hung over her eyes. Her cap, though of good materials, was ill washed and slovenly put on. Her whole dress, though apparently good and serviceable, was very untidy, and looked dirty and slatternly . . . and she appeared very discontented. . . . Her condition had been borne down by the condition of her house."

Source: Edwin Chadwick, *Report on the Sanitary Condition of the Labouring Population of Great Britain*, edited by M. W. Flinn (Edinburgh: Edinburgh University Press, 1965), pp. 189, 192–193.

window curtains and furniture upholstery. By the nineteenth century, box-spring mattresses, a product of industrial manufacturing, were replacing the accumulation of straw and woolen mattresses spread over a rope-web foundation. Despite the cost, by the end of the nineteenth century the wooden bed in a private bedroom had become common in the middle-class home. Inexpensive and durable iron beds lacked the warmth and status of wood and were deemed suitable for servants or institutions.

The Bathroom. The nineteenth-century bathroom is an important example of how emerging notions of privacy intersected with the development of the public infrastructure and technological innovation. Embarrassed by the odor, sound, and filth of their bodily functions, Victorians sought privacy in which to attend to them. Water closets, or flush toilets, had been available to the wealthy since at least the early eighteenth century. Queen Anne of England (reigned 1702–1714) had a water closet constructed in her dressing room at Windsor Castle. These early water closets were privies moved indoors and enclosed in a small closet. They flushed when water placed in a cistern above the toilet was released and washed the waste into pipes leading to a sewer or the household cesspool. In the 1770s two English inventors improved the earliest water closets by adding mechanical flaps to keep sewage odors from reentering the bathroom. By the turn of the nineteenth century, more than six thousand toilets had been produced; but, because they required connection to a sewer and a steady supply of water, only a handful of homeowners could afford such luxury. Throughout the nineteenth century, inventors—including Thomas Crapper (1836–1910), whose name eventually became a slang term for the flush toilet—continued to improve the toilet. Yet, most urban residents continued to relieve themselves in common privies located in tenement courtyards, or they used chamber pots that were emptied into cesspools or—as had been the case since the Middle Ages—into the street. Cesspit cleaners and street sweepers managed to turn this waste into earnings by transporting the raw sewage of urban residents into the countryside to be used as fertilizer. The lack of running water and sewer systems made it impossible for most people to have flush toilets before the late nineteenth century. By the late 1880s, architects were beginning to incorporate flush toilets into designs for houses and apartment buildings. At the same time, the separate bathroom was increasingly found in the dwellings of the wealthy, in hotels, and even in high-priced brothels. The bathroom was usually located far from living spaces, evidence that people still did not bathe often and that they wanted to remove embarrassing reminders of human waste and impurity as far as possible from the centers of domestic activity.

Public Water Works. The infrastructure that made possible clean water for flushing toilets and bathing and methods of carrying away waste required substantial public investment and committed private subscription. The first sewers, often just covered gutters, could not carry away all the waste of a modern city. Though there were several earlier attempts to develop sewage systems, urban authorities did not successfully address the problems caused by contaminated wells, overused privies, and raw-sewage discharge until after the 1830s. By 1855 enough progress had been made for the British Parliament to pass a law requiring that all urban waste be evacuated through sewage pipes. In Paris between 1852 and 1869 the network of sewer lines expanded from 87 miles to 350, and by 1911 it exceeded 750. New water-usage patterns emerged during the nineteenth century, as new ideas about cleanliness and health greatly increased the demand for water. Over the course of the century municipal authorities all over Europe endeavored to construct the municipal water services and the sewage systems on which, among other things, new notions of bathroom privacy depended. During the eighteenth century, clean water had been scarce. Even in the countryside, where rural households acquired water from nearby springs, rivers, brooks, wells, or ponds, water quality was often less than satisfactory. In large cities, clean water was even more difficult to acquire. Eighteenth-century urban residents seldom had direct access to running water. The daily supply was either drawn from wells or fountains and carried home by servants or family members or bought from water carriers, who transported it in pails. During the nineteenth century, even as water became more accessible, it was still expensive, and the number of households that could afford to be connected to public water systems varied from city to city into the early twentieth century. London was relatively well served, but even in this city of more than 2.5 million inhabitants only 300,000 residences were supplied with municipal water in 1850. Even in 1910, the French city of Nevers, with a total population of 30,000, had only 3,000 fee-paying consumers of municipal water. Working-class tenements rarely had running water, and even homes in relatively well-off urban districts had no running water on the upper floors.

Heat. In a scene from Charles Dickens's popular tale *A Christmas Carol* (1843), Ebenezer Scrooge's clerk huddles before a fire fueled by one lump of coal; he is wrapped in a comforter and tries to warm his hands over a candle. It is difficult today to conceive of life before electricity, public utilities, and relatively inexpensive and constant access to efficient heating. Europeans of the nineteenth century and earlier, however, could not completely shield themselves from changing outdoor temperatures. In the countryside, one important source of household warmth remained the body heat of livestock, which frequently shared living space with their owners. In the eighteenth century, energy from combustion depended on wood, either in the form of charcoal, "new wood" cut live from a forest and allowed to dry before it was burned, or timbers floated downriver and cut up for firewood. Though three times as efficient as charcoal, easier to light, and less likely to asphyxiate people in rooms without proper ventilation, coal was not readily available in most places and so did not replace these other sources of household heat until well into the nineteenth century. As late as 1830, coal constituted only one-quarter of the fuel consumed in Paris. (The British Isles were an exception. Wood had been scarce there since at least the mid sixteenth century, and coal was relatively plentiful.) Until the early nineteenth century, fireplaces continued to be the main source of heat in most European homes, despite innovations that made stoves more efficient and less expensive. For middle-class urban households of the nineteenth century, the fireplace had an appeal that went beyond its functional utility. An imposing fireplace provided a natural focal point for family gatherings, and the mantel above it was an ideal place to display family heirlooms—expensive ornamental clocks, candelabra, portraits, or knickknacks. Parlors—and increasingly bedrooms—were equipped with fireplaces, uniting the functional purposes of heating and lighting a residence with domestic intimacy. The cast-iron stove was increasingly used for cooking and often replaced the kitchen fireplace in which earlier generations of cooks had prepared meals. Among the urban working class, cast-iron or ceramic stoves served the double function of heating and cooking.

Light. The various means of domestic lighting at the beginning of the nineteenth century largely remained what they had been in the Middle Ages. Light was neither cheap nor efficient. Wax candles were expensive. Cheaper tallow candles smelled bad. Other kinds of artificial lighting also had disadvantages. Burning wicks in small pools of nut, kale, or rapeseed oil were too expensive for year-round use. Despite nineteenth-century innovations, the hearth provided the most consistent source of affordable evening illumination for the rural poor. Bourgeois homemakers made greater use of wax candles, but even they relied heavily on the indirect light of the fireplace. Placing candles on the dining-room table, for example, appears to have been a rare practice, so the dining room was poorly lit. For wealthy households, however, several innovations enhanced home

A middle-class Spanish family at the dining table after dinner (illustration by K. Edwall; from *La Ilustracion Español y Americana*, February 1889)

lighting. In 1783 the French scientist, inventor, and entrepreneur François Ami Argand improved the oil lamp by introducing a new kind of wick that burned brighter than other wicks. Later he enclosed the flame in a glass chimney and developed a mechanism for raising and lowering the wick to increase or decrease the volume of light. The carcel lamp, patented in 1800, regulated the oil flow to the wick with a clock-like mechanism. The cost of repairs, however, made it impractical and limited its use. Moderator lamps, invented in 1836, used a spring to force oil up the wick. They became popular among the bourgeoisie, but they were too expensive for most urban residents. Ultimately, however, all these lamps were just improved versions of the oil lamp that had been used since antiquity. Developed in 1850, the first kerosene lamp was too dangerous and its fuel too costly. In the 1870s and 1880s, however, safer kerosene lamps were made, and kerosene became much more readily available after oil discoveries in the United States. These improved kerosene lamps provided an effective and safe source of light for middle-class homes. The introduction of gas and electrical home lighting in the late nineteenth century expanded the homeowner's options, providing more consistent and brighter light sources, while at the same time linking households more tightly to urban infrastructures. By the turn of the twentieth century, light from a gas mantle provided twelve times the light from a candle or an oil lamp; an electric light bulb was one hundred times more powerful.

Sources:

Edwin Chadwick, *Report on the Sanitary Condition of the Labouring Population of Great Britain*, edited by M. W. Flinn (Edinburgh: Edinburgh University Press, 1965).

Alain Corbin, *The Foul and the Fragrant: Odor and the Social Imagination* (Cambridge, Mass.: Harvard University Press, 1986).

Katherine Grier, *Culture and Comfort: Parlor Making and Middle-Class Identity* (Washington, D.C.: Smithsonian Institution Press, 1988).

Julie L. Horan, *The Porcelain God: A Social History of the Toilet* (Secaucus, N.J.: Birch Lane Press, 1996).

Dominique Laporte, *History of Shit* (Cambridge, Mass.: MIT Press, 2000).

Michelle Perrot, ed., *From the Fires of Revolution to the Great War*, translated by Arthur Goldhammer, volume 4 of *A History of Private Life*, general editors Philippe Ariès and Georges Duby (Cambridge, Mass.: Harvard University Press, 1990).

R. M. Pritchard, *Housing and the Spatial Structure of the City: Residential Mobility and the Housing Market in an English City since the Industrial Revolution* (Cambridge: Cambridge University Press, 1976).

Donald Reid, *Paris Sewers and Sewermen: Realities and Representations* (Cambridge, Mass.: Harvard University Press, 1991).

Wolfgang Schivelbusch, *Disenchanted Night: The Industrialization of Light in the Nineteenth Century*, translated by Angela Davies (Berkeley: University of California Press, 1995).

Debra L. Silverman, *Art Nouveau in Fin-de-Siècle France: Politics, Psychology, and Style* (Berkeley: University of California Press, 1989).

Jack Nelson Tarn, *Five Per Cent Philanthropy: An Account of Housing in Urban Areas between 1840 and 1914* (Cambridge: Cambridge University Press, 1973).

Georges Vigarello, *Concepts of Cleanliness* (Cambridge: Cambridge University Press, 1988).

Whitney Walton, *France at the Crystal Palace: Bourgeois Taste and Artisan Manufacture in the Nineteenth Century* (Berkeley: University of California Press, 1992).

FOOD

Cereals in the Pre-Industrial Diet. With the exception of a small elite throughout Europe, the overwhelming majority of the population before 1800 subsisted on diets far below current nutritional expectations. Nonetheless, purchases of food generally consumed more than half of the household budget, and cereals, principally wheat, were the staple of the diet. Bread—whether the preferred white bread made of wheat or darker, coarser breads made of rye, barley, buckwheat, or millet—was the least expensive source of calories for pre-industrial populations. Wine and beer were the predominant beverages, supplying 10 percent of daily caloric intake. Any surplus funds in the family budget usually were spent on more beer and wine rather than meat or vegetables (some of which were supplied by a small family garden).

Preserved and Processed Foods. The cereal-dominated diet was dramatically altered over the course of the nineteenth century by industrialized methods of food production and preservation and by the expansion and integration of networks for distributing food products, first in the cities and by 1914 nearly everywhere in western and central Europe as well as in the United States. Prior to the nineteenth century, food preservation technology consisted of salting or dehydrating fish, meat, or vegetables. In 1796 Nicolas Appert, a chef in the French Revolutionary army, devised a new technique to preserve food. To supply a mobile army with dependably edible rations, he invented a method of preserving perishable foods such as jellies, eggs, milk, vegetables, or fruits by bottling them. By 1810 he had switched from glass bottles and jars to tin cans. By 1850 canning factories throughout Europe and America were processing vast quantities of preserved food. Products that once could be shipped only to nearby local markets could be shipped great distances once they were canned. Fresh food could also be preserved by refrigeration and freezing, a technique understood in many parts of the world, including Europe, for centuries. By the nineteenth century, the harvesting of natural ice for food preservation had become a big commercial enterprise. Clean ice proved expensive, however, not least because of the costs of transport. In 1850 Scotsman James Harrison invented the first ice-making machine, and in 1859 Frenchman Ferdinand Carré unveiled at the Great Exhibition in London a device that could make ice cubes. As early as 1851 rail cars refrigerated with natural ice were used to transport butter in the United States, and refrigerated cars were soon used to transport other foods in the United States and Europe. By the early 1880s new techniques of insulation led to the creation of freezer holds on ships, allowing meat to be transported long distances, even across the Atlantic. Argentine beef appeared in European consumer markets. The development of industrialized food production and preservation coupled with revolutions in transport, such as steamships

The weekly market in the Alexanderplatz, Berlin, circa 1863 (Markisches Museum, Berlin)

OPEN-AIR MARKETS

The chaos and confusion in open-air markets was described by Henry Mayhew, who visited a market in Lambeth (a borough of London) late on a Saturday night in 1861.

There are hundreds of stalls and every stall has one or two lights. . . . Then the tumult of the thousand different cries of the eager dealers all shouting at the tops of their voices at one and the same time, are almost bewildering. "So-old again" roars one. "Chestnuts all'ot, a penny a score" bawls another. . . . "Buy, buy, buy, buy, buu-u-y," cries the butcher. . . . "Two pence a pound grapes." . . . "Penny a lot, fine russets" calls the apple woman. And so the babel goes on. . . . This stall is green and white with bunches of turnips, that red with apples, the next yellow with onions, and another purple with pickling cabbages. . . . Each salesman tries his utmost to sell his wares, tempting the passers by with his bargains. The boy with his stock of herbs offers "A double handful of fine parsley for a penny" and the man with a donkey cart filled with turnips has three lads to shout for him to their utmost with their "Ho! Ho! Hi-I-I! What d'you think of this here? A Penny a Bunch—Hurrah for free trade! Here's your turnips!"

Source: Dorothy Davis, *Fairs, Shops, and Supermarkets: A History of English Shopping* (Toronto: University of Toronto Press, 1966), pp. 254–255.

and railroads, expanded the dietary choices for consumers. In turn, the new mass market for food dictated to rural hinterlands which products should be produced and shipped to distant urban markets.

Buying Food. By the end of the nineteenth century, a "retail revolution" associated with industrialization and urbanization had transformed the ways in which food was purchased and consumed. Pre-industrial shoppers purchased their food in a variety of open markets rather than from a single vendor. In eighteenth-century Lyon, for example, a shopper might purchase fruit or vegetables in the Place du Change, meat from butchers at the Boucherie des Terreaux, poultry in the Place St. Nizier, fish at several quays along the Rhône or Saône rivers, and bread from bakeries throughout the city. Despite prohibitions by urban authorities, street peddlers often hawked food in the alleys and streets of European cities. Sometimes these petty retailers sold their foodstuffs directly to artisans' households. In urban centers, there was a thriving market in leftovers: peddlers sold to the poor the leavings from banquets of the rich or the remains of tavern meals.

The Grocery Store. Nowhere during the eighteenth century could one find shops devoted only to selling foods. The modern "grocery store"—which emerged during the 1860s in England and the United States as an outgrowth of dry-goods stores and cooperatives (such as the Rochdale Pioneers in England)—is one of the important innovations of the nineteenth century. Dry-goods stores had begun

selling some processed foods by the 1840s, but several developments were necessary before one store could meet most of the consumer's food needs. All these innovations had occured by the last third of the nineteenth century. New preservation techniques extended the shelf life of foods. Transportation networks carried products to distant markets. The purchasing power of the working classes increased enough to make mass consumption possible. The subsequent development of national brands, lines of processed foods, public advertising campaigns, and new corporate management of stores encouraged the spread of grocery chains.

Working-Class Food. In 1833 the wife of a skilled factory worker in Manchester listed her weekly expenditures: twelve shillings for butter, tea, flour, salt, oatmeal, bacon, potatoes, milk, sugar, pepper, mustard, and one pound of meat for Sunday. Rent, coal, soap, and candles cost another six shillings. For breakfast her family ate porridge, bread, and milk; at mid-afternoon tea they had bread and butter; in the evening they consumed oatmeal porridge, potatoes, bacon, and white bread, which she baked herself. Sundays were special: tea, bread, and butter for breakfast; a little meat at dinner followed occasionally by bread and cheese. Vegetables and eggs were rare additions to the table, purchased when available cheaply.

Family Dining. An increasingly important feature of European culture was the central role of family meals. In keeping with the agrarian timetable, sixteenth-century main meals usually started at eleven in the morning. By the eighteenth century, with a later starting time for the work day (especially in cities), dinner was more often eaten at three in the afternoon. In the nineteenth century—with the increased importance of family time and industrial work routines, as well as the spread of artificial lighting—the main meal was served in the evening in many European households. In France and Italy, however, the workday was divided in the middle by a break long enough for men to return home for a leisurely family meal. Breakfasts in these countries were relatively light: bread, butter, and coffee or tea. In England and America, however, the midday break in the workday was much briefer, and the main meal for nineteenth-century bourgeois families was served in the evening. This change was facilitated by greater availability of artificial light, and it necessitated a hearty morning meal: bacon, eggs, toast, and fruit preserves, or possibly—depending on budget and locale—hot cereals and even beefsteak, kidneys, fresh or smoked fish, omelettes, potatoes, beans, tripe, or clams.

Dinner Parties. The evening meal was not only a time for families to gather but also an occasion for socializing with friends and business associates, especially among the prosperous. During the 1890s, an English family earning the equivalent of about $10,000 per year (compared to the average working-class income of around $400) spent fully a quarter of its income on food and drink. Another quarter went to the serving staff—a cook, a kitchen maid, two housemaids, a serving maid, a governess, a gardener, a

Caricature of middle-class patrons in a Paris restaurant; the book on
the table is the menu (Bibliothèque Nationale, Paris)

coachman, a stable boy, and a manservant. Middle-class families with more modest incomes had fewer servants. This emphasis on food and service demonstrates the social importance of hospitality and how it centered on consumption. According to an English etiquette manual published in 1879, "Dinner parties rank first among all entertainments," and an invitation to attend one conveyed "the greatest mark of esteem." A wealthy family could be expected to host a weekly dinner party for eight or more guests. Less-prosperous bourgeois families also gave dinner parties but perhaps only monthly. By the middle of the nineteenth century, the European middle classes entertained dinner guests in the "French manner." That is, instead of serving all the main dishes simultaneously, dinner was brought to the table as a sequence of courses—as many as nine, beginning with appetizers and concluding with coffee or liqueurs. This method of service required an extensive staff. The more servants attending one's guests, the more impressive the dinner. With fewer dishes left on the table at a time, the table had room for more decorative elements. Extravagant floral displays, as well as china, silverware, and crystal, enhanced the visual display of the meal. The menu was designed to impress guests with its variety, contrast, and order. Grand repasts began with a soup, followed by hors d'oeuvres, and then a course of fish. The fish was typically brought in whole, presented to the

guests and host, and then carved at a side table. The fish course was often followed by a sorbet to clear the palate before service of the entrées: carved meats, a range of poultry or lamb dishes garnished with vegetables, and a "roast" of wild game or fowl. The dessert course included ice creams, whipped creams, fruit preserves, puddings, and a large variety of pastries. Finally, men and women took coffee and liqueurs in separate rooms. Such dinners sometimes lasted late into the night.

Dining Out: The Table d'hôte. Before the nineteenth century the food served in public establishments was generally much less impressive than the meals served at dinner parties in private homes. An innkeeper or a caterer (called a *traiteur* in France) served only a limited variety of foods. Caterers offered table d'hôte, a meal served at a set time for a fixed price, to a clientele of mostly artisans or working-class men, many of whom were regulars. The food was placed in the center of the table, and everyone served himself until the food was gone. A British traveler in Paris during the 1780s, Arthur Young, found his fellow diners rude and the quantity of food insufficient. He complained that "the ducks were swept clean so quickly that I moved from table without half a dinner."

The Modern Restaurant. Modern restaurants began to emerge after 1750, but before 1800 there were none outside

During the first half of the nineteenth century dining out in a restaurant was a relatively new experience, with new rules of sociability. A writer for the 3 February 1839 issue of the *Gazette des tribunaux* wondered what would happen if a diner was unable to pay for his dinner:

As soon as you enter a restaurant, if your face inspires even the slightest confidence, there is the restaurateur ready to offer you his menu's limitless pleasures. For you, his fires light, his turnspit turns, his wine cellar opens, and you—you sit calmly by, enjoying the products of so much bother, all of which are trustingly brought to you on silver plates. And then what happens? Just as you are beginning to digest your dinner, you suddenly notice (in truth or fiction) that you have forgotten your wallet! What recourse does the poor restaurateur have? Will he drag you through the courts, exercise the full range of his legal rights? Will he have you hauled off to jail—you! a man who has dined as the best of men dine?!

Source: Rebecca L. Spang, *The Invention of the Restaurant: Paris and Modern Gastronomic Culture* (Cambridge, Mass.: Harvard University Press, 2000), p. 207.

Paris. By the 1820s Parisian restaurants had introduced several novel features that later characterized restaurants everywhere, including waiters, fixed prices, and menus that allowed diners choices of dishes. In these new restaurants a mixed clientele of total strangers ate in relative isolation within the confined space of the dining room. Menus were unnecessary for the table d'hôte, as there was little choice of offerings. Restaurants, however, introduced complex menus offering a variety of choices for each course. A new sort of literature for the discerning diner, menus advertised their offerings with appetizing, eye-catching descriptions. Restaurants also regularized and standardized cuisine, as discerning eaters evaluated the conformity of a dish to the menu description. Restaurants shaped consumer tastes but also gradually conformed to them, as they adapted their menus to meet consumer demands. For the first time respectable women began eating in public with men, as middle-class wives and daughters began dining in the ornately furnished grand salons of the new restaurants. This curious new practice, which began in Paris, provoked comment from British and American tourists, who interpreted it as a sign of French domestic instability. If diners wanted to avoid intermingling of the genders or dining within earshot of strangers, these eateries also offered smaller, private rooms, called *cabinets particuliers*.

Sources:

Piero Camporesi, *Exotic Brew: The Art of Living in the Age of Enlightenment* (Oxford: Polity Press, 1994).

Dorothy Davis, *Fairs, Shops, and Supermarkets: A History of English Shopping* (Toronto: University of Toronto Press, 1966).

Robert Forster and Orest Ranum, eds., *Food and Drink in History: Selections from the Annales: economies, sociétés, civilizations,* volume 5 (Baltimore: Johns Hopkins University Press, 1979).

Jack Goody, *Cooking, Cuisine, and Class: A Study in Comparative Sociology* (Cambridge: Cambridge University Press, 1982).

Harvey A. Levenstein, *Revolution at the Table: The Transformation of the American Diet* (New York: Oxford University Press, 1988).

Rebecca L. Spang, *The Invention of the Restaurant: Paris and Modern Gastronomic Culture* (Cambridge, Mass.: Harvard University Press, 2000).

Maguelonne Toussaint-Samat, *A History of Food,* translated by Anthea Bell (Oxford: Blackwell, 1992).

Margaret Visser, *Much Depends on Dinner: The Extraordinary History and Mythology, Allure and Obsessions, Perils and Taboos, of an Ordinary Meal* (New York: Grove, 1986).

Visser, *The Rituals of Dinner: The Origins, Evolution, Eccentricities, and Meaning of Table Manners* (New York: Grove Weidenfeld, 1991).

LEISURE AND SPORT

Women, Work, and Leisure. The emergence of the modern dichotomy between leisure and work during the nineteenth century had deep consequences for women of all classes, especially those of the middle class. Domesticity was not defined as productive labor. Working-class women sometimes of necessity did "work" for wages, but running errands, cleaning house, or raising children was not considered work. For middle-class women, managing of the household and supervising the rearing of the children fell outside the classification of "work," while the vital social obligations fulfilled by bourgeois women—such as the time-consuming activities of letter writing or paying and receiving social visits—were considered "leisure." In fact, the middle-class woman's so-called leisure activities had a major influence not only on her family's social status but also on her husband's success or failure in the business world. During the middle decades of the nineteenth century, paying or receiving visits (which were rarely longer than fifteen minutes) became ritualized and carefully staged occasions through which the family's social standing and circle of acquaintances were secured. (A list of a family's social circle might include more than fifty names.) Filling the afternoons of society women, these visits, far from being relaxed and casual, required planning and careful attention to social nuances. Failure to make the requisite condolence calls, congratulatory and charitable visits, and trips to see the wife of a husband's business superior spelled expulsion from polite society. Visits, therefore, were serious and risky affairs. At every moment a woman's dress, demeanor, and status were on display. Hosting visitors in the family parlor offered important opportunities to show off family heirlooms, fashionable furnishings, and other signs of consumer affluence. Evening occasions placed a woman's social talents at center stage. At a dinner party, for example, the hostess's taste, social connections, and domestic management were on display. At the same time, the hostess had to seat guests correctly by status and carefully steer conversations. Unless professional musicians were hired, musical evenings often required the daughters of the household to display their vocal or instrumental talents.

Traditional Sport. Much as the English were at the forefront of the Industrial Revolution, they took the lead in the standardization of sports during the nineteenth century. As early as 1838, William Howitt in his *Rural Life in*

Students at a French lay convent playing croquet, late 1880s (Sirot-Angel Collection)

England declared that a "mighty revolution" was overturning the "sports and pastimes of the common people." Indeed, there appears to have been a fundamental change around the middle of the nineteenth century in the nature and meaning of the games Europeans played. Medieval and early modern Europeans hunted, danced, hawked, fenced, boxed, wrestled, gambled at cards and dice, attended cockfights and bearbaitings, and even played varieties of football. Their games were competitions based in agrarian routines and provided opportunities for collective activity, sociability, and pleasure. The end of the harvest and commercial fairs were celebrated with "sporting" activities that were not isolated from other forms of amusement and formed a part of a wider culture of village revels, which included Carnival or May Day celebrations. The upper classes had their sports as well. Weddings, baptisms, royal coronations, birthdays, or military conquests afforded opportunities for gentlemen to sponsor sports such as horse racing. One notable feature of all these pre-industrial sporting activities is the absence of regulation and uniformity. Well into the nineteenth century, violence, brawling, and bloodshed marked traditional sporting activities, spilling over from daily confrontations on the streets and in the workshops. Cudgeling matches, fistfights, and wrestling attracted large audiences. Fistfighting was perhaps the most popular of these spectacles. A fight "up and down"

permitted the combatants to kick or punch any part of the opponent's body, even to choke the other fighter, which frequently led to death. Males were not the exclusive participants in such brawls. Not only did women shout encouragement and sometimes form the ring, they also fought each other. Writing in the eighteenth century, William Hickey described a public contest between two bare-breasted women. Animal combat also attracted large crowds of bettors and spectators. Throughout the early modern period, spectators from all classes were drawn to bearbaitings, dogfights, and bullbaitings. At a cockfight in London in 1710, Zacharias von Uffenbach noted the presence of both gentlemen and simple folk sitting with "no distinction of place," shouting like "madmen," and betting large sums of money.

Boxing. Despite its rough origins, the sport of boxing was among the first to establish rules, a commercial organization, and a national championship. James Figg (circa 1695 – 1734), who fashioned himself a "Master of the Noble Science of Defense," established a boxing academy in 1719. At his Figg's Emporium in London, he sparred with and trained aspiring pugilists. To give his audience a clear view, Figg held exhibitions of fencing, cudgeling, and bare-knuckle boxing on a raised, circular stage called the ring. His successor, Jack Broughton (circa 1704 – 1789), eliminated sword and cudgel fighting from the program.

Deeply shaken after he accidentally killed an opponent in the ring in 1741, Broughton sought to regulate the sport of boxing and make it safer by drawing up the first written rules for boxing matches. "Broughton's Rules" (1743) forbade blows below the belt, leg holds, and beating a downed fighter. They also divided the fight into rounds separated by thirty-second rest intervals. The length and number of rounds was left undetermined, and a fight ended only when a pummeled fighter became so disoriented that he could not "toe the mark" in the center of the ring, voluntarily gave up and "threw in the towel," or was knocked unconscious. Broughton's rules governed the sport for nearly one hundred years, serving as the basis for the London Prize-Ring Rules of 1858, which were replaced by the Queensberry Rules in 1867.

Boxing Champions. Prizefighting became a national pastime, with legendary champions such as Broughton, the Jewish fighter Daniel Mendoza, "Gentleman" John Jackson, "The Butcher" John Gully, and Tom "The Gas-Man" Hickman. Their exploits were reported in new weekly papers devoted to the sport. Prizefights attracted gamblers from all classes, who lay enormous wagers and promised substantial purses to professional fighters. Many pugilists hailed from the growing urban, laboring classes of Europe, who were eager to establish some autonomy and earn more money than they could in a lifetime of factory work, even at the risk of their lives. The sport flourished into the 1820s, but thereafter suffered from attacks by middle-class reformers and evangelical crusaders who condemned gambling, bloodletting, and drinking as threats to morality and labor discipline. Some middle-class gentlemen continued to box, but after 1867 they followed the "civilized" rules to which John Sholto Douglas, Marquis of Queensberry, lent his name. For the first time, fighters were required to wear padded boxing gloves; rounds were limited to three minutes, and the ten-second count was introduced. Many middle-class boys and men abandoned boxing for sports such as golf, yachting, cricket, rugby, or rowing. Boxing remained an important part of working-class culture, however, into the twentieth century.

Folk Football. Like boxing, football (or soccer) drew wrathful denunciations from middle-class reformers during the middle of the nineteenth century. Such condemnations were not new. Folk football was a rough sport played by villagers in medieval Europe. There were no standard rules, but in all versions the object was to propel a ball forward toward an opponent's goal, and high levels of violence and injury were common. In England the sport was actually banned by royal edict in 1314, 1349, 1389, and 1401. The Puritans of the seventeenth century denounced football as more "a friendly kind of fight than play or recreation, a bloody and murdering practice than a fellowly sport or pastime." Neither royal decrees nor local ordinances could stop villagers from playing football, but the Industrial Revolution did. Once farm laborers and craftsmen migrated to urban centers to find work in factories, the crowded ghettos of industrial cities had little space in which to play football.

With workdays before the mid nineteenth century so long (up to sixteen hours) and exhausting, workers had little time or inclination for such entertainment. Sundays, by law and by necessity, had become days of rest. With their limited spare time, workers retired to pubs and taverns, where they could bowl or play darts and billiards. By 1840 folk football was nearly moribund.

Modern Football. When football was revived in the second half of the nineteenth century and became more like the game Americans call soccer, it was reborn on the playing fields of English "public" schools, where the sons of England's elite were educated. At Eton, Rugby, Harrow, Winchester, Charterhouse, and other similar institutions, games such as football, cricket, or rowing were viewed as training for England's future leaders. In the words of William J. Baker, sports taught these boys "to exert their personalities and thus to wield power over the younger, weaker, or more timid members of their society." Each school played football according to its own rules. Winchester and Charterhouse dribbled the ball with their feet, allowed occasional handling, and permitted no long kicks or tackling (because the playing fields were paved brick). At Eton a brick wall 120 yards long marked one sideline while the field was only 6 yards wide. Up and down this narrow corridor some twenty players attempted to propel the ball toward a garden door at one end or a tree stump at the other. The sport was banned at Eton after a rough incident, but the schoolboys then moved their game to an open field, where a sport much closer to modern soccer developed.

Rugby. At Rugby School players kicked the ball to advance it, but the rules also permitted them to handle the ball, run with a carried ball, and tackle. To score, a player could kick the ball through a goal but could also "run in" the ball across the goal line. When schoolboys from Rugby and Eton attended university, however, disagreement on the rules of the game necessitated some codification. In 1845 Rugby school graduates wrote up a set of rules for their version of football. Published in 1846, these rules became the basis for the "Cambridge Rules" of 1848, which set the standard for intercollegiate competition in the separate sport of rugby. With the formation of the Football Association, established by representatives from several clubs and university sides in 1863, English football divided into rugby and soccer versions. Rugby remained a schoolboy game.

Professional Football. After 1885 association football (soccer) began formally accepting professional players, and henceforth the sport became as much a part of working-class culture as that of the middle class. Entrepreneurs saw opportunities for profit in the game, and football teams were filled with salaried players wearing new uniforms and competing in large stadiums before ever-growing crowds of paying spectators. Professional teams were soon organized into leagues and competed in a variety of tournaments. The first Football Association Cup final was held in 1872 and drew an audience of only 2,000 fans. By 1901 the number of spectators at this annual match had risen to more than

Most young athletes learn the rules of various sports from watching television, playing in neighborhood games, and joining organized teams. But before the rules became standardized, having watched or played a sport in one place did not guarantee that one would know the rules in another. In his popular novel *Tom Brown's School Days* (1857), set at Rugby School in England, Thomas Hughes included a conversation between "new boy" Tom Brown and his schoolmate East that reveals the differences in football rules from school to school and suggests the importance of sport in establishing social hierarchies in the elite English "public" schools:

> "You just will see a match; and Brooke's going to let me play. . . . That's more than he'll do for any other lower-school boy. . . ."
>
> "Who's Brooke?"
>
> "Why that big fellow who called over at dinner. . . . He's the cock of the school, and head of the Schoolhouse side, and the best kick and charger in Rugby."
>
> "Oh, but do show me where they play? And tell me about it. I love football so, and have played all my life. Won't Brooke let me play?"
>
> "Not he," said East, with some indignation; "why, you don't know the rules—you'll be a month learning them. And then it's no joke playing up in a match, I can tell you. . . . Why, there's been two collarbones broken this half, and a dozen fellows lamed. And last year a fellow had his leg broken."

Tom listened with the profoundest respect to this chapter of accidents, and followed East across the level ground till they came to a sort of gigantic gallows of two poles eighteen feet high, fixed upright in the ground some fourteen feet apart, with a cross bar running from one to the other at the height of ten feet or thereabouts.

> "This is one of the goals," said East, "and you see the other across there, right opposite. . . . Well the match is the best of three goals; whichever side kicks two goals wins: and it won't do, you see, just to kick the ball through these posts; it must go over the cross bar; any height'll do, so long as it's between the posts. You'll have to stay in goal to touch the ball when it rolls behind the goal posts, because if the other side touch it they have a try at goal. Then we fellows in quarters, we play just about in front of goal here, and have to turn the ball and kick it back before the big fellows on the other side can follow it up. And in front of us all the big fellows play, and that's where the scrummages are mostly." Tom's respect increased as he struggled to make out his friend's technicalities, and the other set to work to explain the mysteries of "off your side," "drop-kicks," "punts," "places," and other intricacies of the great science of football.
>
> "But how do you keep the ball between the goals?" said he. "I can't see why it mightn't go right down to the chapel."
>
> "Why that's out of play," answered East [after explaining the boundaries]. "As soon as the ball gets past them, it's in touch and out of play. And then whoever first touches it, has to knock it straight out amongst the players up, who make two lines with a space between them, every fellow going on his own side."

Source: Thomas Hughes, *Tom Brown's School Days* (Mahwah, N.J.: Watermill Press, 1988).

110,000. In 1900 a professional footballer earned nearly £ 2 per week, the equivalent of a skilled craftsman's wages. The sport also afforded a degree of social recognition otherwise denied working-class youths. For working-class spectators as well, football served as the basis of a new form of community solidarity. As J. B. Priestly noted, cheering for a team "turned you into a member of a new community, all brothers together for an hour and a half, . . . and there you were cheering together, thumping one another on the shoulders, swapping judgements like lords of the earth, having pushed your way through a turnstile into another and altogether more splendid kind of life. . . ."

Other Sports. An equally important leisure culture was established around games played in the private grounds or clubs of the elite. Cricket was dominated by such clubs. The Marylebone Cricket Club in London, for example, attracted merchants, country gentlemen, and successful professionals eager to participate in the sporting culture but also to set themselves apart from the clerks, managers, and shopkeepers of the petty bourgeoisie. Rowing, bicycling, and yachting also afforded entertainment apart from working-class participation or intrusion. Croquet, badminton, lawn tennis, archery, and golf also offered genteel entertainment suitable for hardy competition and restricted social mingling. The lawn itself served as an important marker of middle-class distinction, a luxurious green space next to the confined, paved courts of urban tenements. Croquet was the first lawn game to catch on widely. Though one version of the game was brought to England from France in the mid seventeenth century, the game that became modern croquet was brought to England from France by retired army officers after the Napoleonic Wars. This adaptation of the *jeu de maille* (mallet game) became extremely popular in England and the United States during the 1860s. Badminton and archery soon followed as popular leisure activities. In 1873, Major Walter Clopton Wingfield adapted the ancient royal game of tennis to the budgets and lawns of the middle classes. Henceforth, versions of lawn tennis played in the privacy of the bourgeois garden provided opportunities for socially appropriate meetings between the genders and for genteel competitions between social equals. In 1875 the All-England Croquet Club changed its name to the All-England Croquet and Lawn Tennis Club and radically altered Wingfield's game, lowering the net, covering the rubber ball with felt, allowing the server a second attempt, and altering the dimensions and shape of the court. Two years later the club held its first lawn-tennis championship match at Wimbledon. Its 1885 tournament drew more than 3,500 spectators.

Gymnastics. Perhaps the most significant alternative to modern, Anglo-American sporting culture was the emergence in Germany and Scandinavia of modern gymanistics. The earliest proponents of German gymnastics, called *Turnen,* were inspired to develop the sport by the educational ideas of the French Enlightenment philosopher Jean-Jacques Rousseau and by Napoleon's defeat of the Prussian army. Preaching Rousseau's admonition that physical exercise engendered not only good health but also moral character and wisdom, German educator Johann Friedrich Guts Muths (1759–1839) promoted the importance of games and rigorous calisthenics as part of the academic day. Guts Muths's regimen included running, jumping, vaulting, and climbing various apparatus as a means of developing muscular strength and coordination. Perhaps the most influential German physical educator of the first half of the nineteenth century, Friedrich Ludwig Jahn (1778–1852) combined a passion for physical fitness and individual liberty with an ardent nationalism and fanatical hatred of the French. Jahn concluded that the future of the still un-unified German people depended as much on the physically fit as on the intellectually able. Jahn took his pupils on demanding hikes and put them through a program of exercise. Expanding on the apparatus originated by Guts Muths, Jahn built a playground, or *Turnplatz,* in a field near Berlin, with a running track, parallel bars, beams, vaults, rings, and other climbing apparatus. Soon adults were also attracted to the activity. Adherents to German gymnastics did not just practice physical fitness. They also aggressively encouraged a liberal egalitarianism, wearing gray uniforms to eliminate marks of class distinction, and a devout patriotic determination, singing patriotic songs and drilling in groups with near-military synchronization. In the end, the political activities of German gymnastic associations involved them in failed attempts to bring a liberal constitution to Germany and resulted in a twenty-year ban on such sporting associations. German gymnastics did not disappear, however. By the 1840s gymnastics had been incorporated into the Prussian school curriculum, and with the foundation of the *Deutsche Turnerschaft* (German Gynastics Club) in 1860, the liberal politics of early gymnasts were supplanted by a devotion to fitness and the possibilities of German empire.

The Olympic Games. The emergence of the modern Olympic games largely resulted from the efforts of a Parisian aristocrat, Pierre, Baron de Coubertin, who started out on a mission to improve the physical fitness of young Frenchmen after the humiliating defeat of France by Prussia in 1870. His campaign had little initial impact on French sport, but he was much more successful when he decided to revive the ancient Greek spectacle of the Olympic Games, which several other nineteenth-century Europeans had attempted with little success. Coubertin's correspondence with international sporting figures and his lectures in European and American cities, however, came at a time when an enthusiasm for sport as character education was growing among the elite of Europe. The first International Olympic Games were held in Athens, Greece, in 1896, and Coubertin served as president of the International Olympic Committee until 1925. Among the sports included at the first modern Olympiad were ancient contests such as the javelin, discus, running events, and wrestling, as well as modern competitions, including cycling, sharpshooting, tennis, and rowing. The Athens Games were marked by true amateurism and little beforehand preparation. The victor of the Athens marathon, Greek runner Spiridon Loues, had never before won a race in his competitive career, and he never raced again. The informality of the first Olympics did not last long. By the London Games of 1908, a spirit of national expectation suffused the games with a sense of urgency and national pride, which had been less pronounced during the earlier rather low-key games in Athens, St. Louis, and Paris. In London more than 300,000 spectators watched the teams of nineteen nations, attired in team uniforms and competing for supremacy on the athletic stage. Even at this early date in the development of the Olympic movement, anxieties about sport as a measure of racial virility and national character were already apparent. As Europe prepared for seemingly inevitable conflict, the Olympics became less a vehicle for world peace and increasingly an alternative forum for national confrontation.

Women and Sports. Throughout most of the nineteenth century, men agreed that women should be excluded from sports. The founder of the modern Olympic Games, Pierre, Baron de Coubertin, said flatly: "The role of woman is what it has always been. . . . She is above all the companion of man, the future mother of a family, and she should be brought up with this fixed destiny in mind." Critics feared that women's participation in sports would undermine male authority in the family and would lead to a collapse of public morals. Of course, spectacles of half-dressed women boxing or wrestling, a common feature of working-class entertainment, seemed to support the notion that women's athletic activities aroused the prurient interest of men. Despite such widespread male disapproval, nineteenth-century European women did participate in individual and team sports. Indeed, the rhetoric of "character building" employed in praise of middle-class male athleticism also provided the justification for women's sports. After all, exercise would "build" hardy mothers. In late Victorian schools, therefore, some attempt was made to offer physical education for young women. In 1876 the London school board required physical exercise for young girls and appointed Concordia Löfving to train teachers in the Swedish system of gymnastic exercises. Löfving was later replaced by another Swede, Martina Bergmann-Österberg. Middle-class women's participation in sports subtly reinforced ideals of domesticity

Start of the 100-meter race at the first modern Olympic Games, Athens, 1896

and class distinction as well. While women were permitted to play tennis or croquet, modesty and fashion could not be ignored. It was considered unfeminine for women to compete strenuously or dress inappropriately. They were not to bare their ankles during competitions, and a fashionable tennis outfit might consist of "a cream merino bodice with long sleeves edged with embroidery; a skirt with deep kilting, over it an old-gold silk blouse-tunic with short wide sleeves and square neck" topped off with a "large straw hat."

Women, Cricket, and Football. Between 1740 and the 1830s, upper-class women in the south of England competed against each other in cricket, while village women from Sussex, Hampshire, and Surrey occasionally played the game as well. By the middle of the nineteenth century such competitions became offensive to the middle-class conception of femininity, and women's cricket nearly disappeared. Though women resumed play in the final decades of the century, female cricketers were never accepted by men because sport had come to be an exclusive marker of masculinity. Women footballers faced similar objections. When the British Ladies Football Club (BLFC) formed in 1894, with the guidance of a Miss Nettie J. Honeyball and the sponsorship of Lady Florence Dixie, it was greeted with derision and soon disbanded.

The first match drew some ten thousand curious spectators. The press subsequently declared that "girls are totally unfitted for the rough work of the football-field. As a means of exercise in a back-garden it is not to be commended; as a public entertainment it is to be deplored." Women footballers, like women cricket players, threatened the masculine monopoly on team sport.

Sources:
William J. Baker, *Sports in the Western World,* revised edition (Urbana: University of Illinois Press, 1988).

Denis Brailsford, *Sport and Society: Elizabeth to Anne* (London: Routledge & Kegan Paul, 1969).

John Ford, *Cricket: A Social History, 1700–1835* (Newton Abbot, U.K.: David & Charles, 1972).

Elliott J. Gorn, *The Manly Art: Bare-Knuckle Prize Fighting in America* (Ithaca: Cornell University Press, 1986).

Alan Guttman, *Games and Empires: Modern Sports and Cultural Imperialism* (New York: Columbia University Press, 1994).

Richard Holt, *Sport and the British: A Modern History* (Oxford: Oxford University Press, 1990).

Holt, "Women, Men and Sport in France, c. 1870–1914: An Introductory Survey," *Journal of Sport History,* 18, no. 1 (1991): 121–134.

Kathleen E. McCrone, "Class, Gender, and English Women's Sport, c. 1890–1914," *Journal of Sport History,* 18, no. 1 (1991): 159–181.

Bonnie G. Smith, *Ladies of the Leisure Class: The Bourgeoises of Northern France in the Nineteenth Century* (Princeton: Princeton University Press, 1981).

SIGNIFICANT PEOPLE

ARISTIDE BOUCICAUT

1810-1877
DEPARTMENT STORE FOUNDER

Early Years. Aristide Boucicaut, founder of the first French department store, was born in the Norman village of Bellême, where his father was a hat maker, and left home at eighteen to work with an itinerant peddler. By 1835 he was living in Paris, where he was employed at the Petit Saint-Thomas, a dry-goods store (known in France as a *magasin de nouveauté*, or novelty store), selling wares such as silks, cloths, ready-to-wear clothing, stitchery, umbrellas, and gloves. Shortly after his arrival in Paris, Boucicaut met and married Marguerite Guérin. After rising to a managerial position at the Petit Saint-Thomas, Boucicaut borrowed 50,000 francs and went into partnership with Paul Videau to purchase Au Bon Marché, a similar novelty store on the Left Bank of the Seine. When the two partners bought the store in 1852, it had only twelve employees and retail sales of about 450,000 francs annually. During the 1850s and 1860s the store expanded in size, and by 1863 Boucicaut was able to buy out Videau with borrowed money. In 1868 he was able to buy the rest of the block in which the store stood, and the following year he began construction on a new building to house the first true department store.

Business Success. Employing engineer Gustave Eiffel and architect L. A. Boileau, Boucicaut began building a department store that eventually covered more than five hundred thousand square feet and took up an entire block of prime Parisian real estate. The architecture of the store was a marvel, employing innovative iron-and-glass construction, with skylights to maximize natural lighting. Aristide Boucicaut died ten years before the building reached its full size in 1887, but he did live to see his dream of a retail empire come to fruition. In the year he died, 1877, sales in his gigantic store grossed more than 73,000,000 francs, dwarfing most of his competitors, and the store employed 1,788 workers. Nearly thirty years later, the retail sales and mail-order purchases at the store topped 188 million francs.

Significance. Though Boucicaut may not have been the father of modern mass marketing, his department store successfully exploited new developments in merchandising, financing, and retail organization. After purchasing Au Bon Marché in 1852, Boucicault expanded the product line and increased the number of departments from four to thirty-six, including ready-to-wear clothing, men's wear, children's products, household furnishings, camping goods, perfume, shoes, leather goods, kitchen wares, and eventually toys and sporting goods. On a particularly brisk sales day in the 1890s, the department store might open its doors to as many as 70,000 shoppers. Au Bon Marché also instituted a large-volume mail-order service. During the winter of 1894, for example, more than 1.5 million catalogues were mailed to prospective customers. The mail-order business not only reached customers in France but as far away as Russia, the United States, and South America. Boucicaut also offered financing to manufacturers and wholesalers, and eventually he vertically integrated his business from production through sales. For example, the company had its own workshops within the store to produce shirts, baby clothes, bedding, coats, cloaks, made-to-measure bridal gowns, and many other products. By 1890, 600 workers were employed in these workshops alone.

Sources:

John William Ferry, *A History of the Department Store* (New York: Macmillan, 1960).

Michael B. Miller, *The Bon Marché: Bourgeois Culture and the Department Store 1869–1920* (Princeton: Princeton University Press, 1981).

EDWIN CHADWICK

1800-1890
REFORMER

Crusader. Edwin Chadwick's contemporaries called him boring, unreasonable, and overbearing, but he was, in fact, an effective crusader for social change. He devoted his considerable talents to solving public-health problems engendered by the Industrial Revolution, and he had the satisfaction of seeing steps taken to address most of the wrongs he sought to correct.

Early Years. Chadwick was born on 24 January 1800 at Longsight, near the city of Manchester. When he was ten, he and his family moved to London, where he was initially trained in the legal profession. He became acquainted with the great utilitarian philosophers of his time, Jeremy Bentham (1748–1832) and John Stuart Mill (1806–1873), and for a time served as Bentham's personal secretary. Medical reformer Neil Arnott, Chadwick's personal physician, introduced him to the social implications of public hygiene. In 1834, Chadwick was appointed to the Poor Law Commission, which the government established to reform the distribution of relief to the poor. In particular, the commission was appointed to discourage the poor from taking advantage of charity. Maintaining that people without work were just lazy, Parliament had decreed that government relief would be distributed only to people so destitute that their sole option was living in unpleasant workhouses, where they were given onerous and distasteful tasks designed to motivate them to seek other employment. After epidemics of cholera and typhoid broke out in 1837 and 1838, the government turned its attention to the health and hygiene of the working classes, assigning the Poor Law Commission to investigate hygienic conditions in the manufacturing towns of the country.

Chadwick's Report. Because he was unable to get along with the three other members of the Poor Law Commission, Chadwick, who was its secretary, basically researched and wrote *Report on the Sanitary Condition of the Labouring Population of Great Britain* (1842) by himself, taking several years to complete it. He sent detailed questionnaires to poor-law guardians throughout the country, and he buttressed the data he collected from them with many eyewitness accounts from doctors who treated the poor. Chadwick also participated personally in inspecting workers' housing in parts of London, Edinburgh, Glasgow, Manchester, Leeds, and Macclesfield. His conclusions represented significant disagreement with the government policy, as well as a departure from his own earlier thinking about the dimensions of poverty, the necessity of poor relief, and how it should be distributed. In fact, his fellow commissioners considered his conclusions too radical and refused to be associated with the report. In particular, Chadwick's approach to sanitary reform called for the greatly increased involvement of local and national governments.

Changing Public Opinion. The main purpose of Chadwick's report was to influence public attitudes toward the poor. Because of his controversial conclusions, however, the government would not sponsor its publication, and to take his case to the public Chadwick had to arrange for private publication. As many as 20,000 copies were subsequently sold or given away. *The Times* and *The Morning Chronicle* also published features on Chadwick's report. His first aim was to establish irrefutable evidence of how poor drainage, inadequate water supplies, and overcrowded housing were linked to disease, high mortality rates, and low life expectancy. Chadwick then turned to the economic costs of ill health among the poor before addressing what he felt to be the most damaging effect of poor hygienic conditions: the connection of inadequate housing to gambling, drunkenness, and immorality. Such thinking was profoundly different from his attitudes in the mid 1830s. Like the other Poor Law Commissioners, he had then considered poverty and the resort to charity a result of moral failings, rather than their cause. By the 1840s he had concluded that moral reform could not be accomplished by making workhouses inhospitable, but rather by government programs to improve the housing of the working class.

Impact. Chadwick's report instigated a struggle in Parliament that lasted nearly ten years, and it was a model for later investigations of housing in France and the United States. The most important legislation resulting from Chadwick's report was the Public Health Act of 1848. Although this law only partially addressed the concerns raised by Chadwick's report, it was a step toward reforming the living conditions of the laboring poor. For historians Chadwick's enormous report has provided valuable information about working-class living conditions during the early period of industrialization.

Sources:

Edwin Chadwick, *Report on the Sanitary Condition of the Labouring Population of Great Britain*, edited, with an introduction, by M. W. Flinn (Edinburgh: Edinburgh University Press, 1965).

John Nelson Tarn, *Five Per Cent Philanthropy: An Account of Housing in Urban Areas between 1840 and 1914* (Cambridge: Cambridge University Press, 1973).

WILLIAM GILBERT GRACE

1848-1915
CRICKET PLAYER

National Sports Star. William Gilbert Grace, a country doctor from Gloucestershire, England, dominated the game of cricket from 1862 until his retirement in 1899 at the age of fifty-one. He was the first English national sports star.

Early Years. Unlike most of his contemporaries, Grace did not come out of the elite British "public" school system, where the ideal of the gentleman sportsman was nurtured. Born in 1848, Grace began playing cricket with his brothers under the tutelage of his father and a cricket-playing uncle. Grace's father, a rural physician, had connections to the Duke of Beaufort that secured the young prodigy entry into the country-house matches of the rural squierarchy. Grace played his first county match against first-rate adult competition at the age of fourteen. His reputation was made when at fifteen he scored his first of many "centuries" (batting for more than one hundred runs) against the Gentlemen of Sussex.

Career. During his cricket career Grace managed to score more than fifty-four thousand first-class runs and is still fifth on the all-time list of cricket batsmen. Nicknamed "the Doctor," Grace was primarily a cricket player, although during the winter off-season he did work as a physician. He devoted hours to training for matches and traveling to sporting venues. Hardly an amateur athlete, he was known to accept large sums of money to endorse commercial products. In the genteel sport of cricket, Grace was an anomaly. Aggressive on the field, he verbally assaulted opponents and often upbraided officials. His personality, his unusually large stature, and his prodigious exploits as a batsman combined to secure his lasting reputation as a larger-than-life sportsman.

A Superstar. Grace's presence in a game was guaranteed to draw large crowds of spectators. Sometimes the usual three-pence admission price was doubled when Grace played. In July 1873 thirty thousand fans attended a three-day match to watch Grace play. One Saturday in July 1878, between fifteen and twenty thousand spectators went to the Old Trafford ground in Manchester to see Grace at bat. The large crowd overwhelmed the gatekeepers and, once inside, spread onto the playing field. At his death in 1915 Grace was described as "the best known of all Englishmen." Perhaps only Queen Victoria herself was better known. Still one of the most successful batsmen in English cricket history, Grace was a charismatic sports idol whose renown has been com-

pared with that of later athletes such as Pelé, Babe Ruth, and Joe Louis.

Sources:

William J. Baker, *Sports in the Western World*, revised edition (Urbana: University of Illinois Press, 1988).

Richard Holt, *Sport and the British: A Modern History* (Oxford: Oxford University Press, 1990).

Eric Midwinter, *W. G. Grace: His Life and Times* (London: Allen & Unwin, 1981).

Simon Rae, *W. G. Grace: A Life* (London: Faber & Faber, 1998).

Keith A. P. Sandiford, "English Cricket Crowds During the Victorian Age," *Journal of Sport History*, 9, no. 3 (1982): 5–20.

MATHURIN ROZE DE CHANTOISEAU

DIED 1806
RESTAURATEUR

Early Years. The son of Armand Roze, a landowner and merchant in Chantoiseau, France, Mathurin Roze added the aristocratic-sounding "de Chantoiseau" to his name before moving to Paris in the early 1760s. There he became involved in several business ventures and reform projects. His preoccupation with the financial health of the kingdom coincided with a concern for the physical well-being of the citizenry of Paris. He opened his first restaurant in 1766, and three years later he published a pamphlet describing a fiscal program designed to increase the money supply while neither increasing taxes nor encouraging inflationary pressures. The plan, which received some attention at court and for which Roze hoped to be acknowledged, instead landed him briefly in jail for distributing an incendiary tract. Despite this setback, Roze revisited the issue in 1789. On the eve of the French Revolution this self-described "Friend of All the World" presented a reworked plan to Louis XVI and the Estates General. It was politely dismissed, but Roze periodically made similar proposals throughout the revolutionary years. Roze also wrote the *Almanach général*, a directory of the most important wholesalers, merchants, bankers, courtiers, artists, and artisans in France, which appeared regularly during the 1770s and 1780s. The almanac also regularly credited a "M. Roze" (himself) with starting the first restaurant.

Restaurateur. In 1768 Roze paid 1,600 livres for the title of "cook-caterer following the Court." This privilege, which freed him from contending with the cook-caterers' guild and their regulations, gave Roze's eatery the imprimatur of royal patronage. According to the almanac, his restaurant specialized in bouillons or "princely consommés." It did not initially promise an abundance of food or a wide variety of dishes; instead, it advertised a healthful restorative for the "weak-chested," the asthmatic, the tubercular, and other physically fragile city residents. In the 1769 edition of the *Almanach général*, Chantoiseau included the following description of his gustatory accomplishments: "Roze, rue Saint Honoré, Hôtel d'Aligre, the first restaurateur, offers fine and delicate meals for 3–6 *livres* per head." He also offered a novel style of presentation; his food was "served not at a *table d'hôte,* but at any hour of the day, by the dish, and at a fixed price." Allowing patrons to eat what and when they wanted distinguished Roze's establishment from earlier, usually lower-class, table d'hôte eateries, which served the same meal to everyone at a set time for a single price, and his innovation supports his claim to have invented the restaurant as it is known today. Roze's involvement in the retail food trade was short-lived. Anne Bellot took over his restaurant during the 1780s.

Later Career. In 1799 Roze and a partner proposed to establish their own credit system and founded a private bank. This venture failed, and the two went bankrupt. When Roze died in March 1806, he was penniless. Yet, the restaurant he had founded had become a fixture of the Parisian landscape, and he was eventually recognized as the first modern restaurateur, a distinction he had claimed for himself.

Source:

Rebecca L. Spang, *The Invention of the Restaurant: Paris and Modern Gastronomic Culture* (Cambridge, Mass.: Harvard University Press, 2000.)

DOCUMENTARY SOURCES

Edwin Chadwick, *Report on the Sanitary Condition of the Labouring Population of Great Britain* (London: Printed by W. Clowes & Sons, 1842)—A report based on survey results and firsthand observations, with extensive quotations from many local investigators, on working-class living conditions throughout England and Scotland; the report contributed to the passage of the 1848 Public Health Act, which established the responsibility of the British government for protecting the nation's health.

Friedrich Engels, *Die Lage der arbeitenden Klasse in England* (Leipzig: Wigand, 1845); translated by Florence Kelley Wischnewetzky as *The Condition of the Working Class in England in 1844* (New York: Lovell, 1887)—A study of Victorian England written after a two-year stay in Manchester, a dreary manufacturing city in the throes of the Industrial Revolution; this critique of early industrialization captures the personal tragedies and institutional failures of the period.

Gustave Flaubert, *Madame Bovary, mœurs de province,* 2 volumes (Paris: Michel Lévy frères, 1857); translated by John Sterling as *Madame Bovary. A Tale of Provincial Life* (Philadelphia: T. B. Peterson & Bros., 1881)—A novel about a frustrated, provincial middle-class French housewife who engages in an adulterous affair to ease the boredom of her ordinary existence; this realistic novel is a commentary on the constraints of middle-class life.

Thomas Hughes, *Tom Brown's School Days* (Cambridge: Macmillan, 1857)—An exceptionally popular juvenile novel about a young boy sent to the Rugby School to develop the good character expected of the English gentleman; the novel is a valuable picture of life at an elite British "public" school during the nineteenth century.

Jacques-Louis Ménétra, *Journal de ma vie* [written 1764–1802] (Paris: Montalba, 1982); translated by Arthur Goldhammer as *Journal of My Life* (New York: Columbia University Press, 1986)—A rare autobiography of an eighteenth-century artisan, who described his travels as a journeyman throughout France, his sexual exploits, and the sociability of artisanal associations during the Old Regime.

Emile Zola, *Le Ventre de Paris* (Paris: Charpentier, 1873); translated by John Stirling as *The Markets of Paris (Le Ventre de Paris)* (Philadelphia: T. B. Peterson & Bros., 1879)—A novel set in Les Halles, the central market of Paris, where market women, fruit and produce sellers, and dealers in leftover food from restaurants and aristocrats' tables compete for space; drawing on Zola's extensive visits to the market, the novel realistically portrays an often-ignored part of nineteenth-century daily life.

THE FAMILY AND SOCIAL TRENDS

by CHRISTOPHER R. CORLEY

CONTENTS

Sidebars and tables are listed in italics.

1750-1800

- During the later European Enlightenment, philosophers reject unquestioned obedience to tradition and religion and advocate new social relationships, especially within the family. These writers, mostly men, argue that women should follow their natural destinies as mothers and domestic managers, roles that became hallmarks of Victorian-era motherhood in the nineteenth century.

1750-1850

- The average marriage age rises steadily in Europe. By the mid nineteenth century the average age for men is twenty-seven, and women average twenty-four.

1762

- Jean-Jacques Rousseau publishes his novel *Emile,* which is almost immediately popular and helps to begin a new wave of interest in the natural development of children.

1780-1850

- An evangelical movement within the Anglican Church helps to affirm a new middle-class identity based on maintaining "separate spheres" for men (public life) and women (home life).

1792

- The French Revolutionary government begins to institute a series of pathbreaking legal changes. It outlaws lettres de cachet, warrants by which an individual could be imprisoned without trial. The age of majority is lowered to twenty-one years, and all children are made eligible for equal inheritance. Marriage becomes a civil act, and divorce is legalized. At nearly the same time, a reaction sets in against women's participation in politics and public life.

- Mary Wollstonecraft publishes *A Vindication of the Rights of Woman.*

1793

- French feminist Olympe de Gouges, author of the *Declaration of the Rights of Woman and the Citizen* (1791), and Marie Antoinette, Queen of France, are both executed for treason.

1798

- Thomas Malthus publishes *An Essay on the Principles of Population,* arguing that human population growth will naturally correct itself through famine and disease.

1800s

- The illegitimacy rate in Europe soars as young people migrate to urban areas and put off marriage until their later years. Some historians have estimated that as many as 15 to 20 percent of all births were out of wedlock.

1803-1804

* DENOTES CIRCA DATE

- French Emperor Napoleon Bonaparte institutes the Civil Code in territories under French control. Although the principle of equal inheritance is maintained, many other legal changes enacted in 1792 and 1793 are overturned, including the ability of women to obtain a divorce and to control the property she brings into a marriage.

1830s

- Labeled "utopian socialists" by more-radical critics, social reformers such as Charles Fourier, Suzanne Voilquin, and Claude-Henri de Rouvroy, Comte de Saint-Simon, plan and attempt to create alternative forms of social organization based on cooperative economies and gender equity.

1830s-1880s

- Throughout Europe legislation is passed to limit work hours and establish minimum ages for children employed in factories and other industries.

1839

- Instigated by Caroline Norton's *Natural Claim of a Mother to the Custody of Her Child* (1837), the Infant Custody Act is passed in the United Kingdom, giving mothers rights to their children under seven years of age.

1846-1850

- During the Great Irish Famine some families die of starvation. Many others are left impoverished and are evicted from their homes by property owners. The famine sparks a major immigration to the Americas.

1848

- Amid Europe-wide political and social upheaval, Karl Marx and Friedrich Engels publish *The Communist Manifesto*. In one important section of their pamphlet, these radical socialists argue that a socialist revolution will require a reorganization of the family, in which the entire community will collectively care for the children.

1850s-1870s

- In England the Langham Place Group, led by Barbara Smith Bodichon, presses for property reform and women's rights over their property.

1860s-1870s

- A Russian medical-reform movement emerges to teach modern birthing techniques to rural midwives, called *povitukhi*. By 1905 more than fifty schools have been established throughout Russia, but most Russian children are still born in unsanitary environments.

1861

- Isabella Beeton's *Book of Household Management* is published. A compilation of her magazine articles about women and domestic work, the book is an instant success.

1866

- Many European women have begun to give birth in hospitals, where sanitary conditions are often far worse than at home, the traditional location for births throughout pre-industrial Europe. In 1866 thirty-four women of every one thousand who give birth in hospitals die, as compared to just under five of every one thousand whose babies are delivered at home.

* DENOTES CIRCA DATE

THE FAMILY AND SOCIAL TRENDS

1867
- Philosopher John Stuart Mill, a member of the British Parliament, conducts an unsuccessful campaign for women's suffrage.

1869
- Mill publishes *On the Subjection of Women*, which becomes one of the most respected examples of nineteenth-century liberal political philosophy.

1870
- After decades of petitions and rallies for change, Parliament passes the Married Women's Property Act.

1870s-1880s
- Growing numbers of children attend state-sponsored schools, especially between the ages of five and ten years old. As a result, literacy rates increase for adults throughout Europe.

1879-1884
- Two major theoretical works on the family and political organization—August Bebel's *Women and Socialism* (1879) and Friedrich Engels's *Origins of the Family, Private Property, and the State* (1884)—argue that the origins of patriarchy lie in the establishment of private property.

1886
- The Contagious Disease Acts are repealed by the British Parliament. British feminists, led by Josephine Butler, have criticized the acts for creating a double standard by which poor women were prosecuted for resorting to prostitution while their male clients were ignored.

1889
- Norwegian playwright Henrik Ibsen's *A Doll's House* has its premiere on the London stage, causing a stir among feminists and antifeminists alike. In Germany and other European countries, Ibsen's conclusion—in which the middle-class heroine leaves her husband—is deemed too controversial and changed in theaters where the play is performed.

1900
- Swedish author Ellen Key publishes *The Century of the Child*, capping more than 150 years of increased attention to children and signaling their centrality in the family for the twentieth century.

1910
- More than 250 British government inspectors handle more than 50,000 complaints registered with the National Society for the Prevention of Cruelty to Children.

* Denotes Circa Date

OVERVIEW

Two Revolutions. The French Revolution of 1789 and the Industrial Revolution had major repercussions in the modern era, not only on political and economic history but also on European family and social life. The French Revolution popularized ideas of human equality and democratic political participation. The Industrial Revolution profoundly altered the ways in which humans produced and consumed goods. It also fostered the rise of the middle class, the primary purchasers of these new ready-made goods. This class—which included merchants, bankers, professional people, tradesmen, and owners of small factories—lived in cities and towns and was generally less prosperous than members of the nobility but more wealthy than urban artisans. Furthermore, unlike successful nonaristocrats of the past, middle-class finances were not linked to landholdings. Instead, the prosperity of the middle class, or bourgeoisie, was tied to the Industrial Revolution, which they supported through investment of their financial assets as well as by purchases of consumer products. During the late eighteenth century, there arose two distinct family cultures. One family model was based on a companionate marriage promoting affective bonds between parents and children. The other was based on the family as an economic unit with a dominant father at its head. These models were often found within the same family, and to some extent they still characterize the modern family today. The family also helped people form ideas of what social and political institutions should be like. From this perspective, the family was not merely acted on and molded by social changes. It also influenced them. For the first time in Western history, eighteenth- and nineteenth-century politicians and philosophers stressed the important responsibilities of parents in raising future citizens, promoting the child's natural qualities, and especially protecting the child's innocence. The nation-states of the nineteenth century attempted to use the family to promote the wealth and future stability of the state with the first widespread use of state officials to regulate and protect family life and childhood.

The Family, the State, and Social Change. In 1877 Frédéric Le Play (1806–1882) wrote: "Private life stamps public life with its character. The family is the foundation of the state." Nearly a century earlier, during the French Revolution, members of the National Assembly attempted to institute lasting change in their society by making sweeping revisions to laws and regulations that had guided French family life and relationships for centuries. Arbitrary imprisonment of children was abolished; egalitarian property rights were made mandatory; children became emancipated adults at twenty-one instead of twenty-five or even thirty; and women were allowed to divorce their husbands. At the same time, politicians in France and other parts of Europe drafted legislation that placed the state at the center of family relationships, rituals, and supervision of children, undermining the woman's place in the family. While most of the revolutionary conversation in France centered on the "rights of man," some women claimed that they too had natural rights and liberties. Olympe de Gouges (1745–1793) wrote *Declaration of the Rights of Woman and the Citizen* (1791), clearly echoing the better-known *Declaration of the Rights of Man and the Citizen* (1789). Napoleon Bonaparte's Civil Code of 1803–1804 reinstated in law many of the old forms of patriarchal dominance in the family while safeguarding liberal ideas of political participation by and equality among men. In England more and more men were given the right to vote, but women remained explicitly excluded until the twentieth century.

Feminism. Over the course of the nineteenth century women began to work collectively for equality in the home and in the workplace. To critique the established gender order of their time, they used the liberal questioning of hierarchies initiated by philosophers and leaders of the Enlightenment and the revolutionary movements of the eighteenth and nineteenth centuries. Organized feminist groups appeared throughout Europe, and their earliest arguments focused on the oppression of women in the home. Property and divorce laws were discussed and debated, as a woman in most European countries had little opportunity to initiate a divorce and had little control over her property after marriage. By the mid nineteenth century, women successfully raised these issues in political arenas, and gradual reforms were implemented. Feminists also worked for increasing opportunities for higher education, professional work, and sexual liberation, and in the years preceding World War I many feminist groups—some violent—took to the streets to demand the right to vote.

The Social Question and Social Legislation. Whether they were traditional conservatives or modern liberals, nineteenth-century political theorists believed that the family lay at the heart of society. Thus, when families failed to live up to the middle-class model established early in the century, the state, which came to be dominated by the middle class, gradually intervened to protect individual members and establish the proper family model. During the 1830s and 1840s European governments increasingly attempted to regulate industry, schools, and family life. In the process government bureaucrats inevitably imposed their own middle- and upper-class assumptions about proper family life on the rest of the population. The state also increasingly took on the role of surrogate parent, especially for the lower classes, which were hit hardest by the economic and social transformations of the industrial age. As lawyer Jules Ferry (1832–1893), who served as premier of the French Third Republic in 1880–1881 and 1883–1885, instructed schoolteachers in 1883, "You are the auxiliary and, in some respects, the substitute for the father of the family. Speak then to his son as you would wish one to speak to your own." State-sponsored labor regulation and relief for the poor created a division in which families who lived according to middle-class ideals were judged deserving of state aid and families who were organized in other ways were deemed unworthy.

Work and Social Life. European family members had traditionally labored together at home, but beginning in the late eighteenth century, the workplace increasingly moved away from the home, becoming for millions of Europeans the factory. This economic shift changed family relationships. Early in the Industrial Revolution many children worked long and brutal hours in miserable conditions at the new factories. The ability of children to earn money increased the possibilities for their independence from adults and helped to populate growing cities with young people who had no traditional family ties or other networks of authority to monitor them. Like children, women had traditionally been instrumental in the production of wealth in the home. Their move to factory work also disrupted family relationships. During the early stages of the Industrial Revolution, many families relied on the work of all members outside the home. Later in the nineteenth century the middle-class values of domesticity and the primacy of a male "breadwinner" bolstered the demands of the new unions that a "family wage" be paid to the male. This change theoretically allowed the woman to remain at home, but often the "breadwinner's" wage was not high enough to support the working-class family. Because of union restrictions and protective legislation, women were forced to work as seamstresses, laundresses, and even prostitutes.

Birth. During the Industrial Revolution there were also changes in who supervised and guided childbirth. In preindustrial Europe, women called midwives guided childbirth in the mother's home. Birth was a female domain. In the nineteenth century, however, professional male doctors licensed by specialized schools began to oversee childbirth. This change was part of a larger professionalization of medicine. As in many other fields, women were pushed out of their historic roles by men, who for the most part were the only ones allowed to pursue advanced education. The place of birth also began to change from the home to the hospital. This change was not always a positive one for mothers. Before modern knowledge of sanitation had become widespread, many women died in disease-ridden hospitals. Another major shift occurred in nursing children. Before the nineteenth century, many mothers had entrusted the breast-feeding of their infants to paid wet nurses. This process was increasingly criticized by philosophers, doctors, and social critics, who advocated breast-feeding by the mother as the natural and therefore proper way to rear children. This change was part of a larger shift toward stressing the "natural" role of parents in the upbringing of their children instead of relying on nurses, maids, and servants.

Demographic Change. During the nineteenth century fertility declined, but population grew. Although fewer children were born, plunging infant-mortality rates allowed more infants to survive. This trend occurred first in northwestern Europe, but by 1900 it was common everywhere on that continent. The plague, which had ravaged Europe periodically since the fourteenth century, all but disappeared during the eighteenth century as gradual advancements were made in medicine, health care, and sanitation. European couples increasingly made conscious decisions to extend the interval between births by practicing birth control, largely through coitus interruptus. By the end of the nineteenth century, growing numbers of couples were using alternative methods of birth control, such as condoms.

Childhood. As they had fewer children, who lived longer lives, parents tended to make a greater emotional investment in each child. In part because of the demographic changes, many historians identify the eighteenth and the nineteenth centuries as the period in which Europeans recognized childhood as a distinct stage in life. Eighteenth-century philosophers reinforced the idea that each child began as a blank slate and needed individual nurturing. The length of childhood was often determined by the social class of the family. Middle-class children enjoyed longer periods of childhood and dependency on their families than ever before. The middle-class home became a place to protect children from the outside world, and mothers rather than wet nurses or governesses became the primary caregivers for children. The first widespread commercialization of childhood also took place as products such as books, clothing, and toys were developed especially for middle-class children. The childhood of a working-class boy or girl was much shorter. Many of them worked from the age of six alongside adults in factories, mills, and mines. These children never experienced the comfort and protection of home, and until the end of the nineteenth century few were exposed to formal education. For them adulthood, characterized by long hours of labor, arrived quickly.

Education. Between 1750 and 1914 a growing portion of the European population had the opportunity for formal education. Increasingly troubled about the historic control of education by local clergy, secular government officials gradually developed state-run schools and government-certified teachers to guide the education of even the poorest children. During the second half of the nineteenth century, states made elementary education mandatory for all citizens regardless of social class, and the slow movement of the working classes to public schools also helped further identify stages in childhood for poor children as well as for their more affluent counterparts. Education was not equally available for boys and girls, however. While middle- and upper-class boys were encouraged to continue their education in the universities, young girls were prepared for lives as mothers and spouses. Only in the later nineteenth century did women have some opportunities to attend universities, where they were segregated from their male counterparts and allowed to train only for professions in "maternal" services, such as teaching and nursing.

Youth. New economic and migration patterns allowed European youths to become more independent than ever before from their parents and other adults. As young people moved into urban areas and entered the workforce in factories and mines, they often practiced new living arrangements, delaying marriage into their late twenties and early thirties. By midcentury, especially after the 1848 revolutions, political leaders were worried that there were too many independent young people living in the urban centers. Reformers created youth-centered institutions, such as scouting, where adolescents could learn civility, patriotism, and the work ethic. Youths also began to create important cultures independent from adults, whether as middle- and upper-class university students or in the late nineteenth century as "bohemians" who rejected traditional lifestyles and sexual mores.

Sexuality. As improved nutrition and health lowered the age of menarche (the first menstrual period), extending women's reproductive years, and as people delayed marriage and moved away from traditional environments such as church-dominated rural villages that regulated sexual mores, time and opportunity for sexual activity outside marriage increased. Illegitimacy rates skyrocketed. Sexuality increasingly became a topic of public interest and debate. By the mid nineteenth century, England, for example, was attempting to regulate prostitution by criminalizing the women. This law provoked an outcry from female middle-class reformers, who argued that such criminalization was another example of the long-held double standard against women while exonerating the sexual appetites of their male clients. By the end of the century, women began to argue for greater sexual freedom by advocating new forms of birth control and more public discussion of women's sexuality.

Marriage. Because it drew people away from their rural roots, industrialization allowed a growing number of Europeans to choose marriage partners on their own, instead of having their decisions dictated by family and village traditions. Because they often married late, they remained single for a long period of time. By the end of the eighteenth century, most men and women married in their mid to late twenties, a pattern that continued through the end of the nineteenth century. In many European countries marriage became a secular institution secured by a civil contract in addition to, or independent of, religious vows.

The Family Unit. The idea that the extended family (more than two generations living in the same household) was the norm before the twentieth century is a myth. Historians are now convinced that, except in some parts of southern Europe and European Russia, most households were nuclear families. By the nineteenth century the European middle classes had succeeded in defining their family model as the most proper for society in general. These changes had important ramifications for the roles of individual family members. By the late eighteenth and nineteenth centuries, families had largely excluded servants and non-kin from their households. Households contained only parents and children. Mothers were instructed to remain in the home to care for their children and provide domestic security that would shield the family from the harshness of public life. Men worked outside the home and maintained the household by providing an income. Childhood was glorified in the late eighteenth and nineteenth centuries as the happiest moment of life, in which humans should develop their natural inclinations through play and education while they were protected from adult life.

TOPICS IN THE FAMILY AND SOCIAL TRENDS

BIRTHS AND DEATHS: DEMOGRAPHIC PATTERNS AND FAMILY STRUCTURES

Population Trends. Historians estimate that between 1700 and 1800 the European population increased from 120 million people to 180 million. By the outbreak of World War I in 1914 the European population had reached 458 million people. This population growth occurred despite the rising average age at first marriage (by 1850, twenty-four for women and twenty-seven for men). The increase was fueled by lower mortality rates arising from better sanitation and improved medical and health care. New foods introduced into Europe also helped people live longer. Nutritious and plentiful new crops from the Americas such as corn and the potato were gradually incorporated into the European diet. Farmers improved agricultural techniques as well, increasing crop yields and thus the food supply. Many political leaders believed that large populations benefited their countries economically and militarily. Until the 1850s and 1860s the populations of nearly all European regions rapidly increased; then population growth began to slow. This new demographic model had occurred in France by 1850, and by 1870 fertility rates were declining throughout Europe. The average Frenchwoman bore 3.38 children in 1850, but by 1900 the rate had fallen to 2.79. In England, the rate fell from 4.95 to 3.40 children, and the Swedish rate fell from 4.27 to 3.91.

The Household. A household is a group of people who live together. They may or may not be biologically related. For the people who reside in them, households serve several important functions, which may change with time and place. Households are economic units; that is, the people who live in them both produce goods and consume them. A household is also a social and cultural unit; economic dependency fosters reciprocal and at times hierarchical relationships. One household may also cooperate with other households to share economic and social tasks. For example, in the nineteenth century agricultural households cooperated with each other during the harvests and at other important periods during the year. Households could be formed in several ways, but by far the most common was marriage. Men and women married for the

first time in their mid to late twenties and established a new household unit separate from their parents or other relatives. This pattern was especially common in western and northern Europe. In central, eastern, and southern Europe, some children married at earlier ages and joined complex households that also included their parents or siblings. In this second model, no new household was created; the composition of the original household just changed.

Gravestone for a rural Yorkshire family documenting the high infant-mortality rate in nineteenth-century Great Britain

English economist Thomas Malthus (1766–1834) contributed to the Enlightenment debate about the perfectibility of human society with works on poverty and overpopulation. Aware of the population growth that Europe had experienced in the late eighteenth century, he theorized that populations cannot grow without at some point reaching a limit defined by available resources, especially food. When this limit is reached, Malthus argued in his first *Essay on Population* (1798), populations would naturally decline through starvation and impaired fertility.

I think I may fairly make two postulata.

First, That food is necessary to the existence of man.

Second, That the passion between the sexes is necessary and will remain nearly in its present state.

These two laws, ever since we had any knowledge of mankind, appear to have been fixed laws of our nature, and, as we have not hitherto seen any alteration in them, we have no right to conclude that they will ever cease to be what they now are, without an immediate act of power in that Being who first arranged the system of the universe, and for the advantage of his creatures, still executes, according to fixed laws, all its various operations. . . .

Assuming then, my postulata as granted, I say, that the power of population is indefinitely greater than the power in the earth to produce subsistence for man.

Population, when unchecked, increases in geometrical ratio. Subsistence increases only in an arithmetical ratio. A slight acquaintance with numbers will show the immensity of the first power in comparison of the second.

By that law of our nature which makes food necessary to the life of man, the effects of these two unequal powers must be kept equal.

This implies a strong and constantly operating check on population from the difficulty of subsistence. This diffi-

culty must fall some where and must necessarily be severely felt by a large portion of mankind.

Through the animal and vegetable kingdoms, nature has scattered the seeds of life abroad with the most profuse and liberal hand. She has been comparatively sparing in the room and the nourishment necessary to rear them. The germs of existence contained in this spot of earth, with ample food, and ample room to expand in, would fill millions of worlds in the course of a few thousand years. Necessity, that imperious of all pervading law of nature, restrains them within the prescribed bounds. The race of plants, and the race of animals shrunk under this great restrictive law. And the race of man cannot, by any efforts of reason, escape from it. Among plants and animals its effects are waste of seed, sickness, and premature death. Among mankind, misery and vice. The former, misery, is an absolutely necessary consequence of it. Vice is a highly probable consequence, and we therefore see it abundantly prevail, but it ought not, perhaps, to be called an absolutely necessary consequence. The ordeal of virtue is to resist all temptation to evil.

This natural inequality of the two powers of population and of production in the earth and that great law of our nature which must constantly keep their effects equal form the great difficulty that to me appears insurmountable in the way to the perfectibility of society. All other arguments are of slight and subordinate consideration in comparison of this. I see no way by which man can escape from the weight of this law which pervades all animated nature. No fancied equality, no agrarian regulations in their utmost extent, could remove the pressure of it even for a single century. And it appears, therefore, to be decisive against the possible existence of a society, all the members of which should live in ease, happiness, and comparative leisure; and feel no anxiety about providing the means of subsistence for themselves and families.

Source: Thomas Robert Malthus, *Population: The First Essay* (Ann Arbor: University of Michigan Press, 1959), pp. 4–6.

The Diversity of Demographic and Family Systems. Historians do not agree on how to characterize household systems and patterns across the different regions of Europe during the industrial era. Some historians believe that the western and northern models (first marriage in the late twenties, nuclear family households of parents and their biological offspring) may have become more common in eastern and southern Europe by the end of the nineteenth century. Others counter that households might just as easily have changed from simple to complex units housing multiple generations depending on local economic circumstances and especially the availability of land and wage labor. Still others identify variations within the same general geographical region. An example from Russia illustrates the difficulty of generalizing about household systems in Europe. In the late nineteenth century Russian male peasants who lived near developing industrial cities

such as Moscow tended to marry earlier than urban youths in other parts of Europe. These males maintained their ties to family networks in the countryside, which encouraged earlier marriages than might otherwise have been feasible for youths who lived away from home. Russian males, as a result, profited from the work available in the cities and maintained complex households in the countryside. In central and western Europe households increasingly excluded extended kin (such as aunts, uncles, and cousins). The opposite seems true in parts of the southern, Mediterranean regions of Europe and in eastern Europe, including parts of Russia. This difference may be attributed in part to the relatively late arrival of industrialization in these areas. Perhaps the only safe generalization, which still has many exceptions, is that over the course of the years between 1750 and 1914 the nuclear-family household became increasingly common.

Spanish and Russian peasant mothers and their children in the 1890s (left: from *La Ilustracion Iberica*, 1894; right: Russian State Archive of Film and Photographic Documents, Krasnogorsk)

Sources:

Massimo Livi Bacci, *The Population of Europe*, translated by Cynthia De Nardi Ipsen and Carl Ipsen (Malden, Mass.: Blackwell, 2000).

D. V. Glass and D. E. C. Eversley, *Population and History: Essays in Historical Demography* (London: Arnold, 1965).

Peter Laslett, Jean Robin, and Richard Wall, eds., *Family Forms in Historic Europe* (Cambridge: Cambridge University Press, 1983).

CHILDHOOD

Births: From Midwife to Physician. In pre-industrial Europe, midwives controlled the birthing process. Birth was women's domain, and midwives used techniques derived from generations of tradition and experience to assist in the delivery of babies, allowing most births to run their natural course and generally not interfering in the process. This practice was still largely followed in late-nineteenth-century Russia, where the uneducated midwife, or *povitukha*, assisted pregnant peasant women. Part of their help included preparing warm baths and special herbs and ointments. In wealthier households, special cloths were hung around the room and the bed for the delivery. Midwives also helped with the housework after the birth. By the nineteenth century, professional male doctors trained in medical schools open only to males began to write manuals on childbirth and gradually pushed the midwives out of the birthing process. During the eighteenth century, male doctors had begun using new inventions—such as forceps—to move the baby manually through the birth canal. These technologies were effective, but such tools and procedures were still in the developmental stage and contributed to the deaths of women and their infants in childbirth—as did doctors' ignorance of the need to sanitize their instruments and the mother's immediate environment.

Nursing. Wet-nursing, the process of having another woman breast-feed one's infant, either in one's home or at the wet nurse's home, was common in pre-industrial western Europe. Often, urban, middle-class mothers sent their babies away from home for some time to live with and be nursed by poorer women in the countryside. Weaning usually occurred during the child's second year, and a child sometimes lived away from its parents until that time. Around 1750 philosophers began to express their disapproval of mothers who sent their children out to nurse, for many wet nurses lived in impoverished, unhealthy environments. They also argued that children imbibed not only the milk but also the morals and integrity of the nurse. For example, Jean-Jacques Rousseau (1712–1778) accused wet nurses of negligence and argued that women who neglected "their first duty" to nurse their own children were bad mothers. His belief that the death rate for wet-nursed children was higher than that for babies nursed by their own mothers is supported by statistics. Wet-nursing was also increasingly criticized by the middle classes for depriving a child of its natural relationship with its mother.

Baby Food. Food for newborns went beyond breast milk in some colder European environments where animal milk might

At the end of her best-selling *Book of Household Management* (1861), Isabella Beeton (1836–1865) included a section titled "The Rearing and Management of Children, and Diseases of Infancy and Childhood." By the nineteenth century, the middle class assumed that the truly caring and moral mother would breast-feed her child instead of sending it to a wet nurse. Like her contemporaries, Beeton praised the soothing effects of beer on infants, a food not recommended by modern medical practitioners.

As Nature has placed in the bosom of the mother the natural food of her offspring, it must be self-evident to every reflecting woman, that it becomes her duty to study, as far as lies in her power, to keep that reservoir of nourishment in as pure and invigorating a condition as possible; for she must remember that the *quantity* is no proof of the *quality* of this aliment.

The mother, while suckling, as a general rule, should avoid all sedentary occupations, take regular exercise, keep her mind as lively and pleasingly occupied as possible, especially by music and singing. Her diet should be light and nutritious, with a proper sufficiency of animal food, and of that kind which yields the largest amount of nourishment; and, unless the digestion is naturally strong, vegetables and fruit should form a very small proportion of the general dietary, and such preparations as broths, gruels, arrowroot, etc . . . , still less. Tapioca, or ground-rice pudding, made with several eggs, may be taken freely; but all slops and thin potations, such as that delusion called chicken-broth, should be avoided, as yielding a very small amount of nutriment, and a large proportion of flatulence. . . . Lactation is always an exhausting process, and as the child increases in size and strength, the drain upon the mother becomes great and depressing. Something more even than an abundant diet is required to keep the mind and body up to a standard sufficiently healthy to admit of a constant and nutritious secretion being performed without detriment to the physical integrity of the mother, or injury to the child who imbibes it; and as stimulants are inadmissible, if not positively injurious, the substitute required is to be found in *malt liquor*. To the lady accustomed to her Madeira and sherry, this may appear a very vulgar potation for a delicate young mother to take instead of the more subtle and condensed elegance of wine; but as we are writing from experience, and with the avowed object of imparting useful facts and beneficial remedies to our readers, we allow no social distinctions to interfere with our legitimate object. . . .

The nine or twelve months a woman usually suckles must be, to some extent, to most mothers, a period of privation and penance, and unless she is deaf to the cries of her baby, and insensible to its kicks and plunges, and will not see in such muscular evidences the gripping pains that rack her child, she will avoid every article that can remotely affect the little being who draws its sustenance from her. . . . As the best tonic, then, and the most efficacious indirect stimulant that a mother can take at such times, there is no potation equal to *porter* and *stout*, or, what is better still, an equal part of porter and stout. . . . Stout alone is too potent to admit of a full draught, from its proneness to affect the head; and quantity, as well as moderate strength, is required to make the draught effectual; the equal mixture, therefore, of stout and porter yields all the properties desired or desirable as a medicinal agent for this purpose.

Source: Isabella Beeton, *The Book of Household Management* (London: S. O. Beeton, 1861), pp. 1034–1035.

keep for longer periods of time than in warm climates. In the Scandinavian countries and eastern Europe mothers often supplemented their own milk with pap. The ingredients of pap varied from region to region, but it was generally a mixture of animal milk and bread crumbs or flour. Parents soaked towels or other cloths in this mixture and allowed babies to suckle the cloth. Sometimes they sucked on the same one for up to a week. Some Russian women added bacon to pap.

Disease Prevention. Increasingly in the nineteenth century, published guides for mothers offered instruction on how to care for their children. By the end of the century, mothers were beginning to learn about diseases and bacteria from the work of Louis Pasteur (1822–1895) and began to boil animal milk to reduce the danger of its causing illness in newborns. The practice of swaddling (wrapping the child tightly in cloth bands), which was common in pre-industrial Europe, came under criticism from eighteenth-century philosophers, who viewed the practice as detrimental to the baby's health and to its natural desire for freedom. Swaddling was gradually abandoned, first in urban areas and then in the countryside, where traditional practices retained their grip longer.

Child Mortality. Compared to modern standards, infant mortality was extremely high in the eighteenth and nineteenth centuries. Between 1840 and 1845, on average, 137 of 1,000 Danish children died in their first year of life. The rates were a bit higher in France and England. By the end of the century, infant mortality was 150 deaths per 1,000 births in many countries, including France, Italy, England, and Sweden. Not only did births occur in unsanitary rooms, but also babies born before the development of modern immunization were vulnerable to a variety of diseases and complications. Once pasteurized milk became available in the later nineteenth century, one cause of infant mortality was substantially reduced. Child mortality rates were highest before weaning (usually during the second year) and declined steadily thereafter.

Infanticide and Child Abandonment. While many children died of natural causes, others perished at the hands of their mothers. Infanticide was a serious concern among lawmakers and local officials in the pre-industrial period. While legislation outlawing infanticide, usually advocating execution for a mother convicted of the crime, was still on the books in the eighteenth and nineteenth centuries, few women were prosecuted for the crime during the industrial age, suggesting that the rate of infanticide was declining, perhaps because of rising living standards and new programs aimed at aiding impoverished mothers. During the nineteenth century European states created offices and bureaus designed to help support poor mothers and to teach them how to care for their children according to middle-class standards. The means by which societies coped with the problem of child abandonment also changed. Young women with no immediate families or other support systems sometimes felt compelled to leave unwanted children under bridges, near streams, or on the doorsteps of religious establishments. In small villages, especially in southern Europe, having an illegitimate child brought shame not only to the mother but to her entire household as well. During the eighteenth and early nineteenth centuries European governments concerned about maintaining growth in their populations established foundling hospitals. Despite the notoriously poor conditions in such establishments, increasing numbers of mothers abandoned their children, many of them illegitimate, at these hospitals. Some mothers placed notes or identification tags on their babies, hoping that they might return one day and reclaim them, but they rarely did. One historian has estimated that by 1800 close to 100,000 children were abandoned annually in Europe.

Child Abuse. Protecting children from abuse became an important issue during the nineteenth century and was part of a larger movement by philanthropists and reformers to protect the interests of children. Early reform movements centered on the child laborer. Michael Thomas Sadler (1780–1835), a member of the British House of Commons, introduced legislation that limited the employment of children in factories. Known as the Factory Act of 1833, this bill regulated the hours children and adolescents could work. In 1853 Prussia passed a child-labor law that established the minimum age for child labor at twelve, and France did the same in 1874. By mid century, many middle-class women had begun to exercise "natural

---

FIGHTING CHILD ABUSE

In 1889 Pauline Kergomard (1838–1925) gave a speech to the International Congress of Women's Charitable Organizations and Institutions in which she explained how the French Association of Child Rescue defined the physical and mental abuse of children and outlined its activities.

Abused (children) are:
  Children who are the subjects of habitual and excessive physical mistreatment;
  Children who, as a result of criminal negligence by their parents, are habitually deprived of proper care;
  Children habitually involved in mendacity, delinquency, or dissipation;
  Children employed in dangerous occupations;
  Children who are physically abandoned.
Children who are morally endangered are:
  Children whose parents live in notoriously uproarious and scandalous state;
  Children whose parents are habitually in a state of drunkeness;
  Children whose parents live by mendacity;
  Children whose parents have been convicted of crimes;
  Children whose parents have been convicted of theft, habitually encouraging the delinquency of minors, of committing an offense against public decency or an immoral act. . . .
While we wait for the law to arm us solidly against the undeserving parents from whom we have already wrenched some victims; while we wait for it to permit us to take all the children who roam the streets to our temporary shelter; while we wait for it to permit us to search the hovels where there is torture and depravity, we have set ourselves the task of:
  Snatching children from the horrible hornets' nest of a police record by saving them from first convictions;

preventing them from being confined or released from confinement too early, which would fatally return them to the streets and bring them back before the courts;
  improving their conditions at the police station or detention center while they await trial.
To this end we have established out headquarters at the *Palais de Justice* and, thanks to the humanitarian feelings of almost all the magistrates . . . we make ourselves known to the accused on their arrival, we negotiate with certain parents who have them sign over custody to us, we send children to farmers in the country (of whom we now have one hundred twenty for this purpose), we release to the Public Assistance Administration those who fall under their jurisdiction. . . .
  Then, too, we have improved the conditions under which children are detained at the Police Station and Detention Center, girls being in greater need for this than boys. Not long ago the girls held in the Detention Center—some were four years old, some sixteen—were all placed together; now there is a separation [by ages]. . . .
  Not long ago they slept three to a cell—without surveillance. Today there is a dormitory where observation is easy.
  Not long ago they had nothing to keep them busy and spent their days telling each other their sad pasts. Today they sew—the Association has furnished them with material and sent a sewing teacher—today they read, because the Association has assembled a library.
  Not long ago they stayed in the Detention Center in the same sordid clothing and unwashed state as the day they were arrested. Today there are baths and changes of clothes.
  Oh! There is a great deal still to be done, but the Association is happy with the results it has achieved.

Source: Lisa DiCaprio and Merry E. Wiesner, eds., *Lives and Voices: Sources in European Women's History* (Boston: Houghton Mifflin, 2001), pp. 317–318.

---

maternal charity," creating reform associations that took a woman's domestic qualities into the public sphere to care for the children of the working classes. In England by 1893 perhaps as many as 500,000 women were involved in charitable organizations predominately geared to the welfare of children. By the end of the century states had begun to take over the care and welfare of children from private reform and philanthropic societies. Governments also began to make it a crime for parents to abuse their children. Many European countries established societies for the protection of children, such as the Societies for the Prevention of Cruelty to Children in England. In 1889 France and Britain passed laws that enabled the state to remove a child from parental control when "fathers and mothers . . . , through their habitual drunkenness, their notorious and scandalous misconduct . . . compromise the safety, health, and morality of their children." By the end of the nineteenth century, then, the state had moved from protecting paternal rights over children to threatening to remove those rights in cases of abuse.

Transformation of Attitudes toward Children. Changes in the treatment of the welfare of children may be one sign of an increase in the degree of emotional attachment parents felt toward their children. By the late nineteenth century the population increases of the previous one hundred years had slowed. Most couples had two or three children instead of four or five. Some historians have argued that this demographic shift conditioned parents to increase their attention to their children and that greater affection resulted. Many later-nineteenth-century writers and artists depicted childhood as the purest stage of human life, devoid of the imperfections later caused by society. In her autobiography, nineteenth-century author George Sand (1804–1876) stated that "childhood is good, it is honest, and the best people are those who retain the most of its innate honesty and sensitivity." One major consequence of this outlook was the parents' increased concentration on their children's early development and education and on shielding children from the outside world by placing them more firmly within the parental control within the home. By 1900 Swedish writer Ellen Key could confidently predict that the twentieth century would be the "century of the child."

Children's Toys and Clothes. Between 1750 and 1914 parents came to assume that children needed specific material objects in order to live fruitful childhoods. Toys, children's clothes, and games all existed in pre-industrial Europe, but during the eighteenth and nineteenth centuries the production and marketing of these products were increasingly targeted exclusively for children and more and more with gender distinctions in mind. Small-toy manufacturers arose throughout Europe, and department stores and their catalogues began to focus on material goods for children. Specialized children's periodicals were also developed during the nineteenth century. From birth until about the age of seven, European boys and girls wore similar clothes, played with the same toys, and received the same education. After seven, however, gender defined their education and material surroundings. Boys left the purview of the mother and entered the masculine world.

Toy (and eventually real) horses, swords, trumpets, guns, and uniforms became the playthings for boys, while girls played with tambourines, dolls, puppets, and balls. Boys' toys inspired an imagination that took them outside the home while girls played with puppets and dolls in the salon and so were conditioned to imagine a future life inside the home.

Sources:
George Alter, *The Family and the Female Life Course: The Women of Verviers, Belgium, 1849–1880* (Madison: University of Wisconsin Press, 1988).

Hugh Cunningham, *Children and Childhood in Western Society Since 1500* (New York: Longman, 1995).

Valerie A. Fildes, *Breasts, Bottles, and Babies: A History of Infant Feeding* (Edinburgh: Edinburgh University Press, 1986).

Rachel Fuchs, *Poor and Pregnant in Paris* (New Brunswick: Rutgers University Press, 1996).

Deborah Gorham, *The Victorian Girl and the Feminine Ideal* (Bloomington: Indiana University Press, 1982).

Colin Heywood, *A History of Childhood* (Cambridge, U.K.: Polity / Malden, Mass.: Blackwell, 2001).

George E. Sussman, *Selling Mother's Milk: The Wetnursing Business in France, 1715–1914* (Urbana: University of Illinois Press, 1982).

EARLY YEARS: ADOLESCENCE AND YOUTH

Paternal Power and the Emancipation of Children. During the eighteenth century, youth was extended further than ever before, both by law and by the assertion of parental authority over children. By the 1760s laws bolstering the father's right to control his children's property and choices of marriage partners were enacted in many parts of Europe. In some places children remained legally under paternal power until the age of thirty. Stories abounded of cruel parents who refused to let their children marry or practice the professions of their choice. The French monarchy was infamous throughout Europe for its lettres de cachet, arrest warrants authorizing the confinement of an individual without trial. Many such warrants were used at a parent's request to punish unruly youths, who were often imprisoned or transported to penal colonies. During the French Revolution, the National Assembly abolished such warrants. Equating excessive paternal authority in the home with excessive royal authority over subjects, the assembly also limited paternal power by declaring twenty-one the universal age of majority for men and women. France and other European nations attempted to harness youthful energy, first by engaging young people in the rituals of citizenship and later by requiring military service from them. French Revolutionaries held a Fête de la Jeunesse (Festival of Youth), at which sixteen-year-old boys were granted the "duty of bearing arms." When young people turned twenty-one, women were expected to begin bearing children for the Republic while men were expected to take up their roles as citizens and defenders of the state. These legal and social changes contributed to the demarcation of a distinct life stage, which by the end of the nineteenth century was widely known as *adolescence*.

Middle-Class Adolescence. While the legal dependency of youths on their parents may have been reduced in the nineteenth century, middle-class adolescents of the period became more dependent. Historians have identified adolescence as a stage of social dependency that was at first peculiar to the mid-

Many Europeans considered the decades before World War I the Belle Epoque (Beautiful Era), a time when society was at its grandest and life for most was wonderful. After World War I, many Europeans identified their youth with this period. Stefan Zweig (1881–1942), an Austrian Jewish writer, epitomized this age in his autobiography, *The World of Yesterday* (1943). Calling his early years a "Golden Age of Security" in which Austrian middle-class families felt assured of their economic and political well-being, he also revealingly described the social anxiety surrounding female adolescence in the 1890s.

This "social morality," which, on the one hand privately presupposed the existence of sexuality and its natural course, but on the other would not recognize it openly at any price, was doubly deceitful. While it winked one eye at a young man and even encouraged him with the other "to sow his wild oats," as the kindly language of the home put it, in the case of a woman it studiously shut both eyes and acted as if it were blind. That a man could experience desires, and was permitted to experience them, was silently admitted by custom. But to admit frankly that a woman could be subject to similar desires, or that creation for its eternal purposes also required a female polarity, would have transgressed the conception of the "sanctity of womanhood. . . ." In order to protect young girls, they were not left alone for a single moment. They were given a governess whose duty it was to see that they did not step out of the home unaccompanied, that they were taken to school, to their dancing lessons, to their music lessons, and brought home in the same manner. Every book they read was inspected, and, above all else, young girls were constantly kept busy to divert their attention from any possible dangerous thoughts. They had to practice the piano, learn singing and drawing, foreign languages, and the history of literature and art. They were educated and overeducated. But while the aim was to make them as educated as possible, at the same time society anxiously took great pains that they remain innocent of all natural things.

Source: Stefan Zweig, *The World Of Yesterday* (Lincoln: University of Nebraska Press, 1964), pp. 77–78.

Members of Wandervogel, a German youth group, on tour in 1912 (Ullstein Bilderdienst)

dle class but slowly penetrated the rest of society by the end of the century. Since middle-class children had more schooling and leisure time than those of the working class, it is understandable that the concept of adolescence emerged in the middle class. Secondary and boarding schools—in part a product of parental concern to prepare children for success in life—were instrumental in this process. The poor faced different circumstances. Even in 1900 many adolescents never attended secondary school, and, consequently, the conception of adolescence as a life stage with its own needs and problems spread more slowly among the poor.

Young Workers. Because many were forced to begin working for a living as early as age seven, boys from the working class often had shorter childhoods than their middle- or upper-class counterparts. Consequently, the period in which they were independent from their parents and unmarried could last many years. The numbers of these boys, who were often migrants searching for work, swelled during the nineteenth century, and they created their own social organizations, sometimes criminal gangs or secret journeymen's brotherhoods in league against their employers. Disgruntled, mobile, and independent youths threatened order and property in urban neighborhoods and even contributed to the rebellions that erupted throughout Europe in the 1830s and 1840s.

Juvenile Delinquency. Modern conceptions of adolescence were also created through judicial institutions. Alarmed by pickpockets, street gangs, and prostitution, the urban middle classes and political elite of nineteenth-century Europe blamed urban youths for what they perceived as an increase in crime. One historian has called the street gang "the school of the poor" that taught young people important social and survival skills. By the late nineteenth century, social reformers called for special courts that would consider only the crimes of children and teenagers. Individualized penalties and specific correctional institutions were gradually developed for youths. For example, in 1854 England passed a Youthful Offenders Act that established special youth-detention centers for children up to age sixteen. German courts for youthful offenders were established in 1910.

Youth Organizations and Movements. In the nineteenth century, European governments and political parties attempted to harness the energy of male youths and to teach them proper values in a variety of ways. Protestant and Catholic churches sponsored youth groups to teach morality, thrift, and the middle-class work ethic within a Christian framework. Most movements were deeply patriotic as well. The Boys' Brigade, the first British youth group dedicated to military and religious training, was founded in 1883 by William Alexander Smith (1854–1914). Other groups emerged in subsequent decades. One of the most influential was the Boy Scouts, founded by Robert Baden-Powell (1857–1941) in the decade before World War I. Designed to foster new citizens' loyalty to their communities and nations, the scouting movement spread to most Western countries in the early decades of the twentieth century. Some other youth groups appear to have formed spontaneously without adult supervision. The German youth group Wandervogel (Migrating Bird), for example, was formed as an informal naturalist and hiking group during the

1890s but did not become an official organization led by adults until 1901.

Sources:

Carol Dyhouse, *Girls Growing Up in Late Victorian and Edwardian England* (Boston: Broadway House, 1981).

John Gillis, *Youth and History: Tradition and Change in European Age Relations, 1770-Present*, expanded edition (New York: Academic Press, 1981).

John Neubauer, *The Fin-de-Siècle Culture of Adolescence* (New Haven: Yale University Press, 1992).

J. R. Wegs, *Growing Up Working Class: Continuity and Change Among Viennese Youth, 1890–1938* (University Park: Pennsylvania State University Press, 1989).

EDUCATION

Increased Access. Throughout most of European history only the children of the elite had access to education. Europeans believed education would be of little use to the masses destined for the difficult life of unskilled labor. Lower-class families most often believed that their hard work, poverty, and lack of education were normal as well. Working-class families needed the labor of all family members, including the children as young as six. Such economic realities allowed little time for school. The religious reformations of the sixteenth and seventeenth centuries, however, had begun to stress literacy as important for salvation. In 1717 Prussia became the first state to mandate primary education. Similar reforms were gradually made throughout Europe, with uneven results for boys and girls. In the eighteenth and nineteenth centuries, many wealthy Catholic families sent their daughters to convents, where they learned to read in addition to attaining skills in needlework and social etiquette. Overall, however, boys were much more likely to be able to read than girls because education was deemed more important for males than it was for females destined to be housewives. It was not until 1882, for example, that the French government made elementary education compulsory for both girls and boys from six to thirteen years old.

Charity and Poor Schools. Religious institutions dominated children's education in the eighteenth century. The Church of England and associated philanthropic societies had already developed poor and charity schools for children in the seventeenth century. By the late eighteenth century, many lower-class boys and girls had opportunities to attend some kind of primary school. Catholic schools dominated Paris and other French cities. Schools were created by private initiative as a way of saving children's souls and of reforming society in general. In the eighteenth and nineteenth centuries many working-class parents may also have seen schools as a useful baby-sitting service and perhaps as a means for social advancement through literacy.

Public Primary Education. Common people received no state-sponsored education until the eighteenth century, when reforms in education were led by central and eastern European states, especially after they were defeated in the Napoleonic Wars. Prussia, where elementary schools had been compulsory for all children since 1717, was followed by the Habsburg Empire, where Empress Maria Theresa cre-

Boys in a Russian technical school, 1905

ated a system of elementary education in 1774. In 1786 Catherine the Great of Russia issued an edict that attempted to form an educational system for all free Russians (those who were not serfs). The major push for state-sponsored free schooling began a century later, however. In France, where Church-sponsored schools were widespread, the foundation of public primary education coincided with the birth of the Third Republic (1870–1940). Secular reformers in countries such as France and Italy attempted to reduce the role of the Catholic Church in educating their youth. In France between 1879 and 1882, schools were established to train schoolteachers, and the government eventually established a primary school in every French village. After 1881 schooling was compulsory in England for girls and boys between five and ten years old. The net result of the elementary-education movement was increased literacy by the end of the nineteenth century in most areas of Europe except the Mediterranean regions of Spain and Italy. By then nine of ten male Scots, two of three French boys and girls, and one of two English children of both sexes could read, while fewer than half of Spaniards and Italians could do so, even in 1900. Everywhere literacy rates differed between town and country. By the mid nineteenth century most urban children could read, but far fewer could do so in rural areas throughout Europe, where elementary instruction arrived only in the early twentieth century, government edicts notwithstanding.

Secondary Education. Secondary schooling was largely a product of the nineteenth century, during which far more children attended primary schools than secondary. In 1902 only 9 percent of all fourteen-year-olds in England attended secondary school, and the percentage declined as children aged. Education reformers and political leaders grappled with the curriculum for adolescents, focusing most of their attention on boys. Some argued that children should be educated as they always

RURAL EDUCATION IN FRANCE

In 1911 and 1912 the French Ministry of Public Education asked teachers throughout the country to reflect on their experiences since the late nineteenth century. The following observations reveal some of the difficulties teachers faced in small, rural villages still tied to their traditional ways.

Rhône. In the eyes of the peasant and the working man the teacher, correctly dressed and decently lodged, is a lady, almost an aristocrat. It should surely be a simple matter to keep children in a brilliantly lighted, well-ventilated room that is heated in winter and kept cool in summer! To have one rest day a week besides Sunday, to have holidays at Christmas and Easter and two long months of liberty in August and September—is not that an enviable existence? So a latent but real jealousy springs up among these workers, who have no idea of the exhausting labors of the school teachers.

Mayenne. From the moment of my arrival at B———, I turned my attention to making myself popular with the children and to winning the hearts of the mothers. The population sought to make things hard for me. I was spied upon, and the children were questioned to see if I had not been guilty of intolerance. The *curé* (priest) organized the campaign. He gave orders to close the doors in my face when I made my first round of visits. He used every means to make life unbearable for me and to keep me shut up at home. But I was not long in gaining a real influence over the community, and ever since I have been guarding it as a treasure. Established as it is in the popular confidence, my school is, so to speak, invulnerable. The violent attacks on the "schoolbooks" slipped by unnoticed. Not a single mother listened to the belligerent suggestions so freely made.

Source: David Thomson, *France: Empire and Republic, 1850–1940* (New York: Harper & Row, 1968), pp. 239–243.

had been, with intense study of the classics, history, languages, and literature. Others, more concerned about the economic success of the nation-state in an industrial age, promoted a "modern" curriculum that would prepare the students to enter the workforce with important mathematical and scientific skills. In Germany, where modern curricula were established through imperial edicts in 1892 and 1900, the gymnasiums (secondary schools that prepared students for university studies) were a model for the new sort of secondary school. For most of the nineteenth century, girls were educated separately from boys, and girls received an education deemed fitting for womanly pursuits at the time. It did not include science, mathematics, or physical education. Amid concerns for the success of the nation-state, physical education did enter the curriculum for boys. Most European countries stressed some form of athletics or sports as a means of developing better citizens and soldiers. Universities were open only to the wealthiest and most-advantaged Europeans, and women were allowed to enter the universities only during the second half of the nineteenth century. British feminists led a campaign for women's access to

JOHN NEWBERY ON CHILD REARING

Originally published in 1744 by John Newbery, *A Little Pretty Pocket-Book* signaled a shift in attitudes toward children that occurred during the Industrial Age and has continued to the present day. Newbery's advertisement for the book stated that it was for "the Instruction and Amusement" of children—a considerable change from earlier children's books filled with religious tenets and admonitions for children to avoid idleness and sin. In a preface addressed to parents, Newbery expressed the Enlightenment view that children should be molded and educated to be happy and productive citizens:

The grand design on the nurture of children, is to make them *strong, hardy . . . virtuous, wise, and happy;* and these good purposes are not to be obtained without some care and management in their infancy.

Would you have your child strong, take care of your nurse; let her be a prudent woman, one that will give him what meat and drink is necessary, and such only as affords a good nutriment, no salt meats, rich tarts, sauces, wine, etc . . . a practice too common amongst some indulgent people. She must also let the child have due exercise; for 'tis this that gives life and spirits, circulates the blood, strengthens the sinews, and keeps the whole machinery in order.

Would you have a hardy child, give him common diet only, cloath him thin, let him have good exercise, and be as much exposed to hardships as his natural constitution will admit. The face of a child, when it comes into the world (says the great Mr. Locke) is as tender and susceptible of Injuries as any other part of the body; yet, by being always exposed, it becomes proof against the severest season and the most inclement weather; even at a time when the body (tho' wrapp'd in flannels) is pierced with cold. . . .

Would you have a virtuous son, instil into him the principles of morality early, and encourage him in the practice of those excellent rules, by which whole societies, states, kingdoms, and empires are knit together. Take heed what company you intrust him with, and be always sure to set him a good example yourself.

Would you have a wise son, teach him to reason early. Let him read, and make him understand what he reads. No sentence should be passed over without a strict examination of the truth of it; and though this may be thought hard at first, and seem to retard the boy in his progress, yet a little practice will make it familiar, and a method of reasoning will be acquired, which will be of use to him all his life after. Let him study mankind, show him the springs and hinges on which they move; teach him to draw consequences from the actions of others; and if he should hesitate or mistake, you are to set him right: but then take care to do it in such a manner, as to forward his enquiries, and pave this his grand pursuit with pleasure. Was this method of reasoning put more in practice by tutors, parents, etc. . . . we should not see so many dismal objects in the world; for people would learn by the misfortunes of others to avert their own.

I doubt not but every parent, every father and mother, would gladly contribute what they could towards the happiness of their children; and yet it is surprising to see how blind they are, and how wide they mistake the mark. What the indulgent parent generally proposes for the happiness of his child, is a good fortune to bear him up under the calamities of life; but daily experience tells us, this is insufficient. . . . Subdue therefore your children's passions; curb their tempers, and make them subservient to the rules of reason. And this is not to be done by chiding, whipping, or severe treatment, but by reasoning and mild discipline. . . . This method, regularly pursued, would soon break his passion of resentment, and subdue it to reason.

The next prudent step to be taken, is to check his inordinate craving and desiring almost every thing he sees; . . . in the first place, I would lay down this as a maxim with him, that he should never have anything he cried for; and therefore, if he was willing to obtain any favor, he must come with a reasonable request, and withdraw without the appearance of any uneasiness in case of a disappointment.

Some over-fond people will think these are harsh precepts. What, say they, are children never to be obliged? I answer, Yes, I would have them obliged and pleased, but not humored and spoiled. They should have what they asked for in a proper manner; but then they should wait my time, without seeming over solicitous, or crying after it. I would make them exercise patience, that they might know the use of it, when the cares of the world came on. And, therefore, I say again, children should never have anything they cried for; no, not on any consideration whatsoever.

Source: John Newbery, Preface to *A Little Pretty Pocket-Book* (New York: Harcourt, Brace & World, 1967), pp. 55–62.

university education by founding their own colleges, which later became part of universities. Among the schools they founded was Girton College, established in 1869, which became affiliated with Cambridge University in 1873, though the female students enrolled there continued to be denied Cambridge degrees until after World War II.

Children's Books. By the eighteenth century, inexpensive songbooks, religious primers, and chapbooks were widely available for children. This commercial development paralleled an intellectual one, for Enlightenment philosophers optimistically looked to children and children's education as the main way that society could progress. John Newbery (1713–1767), a publisher and bookseller in London during the mid eighteenth century, provided the foundation for much of the subsequent children's book trade. Newbery published such well-known books as *A Little Pretty Pocket-Book* (1744) and *Goody Two-Shoes* (1765), which represented a shift in the history of writing for children. While seventeenth-century authors focused on the sinfulness of children and the need for them to recognize their depravity, Newbery's books instead focused on the child's developmental potential. Children's books in the industrial era did not ignore gender and class distinctions. Indeed, they often reinforced them. Girls were instructed to be diligent homemakers for their future husbands, while boys were instructed to prepare earnestly for careers outside the home, often in public service.

Sources:

James Albisetti, *Schooling German Girls and Women: Secondary and Higher Education in the Nineteenth Century* (Princeton: Princeton University Press, 1988).

Linda Clark, *Schooling the Daughters of Marianne: Textbooks and the Socialization of Girls in Modern French Primary Schools* (Albany: State University of New York Press, 1984).

Raymond Grew and Patrick Harrigan, *School, State, and Society: The Growth of Elementary Schooling in Nineteenth-Century France* (Ann Arbor: University of Michigan Press, 1991).

MARRIAGE AND DIVORCE

Choosing a Spouse. Men and women generally had more freedom to choose their marriage partners after 1750 than they had in pre-industrial Europe, though parents and kin still influenced their choices. Future couples usually met one another through common friends or family members. Traditionally, the man proposed, and, if the woman accepted, the agreement was followed by an exchange of gifts and a dinner involving both families. Arranged marriages still existed in the nineteenth century, especially among the aristocracy and upper bourgeoisie, but these engagements decreased in popularity as the importance of love and choice for lifelong domestic partners assumed greater importance. The movement of young people from the countryside to urban areas contributed to the decline of arranged marriages. Free from pressures of family, church, and community, youths living away from home could form and break relationships with relative ease. More and more often these relationships involved cohabitation because economic conditions discouraged young poor people from

HARRIET TAYLOR ON DIVORCE

John Stuart Mill (1803–1873) and Harriet Taylor (1807–1858) married in 1851 after a long relationship, during part of which Taylor was married to another man. Both Mill and Taylor campaigned actively for the equality of women, especially in the realms of marriage and divorce. Taylor's argument for allowing divorce reveals how the issue touched many aspects of male and female relationships.

Women are educated for one single object, to gain their living by marrying—(some poor souls get it without churchgoing. It's the same way—they do not seem to be a bit worse than their honored sisters). To be married is the object of their existence and that object being gained they do really cease to exist as to anything worth calling life or any useful purpose. One observes very few marriages where there is any real sympathy between the parties. The woman knows what her power is and gains by it what she has been taught to consider "proper" to her state. The woman who would gain power by such means is unfit for power, still they do lose this power for paltry advantages and I am astonished it has never occurred to them to gain some large purpose; but their minds are degenerated by habits of dependence. I should think that 500 years hence none of the follies of their ancestors will so excite wonder and contempt as the fact of legislative restraints as to matters of feeling—or rather in the expression of feeling. . . . Would not the best plan be divorce which could be attained by any *without any reason assigned,* and at small expense, but which could only be finally pronounced after a long period? Not *less* time than two years should elapse between suing for divorce and permission to contract again—but what the decision will be must be certain at the moment of asking for it—unless during that time the suit should be withdrawn. . . .

In the present system of habits and opinions, girls enter into what is called a contract perfectly ignorant of the conditions of it, and that they should be so is considered absolutely essential to their fitness for it. . . .

. . . At this present time, in this state of civilization, what evil could be caused by, first placing women on the most entire equality with men, as to all rights and privileges, civil and political, and then doing away with all laws whatever relating to marriage? Then, if a woman had children she must take charge of them, women could not then have children without considering how to maintain them. Women would have no more reason to barter person for bread, or for anything else, than have men. Public offices being open to them alike, all occupations would be divided between the sexes in their natural arrangements. Fathers would provide for their daughters in the same manner as for their sons.

All the difficulties about divorce seem to be in the consideration for the children—but on this plan it would be the women's *interest* not to have children—now it is thought to be the woman's interest to have children as so many ties to the man who feeds her.

Source: John Stuart Mill and Harriet Taylor Mill, *Essays on Sex Equality,* edited by Alice Rossi (Chicago: University of Chicago Press, 1970), pp. 85–87.

marrying. While this practice contributed to increasing rates of illegitimate births, it also fostered the tendency toward individual choice of a marriage partner.

Marriage Agreements. After a couple became engaged, most middle- and upper-class families drew up a formal marriage contract, an agreement indicating what property each spouse would bring into the marriage. This agreement was especially important for women because any property she acquired after the marriage came under her husband's control. Between 1750 and 1914 marriage agreements gradually became secularized. By the nineteenth century most marriage contracts were primarily civil contracts that were blessed by the local church only after the fact. On 20 September 1792 the French National Assembly made marriage a civil act and not a religious one. Most other European cultures held tightly to their religious traditions, however, while embracing the role of civil authority. In Catholic countries, for example, the majority of marriages were celebrated after harvest in the fall, or

between Christmas and Ash Wednesday. The Church prohibited marriages during Advent and Lent, and most people with agricultural livelihoods had difficulty finding time for weddings during particularly intensive periods of labor. Likewise, fewer weddings were celebrated during lengthy periods of poor weather or political upheaval. Marriage celebrations included family and friends and could be quite elaborate, sometimes lasting several days. By the mid nineteenth century, the honeymoon became popular as newlyweds slipped away to a country inn or an urban hotel.

Property Laws. For most of the industrial era, married women had little legal control over their property. Their husband's permission was required for business transactions or to create a last will and testament. All property earned by either spouse during the marriage was controlled by the husband. Article 213 of the Napoleonic Civil Code of 1804 offered a terse explanation of this dependency: "A husband owes protection to his wife, a wife obedience to her husband." Even

Cartoon of a divorce celebration on the cover of a magazine published shortly after the French government legalized divorce (Bibliothèque des Arts Decoratifs, Paris)

nation-states such as Spain, Italy, and most of those in central Europe, which had traditionally allowed women to control some of their property, eventually enacted nineteenth-century legal reforms modeled on the Napoleonic Code. English common law was even more extreme. It dictated that all a woman's property, not just that acquired after the marriage, was under her husband's control. The British *Magazine of Domestic Economy*, founded in 1835, treated this law as a fact of life, observing, "A woman gives up her worldly possessions in exchange for a determinate station." English women could not control the property they acquired during marriage until the passage of the Women's Property Act in 1870. Even after this legal reform, husbands still controlled the property their wives brought into the marriage, and the laws regarding wives' property did not substantially change in other countries until the first decade of the twentieth century. Germany passed a law allowing women to control their property in 1900, and France reformed its property laws along these lines in 1910.

Marital Expectations. Marriage was traditionally conceived as a hierarchical relationship between husband and wife, and this perception changed little during the industrial era. There were changes, however, in what spouses expected from one another, especially concerning sexuality. Women increasingly came to assume that they had control of their own bodies, a change that decreased the emphasis on the sexual duties of husband and wife—the traditional "marriage debt" by which husband and wife were obliged to procreate. One result of this change was the decline in the birthrate, especially after 1860. Some couples abstained more often, while others practiced coitus interruptus. By the later nineteenth century a variety of contraceptives had been developed that further helped to prevent pregnancy.

Divorce. Although courts had granted marital separations for centuries, divorces became available to most people only in the late eighteenth century. The French Revolutionaries passed a divorce law in 1792. The French recognized at least seven grounds for divorce and made it relatively inexpensive and accessible to almost anyone. As a result, approximately thirty thousand French couples applied for divorce between 1792 and 1803. In the French city of Rouen about half of all divorces during this period were granted before 1796. Napoleon's 1804 legal reforms made it much more difficult to gain a divorce, especially for women. Napoleon reinstated Old Regime standards of order and authoritarianism under the paternal head of the family. According to Napoleon's Civil Code, husbands could apply for a divorce if they merely suspected their wives of infidelity, but wives had to prove that their husbands had been unfaithful. After 1816 divorce became impossible in France, and the law banning divorce remained on the books there until 1884. England allowed individual divorces by act of Parliament during the seventeenth and eighteenth centuries, but they were rare and available only to the elite. After 1770 the divorce requests submitted to Parliament multiplied. Finally, in 1857 new laws made divorce available to a wider range of the British

population than ever before. Germany legalized divorce in 1875. In predominantly Catholic states such as Austria, Spain, and Ireland divorce remained illegal into the twentieth century except in rare cases, and then only for non-Catholics. Generally, nineteenth-century divorces, when they did occur, were instigated by women who charged their husbands with desertion or claimed spousal incompatibility. Even when they were legal, divorce was relatively rare by modern standards and overwhelmingly an urban phenomenon. Although there was a gradual rise in the divorce rate across the nineteenth century, even around 1900 only about 7 percent of all marriages ended in divorce (compared to 30–50 percent of all marriages in late-twentieth-century Europe).

Sources:
John Gillis, *For Better, For Worse: British Marriages, 1600 to the Present* (New York: Oxford University Press, 1985).

Roderick Philips, *Putting Asunder: A History of Divorce in Western Society* (Cambridge: Cambridge University Press, 1988).

Marilyn Yalom, *A History of the Wife* (New York: Perennial, 2002).

PARENTING AND FAMILY RELATIONS

Motherhood. For centuries, giving birth to a child and caring for a child were different activities. Parents frequently sent their children out to wet nurses, and wives were often preoccupied with other activities that were considered more important to the household economy than caring for the children. By the nineteenth century, however, child rearing appears to have become the major focus for a married woman. In the eighteenth and nineteenth centuries, only the wealthiest families employed nurses or governesses. The domestic ideal of the middle classes was a mother caring for her children in her home. If the family were wealthy enough, a servant or two might be hired for domestic chores, but the task of raising the children was linked to the mother. Enlightenment philosophers such as Jean-Jacques Rousseau (1712–1778) helped to form this concept of the mother's natural duties in the eighteenth century. By the nineteenth century a myriad of manuals advised mothers about how to realize their natural destinies. Mothers were authority figures for young children of both sexes, but when a child reached the age of seven, gender defined the extent of the mother's role. After the male child reached his seventh year, he was generally under his father's control, while the responsibility for rearing a daughter remained with the mother. Daughters were expected to be subservient to their mothers throughout their lives, while mothers were supposed to prepare their daughters for their future roles as wives and mothers. The aristocracy still maintained a series of intermediaries between themselves and their children, but mothers of all social classes were heavily involved in their daughters' upbringing in their later childhood and teenage years.

Fatherhood. Some historians have suggested that the changes accompanying industrialization during the eighteenth and nineteenth centuries brought about a

A Hamburg merchant and his family, 1847
(Markisches Museum, Berlin)

redefinition of manhood and patriarchal authority. The increase in landless laborers undermined the traditional identification of landownership and manhood, and the increasing mobility of youths leaving home in search of work loosened the bonds of paternal authority. Because the French Revolutionaries linked political tyranny with paternal authority, they decreed in 1792 that fathers no longer held an unlimited paternal authority (*puissance paternelle*) over their children. Also, factory workers and businessmen working away from their homes and their children did not have as much opportunity to interact with their children as they might have had on a farm or in a small family business located in or near the family home—the typical pattern in pre-industrial Europe. Thus, many Europeans in the industrial era thought of their fathers as loving yet distant from their everyday world. Anna Korvin-Krukovskaia (born 1843), a daughter of a Russian nobleman, remembered her father as "essentially good and loving, but he surrounded himself with an air of inaccessibility as a matter of principle."

Parenting and the State. By the late nineteenth century many European nations worried that their populations were dwindling, especially among the "socially respectable" middle and upper classes. Thus, philanthropic and government organizations worked to reinforce concepts of the natural duties of parents. As the philosophy of "Social Darwinism" adapted the theories of Charles Darwin to competitive relations between states, "survival of the fittest" was tied to a healthy and growing population. The Bordeaux Society for Maternal Charity in France, for example, was organized to help women of the lower classes learn how to care for their children and raise them to become proper French citizens and soldiers. By the late nineteenth century, French mothers who had many children were given medals resembling military awards for helping to populate the nation. In the first decade of the twentieth century, the British passed four separate government acts with the express purpose of overseeing the children of poor families in the interest of securing their survival and healthy development. The Education Acts of 1906–1907 mandated daily meals for schoolchildren and medical exams twice a year in schools. In 1907 the British passed the Notification of Births Act, which required all live births to be registered within thirty-six hours and a visit to the new parents soon after by a government health official.

Sources:

Ann Taylor Allen, *Feminism and Motherhood in Germany, 1800–1914* (New Brunswick, N.J.: Rutgers University Press, 1991).

Leonore Davidoff and Catherine Hall, *Family Fortunes: Men and Women of the English Middle Class, 1780–1850* (Chicago: University of Chicago Press, 1987).

Barbara Alpern Engel, *Mothers and Daughters: Women of the Intelligentsia of Nineteenth-Century Russia* (Cambridge: Cambridge University Press, 1985).

Robert Nye, *Masculinity and Male Codes of Honor in Modern France* (Berkeley: University of California Press, 1998).

Ellen Ross, *Love and Toil: Motherhood in Outcast London, 1870–1918* (New York: Oxford University Press, 1993).

THE PREDOMINANCE OF THE MIDDLE-CLASS IDEAL

The Rise of the Bourgeoisie. Divisions among the social classes became exacerbated during the industrial era, during which the prototypical modern family emerged among the middle and professional classes. The bourgeois family is defined primarily by its ability to generate income and by its strict division of gender roles. The ideal middle-class family had a single wage-earning male at its head, a mother who could afford to remain at home to manage the household and raise the children, and at least one servant, who cleaned the home and served the needs of the mother and family. In this model, the place of production was separated from the home. The family, and especially the children, were cushioned from public life and protected by the parents. Nineteenth-century artwork frequently depicts these family relationships, particularly the relationship between mother and children, within the protective confines of the home or outdoors in gardens and other nature scenes.

Separate Spheres. As the workplace and the home became increasingly separated, an ideology of separate spheres developed to define the proper roles of people and spaces within and outside of the home. Eighteenth- and nineteenth-century scientific ideas about the "natural roles" of men and women, combined with the revitalization of evangelical ideas equating godliness with knowing one's proper place and role in society, helped to make separate spheres a normal part of family life. Hannah More (1745–1833), an evangelical English writer, believed that one's biology signaled an obligation to perform specific tasks to please God and to maintain society properly. Women were ideally to remain in the private domain, where they could perform their maternal functions. Women's virtue was defined by their ability to provide a safe home environment for their children and husbands that would nurture a new generation of citizens. These obligations developed into what historians call a "cult of domesticity," in which middle-class society viewed the home as a safe haven from the rest of the industrial world. Middle-class male work and political interests, it was believed, naturally made men public figures. Their identity was structured around their work ethic and their political functions. Working-class people also contributed to the creation of separate spheres. Working males had their own public culture, which was most identifiable in their workplace and union activities but also in the leisure hours they spent drinking at local taverns and pubs.

Family Meal Rituals. Middle-class family life was organized according to a series of mealtime rituals that defined the member's place in the family and helped reaffirm family and social ties. Meals were designed so that the entire family might enjoy them together. Mothers were instructed to provide wholesome meals that would keep the children healthy and keep the husband at home. A French nineteenth-century housewif-

SEPARATE SPHERES

Historian Martine Segalen developed a chart to describe how the nineteenth-century middle class divided activities and even emotional qualities into private and public spheres:

Private Sphere	Public Sphere
Home	Outside world
Leisure time	Working time
Family	Nonfamily relations
Personal and intimate relationships	Impersonal and anonymous relationships
Proximity	Distance
Legitimate love and sexuality	Illegitimate sexuality
Feeling and irrationality	Rationality and efficiency
Morality	Immorality
Warmth, light, and softness, harmony and wholeness	Division and dissonance
Natural and sincere life	Artificial and affected life

Source: Martine Segalen, "The Family in the Industrial Revolution," in *The Impact of Modernity*, volume 2 of *A History of the Family*, edited by André Burguière, Christiane Klapisch-Zuber, Segalen, and Françoise Zonabend, translated by Sarah Hanbury Tenison, Rosemary Morris, and Andrew Wilson (Cambridge, Mass.: Belknap Press of Harvard University Press, 1996), pp. 400–401.

ery manual insisted, "Care should be taken with the honors of the dinner table not only when you have guests but also for your husband's sake, in order to make life at home more civilized." In the preface to *The Book of Household Management* (1861) Isabella Beeton (1836–1865) told her readers, "Men are now so well served out of doors,—at their clubs, well-ordered taverns, and dining houses, that in order to compete with the attractions of these places, a mistress must be thoroughly acquainted with the theory and practice of cookery, as well as be perfectly conversant with all the other arts of making and keeping a comfortable home." Sunday meals were the most important of all weekly gatherings and were often followed by a promenade to the local park. The bourgeois annual calendar was filled with other holidays that had religious origins and were celebrated within the family.

The Happy Home. Family homes are influenced by contemporary social and cultural life. Families in pre-industrial European societies lived in two- or three-room dwellings; several family members often shared the same bedroom and in some cases the same bed. In

Religious evangelicals such as Thomas Gisborne (1758–1846) and Hannah More (1745–1833) in England believed that only a reinvigorated Christianity would help to stem the evils of the Industrial Revolution. For Gisborne one important means of creating a new sense of security was a reaffirmation of the maternal role that he believed was natural to wives and mothers. In his *An Enquiry into the Duties of the Female Sex* (1797) Gisborne emphasizes the proper management of the household, contributing to the new "cult of domesticity" that became popular at the turn of the nineteenth century:

Are you then the mistress of the family? Fulfill the charge for which you are responsible. Attempt not to transfer your proper occupation to a favorite maid, however tried may be her fidelity and her skill. To confide implicitly in servants, is the way to render them undeserving of confidence. If they are already negligent or dishonest, your remissness encourages their faults, while it continues your own loss and inconvenience. If their integrity is unsullied, they are ignorant of the principles by which your expenses ought to be regulated; and will act for you on other principles, which, if you knew them, you ought to disapprove. They know not the amount of your husband's income, or of his debts, or of his other incumbrances; nor, if they knew all these things, could they judge what part of his revenue may reasonably be expended in the departments with which they are concerned. They will not reflect that small degrees of waste and extravagance, when they could easily be guarded against, are criminal; nor will they suspect the magnitude of the sum to which small degrees of waste and extravagance, frequently repeated, will accumulate in the course of the year. They will consider the credit of your character as intrusted to them; and will conceive, that they uphold it by profusion. The larger your family is, the greater will be the annual portion of your expenditure, which will, by these means, be thrown away. And if your ample fortune inclines you to regard the sum as scarcely worth the little trouble which would have been required to prevent the loss; consider the extent of good which it might have accomplished, had it been employed in feeding the hungry and clothing the naked. Be regular in requiring, and punctual in examining, your weekly accounts. Be frugal without parsimony; save, that you may distribute. Study the comfort of all under your roof, even of the humblest inhabitant of the kitchen. Pinch not the inferior part of the family to provide against the cost of a day of splendor. Consider the welfare of the servants of your own sex as particularly committed to you. Encourage them in religion, and be active in furnishing them with the means of instruction. Let their number be fully adequate to the work which they have to perform; but let it not be swelled either from a love of parade, or from blind indulgence, to an extent which is needless. In those ranks of life where the mind is not accustomed to continued reflection, idleness is a never-failing source of folly and of vice. Forget not to indulge them at fit seasons with visits to their friends; nor grudge the pains of contriving opportunities for the indulgence. Let not one tyrannise over another. In hearing complaints, be patient; in inquiring into faults, be candid; in reproving, be temperate and unruffled. Let not your kindness to the meritorious terminate when they leave your house; but reward good conduct in them, and encourage it in others, by subsequent acts of benevolence adapted to their circumstances. Let it be your resolution, when called upon to describe the characters of servants who have quitted your family, to act conscientiously towards all the parties interested, neither aggravating nor disguising the truth. And never let any one of those whose qualifications are to be mentioned, not of those who apply for the account, find you seduced from your purpose by partiality or by resentment. . . .

Source: Thomas Gisborne, *An Enquiry into the Duties of the Female Sex,* in *Nineteenth-Century Europe: Liberalism and its Critics,* edited by Jan Goldstein and John W. Boyer (Chicago: University of Chicago Press, 1988), pp. 101–102.

the industrial era, middle-class families began to build larger homes divided into rooms for specific purposes and individual family members. While the typical pre-industrial home had a central room where most family activities occurred, the Victorian home separated public meeting rooms—the parlor and dining room, for example—from the private bedrooms of the children and parents. Rooms were established just for children, while other rooms became spaces for men or women, such as the library for the male and the kitchen for the female. Homes were also surrounded by gardens that separated the family from the public world and symbolically protected the children within their gates. By the mid nineteenth century "Home Sweet Home" had become established as a middle-class motto. For the first time the home was idealized as a secure place away from the workaday realities of the outside world. New interior styles stressed safety and emotional security. While the bourgeois home separated and secluded its residents from the pressures of public life, poor factory families lived in one- or two-room dwellings, often underground in basements with little or no access to fresh air and virtually no privacy for individual family members. Nineteenth-century reformers were shocked to see the living conditions of the working class. They reported stark, dank, and damp living conditions in dwellings occupied by more than one family. This housing was built by private entrepreneurs or by factory owners in open spaces around the towns. Because workers could barely afford the rents on their apartments, they often rented parts of

A middle-class French family at the dinner table, late nineteenth century (Sirot-Angel Collection)

their small spaces to members of their extended families or friends. While the bourgeois nuclear family was glorified as the new social model, poor families could not afford to live this way. Their extended, multigenerational family models deviated from what their contemporaries perceived as the "normal" practices of life.

Sources:

André Burguière, Christiane Klapisch-Zuber, Martine Segalen, and Françoise Zonabend, eds., *The Impact of Modernity,* volume 2 of *A History of the Family,* translated by Sarah Hanbury Tenison, Rosemary Morris, and Andrew Wilson (Cambridge, Mass.: Belknap Press of Harvard University Press, 1996).

Leonore Davidoff and Catherine Hall, *Family Fortunes: Men and Women of the English Middle Class, 1780–1850* (Chicago: University of Chicago Press, 1987).

Bonnie G. Smith, *Ladies of the Leisure Class: The Bourgeoises of Northern France in the Nineteenth Century* (Princeton: Princeton University Press, 1981).

REPLACING THE MOLD: ALTERNATIVES TO THE MIDDLE-CLASS IDEAL

Middle-Class Feminism. While the origins of feminism can be found in the seventeenth and eighteenth centuries, not until the nineteenth century were coherent alternatives to familial and social relations proposed. Some middle-class women were at the forefront of these challenges to the bourgeois ideal. The opening of a dialogue over the natural rights of men as citizens during the French Revolution created a forum in which men and women could criticize the traditional place of women as domestic creatures not suited for public life. The French writer Olympe de Gouges (1745–1793) critiqued women's place in society in *Declaration of the Rights of Woman and the Citizen* (1791), focusing on their status in the family. Feminists began to argue that women needed to be eman-cipated from their husbands' authority before they could be considered citizens. Despite their demands for liberation, feminists found themselves ever more restricted to the family while even their poorest male counterparts gradually attained the political rights of citizenship. After working within many of the social-democratic reform movements of the early nineteenth century—such as Chartism in England in the 1840s and the revolutionary movements that swept Europe in 1848—middle-class women raised specific public criticisms of their status during the second half of the nineteenth century. They did not explicitly reject the middle-class ideal, but instead they sought to use socially acceptable conceptions of women as nurturers and caregivers to extend women's rights. They formed wide-ranging collective organizations that sponsored newspapers and sought to advance women's status, first within marriage and the family and then in society at large. Divorce and property legislation was among their biggest concerns. In England, Caroline Norton (1808–1877) petitioned the British Parliament for changes in the laws governing women's property and child custody after her husband, George Norton, attempted to take both from her in a divorce case. Her efforts culminated in the Infant Custody Act of 1839, which allowed women custody of children who had not yet reached seven years. Another Englishwoman, Barbara Smith Bodichon (1827–1891), led efforts for property reform that culminated in the passage of the Married Women's Property Act in 1870. This act enabled married women to control their wages and any inheritance they gained after marriage. Similar efforts followed in most other European states, including Russia and the new nation-states of Germany and Italy. Feminists also

THE WORKING-CLASS MOTHER

The 1833 parliamentary testimony of Dr. Hawkins, an English medical practitioner, is typical of the middle-class answer to the burdens that working-class women faced as wives, mothers, and workers: that is, he would make the working-class mother more like her middle-class counterpart.

But let us suppose one of these young females about to assume the character of wife, mother, nurse, house-keeper,—which she too often undertakes prematurely and improvidently. She has no time, no means, no opportunities of learning the common duties of domestic life; and even if she has acquired the knowledge, she has still no time to practice them. In addition twelve hours' labor is an additional absence from home in going and returning. Here is the young mother absent from her child above twelve hours daily. And who has the charge of the infant in her absence? Usually some little girl or aged woman, who is hired for a trifle, and whose services are equivalent to the reward. Too often the dwelling of the factory family is no home; sometimes it is a cellar, which includes no cooking, no washing, no making, no mending, no decencies of life, no inventions to the fireside. I cannot help on these and other grounds, especially for the better preservation of infant life, expressing my hope that a period may arrive when married women shall be rarely employed in a factory.

Source: Edgar Royston Pike, ed., *Hard Times: Human Documents of the Industrial Revolution* (New York: Praeger, 1966), p. 236.

worked to improve educational opportunities for women at all levels of schooling and to increase access and opportunities for professional work outside the home.

The New Woman. By the late nineteenth century middle-class feminist activism, a rise in use of birth control, improved medical knowledge about pregnancy, and an increase in the number of single women working professionally contributed to the idea of what contemporaries called the "new woman." The "new woman" was a single female who rejected the bourgeois model of marriage and the "cult of domesticity." She argued for sexual freedom and equality, defined as the capability to separate sexual activity from the burdens of pregnancy, so that she might enjoy social and sexual relationships in the same way that her male counterparts did. By the early twentieth century she began to argue for the right to vote and an end to the oppression of women in the family and society. Many suffrage organizations reduced their demands for equal political rights when World War I began in 1914, but women in many European countries gained the right to vote in the years immediately following the war.

Gay and Lesbian Relationships. As the discussion of homosexuality grew more common in the nineteenth century, especially among urban and educated people, that lifestyle became another alternative to the bourgeois family model. Karoly Benkert (1824–1882), a Hungarian psychoanalyst, employed the term *homosexual* for the first time in the 1860s. By the 1880s and 1890s the causes and nature of homosexuality, especially lesbianism, were topics of public discourse. This discussion was linked to two

British suffragettes in October 1908, after their release from Holloway Prison, where they were jailed for demonstrations demanding voting rights for women

THE FAMILY AND SOCIAL TRENDS

issues that concerned many Europeans at the time: the growing number of single people and a reduction of the birth rate. Many people identified homosexuality with the new bohemian lifestyle made popular by the youths who dominated the urban landscapes of Europe. The "free" living arrangements identified with homosexual activity concerned political and social analysts because this lifestyle deviated from the family model that dominated middle-class values and much government policy for more than a century.

Sources:

Renate Bridenthal, Susan Mosher Stuard, and Merry E. Wiesner, eds., *Becoming Visible: Women in European History,* third edition, revised (Boston: Houghton Mifflin, 1998).

Genevieve Fraisse and Michelle Perrot, eds., *Emerging Feminism from Revolution to World War,* volume 4 of *A History of Women in the West* (Cambridge, Mass.: Belknap Press of Harvard University Press, 1993).

Karen Offen, *European Feminisms, 1700–1950* (Stanford, Cal.: Stanford University Press, 1999).

Bonnie G. Smith, *Changing Lives: Women in European History Since 1700* (Lexington, Mass.: D. C. Heath, 1989).

SEXUALITY

Birth Control. Although criticized by social and religious moralists since the Middle Ages, attempts to avoid pregnancy always existed, and by the nineteenth century men and women had more-successful contraceptive methods available to them. In the eighteenth century French observers such as Jean-Baptiste Moheau (1745–1794) railed against birth control. He argued that "rich women, for whom pleasure is the greatest objective and the sole preoccupation, are not the only ones who regard the propagation of the species as a trickery of past times: already these deadly secrets, unknown to any animal other than man, these secrets have penetrated into the countryside: nature is cheated even in the villages." Much traditional lore about methods of contraception spread from generation to generation through word of mouth. Methods of varying success—such as herbal contraceptives, potions, and magic—had been available since the Middle Ages, and European men and women continued to use them into the nineteenth century. In general the upper classes were more successful at limiting the size of their families. Early in the eighteenth century, elite women began to stress the dangers of too many pregnancies. Coitus interruptus began to be perceived as less of a crime against nature than in earlier centuries, when the traditional social perception was that sexual relations between spouses and the begetting of children were obligatory religious duties. Some social commentators, such as Thomas Malthus (1766–1834) and Marie-Jean Caritat, Marquis de Condorcet (1743–1794), broke from the moralists' arguments and maintained that parents should exercise restraint in the conception of children if they could not afford large families. One of the Enlightenment philosophers who began to separate sexual relations from procreation, Condorcet wrote that of all the animals of the world, the human alone "has found a way to separate, in the act

which should perpetuate the species, the gratification inherent in that act and the procreation which, in other species, is the involuntary cause of it." After 1850 condoms and diaphragms, which had already been in use among the elite, became increasingly available to people of all classes. Abortion was also widely available, though the French and German penal codes banned it, and there was a widespread criminalization of the practice. By the 1880s western Europeans were engaged in a debate about birth control and women's bodies, and the discussion had extended to eastern Europe and Russia by the first decade of the twentieth century. On the one hand, legislators were often vehemently opposed to birth control because they considered population growth essential to the strength of the nation-state and were concerned about declining birthrates. On the other hand, physicians such as Madeleine Pelletier (1876–1939) as well as feminist organizations argued that birth control was essential to women's health. Feminists argued that all women should have control over their own bodies and that motherhood should be a choice, not an obligation. In Russia some male physicians joined with feminists seeking to reduce criminal penalties for abortion or even to decriminalize it altogether.

The Illegitimacy Explosion. In the nineteenth century the tendency toward late marriages and the mobility of young people contributed to an "illegitimacy explosion." Historians have estimated that between 1 and 4 percent of all eighteenth-century births were illegitimate, but in the nineteenth century the rate hovered near 10 percent. In Paris and other urban areas nearly a quarter of

Tin for a late nineteenth-century French condom
(Musée d'Histoire de la Médecine, Paris)

Josephine Butler (1828–1906) led the campaign to overturn the Contagious Disease Acts of 1864, 1866, and 1869, through which the British Parliament attempted to control prostitution and the spread of venereal diseases such as syphilis by imposing harsh penalties on prostitutes but not on their male customers. Owing in large part to opposition by Butler and others, the acts were repealed in 1886. The following passages are part of Butler's attempts to educate the public about the harsh and unjust consequences of these laws:

I daresay you all know that there are women, alas, thousands of women, in England who live by sin. Sometimes, when you have been late at your market town, you may have passed one such in the street, and have shrunk aside, feeling it a shame even to touch her; or perhaps, instead of scorn, a deep pity has filled your heart, and you have longed to take her hand, and to lead her back to a better and happier life. Now, it is the pity and not the scorn which I would fain have you feel towards these poor women. . . .

The Parliament and the Government of England have done nothing *for* these women, what it has done *against* them you shall now hear.

I have taken it for granted that you all know that there is such an evil as prostitution in the land; but perhaps some of you are not aware that those who lead vicious lives are liable to certain painful and dangerous diseases, called *contagious*, because it is supposed that one person can only take them from another by contact, or touch. A healthy man, by merely walking down a street where there is a small-pox or fever, may sicken and die; but with these contagious [venereal] diseases it is quite different, all men are safe from them so long as they live virtuous lives. . . .

You know it costs a great deal of money to train a man to be a soldier or sailor, and if he is often ill and unfit for service that money is as good as lost. Now, when the Government found that very many soldiers and sailors were constantly in the hospital, owing to contagious [venereal] disorders, they asked themselves what they could do to prevent such a waste of the public funds, and such a weakening of the forces on which the country has to depend for safety in time of war, which was quite right; but instead of teaching or helping them to lead pure lives, they resolved to protect them against contagious diseases—in other words, to make it safe for them to sin. . . .

The Contagious Diseases Act of 1869 provides that in fifteen towns where there are always many soldiers and sailors—such as Canterbury, Aldershot, Portsmouth, and Plymouth—there shall be surgeons appointed to examine with certain instruments the persons of all prostitutes. . . . Those whom the surgeons find to be diseased, they are to send to what are called hospitals, but are really prisons, to be cured, and when they are well, they are dismissed to follow their former pursuits, their certificates of health being put into the hands of the police. . . .

. . . I want you to see . . . how unjust [these laws] are to sinful [women]. For when a woman sins, does she sin alone? Rather for one sinful woman are there not fifty—ay, a hundred, sinful men? And which of them, the ignorant, half-starved prostitutes, or the men, often well-taught and well-fed, who consort with them, are they that carry diseases to virtuous wives, to transmit it to unconscious infants? Surely the men. Then they are not only more guilty, but also more dangerous in their guilt. Yet the punishment of the sin of *two* is made by these laws to fall upon *one* alone, and that one the least to be blamed, and the most to be pitied. . . .

. . . I must just point out that all these police spies, and examining surgeons, and hospitals for diseased women, who are to be cured, not that they may be saved from their vicious life, but that soldiers and sailors may share it without risk, cost a great deal of money, and that all the money comes from the pockets of the people.

Source: Lisa DiCaprio and Merry Wiesner, eds., *Lives and Voices: Sources in European Women's History* (Boston: Houghton Mifflin, 2001), pp. 361–363.

---

all nineteenth-century births were illegitimate. Moreover, 30 to 40 percent of children were likely conceived before the wedding day. Historians no longer believe that the increase in the illegitimacy rate was solely connected to urbanization and industrialization. It does seem clear, however, that the social and economic changes of the industrial era allowed youths more freedom to meet members of the opposite sex and to make—or break—marriage promises. Young Europeans typically delayed marriage until their late twenties, but they were often free from traditional family, church, or village controls at the age of thirteen. By the nineteenth century the average age of menarche (a woman's first menstrual period) fell from sixteen to thirteen, allowing childbearing to begin earlier. One consequence of the creation of a growing, relatively independent, and sexually mature generation of young Europeans was the soaring rate of illegitimate births between 1750 and 1850.

Women and Sexual Pleasure. The "new women" who emerged in the late nineteenth century asserted that sexual gratification was not only for men; women had sexual desires and needs as well. Middle-class women wrote books and gave speeches in which they asserted their right to sexual pleasure without fear of domination by men. Some women advocated lesbianism or wrote novels extolling women's independent sexual experiences. Other women pursued sexual reform in different ways. Russian women, for example, organized conferences on sexual behavior and prostitution in 1908 and 1910. Reformers such as Englishwoman Josephine Butler (1828–1906) attacked the double standard by which society tolerated male sexual relations with prostitutes yet subjected the prostitutes to internment and the wives of their

A woman leaving her child at a Paris orphanage during the mid nineteenth century (Bibliothèque Nationale, Paris)

customers to the risk of venereal disease. Other reformers, such as Nelly Roussel (1878–1922) of France, proposed "birth strikes" in 1904. She advocated withholding sexual relations from men until women were treated more equally in heterosexual relationships.

Sources:
Laura Engelstein, *The Key to Happiness: Sex and the Search for Modernity in Fin-de-Siècle Russia* (Ithaca, N.Y.: Cornell University Press, 1992).

Genevieve Fraisse and Michelle Perrot, eds., *Emerging Feminism from Revolution to World War*, volume 4 of *A History of Women in the West* (Cambridge, Mass.: Belknap Press of Harvard University Press, 1993).

Tamara K. Hareven and Robert Wheaton, eds., *Family and Sexuality in French History* (Philadelphia: University of Pennsylvania Press, 1980).

WIDOWHOOD AND OLD AGE

The New Elderly. In the eighteenth and nineteenth centuries the percentage of the elderly in the European population grew because people were living longer. By 1850, 10 percent of the European population was over sixty. In southern and eastern Europe—regions characterized by complex, multigenerational households—the elderly frequently lived with their children and grandchildren. In western and northern Europe, the elderly were more likely to live by themselves. As the proportion of the elderly in society increased, the concerns and needs of older people were brought to the center of political debate.

Safety Nets: State Pensions and Insurance. Until the late eighteenth century, most elderly people had only their families to support them. Many widows and widowers moved in with their children. Others gave their children their inheritance early as a type of annuity in return for long-term care. Many European countries had pensions for military veterans. Public programs addressing the needs of specific individuals were the norm in the early nineteenth century, but increasingly European nation-states began to guarantee a minimum standard of living for retired civil servants, and then gradually for a larger percentage of the population. In 1853 France began providing pensions for soldiers and government workers when they reached the age of sixty. The Prussian government instituted pensions for factory workers in 1854. During the late nineteenth and early twentieth centuries social-insurance plans for all elderly citizens became popular in many nations. Chancellor Otto von Bismarck (1815–1898) of Germany made his government the first to provide this service in 1889. France, Great Britain, and Austria-Hungary followed suit in the first decade of the twentieth century.

Death in the Family. The death of a parent or a spouse creates an emotional crisis while also initiating a redefinition of family relationships and kinship connections through the transfer of wealth, memory, and identity from generation to generation. Between 1750 and 1914, unless one were destitute, natural deaths most often occurred at home, usually with the family present. Hospitals were unsanitary and mostly occupied by the indigent. The behavior of survivors had become highly ritualized. After death, the corpse was initially placed in a room (usually the parlor) of the family home, where relatives would gather to mourn the passing. In most regions of Europe the family would then contact the local church or funeral home to arrange for burial and invite friends and members of the extended family to take part in a procession carrying the body to the church and then to the cemetery. Mourning continued after the funeral, with prescribed behavior that differed according to gender and age status. According to etiquette books of the period, widows were expected to undergo stages of mourning that could last several years. Widows who did not wear special black dresses, often trimmed with black crape and jewelry composed of jet (black glass or coal), risked social condemnation. After the period of high mourning (usually twelve months) had ended, widows wore simple black dresses with less crape. A widow entering the half mourning period (generally between one and two years after her husband's death) could lighten her wardrobe by wearing shades of black, grey, lavender, and mauve. The mourning period for widowers was significantly shorter, generally six months.

Widows and Widowers. During 1750–1914 women tended to outlive men. In the eighteenth and nineteenth centuries, close to 20 percent of all women might have been widows at any given time, and the widow's financial situation could be difficult. Laws varied from region to region, but in most European traditions the family estate, including property that the husband brought into the marriage, went to a husband's descendants, not his widow, unless the husband had specifically dictated otherwise before his death. Sometimes widows stood to lose legal custody of their children. In some places maternal and paternal family members could assemble and agree to give widows control over their children and her property, granting the widow some economic stability in her old age. Many other poor widows found it too difficult to survive alone and remarried out of financial necessity.

An elderly London woman caring for a child in return for bread and a cup of tea, 1875

Sources:

John Morley, *Death, Heaven and the Victorians* (Pittsburgh: University of Pittsburgh Press, 1971).

Jill Quadagno, *Aging in Early Industrial Society: Work, Family, and Social Policy in Nineteenth-Century England* (New York: Academic Press, 1982).

Peter Stearns, *Old Age in European Society: The Case of France* (New York: Holmes & Meier, 1976).

David Troyansky, *Old Age in the Old Regime: Image and Experience in Eighteenth-Century France* (Ithaca, N.Y.: Cornell University Press, 1989).

SIGNIFICANT PEOPLE

CHARLES FOURIER

1772-1837
SOCIALIST PHILOSOPHER

Plans for the Future. During the eighteenth and early nineteenth centuries many visionary men and women desired to change the political and social structures of their world. Reformers who believed they could chart the future course of society by employing reason and scientific observation called themselves socialists because they were especially interested in engineering new forms of social organization. The core of this movement existed in France, where it was led by people such as Claude-Henri de Rouvroy, Comte de Saint-Simon (1760–1825), Auguste Comte (1798–1857), Pierre-Joseph Proudhon (1809–1865), and Charles Fourier. Although the founders of the early socialist movements were men, women were particularly attracted to these groups and often became leading voices in their development.

Early Life. Charles Fourier was born and raised in the city of Besançon in eastern France. He was the only son, the youngest of four children, and was educated at the local collège of Besançon. His father died when Fourier was only nine years old. When he was eighteen, his mother enrolled him as an apprentice in business and commerce, first in Rouen and later in the much larger city of Lyons. Working at various jobs, as well as serving in the military during the tumultuous years of the French Revolution (1789–1799), Fourier never succeeded in the business world. When his mother died in 1812, she left him a considerable inheritance, which allowed him to leave work and retire to the countryside to write.

Social Radical. Like most socialists, Fourier observed that industrialization had created vast progress and unimaginable wealth, but the wealthy profited disproportionately to the rest of society. In response he spent the last thirty years of his life creating a blueprint for social and economic equality. His writings did not become widely known, but by the mid 1820s he had managed to attract some devoted students. He moved to Paris in 1826 and three years later published his most accessible work, *Le Nouveau Monde industriel et sociétaire* (The New Social and Industrial World). In 1832 his followers began publishing two journals, *Le Phalanstère* and *La Phalange*, which further disseminated his views.

Philosophy. In his works Fourier criticized contemporary civilization and urged change according to a scientific model of human organization. He believed that the universe operated according to fixed natural and social laws that humans needed to discover and live by in order to enjoy fruitful lives. Society would operate best, he said, when people created communities called *phalanges* (phalanxes) that were organized according to individual personalities and emotions. Fourier calculated that there were just over eight hundred individual characteristics among twelve basic human passions. The perfect community would include all these human characteristics in people of different ages, genders, and abilities. Such communities would comprise between 1,600 and 2,000 men, women, and children, who would work and live together in a single building called a *phalanstery*. There residents would be grouped not according to family organization but according to age and wealth. They would work according to their natural inclinations and be paid according to their own contributions to the labor of the group.

Marriage and Family Life. Fourier believed that the evils of modern civilization originated in the repressive bourgeois family structure. He charged that men treated their spouses as if they owned them and worked only for them, while mothers and children had little freedom to express their deepest sentiments. He believed that humans should create more-equitable relationships between the sexes and that equality could exist only if people were freed from the restraints of marriage. To accomplish such equality, he advocated free love and the collective raising of children within the community. He sharply criticized the French Revolutionaries for not going far enough in their marriage reforms. He was ahead of his time when he wrote that "the extension of the privileges of women is the fundamental cause of all social progress."

Later Years. A utopia, by definition, does not exist. Fourier and the other socialists of his time attempted to attract wealthy patrons to finance the creation of new communities to serve as models of social organization that they hoped would attract new members and eventually spread to the rest of society. Fourier's only attempt to found a phalanx, near Rambouillet in 1832, failed. By 1833 Fourier was extremely ill, and he died on 10 October 1837.

Legacy. Fourier's philosophy gained admirers throughout Europe, from Russia to Spain, and in the United States, where more than forty communities based on Fourier's ideas were attempted in the early nineteenth century. One such community was Brook Farm (1841–1847) in Massachusetts, the well-known Transcendentalist community whose founding members included George Ripley, Ralph Waldo Emerson, and Nathaniel Hawthorne. Though all these communities failed, historians generally credit Fourier and his contemporary socialists for their early feminist critiques of society and for inspiring the more-radical socialist philosophy of Karl Marx and Friedrich Engels decades later.

Sources:

Jonathan Beecher, *Charles Fourier: The Visionary and His World* (Berkeley: University of California Press, 1986).

Nicholas V. Riasanovsky, *The Teaching of Charles Fourier* (Berkeley: University of California Press, 1969).

Michael Spencer, *Charles Fourier* (Boston: Twayne, 1981).

FRIEDRICH WILHELM FROEBEL

1782-1852
EDUCATOR

Life. The Romantic movement of the early nineteenth century included many advocates for the nurturing and education of children. One of the most important was the German educator and philosopher Friedrich Froebel. His mother died while he was still an infant in Oberweissbach, a small village of Thuringia. He had a rather strict Lutheran upbringing by his pastor father. After beginning his education at the local village school, Froebel was only ten years old when he was sent to live with an uncle and attend another village school in Stadt Ilm. When he turned fifteen, he became an apprentice forester but decided he disliked the trade after two years. From 1799 to 1816 he studied at the Universities of Jena, Göttingen, and Berlin while also working briefly at various jobs as a teacher and secretary. He also served in the Prussian army during the Napoleonic Wars. Having become interested in education at the University of Jena, Froebel established his own school, the Universal German Educational Institution, in 1816, hoping it might become a model for a rejuvenation of education in Prussia. During the 1820s he was active publishing his educational theories, and in 1831 he ceded control of the school and traveled with his wife to Switzerland, where he helped found and develop a school for poor children. In 1836 he returned to Prussia with his ill wife. In these decades Froebel formulated his idea for a school for very young children. In 1837 in Blankenburg he founded the Child Nurture and Activity Institute, which he later renamed the Kindergarten (child garden), using the school as a model to encourage the opening of more such schools during the 1840s.

Educational Philosophy. Froebel outlined the major components of his thought in *Menschenerziehung* (The Education of Man), published in 1826 and subsequently translated into several different languages, including English. (The book was widely available in the United States by the 1880s.) Deeply influenced by Enlightenment philosophers, especially Immanuel Kant (1724–1804), Froebel believed that the self was developed through a combination of sensory experiences that begin immediately after a child's birth. This development, he explained, was a continuous process that grew increasingly complex as the individual aged. Children, he said, needed special attention throughout their early years to insure later success. Believing that children learned by establishing relationships between themselves and the world, Froebel taught that doing so successfully was essential because the world was the ultimate, ever-changing manifestation of divine love.

Stages of Childhood. While philosophers and educators had generally treated birth through age seven as a single life stage, Froebel argued that children passed through three stages between birth and age six: infancy, early childhood, and childhood. Because the child changed and developed so quickly during these years, parents and teachers had to be especially aware of the child's surroundings and the kinds of sensory experiences to which the child was exposed. Texture, color, and light were all important for the young child, and play was the main activity through which the child could develop relationships to its surroundings. Froebel instructed parents and teachers to develop specific skills in their children even before the child could walk, such as having the child learn to grasp, hold, and pull on items in the infancy stage. Children left infancy when they became more interested in objects than in themselves, and they left the stage of early childhood as their intellectual capabilities developed, usually between the ages of four and six years.

The Kindergarten Movement. Froebel's name for his schools, Kindergartens, with its implications of cultivation and domestication, distanced himself from advocates of Jean-Jacques Rousseau's emphasis on developing the child in nature; yet, Froebel also rejected the established institution of the school. He taught that a child should be allowed the freedom to play and express himself or herself within protective confines created by specially trained adults who were deeply aware of the child's needs. He popularized his ideas by appealing to groups of women to take seriously and professionalize their role as educators, maintaining contacts with these groups through a series of letters that outlined his general philosophy. The revolutionary fervor of 1848 hurt the Kindergarten movement in Prussia, where government officials believed erroneously that it was attached to radical socialism and outlawed it in 1851, the year before Froebel's death. Despite the ban, the movement eventually spread across Europe and to North America. Proponents of Froebel's philosophy emerged in England as early as 1856, and the Froebel Society was established there in 1874 to train teachers and parents in early-childhood education.

Sources:

Robert Downs, *Friedrich Froebel* (Boston: Twayne, 1978).

Irene Lilley, ed., *Friedrich Froebel: A Selection from His Writings* (Cambridge: Cambridge University Press, 1967).

Jennifer Wolfe, *Learning from the Past: Historical Voices in Early Childhood Education* (Mayerthorpe, Alberta: Piney Branch Press, 2000).

MARIA MONTESSORI

1870-1952

EDUCATOR AND PHYSICIAN

Groundbreaker. Maria Montessori was born into a middle-class, well-educated family in Chiaravalle, Italy, and she lived most of her life in Rome. Her parents, especially her mother, supported her educational goals, and she attended a technical school primarily designed for students planning careers in the sciences. Most nineteenth-century career women were teachers or nurses, but Montessori wanted to become a scientist and entered the University of Rome. She eventually turned to medicine, and in 1896 she became the first modern Italian woman to receive a doctorate in medicine at the University of Rome. During the late 1890s she worked in Rome at institutions for the mentally disabled. During her work with the disabled she became interested in how children learn and respond to their environments.

A New Woman. Having defied the traditional path of most bourgeois women of her day, Montessori was one of a new generation of middle-class women who challenged the traditional gender roles established during the nineteenth century. By the final years of that century these "new women" were rejecting domesticity and motherhood as their only occupations. They dressed differently than bourgeois women, rode bicycles, studied subjects considered improper for them, and tried to embark on careers few other women had entered before. In 1899 Montessori traveled throughout Italy for two weeks, delivering a lecture called "The New Woman" in order to raise money to fund shelters for the poor. In her lectures, attended by capacity crowds of admirers, she criticized the male scientific perception of women.

The Montessori Method. By the turn of the century, Montessori had become well known for her work with the mentally handicapped. Over the next few years, she changed course and focused on the education of healthy children. In 1907 she opened her first Casa dei Bambini (Children's House) for young children in a poor, working-class neighborhood of Rome. She went on to publish educational treatises based on her work and research with her students, beginning with *Il metodo della pedagogia scientifica* (The Montessori Method) in 1909. In it she provided a new model for education, rejecting the systems of rote memorization popular at the time and arguing that children learn best when they are allowed to develop their skills freely through useful activities. Montessori wrote that the teacher should not devise tasks for the children to complete but instead should allow them to develop their own tasks and own methods of learning. Rather than guiding children from one activity or subject to the next, teachers should provide materials for various learning activities and allow students to experiment with the ones that interest them until they felt satisfied that they understood them. Spontaneity was crucial to her method, and teachers had to be prepared to adapt to the children's interests at a given moment. By 1912 stories about her work were being featured in magazines and newspapers throughout Europe and the United States. Before the outbreak of World War I in 1914 hundreds of admirers had established schools in which they employed her methods.

Sources:

Elizabeth Hainstock, ed., *The Essential Montessori* (New York: Plume, 1997).

Rita Kramer, *Maria Montessori: A Biography* (New York: Putnam, 1977).

E. Mortimer Standing, *Maria Montessori: Her Life and Work* (London: Hollis & Carter, 1957).

JEAN-JACQUES ROUSSEAU

1712-1778

PHILOSOPHER

Early Life. Jean-Jacques Rousseau was born in Geneva, where he spent his difficult childhood. His mother died while he was young, and his father neglected him. When he was sixteen years old he left Geneva. After traveling throughout northern Italy and returning for a time to Switzerland, he settled in Paris during the early 1740s. In Paris he became acquainted with many other French philosophes, notably Denis Diderot (1713–1784), the editor of the celebrated *Encyclopédie*. Rousseau's early interest was music, but by the late 1750s he had turned to philosophy and politics, after winning an essay competition sponsored by the Academy of Dijon. In 1758 he left Paris for rural life on a friend's country estate near Montmorency.

Writings. During the 1750s and 1760s Rousseau produced his best-known books, including his *Lettre à d'Alembert* (Letter to d'Alembert, 1758), *Julie: ou, la nouvelle Heloïse* (Julie, or, The New Heloïse, 1761), *Du Contrat social* (On the Social Contract, 1762), and *Emile* (1762). Critical of religion and government, *On the Social Contract* and *Emile* angered the French monarchy, and Rousseau was exiled. He traveled to Switzerland, where his books had also offended authorities, who had ordered his arrest. Fleeing to England, he remained there until 1767, when he returned to France and lived under the protection of powerful friends until his death in 1778.

Marriage. Rousseau had a series of liaisons with women who came from various social classes and who were either much younger or older than he, and he did not marry until 1768, when he was wed to Thérèse le Vasseur, a servant with whom he had begun a relationship in 1745. By the time they were married the two had already had five children. Rousseau had neglected all his offspring, abandoning them at various orphanages.

The "Noble Savage." Many philosophers of Rousseau's day considered intellectual questions about the family and the individuals in it: What was a family like in a "state of nature," a state of existence before civilization? How did mothers and fathers act? How were children raised? Deeply critical of his society, Rousseau believed that social and political inequalities corrupted people, claiming in *On the Social Contract:* "man is born free but everywhere is in chains." Rousseau argued that human government is a contract between the people who run the government and those who are governed by it. People enter the contract because life without government would be too difficult, and they expect the government to respect their individual rights while providing security and happiness.

On Childhood. By the nineteenth century Rousseau's philosophy of education was making a huge impact on literate Europeans' perspectives of childhood and on the place of the child in the middle-class family. In his novel on education, *Emile* (1762), Rousseau criticized his society's vision of children as small adults rather than seeing childhood as a separate stage of life in which children's needs and passions are different from those of adults. "We know nothing of childhood," he wrote. "The wisest writers devote themselves to what a man ought to know without asking what a child is capable of learning." Rousseau was deeply influenced by British philosopher John Locke (1632–1704), who argued that newborn children's minds were like blank slates, and they learned everything—including morality and perceptions of good and evil—through sensory experience. Because the child is born naturally good and learns everything from sensory experience, Rousseau believed that mothers should play an active role in their children's upbringing from birth to age five and should not send them to wet nurses. After a child turns

five, a tutor should take over from parents, he argued. In *Emile*, Rousseau is represented by the tutor of a fictional orphan boy, Emile. Teacher and student share a solitary existence. Emile is not allowed to venture into society, for society—as well as friends, books, and religion—would corrupt him. When Emile turns twelve, the tutor teaches him reason, logic, and the trade of an artisan cabinetmaker so he can earn a living. At fifteen he is old enough to study history and begin social relationships. He is introduced to religion when he reaches eighteen, and he is finally allowed to enter society when he is twenty.

Sophie and Emile. In Rousseau's novel, Sophie, Emile's future partner, is raised in the country as well. She is the perfect mate for Emile because she is from a well-off but unpretentious rural family. She is smart, but not too intelligent for Emile, and her skills lie in the domestic duties for which Rousseau believed women were naturally suited: sewing, cooking, and housekeeping. Rousseau believed that women wrongly dominated human life, and he criticized women in his society for their "false modesty" and "unnatural" control over men. He wrote that a woman's natural sphere of influence was the home while a man's was the government. Thus, Sophie's only role in the novel is to obey and to please Emile. *Emile* is an excellent example of how Enlightenment philosophers, who were liberal in many regards, were often conservative in their views about relationships between men and women. While Enlightenment thinkers criticized many other aspects of European culture and society, they tended to consider the gender relations of their time natural and immutable.

Sources:

Maurice Cranston, *The Noble Savage: Jean-Jacques Rousseau, 1754–1762* (Chicago: University of Chicago Press, 1991).

Patrick Riley, ed., *The Cambridge Companion to Rousseau* (Cambridge: Cambridge University Press, 2001).

SIGRID UNDSET

1882-1949
NOVELIST AND SOCIAL COMMENTATOR

Life. The Norwegian writer Sigrid Undset was born in Kalundborg, in western Denmark, the eldest of three daughters. Her father was an archaeologist, and the family lived a comfortable upper-middle-class lifestyle. In 1884 the family moved to Kristiania (now Oslo), Norway. After Undset's father died in 1893, her mother raised her daughters in more difficult conditions. From 1899 until 1909 Undset attended a commercial school in Kristiania and then worked as a secretary in an office. During this decade she began to write, and in 1907 and 1908 she published her first two books, the novel *Fru marta Oulie* (Mrs. Marta

Oulie) and *Den lykkelige alder* (The Happy Age), a collection of short stories about middle-class women in contemporary Norway.

Early Themes. Undset's early fiction is a window into the experiences of middle-class Norwegians at the turn of the century. In *Mrs. Marta Oulie* Undset depicts the life of a middle-class housewife who has become involved in an affair with her husband's friend. After her husband becomes ill and dies, she is so guilt-ridden that she refuses to continue her relationship with her lover. One of the stories in *The Happy Age* focuses on the difficulties faced by poor teenage girls as they interact with wealthier school friends. Two other stories describe the economic insecurity and unfulfilling work experiences of young middle-class women who have left home in search of careers. The women dream of better, more gratifying lives; yet, they avoid extended relationships with men and offers of marriage because they fear that their dreams might never come true. One character commits suicide when she realizes the difficulties of her depressing situation.

Feminism. From 1909 until the outbreak of World War I, Undset studied in Italy, visiting Paris and continuing to write fiction. *Jenny* (1911) reveals Undset's interest in turn-of-the-century feminist issues and her belief that women should be allowed to pursue interesting professions and enjoy family life. Turn-of-the-century middle-class Europeans, however, frowned upon these goals. Undset's title character eventually commits suicide after struggling between identifying herself through her work and through her personal and sexual relationships. The novel sold well but aroused intense feelings. Social conservatives were shocked by its explicit discussion of sexuality, eroticism, and pregnancy, while feminists questioned the meaning of having the main character abandon her career for her relationships and then kill herself.

Marriage and Family. While studying abroad, Undset met her future husband, Anders Svarstad, whom she married in 1912, after he left his first wife and children. They separated in 1919, when she was pregnant with their third child. Undset and her children settled in Lillehammer, Norway, where they lived until 1940.

Nobel Prize. During the 1920s Undset published a trilogy of historical novels, *Kristin Lavransdatter* (1920–1922), on the basis of which she was awarded the 1928 Nobel Prize in literature. In 1924 she converted to Catholicism. Her faith plays an important role in the historical and contemporary novels she wrote during the 1920s and later. Undset fled Norway after the Germans invaded in 1940 and spent the war in Sweden and the United States. She returned home in 1945 and died there in 1949.

Sources:

Carl Bayerschmidt, *Sigrid Undset* (Boston: Twayne, 1970).

Tim Page, ed., *The Unknown Sigrid Undset* (South Royalton, Vt.: Steerforth Press, 2001).

MARY WOLLSTONECRAFT

1758-1797
FEMINIST

The Birth of Feminism. In the revolutionary fervor that swept the Atlantic world during the late eighteenth century, women began to demand the same rights that liberal revolutionaries had claimed for men. The American Revolution of 1776, the French Revolution of 1789, and the Haitian Revolution of 1791 had all been inspired by the liberal Enlightenment philosophies of the eighteenth century that questioned whether a tiny aristocracy should rule over an entire people without their consent. The United Kingdom was also in the throes of debates about government. As the aristocracy's domination of Parliament came under intense scrutiny, British women joined the cry for the same "natural rights" of freedom, property, and the pursuit of happiness that the philosophers and revolutionaries demanded for men.

Early Years. Mary Wollstonecraft was born in the Spitalfields district of London. On her grandfather's death in 1765, her father used a substantial inheritance to take up farming, moving his family frequently as he failed at a succession of farming ventures in Barking (now part of Greater London), Yorkshire, and Wales, finally settling again in London in 1777. Mary was largely self-taught and developed an interest in writing at an early age. When her family returned to London in 1777, she attempted to leave home and become independent, but after her mother died in 1780, she returned to care for her siblings and her father. In order to provide for her family, she founded a school at Newington Green in London. The school failed in 1786, and Wollstonecraft began to write in order to pay her debts. By the late 1780s, Wollstonecraft had become acquainted with several members of the liberal intelligentsia in London, including philosophers William Godwin (1756–1836) and Thomas Paine (1737–1809). Living alone in London, Wollstonecraft supported herself by writing and working for bookseller Joseph Johnson (1738–1809).

The Vindications. When the French Revolution began in 1789, Wollstonecraft and her liberal circle of friends looked across the English Channel with admiration. After Edmund Burke (1729–1797) wrote his conservative *Reflections on the Revolution in France* (1790), Wollstonecraft responded with a defense of the the revolutionary ideals in *A Vindication of the Rights of Men* (1790). In 1792 she traveled to France to see the effects of the revolution firsthand. Before crossing the Channel, Wollstonecraft published *A Vindication of the Rights of Woman* (1792). In this work Wollstonecraft, who is often hailed as one of the first feminists, rejected the traditional assertion that sexual difference made men and women naturally unequal (a view upheld even by liberal philosophers such as Jean-Jacques Rousseau) and criticized the practice of educating boys and girls differently. Yet, true to the views of her time, Wollstonecraft still maintained that women's chief role was motherhood, explaining that women needed education to become better mothers and thereby improve society as a whole. Only well-educated women, she wrote, could be true partners to their husbands. With these arguments, Wollstonecraft foreshadowed the development of the ideal of "republican motherhood," which dominated the debate over women's role on both sides of the Atlantic during the early nineteenth century.

Unconventional Relationships. In France, Wollstonecraft fell in love with American Gilbert Imlay (1754–1828), with whom she had an illegitimate child, Fanny (1794–1817). The relationship began to fall apart in 1795, when she reacted to Imlay's infidelities by attempting suicide. She finally broke with Imlay in 1796. Though extramarital sex and bearing a child out of wedlock were strongly condemned by middle-class moralists, Wollstonecraft's letters reveal that she wanted to marry Imlay and was not blatantly flaunting convention. Back in England, she became pregnant with William Godwin's child and married him in 1797. Their marriage was also unconventional, as they attempted to lead individual lives. Five months after their wedding, Wollstonecraft died shortly after giving birth to their only child, Mary (1797–1851), who later became well known as Mary Shelley, the author of *Frankenstein* (1818).

Sources:

Miriam Brody, ed., *A Vindication of the Rights of Woman* (New York: Penguin, 1992).

Diane Jacobs, *Her Own Woman: The Life of Mary Wollstonecraft* (New York: Simon & Schuster, 2001).

Janet Todd, *Mary Wollstonecraft: A Revolutionary Life* (New York: Columbia University Press, 2000).

DOCUMENTARY SOURCES

Isabella Beeton, *The Book of Household Management* (London: S. O. Beeton, 1861)—A compilation of articles Beeton published in the *Englishwoman's Domestic Magazine,* instructing women on the intricacies of housewifery and motherhood.

Friedrich Engels, *Die Lage der arbeitenden Klasse in England* (Leipzig: Wigand, 1845); translated by Florence Kelley Wischnewetzky as *The Condition of the Working Class in England in 1844* (New York: Lovell, 1887)—Written by one of the founders of the communist movement, this work describes the poverty and despair workers faced in Manchester, the great industrial city of northern England.

Emile Guillaumin, *La Vie d'un simple* (Paris: Stoke, 1904); translated by Margaret Holden as *The Life of a Simple Man* (New York: Stokes, 1920)—A novel that depicts in realistic detail the family life and material conditions of a nineteenth-century French sharecropper.

Edward Humphries, "A Ranker's Ramblings, the Unpublished Memoirs of Major E. S. Humphries" (n.d.)—An autobiography by a British army officer, who described his teenage employment as an errand boy in London in 1904; first published in *The Annals of Labor: Autobiographies of British Working-Class People, 1820–1920,* edited by John Burnett (Bloomington: Indiana University Press, 1974), pp. 209–214.

Henrik Ibsen, *Et Dukkehjem* (Copenhagen: Gyldendalske Boghandels, 1879); translated by William Archer as *A Doll's House* (London: Unwin, 1889)—A well-known play about middle-class marriage and the difficult choice a woman makes between social expectations and self-fulfillment.

Stéphanie Jullien, "Letters" (written in 1833)—Written by a bourgeois Parisian, these letters reveal the intense anguish involved in selecting a marriage partner; first published in *Victorian Women: A Documentary Account of Women's Lives in Nineteenth-Century England, France, and the United States,* edited by Erna Olafson Hellerstein, Leslie Parker Hume, and Karen Offen (Stanford University Press, 1981), pp. 144–149.

"A Manchester Housewife's Weekly Budget" (written in 1833)—The income and expenses for a working-class English family; published in *Hard Times: Human Documents of the Industrial Revolution,* edited by Edgar Royston Pike (New York: Praeger, 1966), pp. 52–54; also includes several other useful documents from the British Parliament's investigation into the lives of the working classes.

Magdelan Pember Reeves, *Round About a Pound a Week* (London: Bell, 1913)—Based on Reeves's 1909 lecture on "The Economic Disintegration of the Family," this book depicts the everyday life of the British working poor, describing housing, budgets, food preparation, and child-care practices.

Alexander Schneer, *Über die Zustände der arbeitenden Klassen in Breslau* [On the Conditions of the Working Class in Breslau] (Berlin, 1845)—A collection of interviews with local doctors and government officials about the lifestyles, living conditions, and health of the German working classes; translated selections of this work were first published in *Documents in European Economic History, Volume 1: The Process of Industrialization,* edited by Sidney Pollard and Colin

Holmes (New York: St. Martin's, 1968), pp. 497–501, which also includes other useful documents relating to the social lives of the European working classes.

Flora Tristan, *Le Tour de France: Journal inédit (1843–1844)* (Paris, 1973)—Observations by French feminist and social reformer about working-class life in France; excerpts in English were first published in *Victorian Women: A Documentary Account of Women's Lives in Nineteenth-Century England, France, and the United States* (1981), pp. 471–473.

The civil marriage ceremony of Mathurin Moreau, performed by the groom's father in Paris, 1881; among the guests are the future Tsar Nicholas II of Russia (seated third from left) and (standing behind him) the future King Edward VII of Great Britain and novelist Emile Zola; painting by Henri Gervex (Bibliothèque des Arts Décoratif, Paris)

RELIGION AND PHILOSOPHY

by TERRY BILHARTZ

CONTENTS

Sidebars and tables are listed in italics.

1750
- Hasidism, a pietistic branch of Judaism, is established by Israel ben Eliezer, whose followers call him Baal Shem Tov (Master of the Good Name).

1753
- In Great Britain an Act of Parliament permits the naturalization of Jews.

1758
- Pope Benedict XIV dies and is succeeded by Cardinal Carlo della Torre Rezzonico as Clement XIII.

1759
- In an attempt to reduce the influence of the Roman Catholic Church in the realm of secular politics, Portugal expels the Society of Jesus (Jesuits).

1762
- Jean-Jacques Rousseau publishes *Du Contrat social* (On the Social Contract), in which he asserts that government receives its authority by the consent of its people, not from divine rights conferred by God.

1765
- Robert Raikes founds Sunday Schools in England.

1766
- Tsarina Catherine the Great grants freedom of worship in Russia.

1767
- The Jesuits are expelled from Spain.

1769
- Pope Clement XIII dies and is succeeded by Cardinal Lorenzo Ganganelli as Clement XIV.

1772
- The Inquisition, which has been attempting to enforce Roman Catholic orthodoxy, is abolished in France.

1773
- Under pressure from nation-states that oppose the influence of powerful Jesuits, Pope Clement XIV dissolves the Jesuit order, the Society of Jesus.

1775
- On the death of Pope Clement XIV, Cardinal Giovanni Angelo Braschi is elected Pope, taking the name Pius VI.
- New Testament textual criticism begins with the work of Johann Jakob Griesbach.

* DENOTES CIRCA DATE

1776
- Social philosopher Adam Smith publishes *The Wealth of Nations,* in which he outlines the evolution of economic systems from primitive hunting to free-market capitalism.

1779
- In his posthumously published *Dialogues concerning Natural Religion* philosopher David Hume asserts the impossibility of proving the existence of God through the use of human reason.

1781
- Joseph II of Austria grants a patent of religious tolerance and freedom of the press in Austria.
- Philosopher Immanuel Kant publishes his *Kritik der reinen Vernunft* (Critique of Pure Reason), in which he argues that while human reason cannot establish that God exists, it also cannot prove His nonexistence.

1782
- In Vienna, Pope Pius VI fails to persuade Joseph II to rescind the program of toleration in Austria.
- Clergyman-scientist Joseph Priestley publishes *A History of the Corruptions of Christianity,* in which he argues that Jesus was a mortal man who preached the resurrection of the body, not the soul, which is a nonexistent abstraction.

1784
- The Bengal Asiatic Society is founded to study Sanskrit, leading to the broader dissemination of Hindu religious ideas in Europe.
- John Wesley's *Deed of Declaration* establishes the charter of Wesleyan Methodism.

1788
- Immanuel Kant publishes his *Kritik der praktischen Vernunft* (Critique of Practical Reason), in which he asserts that the idea of the existence of God enters the human mind through an inner voice of conscience he calls the "categorical imperative."

1789
- Philosopher Jeremy Bentham publishes *Principles of Morals and Legislation,* in which he argues that humankind is primarily motived by pleasure and pain and that the best law is the one resulting in the "greatest happiness of the greatest number."

1790
- Jews in France are granted civil liberties.

1791
- Thomas Belsham founds the Unitarian Society.

* DENOTES CIRCA DATE

1792

- The Baptist Missionary Society is founded in London.

1793

- William Carey leaves England for India, where he serves as the first Protestant missionary.

1794

- William Paley publishes *Evidences of Christianity*, arguing for the historical truth of the Gospels.

1795

- Freedom of worship is granted in France.
- The London Missionary Society is founded.

1797

- William Wilberforce publishes *A Practical View of the Religious System*, his defense of the Anglican faith against the arguments of freethinkers and atheists.

1798

- French troops invade Rome and capture Pope Pius VI.

1799

- Friedrich Schleiermacher publishes *Über die Religion: Reden an die Gebildeten unter ihren Verächtern* (On Religion: Speeches to its Cultured Despisers), arguing that true religion is "taste for the infinite" based primarily in feelings rather than reason and established belief systems.
- Pius VI dies in captivity in France.

1800

- Cardinal Barnaba Chiaramonti is elected Pope, taking the name Pius VII.

1801

- Napoleon I and Pope Pius VII negotiate a concordat defining the relationship between Church and State in France.

1802

- The Huguenot (Protestant) Church is given legal standing in France.

1802-1803

- Georg Wilhelm Friedrich Hegel and Friedrich Schelling publish the *Kritisches Journal der Philosophie* (Critical Journal of Philosophy).

* DENOTES CIRCA DATE

1804
- The British and Foreign Bible Society is founded in London.

1808
- Napoleon abolishes the Inquisition in Spain and Italy.
- French troops occupy Rome, prompting Pope Pius VII to excommunicate Napoleon, who responds by imprisoning the Pope.

1811
- During the "Great Schism" in Wales two-thirds of Welsh Anglicans leave the Established Church.

1812
- Jews in Prussia are granted civil equality.

1813
- The Russian Bible Society is formed.

1814
- After the fall of Napoleon, Pope Pius VII returns to Rome, where he restores the Inquisition and reestablishes the Jesuit order.

1815
- The Congress of Vienna settlement restores to the papacy much of the Church land confiscated in France during the Revolutionary and Napoleonic eras.

1815-1817
- Juan Llorente publishes his *Historia critica de la inquisition de España* (History of the Inquisition in Spain), an anticlerical work blaming the Catholic Church for the deaths of some thirty thousand so-called heretics (a figure modern historians consider inflated).

1817
- Lutheran and Reformed (Calvinist) Churches in Prussia form an Evangelical Union.

1818
- Hegel becomes professor of philosophy at the University of Berlin.

1821-1822
- Friedrich Schleiermacher publishes *Der christliche Glaube* (The Christian Faith), in which he develops his idea that religious faith is based on the intuitive awareness of a higher power that gives meaning to an otherwise meaningless existence.

* DENOTES CIRCA DATE

1822
- The Royal Asiatic Society for the study of Eastern languages is founded, contributing to the growth of Western interest in Asian religions.

1823
- Pope Pius VII dies and is succeeded by Cardinal Annibale della Genga, who takes the name Leo XII.

1825
- French law makes sacrilege a capital offense.

1827
- In England, John Nelson Darby, a former Anglican clergyman, founds the Plymouth Brethren, a Protestant group that does not recognize clergymen as distinct from lay people, and becomes active in foreign missionary work.
- John Keble publishes *The Christian Year,* devotional poems for each of the holy days mentioned in the Anglican Book of Common Prayer.

1828
- Following the repeal of the British Test and Corporation Acts, Catholics and Nonconformists are allowed to hold public office in Great Britain.

1829
- The Catholic Emancipation Act allows British Roman Catholics to serve in Parliament and hold almost any other public office.
- On the death of Pope Leo XII, Cardinal Francesco Castiglione is elected Pope, taking the name Pius VIII.

1831
- Pope Pius VIII dies and is succeeded by Cardinal Mauro Capellari as Gregory XVI.

1833
- John Keble's sermon *On the National Apostasy* criticizes the British Parliament's control over the Anglican Church and sets in motion the Oxford Movement.
- The Greek Orthodox Church becomes independent from control by the patriarch of Constantinople.

1835-1836
- David Friedrich Strauss publishes *Das Leben Jesu kritisch bearbeitet* (The Life of Jesus Critically Examined), in which he calls the Gospels "historical myth."

1838
- Auguste Comte gives the social science of sociology its name.

* DENOTES CIRCA DATE

1839-1842

- The Opium Wars, which begin when the Chinese try to suppress British opium trade in their country, end with victory for the British, one consequence of which is increased access of missionaries to inland areas of China.

1843

- Søren Kierkegaard publishes the first of the works that establish his reputation as the founder of European Existentialism.

- John Stuart Mill publishes *A System of Logic,* an ambitious attempt to define the methods of the physical and social sciences.

1845

- Friedrich Engels publishes *Die Lage der arbeitenden Klasse in England* (The Conditions of the Working Class in England), an exposé of the ill effects of industrialization.

- Anglican clergyman John Henry Newman, a leader of the Oxford Movement, becomes a Roman Catholic.

1846

- The Evangelical Alliance is founded in London.

- Pope Gregory XVI dies and is succeeded by Cardinal Giovanni Maria Mastai-Ferretti as Pius IX.

1847

- A famine in Ireland sets in motion a major wave of immigration to the United States.

1848

- Karl Marx and Friedrich Engels publish the *Manifest der kommunistischen Partei* (Manifesto of the Communist Party), calling on workers to rise up against their capitalist bosses.

1850

- Prussia establishes a church council to manage Protestant churches.

1854

- Pius IX declares the dogma of the Immaculate Conception of the Blessed Virgin Mary to be an article of faith.

1858

- Bernadette Soubirous says the Blessed Virgin Mary appeared before her at Lourdes, France.

- Lionel de Rothschild becomes the first Jewish member of the British Parliament.

1859
- Charles Darwin publishes *On the Origin of Species by Natural Selection*, propounding a theory of evolution that is widely interpreted as antithetical to the biblical explanation of creation.
- The first Anglican missionary work begins in Japan.

1864
- Pope Pius IX publishes his *Syllabus of Errors*, condemning liberalism, socialism, rationalism, and other modern ideas.

1865
- James H. Taylor founds the China Inland Mission.

1866
- Lay readers are permitted to conduct nonsacramental services in the Church of England.

1867
- Karl Marx publishes volume one of his *Das Kapital*, predicting a worldwide workers' revolution that will create a classless, communist society.

1868
- Austrian schools are freed from Church control.

1869
- The Vatican Council opens in Rome.

1870
- The Vatican Council promulgates the dogma of papal infallibility.

1871
- In protest against the proclamation of papal infallibility, a splinter group of Old Catholics leaves the Roman Church and holds its first congress in Munich.
- The Anglican Church in Ireland is disestablished but is allowed to keep the cathedrals and other church buildings it acquired during the English Reformation of 1537, which established Anglicanism as the state church of Ireland.

1872
- Resenting the influence of Rome on German Catholics, Otto von Bismarck breaks off diplomatic relations with the Vatican and expels the Jesuits from Germany.

1875
- Pulpit laws in Prussia ban priests from speaking about politics in their sermons.

* DENOTES CIRCA DATE

1878
- Pope Pius IX dies and is succeeded by Cardinal Gioacchino Vincenzo Raffaele Luigi Pecci as Leo XIII.

1879
- Anti-Jesuit laws are passed in France.
- The national body of the Swedish Baptist General Conference is formed.

1880
- Frances Xavier Cabrini founds the Order of the Missionary Sisters of the Sacred Heart.

1881
- The Vatican archives are opened to scholars.

1883
- The Fabian Society is founded in London with the purpose of creating a democratic socialist state.

1885
- Julius Wellhausen proposes two earlier narratives, identified as "J" and "E," as sources for the Book of Genesis.

1886
- Marx's *Das Kapital* is published in English.

1886–1889
- Adolf von Harnack publishes *Lehrbuch der Dogmengeschichte* (History of Dogma), in which he calls for a return to Christian doctrine as it is stated in the New Testament.

1891
- Pope Leo XIII issues his "Rerum novarum" (Of New Things), an encyclical recognizing the plight of the working classes.

1896
- Theodor Herzl calls for the establishment of a Jewish homeland, founding the modern Zionist political movement.

1899–1901
- During the Boxer Rebellion, an uprising against foreigners in China, thousands of European missionaries and their converts are killed.

1901
- William Wrede publishes *Das Messiahgeheimnis in den Evangelien* (The Messianic Secret in the Gospels), in which he asserts that Jesus was not identified as the Messiah until after his death.

* DENOTES CIRCA DATE

1903
- On the death of Pope Leo XIII, Cardinal Guiseppe Sarto is elected Pope and takes the name Pius X.

- Anti-Jewish pogroms take place in Russia.

1904
- France establishes the separation of Church and State.

1904-1905
- Max Weber publishes *Die protestantische Ethik und der Geist des Kapitalismus* (The Protestant Ethic and the Spirit of Capitalism), in which he links Protestant theology and the rise of capitalism.

1905
- The Baptist World Alliance is formed.

1906
- Jesuit general Franz Wernz reforms the order's plan of studies.

- Albert Schweitzer publishes *Von Reimarus zu Wrede* (The Quest for the Historical Jesus), theorizing that Jesus's religious views were shaped by a belief that the end of the world was imminent.

1907
- A papal encyclical condemns modernism.

1910
- The World Missionary Conference is held in Edinburgh.

1912
- The Church of Scotland revises its prayer book.

1914
- Pope Pius X dies and is succeeded by Cardinal Giocomo della Chiesa, who takes the name Benedict XV and reigns until 1922.

* DENOTES CIRCA DATE

OVERVIEW

European Religious Prospects. By the eighteenth century, European Christianity in general, and the Roman Catholic Church in particular, had largely recovered from the political and moral difficulties that had confronted it during the turbulent Reformation and Counter Reformations movements of the sixteenth century. Spurred by the missionary zeal of the Jesuits and the colonial expansion of Catholic Spain, Portugal, and France, the Roman Catholic Church had gained new believers to compensate at least partially for those it earlier had lost to the Protestants, and even was in the process of winning back growing minorities within the Eastern Orthodox Churches. By 1750 the Roman Catholic Church had faithful worshipers living on five continents and on the major islands that encircled them. Protestants were also spreading around the globe, although their numbers were much lower than those of the Catholic Church. Except for the Russian Church, Eastern Orthodox churches lacked vitality and had little growth. Eighteenth-century Catholics could easily envision the demise of the Protestant influence and the return of the Eastern Churches under the authority of the Pope. This bright Catholic future, however, never materialized, in part because European Christendom was challenged by several late-eighteenth-century intellectual and political developments that undercut the influence of all Christian traditions, in particular the Roman Catholic Church.

The Recession of Christianity, 1750–1815. Several factors contributed to diminishing Christian influence in traditionally Christian lands. During the second half of the eighteenth century the Society of Jesus (Jesuits) were confronted by hostile secular governments that feared and resented Jesuit influence within their borders. In 1759 the Portuguese expelled the Jesuits from their territories, and within a decade France, Spain, and Naples had done so as well. Under growing pressure from European nation-states, Pope Clement XIV (reigned 1769–1774) officially dissolved the Society of Jesus in 1773. For the next three decades the Jesuits persisted only in those Protestant and Eastern Orthodox lands that refused to publish the papal brief. In 1814 Pope Pius VII (reigned 1800–1823) restored the Jesuit order. During the period of the Jesuits' suspension, the Roman Catholic Church lost ground not only in Europe but also in Asia, Africa, and the Americas. Mean-while, the influence of Rome also suffered as a group of powerful monarchs known as "enlightened despots" endeavored to improve the living conditions of their subjects by reconstructing their states according to the dictates of reason. Their determination to bring about reform, with or without the support of the Church, inevitably undercut ecclesiastical authorities. These "enlightened despots" included Charles III of Spain (reigned 1759–1788), who curbed the Inquisition that had been investigating and punishing suspected heretics in Spain since the Middle Ages and suppressed the Jesuits; Joseph II of Austria (reigned 1765–1790), who confiscated church lands, placed the training of priests under state control, and prohibited the publication of papal bulls without his permission; and the deistic Frederick II of Prussia (reigned 1740–1786), who granted religious freedom to his subjects. These rulers advanced not only ideals of religious toleration, which to the established churches were signs of secularization, but also advocated greater state oversight of the church.

Deism and Romanticism. Alongside adverse political developments were emerging intellectual currents that challenged widely accepted Christian notions. During the Enlightenment, Europeans became increasingly confident in the ability of the human mind to understand the laws of nature. As faith in human reason soared, belief in divine revelation waned. The new emerging religion of this Age of Reason was Deism, a natural religion that viewed God as the Great Architect who created a universe and governed it by rational, universal laws that could be discerned by the human mind. To obtain happiness, the Deists believed, humans must liberate themselves from the superstitions of the past and obey the laws of nature. Although Deists believed in the existence of God and in an afterlife that rewarded virtue and punished sin, they rejected Christian doctrines such as the Incarnation, the Resurrection, and the Atonement. While some Deists, such as Joseph Priestley (1733–1804) and William Paley (1743–1805) in England, were churchmen who attempted to salvage some Christian doctrines, other influential Deists—including the most widely read author of the Enlightenment, the Frenchman Voltaire (1694–1778)—were openly hostile to all forms of Christianity. Another intellectual current that undercut Christianity was Romanticism. This literary and artistic movement—in many ways a reaction against the universalism and cold rationalism of the Enlightenment—elevated emotion over reason, focusing on the glories of the individual self and on the virtue of freedom from social constants. While not all Romantics were anti-Christian, Romantic writers such as Jean-Jacques Rousseau (1712–1778) rejected historic Christian understandings of the divine, embracing instead a pantheistic mysticism that revered not a personal deity but an impersonal, sacred universe. By the end of the eighteenth century, traditional Christian worldviews were being challenged both by Rationalists, who sought truth through reason alone, and by Romantics, who trusted intuitive, visionary experiences more than ancient scriptures or church traditions.

Religion in an Age of Revolutions. The French Revolution and the Napoleonic Wars that followed it also adversely influenced European ecclesiastical affairs. In 1789 a debt crisis forced Louis XVI (reigned 1774–1792) to call into session the Estates General to find a solution to the economic ills that were threatening France. This body, which had not met in two centuries, consisted of France's three major social groups: the First Estate (the clergy), the Second Estate (the nobility), and the Third Estate (the commoners). Although more commoners gathered in Paris than members of the other two estates combined, Louis's announcement that—in accord with traditional procedures—each estate would vote separately meant that control would be given to a minority coalition of clerics and nobles. Unwilling to accept domination by the privileged classes, the Third Estate declared itself the National Assembly and invited the other Estates to join it. This National Assembly promptly made drastic changes in the structures of Church and State. It abolished the payment of the tithe (one tenth of one's income) to the Roman Catholic Church, a decision that ended a financial burden on French peasants but also deprived the Church of one of its chief sources of funds. Later, the National Assembly confiscated church lands, dissolved the monasteries, and proclaimed that parish priests would be elected by all the citizens, including Protestants and Jews as well as Catholics. In time, the French Revolution turned more violent and anti-Christian. During the so-called Reign of Terror, the king, queen, and some sixteen thousand nobles were executed, and Christianity was officially denounced as a superstition. However, the attempt of the radicals to establish a state religion with festivals honoring the events of the Revolution failed, and in 1795 a new constitution was established that promised religious freedom.

From Napoleon to the Congress of Vienna. In 1799 Napoleon took charge of France and ruled the nation first as consul and later as a hereditary emperor until his forced abdication in 1814. During his years in power, he masterfully manipulated the Roman Catholic Church for his political purposes. In 1801 he negotiated a concordat between himself and Pope Pius VII that restored some confiscated lands to the Church but also gave the government a veto authority over the appointment of bishops.

Following this agreement, he unilaterally announced that no papal decrees would be published in France without his permission. His relations with the Pope soon deteriorated, and in 1808 French troops occupied Rome. When Pius VII retaliated by excommunicating Napoleon, the French emperor had the Pope imprisoned. After the fall of Napoleon, Pius was freed and returned to Rome. In 1815 the Congress of Vienna convened to undo what had been attempted during the French Revolution and the Napoleonic years. French borders returned to pre-Revolution boundaries; the house of Bourbon was reinstated in France; and most of the monarchs whom Napoleon had deposed were restored to their thrones. In ecclesiastical affairs, most papal territories were returned to the Pontiff. After a generation of unrest, power on the Continent was again securely in the hands of ultramonarchists and political conservatives.

The Triumph of Nationalism and Liberalism. Notwithstanding the bloody Crimean (1854–1856) and Franco-Prussian (1870–1871) Wars, the century after the Congress of Vienna was largely marked by peace in Europe. The absence of full-scale war, however, did not mean a lack of national unrest. Punctuating the period were chronic nationalistic uprisings and liberal and socialistic crusades. For several years after the settlement in Vienna, these movements were opposed and largely repressed by political conservatives led by Chancellor Klemons von Metternich of Austria (1773–1859). Although Metternich enjoyed some early successes, however, the tide of history was against him. In 1829 the Greeks won their independence from the Turks. In 1830 Belgium secured its independence from the Netherlands, thus dividing this region into Catholic Belgium and Protestant Holland. In 1848 riots and revolts among left-wing revolutionaries broke out in Italy, Belgium, France, England, and Switzerland. Although most of the revolts were suppressed, the spirit of reform ultimately produced significant changes across Europe. In that year Switzerland gained a new constitution; Metternich was ousted in Austria; and a revolution led by Louis-Napoleon Bonaparte, nephew of Napoleon I, established the Second Republic in France, where President Bonaparte proclaimed himself Emperor Napoleon III in 1852. In the same year Hungary proclaimed its independence from Austria but was brought back under Austrian control in 1849. By 1860 Italy was mostly unified at the expense of the Papal States, and Germany was united in 1871 under William of Prussia (1797–1888), who became Emperor William I of Germany.

The Retrenchment of Catholicism. The tumultuous events that followed the Revolution of 1848 convinced Pope Pius IX (reigned 1846–1878) that the forces of liberalism and modernism were hostile to the Catholic Church. His distrust was magnified during the 1860s and 1870s, when Chancellor Otto von Bismarck of Prussia (1815–1898) took strong actions against the Catholic Church, breaking diplomatic ties with the papacy, expelling several monastic orders from the land, and cutting the subsidies historically given to the Church. Even as Rome was losing some of its temporal power, however, the papacy under the leadership of Pius IX was advancing its authority in ecclesiastical matters. In 1864 Pius boldly challenged the liberal currents of the time with the publication of the *Syllabus of Errors,* a list of eighty modern ideas that Catholics were instructed to reject. In 1870 the Vatican Council further enhanced the authority of the papacy when it defined for Catholics the dogma of papal infallibility.

Protestant Diversification and Expansionism. Another consequence of political developments during the second half of the nineteenth century was the simultaneous growth of "free churches" supported by voluntary contributions and the demise of state-supported established churches. This trend toward the separation of Church and State worked to the advantage of several upstart Protestant bodies, particularly the Methodists, Baptists, and other evangelical groups. The intellectual currents of the day accentuated the fragmentation of the Protestant tradition, as Protestants reacted in various ways to the major controversies of the age—such as socialism, Darwinism, Social Darwinism, and biblical criticism. Some Protestants retreated into the safety of the historic creeds and confessions; others placed their trust in the value of personal religious experiences; still others sought to defend their faith by accommodating it to the scientific theories and philosophies of their time. As Protestantism became more diverse, it also enjoyed extraordinary growth. New interdenominational societies were formed to take the Protestant message to all peoples of the world. Notwithstanding the hostile forces that threatened historic Christianity, during the century between the Congress of Vienna and World War I the Protestant tradition grew in vitality and numbers and became more entrenched in Europe and around the globe.

TOPICS IN RELIGION AND PHILOSOPHY

THE EASTERN ORTHODOX TRADITION

Orthodox Churches in Southeastern Europe. During the nineteenth century, the once great Ottoman Empire became known as "the sick man of Europe." By 1914 this empire had lost all of its European possessions except a small region around Constantinople (now Istanbul). Two factors contributed to the decline of these Muslim Turks: the growing strength of Russia and the intensification of nationalism among the peoples of southeastern Europe. One manifestation of this nationalism was the attempt to make the Christian Eastern Orthodox churches into national churches, independent from the Ecumenical Patriarch in Constantinople, who was under the control of the Turkish rulers. For this reason the patriarchs of Constantinople were often despised as outsiders in southeastern Europe, as were the Greek bishops and clergy that the patriarchs sent to administer the rites of the Orthodox Church. During the century before World War I, political independence movements in this region often were preceded by mass movements to throw off the patriarchal yoke and to achieve ecclesiastical independence. In Greece in 1833, for instance, the national assembly, with the support of thirty Orthodox bishops, declared that the Church of Greece had no head but Christ. In subsequent years, as Greece extended its borders, the Church of Greece expanded its areas of jurisdiction, thus decreasing the territories formerly under the Ecumenical Patriarch. As it grew weaker, the Ottoman government recognized the Bulgarian Church (1870), the Serbian Church (1879), and the Church of Rumania (1885) as autocephalous (self-governing) churches. The Ecumenical Patriarch was so indignant at this severing of the body of Christ that communion between the national churches and the Ecumenical Patriarch was not fully restored until the mid twentieth century.

The Russian Orthodox Church. The history of nineteenth-century Russian Christianity is complex. As the Russian tsars flip-flopped in their attitudes toward liberalism and the West, the Russian Orthodox Church, which was closely associated with the state, also shifted in its religious and political emphases. Under Tsar Alexander I (reigned 1801–1825), the pietistic movement on the Continent and in England influenced developments within the Russian Orthodox Church. In 1813 the Russian Bible Society was formed as a sister body to the British and Foreign Bible Society. Both associations were committed to translating the Bible into vernacular languages and to distributing copies of it widely. Later in Alexander's reign, the Jesuits were banished from the capital; the ministry of religious affairs and public education was created; and the Holy Synod was

Russian Orthodox monks and novices at Kerzhensky Monastery, circa 1880 (Hulton-Deutsch Collection/CORBIS)

given supervision over all forms of religion throughout the empire. However, the next tsar, the conservative Nicholas I (reigned 1825–1855), was less willing to be associated with Western ideas or institutions. Under Nicholas the work of the Russian Bible Society was suppressed, and the Russian Orthodox Church was touted as the divinely commissioned Church and the guardian of true Christianity. In the first decade of the next tsar, Alexander II (reigned 1855–1881), Russia again turned toward the West, accepting several liberal measures, including the emancipation of the serfs. At this time influential clergy lobbied the tsar to ease State control of the Church. These ecclesiastical reforms, however, were never granted. Instead, during Alexander's last fifteen years and throughout the reign of his successor, Alexander III (reigned 1881–1894), measures were taken

to isolate Russia from Western influences. Increasingly, Russia became dominated by "Slavophiles," lovers of Holy Russia who insisted that Russian civilization was superior to Western culture. In religious matters, the Slavophiles insisted that the Russian Orthodox Church was the true Mother Church and that—just as Constantinople had earlier replaced Rome as the center of Christianity—so Moscow had now emerged as the "third Rome" and was commissioned by God to uphold Christian orthodoxy.

Russian Philosophers and Theologians. Among the great religious thinkers of nineteenth-century Russia were Alexis S. Khomiakov (1804–1860) and Vladimir S. Soloviev (1853–1900). Khomiakov, an aristocrat by birth, was a Slavophile lay theologian who argued that the Orthodox Church was the perfect synthesis of the imperfect Catholic

KHOMIAKOV ON THE ONE CHURCH

Russian Alexei Khomiakov described the Orthodox Church as the perfect synthesis of the Catholic and Protestant traditions, arguing in his essay "The Church is One" (written in 1844–1845) that the division of Christianity is an earthly illusion not recognized by God:

THE UNITY OF THE CHURCH follows of necessity from the unity of God. . . . the unity of the Church is not imaginary or allegorical, but a true and substantial unity, such as is the unity of many members in a living body. The Church is one, notwithstanding her division as it appears to a man who is still alive on earth. It is only in relation to man that it is possible to recognize a division of the Church into visible and invisible; her unity is, in reality, true and absolute. Those who are alive on earth, those who have finished their earthly course, those who, like the angels, were not created for a life on earth, those in future generations who have not yet begun their earthly course, are all united together in one Church, in one and the same grace of God; for the creation of God which has not yet been manifested is manifest to Him; and God hears the prayers and knows the faith of those whom He has not yet called out of non-existence into existence. Indeed the Church, the Body of Christ, is manifesting forth and fulfilling herself in time, without changing her essential unity or inward life of grace. And therefore, when we speak of "the Church visible and invisible," we so speak only in relation to man.

Source: Alexei Khamiakov, *The Church Is One* (London: Fellowship of St. Alban & St. Sergius, 1968).

and Protestant Churches. According to Khomiakov, the Roman Catholic Church had achieved unity without freedom, and Protestantism possessed freedom without unity. The Orthodox tradition alone displayed *sobornost*, the community of divine love that combines both unity and freedom. Equally influential was the deeply religious, systematic philosopher Soloviev. Although a member of the Russian Orthodox Church, Soloviev longed to see a reunion of the Orthodox, Catholic, and Protestant traditions. In his younger days this Christian mystic was hopeful that, with its ability to blend Western and Eastern principles, Russia would lead humanity into an age of divine love in which nations would relate to each other on the basis of Christian principles. In his later years Soloviev replaced this optimistic vision of the future with the teaching that the coming world emperor would be the Antichrist, who would rule by vanity rather than love. In these sobering works Soloviev advanced the view that Christians should retire to the desert, achieve Church reunion, and prepare for the second coming of Christ to bring in the millennial reign of peace. These teachings influenced a later generation of Russian Christians, who were forced into exile following the triumph of the Bolsheviks in the Revolution of 1917.

Sources:

Demetrious J. Constantelos, *Understanding the Greek Orthodox Church* (Boston: Hellenic College Press, 1990).

George Bernard Hamilton, *The Religion of Russia: A Study of the Orthodox Church in Russia from the Point of View of the Church in England* (London: Society of Saints Peter and Paul, 1915).

Fred Mayer, *The Orthodox Church in Russia* (New York: Vendome Press, 1982).

THE EMERGENCE OF METHODISM

Methodist Piety and Good Works. Methodism had its origins in a prayer and Bible-study group founded by the recently ordained Anglican clergyman John Wesley (1703–1791) at Oxford around 1729. Detractors of the group called the group "Methodists" because of their systematic approach to their devotions, and the term was subsequently applied to all Wesley's followers. While he and his brother Charles were serving as Anglican missionaries in the American colony of Georgia during the years 1735–1737, Wesley, who advocated spiritual self-discipline and the performance of charitable acts, met and was deeply influenced by the Moravians, a German pietist sect that stressed the individual's personal relationship to God. In 1739 Wesley began a lifetime of itinerant preaching, traveling some 250,000 miles on foot and horseback throughout England, Wales, Scotland, and Ireland by the time of his death in 1791.

Methodist Organization. Wesley organized the people who converted to Christianity into fellowship groups known as Methodist societies. Like the members of the club at Oxford, these Methodists were encouraged to gather together during the week for a time of preaching, praying, singing, and testifying and then to attend the Anglican services on Sunday at their parish churches, where they would worship according to the Book of Common Prayer and receive the sacraments of the Church of England. The Methodist societies welcomed into their fellowship anyone who expressed the desire to "flee from the wrath to come" and to follow the three general rules: avoid evil, do good, and employ the means of grace to grow spiritually. Later, Wesley also divided the societies into "classes," smaller groups of about a dozen people each. In these intimate spiritual-support groups members met once a week to share their spiritual struggles and victories and to answer the weekly question: "How goes it with your soul?" Occasionally, the opposition against Wesley and the Methodists turned violent. Despite such threats, however, this renewal movement within the Church of England grew so rapidly that it encouraged Wesley to commission lay preachers and assistants to help him in his work. Beginning in 1744, Wesley began to meet with his preachers at Annual Conferences, where the preachers discussed issues of theology and mission and received preaching assignments from Wesley for the following year.

Women and Methodism. Most of the leaders of the early small Methodist groups were women. Some English-

The 1779 Methodist Annual Conference, at City Road Chapel, London, with John Wesley
preaching from the high pulpit and Charles Wesley seated at the lower lectern
(Methodist Church Archives and History Committee)

men insisted that Wesley and his associates were under-mining family values by allowing women to spend large amounts of time away from home attending Methodist meetings and performing Methodist "good works" such as visiting the sick. Wesley initially had some doubts about allowing women to preach, but in 1787, over the objections of some male preachers, he officially authorized the first female Methodist preacher, Sarah Mallet. After Wesley's death in 1791, however, the opposition against women preachers was rekindled, and in 1803 the Methodist practice of authorizing female preachers was halted and not resumed until the late nineteenth century.

From Movement to Church. Wesley never intended to start a new denomination. His aim was to awaken the masses from their spiritual slumber and bring vitality to the Church of England. Throughout most of his life, he reprimanded those who wished to break away from Anglicanism. He never left the Church of England, nor was he ever disowned by it. Nonetheless, Anglican authorities disapproved of Methodist "irregularities" such as preaching without regard for parish boundaries and ultimately refused to recognize Methodist services as Anglican worship. English law allowed non-Anglicans to hold worship services only if their religious group was officially registered. Wesley thus found himself in a difficult situation. If the Methodists registered, they would be acknowledging that they were not Anglicans; but if they did not register, they would be breaking the law. In 1787 Wesley made the difficult decision to instruct his preachers to register, the first step toward legal separation. By the time of his death in

1791, the British Methodists were well on their way toward establishing themselves as an independent church, just as the American Methodists had done, with Wesley's blessing, in 1784.

The Legacy of Methodism. Methodism influenced and was influenced by the Industrial Revolution. One result of the rapid industrialization of Great Britain during the late eighteenth century was the mass movement of people toward the emerging industrial centers. Uprooted people in economic peril tended to lose their connections with the parish church. Methodism, with its informal and vibrant piety and its practice of taking religious services to the people, was better positioned to meet the spiritual needs of these uprooted masses than the structured Anglican establishment. Wesley was a Tory and had little to do with social reform, but he did support the abolition of slavery. He also campaigned to stop the production of distilled spirits and the excessive breeding of horses because he believed that reserving grain for making liquor and feeding aristocrats' horses showed the upper class's contempt for the poor. The Methodist movement appealed to the industrial masses and brought thousands of British workers into the church. Historians have fiercely debated the political consequences of this proletarian revival. Some credit, or blame, the Methodists for preventing a British revolution like the one that occurred in France. Others insist that Methodism slowed reform by diverting discontent into religious rather than political activity. Yet, others argue that Methodism assured the ultimate success of social reform by providing a method for nonviolent change that was in keeping with the British temperament. Most historians agree, however, that Methodists' humanitarian concerns, coupled with their passion for order, exerted a powerful influence on the social and political landscape of eighteenth- and nineteenth-century England.

Sources:

A. D. Gilbert, *Religion and Society in Industrial England: Church, Chapel and Social Change, 1740–1914* (New York: Longman, 1976).

Francis J. McConnell, *John Wesley: A Biography* (New York: Abingdon Press, 1939).

Bernard Semmel, *The Methodist Revolution* (New York: Basic Books, 1973).

E. P. Thompson, *The Making of the English Working Class* (New York: Pantheon, 1964).

Charles Yrigoyen Jr., *John Wesley: Holiness of Heart and Life* (New York: General Board of Global Ministries, 1996).

MODERN JUDAISM

Origins. In premodern times, the world of European Jewry was violent, segregated, and insecure. Jews were required to live in separated neighborhoods known as "ghettos," had limited civil liberties, and often were prohibited from land ownership or craft-guild membership. Jewish institutions thrived in this segregated environment. In Jewish ghettos, economic activities shut down on the Sabbath; marriages and bar mitzvah ceremonies were community affairs; and children received sacred and practical instruction in Jewish schools. While ghetto life limited Jewish economic and political advancement in the Christian world, it provided Jews with a sense of community and a special appreciation for their heritage. During the late eighteenth and early nineteenth centuries, Jews across Europe slowly won new civil and political freedoms. Once emancipated from the ghetto, some Jews began to question the appropriateness of old Jewish customs. Many aspired to become integrated into society without losing their Jewish identity. Others insisted that integration was heresy. The age of emancipation brought calls for both reform and retrenchment, and in this environment, several new forms of Judaism arose.

Orthodox Judaism. The term *Orthodox Judaism* most commonly applies to traditionalist movements resistant to the influences of modernization that arose in response to emancipation. Of the major Jewish denominations, Orthodoxy is the least centralized. Without a single governing body, this group is unified by a commitment to certain common principles, particularly to the Torah, both Written and Oral, as the exact word of God revealed without human influence. Viewing the revealed Torah not as a value system but as the divine standard, the Orthodox retain traditional Jewish laws and customs, such as observing ancient dietary and dress regulations, prohibiting women from leading in worship, segregating the sexes during worship, conducting all rituals in the Hebrew language, and insisting on the circumcision of Jewish males on the eighth day after birth by an authorized *mohel*, a person trained to perform both medical and religious aspects of the procedure. Theologically, most Orthodox Jews embrace

In early modern times the Christian majority in Europe often justified the political and economic restrictions placed on European Jews by invoking the necessity for maintaining religious conformity. As the concept of religious toleration became more accepted, however, a new argument for Jewish repression developed. After a French linguist, Joseph-Ernest Renan (1823–1892) advanced the idea that the "Aryans" and the "Semites" were different races, a group of German writers drew on his theory to assert that Jews were members of a distinct and inferior race. By the 1870s this anti-Semitism had spread across Germany, Austria-Hungary, France and Russia, often resulting in the persecution of Jews. One of the worst outbreaks of anti-Jewish violence took place in 1881 in Russia. A major consequence of these anti-Jewish *pogroms* (a Russian word meaning "devastation") was a mass exodus of Jews from Russia to other regions, especially to the United States.

Source: Solomon Grayzel, *A History of the Jews* (New York: Penguin, 1968).

the thirteen principles of faith written by Rabbi Moses Maimonides (1135–1204) in the twelfth century. These principles include a belief in the coming of a Messiah and a final revival of the dead.

Reform Judaism. Originating in Germany in the early nineteenth century, Reform Judaism is less constrained by traditional forms than the other major Jewish denominations. Reform Jews view the words of the Torah as divinely inspired but not eternally binding. That is, they believe that the words of the Torah express timeless truths but are also the products of earlier cultures. Most early reformers embraced five common principles: 1) Judaism is capable of continuous development and should adapt its teachings to the needs of the times; 2) ancient rituals and dietary laws need not be observed; 3) circumcision should be voluntary; 4) the Talmud is not the authoritative interpretation of the sacred tradition; and 5) the coming of a personal Messiah to lead the Jews back to Palestine is no longer anticipated. Later, in the twentieth century, some Reform Jews decided that the early reformers had overreacted against entrenched Orthodoxy and reclaimed some traditional customs, such as maintaining a prayer life, observing the Sabbath, and recognizing that the Written and Oral Law are important sources that should be adapted to the needs of each generation. Doctrinally, Reform Jews insist that the heart of Judaism is the belief in the One God, who rules the world through law and love. Reform Jews anticipate not the coming of a personal Messiah but of a messianic age in which truth, justice, and peace will dwell among all peoples.

Cornerstone-laying ceremony for a synagogue in Kremisier, Moravia, 1908 (Statni Zidovske Muzeum, Prague)

Conservative Judaism. Conservative Judaism is a hybrid tradition midway between the Orthodox and Reform movements. The Conservative movement originated in the mid nineteenth century and is often interpreted as a "counter reformation" necessitated by the alleged excesses of the Reform movement. Like Orthodox Jews, the Conservatives believe the Torah and the Talmud to be divinely inspired. They also recognize, however, a human role in the formation of these texts and thus accept them as historical documents influenced by other cultures. Conservatives embrace several reforms, such as discarding the ancient dress requirements, but they keep other traditions, such as the use of Hebrew in religious rituals and restrictions on diet and Sabbath activities.

Sources:
Calvin Goldscheider and Jacob Neusner, eds., *Social Foundations of Judaism* (Englewood Cliffs, N.J.: Prentice Hall, 1990).

Solomon Grayzel, *A History of the Jews* (New York: Penguin, 1968).

THE OXFORD MOVEMENT

Objectives and Emphases. Also known as "Tractarianism" because its views were published in ninety religious pamphlets called *Tracts for the Times* (1833–1841), the Oxford Movement was launched in the early 1830s by Anglican clergymen at Oxford University. The primary objective of the movement was to bring spiritual renewal to the Church of England by reviving certain Roman Catholic doctrines and rituals that Anglicans had dropped during the struggles of the Protestant Reformation. The participants in the movement longed for a return to the ancient days before the universal church had been torn by the stresses of nationalism. Viewing the universal church as a divinely created and ordered society that was intended to transcend politics, geography, and time, these Oxford clergymen wanted the Church of England to be free from state authorities in matters of doctrine and discipline. To achieve "reunion" and to recover the lost heritage of the early Christian Church, the proponents of the movement insisted that the holy sacraments be administered by priests ordained by bishops who themselves were divinely authorized for ministry through a line of succession that dated back to the apostles. In addition to this assertion that ecclesiastical authority is passed through a line of apostolic succession, these "high church" clergymen emphasized other Catholic doctrines that Anglicans had neglected or rejected in recent centuries, including baptismal regeneration (the belief that baptism brings about the rebirth of the soul in Jesus Christ), auricular confession (telling one's sins to a priest), and the real presence of Christ in the bread and wine served at Eucharist, or Holy Communion.

Origins and Leaders. The chief architects of the movement included the clergymen John Keble (1792–1866), John Henry Newman (1801–1890), and Edward Pusey (1800–1882). Keble achieved renown in 1827 with the publication of *The Christian Year,* a book of devotional poems fitted to the holy days mentioned in the Book of Common Prayer. This well-received publication—which was republished in more than 150 editions during the next half century—helped him to acquire a professorship of poetry at Oxford University in 1831. In 1833, responding to a controversial attempt by the British government to suppress ten redundant bishoprics in Ireland, Keble preached an explosive sermon, *On the National Apostasy,* decrying the power of Parliament over the Church. Calling for an autonomous, holy, and catholic (universal) Church, Keble insisted that the Church was a divine society with heavenly authority, not a plaything of politicians.

Tracts for the Times. A few days after Keble preached his sermon, he was one of a small group of Oxford divines who gathered to pledge themselves to uphold "the apostolic succession and the integrity of the Prayer-Book." From this meeting, the Oxford Movement was launched. To popularize the effort, the vicar of the university church in Oxford, Newman, began editing a series of pamphlets, *Tracts for the Times,* to encourage a return to the beliefs and customs of the early Church. Of these ninety tracts, Newman wrote or co-authored nearly one-third. Under Newman's leadership, the Tractarians advocated an Anglicanism that was a middle way between Roman Catholicism and Protestant evangelicalism. In 1841 Newman published the controversial ninetieth tract, which moved him beyond the position of other Tractarians. In this tract Newman argued that the Thirty-nine Articles, which encapsulated the official doctrines of the Church of

E. B. Pusey and John Keble, leaders of the Oxford Movement (right: portrait by George Richmond)

England, were not contrary to Roman Catholic doctrine and practice. He argued for the validity of sacraments other than baptism and Holy Communion and for the real presence of Christ in the Eucharist, as well as acknowledging the existence of purgatory—all Catholic beliefs that most Anglicans (as well as Protestant denominations) considered contrary to their dogma. This tract caused such controversy that Bishop Richard Bagot of Oxford promptly commanded the termination of the series. In time Newman and other Tractarians of his persuasion left the Church of England and were admitted into the Roman Catholic Church.

After Newman's Conversion. After Newman left the Tractarians in 1841, another Anglican clergyman and Oxford scholar, Edward Pusey, assumed a more important role in that Anglo-Catholic movement, becoming so closely associated with it that opponents sarcastically dubbed the Oxford Movement "Puseyism." In addition to writing several pamphlets for the *Tracts for the Times* series, Pusey helped to edit and translate *The Library of the Fathers of the Holy Catholic Church* (1838–1885), which encouraged Anglicans to study and appreciate the values of the early patristic fathers. In 1865–1870 he and Newman engaged in a "pamphlet war," in which Pusey defended the principles of the Tractarian movement and Newman, who had become a Roman Catholic priest in 1845, espoused Catholic dogma. By the end of the nineteenth century the Tractarians were placing an increased emphasis on the need for Christians to respond to the social problems caused by the Industrial Revolution. This demand for a "Social Gospel" led to the establishment in 1889 of the Christian Social Union, headed by Brooke Westcott (1825–1901) and Henry Holland (1847–1918).

Sources:

Owen Chadwick, *The Mind of the Oxford Movement* (Stanford, Cal.: Stanford University Press, 1960).

Peter Benedict Nockles, *The Oxford Movement in Context: Anglican High Churchmanship, 1760–1857* (New York: Cambridge University Press, 1994).

Bernard M. G. Reardon, *Religious Thought in the Victorian Age* (New York: Longman, 1980).

PIETISM

Origins. Just as the American colonies experienced an early eighteenth-century revival, the so-called Great Awakening, European Christians experienced a fervent form of religious experience known as Pietism, which had its origins in the late seventeenth century and continued well into the eighteenth. Characterized less by religious dogma or sacramentalism than by heartfelt devotion, ethical purity, and charitable activity, this movement can be traced back to evangelical Lutherans Philipp Jacob Spener (1635–1705) and August Hermann Francke (1663–1727). Another major proponent of Pietism was Count Nikolaus Ludwig von Zinzendorf (1700–1760), a Pious German nobleman. In the early eighteenth century he befriended a group of persecuted religious refugees, the Unitas Fratrum (Unity of Brethren), who had been forced to flee their

Count Nikolaus von Zinzendorf, leader of the pietistic Moravian Brethren (portrait by Alexander Simon Belle; from A. J. Lewis, *Zinzendorf, The Ecumenical Pioneer*, 1962)

native Moravia, and gave them asylum on his lands. Zinzendorf joined their sect and emerged as its bishop in 1737. Though the Moravians embraced central Lutheran doctrines—such as the authority of the Bible, salvation by faith alone, and the priesthood of all believers—the relationship between the Moravians and German Lutherans was never secure, and the Moravians formally broke with the mother church after Zinzendorf's death. Known as the Moravian Brethren, this pietistic sect never achieved great size, but it exerted a larger influence on Protestantism than its numbers warranted.

Influence on Protestantism. One of the most significant contributions of Pietism to Protestant Christianity was its missionary impulse. Before Pietism, Protestant reformers paid scant attention to the non-Christian world. Under the influence of Zinzendorf and other pietistic leaders, however, Protestants trained and sent Christian missionaries to the Caribbean, Africa, India, South America, and North America. Pietistic groups were involved in many humanitarian endeavors, establishing orphanages, building schools, and organizing centers to care for lepers, the blind, unwed mothers, and the insane. The clerics of state churches often accused the Pietists of being overly emotional, subversive, and even heretical. Given their antitraditionalism, much of this criticism was understandable. Pietism nonetheless exerted a broad influence on European Protestantism. Through John Wesley, the pietistic concern for experiential religion penetrated the Church of England and the new Methodist Church that separated from the

Anglicans at the end of the eighteenth century. In Norway the unordained itinerant preacher Hans Nielsen Hauge (1771–1824) traveled more than ten thousand miles in six years, denouncing the orthodoxy of the state church and proclaiming the need for heartfelt religious conversion. Although arrested and imprisoned for ten years for preaching as a layman, Hauge helped to create a lay movement that ultimately brought vitality to the Norwegian church. Pietism also contributed to the development of the Inner Mission Society, which was founded in Germany in 1849 and later spread to Scandinavia, and to the establishment of the Swedish Mission Covenant Church (1878). The movement also was influential in its birthplace, Germany, where it had nationalistic as well as religious consequences, as religious emotions were easily extended from devotion to God the Father to loyalty to the Fatherland. The pietistic movement also indirectly impacted the direction of nineteenth-century philosophical thought, as it influenced three important post-Enlightenment thinkers: Immanuel Kant (1724–1804), Johann Wolfgang Goethe (1749–1832), and Friedrich Schleiermacher (1768–1834).

Beyond Protestantism. The mysticism and warm piety that were central to Protestant forms of Pietism also appeared in other religious traditions. In Roman Catholic France, for instance, a Jansenist movement that advanced the Augustinian emphasis on the need to experience the divine gained a popular following among the French masses. In eighteenth-century Judaism, Israel ben Eliezer (1700–1760), called by his followers Baal Shem Tov (Master of the Good Name), founded the Hasidic movement, which sought to move beyond ritual to a sense of union with God. Like Enlightenment thinkers, Pietists attacked ingrained systems of religious orthodoxy and promoted the rights of individuals. Pietism differed from Enlightenment thought, however, in that it prompted respect for biblical scripture and spiritual renewal, while the rationalism of the Enlightenment produced religious skepticism and secularism.

Sources:
Dale W. Brown, *Understanding Pietism* (Grand Rapids: Eerdmans, 1978).

Richard L. Gawthrop, *Pietism and the Making of Eighteenth Century Prussia* (New York: Cambridge University Press, 1993).

F. Ernest Stoeffler, *German Pietism During the Eighteenth Century* (Leiden: Brill, 1973).

SECULAR PHILOSOPHY

Cartesian Rationalism. The Cartesian Rationalism of the seventeenth century was fundamental to Enlightenment thought and thus to many nineteenth-century philosophies. Cartesian Rationalism was developed by René Descartes (1596–1650), a distinguished seventeenth-century French mathematician, who united algebraic and geometric mathematics by developing a method to transform algebraic formulas into plotted curves and to convert curves into algebraic equations. Before Descartes, algebra was the mathematics of discrete quantities, a method particularly suited to those who viewed reality as a composite of parts, while geometry was the mathematics of the spatial void,

suited to the Platonists, who viewed nature as a unity rather than as a collection of countable parts. Descartes' new method abolished this distinction, thus making it possible to view the world as a cosmic machine of interacting parts that act in harmony with each other in ways that can be comprehended by the rational mind.

Descartes' Proof of God. Although he was also an ardent Roman Catholic, Descartes was a true mathematician, trusting only what could be rationally proved by mathematical reasoning. His philosophy began with the dictum "I think, therefore I am." From this truth, which he considered to be self-evident, Descartes reasoned that as a thinking being he could conceive in his mind the possibility of a "more perfect being." According to Descartes, since his mind could not have produced such an idea, there must exist a God that placed this idea of divine perfection into his mind. From these opening axioms—Mind exists, and God exists—Descartes deduced that since, as a perfect being, God would not deceive, sense perceptions given to rational beings can be trusted to give humans meaningful insights into the real world. Thus, from a starting place of universal doubt, Descartes constructed a philosophical system that not only affirmed the existence of God but also expressed confidence that Nature, like geometric curves and shapes, could be reduced into mathematical forms.

John Locke. While Descartes' philosophical ideas were gaining influence on the Continent, in England an Oxford professor named John Locke (1632–1704) was developing a philosophical method known as Empiricism—a term taken from the Greek word for "experience." Unlike Descartes, Locke rejected the Cartesian notion that humans are born with innate ideas implanted in their minds. Instead, Locke insisted that the mind is like a blank slate at birth and that sense perception is the source of true knowledge. Like Descartes, however, Locke argued that the order of the world corresponded to the order of the mind and that absolute certainty could be reached by combining Empiricism with the Cartesian method.

David Hume. An eighteenth-century critic of Locke and Descartes was the Scottish philosopher David Hume (1711–1776), who argued that knowledge was much more limited than the rationalists claimed. For instance, notwithstanding Locke's claim that knowledge based on experience could be trusted, Hume insisted that the scope of knowledge is limited because humans cannot experience such things as cause and effect. For example, Hume argued that when billiard balls collide, human eyes can witness the movement of balls in predictable patterns, but this observation does not prove that the motion of one ball caused the motion of the other balls. Rather, in this billiard-ball experiment all that is truly observed with the senses is a series of phenomena that human minds have linked together by the mental concept of cause and effect. To Hume, the principle of causation (that is, every event must have a cause) was neither self-evident nor demonstrable by experience. Causation, he said, has no basis in observation; rather it is the result of mere mental constructs. Similarly,

Cartoon tracing Charles Darwin's evolution from a worm (Darwin Archive, Cambridge University Library)

Hume doubted the ability of humans to experience real things, insisting instead that the senses perceive only the attributes of substances and not the substances themselves. Hume's critique of the rationality of cause and effect and his insistence that humans cannot speak rationally about real substances challenged the philosophical premises of both the Cartesians and the Empiricists. His ideas also challenged the religious thinkers of his day by undercutting the traditional ontological and "first-cause" arguments for the existence of God.

Applied Science and the Idea of Progress. The Industrial Revolution and the advances in applied science that accompanied it persuaded many social commentators that the past was radically different from, and inferior to, the present. For growing numbers of nineteenth-century thinkers, history appeared to be the story of human progress. To these observers, the modern mind finally had learned to manipulate the forces of nature for human benefit. Steam power ended reliance on muscle power; electricity liberated workers from dependence on the sun; railroads

and the telegraph challenged the constrictions of time and distance; the discovery of germs and the development of organic chemical fertilizers reduced disease rates and increased food supplies, thus expanding the human life span. Although not all people shared equally in the benefits of the age, growing numbers were enjoying levels of wealth and comforts formerly known only to kings. To these people progress was not only real but part of the structure of the universe.

Origins of Secular Philosophies. The optimism of the age negatively impacted religious thinking in two fundamental ways. On the one hand, the acceptance of the idea of progress caused some people to rethink the relevance of religious views that had been passed down from less advanced times. In addition, the idea of progress encouraged many to turn to science rather than to religion to find solutions for human predicaments. Ludwig Feuerbach (1804–1872) expressed these sentiments in *Das Wesen des Christentums* (1841; The Essence of Christianity), when he declared that religions were man-made institutions that existed only to satisfy human needs. "Do you want to improve the people?" Feuerbach asked. "Then instead of preaching against sin, give them better food. Man is what he eats." Alongside Feuerbach, other social thinkers formulated secular belief systems that challenged the prevailing religious worldviews. Among the most influential of these new secular philosophies of progress were Utilitarianism, Positivism, Evolutionary Materialism, and Marxism.

Utilitarianism. Utilitarianism is a moral theory first developed by the English philosopher and social reformer Jeremy Bentham (1748–1832), who presented his views in *An Introduction to the Principles of Morals and Legislation*, written in 1780 and published in 1789. The centerpiece of this work is the principle of *utility*. According to Bentham, an action conforms to the utilitarian principle if and only if it promotes more pleasure or happiness than pain or unhappiness. Good laws are those that increase pleasure and eliminate pain for the greatest numbers of people; bad laws do the opposite. Good laws add to human happiness, while bad laws subtract from it. Since the aim of government is to provide "the greatest happiness for the greatness number," laws and customs that fail to increase pleasure should be discarded, even if they rest upon accepted traditional values.

John Stuart Mill. One of Bentham's disciples was John Stuart Mill (1806–1873), who from 1830 until his death championed the utilitarian principles of happiness, individual liberty, equality, and the primacy of reason. His major works include *A System of Logic* (1843), an ambitious attempt to define the methods of science and to demonstrate the applicability of these methods to social as well as natural phenomena, and *Utilitarianism* (1861), a classic defense of the view that the primary human objective ought to be the maximization of happiness for the greatest number of people. Two influential later works were *The Subjection of Women* (1869) and *Three Essays on Religion* (published posthumously in 1874). In the former, Mill argued that if freedom is good for men, it is also good for women, an idea considered radical for its time. In the latter, Mill asserted that while the universe could not be governed by an omnipotent and loving God, it is likely that a less omnipotent force is present in the world. This position satisfied neither his supporters, who expected him to express a more visceral agnosticism, nor his critics, who denounced any form of religious skepticism.

Positivism. While Mill was advocating Utilitarian principles in England, Auguste Comte (1798–1857) in France was developing a philosophy known as Positivism. Like Utilitarianism, Positivism invoked the name of science—as the sole legitimate source of authority—to advocate sweeping changes in social institutions. As a young man, Comte concluded that the human mind naturally passes through three main phases. According to his "Law of Three Stages," the immature thinker attributes the cause of things to the spirit world; in the second stage the mind appeals to philosophy and to abstract forces of Nature to find understanding; and in the third stage the mature mind gains understanding through the scientific process of observing and correlating the concrete facts of existence. Comte detailed the implications of his "Law of Three Stages" in a lengthy series of publications that include *Cours de philosophie positive* (1830–1842; Course in Positive Philosophy) and *Système de politique positive* (1851–1854; System of Positive Politics). In these works Comte argued that the history of humanity could be divided into three periods: 1) the age of theology, when human speculations were drawn from superstitions and religious prejudices; 2) the age of metaphysics, when the search for reality took the form of rational speculation unsupported by facts; and 3) the age of positivism, when dogmatic assumptions were being replaced by factual and scientific knowledge. Convinced that truth could be known only through observation and experimentation, Comte sought to create a science of society that would usher in the age of positivism. He named this new science "sociology."

Evolutionary Materialism. In 1859 the English biologist Charles Darwin (1809-1882) published *On the Origin of Species by Means of Natural Selection,* setting forth a theory to explain changes that have taken place in species of animals over time. Darwin observed two facts of nature: more organisms of all species are born than the environment can support, and no two organisms are identical. From these observations he deduced that within nature a struggle for survival must occur among unlike organisms, and that the organisms best fitted to the environment would be more likely than their less-suited competitors to survive, reproduce, and pass on their genetic makeup. Over time, species evolve through a natural weaning process that eliminates those organisms least fitted to the environment. This provocative insight had an immediate impact on how scientists looked at the natural world, and it also had a major influence on the emerging social sciences.

Social Darwinism. The individual most responsible for transforming Darwinism into Social Darwinism (or Evolutionary Materialism) was the English social philosopher Herbert Spencer (1820–1903), whose ten-volume *System of Synthetic Philosophy* (1855–1896) is an attempt to bring together biology, psychology, sociology, and ethics into a single grand evolutionary system. Central to this work were the modified Darwinian ideas that within natural (male-dominated) human societies: 1) more men exist than the market can support; 2) men are gifted with varying degrees of ability; 3) a struggle for survival, therefore, must take place among unlike men; and 4) if government and religious institutions do not interfere with the law of nature, the fittest men will survive, reproduce, and pass on their superior genetic traits, which will lead to social progress. Conversely, however, if "do-gooders" interrupt the natural-selection process by giving preferences to the less fit, Spencer argued, social stagnation or even racial suicide would follow. Like Bentham, Comte, and Marx, Spencer affirmed the idea of progress, but his "perfect world" glorified individual, not collectivist, goals. Moreover, like the other "scientific" philosophies of progress,

Karl Marx and Friedrich Engels, circa 1861, with Marx's daughters Jenny, Eleanor, and Laura

Spencer's philosophical system of Evolutionary Materialism reserved no place for the conception of God because God was not knowable as a "positive" fact.

Marxism. Marx rejected the possibility of a gradual transformation of society for the good. His socialist predecessors had called for holding property and means of production under control of society as a whole and distributing income equally to all, and they believed that the reorganization necessary to reach such goals could be brought about peacefully. Marx, however, insisted that such "utopian" thinking was both deluded and dangerous and asserted that "socialism cannot be brought into existence without revolution." From the German philosopher Georg Wilhelm Friedrich Hegel (1770–1831), Marx accepted the premise that conflict precedes progress. Unlike Hegel, however, Marx was convinced that humans are motivated primarily by their basic economic needs (food, shelter, and clothing), not by rational thinking. Whereas Hegel insisted that ideas drive history, Marx declared that ideas are rationalizations of economic impulses and that the engine of history is not the clash of ideologies but the clash of economic classes. According to Marx's theory of history, civilization began in a state of primitive communism (in which members of a group own all property in common and share equally in the fruits of their labors) and then had progressed through stages characterized by slavery, feudalism, and capitalism. Marx pointed out that each new epoch was preceded by class warfare: the successful protest of slaves gave birth to

feudalism; the successful protest of serfs led to capitalism. Then he prophesied one final turn of history; exploited workers would rise up to destroy capitalism and establish an advanced system of communism, which, Marx promised, would be characterized by a "classless society" and by the "withering away" of the state. Marx's call to arms was sounded in the *Manifest der kommunistischen Partei* (Manifesto of the Communist Party), which he wrote with Friedrich Engels in 1848, the year of widespread uprising throughout Europe: "The proletarians have nothing to lose but their chains. They have a world to win. Workers of the world unite!"

Das Kapital. In volume one of his major work, *Das Kapital* (1867–1894), Marx offered a detailed commentary on the causes and manifestations of the coming revolution. In the "Historical Tendency of Capitalist Accumulation," a section based more on theory than on research in primary sources, Marx asserted that history demonstrates "a progressive diminution in the number of capitalist magnates"; "a corresponding increase in the mass of poverty, oppression, enslavement, degeneration and exploitation"; and "a steady intensification of the wrath of the working class." Thus, Marx boldly asserted, by concentrating wealth in the hands of the few and by exploiting the misery of workers, capitalists were "digging their own graves" and preparing the world for the coming worldwide communistic revolution. Although Marx claimed that these predictions were based on science, in actuality his expressions were the words of a poet and moral philosopher who was more interested in proclaiming his understanding of truth than in investigating it.

Sources:

M. M. Bober, *Karl Marx's Interpretation of History* (New York: Norton, 1965).

T. B. Bottomore, ed. and trans., *Karl Marx: Selected Writings in Sociology and Social Philosophy* (London: Watts, 1956).

James E. Crimmins, ed., *Utilitarians and Religion* (Bristol, U.K.: Thoemmes Press, 1998).

Patrick Gardiner, ed., *Theories of History* (Glencoe, Ill.: Free Press, 1959).

Paul Johnson, "Karl Marx: 'Howling Gigantic Curses,'" in his *Intellectuals* (London: Weidenfeld & Nicolson, 1988).

Ronald H. Nash, ed., *Ideas of History* (New York: Dutton, 1969).

Ronald L. Numbers and John Stenhouse, eds., *Disseminating Darwinism: The Role of Place, Race, Religion and Gender* (New York: Cambridge University Press, 1999).

Richard E. Olsen, *Karl Marx* (Boston: Twayne, 1978).

Allen W. Wood, *Karl Marx* (London: Routledge & Kegan Paul, 1981).

THEOLOGICAL LIBERALISM

Origins. During the eighteenth century, Enlightenment thinkers were confident that the human mind could discern all forms of truth through the use of reason alone. To these thinkers the study of nature, not supernatural revelation, promised the most reliable answers to the fundamental questions of human existence. These scholars, who came to be known as "neologians" or "innovators," questioned the doctrines of biblical inspiration that had been articulated since the Age of Reformation. They also challenged the supernaturalism of Christianity in all its forms, including

The "Father of Liberal Theology," Friedrich Schleiermacher, delivering his last sermon, 2 February 1834 (Deutsche Staatbibliothek, Berlin)

Leading Liberal Thinkers. The theologian dubbed the "father of Liberal Theology" was Friedrich Schleiermacher (1768–1834), who was followed by later scholars such as Albrecht Ritschl (1822–1889) and Adolf von Harnack (1851–1930). According to Ritschl, true faith was derived from making "value judgments" about reality, not from intellectually assessing data about the world. For Ritschl the importance of Jesus was his value to the Christian community. If the community believed that Jesus was divine, that belief was what mattered, not any particular set of historical facts about him. Ritschl defined Christians as those who strove to organize humankind in accordance with Jesus' command to love one another. Self-giving love, not the profession of a set of doctrines, should be the individual's chief religious priority. For Ritschl, as for other religious liberals, Christian love transcends truth, so rational inquiry was essentially unnecessary. Also focusing on the ethical teachings of Jesus, Harnack asserted that the purity of the religion of Jesus had been corrupted as Christianity spread from its Jewish origins to become a world religion. The task of the theologian, Harnack insisted, was to return to the original message of Jesus, which had nothing to do with the theological controversies that produced the dogmas of the Trinity and the definitions of the dual natures of Christ. In *Das Wesen des Christentums* (1900; What Is Christianity?), Harnack summarized the essence of Christianity as including the Fatherhood of God, the Brotherhood of Man, and the infinite value of the human soul.

Criticism. The "Social Gospel" ideals of the liberal theologians aided the humanitarian movements for politi-

the historic Christian doctrines of the Trinity, the deity of Christ, the virgin birth, the miracles of Jesus, the resurrection, and the atonement. Historic Christianity underwent another round of criticism in the nineteenth century after the rapid expansion of international trade, recreational travel, and Christian missionary efforts brought Western Christians into closer contact with other world religions, which had their own highly developed ethical value systems. Knowledge of these traditions encouraged scholars to re-examine the relationship between culture and religion, to compare the similarities and differences between the various religious traditions, and to analyze critically the sacred texts of each. The new methods of textual criticism were applied to the study of the Bible as well as other ancient texts. One reaction to these assaults against revealed religion was a movement within the churches that attempted to redefine the essence of Christianity in ways to make it appear compatible with the prevailing intellectual currents of the times. This movement to salvage something of the Christian tradition from the assaults of the Enlightenment is known as Theological Liberalism.

COMTE'S RELIGION OF HUMANITY

Although Comte did not believe in God, he promoted the creation of a "religion of humanity," whose adherents would worship the sacredness of humanity itself. At the heart of this secular religion was a belief in the oneness of the human race. Influenced by his Roman Catholic upbringing, Comte also proposed that the religion of humanity should have a calendar of secular saints' days, a catechism, and a priesthood of scientists, with Comte himself serving as pontiff. Comte's church never emerged as a major institution; yet, the central ideas of Positivism—including the premises that nature is orderly and knowable; all natural phenomena have natural causes; nothing is self-evident; all knowledge should be derived from experience; and the methods of science can be applied to the study of societies—influenced the development of several disciplines, including history, sociology, and analytical and linguistic philosophy.

Source: Auguste Comte, *A General View of Positivism,* translated by J. H. Bridges (London: Trübner, 1865).

cal reform that arose in industrializing nations during the late nineteenth and early twentieth centuries. Some Christians, however, viewed such liberal redefinitions of Christianity as an assault against the historic faith. In the early twentieth century a group of "Neo-Orthodox" theologians emerged to critique the central ideas of the liberal thinkers. Their views on the shortcomings of Theological Liberalism are summarized in an often quoted statement by H. Richard Neibuhr (1894–1962), who bemoaned that Liberalism struck at the roots of Christianity by suggesting that "A God without wrath, led men without sin, into a kingdom without judgment through the ministrations of a Christ without a cross."

Sources:

Karl Barth, *Protestant Thought from Rousseau to Ritschl*, translated by Brian Cozens (New York: Harper, 1959).

Warren F. Groff and Donald E. Miller, *The Shaping of Modern Christian Thought* (Cleveland: World, 1968).

THE VATICAN COUNCIL OF 1869-1870

Challenges to the Church. Not since the Reformation of the sixteenth century had the Roman Catholic Church felt as threatened as it did during the second half of the nineteenth century. By the mid nineteenth century, many of the conservative governments that had allied themselves with the papacy following the Congress of Vienna in 1815 were threatened by revolutionaries who wanted to remake the established order. To many liberals, socialists, and nationalists imbued with the spirit of reform, the Roman Catholic Church appeared as an obstacle to progress. Equally disturbing to Christianity in general, and to the Roman Church in particular, was the spread of new scientific doctrines that questioned traditionally accepted truths concerning the age of the earth and the origins of life. Furthermore, the emergence of new approaches to the study of the past led many people, even in Catholic countries, to question the validity of historical dogmas and the authority of the Pope. Alongside these intellectual challenges were practical problems that confronted the papacy. Between 1859 and 1866, Italian patriots determined to unify Italy were able to secure four fifths of the lands once controlled by the papacy, leaving only Rome and its environs in papal hands. In the midst of these troubling times, Pius IX answered the anti-clerical forces that challenged the Church by calling of the Vatican Council.

Preparations. Also known as the twentieth ecumenical council of the Roman Catholic Church, the Vatican Council of 1869–1870 was the first such gathering held since the adjournment of the Council of Trent in 1563. The three-century interval between that meeting and the Vatican Council of 1869–1870 was the longest gap between councils in the more than 1,500 years since the Roman Emperor Constantine convened the first Christian council at Nicaea in the year 325. In December 1864, five years before the opening of the Vatican Council, Pope Pius IX (reigned 1846–1878) published his well-known *Syllabus of Errors,* a list of eighty modern ideas that the Pope considered dangerous to the life of faith, including

PAPAL INFALLIBILITY

The *First Dogmatic Constitution on the Church of Christ,* approved by the Vatican Council on 18 July 1870, includes the following language about the authority of the Pope:

On the infallible teaching authority of the Roman Pontiff

Therefore, faithfully adhering to the tradition received from the beginning of the Christian faith, to the glory of God our savior, for the exaltation of the Catholic religion and for the salvation of the Christian people, with the approval of the Sacred Council, we teach and define as a divinely revealed dogma that when the Roman Pontiff speaks EX CATHEDRA, that is, when, in the exercise of his office as shepherd and teacher of all Christians, in virtue of his supreme apostolic authority, he defines a doctrine concerning faith or morals to be held by the whole Church, he possesses, by the divine assistance promised to him in blessed Peter, that infallibility which the divine Redeemer willed his Church to enjoy in defining doctrine concerning faith or morals. Therefore, such definitions of the Roman Pontiff are of themselves, and not by the consent of the Church, irreformable.

pantheism, socialism, communism, liberalism, secret societies, civil marriage, and indifference to religion. At the same time, Pius began working with the cardinals on preparations for an ecumenical council. War between Austria and Prussia in 1866 and the subsequent withdrawal of the French troops occupying Rome and protecting the Vatican temporarily interrupted these preparations, but after the return of the French army in 1867, planning for the council resumed. Invitations were sent not only to Roman Catholic bishops and heads of religious orders but also to Protestant and Eastern Orthodox bishops. Since the invitations included the demand that all who attended should acknowledge the supremacy of the Pope, none of the non–Roman Catholics accepted the invitation. Secular princes, who had attended previous councils, were not invited, and for the first time bishops from outside Europe were included.

Purpose and Pronouncements. The central purposes for the council were to define and condemn contemporary "errors" that threatened the Church and to give further definition to Catholic doctrines. Many of the attendees wanted to give formal approval to two dogmas: the infallibility of the Pope in spiritual matters and the bodily assumption of the Virgin Mary (the doctrine that Mary's body as well as her soul ascended to Heaven). Papal infallibility emerged as the dominant concern of the council, and its final resolution was the greatest accomplishment of the Vatican Council. After great debate, the declaration was favored by a large majority, with 522 voting for the declaration and only 2 against. More than 100 other

Opening of the Vatican Council of 1869–1870 (Museo Central del Risorgimento, Rome)

bishops, however, abstained from voting. Papal infallibility was particularly controversial among French, Austrian, and German bishops, who were reluctant to allow a Pope to determine Church dogma without the concurrence of an ecumenical council, and among the American bishops who feared a negative reaction to the notion of papal infallibility in democratic America. The second issue was not decided because the council ended suddenly and prematurely, following the outbreak of the Franco-Prussian War in July 1870. The dogma of the bodily assumption of the Virgin was not formally approved by the Roman Catholic Church until 1950, when it was affirmed by papal bull rather than conciliar action.

The Work of the Council. Between its opening on 8 December 1869 and the final meeting of the full council on 18 July 1870, the Vatican Council discussed and approved a profession of faith and two constitutions known as the *Dogmatic Constitution on the Catholic Faith* and *First Dogmatic Constitution on the Church of Christ.* The profession affirmed traditional Catholic doctrines, including beliefs that separated Catholics from Protestants, such as the acceptance of the seven sacraments (as opposed to the two, baptism and holy communion, recognized by Protestants), the doctrine of transubstantiation (the belief that the bread and wine served at communion become the body and blood of Christ), and the belief in the existence of purgatory and in the power of indulgences. The *Dogmatic Constitution on the Catholic Faith* condemned the doctrines of rationalism that "plunged the minds of many into the abyss of pantheism, materialism and atheism," affirmed the authority of Scripture and the authority of only the Catholic Church to interpret it, and

forbade the acceptance of scientific conclusions that were contrary to doctrines of faith; it also included a list of anathemas for embracing condemned beliefs. The final and most important work of the Vatican Council was the *First Dogmatic Constitution on the Church of Christ.* This decree, which was promulgated by the Pope "with the approval of the sacred council," affirmed that because Christ had given Peter charge over the Church, Peter's successors, the bishops of Rome (who later became known as Popes), held primacy over the Universal Church. The decree also asserted that there was no valid appeal to decisions by the Roman pontiffs, thus affirming the superiority of the pope over ecumenical councils. The climax of the document was the declaration that the Pope, when speaking *ex cathedra* (in the exercise of his office), possesses the "infallibility with which the divine Redeemer willed that His Church should be endowed for defining doctrine regarding faith and morals."

The Legacy of the Vatican Council. In taking this action, the Vatican Council ended all debate within the Roman Catholic Church regarding the supreme authority of the Pope, both as the administrative head of the Church and as the custodian of the faith. This action made less likely future reconciliation between Catholics and the Eastern Orthodox and Protestant traditions. By rejecting the validity of State interference to Church affairs, the Vatican Council also sharpened the conflict between the Roman Catholic Church and the nation-states of the nineteenth century. It caused a minor schism in areas of Germany, Austria, and Switzerland, where opponents of the council broke from Rome to found the Old Catholic Church. The Roman Catholic

Church, however, emerged from the Vatican Council as a more tightly coordinated body under the authority of a single administrative and spiritual head. The confident and definitive pronouncements of the Vatican Council gave solace to Catholics who sought to defend their faith against the hostile forces of rationalism, materialism, atheism, and Protestantism, but at the same time it gave ammunition to those who charged that the Church was out of step with the modern world.

Sources:
James J. Hennesey, *The First Council of the Vatican* (New York: Herder & Herder, 1963).

Margaret O'Gara, *Triumph in Defeat: Infallibility, Vatican I, and the French Minority Bishops* (Washington, D.C.: Catholic University of America Press, 1988).

WEST MEETS EAST

The Catholic Missionary Impulse. Roman Catholic missionary work in Asia dates to the arrival of the renowned Jesuit missionary Matthew Ricci (1552–1610) in China in 1583. After impressing the emperor with his clock-making skills, Ricci eventually secured permission to remain in the imperial capital, where he was able to establish a Christian base and introduce Christian literature to the Chinese people. Like all pioneer missionaries to the East, Ricci faced the challenge of finding Eastern

equivalents for Christian terms and managed to introduce the Christian message in terms understandable to the Chinese world view. As long as Ricci's approaches to missionary outreach were followed, the Jesuit mission in China flourished. By the early eighteenth century, however, new missionaries to China reported to Rome that the converts of the Jesuits embraced a pagan form of Christianity. In a series of papal bulls, Rome ultimately insisted that missionaries must not accommodate the gospel to the "superstitions" of the Chinese people. Some of the orders sent from Rome angered the Chinese emperors, who threatened to banish all Catholics who refused to follow the rules established by Father Ricci. For the next two hundred years, the tenuous relations between the Church and Chinese state officials hindered the success of Catholic missionary work in China.

The Protestant Missionary Impulse. Just as the sixteenth century was a century of Catholic geographic expansion, the nineteenth century was a century of Protestant globalization. This era of extensive Protestant missionary outreach coincided with the colonial expansion of the West into the East, and at times the relationship between missionary penetration and colonization was hostile rather than friendly. For years the powerful British East India Company barred missionaries from

European missionaries wearing Eastern attire in China, mid nineteenth century

the lands under its control. Nonetheless, by the end of the nineteenth century European Protestant missionaries were widespread in less-industrialized regions of Asia.

Women and Ecumenicalism. Before the nineteenth century, Protestant efforts to export Christianity were largely financed either by the state or by a single religious denomination. Early in the eighteenth century, for example, a Danish king affected by Pietism sent missionaries to India. Similarly, various Protestant churches created missionary societies to export their particular brand of Christianity. The Church of England established the Society for Promoting Christian Knowledge in 1698 and the Society for the Propagation of the Gospel in Foreign Parts in 1701. Later in the eighteenth century, the Moravians and the Methodists also founded missionary societies. During the heyday of the nineteenth-century missionary impulse, however, the voluntary, ecumenical missionary society, rather than the state-supported or denominationally controlled institution, took the lead in spreading Protestant doctrines beyond the boundaries of Europe. To a greater degree than before, women played a major role in these privately financed, nondenominational efforts to spread Christianity. Women at home contributed their time and money to fund worldwide missionary activity. Overseas, they assumed teaching duties and preaching roles often forbidden to them at home. Thus, the missionary movement contributed not only to ecumenicalism among mainstream Protestant denominations but also to the feminist movement among Western Protestants.

The Spread of Protestantism in Asia. The individual most commonly recognized as the "father of modern Protestant missions" was William Carey (1761–1834), an Englishman born into an Anglican household and converted to Baptist teachings in 1783. In 1792 Carey founded the Particular Baptist Society for Propagating the Gospel Among the Heathen (later, the Baptist Missionary Society). The next year, Carey himself left England for India. During his lifelong career in India, Carey organized Christian churches and translated portions of the Bible into some thirty-five languages. His labors inspired many other Europeans to follow his example. In 1795, for example, the English Methodists, Presbyterians, and Congregationalists united forces to found the London Missionary Society; the following year the Scottish Missionary Society and the Glasgow Missionary Society were begun. In 1799 evangelicals within the Church of England started the Church Missionary Society. Four years later Protestants across Britain created the British and Foreign Bible Society, the first of many Bible associations with the purpose of supplying copies of the Bible to households around the globe. By the early decades of the nineteenth century, dozens of organizations were raising funds, training preachers, printing Bibles, circulating religious tracts, and sending missionaries to remote areas distant from their European origins.

THE GOD WORSHIPERS

One unexpected consequence of the spread of Christian teachings into China was the rise of a powerful religious movement that drew on Christian teachings but was not truly Christian. After coming into contact with Christian literature, a charismatic Chinese rebel named Hung Hsiu-ch'uan (1814–1864) proclaimed himself a son of God who was called to reform China. In 1846 he and a friend formed the Association of God Worshipers, a semi-Christian group that taught that all property should be held in common, that the sexes were equal, and that the state must prohibit prostitution, adultery, slavery, opium, alcohol, and the binding of women's feet. By 1850 Hung's followers included more than one million disciplined soldiers, who set out to make Hung the new emperor of China, launching the so-called Taiping Rebellion. In 1853 they conquered Nanking, making it their "Heavenly Capital." Their attempt to take Beijing failed, but they continued to hold Nanking until 1864, when the city fell to government troops. As the outcome became apparent, Hung committed suicide. The God Worshipers continued to fight sporadically, and by the time their movement was finally crushed in 1873, more than twenty million Chinese had been slaughtered.

Source: Jonathan D. Spence, *The Taiping Vision of a Christian China, 1836–1864* (Waco, Tex.: Baylor University Press, 1998).

The Impact in China. In 1807 the London Missionary Society sent Robert Morrison (1782–1834) to Canton. As the first Protestant missionary to China, Morrison enjoyed few immediate successes. Distrusted both by the Chinese and officials of the British East India Company, Morrison won few converts. His major achievement was working with another missionary, William Milne, to translate the Bible into Chinese, a task they completed in 1821. Significant Protestant inroads in China were not realized until four decades later. In 1839 a war broke out between England and China, when the Chinese government attempted to suppress the trade in opium, which was being sold by British merchants, who used their profits to buy tea for sale in Europe. This Opium War ended with a British victory in the Treaty of Nanking (1842), which gave Hong Kong to the British and opened five important ports to British trade. The treaty also allowed Protestant missionaries greater access to the interior of China. In 1865 J. Hudson Taylor (1832–1905) founded the China Inland Mission, an organization that accepted missionaries of all denominations. Through its influence, hundreds of churches were established throughout China. Many Chinese feared and resented the growing influence of foreigners in their country. In 1899 a violent uprising against foreigners, which became known as the Boxer Rebellion (1899–1901), took the lives of thousands of European missionaries and their Chinese converts before the Western powers succeeded in crushing the rebellion.

Asian Religions in Europe. Increased contact between Europe and Asia not only resulted in the exportation of Western religious traditions to the East but also increased Westerners' awareness of previously little-understood Eastern religious traditions. Thus, during the nineteenth century, comparative religions arose as a scholarly discipline, especially after the publication in 1847 of *The Religions of the World* by F. D. Maurice (1805–1872). Soon, the extensive and mysterious texts of Hindu and Buddhist scriptures were being studied in Western universities. After Max Muller's multivolume edition of Eastern scriptures (1875–1901) was published, Eastern concepts such as *karma, reincarnation,* and *nirvana* entered the religious vocabulary of Europeans. By the end of the nineteenth century, a growing minority of Westerners who were dissatisfied with the Judeo-Christian traditions was turning to the religions of the East for spiritual solace.

Sources:
Stephen Neill, *Colonialism and Christian Missions* (New York: McGraw-Hill, 1966).

Neill, *A History of Christian Missions,* second edition, revised by Owen Chadwick (Harmondsworth, U.K.: Penguin, 1986).

Jonathan D. Spence, *The Taiping Vision of a Christian China, 1836–1864* (Waco, Tex.: Baylor University Press, 1998).

SIGNIFICANT PEOPLE

GEORG WILHELM FRIEDRICH HEGEL

1770-1831
IDEALIST PHILOSOPHER

Education and Career. Georg Wilhelm Friedrich Hegel is often called the last great German Idealist philosopher; that is, his philosophy is based on the idea that underlying all historical experience is an abstract spirit transcending material forms. Born into an upper-middle-class Stuttgart family, Hegel began preparing for the Lutheran ministry at an early age. He studied theology at the University of Tübingen (1788–1793), where his friends included philosopher Friedrich Schelling (1775–1854) and poet Friedrich Hölderlin (1770–1843). During his student years, he became acquainted with and influenced by the writings of Immanuel Kant (1724–1804). In time, however, Hegel became dissatisfied not only with Kant but with the field of theology, preferring instead to study not religion but the whole of reality. After leaving Tübingen, Hegel worked as a tutor in Bern and Frankfurt until 1799, when an inheritance from his father gave him the financial freedom to begin his academic career.

He became an unsalaried lecturer (who was paid directly by his students) at the University of Jena, where he became a salaried associate professor of philosophy by 1805. In 1808 he became rector and philosophy professor at a secondary school in Nuremberg, where he remained until 1816, when he accepted the chair of philosophy at the University of Heidelberg. Two years later, he left Heidelberg to assume the chair of philosophy at the prestigious University of Berlin, where he taught until his death in 1831. Hegel's major publications include *Die Phänomenologie des Geistes* (1807; Phenomenology of Spirit), *Wissenschaft der Logik* (1812–1816; The Science of Logic), *Grundlinien der Philosophie des Rechts* (1820; Philosophy of Right), and his posthumously published *Vorlesungen über die Philosophie der Religion* (1832; Lectures on the Philosophy of Religion) and *Vorlesungen über die Geschichte der Philosophie* (1833–1836; Lectures on the History of Philosophy).

Hegelian Thought. Hegel's objective was to formulate a new way of thinking that would allow one to view the totality of reality, the human, the natural, and the divine. Like Kant, Hegel rejected the mechanistic, amoral universe of Enlightenment thinkers, insisting instead that a benevolent, impersonal God created the universe and controls it. Although Hegel was convinced that Christianity was the "absolute religion," he insisted that the divine was revealed not only at the individual level through the Incarnation in Jesus Christ but also throughout the course of world history. Unlike Kant, who divided the world into what could be known through reason and what could not, Hegel insisted that human reason can understand reality and, moreover, that reason and reality were one. As Hegel asserted, "What is rational exists, and what exists is rational." By this thinking, the events of history are not accidents; when properly understood, they are manifestations of the universal divine idea. While human conditions continuously change, Hegel believed, each change moves the world closer to the universal goal of history: the achievement of human freedom. Thus, history is the story of the progress of humanity toward true freedom.

The Dialectic Method. Hegel explained the ongoing, progressive path of history through his "law of the Dialectic." According to Hegel, every age is governed by a dominant idea, which he labels the spirit or the "thesis" of the age. In time, this thesis is challenged by a new concept, its "antithesis," which is incompatible with the "thesis." To resolve the conflict between the "thesis" and the "antithesis," a blending of opposites occurs, thereby producing a higher "synthesis," which becomes the new dominant idea, or thesis, of the next age. History consists of the constant flow of ideas and their opposites, which when reconciled, reach purer forms. The new synthesis does not come without strife, but conflicts commonly regarded as tragedies do not demonstrate the triumph of evil. They are necessary steps forward toward the universal goal, human freedom. To Hegel, however, the highest form of freedom was not the absence of self-restraint, for the true ethical unit was not the isolated individual but the state in which the individual lives. Consequently, the movement of history is not toward individual freedom but toward the freedom of the community as a whole. Therefore, Hegel's philosophy exalts the state because only through it can humankind find meaning and be truly free.

The Hegelian Legacy. Hegel's assertions have attracted the attention of many social thinkers. Following his death, his adherents became divided into left-wing and right-wing factions. On the left, Karl Marx (1818–1883) modified Hegel's theory of the dialectic to explain his views on the historical cycle of class wars and to argue for the historical movement of civilization from primitive communism, to slavery, to feudalism, to capitalism, and ultimately to advanced communism. Thinkers on the right expanded Hegel's reverential ideas about the state to justify nationalistic notions of blind obedience to government authorities. Still others, including Søren Kierkegaard (1813–1855), the founder of Existentialism, reacted to the popularity of Hegel's system by condemning the arrogance of viewing human actions as the unfolding of God's plan for humanity. Hegel's provocative insights significantly shaped the direction of modern thought among not only philosophers but also historians, theologians, sociologists, and political theorists.

Sources:

Ermanno Bencivenga, *Hegel's Dialectical Logic* (New York: Oxford University Press, 2000).

Patrick Gardiner, ed., *Theories of History* (Glencoe, Ill.: Free Press, 1959).

IMMANUEL KANT

1724-1804

IDEALIST PHILOSOPHER

Education and Career. Few thinkers have exerted so great an influence on the modern world as Immanuel Kant, a child of the Enlightenment who challenged the limits of pure reason. The son of a pietistic craftsman, Kant was born in Königsberg, East Prussia (now Kaliningrad, Russia). In school he studied Greek, Latin, Hebrew, and French, as well as mathematics and theology. At sixteen he entered the University of Königsberg, where he studied for seven years, developing his interests in science and philosophy. Following the death of his father in 1746, financial hardship forced him to leave the university without earning a degree. He found employment as a private tutor in the family of a pastor in the Reformed Church and in his spare time continued to study and work on a dissertation. At age thirty-one, he returned to the university, successfully defended his dissertation, and was awarded his degree. For the next fifteen years, he worked in the library and taught science and mathematics as an unsalaried lecturer who was paid for his services directly by his students. In 1770, at the age of forty-six, he was appointed to a regular chair of logic and metaphysics at the University of Königsberg, where he spent the next twenty-seven years teaching and writing his most significant philosophical works. Kant was a short, frail man with a deformed right shoulder, but he experienced good health until his later years. After retiring from his teaching duties in 1797, he continued to live and to write in Königsberg, until his death in 1804.

Intellectual Influences. In addition to the intellectual influences of his pietistic religious upbringing, the young Kant was affected by, but remained largely unimpressed with, the popular philosophies of his day: Cartesian Rationalism and Empiricism. Before reading Empiricist David Hume (1711–1776), Kant had accepted the prevailing eighteenth-century philosophies that embraced sense experience as the basis of metaphysical truth and asserted the ability of the rational mind to deduce the known from the unknown. After discovering Hume's criticisms of these Rationalist ideas, however, Kant announced that he was awakened from his "dogmatic slumber." If Hume were correct, he decided, the study of metaphysics—the division of philosophy concerned with the fundamental nature of reality and being—was a worthless venture. Kant therefore devoted the remainder of his career to building a critical philosophy that could counter Hume's skeptical arguments and restore the validity of metaphysical reasoning. In 1781 Kant published his influential *Kritik der reinen Vernunft* (Critique of Pure Reason), in which he addressed "What can be known?"—the fundamental question of epistemology, the philosophical study of the origin, nature, methods, and limits of knowledge. Kant called this exploration into human knowledge a "Copernican Revolution" in philosophy because it offered a radically different approach to the accepted way of dealing with sense data. According to Kant, one must no longer assume that "knowledge must conform to objects"; instead, he argued, "objects must conform to our knowledge." Kant meant that the starting point of knowledge is not external objects internally known to humans by sense data received passively by the mind; rather, the starting point is the human mind, which actively imprints pure forms (categories) on the sense data and thus makes sense of what one knows as objects.

Kantian "Structures" and "Categories." Like the Empiricists before him, Kant rejected the Cartesian concept of innate ideas. Yet, unlike the Empiricists, who considered the newborn mind a "blank slate" that achieved all its knowledge through the senses, Kant insisted there are two universal structures of the mind (time and space) and twelve categories (including such concepts as causality and existence) that are not perceived via the senses. The mind uses these structures and categories to organize the data received by the senses. Without these mental concepts, Kant argued, nothing is thinkable: sense data without the universal structures of time and space and without categories such as causality and existence are chaotic and unintelligible noise. Thus, Kant drew a distinction between the reality a person experiences and reality itself. Human knowledge does not involve knowing the essence of things; rather it involves knowing things as one's mind can grasp them. Insisting that there was no such thing as pure objective knowledge, Kant rejected the objective certainty of the Cartesians and Empiricists as mere illusions.

Religious Implications. The religious ramifications of this argument were profound. Since existence cannot be derived from experience but is instead a necessary, yet undemonstrable, category of the mind, there is no way to prove the existence of God or the human soul. Similarly, the mind cannot really conceive of the concept of eternity (the absence of time) because the concept of time is one of the universal structures of the human mind. In these statements Kant was not denying the existence of God, the soul, or immortality; he was denying that they could be known through reason. Consequently, he wrote, the traditional, rational arguments of theology for the existence of God should not be viewed as conclusive proofs but rather as speculative reasoning. Although Kant has often been suspected of agnosticism, this conclusion is not validated in his writings. In the preface to the second, 1787 edition of his *Critique of Pure Reason*, Kant stated that he "found it necessary to deny reason in order to make room for faith." That is, he demolished the arguments for the proof of the existence of God, not to destroy belief in God but to make belief possible. The same logic that demonstrates the inability of reason to prove God's existence also proves the invalidity of the counterassertion that God does not exist. To Kant, reason did not lead to atheism.

Critique of Practical Reason. In a response to the criticisms directed at his *Critique of Pure Reason*, Kant wrote *Kritik der praktischen Vernunft* (1788; Critique of Practical Reason), a work that addressed not the epistemological question "What can we know?" but the ethical question "What ought we to do?" Kant argued that while pure reason cannot prove God's existence, the idea of God is necessary in order to systematize knowledge. Kant insisted that the idea of God is not invented; instead it comes to all rational beings through practical reason, not pure reason. To Kant, practical reason is that sense of moral obligation that all humans are capable of feeling. Kant calls this inner voice of conscience the "categorical imperative." By *categorical* he meant "universal" (it applies to all humanity), and *imperative* means "nonoptional command." Kant argued that because humans can choose to obey the categorical imperative, they are free beings; that since the highest perfection that can be attained in this life is only partial, immortality must exist; and that since the idea of moral law is within all rational beings, a lawgiver who embodies the perfection implied by that moral law must exist. God is that morally perfected lawgiver. Hence, Kant insisted that the moral nature of humanity testifies to the existence of a divine reality, immortality, and human freedom. Kant's ethical theory rests on three insights. 1) An action has moral worth if it is done for the sake of duty. That is, one should act not for self-gain or even for altruistic reasons such as pity or compassion; one should act because it is the right thing to do and pay no regard to the consequences of one's action. 2) An action is morally correct if it is an appropriate action for all humans at all times. That is, what is fair for one is fair for all because moral law applies universally without exceptions. 3) Humans should act morally toward other humans, respecting them as autonomous beings who deserve the right to think and act for themselves and never treating another person as a means to an end.

Kant's Legacy. Kant influenced modern thought in a variety of ways. His works fostered the development of the tradition known as philosophical Idealism, which was advanced by Johann Fichte (1762–1814), Friedrich Schelling (1775–1854), and Georg Wilhelm Friedrich Hegel (1770–1831). Kant also provided insights that informed the theological thinking of Friedrich Schleiermacher (1768–1834). Moreover, his argument that there is no purely objective knowledge and that one has to deal with the world not as it is but as it appears has led to many modern theories in fields ranging from the physical sciences to psychology and literary studies.

Sources:

Monroe C. Beardsley, ed., *The European Philosophers from Descartes to Nietzsche* (New York: Modern Library, 1960).

James M. Byrne, *Religion and the Enlightenment: From Descartes to Kant* (Louisville, Ky.: Westminster John Knox Press, 1997).

Warren R. Groff and Donald Miller, *The Shaping of Modern Christian Thought* (New York: World, 1968).

Otfried Hoffe, *Immanuel Kant,* translated by Marshall Farrier (Albany: State University of New York Press, 1994).

Roger J. Sullivan, *Immanuel Kant's Moral Theory* (New York: Cambridge University Press, 1989).

SØREN KIERKEGAARD

1813-1855
EXISTENTIALIST THEOLOGIAN

Family Background. The youngest of seven children, Søren Kierkegaard was born in Copenhagen, Denmark, on 5 May 1813. Already fifty-seven years old at the time of Søren's birth, his father was a pious, well-educated, prosperous Danish tradesman who had risen from poor, farming origins. Despite his success, he suffered from bouts of depression and was fearful that God would punish him for his youthful sins by taking all of his children before they reached maturity. Of Søren's six siblings, all but one died young. From his father, Søren inherited several important features: the wealth that would enable him to devote his life to writing, the genetic disposition toward mental illness that brought him both suffering and insight, and a strict religious faith that stressed the seriousness of sin and guilt and the importance of individual accountability.

Early Life. Kierkegaard was a gifted man with a sharp mind and a twisted body, for which he was ridiculed throughout his life. At age seventeen he was drafted into the Royal Guard but then dismissed as unfit for military service. He enrolled at the University of Copenhagen, where he excelled in the study of ancient languages, philosophy, and theology and earned a master's degree in 1840. In the same year he became engaged to Regine Olsen, a young woman from an upper-class Copenhagen family. After experiencing another of his recurring bouts of melancholy, however, Kierkegaard decided that it would be selfish to marry. In 1841 he broke off the engagement and left Copenhagen for Berlin. Five months later he returned to Copenhagen and began a prolific writing career, eventually producing works of philosophy, religion and theology, psychology, literary criticism, and fiction.

Major Literary Works. A somber, unorthodox, and brilliant writer, Kierkegaard often used humor, satire, and parody to provoke. In 1843 alone, he published six books, including his first major work, *Enten-Eller* (Either/Or), in which he asserted that everyone must make a critical decision about how to live. All humans, he wrote, begin life as aesthetes, that is, as egotists who seek immediate sensory gratification. The decision to remain an aesthete, Kierkegaard insisted, would ultimately lead to despair because within the human spirit there is a sense of the eternal that cannot be satisfied by sensory experience alone. The despair that results from the inner conflict between what is temporal and what is infinite, however, is good, because this dread can motivate the aesthete to become ethical. To Kierkegaard, the ethical individual is the one who moves beyond despair and who chooses to enter the ethical plane, thereby finding meaning and fulfillment in fighting for a universal cause that one knows is good. Several months after publishing *Either/Or*, Kierkegaard produced *Frygt og baeven* (Fear and Trembling), in which he analyzed his guilt over having violated social norms by ending his engagement. The chief protagonist of this book is the patriarch Abraham. In the biblical story God asked Abraham to sacrifice his son Isaac, but after Abraham demonstrated his willingness to kill his son on the altar, God gave him a ram to sacrifice instead and returned Isaac to Abraham. According to Kierkegaard, the person of faith is like Abraham, who was willing to sacrifice his most prized possession, trusting in the absurd proposition that God is able to do the impossible. Thus, the wise are those who learn to renounce the things of this world and, through the absurdity of faith, trust God to restore their relationship with the world.

Contribution and Legacy. In his 1843 publications, thirty-year-old Kierkegaard presented themes that he developed during the remaining twelve years of his short life. A central motif in much of Kierkegaard's thought is the paradox that involves knowing the difference between being a Christian and living within Christendom. Disputing the teachings of German philosopher Georg Wilhelm Friedrich Hegel (1770–1831), who asserted that anyone with rational faculties could come to understand the mind of God, Kierkegaard insisted that God could not be known through reason but rather only through a faith that comes in the scriptures and in Jesus Christ. To Kierkegaard, one must either choose or reject the claims of Christianity, and this decision must be made on faith, because there is no historical evidence that leads one directly to believe in the God-man Jesus. For Kierkegaard faith is not reasonable; neither does it lead to a tranquil life. Instead, true faith embraces what the natural mind considers to be offensive and absurd. To have faith, Christians must suspend reason in order to believe in something higher than reason. Moreover, faith comes at a great personal cost, for it demands a life of self-denial. Forms of Christianity that do not demand sacrifice are not Christian, Kierkegaard asserted; they are merely forms of paganism. Thus, he denounced those who emphasize the light, joyous, communal aspects of Christianity and advocated a radical form of Christianity that stands opposed to the world, time, and reason while forever stressing the seriousness of sin and the responsibility of the individual to secure redemption through faith in the absurd. Because of his emphasis on the need to make a decision and commit oneself totally to it, Kierkegaard is remembered as the spiritual father of European existentialism.

Sources:

Steven M. Emmanuel, *Kierkegaard and the Concept of Revelation* (Albany: State University of New York Press, 1996).

David Jay Gouwens, *Kierkegaard as Religious Thinker* (New York: Cambridge University Press, 1996).

Bruce H. Kirmmse, *Kierkegaard in Golden-Age Denmark* (Bloomington: Indiana University Press, 1990).

KARL MARX

1818-1883
COMMUNIST PHILOSOPHER

Early Years. One of nine children, Karl Marx was born on 5 May 1818, in Trier, Prussia. Although both his paternal and maternal grandfathers were Jewish rabbis and Talmudic scholars, after a Prussian decree in 1815 banned Jews from the higher ranks of society, his father, an ambitious and successful lawyer, renounced his Jewish heritage and became a Protestant. At age six Karl and his siblings were baptized as Christians in the Evangelical Established Church. Nine years later Karl was confirmed into the church, and for a time he embraced the Christian faith. He was educated at a recently secularized Jesuit high school, and in 1835 he entered Bonn University, leaving after a year to enroll at the University of Berlin. He studied the classics and philosophy, becoming acquainted with the Hegelian "dialectic" system that explained history as a process driven by the clashing of contrary ideas. After neglecting his studies for radical student activities, Marx submitted his dissertation to the University of Jena, where academic requirements were more lax than in Berlin, and earned a doctorate in 1841. Unable to find an academic post, Marx became editor of a radical Cologne newspaper in 1842. After it was suppressed in early 1843, Marx secured employment in Paris as a journalist. Before leaving Germany he married his childhood girlfriend, Jenny von Westphalen.

Communism. In Paris, Marx became involved in the Communist League and met Friedrich Engels (1820–1895), who became his lifelong friend and frequent collaborator. He was expelled from France in 1845 and went to Brussels, where he was soon joined by Engels. Over the next two years Marx began to develop his theory of history and collaborated with Engels on several works, including their *Manifest der kommunistischen Partei* (1848; Manifesto of the Communist Party), which they wrote at the request of the Communist League of London. When the 1848 revolutions began, Marx returned to Paris just in time to avoid expulsion from Belgium. From there he went to the Rhineland, where he and Engels participated in efforts to establish democracy there. When the revolution failed, he was banished in May 1849. After returning to Paris, he was expelled from France, and in August he reached London, where he settled and spent the remaining thirty-four years of his life. In England, Marx was involved in revolutionary politics, helping to organize the International Working Men's Association in 1864, but most of his time in London was spent in the British Museum collecting material for his major work, *Das Kapital.* Marx published one volume of *Das Kapital* in 1867, and the remaining two volumes were published posthumously in 1885 and 1894, after Engels compiled and edited them from Marx's unfinished manuscripts.

Marx's Legacy. Marx viewed communism as the most advanced stage in the evolution of human society. He predicted that workers were increasingly exploited and impoverished by their capitalist bosses, the angry laboring class would rise up in violent revolution against their wealthy oppressors and create an advanced communist system in which a new classless society would bring about the "withering away" of the state. Modern scholars have questioned several of Marx's basic assumptions. For instance, some have pointed out that workers' living conditions produced by the Industrial Revolution were often no more deplorable than those they experienced in rural pre-industrial economies. Moreover, contrary to Marx's predictions, communist revolutions did not begin in the most industrialized capitalist counties. Other critics of Marxism have questioned the ethics of an ideology that leaves no room for competing belief systems and that embraces violence as the means to secure a noble end. Yet, Marx's philosophy inspired the creation of socialist parties in many European countries, and forms of it were institutionalized in two of the largest countries in the world, Russia and China. Both critics and adherents of Marxism agree that this nineteenth-century philosophy had a major impact on the twentieth-century world.

Sources:

M. M. Bober, *Karl Marx's Interpretation of History* (New York: Norton, 1965).

T. B. Bottomore, ed. and trans., *Karl Marx: Selected Writings in Sociology and Social Philosophy* (London: Watts, 1956).

Paul Johnson, "Karl Marx: 'Howling Gigantic Curses,'" in his *Intellectuals* (London: Weidenfeld & Nicolson, 1988).

Richard E. Olsen, *Karl Marx* (Boston: Twayne, 1978).

Allen W. Wood, *Karl Marx* (London: Routledge & Kegan Paul, 1981).

JOHN HENRY NEWMAN

1801-1890
CARDINAL

Early Years. Born into an upper-middle-class family in London in 1801, John Henry Newman was "converted" into evangelical Christianity in 1816. At that time he considered the teachings of the Roman Catholic Church to be heretical. The following year, he entered Trinity College, Oxford, from which he graduated with honors in 1820. Remaining at Oxford, he became a fellow at Oriel College in 1822 and was ordained an Anglican priest in 1825. After serving as curate of St. Clement's Church, Oxford, Newman became vicar of St. Mary's, the university church, in 1828. By this time he had jettisoned his youthful evangelical, low-church views for high-church Anglicanism.

From Anglican to Catholic. In 1833 Newman was among the first Anglican clergyman to join with John

Keble (1792–1866) in launching the Oxford Movement, a renewal effort to revitalize the Church of England by restoring the historical practices of the early Christian Church. For the next eight years Newman served as editor of *Tracts for the Times,* writing several tracts in this series, including the last and most controversial, "Tract 90." In it Newman challenged Anglican orthodoxy by providing a Roman Catholic interpretation of the Thirty-nine Articles, the official statement of the doctrines of the Church of England. Following the controversy surrounding this publication, Newman resigned as editor of the series and *Tracts for the Times* was terminated. Over the next four years Newman gradually came to the conviction that Roman Catholicism offered the truest expression of divine truth. In 1845, he left the Church of England and was received into the Roman Catholic Church. The next year, after deciding to become a Catholic priest, he left England for Rome, where he was ordained into the priesthood in May 1847.

Catholic Educator. Newman received a commission from Pope Pius IX (reigned 1846–1878) to introduce in England the institution of the Oratory, a religious community of secular priests who, in addition to performing pastoral duties such as celebrating mass and hearing confessions, are given enough free time to study, write, and teach (often at a school connected to the Oratory). After returning to England in late 1847, Newman founded an Oratory in Staffordshire, which was soon relocated to Egbaston, outside Birmingham, where he spent most of the remaining years of his life. In 1851 he was appointed rector of a new Catholic University of Ireland to be established in Dublin. Though a few students eventually enrolled, the school failed and Newman resigned as rector in 1858. Having already opened a branch of the Oratory in London, which like the Birmingham Oratory provided instruction similar to that received in English public schools, Newman proposed the establishment of an Oxford Oratory, a plan that failed after opposition by his former fellow Tractarians.

Catholic Writer. A bold and daring writer who seemed to relish controversy, Newman attempted to counter the English anti-Catholic propaganda of the period by writing letters to British newspapers under the pen name "Catholicus" and by publishing a series of apologetic sermons, *Lectures on the Present Position of Roman Catholics* (1851). In 1859 he became editor of a Catholic magazine, *The Rambler,* but two months later, after he wrote and published an essay that questioned the doctrine of papal infallibility, he was asked to resign. Later, after the Vatican Council of 1869–1870, Newman accepted its definition of papal infallibility and wrote a defense of that dogma in his *Letter Addressed to His Grace the Duke of Norfolk* (1875). Newman's best-known work is his *Apologia pro Via Sua* (1864; Apology for His Life), a spiritual autobiography in which he argued that reason alone is an inadequate guide in matters of religious faith.

Cardinal Newman. In 1879 Pope Leo XIII (reigned 1878–1903) made Newman a cardinal in the Roman Catholic Church. He continued his duties at the Birmingham Oratory until his health began to fail in 1886. Following his death on 11 August 1890, Cardinal Newman was praised by fellow Catholics for his unworldliness and humility. The Church declared him "Venerable" on 22 January 1991.

Sources:
Walter Jost, *Rhetorical Thought in John Henry Newman* (Columbia: University of South Carolina Press, 1989).

Ian Turnbull Ker, *John Henry Newman: A Biography* (Oxford: Oxford University Press, 1988).

PIUS IX

1792-1878
POPE

Early Years. The individual who would serve as Pope longer than any other man in history was born Giovanni Maria Mastai-Ferretti in Senigallia, Italy. As a child, he was bright but sickly, subject periodically to epileptic seizures. After receiving a classical education in Volterra, he went to Rome in 1809 to study theology and philosophy but returned home the following year because of political unrest. In 1814 he went back to Rome, where he sought admission to the Pope's Noble Guard. After authorities declared him physically unfit to serve, however, he entered a Roman seminary to study theology. Ordained in 1819, he was appointed the spiritual director of a Roman orphanage, where he remained until 1823, when he was sent as a church auditor on a mission to South America. After his return to Rome in 1825, he was appointed canon of the Church of Santa Maria and director of the San Michele hospital. In 1827 he was made archbishop of Spoleto. Four years later, when a band of four thousand Italian revolutionaries broke from the Austrian army and threatened Spoleto, Archbishop Mastai-Ferretti intervened, persuading the revolutionaries to disband and convincing the Austrian authorities to pardon the rebels and to provide them with funds to return to their homes. Following this display of leadership and diplomacy, Pope Gregory XVI (reigned 1831–1846) transferred Mastai-Ferretti to the more-important diocese of Imola, and in 1840 Gregory named Mastai-Ferretti a cardinal. In 1846, following Gregory's death, the cardinals who assembled to elect a new Pope were divided into a conservative faction that favored absolutism in ecclesiastical affairs and a liberal faction that favored moderate political reforms. In a close vote, the liberal leader, Cardinal Mastai-Ferretti, was elected the new Pope. He took the name Pius IX, and his coronation took place on 21 June 1846.

Administering the Papal States. During the early years of his pontificate, Pius IX established conciliatory policies toward the nationalists, who clamored for the political unification of Italy, though he himself did not support their revolutionary goals. His first major act was to grant amnesty to political exiles and prisoners in the Papal States. Unlike his conservative predecessor, Gregory XVI, Pius IX also announced his willingness to accept moderate political reforms, and in 1847 he established an advisory council of laymen from the various papal provinces in Italy, created a civil guard, and set up a cabinet council. He rejected, however, the more radical ideas of those Italians who demanded constitutional government and a declaration of war against Austria. Pius IX demonstrated his conservative leanings in his encyclical of 9 November 1846, in which he condemned intrigues against the Holy See, the spirit of sectarian bitterness, secret societies, Bible associations, false philosophy, communism, and the licentious press.

The Revolutions of 1848. The radicals were not satisfied with Pius's moderate reforms, and—as revolutions swept Europe in 1848—street riots forced him to accept a constitutional government for the Papal States, although he still rejected demands for war against Catholic Austria. Later that year, after his prime minister was assassinated, Pius IX and many cardinals fled from Rome to Gaeta in the kingdom of Naples, where he remained in exile until 1850. Then, after French troops restored order in his territory, Pius returned to Rome, by this point an avowed foe of liberalism and reform.

Italian Unity. Ultimately, Pius was unable to withstand the forces of nationalism. In 1860 all the territory of the Papal States except Rome became part of the new kingdom of Italy. Ten years later, after the withdrawal of the protective French troops, Rome became the capital of a completely unified Italy. The success of the Italian nationalists greatly reduced the temporal power of the papacy. The new government passed the Law of Guarantees (1871), granting the pope the rights of a sovereign (such as conducting his own diplomatic negotiations), an annual pension, and authority over the Vatican and a small district around it. Because acknowledging this law was tantamount to giving up claim to political sovereignty over nearly all papal territory, Pius refused to do so. (The papacy finally recognized the law in the Concordat of 1929.) Considering himself a prisoner within the confines of Rome, Pius IX retired to the Vatican, where he remained until his death on 7 February 1878.

Advancing Religious Authority. Although the Roman Catholic Church lost temporal power during the pontificate of Pius IX, under his leadership the papacy significantly advanced its authority in ecclesiastical matters. In 1854 Pius proclaimed the dogma of the Immaculate Conception of Mary, which asserts that as the Mother of God, Mary was pure from all sin, including original sin. This proclamation marked the first time a pope defined a dogma without the support of a council. Ten years later Pius IX challenged the liberal currents of the times in an 1864 encyclical that condemned sixteen propositions declared to be dangerous to the faith. Accompanying this encyclical was his well-known *Syllabus of Errors*, which listed eighty previously censured ideas that Catholics were instructed to reject. Some of the condemned errors included the heresies of pantheism, naturalism, rationalism, and communism. The list also condemned freemasonry, the idea that Protestantism was an acceptable form of Christianity, and liberal innovations such as the separation of Church and State, freedom of worship, freedom of the press, and public schools outside church supervision. In 1870 the Vatican Council called by Pius IX promulgated the dogma that "when the Roman Pontiff speaks EX CATHEDRA, . . . he possesses . . . that infallibility which the divine Redeemer willed his Church to enjoy in defining doctrine concerning faith or morals." Although some German, Dutch, and Austrian Catholics rejected this dogma and withdrew from Rome to form the "Old Catholic Church," this pronouncement of papal infallibility did not provoke violent reactions from state authorities, largely because—with the declining temporal power of the Roman Catholic Church—the papacy was no longer a threat to the sovereigns of nation-states.

Sources:

Edward Hales, *Pio Nono: A Study in European Politics and Religion in the Nineteenth Century* (London: Eyre & Spottiswoode, 1956).

Samuel William Halperin, *Italy and the Vatican at War* (Chicago: University of Chicago Press, 1939).

Michael Ott, "Pope Pius IX," in *The Catholic Encyclopedia*, volume 12 (New York: Appleton, 1911).

FRIEDRICH SCHLEIERMACHER

1768-1834
PROTESTANT THEOLOGIAN

Early Life. Friedrich Schleiermacher was born in Breslau, Lower Silesia (now Wrocław, Poland). His great-grandfather, grandfather, and father were all pastors in the Reformed (Calvinist) tradition. A decade after Friedrich's birth, his father, a chaplain in the Prussian army, experienced a pietistic awakening after coming into contact with a Moravian community, a German Protestant sect. He and his wife were so impressed with the Moravians that in 1783 they sent Friedrich to a Moravian school in Niesky, near Görlitz. There he studied ancient languages, mathematics, and botany, as well as acquiring an appreciation for the importance of a transforming, inner religious experience. When he was sixteen, he entered the Moravian seminary in Barby. A young scholar with keen intellect and great curiosity, Schleiermacher smuggled into his dormitory philosophical books forbidden by the Moravian schoolmasters and read them surreptitiously. In

1787, against his father's wishes, he left the seminary and entered the University of Halle, where he explored the teachings of the great ancient and modern philosophers, becoming particularly impressed with the insights of the German critic of rationalism Immanuel Kant (1724–1804). After failing one section of the examination to become a Reformed minister in 1790, Schleiermacher worked as a tutor for several years before passing the examination in 1794. Schleiermacher then was ordained and served for several years as an associate pastor in a Reformed Church in Landsberg. In 1796 he moved to Berlin to become a hospital chaplain. In Berlin, Schleiermacher was introduced to a circle of poets and philosophers that included Friedrich von Schlegel (1772–1829), a leading member of the budding Romantic movement. Schlegel encouraged Schleiermacher to begin his writing career, as a poet as well as a theologian.

On Religion. In 1799 Schleiermacher anonymously published his first book, *Über die Religion: Reden an die Gebildeten unter ihren Verächtern* (On Religion: Speeches to its Cultured Despisers), a Christian apologetic addressed primarily to young Berlin intellectuals who were dissatisfied with both orthodox Christian theology and the rationalism and moralism of Enlightenment thought. Schleiermacher argued that they were not rejecting true religion, for authentic religion was not a collection of dogmatic teachings, a Kantian system of ethics, or a philosophy deduced from abstract metaphysical reasoning. On the contrary, Schleiermacher insisted, true religion was a "taste for the infinite" that was grounded primarily in feelings and was only secondarily concerned with belief systems and actions. Few of Schleiermacher's contemporaries embraced this work with enthusiasm. Most Romantics disapproved of its Christian tone, while church authorities criticized its pantheistic leanings. Yet, modern scholars recognize that this work is the origin of provocative ideas that characterize Schleiermacher's profound and influential mature thought.

Pastor and Teacher. In 1802 Schleiermacher became pastor of a small congregation in Stolpe, Pomerania, where he worked at translating Plato's dialogues and continued writing poetry. In 1804 Schleiermacher began his teaching career when he became a professor of ethics and pastoral care at the University of Würzburg, a newly formed liberal institution that embraced students of all sects and included both Protestants and Catholics on its faculty. Later that year he accepted a call to become the first Reformed professor at the predominately Lutheran University of Halle, a position that he held until the school was disrupted by Napoleon's invasion of Halle in 1806. Schleiermacher made his way to Berlin, where he lived for the remaining twenty-seven years of his life, serving as a successful preacher at Holy Trinity Church. In 1809 he married a young widow, Henriette von Muhlenfels. That same year, he was appointed to a professorship of theology at the University of Berlin, where he became dean of the theology faculty in 1810. An ardent patriot and German nationalist, Schleiermacher called for independence from the French as the first step in achieving a unified Germany. He also advocated merging the German Reformed and Lutheran branches of the Prussian church, although this union, he insisted, must not be imposed by state authorities.

Major Works. During his years in Berlin, Schleiermacher also wrote his most influential works. The class lectures that he delivered between 1819 and 1832 at the University of Berlin were not published during his lifetime, but later they were reconstructed from students' notes and published in 1864 as *Das Leben Jesu* (The Life of Jesus). In these lectures, Schleiermacher presented Jesus as fully human, but distinct from all other human beings in his consciousness of God's presence within him. In his study of the Gospels, Schleiermacher stressed the differences between the Synoptic Gospels (Matthew, Mark, and Luke)—which were given that name because the are remarkably alike in structure, content, and wording—and the Gospel of John, which is arranged differently from the others. Unlike most New Testament scholars before or since, Schleiermacher argued that John provided more insight into the life of Jesus than did the Synoptics. His arguments that the Synoptic Gospel writers drew on two common sources, a narrative and a collection of sayings of Jesus, paved the way for future New Testament scholars to formulate the widely accepted "two-source hypothesis" that the Gospels of Matthew and Luke were independent works, each based on two earlier texts, the Gospel of Mark and a lost collection of Jesus' sayings commonly referred to as the "Q source."

The "Father of Modern Protestant Theology." In addition to his New Testament scholarship, Schleiermacher wrote his widely acclaimed *Der christliche Glaube* (The Christian Faith), published in two volumes in 1821 and 1822. In this work Schleiermacher developed more fully his idea that the heart of religion was the intuitive awareness of a power beyond humankind, without which meaningful existence was impossible. For Schleiermacher, Christian doctrines were important because they expressed a community's immediate awareness of God, but these historic verbal formulations were not eternal, unchanging truths that could be derived from rational knowledge. Following Kant, Schleiermacher insisted that humans cannot objectively know God in himself, but only as he is in relationship to humanity. To Schleiermacher, sin was the claim to self-sufficiency, and it is original in the sense that this tendency is common to all. Through sin, humans become alienated from God and come to fear him as judge, knowing that they are deserving of His wrath. Grace, however, is the antithesis to sin; it is the consciousness of being in harmony with God. Grace comes to believers through the redemptive work of Jesus Christ, the perfect being who fully realized the consciousness of God within himself, and through whom the community of faith becomes aware of its need for and its union with God. The

Holy Spirit, according to Schleiermacher, is the consciousness of God in Jesus Christ operating through the community of the Church, which itself consists of those in whom the consciousness of God is dominant. Schleiermacher's assertion that humanity is dependent, weak in body and spirit, and in need of forgiveness and grace is in many ways a restatement of historic Protestant Christian beliefs; yet, his approach to theological thinking was innovative because his starting point for constructing Christian theology was not the Bible, creeds, ethics, or reason but rather the living experiences of those who found redemption in Jesus. By interpreting Jesus as the bearer of a perfect God-consciousness, Schleiermacher attempted to insulate Christianity from the criticisms of the secularized intelligentsia of his day, not by appealing to Enlightenment rationalism or to Kantian morality, but by showing that religion is a universal human experience, which philosophy and science must recognize. For this contribution to religious thought, Schleiermacher has been labeled the "father of modern Protestant theology."

Sources:

Dawn DeVries, *Jesus Christ in the Preaching of Calvin and Schleiermacher* (Louisville, Ky.: Westminster John Knox Press, 1966).

Julia A. Lamm, *The Living God: Schleiermacher's Theological Appropriation of Spinoza* (University Park: Pennsylvania State University Press, 1996).

Edward T. Oakes, ed., *German Essays on Religion* (New York: Continuum, 1994).

JOHN WESLEY

1703-1791
FOUNDER OF METHODISM

Birth and Early Life. Samuel and Susanna Wesley had nineteen children, ten of whom survived to adulthood. John Wesley, their second son, was born in the small town of Epworth in Lincolnshire, England. John's great-grandfather, grandfather, and father were all clergy in the Church of England, as were his older brother, Samuel Jr., and younger brother, Charles. While John was still a toddler, his mother taught him to read, and soon he developed a great love for two books, the Bible and the Anglican Book of Common Prayer. At eleven he was enrolled in Charterhouse, an exclusive boys' school then located in London, which prepared him for entry into Christ Church College, Oxford. An avid reader, Wesley graduated in 1724, having studied the classics, science, theology, and history and having become proficient in reading the New Testament in the original Greek. He was elected a fellow of Lincoln College, Oxford, in 1826 and was awarded a master's degree the following year. After he was ordained an Anglican priest in 1728, Wesley returned the following year to Oxford, where he taught for several years. During this time he helped to organize a small group of students who committed themselves to the spiritual disciplines of prayer, Bible study, fasting, receiving the sacrament of Holy Communion, and performing acts of kindness, including caring for the poor and visiting prisoners. Critics gave this little group several sarcastic names, including "Bible moths," "the Holy Club," and "the Methodists" (because they practiced a peculiar "method" of piety). The third term of derision stuck, and the movement with which Wesley was associated was called Methodism.

A Spiritual Pilgrimage. In 1735 Wesley and his brother Charles volunteered to go to America as missionaries. Wesley later said that he left for America with three goals in mind: to convert the Native Americans to Christianity, to minister to the English-speaking Anglicans in Georgia, and to gain an assurance of his own salvation. Two years later he returned to England, having failed, in his estimation, to have achieved any of his goals. During this time he had come into contact with a group of Moravians, a German pietistic sect that taught a simple personal faith within a morally disciplined fellowship. Wesley had been particularly impressed with the courage members of this group demonstrated during a storm at sea, an inner peace that rested on a sense of an assurance of their eternal safety. Back in England, the spiritually depressed Wesley sought the counsel of a Moravian friend, Peter Möhler, who convinced him to continue to preach assurance until he experienced this faith himself.

The Aldersgate Experience. On 24 May 1738 Wesley attended a religious meeting in Aldersgate Street, London. At about a quarter before nine, while someone was reading Martin Luther's preface to his commentary on the *Epistle to the Romans*, Wesley felt his heart "strangely warmed." According to his later writings, this "Aldersgate experience" did not insulate him from temptation, doubt, and despair, but it did convince him that holiness was not obtained by human striving but by trusting in the grace of God in Christ. This religious experience shaped all his later life and work.

Itinerant Preaching. After George Whitefield, a fellow evangelical Anglican minister, convinced him to preach to coal miners out of doors near Bristol in April 1739, Wesley decided "The world is my parish" and began a life of itinerant preaching, holding indoor and open-air services in homes, marketplaces, entrances to mines, and chapels, as well as in local Anglican parish churches. During the next half century, Wesley traveled widely in England, Wales, Scotland, and Ireland. He felt called by God to organize the people he converted during his preaching tours into fellowship groups known as Methodist societies, but he did not start out with the intention of forming a separate church. By 1784, however, the American Methodists had become an independent denomination, and British Methodists were well on their way to independent status by the time of his death on 2 March 1791.

Publications. A prodigious writer and editor, Wesley produced some thirty volumes of theological, ecclesiastical, social, political, and even medical commentaries. His most important works include 132 published sermons (1730–1791), his *Explanatory Notes Upon the New Testament* (1755), and his hymn books, which include some hymns by him and some six thousand by Charles Wesley.

Sources:

Francis J. McConnell, *John Wesley: A Biography* (New York: Abingdon Press, 1939).

Bernard Semmel, *The Methodist Revolution* (New York: Basic Books, 1973).

Charles Yrigoyen Jr., *John Wesley: Holiness of Heart and Life* (New York: General Board of Global Ministries, 1996).

DOCUMENTARY SOURCES

Friedrich Engels and Karl Marx, *Manifest der kommunistischen Partei* [Manifesto of the Communist Party] (London: Office der "Bildungsgesellschaft für Arbeiter" von J. E. Burghard, 1848)—A call for the workers of the world to rise up against their capitalistic oppressors.

Adolf von Harnack, *Das Wesen des Christentums* [What is Christianity?] (Leipzig: Heinrichs, 1900)—A liberal theological work advancing the idea that the true essence of Christianity embraces the fatherhood of God, the brotherhood of man, and the value of the human soul.

Immanuel Kant, *Kritik der reinen Vernunft* [Critique of Pure Reason] (Riga: Hartknoch, 1781)—An influential philosophical answer to the important epistemological question "What can be known?"

Alexei Khomiakov, "The Church is One" (written 1844–1845)—An argument for the divine unity of the church under the guardianship of the Russian Orthodox Church.

Søren Kierkegaard, *Enten-Eller* [Either/Or] (Copenhagen: Reitzel, 1843)—The first major work by the founder of Christian existentialism, which implores humanity to find meaning in life by fighting for a cause that is morally right.

John Stuart Mill, *A System of Logic, Ratiocinative and Inductive, Being a Connected View of the Principles of Evidence, and the Methods of Scientific Investigation,* 2 volumes (London: Parker, 1843)—An ambitious attempt to define scientific method and demonstrate its applicability in analyzing social as well as natural phenomena.

John Henry Newman, No. 90 in *Tracts for the Times,* nos. 1–90 (London: Rivington / Oxford: Parker, 1833–1841)—An influential and controversial tract offering a Roman Catholic interpretation of the Thirty-nine Articles of Anglican doctrine.

Pius IX, *Syllabus of Errors* (Vatican City, 1864)—A condemnation of modernism identifying eighty heretical beliefs deemed dangerous to the Roman Catholic faith.

Friedrich Schleiermacher, *Der christliche Glaube* [The Christian Faith], 2 volumes (Berlin: Reimer, 1821, 1822)—A work widely regarded as the most important formulation of Protestant systematic theology since John Calvin's *Institutio Christianae religionis* (1536; Institutes of the Christian Faith); Schleiermacher's book rests on the premise that the essence of religion is found in human experiences of the divine.

Herbert Spencer, *System of Synthetic Philosophy* (London, 1855–1896)—A massive attempt to bring together biology, psychology, sociology, and ethics into a single grand evolutionary system, which begins with *The Principles of Psychology* (1855) and ends with the final parts of *The Principles of Sociology* (1874–1896); known as the "father of Social Darwinism," Spencer attempted to apply Darwin's biological theories to the social sciences.

Vatican Council, *First Dogmatic Constitution on the Church of Christ* (Vatican City, 1870)—The decree asserting the dogma of papal infallibility.

John Wesley addressing followers from his father's gravestone in Epworth churchyard after the Anglican pastor of the church refused to allow Wesley to preach in the sanctuary, 6 June 1742 (City Road Chapel, London)

CHAPTER TEN

SCIENCE, TECHNOLOGY, AND HEALTH

by JEFF HORN

CONTENTS

Sidebars and tables are listed in italics.

1751-1772
- Denis Diderot and Jean Le Rond d'Alembert's twenty-four-volume *Encyclopédie* is published in France.

1753
- British colonist and scientist Benjamin Franklin invents the lightning conductor in Philadelphia.

1754
- The Royal Society of Arts is founded in London.

1764
- English inventor James Hargreaves invents the spinning jenny, which he patents in 1770.

1769
- In England, inventor Richard Arkwright develops and patents a water-powered spinning frame to produce thread for the textile industry.

1772
- English chemists Daniel Rutherford and Joseph Priestley independently isolate the element nitrogen.

1775
- Priestley discovers hydrochloric and sulfuric acids.

1776
- Scottish engineer James Watt begins manufacturing his version of the steam engine, which he invented in 1765 and patented in 1769.

1779
- English inventor Samuel Crompton develops the spinning mule, which enables the production of large quantities of high-quality yarns and threads.

1780s
- Italian physician Luigi Galvani, a professor of anatomy who experiments with electricity and muscles, notices that frogs' legs contract if an electrical jolt is applied to them.

1783
- In Annonay, France, brothers Jacques-Etienne and Joseph-Michel Montgolfier inaugurate hot-air-balloon travel.

1784
- Englishman Henry Cort develops the puddling process for smelting iron.

* Denotes Circa Date

1784

• French chemist Claude-Louis Berthollet develops a method for chlorine bleaching of textiles.

1785

• British inventor and clergyman Edmund Cartwright invents the power loom; it is patented in stages over the next three years.

1794

• The first telegraph line, for transmitting military information, is set up between Paris and Lille.

• The National Institute is created in Paris.

• The metric system is introduced in France.

1798

• English physician Edward Jenner develops a vaccination against smallpox.

1799

• Scottish chemist Charles Tennant combines chlorine and lime to create a bleaching powder for use on textiles.

1800

• Italian physicist Alessandro Volta invents a means of storing electricity in a battery composed of zinc and copper plates.

• English scientist William Nicholson uses electricity to break water into its constituent elements—oxygen and hydrogen.

• English engineer Richard Trevithick constructs the model for a new, high-pressure steam engine, making possible the development of steamboats and railroad locomotives.

1803

• English chemist and physicist John Dalton develops an explanation of the atomic nature of matter.

1810

• French chef Nicolas Appert develops a technique for preserving food in tin cans.

1820

• Danish physicist Hans Christian Ørsted discovers electromagnetism.

1821

• In England, chemist Michael Faraday develops the principle of the electric motor and describes the fundamentals of electromagnetism.

* DENOTES CIRCA DATE

1822
- Joseph Nicéphore Niépce invents the heliograph, the first permanently captured optical image.

1823
- Mechanics' institutes are founded in London and Glasgow to provide training for artisans and the working classes.

1825
- English inventor George Stephenson develops an effective steam locomotive, based on his first prototype of 1814.

1829
- British chemist James Smithson leaves his fortune to found the Smithsonian Institution in Washington, D.C.

1831-1836
- English naturalist Charles Darwin sails on the HMS *Beagle,* a surveying vessel, to the Pacific Islands, South American coast, and Australasia.

1837
- English scientists Charles Wheatstone and William F. Cooke patent an early form of the electric telegraph.

1839
- French painter Louis Daguerre perfects his daguerreotype, the first practical form of photography.

1851
- An International Exhibition opens in London, featuring the Crystal Palace, a building in which more than thirteen thousand manufactured objects are displayed.

1855
- English nurse Florence Nightingale introduces battlefield nursing care during the Crimean War (1853–1856).

1856
- The first artificial dye is fabricated by English chemist William Henry Perkin.

1857
- Austrian monk and botanist Gregor Mendel performs experiments on heredity by hybridizing varieties of peas.
- French scientist Louis Pasteur proves that living organisms cause fermentation.

* DENOTES CIRCA DATE

1859
- Darwin publishes *On the Origin of Species by Means of Natural Selection, or the Preservation of Favoured Races in the Struggle for Life*, based on his observations during his 1831–1836 voyage aboard the *Beagle*.
- In Belgium, inventor Etienne Lenoir builds an internal-combustion engine.

1864
- Pasteur invents the process of pasteurization of wine.

1865
- At Cambridge University, Scottish physicist James Clerk Maxwell illustrates that light is an electromagnetic phenomenon.

1867
- Swedish manufacturer Alfred Bernhard Nobel patents dynamite.
- English surgeon Joseph Lister introduces antiseptic practices in hospitals.

1869
- Russian chemist Dmitry Ivanovich Mendeleyev formulates the modern form of the periodic table of elements.

1871
- Darwin publishes *The Descent of Man, and Selection in Relation to Sex*, focusing on the evolution of humankind and pointing out its physiological and psychological similarities to the great apes.

1877
- German engineer Nikolaus Otto, who built his first gasoline-powered engine in 1861, invents the four-stroke internal-combustion engine.

1879
- American inventor Thomas Alva Edison and English chemist Joseph Wilson Swan each develop a carbon-filament electric light.

1884
- In England, American-born inventor Hiram Stevens Maxim, a naturalized British subject, develops the first practical single-barrel, rapid-fire machine gun.

1885
- German engineer Karl Friedrich Benz builds his first gasoline-powered vehicle.

1886
- German engineers Gottlieb Wilhelm Daimler and Wilhelm Maybach produce their first automobile.

* DENOTES CIRCA DATE

1888
- German physicist Heinrich Rudolph Hertz and English physicist Oliver Joseph Lodge independently identify the link between radio waves and light waves.

1895
- French chemists and brothers Louis and Auguste Lumière invent a motion-picture camera.
- German physicist Wilhelm Conrad Roentgen discovers X-rays.

1896
- Italian physicist Guglielmo Marconi patents the wireless telegraphy.
- In Paris, physicist Antoine-Henri Becquerel reports his discovery of radioactivity during his experiments with uranium.

1897
- English physicist Joseph John Thomson discovers the electron.

1898
- French scientist Pierre Curie and his Polish wife, Marie, a physical chemist, discover the elements radium and polonium.

1900
- German physicist Max Planck defines the general principles of quantum theory.
- Austrian psychoanalyst Sigmund Freud publishes *Die Traumdeutung* (The Interpretation of Dreams).

1905
- German physicist Albert Einstein publishes his special theory of relativity while working as a patent clerk in Switzerland.

1909
- German chemist Fritz Haber develops a process to create synthetic ammonia.

1913
- Danish physicist Niels Bohr applies quantum theory to subatomic physics.

* DENOTES CIRCA DATE

OVERVIEW

The Enlightenment. The cultural movement known as the Enlightenment emerged in the late seventeenth century as a reaction against two dominant institutions: the Roman Catholic Church and the absolutist French monarchy of Louis XIV (reigned 1643–1715). Stressing the primacy of reason over faith, Enlightenment thinkers drew on the advances of an earlier European Scientific Revolution, particularly the great shift in the Western conception of nature that took place in the seventeenth century, when scholars began to abandon the practice of explaining the natural world by reading and interpreting the works of ancient writers such as Aristotle and instead based their theories on firsthand observations of natural phenomena. Enlightenment thinkers developed the view that the universe functioned like a machine and followed a set of laws that humans were capable of discovering. Their search for knowledge was wedded firmly to the goal of spreading existing learning as widely as possible, and their ultimate objective was to improve the human condition by elevating people's ability to understand and control the natural environment. These goals were the foundations for the greater interaction between science and technology that sparked the Industrial Revolution.

Isaac Newton. Although many thinkers made major contributions to the Scientific Revolution and the Industrial Revolution that followed, few were as influential as English mathematician Isaac Newton (1624–1727), who, around 1665, invented calculus, a branch of mathematics capable of explaining the physics of the universe. (Newton did not publish his methods for more than twenty years, about a decade after the German mathematician Gottfried Wilhelm Leibniz [1646–1716], working independently, developed his own version of calculus.) Newton's important investigations of optics resulted in new theories concerning the properties of light and color, as well as the reflecting telescope. Newton reconfigured the European understanding of the movement of heavenly bodies and developed three laws of motion, definitively overturning previous religious and scientific conceptions of the universe, which were mostly based on the concepts put forth by the fourth-century B.C.E. Greek philosopher Aristotle. Newton's explanation of the universe was standard in the scientific community until the breakthroughs in relativity

and uncertainty by physicists Albert Einstein (1879–1955) and Werner Heisenberg (1901–1976) during the first half of the twentieth century.

Avoiding Conflict. Newton's ability to avoid involvement in conflict between Christianity and the "new" sciences is one reason for his prominent place in the history of science and of Western thought. He argued that God was a sort of cosmic watchmaker who crafted the universe and that the laws of motion were the media through which God maintained the universe. Newton's discoveries and his religious perspective also seemed to demonstrate that the human understanding of the natural world could continually progress, an idea that was contrary to traditional Judeo-Christian religious teachings. Moving beyond old religious conceptions of the natural world was a major element of the scientific agenda during the Age of Enlightenment. Newton's ideas took many years to spread, in part because so few of his contemporaries could understand them. The educated general public had to wait until the early eighteenth century, when writers such as John Locke (1632–1704) and Voltaire (1694–1778) published popular explanations of Newton's ideas. While Newton's calculus, optical theories, and laws of motion percolated slowly through the educated strata of Western society, his religious views were more rapidly adopted by Protestants and Catholics who questioned religious authorities' claims to exclusive knowledge of God's creation. By moderating the potentially atheistic claims of cosmology (the science of the heavens or space), Newton's prestige helped to protect this fledgling science during the initial phases of the Industrial Revolution.

Technology. Although "pure" science made several important breakthroughs during the Scientific Revolution, the direct application of these theories and discoveries lagged far behind. Purely technological developments, particularly those related to industrial crafts, such as iron founding or clock making, and "practical" sciences, such as ballistics (used in military applications) or cartography (stemming from exploration, colonization, and trade), flourished independently from "abstract" scientific investigations, such as those of Newton or French philosopher-mathematician René Descartes (1596–1650), whose invention of analytic geometry united the previously separate disciplines of algebra and geometry, enabling mathematicians and scientists to express geometric concepts in algebraic terms. Until the outbreak of the French Revolution in 1789, science and technology—with only a few exceptions—remained fundamentally separate enterprises, as they had been in the Middle Ages. What ultimately linked the two was a growing insistence that experiments should test scientific ideas, a concept proposed as early as the seventeenth century, most notably by English philosopher Francis Bacon (1561–1626).

Diffusion of Knowledge. Compared to the eras directly before and after it, the Enlightenment was a period of relatively few scientific "breakthroughs." The eighteenth century was fundamentally a period in which ideas were diffused and the consequences of earlier scientific discoveries were explored. The culmination of these efforts was the *Encyclopédie* (1751–1772), the great collaborative enterprise of French *philosophes* (lovers of knowledge) headed by Denis Diderot and Jean Le Rond d'Alembert. A compendium of existing knowledge, this twenty-four-volume encyclopedia was published despite significant opposition from powerful individuals in the Church hierarchy and the French government. The *Encyclopédie* did more than spread learning; it also helped to rationalize and categorize existing knowledge. Other such projects of diffusion and organization included the work of Linnaeus and his followers, beginning in the eighteenth century, on the classification of plants and animals. The organization and publication of scientific knowledge gave the average person the sense that the improvement of the human condition was possible. The technological changes and industrial transformations that took place in the nineteenth century were driven by this belief in progress and had a concrete impact on the daily life of western Europeans and ultimately the rest of the world.

The Industrial Revolution. During the Industrial Revolution, which began around 1780 in Great Britain and soon spread to the rest of Europe, new machines and innovative organizations of production dramatically improved the efficiency of making goods. Practitioners of revolutionary technologies or modes of production acquired advantages in key sectors of industry and rapidly accumulated wealth. As demand for goods quickened, production bottlenecks encouraged tinkerers and experimenters to develop new mechanical solutions, thereby helping to accelerate technological improvements. Manufacturers who took advantage of these changes (as in the cotton-textile industry) had a competitive advantage over rivals. Industry was slowly revolutionized.

Practical and Pure Science. While the technological advances of the first decades of the Industrial Revolution were achieved with little or no input from "pure" science, during the early years of the nineteenth century, advances in that realm—which were often, but not always, applicable to industry—developed from a growing interaction among scientists, industrialists, and the state. No longer was science the province of gifted amateurs, particularly in

electricity and chemistry. As nineteenth-century scientists made new discoveries and explored the links between the various disciplines, they increasingly did their research and trained their successors at new scientific institutions supported by industry and the state. (For a time biology remained the province of talented nonprofessionals who during the second half of the nineteenth century developed the theories of natural selection and evolution by the scientific method of carefully gathering data and applying inductive reasoning to it.) The contributions of nineteenth-century scientists to technological advances brought the prestige of science to new heights, a reputation that lasted well into the twentieth century.

Technological Advances. During the nineteenth century, European investment in technical education for significant proportions of the population and scientific education for the elite helped to create a situation in which an industrial economy could flourish. Western nations increasingly used their technological advantages to acquire vast colonial empires and tied together their holdings with important inventions of the Industrial Revolution, such as the telegraph, the steamship, and especially the railroad. As the economy became increasingly global, the intervention of the state took on growing importance in the process of industrialization. While Western and Westernized nations expanded their control over non- or less-industrialized regions, there were also important shifts in the balance of power in Europe. Although Great Britain began the Industrial Revolution, other nations caught up with and, in some cases, surpassed British manufacturing capabilities.

The Second Wave. The Second Industrial Revolution, which began during the last third of the nineteenth century, took place mainly in the newly formed German Empire and the continent-spanning United States. Many of the scientific advances that sparked economic development were made in Germany and the United States, where educational investment and managerial innovations surpassed those of France, Great Britain, and other European countries. During this Second Industrial Revolution, scientific and technological advances were used to create more-efficient means of manufacturing all sorts of products that could be sold at prices affordable to a wide range of consumers. Important developments occurred in nearly every scientific field at the end of the nineteenth and early twentieth centuries, transforming human understanding of natural phenomena and contributing directly to industrialization. For example, scientific discoveries about electricity and radio waves had enormous commercial potential.

Health. During the late eighteenth century, advances in scientific understanding of the sources of disease permitted a drastic improvement of health care. The causes of illnesses such as smallpox, malaria, and tuberculosis were identified, and effective means to combat them were developed. Eventually, some of these diseases were virtually eliminated in the Western world—a result that would have been inconceivable without the input of scientific establishments created during the Industrial Revolution. Europeans in the early twentieth century lived significantly longer lives than previous generations, without fear of many crippling diseases and health disorders that had bedeviled Western society for millennia. As new scientific and technological developments continued to improve the health and material condition of humanity, however, other advances of the First and Second Industrial Revolutions greatly enhanced the killing capacity of human beings, as illustrated by the carnage of World War I.

TOPICS IN SCIENCE, TECHNOLOGY, AND HEALTH

APPLIED AND PURE SCIENCE: CHEMISTRY

Emergence from Alchemy. Many of the major scientific advances of the eighteenth century were in chemistry. Chemistry was originally the realm of alchemists, including Isaac Newton (1624–1727), who are often associated in the modern mind with the "mystical" search for the "philosopher's stone" reputed to turn base metals to gold and to ensure immortality. Yet, modern scholars have credited these alchemist/chemists with advancing chemical knowledge and contributing to the development of modern scientific methods and equipment. By the Enlightenment, chemistry had emerged as a discipline based on rational scientific inquiry. It also had a conspicuous and direct economic benefit. The various European states, along with individual manufacturers and merchants, helped to advance the development of chemistry as a science by demanding certain products and often providing the resources for systematic investigations into their development. Many "pure" scientists joined in the quest to develop gunpowder that was more combustible and did not smoke, new colors of dyes for textiles, and bleaches that would make the production of white cloth economical. The successful research of eighteenth-century chemists cemented the growing alliance among scientists, entrepreneurs, and the state, which in turn led to even greater advances in the nineteenth century. Practical investigations associated with mining and the production of textile dyes contributed to a body of knowledge that scientists could use to help in their explanations of the universe. For example, in 1803 John Dalton (1766–1844), a schoolteacher in Manchester, England, proposed a doctrine he called "atomism," basing his theory on the findings of French chemists Antoine-Laurent Lavoisier (1743–1794), Claude-Louis Berthollet (1748–1822), and Jean-Antoine Chaptal (1756–1832). Dalton's atomism was the beginning of modern atomic theory.

Antoine-Laurent Lavoisier, originator of the theory of "atomism," and his wife, 1788 (portrait by Jacques-Louis David; Metropolitan Museum of Art, New York)

Atomism. Experimentation with gases convinced Dalton that elements were made up of "atoms," which he defined as indivisible, and that substances were made up of varying proportions of elements. He devised a new system of chemical notation in equations (as in H_2O) and formulated physical laws to describe the ratios. Although atomism was accepted only slowly, by the middle of the nineteenth century it had revolutionized chemistry and transformed how Western cultures looked at the physical world. After decades of research into the relationship of gases and combustion, in 1774 English clergyman Joseph Priestley (1733–1804) identified a substance that became known as oxygen. Priestley figured out that in sunlight green plants use carbon dioxide and produce oxygen. He also ascertained that combustion in air results from oxidation; for example, he recognized that in fires the substance that burns is oxygen. Lavoisier expanded on Priestley's breakthrough, giving oxygen its name and realizing that all chemical reactions may be placed in a rational system composed of elements. According to Lavoisier, there were three basic chemical compounds: acids comprise oxygen plus nonmetals; bases are oxygen plus metals; and salts are acids plus bases. This new system of chemical taxonomy paved the way for vast practical advances at the end of the eighteenth century. Russian chemist Dmitry Ivanovich Mendeleyev (1834–1907) built on Lavoisier's work by creating the modern periodic table of the elements in 1869. After identifying substances in the eighteenth century, chemists of the nineteenth century began to comprehend their structures. The insights of Priestley, Lavoisier, and other chemists of the early Industrial era laid the foundations for chemical research into plants and animals at the molecular level, marking the beginning of organic chemistry. Undertaken in Paris by Lavoisier's successors and in the German-speaking world by Justus von Liebig (1803–1873), such research required a careful, systematic approach. Liebig established the model for the modern research laboratory at Giessen in 1825. His "hands-on" approach to teaching and his search for productive uses of scientific advances rapidly spread to other German universities and research centers. German predominance in European chemical research led to an economic advantage later in the century.

New Approaches. The findings of French and German chemists, including Louis Pasteur (1822–1895), revealed that to understand the nature of a molecule it is not enough to ascertain its chemical formula, which indicates only the kinds and numbers of atoms in that molecule. It is also necessary to discover the structure of a molecule, that is, to understand how its atoms are linked. Having discovered how to determine the configuration of molecules, chemists developed the ability to substitute atoms and transform one substance into another. In 1870 there were about fifteen thousand known organic compounds; by 1910 there were one hundred fifty thousand. The first practical application of the new science of organic chemistry was the discovery of synthetic dyes. In 1856 Englishman William Henry Perkin discovered how to fabricate the first artificial dye. Made from coal tar, a residue of the gas industry, Perkin's aniline dyes were embraced by the German textile industry, whose scientists developed more than one thousand different synthetic dyes before 1914. German synthetic dyes were so popular that they drove natural colorings from the mar-

ket, and dye prices fell by two-thirds. In 1913 Germany manufactured 90 percent of the dyes used worldwide. By making Germany the major manufacturer of lucrative synthetic dyes, German chemists formed such close ties with industry that they were able to attract the financial and institutional support for other sorts of research, which yielded dramatic new dividends.

Sources:

J. D. Bernal, *The Scientific and Industrial Revolutions,* volume 2 of *Science in History,* third edition (Cambridge, Mass.: MIT Press, 1971).

Eric Dorn Brose, *Technology and Science in the Industrializing Nations, 1500–1914* (Atlantic Highlands, N.J.: Humanities Press, 1998).

William Clark, Jan Golinski, and Simon Schaffer, eds., *The Sciences in Enlightened Europe* (Chicago: University of Chicago Press, 1999).

Charles Coulston Gillispie, *Science and Polity in France at the End of the Old Regime* (Princeton: Princeton University Press, 1980).

Ian Inkster, *Science and Technology in History: An Approach to Industrial Development* (New Brunswick, N.J.: Rutgers University Press, 1991).

James E. McClellan III and Harold Dorn, *Science and Technology in World History: An Introduction* (Baltimore: Johns Hopkins University Press, 1999).

Joel Mokyr, *The Lever of Riches: Technological Creativity and Economic Progress* (New York: Oxford University Press, 1990).

Mary Jo Nye, *Before Big Science: The Pursuit of Modern Chemistry and Physics, 1800–1940* (Cambridge, Mass.: Harvard University Press, 1996).

APPLIED AND PURE SCIENCE: PHYSICS

Electricity. The investigation of electricity was popular in the mid eighteenth century. In 1753 British colonist Benjamin Franklin (1706–1790) developed the lightning rod in Philadelphia to prevent damage from lightning strikes. In 1780 Italian scientist Luigi Galvani (1737–1798), a professor of anatomy in Bologna, noticed that frogs' legs contracted if an electrical spark was applied, a phenomenon he called "animal electricity." His interest was shared by Alessandro Volta (1745–1827), a physics professor at Pavia, who around 1795 proved that it was possible to generate electricity by connecting two different types of metal, later producing the first electrical-current battery in 1800. In England, electrical currents were run through substances such as alkalis or salts to examine their chemical composition. In 1800 engineer William Nicholson (1753–1815) was the first person to use electricity to break water into its constituent elements, oxygen and hydrogen. In 1807, using the same methods, English scientist Humphry Davy (1778–1829) announced his discovery of two new heretofore unknown elements, potassium and sodium, which he had isolated from compounds, thus showing how other elements could be identified. These developments linked electricity with chemistry, providing evidence that the various branches of science were fundamentally linked, an idea that proved extremely important in the twentieth century.

Electromagnetism. During the nineteenth century, scientists gradually uncovered linkages between electricity and magnetism. In 1821 Englishman Michael Faraday (1791–1867) conducted a series of deliberately planned investigations, discovering that a magnet needed

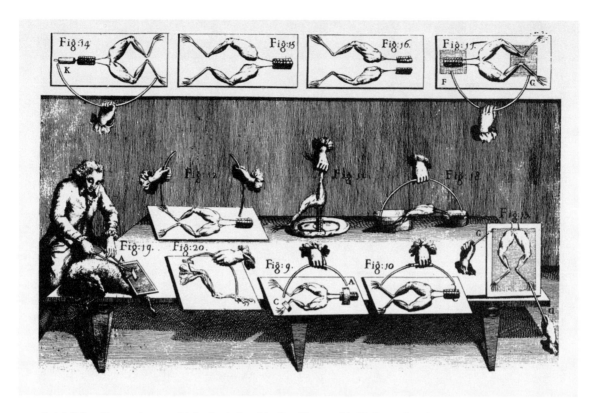

Luigi Galvani's experiments with "animal electricity," as illustrated in his *De viribus electricitatis in motu musculari commentarius* (A Commentary on the Strength of Electricity in Moving Muscles, 1792; British Library, London)

to be moved near an electric conductor to attract current. The results of Faraday's experiments were the basis for the new science of electromagnetism, as well as the foundation for the new electrical industry that emerged rapidly toward the end of the nineteenth century. In 1837 English scientists Charles Wheatstone and William F. Cooke patented a practical application of current electricity, an electric telegraph. In the same year American inventor Samuel F. B. Morse (1791–1872) patented a similar device. Morse also contributed to telegraphy by formulating an alphabetic code of dots and dashes. It was first tested in a long-distance transmission in 1844, when the first U.S. telegraph line was completed between Baltimore and Washington, D.C. The telegraph industry developed rapidly. London and Paris were linked in 1854, and the transatlantic telegraph cable was laid in 1858. Such rapid communication tied the world together as never before. The telegraph showed the potential of electricity, but most other practical applications of Faraday's findings in electromagnetism took more than fifty years to implement because of difficulties involved in working out effective systems to generate electrical current through mechanical action and questions of how to operate machinery using electricity.

Radio. Faraday's findings were rendered into convincing mathematical equations in 1865 by Cambridge University professor James Clerk Maxwell (1831–1879), who showed that light was an electromagnetic phenomenon. Electromagnetic oscillations give off potentially audible waves similar to light waves, which vibrate at much lower frequencies. Demonstrated conclusively in 1888 by two physicists working independently, German Heinrich Rudolph Hertz (1857–1894) and Englishman Oliver Joseph Lodge (1851–1940), this finding was the basis for radio communications. A practical wireless telegraphy emerged in the following decade, after discoveries by Lodge and Italian Guglielmo Marconi (1874–1937).

Electric Lighting. Maxwell's wave theory was put into practice by an international group of scientists, who made the use of electrical power a part of everyday life. In 1867 William Siemens (1823–1883) found that electrical current from one machine could stimulate an electromagnet in another. This dynamic principle of electricity was the foundation of the dynamo, which made possible the widespread production of relatively inexpensive electricity. This discovery stimulated a rush to find practical uses for it. In 1879 American inventor Thomas Alva Edison (1847–1931) and English chemist Joseph Wilson Swan (1828–1914) independently developed the incandescent light bulb. Two years later, Edison discovered how to transmit electrical energy over long distances without significant loss of current. It took decades to put this technology into practice, however, because networks of generators had to be built and linked together. Once the generators were constructed and the wires were strung, however, electricity gradually became available to almost everyone, regardless of where they lived. Not at the forefront of the scientific advances underlying the electrical industry, German industrial leaders were among the first to capitalize on

The following excerpts from Michael Faraday's *Select Researches in Electricity* (1839–1855) describe some of the experiments involved in his demonstrating the links between electricity and magnetism.

The progress of the electrical researches which I have the honour to present to the Royal Society, brought me to a point at which it was essential for the further prosecution of my inquiries that no doubt should remain of the identity of distinction of electricities excited by different means. . . . It is a fact, too, that many philosophers are still drawing distinctions between the electricities from different sources; or at least doubting whether their identity is proved. . . .

Notwithstanding therefore, the general impression of the identity of electricities, it is evident that the proofs have not been sufficiently clear and distinct to obtain the assent of all those who are competent to consider the subject. . . . I have satisfied myself that they are identical, and I hope the experiments which I have to offer, and the proofs flowing from them, will be found worthy of the attention of the Royal Society. . . .

The current produced by magneto-electric induction can heat a wire in the manner of ordinary electricity. At the British Association of Science at Oxford, in June of the present year, I had the pleasure, in conjunction with Mr. Harris, Professor Daniel, Mr. Duncan, and others, of making an experiment, for which the great magnet of the museum, Mr. Harris's new electrometer and the magneto-electric coil were put in requisition. The latter had been modified in the manner I have elsewhere described [*Annales de Chimie*, I: 77], so as to produce an electric spark when its contact with the magnet was made or broken. The terminations of the spiral, adjusted so as to have their contact with each other broken when the spark was to pass, were connected with the wire in the electrometer, and it was found that each time the magnetic contact was made and broken, expansion of the air within the instrument occurred, indicating an increase, at the moment, of the temperature of the wire. . . .

Other experiments were then made, in which all the battery was used, and its charge (being fifty turns of the machine) sent through the galvanometer: but it was modified by being passed sometimes through a mere wet thread, sometimes through thirty-eight inches of thin string wetted by distilled water, and sometimes through a string of twelve times the thickness, only twelve inches in length, and soaked in dilute acid. With the thick string the charge passed at once; with the thin string it occupied a sensible time, and with the thread it required two or three seconds before the electrometer fell entirely down. The current therefore must have varied extremely in intensity in these different cases, and yet the deflection of the needle was sensibly the same in all of them. If any difference occurred, it was that the thick string and thread caused greatest deflection; and if there is any lateral transmission, as M. Colladon says, through the silk in the galvanometer coil, it ought to have been so, because then the intensity is lower and the lateral transmission less.

Hence it would appear that if the same absolute quantity of electricity passes through the galvanometer, whatever may be its intensity, the deflecting force upon the magnetic needle is the same. . . .

The battery of fifteen jars was then charged by sixty revolutions of the machine, and discharged, as before, through the galvanometer. The deflection of the needle was now as nearly as possible to the eleventh division, but the graduation was not accurate enough for me to assert that the arc was exactly double the former arc; to the eye it appeared to be so. The probability is, that the deflecting force of an electric current is directly proportional to the absolute quantity of electricity passed, or whatever intensity that electricity may be.

Source: Michael Faraday, *Experimental Researches in Electricity* (London: Dent, 1912), pp. 1–2, 22–23, 28–29.

the practical potential of electricity. They quickly became the world leader in the manufacture of motors, equipment for the generation and transmission of electricity, and appliances such as lightbulbs and lamps. Although the United States was a much greater producer of electricity, German exports of electrical equipment were almost 300 percent more than those of the United States, as well as 250 percent greater than those of Great Britain.

Telephones. The development of the telephone is a good example of a process of technological invention that emerged in the mid nineteenth century. That is, scientific understanding of the theory preceded the emergence of demand. Inspired by the experiments of German physicist Hermann von Helmholz (1821–1894) with reproducing sound, Scotsman Alexander Graham Bell (1847–1922), residing in the United States, developed the telephone in 1875–1876, while exploring the nature of sound and speech. Bell filed the patent application for his invention first, but another American, Elisha Gray (1835–1901), invented his own version of the telephone at nearly the same time. In fact, the telephone used concepts and machinery available since the development of the telegraph, and Italian Innocenzo Manzetti (1826–1877) had demonstrated an earlier prototype in 1865. None of these inventions was of widespread practical use, however, until the invention of the switchboard, which was installed in 1878 in New Haven, Connecticut, to operate the world's first telephone exchange. Telephones were adopted more gradually in Europe and did not become widespread until after World War II.

Guglielmo Marconi with the 1896 version of his wireless, which could transmit radio waves for a distance of nine miles (The Marconi Company Limited, Chelmsford, Essex)

Sources:

J. D. Bernal, *The Scientific and Industrial Revolutions,* volume 2 of *Science in History,* third edition (Cambridge, Mass.: MIT Press, 1971).

Eric Dorn Brose, *Technology and Science in the Industrializing Nations, 1500–1914* (Atlantic Highlands, N.J.: Humanities Press, 1998).

William Clark, Jan Golinski, and Simon Schaffer, eds., *The Sciences in Enlightened Europe* (Chicago: University of Chicago Press, 1999).

Charles Coulston Gillispie, *Science and Polity in France at the End of the Old Regime* (Princeton: Princeton University Press, 1980).

James E. McClellan III and Harold Dorn, *Science and Technology in World History: An Introduction* (Baltimore: Johns Hopkins University Press, 1999).

Mary Jo Nye, *Before Big Science: The Pursuit of Modern Chemistry and Physics, 1800–1940* (Cambridge, Mass.: Harvard University Press, 1996).

THE FIRST INDUSTRIAL REVOLUTION: COTTON LEADS THE WAY

The Science of Observation. The scientific method of the eighteenth century was a decisive break with the past. Rather than accept the teachings of organized religion and deduce information from traditional learning, natural philosophers (who would now be called scientists) in the Age of Enlightenment based their conclusions on firsthand investigation of nature and natural phenomena. They used rigorous observational and experimental approaches to examine what had happened, even when they did not yet understand why it had occurred. As a result of this new scientific interest in the natural world, a large number of nonscholars of all social classes observed the heavens, experimented with machines, and classified plant and animal species. Their willingness to investigate, their ability to apply the new scientific method, and their emphasis on "what" rather than "why" all played a key role in the technological breakthroughs of the Industrial Revolution. In fact, the fundamental technological developments of the First Industrial Revolution, which began during the sec-

ond half of the eighteenth century and continued well into the next, were made by craftsmen in their workshops, not by university-trained scientists. Although scientific developments of the seventeenth and eighteenth centuries encouraged and permitted such tinkering, there was no direct link between the theoretical advances of the Scientific Revolution and the technology that sparked the Industrial Revolution.

Cotton and Technology. During the second half of the eighteenth century critical technological developments changed the manufacturing process so significantly that the transformation became known as the "Industrial Revolution." Most new machines or processes were invented in response to specific problems that slowed down production. In that sense, these advances were driven by economic "demand" rather than scientific "supply." The Industrial Revolution began in the textile industry, particularly in cotton-cloth manufacturing. Because cotton is stronger and easier to work with than wool, linen, or silk, cotton textiles are more easily produced by machines, and cotton was widely available. Cotton had an enormous potential market, greater than that for any other textile.

Spinning. The first block to expanding production was a difficulty in manufacturing enough cotton thread to keep up with demand. This problem was addressed by Richard Arkwright (1732–1792) with his water-powered spinning frame (1769), by James Hargreaves (died 1778) with his hand-powered spinning jenny (patented in 1770), and Samuel Crompton (1753–1827) with his spinning mule (1779). Crompton's machine combined both power sources in impressive fashion; a spinning mule did two hundred to three hundred times the work of a spinning wheel. This mechanization put pressure on weavers to keep up with thread production. In 1785 Edmund Cart-

A woman operating a steam-powered loom
(Ironbridge Gorge Museums Trust)

The Factory System. While before the Industrial Revolution much work was done at home, the use of specialized machinery led to the concentration of workers at one site and also imposed geographical constraints, primarily the need for a nearby power source, either water or coal. Thus, factories clustered near rivers or coal deposits, and industrialization was more regional than national. This new sort of production permitted increased division of labor and more efficient and more hierarchical management, thereby lowering manufacturing costs. As a result, more and more people could afford manufactured goods, and the demand for them increased.

Iron and Coal. Improvements in iron production made the rapid mechanization of industry feasible, and as in the textile industry, Great Britain led the way. The key to British predominance in iron making stemmed from their use of coal, rather than charcoal, in smelting—a practice that at first seemed a disadvantage. Iron makers preferred charcoal because, as a vegetable fuel, it did not pass on impurities to the smelted iron. In eighteenth-century England, however, widespread wood shortages made charcoal expensive, so the British used coal as a replacement fuel and got much of their iron from their North American colonies. The loss of the thirteen colonies after the War of American Independence (1775–1783) increased the demand for a way to prevent coal from creating impurities in smelted iron. Iron masters experimented until they discovered how to apply heat indirectly using a reverberatory furnace, which separated the coal from direct contact with the iron. This process, known as "puddling," was developed by Englishman Henry Cort in 1784 and perfected in the 1790s. Further improvements made coal-smelted iron equal, or higher, in quality to that produced with charcoal and allowed rapid expansion of English iron production in the late 1790s and even faster growth during the first decades of the nineteenth century, as machines made from iron became more and more essential to economic development.

Steam Power. The experiments of artisans and iron makers with coal and new machinery had an enormous impact on British technological creativity. The most important example was the steam engine. First developed in the late seventeenth century and improved over the course of the eighteenth century, the coal-powered steam engine ultimately replaced dependence on human or animal power. Since the first steam engines were highly inefficient, however, they were used only in places where cheap coal was readily available, usually to pump water out of coal mines. Several skilled British engineers, particularly those with experience designing and building precision tools, were responsible for improving the steam engine. In the 1760s John Smeaton (1725–1792), an instrument maker from Leeds, upgraded existing steam-engine designs and doubled their efficiency. Scottish engineer James Watt (1736–1819), an instrument maker from Glasgow, spent two decades tinkering with the engine, solving several technical problems. His improvements saved a huge

wright (1743–1823) responded by developing the power loom. Although for several decades the power loom did not produce cloth any faster than a weaver, one worker could run two, and later many, looms, thereby increasing production greatly. In the 1780s Arkwright greatly improved earlier carding machines, which combed and straightened cotton. Another important contribution to cotton processing came in 1793, when American inventor Eli Whitney (1765–1825) developed the cotton gin to get seeds and dirt out of raw cotton.

Bleaching. Finished yarn could be bleached with chlorine using a process developed by French chemist Claude-Louis Berthollet (1748–1822) in 1784. In 1799 English chemist Charles Tennant (1768–1838) greatly improved on a Continental European discovery by combining chlorine with lime to make bleaching powder that was easier, more effective, and cheaper to use.

Growth. Although wool production remained the largest textile industry throughout the eighteenth century, the cotton industry expanded quickly. British cotton production increased approximately tenfold between 1760 and 1800 and accelerated even more rapidly in the nineteenth century. By 1830 cotton goods constituted half of all British exports.

Sources:

Eric Dorn Brose, *Technology and Science in the Industrializing Nations, 1500–1914* (Atlantic Highlands, N.J.: Humanities Press, 1998).

Ian Inkster, *Science and Technology in History: An Approach to Industrial Development* (New Brunswick, N.J.: Rutgers University Press, 1991).

James E. McClellan III and Harold Dorn, *Science and Technology in World History: An Introduction* (Baltimore: Johns Hopkins University Press, 1999).

Joel Mokyr, *The Lever of Riches: Technological Creativity and Economic Progress* (New York: Oxford University Press, 1990).

The first steamship to cross the Atlantic Ocean was the *Savannah*, which made the voyage in 1819 taking twenty-eight days, about the same amount of time as the same journey aboard a sailing ship. Because a steamship required coal to fuel its boilers, it was more expensive to operate than a sailing ship, and thus there was little incentive to abandon sail for steam. In 1837, however, British engineer Isambard Kingdom Brunel (1806–1859) designed *Great Western*, which was not only the largest ship in the world but also the fastest. It was capable of transporting 148 passengers at an average speed of 9 knots. On its maiden voyage in 1838, the *Great Western* took fifteen days to sail from Bristol to New York and fourteen days for its return voyage, half the time of the same journey under sail. It became the first steamship with regular transatlantic passenger routes, remaining in service until 1856. Like earlier steamships, the *Great Western* was made of wood and propelled by wooden paddles. Brunel's next steamship, the *Great Britain* (1843), had an iron hull and was the first transatlantic vessel equipped with a screw propeller, an innovation that revolutionized ocean travel by making it faster and more fuel efficient. Larger than the *Great Western*, the *Great Britain* could reach speeds of 14.5 knots and remained in service until 1884.

Early steamships had to stop periodically to take on more fuel. With his next design, the *Great Eastern* (1858; originally the *Leviathan*), Brunel attempted to solve the problem by building a ship five times larger than any ship in existence. Capable of carrying enough coal to take it from England to Australia without stops for refueling, the iron-hulled *Great Eastern* had two paddle wheels in addition to its screw propeller and was capable of carrying 4,000 passengers. The *Great Eastern* was so large that its passenger accommodations and cargo holds were never completely filled, and it was never as fuel efficient as Brunel had hoped. In 1864 it was sold to the company formed to lay the first transatlantic telegraph cable. Like all early steamships, these vessels were also equipped with sails, so that on windy days they could turn off the engines to save on fuel.

Source: L. T. C. Rolt, *Isambard Kingdom Brunel: A Biography* (London: Longmans, Green, 1957).

pressure to run steam-powered vehicles. In 1800 Englishman Richard Trevithick (1771–1833) developed a smaller, high-pressure steam engine powerful enough for steamboats and railroad locomotives, the most important advances in transportation of the early industrial era.

Railroads. Using Trevithick's high-pressure steam engine, which was constantly improved by talented British engineers, the railroad emerged as a viable technology in 1814, when steam locomotives were used to haul coal at mines. The inventor of locomotives for several mines was George Stephenson (1782–1848), who in 1825 designed the *Active* (later renamed *Locomotion*), which pulled the first passenger train from Darlington to Stockton at a speed of fifteen miles per hour. In 1829 Stephenson's *Rocket* reached thirty-six miles per hour, wining a race to determine which locomotive would be used on the new rail line between Liverpool and Manchester, which opened in 1830. In its first year this line carried more than four hundred thousand passengers, making the transportation of people more profitable than carrying freight, a situation that existed until the 1850s. The financial success of this line, in the heart of the rapidly industrializing region of Lancashire, spurred new railroad building. Within twenty years a web of railroad tracks traversed the British Isles; other networks spread rapidly through western Europe and North America. By 1870 extensive railroad systems covered most of the European continent, as well as the United States, Canada, Australia, and India. On the eve of World War I (1914–1918) railroads tied together disparate parts of the world, creating the beginnings of global economic structure. As the maximum

A sawmill powered by one of Watt's steam engines
(Ironbridge Gorge Museums Trust)

amount of coal and permitted the engine to be moved. British entrepreneurs and craftsmen rapidly adapted the version of the engine Watt perfected in 1778 to run all sorts of industrial machines. Constantly improved, the steam engine was essential to industrial mechanization and to the emergence of the factory system. Despite their mobility, Watt's engines were still too large and produced too little speed of the railroad train increased from fifty miles per hour in 1850 to nearly one hundred miles per hour by 1914, so too did the pace of modern life.

Economic and Social Effects. Railroads lowered the cost of transporting heavy goods, allowing remote areas to become part of a global economy. Railroads carried manufactured goods and raw materials more easily and more cheaply than ever before. As markets widened and production costs fell, larger factories could be built, allowing greater potential profits. The ease and relative affordability of railroad transportation allowed industrialists to build factories farther away from sources of raw materials and closer to consumers. As a result, cities grew, and in many industrialized countries the urban working class replaced farmers as the largest single occupational group.

Sources:
Eric Dorn Brose, *Technology and Science in the Industrializing Nations, 1500–1914* (Atlantic Highlands, N.J.: Humanities Press, 1998).

Ian Inkster, *Science and Technology in History: An Approach to Industrial Development* (New Brunswick, N.J.: Rutgers University Press, 1991).

James E. McClellan III and Harold Dorn, *Science and Technology in World History: An Introduction* (Baltimore: Johns Hopkins University Press, 1999).

Joel Mokyr, *The Lever of Riches: Technological Creativity and Economic Progress* (New York: Oxford University Press, 1990).

THE FIRST INDUSTRIAL REVOLUTION: WHY IT STARTED IN BRITAIN

British Dominance. The creation and spread of the modern factory system that began within the British textile industry and later spread to other English industries was a tangible sign of a future Europe-wide Industrial Revolution. As the factory system spread gradually through England, British manufactured goods tended to be cheaper than those manufactured on the Continent and in many cases better made. During the first half of the nineteenth century the British dominated the market for consumer goods produced in factories. Other countries, notably France, the Netherlands, and what later became Belgium, had many of the same social, economic, and technological preconditions for industrialization; however, Britain had many important advantages. Rapid population growth provided plenty of workers and a growing demand for manufactured goods. In terms of natural resources, Britain had a productive agricultural sector, large deposits of high-quality iron and coal, and readily available running water to power machines and facilitate transportation. (No place in Great Britain is more than seventy miles from the sea or more than thirty miles from a navigable river.) The surrounding seas and a relatively stable government protected the British Isles from the destruction of lives and property associated with events such as the revolutionary and Napoleonic wars that devastated the Continent during the late eighteenth and early nineteenth centuries, thereby encouraging investment in British industry. British colonies also furnished raw materials and markets. Britain had been a leading mercantile nation for centuries and had significant capital and institutions—such as the Bank of England, established in 1694—in place to manage a new industrial economy. British workers were educated and well disciplined. British science was no more advanced than that of its Continental rivals, but their technology gave the British an advantage, particularly in their productive use of coal, which benefited metallurgy and machine building. Through decades of trial and error, British artisans had acquired skills in burning coal that could not be passed easily to competitors. The same methodical experimentation carried over into technological advances. British craftsmen excelled at taking other people's often rudimentary ideas and tinkering with them until they could be applied profitably.

British Labor. Because it was relatively well educated and possessed many craft skills, the British labor force played a key role in industrialization, adopting innovations in technology and in the organization of production far more systematically than factory workers on the other side of the English Channel. Generally more disciplined and better educated than Continental workers, British labor also adapted to the time clock and the demands of the machine better than their counterparts during the era of the French Revolution and the Napoleonic regime (1789–1815). In Britain the willingness of the elite to invest in machines and the presence of a large, skilled labor force desperate for jobs were important reasons for the British lead in productivity during the early industrial era.

Accomplishments. In scientific, technological, and economic terms, Britain dominated the First Industrial Revolution as no other relatively small country ever had dominated an era before. By 1841 nearly 50 percent of the British population worked in industry, and by 1860 these workers produced 20 percent of all industrial goods in the world, up from 2 percent in 1750. Britain furnished half the world's iron and cotton textiles, and two-thirds of the coal used worldwide came from British mines. Adjusting for inflation, the gross national product (GNP) of Britain increased fourfold between 1780 and 1850. As Great Britain emerged as the "workshop of the world," its standard of living increased about 75 percent during the same period. Despite heavy emigration and national disasters such as the Irish Potato Famine of the 1840s, the population of the British Isles grew from 9 million in 1780 to 21 million in 1851. Much of this population growth was in the cities; in the 1840s Great Britain became the first country to have more than half of its people living in urban areas.

The Crystal Palace. Britain displayed its dominance in 1851 at an international exhibition in London. It was housed in the Crystal Palace, constructed specifically for the event from glass and iron. More than one-third of a mile in length and towering over the majestic trees in the park, this structure could not have been built twenty years earlier, thus highlighting the rapid progress of British technological capabilities and presaging the emergence of the skyscraper later in the century, after steel became economical enough for widespread use in building construction. Most of the more than 6 million visitors, nearly 30 percent of the British population, to the "Exhibition of the Works of Industry of All Nations" arrived by train, another British technological marvel. After the exhibition, the Crystal Palace was dismantled and re-erected in Sydenham, where it served as an architecture museum until it was destroyed by fire in 1936.

Change. By 1851 the end of British manufacturing dominance was already in sight. Many British visitors at the Crystal Palace were startled by the high quality and reasonable prices of manufactured goods and luxury items from the Continent and the United States. Recognizing the major effect of advanced scientific knowledge and technological ability on economic development, other countries had begun to industrialize, some following the British model. Moreover, the trained scientist was beginning to overshadow the amateur tinkerer. (The first recorded use of the English word *scientist* occurred in 1840.) After 1850, scientists working for entrepreneurs, universities, or directly for the state, dominated industry by applying the advances of science to the needs of manufacturing.

Sources:

J. D. Bernal, *The Scientific and Industrial Revolutions,* volume 2 of *Science in History,* third edition (Cambridge, Mass.: MIT Press, 1971).

Eric Dorn Brose, *Technology and Science in the Industrializing Nations, 1500–1914* (Atlantic Highlands, N.J.: Humanities Press, 1998).

William Clark, Jan Golinski, and Simon Schaffer, eds., *The Sciences in Enlightened Europe* (Chicago: University of Chicago Press, 1999).

Charles Coulston Gillispie, *Science and Polity in France at the End of the Old Regime* (Princeton: Princeton University Press, 1980).

Ian Inkster, *Science and Technology in History: An Approach to Industrial Development* (New Brunswick, N.J.: Rutgers University Press, 1991).

James E. McClellan III and Harold Dorn, *Science and Technology in World History: An Introduction* (Baltimore: Johns Hopkins University Press, 1999).

Joel Mokyr, *The Lever of Riches: Technological Creativity and Economic Progress* (New York: Oxford University Press, 1990).

Mary Jo Nye, *Before Big Science: The Pursuit of Modern Chemistry and Physics, 1800–1940* (Cambridge, Mass.: Harvard University Press, 1996).

GOVERNMENT AND NEW TECHNOLOGIES

Rights to Advanced Technologies. During the industrial age, governments wanted to preserve their national advantages in machinery, worker expertise, and scientific knowledge. Individuals or groups who developed new techniques and new, or more-efficient, machines wanted to maintain their exclusive rights to their inventions while also profiting from them. Because the scientific community was international in scope, however, researchers in different parts of the world sometimes reached similar conclusions at almost the same time. Because interests of governments, inventors, and scientists were often in conflict and because of differences among nations and regions in resources and infrastructures, some scientific advances or technological innovations spread more rapidly and more widely than others, affecting not only a nation's economy but also its military preparedness.

Patents. Throughout the industrialized world, legal protections known as patents for inventors encouraged technological innovation. The first recorded patent was granted in Florence in 1421, and the practice spread throughout Europe. The first government regulations of patents (sys-

temizing an existing practice) were part of a 1624 English law on monopolies. France passed its first patent law in 1791, and other nations adopted similar laws during the nineteenth century. The number of patents issued by various governments grew steadily during the eighteenth century and accelerated rapidly in the early nineteenth century.

National Advantages. Other significant incentives for inventors included state-sponsored prizes for important discoveries, awards for successful inventions, and jobs that allowed innovators to support themselves, providing significant material incentives and thus encouraging tinkering and the application of "pure" science to practical problems. Governments naturally sought to develop scientific and technological advantages over other nations. Maintaining such advantages required more than preventing knowledge from spreading, particularly during the initial stages of the Industrial Revolution; it also included keeping at home men possessed of special craft skills and banning the exportation of the machines they made or used. The British government helped to establish and maintain its dominance of the early Industrial Revolution by legally prohibiting the export of many important machines until 1843 and banning the emigration of certain key categories of workers between 1719 and 1825. Legal restrictions, however, could impede, but not stop, the flow of workers, machines, and ideas across national borders. Many countries—most notably France, Spain, England, and Sweden—employed large numbers of industrial spies to gather information about new technologies and scientific advances and to entice workers with needed craft skills away from industrial competitors. During the eighteenth century, hopes for personal gain, religious impulses, and a desire to travel led more than one thousand British subjects to overcome legal constraints and take their skills and knowledge to France. Others went to the British colonies, the Netherlands, Russia, British-controlled territories in German central Europe, and many other places. Despite similar legal prohibitions, French workers immigrated to Italy, Spain, Russia, and the Netherlands, spreading advanced techniques and machines that could permit productive manufacturing.

Education. Governments also spurred industrialization by founding or encouraging the creation of institutions designed to inculcate scientific knowledge needed for innovation. During the early industrial period, scientific knowledge was disseminated more widely in Britain than elsewhere in Europe, in part through lectures and books for the highly literate British public. Furthermore, unlike its Continental counterparts, British scientific teaching focused a great deal on how things such as machinery moved (mechanics), a subject that had many practical applications. In 1818 the first of hundreds of Mechanics Institutes were established in Britain. Aimed at providing rudimentary scientific principles to potential tinkerers, especially artisans and middle-class amateurs, Mechanics Institutes spread throughout Britain and North America. At the height of their popularity, more than one hundred thousand students were enrolled. As literacy rates rose dra-

The analytical laboratory in the School of Chemistry at the University of Paris, late nineteenth century (Collection of the Canadian Center for Architecture, Montreal)

matically all over Europe in the eighteenth century, scientific or technological training during the early industrial era lagged behind on the Continent and was limited in both availability and quality. While established universities played a role teaching mathematics and advancing medical knowledge, organized religion limited what could be taught there. In most of western Europe the best training in scientific matters came from private institutions, particularly the dissenting academies in England. In fact, the importance of these academies and the Mechanics Institutes in the spread of scientific knowledge were symptoms of the deficiencies in the British educational system that caused Britain to fall behind other European countries during the second half of the nineteenth century.

British Learned Societies. The British state was always less active in the direct promotion of scientific achievement and technological advances than France or, later, Germany, but the British government did facilitate the interaction of scientists, technicians, and entrepreneurs in official institutions such as the Royal Society of Arts, established in Lon-

don in 1754. The existence of such state-sponsored groups also encouraged the formation of new, unofficial learned societies devoted to specific disciplines, where specialists and amateurs mixed freely, sharing scientific knowledge. In England many state and private institutions focused on the application of science to manufacturing. The Royal Society of Arts had a decidedly practical orientation, as did other groups throughout the country, including the Lunar Society in Birmingham (founded circa 1765), the Linnaean Society (established in 1788), the Geological Society (1807), and the Royal Astronomical Society (1831). As was common with other such groups, members of the Lunar Society included not only important scientists such as chemist Joseph Priestley (1733–1804) but also inventors such as James Watt (1736–1819) and industrial entrepreneurs including Matthew Boulton (1728–1809), who manufactured and marketed Watt's steam engine. Such close interaction between laboratory and workshop was uncommon on the Continent. The British societies often published journals in which discoveries, theories, and experiments were described not only to members but also to national and even worldwide audiences.

Continental Universities. On the Continent, however, states encouraged theoretical advances in "pure" science and their application to the needs of the industrial economy through the creation of polytechnic schools. Many states founded organizations to oversee all intellectual activity, in particular, science and technology. The prototypes for these establishments, the Ecole polytechnique and the National Institute, were created in Paris in 1794 and were staffed by leading scientists. Although such efforts bore remarkably little fruit in the eighteenth century, they flourished in the nineteenth century as scientific advances began to have practical application in industry. Other states mimicked the British Mechanics Institutes by adapting their institutions to provide a similar sort of education. Technological training in German-speaking states was broader than anywhere else—the various German polytechnic schools instructed about five thousand students a year by 1850. After 1850 these schools expanded into full-scale *technische Hochshulen* (technical colleges), which facilitated the emergence of a large, influential, scientific elite with close ties to business and government. The most influential educational change with the greatest long-term significance, however, was the French and Prussian governments' thorough reform of their university systems during the first decade of the nineteenth century to give the natural sciences, and scientific research in general, a far more prominent position in the curriculum. The percentage of university graduates in France and Prussia who were trained as physicians, teachers, bureaucrats, and professionals was much higher than in Britain. German universities became centers of scientific and technological research, following the methods of chemist Justus von Liebig (1803–1873), who established the model for the modern research laboratory at Giessen in 1825. The university curriculum reforms contributed greatly to the industrialization of France and especially German-speaking central Europe. Indeed, over the course of the nineteenth century, the Germanic nations eventually surpassed the British in scientific and technological prowess. The Second Industrial Revolution was born in German universities. By the time British universities copied the German educational model in the last decades of the nineteenth century, Great Britain had lost its technological advantage in Europe.

Sources:

George Basalla, *The Evolution of Technology* (Cambridge & New York: Cambridge University Press, 1988).

Eric Dorn Brose, *Technology and Science in the Industrializing Nations, 1500–1914* (Atlantic Highlands, N.J.: Humanities Press, 1998).

N. F. R. Crafts, *British Economic Growth during the Industrial Revolution* (Oxford: Clarendon Press / New York: Oxford University Press, 1985).

J. R. Harris, *Industrial Espionage and Technology Transfer: Britain and France in the Eighteenth Century* (Aldershot, U.K. & Brookfield, Vt.: Ashgate, 1998).

Ian Inkster, *Science and Technology in History: An Approach to Industrial Development* (New Brunswick, N.J.: Rutgers University Press, 1991).

Margaret C. Jacob, *Scientific Culture and the Making of the Industrial West* (New York: Oxford University Press, 1997).

Christine MacLeod, *Inventing the Industrial Revolution: The English Patent System, 1660–1880* (Cambridge & New York: Cambridge University Press, 1988).

Peter Mathias, *The First Industrial Nation: An Economic History of Britain 1700–1914*, second edition (London & New York: Methuen, 1983).

James E. McClellan III, *Science Reorganized: Scientific Societies in the Eighteenth Century* (New York: Columbia University Press, 1985).

Sidney Pollard, *Peaceful Conquest: The Industrialization of Europe 1760–1970* (Oxford & New York: Oxford University Press, 1981).

W. D. Rubinstein, *Capitalism, Culture, and Decline in Britain, 1750–1990* (London & New York: Routledge, 1993).

THE SECOND INDUSTRIAL REVOLUTION

Tariffs and New Markets. By 1815 industrialization in Great Britain had made it a world economic power and given it political predominance in Europe. Yet, its vast financial, commercial, and industrial resources were far out of proportion to its population, supply of raw materials, or scientific prowess. With the end of the distractions of the revolutionary and Napoleonic wars in 1815, industrialization accelerated in Great Britain. Innovative products were developed, and new markets were exploited to their fullest potential. Limited by high tariff walls erected by many of its traditional trade partners on the Continent, nineteenth-century British economic expansion focused on the British Empire and on markets such as Latin America, China, and Africa. Despite a slowdown in the rate of productivity after 1870, at the dawn of the twentieth century, the British remained the wealthiest society on the planet, with economic power still far out of proportion to its population and resources.

French Response. The French reaction to British industrial supremacy was to erect tariff walls to protect domestic industries in areas dominated by Great Britain and to focus on manufacturing those products in which it had advantages, such as luxury items. In addition to creating incentives that lured British entrepreneurs and artisans to France, the French government promoted scientific advances and technological improvement by founding educational institutions, including some specifically for the study of science and technology. This effort began during the revolutionary decade (1789–1799) and escalated under the scientifically minded Bonapartist regime. It took twenty years for local technological institutions to train a generation imbued with mechanical knowledge and scientific principles and prepared to bring about industrial innovation. In the late 1820s French industrial development surged. In fact, French economic growth per capita between 1750 and 1914 was roughly comparable to that of Great Britain. French efforts also focused on spreading scientific knowledge deeply in the population. The Guizot Law (1833) mandated the creation of an elementary school, with a teacher paid from local tax revenues, in every canton, and in 1881 the French pioneered free, state-funded, universal primary education. Soon adopted in most European nations (but much more slowly in the Anglo-Saxon world), universal primary education furnished the burgeoning industrial economy of Continental Europe with workers who had learned mechanical princi-

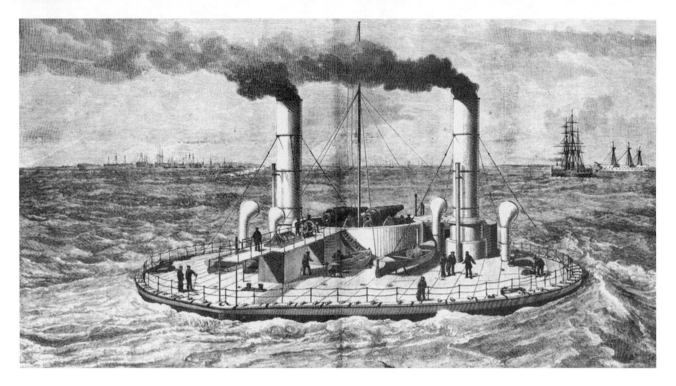

An ironclad, steam-powered Russian battleship, early 1870s (from Asa Briggs, *The Power of Steam*, 1982)

ples as well as reading and writing and were capable of operating increasingly complex machinery and, in some cases, supervising other workers.

Central Europe. Following the defeat of Napoleon Bonaparte in 1815, Austria and Prussia inaugurated explicit pro-industrialization policies that resembled those of France. Most German-speaking states erected tariffs against British imports, while Prussia and several other states took tariff policy to the next level by establishing a free-trade union called the Zollverein in 1834, thus encouraging trade among themselves to the disadvantage of non-Germanic states. While Germanic states emulated and extended an educational model developed in France, in economic planning they imitated the industrial system established by Great Britain. Facilitated by unification in 1871 and the subsequent formation of useful institutions such as a national bank, German industrial production grew rapidly. As in Britain, machine-made textiles were woven on precision machinery made from iron and powered by coal. During the years 1871–1900 industrial growth rates for Germany were double those of Great Britain. Interaction among government, educators, and successful industrialists led to further expansion of technical colleges and universities, which in turn helped more and more members of the fast-growing population to develop scientific and technological expertise, thereby laying the foundations for the Second Industrial Revolution.

Military Technology. The scientific and technological prowess of the European nations permitted them to expand their political and economic power on a global scale. By 1914 Western powers ruled 84 percent of the land masses in the world. Railroads had played a key role

in making remote areas part of a global economy. Thanks to improved Western technology, access to such areas also ensured the subordination of local populations. Western powers used their military superiority to build enormous empires at minimal economic cost. The flat-bottomed steamship, developed in 1823 by the British Royal Navy, played a key role in the extension of British power in Southeast Asia. The power of new Western military technology was displayed in the crushing defeats of China during the Opium Wars of the 1840s. Constantly improved steel-hulled ships, armed with breech-loading rifled artillery with a range of up to twenty miles, could assert Western power in coastal areas. High-powered explosives rendered the wooden naval vessel obsolete, ensuring that only steel-producing countries could build competitive navies. Innovations in firearms permitted relatively small numbers of Western trained-and-equipped troops to defeat huge numbers of less-well-armed native opponents. Following the development of percussion caps by Scottish clergyman Alexander Forsyth (1769–1843) in 1807, a musket could be fired in almost any weather. Spiraling grooves inside the barrel (rifling) improved the range and accuracy of firearms, but not until the shift from muzzle-loading to breech-loading weapons during the 1860s were rifled weapons practical for widespread military use. As rifles became more accurate and capable of firing projectiles over longer distances, the technology of bullets developed as well. In 1848 French army captain Claude-Etienne Minié (1804–1879) combined earlier innovations to fashion a bullet with a hollow base (allowing it to travel more swiftly) and an oblong shape (allowing it to spin inside the barrel). These new bullets then were packaged in a cartridge with the proper charge of gunpowder. Reloading speed, accuracy, and distance were complemented again in the 1860s by repeating rifles, which could fire six rounds a minute. The appearance of the bolt-action rifle at the end of the century permitted even more-rapid fire. Gunpowder was improved after 1885, when French engineer Paul Vieille (1854–1934) discovered nitrocellulose, which, along with its relative nitroglycerine, burned without smoke or ash. Smokeless gunpowder reduced the need to clean the barrel, provided more energy, and was not as moisture permeable as earlier powder. By the 1890s a European infantryman, lying prone and concealed, could fire fifteen smokeless rounds in fifteen seconds in any weather at targets up to a half mile away.

Machine Guns. Smokeless explosives made possible the single-barrel, rapid-fire machine gun. In 1884 British inventor Hiram Stevens Maxim (1840–1916), who was born in the United States, patented such a weapon, which fired eleven bullets per second. Light enough to be carried by an infantryman, the Maxim gun and similar weapons gave Europeans an extraordinary firepower advantage against native cultures. In "The Modern Traveller," a poem published just before the dawn of the twentieth century, British author Hilaire Belloc (1870–1953) summed up the Western technological advantage:

I shall never forget the way
That Blood stood upon this awful day
Preserved us all from death.
He stood upon a little mound
Cast his lethargic eyes around,
And said beneath his breath:
"Whatever happens, we have got
The Maxim Gun, and they have not."

During World War I Europeans turned against each other the killing power they had tested in their acquisition of vast colonial empires in Africa and Asia during the nineteenth century. At the same time they introduced new military weapons and technologies, including tanks, poison gas, and submarines.

Steel and Chemicals. Just as iron was the basis for the First Industrial Revolution, the material foundation of the Second Industrial Revolution was steel. Steel is a form of iron that includes 1 to 2 percent carbon. It is stronger than wrought iron, which has less than 1 percent carbon, and more malleable than cast, or pig, iron, which has 2 to 4 percent carbon. The knowledge of how to make steel had existed for centuries, but the process was too expensive for widespread use. During the 1850s Englishman Henry Bessemer (1813–1898) and American William Kelly (1811–1888) built on earlier technical improvements to develop almost simultaneously an economic means of producing steel. Each man used hot-air blasts to reduce the carbon content of iron. In 1877 two Englishmen, Sidney Gilchrist Thomas (1850–1885) and his cousin Percy Gilchrist (1831–1935), improved this method by introducing limestone slag to the converter to neutralize phosphorus, which makes steel

brittle. In the 1860s two German immigrants to England, brothers Friedrich Siemens (1826–1904) and William Siemens (1823–1883), and in France Pierre Martin (1824–1915) used heated coal gas to perform the same work in a large "open-hearth furnace." During the 1880s the Siemens-Martin "open-hearth" process was improved by incorporating it with the Gilchrist-Thomas technique. These refinements allowed large quantities of iron to be transformed into steel and reduced the price of steel to approximately that of iron. Cheap steel permitted the development of the new machines and technologies that became the basis for twentieth-century industrial economy.

German Steel and Chemicals. By combining the Siemens-Martin and Gilchrist-Thomas processes, Germany acquired a major advantage over its European competitors. By 1914 Germany produced almost as much steel as England, France, Italy, and Russia combined. While inexpensive steel was the basis for a new industrial era, the chemical industry was largely responsible for its expansion. Subsidized by the profitable production of textile dyes and dominated by powerful cartels, the chemical industry formulated many of the substances and products that shaped twentieth-century life in the Western world. "Spin-offs" from the chemical industry include medicines, effective fertilizers, improved glass, photographic film, synthetic fibers, plastics, and powerful explosives. These refinements came not only from company labs but from university scientists whose work was subsidized by the chemical industry. Among them was German chemist Fritz Haber (1868–1934), whose research was funded by BASF (Badenese Aniline & Soda Factory). Haber produced synthetic ammonia in 1909, thereby perfecting the vital "contact process" of separating compounds into their various elements, as well as making possible the large-scale production of synthetic fertilizer.

The Internal-Combustion Engine. By the 1880s the steam engine had reached its full technological potential. Factory managers were frustrated by the large size of these engines and the dirt they produced. From the search for a more efficient and cleaner alternative, the internal-combustion engine was created. The first workable prototype was invented by Etienne Lenoir (1822–1900) of Belgium in 1859. In his two-stroke engine, a mixture of coal gas and air exploded to depress a piston much more forcefully than steam. Several engineers worked on making this model more effective. In 1876 Nikolaus A. Otto (1832–1891) of Germany made a four-stroke engine that compressed the gas before combustion to increase the force exerted on the piston. Another German, Gottlieb Wilhelm Daimler (1834–1900), introduced the first high-speed model in 1885, using gasoline fuel derived from petroleum for rapid vaporization. He also invented the carburetor, which vaporized the fuel while mixing it with air for combustion. Use of the internal-combustion engine, which was cheaper and cleaner than the steam engine, spread rapidly. These new engines also required less labor to operate, ran at dif-

The 1900 model Benz sports car followed by an 1898 Benz-Comfortable (Deutsches Museum, Munich)

ferent speeds, and could be stopped and started more easily than steam engines.

The Automobile. Another German engineer, Karl Friedrich Benz (1844–1929), developed the first practical internal-combustion automobile in 1885–1886. The pneumatic tire, created for bicycles, was easily adapted for use on the motor car. A host of other improvements followed around 1900, including the radiator, the differential, the crank starter, the steering wheel, and pedal brakes. France quickly emerged as the largest producer of self-propelled "horseless carriages." In France a host of small companies produced small numbers of high-quality automobiles as luxury goods, but U.S. manufacturers, notably Henry Ford (1863–1947), saw the potential in marketing less-expensive cars to a wide range of consumers. By 1906 the United States surpassed France in automobile production, and by 1910 the Americans made more automobiles than the rest of the world combined. U.S. predominance in automobile production was based on factors such as high European taxes that favored the use of horses and the emergence of a highly effective manufacturing system, the assembly line, usually associated with production of the Model T by the Ford Motor Company, which built a standardized, inexpensive car with interchangeable parts made from sheet

steel. European automobile manufacturers adopted these methods after World War I.

Powered Flight. Manned flight began in France in 1783 with hot-air and hydrogen balloons. With an internal-combustion engine driving a propeller, the dirigible (basically a steerable balloon), was created in 1884. Gliders provided a model for heavier-than-air flight, but the airplane could not be developed until the emergence of more efficient and lighter engines. After the American brothers Orville Wright (1871–1948) and Wilbur Wright (1867–1912) succeeded in making their first powered airplane flight in 1903, improvements in engine design and overall construction soon permitted controlled turns and flights lasting hours. France was responsible for many developments in this field, in large part because of their leadership in the production and use of aluminum. By the start of World War I, airplanes had crossed the English Channel; the seaplane had been developed; and pilots had the ability to take off and land on ships. Wartime demands for reconnaissance prompted rapid development of the airplane industry, preparing for further expansion in the boom era that followed the war.

The Assembly Line. The United States was a major beneficiary of the economic climate that surrounded the

Second Industrial Revolution. In the period from 1870 to 1913—thanks to major improvements in output per man-hour—the United States caught and surpassed the total industrial output (if not always the technological prowess) of Europe in almost every domain, including steel, aluminum, electricity, and automobiles. Despite U.S. economic predominance by the eve of World War I, with only a few exceptions, nearly all key technological and scientific breakthroughs came from Europe. The Americans, however, developed an important new approach to industrial production, known as the "American system," with federal financial support in the arms-making industry. Its goal was to produce weapons with interchangeable parts, a concept based on employing a sequential series of operations utilizing specially designed, single-purpose machines. Once developed, this system was used to manufacture consumer goods such as sewing machines, bicycles, and then automobiles. A century-long process allowed a genuine system of mass production to emerge. Europeans had developed versions of interchangeable parts and specialized machinery at least a century earlier, but they did not use them in an industrial assembly-line system until after World War I.

Relativity. Pure science also made dramatic strides during the late nineteenth century, culminating in significant revisions of the Newtonian understanding of the universe. Radioactivity was discovered by French physicist Antoine-Henri Becquerel (1852–1908) in 1896 and named by Polish-born French scientist Marie Curie (1867–1934) in 1898. In that same year she and her husband, Pierre (1859–1906), isolated the radioactive elements radium and polonium. Between 1900 and 1914 German scientists Max Planck (1858–1947) and Albert Einstein (1879–1955) and Danish scientist Nils Bohr (1885–1962) transformed the study of physics. In their wake, the concept of a universe based on absolute and fixed principles was replaced by the fundamentals of modern physics—relativity and uncertainty. In 1900 Planck explained that energy was "quantum" in nature; that is, energy is emitted and absorbed in minute, discrete amounts. Five years later Einstein published his special theory of relativity to explain the relationship of space and time. He stated that space and time are not absolute and vary according to motion; thus, for example, a clock in a moving system will tick off the minutes more slowly than a clock in a stationary system. In that same year, Einstein devised his famous formula $E=mc^2$—that is, energy (E) equals mass (m) times the speed of light (c) squared. The implications of this formula are that all mass is congealed energy, and all energy is liberated matter. Since the speed of light is approximately 186,000 miles per second, a tiny amount of mass equals an enormous amount of energy. Because it explains why splitting an atom releases vast amounts of energy, this relationship became the theoretical basis for atomic weapons and nuclear power. In 1913 Bohr applied quantum theory to subatomic physics, and between the World Wars, he and Werner Heisenberg (1901–1976) turned these crucial observations into a whole new explanation of subatomic movement (quantum

mechanics). Since it is impossible to predict the movement of an electron, Bohr and Heisenberg said, all calculations are based on a statistical probability, not an absolute certainty. The revolution in physics that climaxed with this "uncertainty principle" completed the shift from the fixed absolutes of a Newtonian universe to a more ambiguous and bewildering conception of it.

Sources:
George Basalla, *The Evolution of Technology* (Cambridge & New York: Cambridge University Press, 1988).

N. F. R. Crafts, *British Economic Growth during the Industrial Revolution* (Oxford: Clarendon Press / New York: Oxford University Press, 1985).

John Ellis, *The Social History of the Machine Gun* (London: Croom Helm, 1975).

J. R. Harris, *Industrial Espionage and Technology Transfer: Britain and France in the Eighteenth Century* (Aldershot, U.K. & Brookfield, Vt.: Ashgate, 1998).

Daniel R. Headrick, *The Tools of Empire: Technology and European Imperialism* (New York: Oxford University Press, 1981).

David A. Hounshell, *From the American System to Mass Production, 1800–1932: The Development of Manufacturing Technology in the United States* (Baltimore: Johns Hopkins University Press, 1984).

Margaret C. Jacob, *Scientific Culture and the Making of the Industrial West* (New York: Oxford University Press, 1997).

Christine MacLeod, *Inventing the Industrial Revolution: The English Patent System, 1660–1880* (Cambridge & New York: Cambridge University Press, 1988).

Peter Mathias, *The First Industrial Nation: An Economic History of Britain 1700–1914,* second edition (London & New York: Methuen, 1983).

James E. McClellan III, *Science Reorganized: Scientific Societies in the Eighteenth Century* (New York: Columbia University Press, 1985).

Joel Mokyr, ed., *The British Industrial Revolution: An Economic Perspective,* second edition (Boulder, Colo.: Westview Press, 1999).

Sidney Pollard, *Peaceful Conquest: The Industrialization of Europe 1760–1970* (Oxford & New York: Oxford University Press, 1981).

W. D. Rubinstein, *Capitalism, Culture, and Decline in Britain, 1750–1990* (London & New York: Routledge, 1993).

TREATING BODIES AND MINDS: HEALTH CARE

Dirt and Disease. Population growth, urbanization, and industrialization vastly increased health problems in Europe between 1750 and 1914. Dirt from coal smoke darkened buildings and their surroundings, already muddy from unpaved streets. Crowding exacerbated sanitation problems in the cities and industrial districts. Coal fumes joined the smells of garbage and human and animal waste, which littered the streets, particularly in poorer areas, and contaminated the drinking water, already in short supply in most cities. Disease preyed on malnourished urban populations, leading to spectacular declines in life expectancy among the lower classes, especially during catastrophic natural disasters such as the European Potato Blight of the late 1840s. In 1840 in Manchester, England, high rates of infant mortality lowered the average life span among the working class to only seventeen years, whereas the average for all England was forty years. Scientists were slow in understanding how poor sanitation affected human health, and even after scientists applied their knowledge to solving these problems, it took a long time for governments to implement solutions. By the eve of World War I, however,

From his observations while working in London and Edinburgh hospitals, British physician Joseph Lister concluded that cleanliness was essential to preventing postsurgical infections. The following excerpt from his "On the Antiseptic Principle of The Practice of Surgery" (1867) describes how he was influenced by the "germ theory" of French scientist Louis Pasteur to devise a method for reducing the number of such infections.

In the course of an extended investigation into the nature of inflammation, and the healthy and morbid conditions of the blood in relation to it, I arrived several years ago at the conclusion that the essential cause of suppuration in wounds is decomposition brought about by the influence of the atmosphere upon blood or serum retained within them, and, in the case of contused wounds upon portions of tissue destroyed by the violence of the injury.

To prevent the occurrence of suppuration with all its attendant risks was an object manifestly desirable, but till lately apparently unattainable, since it seemed hopeless to attempt to exclude the oxygen which was universally regarded as the agent by which putrefaction was effected. But when it had been shown by the researches of Pasteur that the septic properties of the atmosphere depended not on the oxygen, or any gaseous constituent, but on minute organisms suspended in it, which owed their energy to their vitality, it occurred to me that decomposition in the injured part might be avoided without excluding the air, by applying as a dressing some material capable of destroying the life of the floating particles. . . .

The material which I have employed is carbolic or phenic acid, a volatile organic compound, which appears to exercise a peculiarly destructive influence upon low forms of life, and hence is the most powerful antiseptic with which we are at present acquainted. . . .

There is, however, one point more than I cannot but advert to, viz., the influence of this mode of treatment upon the general unhealthiness of an hospital. Previously to its introduction the two large wards in which most of my cases of accident and of operation are treated were among the unhealthiest in the whole surgical division of the Glasgow Royal Infirmary, in consequence apparently of those wards being unfavorably placed with reference to the supply of fresh air; and I have felt ashamed when recording the results of my practice, to have so often to allude to hospital gangrene or pyaemia. It was interesting, though melancholy, to observe that whenever all or nearly all the beds contained cases with open sores, these grievous complications were pretty sure to show themselves; so that I came to welcome simple fractures, though in themselves of little interest either for myself or the students, because their presence diminished the proportion of open sores among the patients. But since the antiseptic treatment has been brought into full operation, and wounds and abscesses no longer poison the atmosphere with putrid exhalations, my wards, though in other respects under precisely the same circumstances as before, have completely changed their character; so that during the last nine months not a single instance of pyaemia, hospital gangrene, or erysipelas has occurred in them.

As there appears to be no doubt regarding the cause of this change, the importance of the fact can hardly be exaggerated.

Source: Charles W. Eliot, ed., *Scientific Papers: Physiology, Medicine, Surgery, Geology* (New York: Collier, 1897), pp. 271, 281–282.

Europeans of all classes were living longer and healthier lives than they had 150 years earlier, paving the way for much greater and more widespread improvements after the war.

Smallpox Prevention. For millennia, many natural substances had been known to be effective against disease. The practice of inoculation—the injection of a weakened form of a disease to prevent a more drastic occurrence of it—had been practiced since the Renaissance. In 1798 English physician Edward Jenner (1749–1823) took the first step in controlling the deadly disease smallpox by injecting cowpox, a milder form of the disease, into a healthy individual as a means of creating a resistance to it and preventing the more-virulent smallpox. The effectiveness of Jenner's new vaccination was hotly debated by his contemporaries because nearly everyone believed that people contracted diseases when they breathed odors of decay or putrefying excrement (the miasmatic theory of disease). Yet, vaccination slowly became standard practice throughout western Europe. The British Parliament signaled its acceptance with the Vaccination Act of 1853. The development of a smallpox vaccination was the culmination of centuries of trial and error rather than the product of a scientific understanding of why this method worked. Only in the later nineteenth century did directed scientific inquiry discover how antigens (bacteria or viruses) cause diseases.

Malaria. One disastrous and unforeseen result of imperial expansion was the spread of malaria among European colonists. This disease decimated people of European descent who entered the interior of Africa. It is likely that malaria (from the Italian *mal'aria*, or bad air) has killed more humans than any other disease. In 1880 French scientist Alphonse Laveran (1845–1922) isolated the protozoan that causes the disease. In 1897–1898 British physician Ronald Ross (1857–1932) and the Italians Giovanni Batista Grassi (1853–1925) and Amico Bignami (1862–1929) identified that the disease is spread by the *Anopheles* mosquito. Before scientists had finally determined the cause of malaria, trial and error

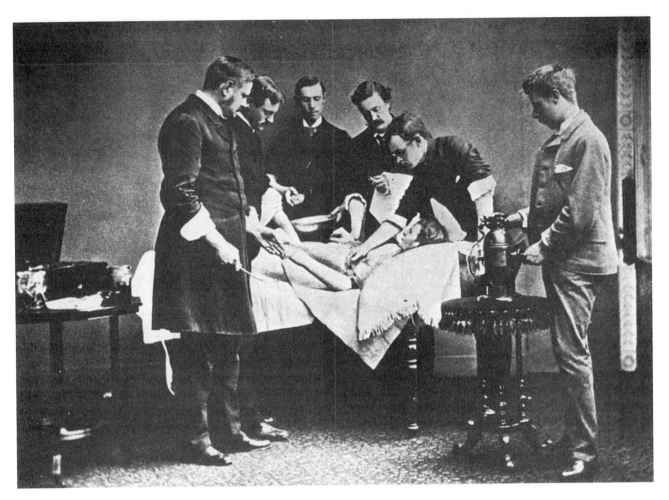

Surgeons performing an operation at the Royal Infirmary in Aberdeen, Scotland, circa 1882
(photograph by G. W. Wilson; Gersheim Collection, Harry Ransom Humanities
Research Center, University of Texas at Austin)

had already produced an effective treatment for it. In the seventeenth century Jesuit priests had brought to Europe a treatment for one strain of malaria—the bark of the cinchona tree, which grows only in the Andes Mountains of South America. The practical breakthrough in treating malaria came in 1820 when two French chemists, Pierre-Joseph Pelletier (1788–1842) and Joseph-Bienaimé Caventou (1795–1877), finally determined how to extract a key alkaloid (quinine) from cinchona bark. By 1830 the drug was being manufactured in sufficient quantity for general use. Quinine was tested during the French invasion of Algeria (1830), but not until 1845 did doctors realize that the bloodstream needs to be saturated with quinine for best effect. Once dosages had been standardized, the interior of Africa was opened to exploitation by people of European descent.

Public-Health Policy. European outbreaks of cholera in 1832 and 1848–1849, along with the omnipresence of many other diseases in urban industrial Europe, pushed states and concerned individuals to devote increased attention to problems of public health. English Poor Law commissioner Edwin Chadwick (1800–1890) took the lead in publicizing urban decay and its attendant health risks. In response, Britain took the first steps toward cleaning up its cities by passing the Public Health Act of 1848, which set up a national-health board with broad authority to create modern sanitary systems. Chadwick and others emphasized the need for clean drinking water. During the 1840s and 1850s close observation by public-health officials, many of them doctors, revealed the limitations of the miasmatic theory of disease. Instead, they suggested that the vector of contagion for a disease was passed through excrement or decaying matter rather than by its odor. This observation set the stage for the bacterial revolution, which transformed the health of Europe and ultimately the world.

Germ Theory. The "germ theory of disease," advanced by French chemist Louis Pasteur (1822–1895) during the mid nineteenth century, was embraced and applied almost immediately, with Germany leading the way. During the mid 1870s German physician Robert Koch (1843–1910) isolated pure strains of bacteria and detailed their characteristics. He later isolated the agents of tuberculosis (1882) and cholera (1883), while other researchers, most of whom were Germans working for large companies, identified the sources of many other diseases. This work made possible the development of effective vaccines and gave birth to the modern science of immunology. Around 1867, Pasteur's germ theory also inspired English surgeon Joseph Lister (1827–1912) to add a chemical disinfectant to wound dressings to prevent infection from airborne bacteria.

Antiseptic Principle. Lister's antiseptic principle was extended by German surgeons, who began to apply antiseptics to all materials in an operating room—including hands, instruments, and clothing—with clear and direct impact on a patient's chance of survival. These methods significantly lowered the death rates for surgical patients and women in childbirth. Thanks to the bacteriological revolution, diphtheria, typhoid, typhus, cholera, bubonic plague, and yellow fever were largely eliminated in Europe. By 1890 the mortality rate in European urban areas was lower than in rural areas, and life expectancy had risen impressively. By 1913 both infant and child mortality had fallen to less than half of what they had been 150 years before.

Healthy Minds. In the late nineteenth century, some doctors took advantage of public support for new ideas associated with scientific medicine to focus on the workings of the human mind. Sexuality was investigated by such important figures as British physician Havelock Ellis (1859–1939). His landmark seven-volume study of sexual issues, the nature of gender, and the practice of homosexuality, *Studies in the Psychology of Sex* (1897–1928), helped to create a new field called "sexology." In *Die Traumdeutung* (1900; The Interpretation of Dreams) Austrian psychoanalyst Sigmund Freud (1856–1939) legitimized the study of dreams, emphasizing their sexual meanings.

Psychiatry. Freud wrote extensively on the nature of sexual desire, arguing that its repression could produce severe psychological consequences. Italian physician Cesare Lombroso (1835–1909) delved into the nature of the criminal mind; French psychologist Alfred Binet (1857–1911) developed tests to measure the capacity of the intellect; and Russian physiologist Ivan Pavlov (1848–1936) discovered how behavior could be modified by conditioned responses. Taken together, these inquiries and their results helped to found the modern scientific fields of psychology and psychiatry, which treated troubled or mentally ill individuals. The findings of these men also revealed the dark underside of the human psyche and undermined faith in human progress.

Institutions and Commercial Applications. In addition to improving public health through the regulation of water supplies and sewer systems and the construction of public baths and toilets, nation-states also increased access to medical education and treatment and supported medical research in institutions of higher learning or specialized facilities. Individuals and private charities also contributed to health research. Most new medicines, however, emerged from the close ties between big business and scientific researchers. Although Pasteur worked at public educational institutions of learning, his breakthroughs came in response to requests for assistance from

THE UNCONSCIOUS MIND

At the turn of the twentieth century Sigmund Freud's theories about the workings of the unconscious mind began a revolution in the way mental-health workers treated their patients. The concept of the *unconscious* was not new, but earlier theorists tended to see it as subordinate to conscious mental processes. For example, Freud's slightly older American contemporary William James described the unconscious as a "fringe" around the edges of conscious thought. For Freud, however, the unconscious was like the underwater part of an iceberg while the conscious was like the much smaller tip that extends above water. The unconscious, Freud said, is the realm of powerful, primitive, often sexual impulses that are frequently contrary to the morals and mores of the individual and society. In addition, he said that the unconscious is the place to which the individual banishes painful mental conflicts and memories. Freud called this process of "forgetting" *repression* and explained that the psyche also practices repression to keep painful thoughts and socially unacceptable urges from resurfacing in the conscious mind. According to Freud, as the psyche represses more and more, the individual begins to experience anxiety, hysteria, or various other forms of mental illness. Deciding that uncovering his patients' unconscious thoughts was essential to effective treatment, Freud observed that they tended to come out in slips of the tongue, everyday mistakes, and dreams, where they were often distorted or veiled in a kind of psychic symbolism. Thus, he developed an elaborate system of dream interpretation. He also devised a form of "talk therapy" called *psychoanalysis*. Having theorized that repressed thoughts come out in dreams because the psyche relaxes its guard against them during sleep, Freud tried to create a dreamlike state in his patients by having them lie on a sofa and encouraging them to free-associate, saying anything that came to mind no matter how irrelevant, inappropriate, or immoral it seemed. Versions of Freud's talk sessions are still part of the modern mental-health repertoire. Though the specifics of his theories have been challenged and in many cases disproved, they created a context in which later, more scientific, psychological studies could take place and provided metaphors that psychologists still employ in their discussions of human thought processes.

Source: Peter Gay, *Freud: A Life for Our Time* (New York & London: Norton, 1988).

brewers and the silk industry. The German researchers who identified diphtheria and tuberculosis worked for drug companies, which reaped vast profits from sales of vaccines to prevent these diseases. The invention of a tablet-making machine in Germany by a team of talented mechanics during the 1890s led to the marketing of name-brand drugs in precise doses, replacing concoctions mixed by local druggists. The combination of government patronage, private donations, and corporate sponsorship during the second half of the nineteenth century helped to create important improvements in the health of the European population. At the end of the initial era of industrialization (1750–1914) Europeans' bodies, on average, were healthier than ever before, but, according to doctors such as Freud, their minds had never been more ill.

Sources:

Theodore S. Hamerow, *The Birth of a New Europe: State and Society in the Nineteenth Century* (Chapel Hill: University of North Carolina Press, 1983).

Colin Heywood, *Childhood in Nineteenth-Century France: Work, Health and Education among the 'classes populaires'* (Cambridge & New York: Cambridge University Press, 1988).

Joan Lane, *A Social History of Medicine: Health, Healing and Disease in England, 1750–1950* (London & New York: Routledge, 2001).

Roy Porter, *The Greatest Benefit to Mankind: A Medical History of Humanity from Antiquity to the Present* (London: HarperCollins, 1997).

SIGNIFICANT PEOPLE

KARL FRIEDRICH BENZ

1844-1929
AUTOMOBILE MANUFACTURER

Early Career. Karl Friedrich Benz was born in the then independent German state of Baden-Württemberg in the city of Karlsruhe, where he attended the polytechnic institute. He worked as an engineer and factory manager before founding his first firm, a machine shop, in 1871. In 1883 Benz established a company in Mannheim that produced stationary internal-combustion engines for industrial use.

Automobile Production. Benz designed and built his pioneering motor carriage at Mannheim in 1885. Patented the following year, it had three wheels and was powered by a water-cooled, two-cycle, one-cylinder engine that ran on benzine; an electrical current started the engine. Benz resisted designing a four-wheeled vehicle until 1893. The following year he introduced the Velo, the first automobile to be mass produced.

Later Career. Benz resigned from active direction of his company in 1903 in a dispute over whether the firm should build motorcycles or develop faster-running engines. When the Daimler and Benz firms merged in 1926, Benz became a member of the advisory board, serving until his death in 1929.

Sources:
David Burgess-Wise, William Boddy, and Brian Laban, *The Automobile: The First Century* (London: Orbis, 1983).

Beverly Rae Kimes, *The Star and the Laurel: The Centennial History of Daimler, Mercedes, and Benz, 1886–1986* (Montvale, N.J.: Mercedes-Benz of North America, 1986).

Friedrich Schildberger, *History of Mercedes-Benz Motor Vehicles and Engines,* fifth edition (Stuttgart: Daimler-Benz, 1972).

SIR MARC ISAMBARD BRUNEL

1769-1849
ENGINEER

Underwater Tunneling. One of the major engineering achievements of the nineteenth century was the development of the technology to construct tunnels under rivers. People had been building land tunnels since ancient times, but efforts to tunnel through ground under water failed because the soft, water-bearing strata tended to collapse. Marc Brunel solved the problem by inventing the tunneling shield (patented in 1818) and went on to build the first underwater tunnel in the world under the River Thames in London (1825–1843).

Early Life. The son of a prosperous farmer, Marc Isambard Brunel was born in Hacqueville, a small village in northern France, and demonstrated his talent for mathematics, mechanics, and drawing at an early age. By the time he was eleven, he had expressed his desire to become an engineer, but his father wanted his son to become a priest and enrolled the boy at a seminary in Rouen. The head of the seminary helped Brunel to acquire training elsewhere in preparation for a career as a naval engineer. Brunel served in the French navy for six years, returning to France in 1793. His Royalist sympathies soon came to the attention of the French Revolutionary government, and he fled to the United States.

Chief Engineer. For the next several years Brunel worked as an architect and civil engineer in New York City and was eventually appointed chief engineer for the city. He also won the competition for designing the Capitol building in Washington, D.C., but another design was used because Brunel's was considered too expensive. During this time he perfected a machine to make pulleys for ships mechanically, instead of by hand, and in 1799 he went to England to submit his plans to the British government.

Engineering in England. The British government had Brunel install forty-three of his machines at the Portsmouth dockyard, where he created one of the first completely mechanized production processes in the world. When complete, his system could be run by ten men and could produce pulleys better and faster than more than one hundred men making them by hand. During the early nineteenth century Brunel designed the first floating landing piers, which were build in Liverpool.

Financial Failures. During his early years in England, Brunel also invented boot-making and knitting machines, an improved printing press, and devices to saw and bend timber, but his attempts to capitalize on these innovations were unsuccessful. His sawmills at Battersea in southwest London were badly damaged by fire in 1814, and the business soon went bankrupt. His army-boot factory, which supplied British troops with strong, comfortable boots during the Napoleonic Wars, went out of business after the war ended in 1815, and the government stopped buying his boots. In 1821 Brunel spent several months in debtors' prison. By then, however, he had patented an invention that ensured his financial stability.

The Tunneling Shield. By the time Brunel turned his attention to the problem of tunneling through water-bearing ground, two attempts to tunnel under the Thames, in 1801 and 1807, had failed when excavators hit quicksand. Around 1818, Brunel noticed how the shipworm bored through wood while its shell plates pushed the sawdust behind it and was inspired to build a large protective iron casing that screw jacks pushed through soft ground while miners inside it dug through shutters that could be opened and closed.

The Thames Tunnel. Brunel's shield was tested for the first time on the tunnel he designed to pass under the Thames between Rotherhithe and Wapping on the east side of London. Construction began in 1825 and, after several major delays, was finally completed in 1843. Partway through the project, Brunel replaced his first tunneling shield with a much larger one. Neither shield failed at any point in the project, demonstrating

the safety of Brunel's invention. The tunnel started out as a pedestrian tunnel, and within four months of its completion more than a million people passed through it. It was converted to a railroad tunnel during the 1860s and became part of the London Underground (subway) system in 1913. In recognition of his achievement, Brunel was knighted in 1841. His only son, Isambard Kingdom Brunel (1806–1859), began his career as resident engineer for the Thames Tunnel and went on to design bridges and railroads, as well as the first transatlantic steamships in regular service.

Sources:

Richard Beamish, *Memoir of the Life of Sir Marc Isambard Brunel* (London: Longman, Green, Longman & Roberts, 1862).

Celia Brunel Noble, *The Brunels, Father and Son* (London: Cobden-Sanderson, 1938).

GOTTLIEB WILHELM DAIMLER

1834-1900
AUTOMOBILE MANUFACTURER

Early Career. Forever linked in the public mind and in historical memory with Karl Friedrich Benz (1844–1929), whom he never met, Gottlieb Wilhelm Daimler was born in Schorndorf, Baden-Württemberg. He trained to be a gunsmith before studying engineering at the Stuttgart polytechnic institute. In 1872, after working for several engineering firms, Daimler became technical director for a company founded by Nikolaus A. Otto (1832–1891), who in 1876 invented the four-stroke internal-combustion engine. In 1882 Daimler founded his own firm and sought to develop an engine that could propel road vehicles.

Horseless Carriages. In 1886 in Karlstadt, Daimler and his chief engineer, Wilhelm Maybach (1846–1929), added a one-cylinder engine to a conventional four-wheeled carriage. By 1889 they had developed a carburetor that used gasoline as fuel, a four-speed gearbox, and a belt-driven mechanism to turn wheels. Their vehicle incorporating these devices traveled at eleven miles per hour. Daimler developed a booming business based on sales of engines to power airships and armored cars, but, once his firm shifted from producing engines to manufacturing automobiles, he was not an effective businessman. Despite the impressive performances of its cars in early road races, Daimler auto production remained relatively small compared to some of the larger French and American automobile manufacturers, for whom high quality was a less significant selling point than low price. In 1926, when Daimler's company merged with Benz's, total German auto production was only 50,000 per year, compared with 4.5 million in the United States.

The Mercedes. Daimler is chiefly remembered for development of the Mercedes, which was inspired by Emil Jellinek, an Austrian diplomat in France. Jellinek wanted a higher-powered automobile engine front-mounted on a longer, lower, and wider frame. Daimler manufactured a vehicle based on this design in 1901, after Jellinek promised to purchase the entire production of thirty-six cars. Jellinek insisted that the model be named after his daughter Mercedes because he was concerned that the German-sounding name Daimler would harm sales in France. Eventually, all Daimler cars were called Mercedes.

High Quality. Daimler's and Benz's success in developing the automobile was based on the impressive quality of German parts, made by a skilled German labor force using precision cutting machines. Their engineering achievements, however, were not matched by equivalent economic success until long after both men had died. After the merger in 1926, and particularly after World War II, changing market conditions created a major demand for high-quality cars, and Daimler-Benz finally became a major worldwide car manufacturer, producing the Mercedes-Benz automobile. In 1998 Daimler-Benz, the largest industrial firm in Germany, merged with American Chrysler Corporation to form DaimlerChrysler.

Sources:

Anthony Bird, *Gottlieb Daimler: Inventor of the Motor Engine* (London: Weidenfeld & Nicolson, 1962).

David Burgess-Wise, William Boddy, and Brian Laban, *The Automobile: The First Century* (London: Orbis, 1983).

Beverly Rae Kimes, *The Star and the Laurel: The Centennial History of Daimler, Mercedes, and Benz, 1886–1986* (Montvale, N.J.: Mercedes-Benz of North America, 1986).

Friedrich Schildberger, *History of Mercedes-Benz Motor Vehicles and Engines,* fifth edition (Stuttgart: Daimler-Benz, 1972).

CHARLES DARWIN

1809-1882
BIOLOGIST

Changing Careers. Born in Shrewsbury, England, Charles Robert Darwin was the grandson of the innovative potter Josiah Wedgwood (1730–1795) and the noted scientist Erasmus Darwin (1731–1802). Educated initially in the classics, Charles Darwin entered the University of Edinburgh at age sixteen to study medicine but left two years later, before completing a degree. His family intervened, sending him to Christ's College, Cambridge, in 1827 to study theology. Instead, however, Darwin turned to the field of study beloved of his grandfather Erasmus: the collection of plant, animal, and geological specimens.

Naturalist. Recognizing Darwin's true vocation, Cambridge botanist John Stevens Henslow helped to get the young man a position as a naturalist on a surveying mission aboard the HMS *Beagle*. Between 1831 and 1836 the *Beagle* visited many exotic locations in and around South America, including the Galapagos Islands, and then continued across the South Pacific, eventually circumnavigating the globe. The voyage exposed Darwin to the flora, fauna, and geology of these little-known regions, providing him with a store of knowledge that he drew on for the rest of his life. On his return to England, Darwin immediately began to write up his findings in bits and pieces, earning an impressive reputation among the scientific community. He waited to publish a theoretical explanation of his research until he could gather additional evidence and refine his ideas. Meanwhile, he lived a quiet country life, using his inherited wealth. He married his cousin Emma Wedgwood, raised a family of eight children, and devoted himself to science.

Evolution. Darwin was ultimately prompted to publish the essence of his theory by the news in 1858 that a younger man, English naturalist Alfred Russel Wallace (1823–1913), was about to circulate a paper that set forth views analogous to his own. On 1 July Darwin's and Wallace's papers on evolution were read to the Linnaean Society, and they were proclaimed co-originators of the theory of evolution. Darwin's paper was the basis for his epoch-making *On the Origin of Species by Means of Natural Selection; or, the Preservation of Favoured Races in the Struggle for Life* (1859). Darwin's basic goal was to describe how different animals could have descended from common ancestors, leading to the vast diversity of existing plants and animals. He argued that species changed, sometimes over millions of years. The process by which this evolution took place caused variations to occur randomly among individuals in a species. These variations gave rise to advantages and disadvantages that influenced survival rates. Through a process called *natural selection,* the most original of Darwin's views, the individuals of a species that were best adapted to their environment reproduced at a greater rate, thereby accelerating divergence from the norm and, over the long run, leading to changes in the whole species. Darwin also described a process he called *specialization,* through which variations in a species emerged as adaptations to diverse environmental conditions. Darwin applied his theories to humankind in *The Descent of Man, and Selection in Relation to Sex* (1871), in which he postulated that humans evolved from a hairy, ape-like animal closely related to the progenitors of the orangutan, chimpanzee, and gorilla. The common origin of these monkeys and human beings, he said, explained resemblances in physical features and even some methods of social interaction.

A Moral Controversy. The idea that species evolved through natural selection aroused a storm of protest in 1859 because it contradicted the version of creation in the Book of Genesis and Judeo-Christian convictions regarding the age of the earth. Darwin argued that the earth was millions of years old, not six thousand years old, as the Roman Catholic Church postulated. Although the scientific community adopted Darwin's conclusions rapidly, the general population of the Western world remained much more skeptical. The outcry in 1871 was even greater as a host of religious figures and moralists expressed horror at the notion of mankind's descent from an animal and the close relationship between humans and monkeys. Debate over "the descent of man," natural selection, and evolution was perhaps the most bitterly contested intellectual battle of the nineteenth century.

Social Darwinism. Darwin's views on the evolution of species were applied by men such as English philosopher Herbert Spencer (1820–1903) to groups within humankind—classes, nations, or "races"—an application Darwin explicitly repudiated. Known as "Social Darwinists," these philosophers believed that "survival of the fittest" determined social, economic, and political status, contributing to the growth of ultranationalism, imperialism, and "scientific racism" in the late nineteenth century. Though Social Darwinism has been largely repudiated, Darwin's own explanation of biological diversity through evolution is now accepted by an overwhelming majority of the scientific community.

Sources:

Philip Appleman, ed., *Darwin: A Norton Critical Edition* (New York: Norton, 1970).

Peter J. Bowler, *Charles Darwin: The Man and His Influence* (Oxford & Cambridge, Mass.: Blackwell, 1990).

Janet Browne, *Charles Darwin: A Biography* (New York: Knopf, 1995).

CAROLUS LINNAEUS

1707-1778
NATURALIST

Swedish Roots. Best known by the Latin version of his name, Carolus Linnaeus was born Carl Linné in the village of Stenbrohult in Småland, a poor province in southern Sweden. He was the eldest son of a curate-farmer and a parson's daughter. (His father, Nils, had devised the Latin surname Linnaeus after a linden tree on the family property.) Carl attended the universities of Lund and Uppsala. He became a medical doctor in 1735 and opened a practice that specialized in treating venereal disease, and in 1739 he was one of six founding members of the Swedish Academy of Science. In 1741 Linnaeus was appointed a professor of medicine at Uppsala University and rose steadily in the ranks of the Swedish royal service, as chief physician to the navy and as a high-ranking adviser to several rulers and ministries. He was ennobled for these contributions and his writings in 1761, at which time he added *von* to the Swedish form of his name (Carl von Linné).

Botanist. Linnaeus had developed an interest in botany during his university years, despite the inferior botanical collections and libraries at Lund and Uppsala. Almost alone in his interest in botany, he was largely self-taught and originally based his work on only a few examples. His system of categorizing plants was formulated not only from firsthand observation but also from his extensive teaching, public lecturing, and tutoring. His students helped collect examples of flora and fauna, beginning first around the Baltic Sea and then all over Europe. They also participated in refining the system of classification that made their teacher famous. After extensive discussion and experimentation, Linnaeus and his students created a system of binomial classification for living beings, especially plants, based on their reproductive characteristics. He hoped to create a system in which the essences of plants identified by Aristotle could be defined according to logical rules. Linnaeus believed that understanding and identifying the characteristics of plants and animals would reveal fundamental truths about nature and glorify God. He hoped that such a system would reflect the genuine order of nature—that it would be truly "natural," not simply an artificial creation of the mind.

Organizing Nature. In his *Systema Naturae* (System of Nature), published in Latin in 1735, Linnaeus suggested a five-tiered approach to organizing the plant kingdom. Moving from the general to the specific, these categories were *classes, orders, genera, species,* and *varieties.* For indexing purposes, each species was designated by its genus and species names. By explaining the nature of the various categories and clarifying how to delineate them, Linnaeus made the cataloguing of plants accessible not only to the learned but also to amateurs. To encourage the use of his system, he often named a species after the person who first identified it. The Linnaean system accelerated the organization and categorization of European natural history. Following in the footsteps of English scientist Isaac Newton (1624–1727), Linnaeus, a deeply religious man, saw the world as a balanced system created by God, but he also saw possibilities for change over time. In *Oratio de telluris habitabilis incremento* (1744; Lecture on the Increase of the Habitable Earth) Linnaeus suggested that new plants and animals might have evolved over time through hybridization. Because of this view he began a major controversy with the most widely read naturalist of his time, Frenchman Georges-Louis Leclerc, Comte de Buffon (1708–1788), head of the French Royal Gardens in Paris. Buffon, who concentrated on collecting fossil evidence and making physical experiments, rejected the notion that the classification of living beings could reveal the "truths" of nature. He saw the occupation as solely for the benefit of human understanding and argued that organisms did not change over time. Despite their differences, Buffon and Linnaeus both helped to set the stage for the evolutionary theory of Charles Darwin during the second half of the nineteenth century.

Sources:

Wilfrid Blunt, *The Compleat Naturalist: A Life of Linnaeus* (New York: Viking, 1971).

Lisbet Koerner, *Linnaeus: Nature and Nation* (Cambridge, Mass.: Harvard University Press, 1999).

Sven Widmalm, "Instituting Science in Sweden," in *The Scientific Revolution in National Context,* edited by Roy Porter and Mikulas Teich (Cambridge: Cambridge University Press, 1992), pp. 240–262.

FLORENCE NIGHTINGALE

1820-1910
NURSE

Middle-Class Upbringing. Florence Nightingale was born into a solidly upper-middle-class family. She and her elder sister, Panthenope, were educated by governesses until her Cambridge-educated father took over the task, teaching his children about the classics, the Bible, and contemporary politics. At age twenty Florence Nightingale overcame her parents' objections and was allowed to receive tutoring in her preferred subject, mathematics, at which she excelled. Becoming a tutor herself, she grew particularly interested in the application of statistical methods to social and political problems.

Answering a Call. In 1837, Nightingale believed God called her to a life of service. Strongly influenced by the example of the Sisters of Saint Vincent de Paul, whom she encountered during a visit to Egypt, she sought to become a nurse, even though that profession was not considered appropriate for an educated woman. In 1851 she received three months of nursing training at the Institute for Protestant Deaconesses at Kaiserwerth, near Düsseldorf in Prussia. She then worked for a time at a hospital run by the Sisters of Mercy near Paris before returning in 1853 to London, where she found work on Harley Street, the center of medicine in London, becoming the (unpaid) superintendent at the Establishment for Gentlewomen during Illness.

Crimea. Only a few months later, in March 1854, England and France joined the Ottoman Turks in the Crimean War against Russia. After newspaper accounts criticized the poor care given to British soldiers in the field, Secretary of War Sidney Herbert (1810–1861), a friend of Nightingale's, asked her to oversee the establishment of nurses in the field hospitals. She and thirty-eight nurses (of whom eighteen were Anglican or Roman Catholic nuns) arrived near Constantinople (now Istanbul) in early November 1854. Despite the resentment and outright opposition of doctors and military commanders, Nightingale set out to reform the sanitation, food, water supplies, and organization of the hospitals. Not only did she oversee personnel, she also performed nursing work. Because of her habit of inspecting hospitals at night, she became known as the "Lady with the Lamp." Using her mathematical skills, Nightingale established a system of keeping records and collected data that enabled her to calculate mortality rates. The results of her calculations showed that British soldiers were seven times more likely to die of diseases such as cholera or typhus in field hospitals than they were to perish in battle—a statistic she attributed to appalling sanitary conditions in the hospitals. Her reforms and the acquisition of better medical equipment caused the mortality rate to fall from 60 percent at her arrival to 43 percent in February 1855 and then to 2.2 percent by May. This success made Nightingale a national hero in England and changed the practice of medicine. Nursing became an accepted and even a prestigious profession for women, who began to play an increasing role in the health field.

Medical Reform. When she returned to England in February 1856, Nightingale took up the cause of military-hospital reform because her statistics showed that, even during peacetime, soldiers aged twenty to thirty-five suffered twice the mortality rate of civilians. Largely as a result of her efforts, Queen Victoria and Prince Albert, along with Prime Minister Henry John Temple, Viscount Palmerston (1784–1865), created the Royal Commission on the Health of the Army, which implemented important improvements in the medical care of the British armed forces at home and abroad. After an illness contracted in the Crimea kept Nightingale from working as a nurse, she became an influential voice on public-health reform. She wrote extensively on the need for proper training of nurses and midwives and sanitary reform in India, the correct design of hospital wards and buildings, and ways to improve public-health standards, particularly in rural areas. Grateful benefactors from the Crimean War era created the Nightingale Fund, which was used in 1860 to establish the Nightingale Training School and Home for Nurses, located at St. Thomas' Hospital in London. Nightingale also influenced the founding in 1861 of a system of district nursing in Liverpool, which was widely imitated. At the end of her long life, in the course of which she was frequently ill, Nightingale's contributions to public health were recognized by King Edward VII, who awarded her the Order of Merit in 1907. She was the first woman to be so honored. Although best known for her role as the "Lady with the Lamp," Nightingale contributed to a wide range of health reforms, and she consistently applied her mathematical training and organizational skills to practical problems.

Sources:

Vern L. Bullough, Bonnie Bullough, and Marietta P. Stanton, eds., *Florence Nightingale and Her Era: A Collection of New Scholarship* (New York: Garland, 1990).

Sue M. Goldie, ed., *I Have Done My Duty: Florence Nightingale in the Crimean War, 1854–56* (Iowa City: University of Iowa Press, 1987).

Elspeth Huxley, *Florence Nightingale* (London: Weidenfeld & Nicolson, 1975).

Martha Vicinus and Bea Nergaard, eds., *Ever Yours, Florence Nightingale: Selected Letters* (London: Virago, 1989).

LOUIS PASTEUR

1822-1895
CHEMIST

Education and Teaching Career. The son of a tanner, Louis Pasteur was born under humble circumstances in Dôle, France. After receiving excellent preparation and encouragement in the local schools of Arbois, where his family had moved, Pasteur earned the French equivalents of B.A. (1840) and B.S. (1842) degrees at the Royal College in Besançon. In 1843 he entered the Ecole Normale Supérieure in Paris, where he became interested in chemistry. On completion of his doctorate in 1847, Pasteur taught in Dijon, Strasbourg, and Lille. He returned to Paris in 1857, becoming director of scientific studies at the Ecole Normale Supérieure.

Brewing, Fermentation, and Pasteurization. Pasteur's initial interest was crystallography (the use of a microscope to study shapes of crystals). In the late 1840s he made an important discovery—that organic molecules are asymmetrical, an insight that underlay his later work on alcoholic fermentation. While teaching in Lille, Pasteur forged a strong working relationship with the brewing industry. In 1856 the father of one of his students, a brewer, asked Pasteur to investigate why certain brews spoiled when others stored under the same conditions did not. Using his microscope, Pasteur swiftly found that fermentation was not the simple process of sugar breaking down into alcohol, as the eighteenth-century French chemist Antoine-Laurent Lavoisier (1743–1794) had postulated. Close examination of the molecules revealed that they were asymmetrical; that is, organic. Pasteur concluded that yeast transformed sugar into alcohol and that the presence of other microorganisms could contaminate the fermentation process. His solutions to the brewers' problems were simple. He suggested that wine, beer, vinegar, and milk should be heated to moderately high temperatures for several minutes to kill microorganisms and that then the liquid should be sterilized to prevent further fermentation or other sorts of degradation. This operation is now called pasteurization. Pasteur also recommended that developing and using pure cultures of microbes and yeasts would help to create a more predictable fermentation process, making possible dramatic improvements in quality control.

Germ Theory. Because of Pasteur's success, the French Department of Agriculture made him head of a commission to investigate a catastrophic disease that was ravaging silkworms and had nearly destroyed the French silk industry. Knowing nothing about silkworms and little about biology in general, Pasteur underwent a period of intensive self-education before beginning his research. By 1868 he had isolated the bacilli of two diseases, identified environmental factors that contributed to them, and determined how to tell if a silkworm was free of disease. His solution was to teach silk farmers how to use a microscope to select disease-free worms for breeding. This practical advice helped the French and Italian silk industries to recover and contributed to the understanding of how environment influenced the spread of disease. This research also supported Pasteur's "germ theory" of disease (first articulated in 1865)—the notion that most dangerous diseases could be attributed to specific microorganisms—which was rejected by most medical practitioners during this period. Yet, he continued to isolate the bacteria that caused specific diseases and develop vaccines against them. In 1881–1882 he proved that anthrax (a deadly cattle and sheep disease) was caused solely by the anthrax bacillus and developed a vaccine against it. At the same time he developed a vaccine to fight chicken cholera.

Rabies Vaccine. In 1885 Pasteur followed his spectacular and highly publicized success with anthrax immunization by developing a vaccine against canine rabies, another deadly disease. The following year he used it successfully to cure a boy who had been bitten by a rabid dog. Infected individuals from all over the world came to his laboratory for treatment. The success of Pasteur's vaccines eventually proved the veracity of his germ theory to the medical profession and the general public. In 1888 he suffered a stroke, which made laboratory work difficult, but his biomedical work was continued at a private nonprofit organization, the Pasteur Institute, founded the previous year. Eight scientists from the Pasteur Institute have been awarded the Nobel Prize in physiology and medicine. In 1983 the AIDS virus was first isolated there.

Impact. Pasteur's findings made possible dramatic improvements in human healthcare. By determining how diseases spread and suggesting practical solutions to protect consumers and treat patients, Pasteur, his colleagues, and successors managed to bring under control many dangerous diseases—including yellow fever, diphtheria, tetanus, polio, and tuberculosis—and to eradicate others. Pasteur's career also illustrates the fruitfulness of the emerging partnership among the scientific community, industry, and the government.

Sources:

Patrice Debré, *Louis Pasteur,* translated by Elborg Forster (Baltimore: Johns Hopkins University Press, 1998).

Gerald L. Geison, *The Private Science of Louis Pasteur* (Princeton: Princeton University Press, 1995).

JAMES WATT

1736-1819
INVENTOR

Early Years. Born in Greenock, Scotland, James Watt was largely self-educated before he went to London in 1755 to learn the trade of mathematical-instrument manufacturing. Two years later he returned home to become instrument maker for the University of Glasgow. Watt became interested in steam power after he was called on to repair a Newcomen steam engine (steam used to pump water from mines). During the 1760s, with financial support from English inventor John Roebuck (1718–1794), Watt experimented with improving the efficiency of this steam engine, which operated on the negative pressure of a vacuum created when steam in a cylinder was cooled and condensed by the introduction of water. With his first engine (patented in 1769), Watt overcame the wasteful use of steam in the Newcomen design by employing a separate condensing chamber that eliminated the need to cool and reheat the cylinder for every stroke of the engine, thereby maximizing efficiency.

Businessman. A new phase in Watt's career began in 1775, after Matthew Boulton (1728–1809) purchased Roebuck's interest in Watt's engine, and the two partners began to manufacture steam engines at the Soho Engineering Works in Birmingham. Their first engine, installed in 1776, pumped water from a coal mine. Highly trained metal craftsmen at the Soho Works also contributed to the improvement of Boulton and Watt's engines. Their efficiency was greatly enhanced after 1776, when John Wilkinson (1728–1808) invented a new lathe that was capable of making pistons and cylinders with much greater precision than earlier machines. Over the next several years Watt developed and patented several other innovations, including the gears to convert the reciprocal, up-and-down movement of pistons into a continuous circular motion that could drive machines such as the loom. He also designed a system in which steam was admitted alternately to both ends of a cylinder, thus creating pressure on the piston in both strokes of the cycle and creating greater and more-continuous power. Finally, drawing on the design of a device used earlier to control windmill speed, Watt developed a steam governor that automatically regulated the speed of an engine by linking output to input, a concept fundamental to automation. Boulton and Watt also benefited from the powerful British patent system, which gave them a monopoly on their inventions. They guarded their rights fiercely.

Scientist. Boulton and Watt conceived of themselves as scientists, joining and participating faithfully in several different learned societies and indulging their interests in many subjects. This activity enhanced their national and international reputations as well as sales of their engines. In 1800 Boulton and Watt's patent rights expired, and Watt retired from business, ostensibly to devote himself solely to science. At this time England had more than five hundred operational Boulton and Watt engines. Several dozen more had been sold on the Continent, and a significant number of copies had been made in places where English patent rights could not be protected. Watt's designs and his willingness to oversee the quality of the machines he and Boulton built earned him a reputation as a scientist and inventor. Because of this renown, subsequent generations remembered him as the inventor of the steam engine, even though such engines had been in existence for generations before Watt took out his first patent. In fact, he vastly improved the efficiency of the steam engine, making it practical for use in industry, thus facilitating the mechanization so fundamental to the Industrial Revolution. Watt also originated the concept of horsepower as a measurement of energy output. As a sign of his importance to the study of efficiency and power, a unit of electrical measurement, the watt, was named after him.

Sources:

Margaret C. Jacob, *Scientific Culture and the Making of the Industrial West* (New York: Oxford University Press, 1997).

A. E. Musson and Eric Robinson, *Science and Technology in the Industrial Revolution* (Manchester, U.K.: Manchester University Press, 1969).

Jennifer Tann, *The Selected Papers of Boulton & Watt* (Cambridge, Mass.: MIT Press, 1981).

Tann and M. J. Brecklin, "The International Diffusion of the Watt Engine, 1775–1825," *Economic History Review*, 31 (1978): 541–564.

DOCUMENTARY SOURCES

Nicolas-François Appert, *L'art de conserver pendant plusieurs années, toutes les substances animales et végétales* [The Art of Preserving all Kinds of Animal and Vegetable Substances for Several Years] (Paris, 1810)—A book by the French chef who discovered the technique of canning food.

John Dalton, *A New System of Chemical Philosophy*, 2 volumes (London: Bickerstaff, 1808, 1827)—A compilation of writings by a pioneering chemist whose doctrine of "atomism" is considered the beginning of modern atomic theory.

Charles Darwin, *The Descent of Man, and Selection in Relation to Sex* (London: John Murray, 1871)—The extension of Darwin's theory of natural selection to describe the evolution of humans from primates.

Darwin, *On the Origin of Species by Means of Natural Selection; or, the Preservation of Favoured Races in the Struggle for Life* (London: John Murray, 1859)—A groundbreaking treatise on natural selection and evolution of species.

Denis Diderot and Jean Le Rond d'Alembert, eds., *Encyclopédie*, 24 volumes (Paris, 1751–1772)—A collection of scientific knowledge amassed during the Enlightenment.

Michael Faraday, *Experimental Researches in Electricity*, 3 volumes (London: Taylor, 1839–1855)—A compilation of an English scientist's important discoveries about the relationship of electricity and magnetism.

Luigi Galvani, *De viribus electricitatis in motu musculari commentarius* [A Commentary on the Strength of Electricity in Moving Muscles] (Modena, 1792)—An Italian physician's descriptions of his experiments with applying electricity to the muscles of frogs.

Edward Jenner, *Inquiry into the Cause and Effects of the Variolae Vaccinae* (1798)—A treatise on the discovery and usefulness of vaccinations.

Carolus Linnaeus (Carl Linné), *Philosophia botanica* [Botanical Philosophy] (1751)—Linneaus's assertion that the classification of the natural world could be followed back to God's original hand in creating the world.

Linnaeus, *Systema Naturae* [System of Nature] (Leipzig, 1735)—The first formulation of the modern scientific system of classifying plants, animals, and minerals according to *classes, orders, genera, species,* and *varieties.*

Joseph Lister, "On the Antiseptic Principle of The Practice of Surgery," *Lancet*, 2 (1867): 353–356—A treatise on antiseptic procedures to be followed in medical surgeries.

James Clerk Maxwell, *A Treatise on Electricity and Magnetism*, 2 volumes (Oxford: Clarendon Press, 1873)—An application of mathematics to problems raised by Faraday's revelation of the links between electricity and magnetism; this book set the stage for important twentieth-century advances in physics.

Dmitry Ivanovich Mendeleyev, *The Principles of Chemistry* (1868–1870)—A textbook by the Russian chemist who developed the periodic table of elements.

William Nicholson, *Introduction to Natural Philosophy*, 2 volumes (London: Printed for J. Johnson, 1782)—A textbook by the founder of the *Journal of Natural Philosophy, Chemistry, and the Arts* (1797–1813).

Joseph Priestley, *The History and Present State of Electricity, with Original Experiments* (London: Printed for James Dodsley, Joseph Johnson & B. Davenport, and Thomas Cadell, 1767)—Pioneering explanations of electrical properties by a scientist and clergyman.

GLOSSARY

Alchemy: A medieval scientific endeavor that attempted to transmute base metals into gold, to discover a universal cure for disease, and to establish a means of achieving immortality. Modern chemistry evolved from alchemy.

Allarde Law: The French Revolutionary reform law, passed in 1791, that abolished the medieval guild system in France.

Anglicanism: The established Church of England.

Antibody: A protective protein molecule that is produced in blood cells called lymphocytes as an immune response to an antigen, a molecule in a foreign substance such as a bacterium, virus, pollen, mold, venom, or food. The ability to create antibodies is an important part of the immune system.

Antiseptics: Physical or chemical agents (often called disinfectants) that prevent putrefaction or infection in organic tissue by destroying or repelling microorganisms.

Argand Lamp: An oil lamp invented by French chemist François Ami Argand in 1783. Influenced by A. L. Lavoisier's theories of combustion, Argand developed a lamp with an innovative wick design capable of doubling the intake of oxygen to the flame. When placed inside a glass cylinder and regulated by a mechanism for raising and lowering the wick, the flame provided a more regular and brighter light than earlier oil lamps.

Atonement: The Christian doctrine that the suffering and death of Jesus were instrumental in redeeming humanity and bringing about its reconciliation with God.

Australasia: The collective name for Australia, New Zealand, Tasmania, and Melanesia.

Bastille Day: The celebration of the storming of the Bastille on 14 July 1789, a controversial remembrance of opposition to royal authority. In 1880 this day became the official celebration of French national unity.

Berlin Conference of 1884–1885: A conference of European leaders hosted by Otto von Bismarck to negotiate the partitioning of Africa into European colonies. African leaders were not invited.

Bloomers: Knee-length pantaloons worn under a tunic, designed in 1851 by Amelia Jenks Bloomer as practical clothing for the progressive woman. Bloomers provoked much comment and derision when they were introduced.

Breech-loaded weaponry: Firearms in which ammunition cartridges—each containing a complete round of gunpowder and a projectile—are loaded in an opening at the base of the barrel.

Cameralism: The theory that economic and political management should be directed primarily at benefiting the state treasury; prevalent in eighteenth-century Prussia.

Capitalism: An economic system in which the means of production are owned by individuals or private corporations. In this system the production of goods and the distribution of income are guided by the operation of a free market. *See also* **Communism.**

Chapbooks: Popular, cheap pamphlets including ballads, poems, fairy tales, folk stories, and religious tracts, often sold by traveling merchants. By the late eighteenth century, chapbooks were published especially for children.

Cité Napoléon: The first low-rent apartment complex in Paris, opened in November 1851.

Classicism: The dominant artistic style for much of the eighteenth century. Closely modeled on ancient Greek and Roman principles, Classical art, architecture, music, and literature embodied what were understood to be the universal values of rationality, order, regularity, and symmetry.

Communism: A political and economic system in which the state or community owns the means of production and income is distributed according to need. *See also* **Capitalism.**

Conciliar: The Roman Catholic tradition of acknowledging the promulgations of the ecumenical councils as the final voice of authority in ecclesiastical matters.

Concordat: An agreement on religious matters between the Pope of the Roman Catholic Church and a secular government.

Constitution: The manner in which a state is organized and governed; also the specific, written body of rules or laws of the nation.

Core: The heart, or major region, of a nation, empire, or culture, based on population density, transport foci, and the seat of power.

Cubism: A style of early twentieth-century painting originated by Georges Bracque and Pablo Picasso. Breaking objects into fragmented geometric shapes, Cubism was a move toward greater subjectivism and abstraction in painting.

Dak: The indigenous postal system of India, which used runners to convey messages to royal courts, military outposts, and commercial centers.

Demimonde: The less-than-respectable world of courtesans, actresses, and worldly divorcées, which titillated and scandalized high society in the nineteenth century.

Despot: An absolute ruler, or tyrant, whose government is typically arbitrary and oppressive.

Dialectic method: A system of logic based on Georg Wilhelm Friedrich Hegel's concept that ideas are advanced by the resolution of contradictory elements (thesis and antithesis).

Diet: A national or provincial legislature.

Dogma: A body of formally and authoritatively affirmed religious beliefs.

Door and Window Tax: A tax on household openings instituted in France in 1798 and abolished in 1917. Because this tax increased with each door or window, it served as a sort of progressive property tax.

Dynamo: A machine that uses electromagnetism—electric currents passing through conductors and producing magnetic fields around them—to convert mechanical energy into electrical energy.

East India Company: A British joint-stock company chartered by Elizabeth I in 1600 to trade in Asian goods and commodities. In 1619 the **Mughal** emperor Jahangir gave British merchants permission to establish coastal factories, and by 1765 the company had emerged as a colonial power in India, collecting revenue and administering the legal system in Bengal, Bihar, and Orissa. By 1858, when power in India was transferred to the Crown, the company had extended British commercial influence and political power over the bulk of India. The company was dissolved in 1873.

Emancipation: The legal action of removing children from the authority of their parents. Emancipated children can manage their finances and freely enter into legal contracts, including marriage.

Empiricism: An **epistemology** dominant in the eighteenth century. Based on the premise that human beings acquire all knowledge through the experiences of the five senses, Empiricism was an outgrowth of the seventeenth-century Scientific Revolution, which affirmed that knowledge of the natural world arrived through observation, experiment, and mathematical measurement.

Environmental determinism: The belief that the culture and society of a people are determined by their environment (landforms, bodies of water, and climate).

Epistemology: The study of the origin, nature, methods, and limits of knowledge.

Ethics: The study of appropriate standards for conduct and moral judgment.

Evangelicalism: Religious doctrines that emphasize salvation by faith, personal conversion, and the authority of Scripture, while promoting the spreading of the Christian gospel through fervent preaching and missionary activities.

Evolution: The theory that all species change over time, rather than remaining the same as they were at the time of creation. The foremost evolutionist was Charles Darwin, who asserted that through a process of "natural selection" the individuals of a species best adapted to their environment reproduce at a greater rate than those not so well equipped for survival, thereby accelerating divergence from the norm and, over the long run, changes in the species.

Expressionism: An artistic style of the late nineteenth and early twentieth centuries that returned to the **Romanticist** notion that a higher spiritual existence was attainable not through rationalism but rather through feeling. Like the Romantics, Expressionists sometimes sought to explore the psyche and the meaning of identity. Unlike their predecessors, however, Expressionists departed from faithfully representing visual reality.

Genre de vie: A term coined by Paul de La Blache to describe an ecological perspective on a people's way of life, based on the influence of culture and environment.

Great European Plain: An area of western, central, and eastern Europe (including Russia) that extends from southwestern France to the Ural Mountains. It contains the medieval and modern core of Europe.

Grecian-bend corset: An undergarment that thrust forward the bust and accentuated a woman's buttocks with the use of a bustle and padding.

Greenwich Mean Time (GMT): The baseline for measuring time internationally; by the mid 1850s, most public clocks in Britain were set to the time as read at the Greenwich Observatory outside London, and in 1880 GMT became the official time for the United Kingdom as a whole. In 1884, as a result of the International Meridian Conference held in Washington, D.C., GMT was established as the basis for a system of international time zones. Sydney, Australia, for example, is nine hours ahead of GMT, while New York City is five hours behind.

Gregorian Calendar: The calendar introduced by Pope Gregory XIII in 1582 to replace the **Julian Calendar**, which overestimated the length of the solar year and had gradually fallen behind solar time. Also known as the new-style calendar, the Gregorian Calendar suppressed ten days (or, after 1700, eleven days) and makes no century year a leap year unless it is exactly divisible by 400, thus bringing calendar time into accord with solar time. The Gregorian

Calendar was adopted by Great Britain and its American colonies in 1752.

Gymnasium: A German secondary school similar to the American high school, developed in the nineteenth century.

Hambach Festival: An 1832 event that may have been the first German mass meeting. Some thirty thousand Germans met at Hambach on the Rhine to celebrate German cultural unity. The festival is commemorated in German consumer culture with Hambach hats, jackets, aprons, pipe bowls, and other items.

Heartland: The inner area of northern Eurasia, including portions of eastern Europe, which is not accessible to the sea. According to Halford Mackinder, in the railroad and air age a major power that consolidated this huge territory would be the global superpower.

Hegemony: Political dominance of a class, social group, or institution; produced not only by the use (or threat) of force, but also by the dominance of certain ideas, social norms, and ways of life that are created by intellectuals and political leaders and accepted by the population as a whole.

Immunology: The scientific study of the ways in which the body resists the invasion of other organisms, such as bacteria, viruses, and fungi.

Imperialism: The policy of extending state control over areas of the world outside the traditional boundaries of the nation, either by direct territorial acquisition or by indirect domination of the political or economic life of an area.

Impressionism: A nineteenth-century artistic style that abandoned the traditional definition of art as the representation of the external appearance of nature. Painters working in this style consciously asserted that the act of representation was more important than the subject matter of the painting, which often had little or no significance in and of itself.

Incarnation: The Christian doctrine that God took human form in the person of Jesus Christ.

Infanticide: The act of killing a newborn baby or infant.

Inoculation: Also called vaccination or immunization, a method of building a defense system in the body against a specific disease by injecting microorganisms of that disease that have been modified or killed.

Internal-combustion engine: A machine that creates mechanical energy from the release of chemical energy by a fuel (usually gasoline) burned in a combustion chamber (often called a carburetor).

Irredenta: An area outside a nation-state's borders that is claimed because the population is of the same ethnicity or national origins.

Julian Calendar: Also known as the old-style calendar (introduced in Rome in 46 B.C.E.), this calendar established the twelve-month year of 365 days with each fourth year (leap year) having 366 days. Each month has 31 or 30 days, except for February, which has 28 days (except in leap years, when it has 29). Because the Julian Calendar overestimated the length of the solar year, season dates regressed almost one day per century. The error was corrected in the **Gregorian Calendar**, which most European countries adopted in 1582.

Lettre de cachet: An arrest warrant issued by the French monarchy to authorize the confinement of an individual without trial. In the late eighteenth century, many people petitioned to have lettres de cachet issued for unruly children or wives.

Menarche: A woman's first menstrual period. In the late eighteenth and nineteenth centuries, the average age of menarche fell as nutrition and general health improved.

Metaphysics: A division of philosophy that is concerned with the fundamental nature of reality and being. *See also* **Epistemology** and **Ontology.**

Modernism: A late nineteenth- and early twentieth-century artistic style characterized in painting by fragmentation and abstraction, in music by dissonance and discord, and in literature by stylistic experimentation and moods of decadence, pessimism, and nostalgia. Marked by an extreme subjectivism, Modernist art expresses the loss of confidence in progress and improvement so prominent in Enlightenment thought.

Mughal Empire: A powerful dynasty that ruled over India from its bases in Delhi and Agra. The dynasty was founded by Zahir-ud-din Muhammad Babur, a Chaghatai Turkish ruler descended from Timur (Tamerlane) and Genghis Khan, in 1526. By 1700, the Mughals exercised control over almost all India, but their authority was rapidly undercut by infighting, Afghan invasions, and the rise of European powers. In 1858 the British abolished the position of the Mughal emperor.

Munshi: An expert in the Indian, Arabic, Persian, and Urdu languages. The **East India Company** employed munshis to teach European officers the languages of Indian diplomacy and commerce, to aid in the drafting of correspondence in Indian languages, and to work as translators and cultural guides.

Nationalism: The political belief that a nationality can flourish only with its own independent state.

Naturalism: An artistic and literary school dedicated to the "scientific" representation of objective reality. Naturalists consciously embraced the philosophy of **Positivism,** from which it took the premise that all reality operates according to immutable natural laws and, thus, the fates of all human beings are determined by heredity and environment. *See also* **Realism** and **Environmental determinism.**

Neo-Europe: An area or nation located outside Europe that is dominated demographically by people of European stock.

Oceania: Collective name for the lands of the Central and South Pacific.

Ontology: A branch of **metaphysics** concerned with the nature of and relations of being.

Optics: The branch of the physical sciences dealing with the nature and behavior of light.

Oxidation: A chemical reaction in which oxygen combines with another element or a compound to form a new compound. For example, combustion is a rapid form of oxidation; rust is formed by the slow oxidation of iron.

Papal infallibility: The Roman Catholic doctrine that a Pope's pronouncements on matters of faith and morals are free from error.

Pathogens: Disease-causing agents such as bacteria, viruses, or fungi.

Philosophes: Eighteenth-century French intellectuals whose writings embodied the principles of the Enlightenment. Believing that science and human reason could bring about progress, they were committed to the reform of politics and society.

Pietism: A religious movement stressing Bible study and religious devotion with the goal of personal conversion.

Pogrom: An organized massacre of (or attack on) Jews.

Positivism: The philosophical view that knowledge can be based only on scientifically observable facts.

Quantum Theory: An explanation of how subatomic, indivisible particles called *quanta* constitute matter and create energy.

Realism: An artistic and literary reaction against Romanticism. Based on objective observation rather than subjective imagination, Realistic art and literature often depicted ordinary or everyday people and events, attempting to do so without artistic or authorial commentary.

Republic: Any state in which supreme power is held by the elected representatives of the people (as opposed to a monarch).

Rifled weaponry: Firearms in which the interior of the barrel has spiral grooves that spin a projectile as it is fired, thereby stabilizing its path and greatly increasing its range and accuracy.

Romanticism: A late eighteenth- and early nineteenth-century style of art, literature, and music. Romantics rejected the **Classical** values of reason, order, and universalism in favor of sentiment, emotion, imagination, and subjectivity. Romantic artists, writers, and musicians were viewed (and often portrayed themselves) as individualistic, creative geniuses, and their expressions of inner vision included appreciation of the beauty and power of nature, the brotherhood of man, the value of human freedom, or the sentiment of **nationalism.**

Rotten Borough: An election district that has fewer inhabitants than other election districts with the same voting power.

Saint Monday: An unauthorized day of rest that workers in early-modern Europe frequently took to continue, or recover from, drunken weekend revelry with their fellows.

Sans-culottes: Literally, "without breeches"; revolutionary artisans and shopkeepers in France known for their distinctive dress. In particular, they did not wear the knee breeches popular among aristocrats in the eighteenth century.

Settler Colony: A colony dominated demographically by European settlers so as to create a **Neo-European** cultural region; examples of such colonies include Canada, the thirteen colonies that became the United States, Australia, and New Zealand.

Social Darwinism: The adaptation of Charles Darwin's biological theory of evolution by natural selection to apply to social, economic, and political change. Social Darwinists used the doctrine of the "survival of the fittest" to argue that Europeans were racially superior to non-Europeans (promoting **imperialism**); that the upper and middle classes were superior to the working class (favoring classism and **capitalism**); and that one's own nation was superior to neighboring nations (justifying national chauvinism).

Socialism: The theory that the community, not private individuals, should own and operate the means of production and distribution, with all members of the community sharing in the work and the products of their labor.

Sojourner Colony: A colony in which a European resides only for purposes of employment, returning to the motherland at the end of his career. Examples of such colonies, which remain predominantly non-European, include India and Nigeria.

Sumptuary Laws: Legislation that attempted to enforce social distinctions by defining how social classes should dress or tried to enforce moral standards by restricting the wearing of clothing thought to be too revealing or suggestive; such laws, which helped to protect the native textile industry by reducing the demand for imported luxury fabrics, were common in early-modern Europe.

Symbolism: A late nineteenth- and early twentieth-century style in painting and literature that embraced extreme subjectivism and employed representational images, or symbols, through which the meaning of the painting or the inner vision of the artist could be derived.

Torah: The first five books of the Hebrew Bible. Derived from the Hebrew word meaning "to teach," *Torah* is sometimes the word used to mean the entire doctrine of Judaism.

Tory: A member of the British Parliamentary Party supporting the traditional, established, political, and religious order. The Tories became the Conservative Party in the 1830s.

Veillées: French village social gatherings that combined agricultural tasks with dancing, games, and courting activities; most rural Europeans villages had similar gatherings.

Whig: A member of the British Parliamentary Party supporting reform of the British government, especially concerning the voting franchise.

GENERAL REFERENCES

GENERAL

Fernand Braudel, *A History of Civilizations* (New York: Penguin, 1994).

Phyllis Deane, *The First Industrial Revolution* (Cambridge: Cambridge University Press, 1965).

Eric J. Hobsbawm, *The Age of Empire, 1875–1914* (New York: Pantheon, 1987).

John Merriman, *A History of Modern Europe: Volume Two, From the French Revolution to the Present* (New York: Norton, 1996).

GEOGRAPHY

Atlas of World History (New York: Oxford University Press, 1999).

Tibor I. Berend and Gyorgy Ranki, *The European Periphery and Industrialization, 1780–1914* (Cambridge & New York: Cambridge University Press, 1982).

Jeremy Black, *Maps and History: Constructing Images of the Past* (New Haven: Yale University Press, 1997).

Brian W. Blouet, *Halford Mackinder: A Biography* (College Station: Texas A & M University Press, 1987).

Margarita Bowen, *Empiricism and Geographical Thought: From Francis Bacon to Alexander von Humboldt* (Cambridge: Cambridge University Press, 1981).

Fernand Braudel, *The Identity of France. Volume One: History and Environment* (New York: Harper & Row, 1988).

Anne Buttimer, *Society and Milieu in the French Geographic Tradition* (Chicago: Association of American Geographers, 1971).

"The First German National Atlas," *Rheinischer Merkor* (11 April 2002): 10.

Fay Gale and Graham Lawton, eds., *Settlement and Encounter* (Melbourne: Oxford University Press, 1969).

Ernest Gellner, *Nations and Nationalism* (Ithaca, N.Y.: Cornell University Press, 1983).

Richard Hartshorne, *The Nature of Geography: A Critical Survey of Current Thought in the Light of the Past* (Lancaster, Pa.: Association of American Geographers, 1939).

David Harvey, *Consciousness and the Urban Experience: Studies in the History and the Theory of Capitalist Urbanization* (Baltimore: Johns Hopkins University Press, 1985).

Paul M. Hohenberg and Lynn Lees, *The Making of Urban Europe, 1000–1950* (Cambridge, Mass.: Harvard University Press, 1985).

David P. Jordan, *Transforming Paris: The Life and Labors of Baron Haussmann* (Chicago: University of Chicago Press, 1995).

L. Kellner, *Alexander von Humboldt* (London & New York: Oxford University Press, 1963).

David Landes, *The Unbound Prometheus: Technological Change and Industrial Development in Western Europe from 1750 to the Present* (Cambridge: Cambridge University Press, 1969).

David Livingstone, *The Geographical Tradition* (Oxford: Blackwell, 1992).

Roy E. H. Mellor, *Nation, State, and Territory: A Political Geography* (London & New York: Routledge, 1989).

Mark Monmonier, "The Rise of the National Atlas," *Cartographica*, 3 (1994): 1–15.

Christopher Moseley and R. E. Asher, eds., *Atlas of the World's Languages* (London & New York: Routledge, 1994).

Richard Muir, *Political Geography: A New Introduction* (New York: John Wiley, 1997).

Lewis Mumford, *The City in History: Its Origins, Its Transformations, and Its Prospects* (New York: Harcourt, Brace & World, 1961).

Mumford, *The Culture of Cities* (New York: Harcourt, Brace, 1938).

Mumford, *Techniques and Civilization* (New York: Harcourt, Brace, 1934).

W. H. Parker, *Mackinder: Geography as an Aid to Statecraft* (Oxford: Clarendon Press, 1982).

James R. Penn, *Encyclopedia of Geographical Features in World History: Europe and the Americas* (Santa Barbara, Cal.: ABC-CLIO, 1997).

Lester Rowntree and others, *Diversity Amid Globalization* (Upper Saddle River, N.J.: Prentice Hall, 2000).

Hugh Seton-Watson, *Nations and States: An Inquiry into the Origins of Nations and the Politics of Nationalism* (Boulder, Colo.: Westview Press, 1977).

John R. Short, *An Introduction to Political Geography* (London & Boston: Routledge & Kegan Paul, 1982).

Helmut de Terra, *Humboldt: The Life and Times of Alexander von Humboldt, 1769–1859* (New York: Knopf, 1955).

Tim Unwin, ed., *Atlas of World Development* (New York: John Wiley, 1994).

Paul Vidal de La Blache, *Principles of Human Geography*, translated by Millicent Todd Bingham (New York: Holt, 1926).

THE ARTS

Gerald Abraham, *The Concise Oxford History of Music* (London & New York: Oxford University Press, 1979).

George J. Becker, *Master European Realists of the Nineteenth Century* (New York: Ungar, 1982).

Barry Bergdoll, *European Architecture, 1750–1890* (Oxford: Oxford University Press, 2000).

Albert Boime, *Art in an Age of Revolution, 1750–1800* (Chicago: University of Chicago Press, 1987).

Richard Brettell, *Modern Art, 1851–1929: Capitalism and Representation* (Oxford: Oxford University Press, 1999).

Timothy J. Clark, *The Painter of Modern Life: Paris in the Age of Manet and His Followers* (New York: Knopf, 1984).

Matthew Craske, *Art in Europe, 1700–1830: A History of the Visual Arts in an Era of Unprecedented Urban Economic Growth* (Oxford: Oxford University Press, 1997).

Philip Gaskell, *Landmarks in European Literature* (Edinburgh: Edinburgh University Press, 1999).

Arnold Hauser, *The Social History of Art*, volume 2 (New York: Knopf, 1952).

François Loyer, *Architecture of the Industrial Age, 1789–1914*, translated by R. F. M. Dexter (Geneva: Skira, 1983).

Anne McCauley, *Industrial Madness: Commercial Photography in Paris, 1848–1871* (New Haven: Yale University Press, 1994).

Robin Middleton and David Watkin, *Neoclassical and Nineteenth-Century Architecture* (New York: Abrams, 1981).

Fritz Novotny, *Painting and Sculpture in Europe, 1780–1880* (New Haven: Yale University Press, 1978).

Henry Raynor, *Music and Society since 1815* (New York: Schocken Books, 1976).

Raynor, *A Social History of Music from the Middle Ages to Beethoven* (New York: Schocken Books, 1972).

Robert Rosenblum, *Nineteenth-Century Art* (Englewood Cliffs, N.J.: Prentice-Hall / New York: Abrams, 1984).

Martin Travers, *An Introduction to Modern European Literature* (New York: St. Martin's Press, 1998).

William Vaughan, *Romantic Art* (New York: Oxford University Press, 1978).

COMMUNICATION, TRANSPORTATION, AND EXPLORATION

C. A. Bayly, *Empire and Information: Intelligence Gathering and Social Communication in India, 1780–1870* (Cambridge & New York: Cambridge University Press, 1996).

J. C. Beaglehole, *The Exploration of the Pacific* (London: Black, 1934).

Beaglehole, *The Life of Captain James Cook* (London: Black, 1974).

John Bierman, *Dark Safari: The Life behind the Legend of Henry Morton Stanley* (New York: Knopf, 1990).

Boyd Cable, *A Hundred Year History of the P. & O., Peninsular and Oriental Steam Navigation Company, 1837–1937* (London: I. Nicholson & Watson, 1937).

Roger Chartier, Alain Boureau, and Cécile Dauphin, eds., *Correspondence: Models of Letter-Writing from the Middle Ages to the Nineteenth Century*, translated by Christopher Woodall (Princeton: Princeton University Press, 1997).

Lewis Coe, *The Telegraph: A History of Morse's Invention and Its Predecessors in the United States* (Jefferson, N.C.: McFarland, 1993).

M. J. Daunton, *Royal Mail: The Post Office since 1840* (London & Dover, N.H.: Athlone, 1985).

David Livingstone and the Victorian Encounter with Africa (London: National Portrait Gallery, 1996).

Clarence B. Davis and Kenneth E. Wilburn Jr., eds., *Railway Imperialism* (New York: Greenwood Press, 1991).

D. A. Farnie, *East and West of Suez: The Suez Canal in History, 1854–1956* (Oxford: Clarendon Press, 1969).

David Fitzpatrick, *Oceans of Consolation: Personal Accounts of Irish Migration to Australia* (Ithaca, N.Y.: Cornell University Press, 1994).

Michael Freeman and Derek Aldcroft, *The Atlas of British Railway History* (London & Dover, N.H.: Croom Helm, 1985).

Henry Fry, *The History of North Atlantic Steam Navigation with Some Account of Early Ships and Shipowners* (New York: Scribners, 1896).

Charles P. Graves, *A World Explorer: Henry Morton Stanley* (Champaign, Ill.: Garrard, 1967).

Paul Greenhalgh, *Ephemeral Vistas: The Expositions Universelles, Great Exhibitions and World's Fairs, 1851–1939* (Manchester: Manchester University Press, 1988).

Charles W. Hallberg, *The Suez Canal: Its History and Diplomatic Importance* (New York: Columbia University Press, 1931).

Daniel R. Headrick, *The Tentacles of Progress: Technology Transfer in the Age of Imperialism, 1850–1940* (Oxford & New York: Oxford University Press, 1988).

Headrick, *The Tools of Empire: Technology and European Imperialism in the Nineteenth Century* (Oxford & New York: Oxford University Press, 1981).

Headrick, *When Information Came of Age: Technologies of Knowledge in the Age of Reason and Revolution, 1700–1850* (Oxford & New York: Oxford University Press, 2000).

Arthur Helps, *The Life and Labours of Mr. Brassey* (London: Bell & Daldy, 1872).

Peter H. Hoffenberg, *An Empire on Display: English, Indian, and Australian Exhibitions from the Crystal Palace to the Great War* (Berkeley: University of California Press, 2001).

Gerald J. Holzmann and Bjorn Pehrson, *The Early History of Data Networks* (Los Alamitos, Cal.: IEEE Computer Society, 1995).

Anne Hugon, *The Exploration of Africa: From Cairo to the Cape* (New York: Abrams, 1993).

Richard R. John, *Spreading the News: The American Postal System from Franklin to Morse* (Cambridge: Harvard University Press, 1995).

Denis Judd, *Livingstone in Africa* (London: Wayland, 1973).

Ian J. Kerr, *Building the Railways of the Raj, 1850–1900* (Delhi: Oxford University Press, 1995).

Ferdinand de Lesseps, *The History of the Suez Canal: A Personal Narrative*, translated by Sir Henry Drummond Wolff (Edinburgh & London: Blackwood, 1876).

Mohini Lal Majumdar, *Early History and Growth of Postal System in India* (Calcutta: Rddhi-India, 1995).

Keith Middlemas, *The Master Builders: Thomas Brassey, Sir John Aird, Lord Cowdray, Sir John Norton-Griffiths* (London: Hutchinson, 1963).

Hiram Morgan, ed., *Information, Media and Power Through the Ages* (Dublin: University College Dublin Press, 2001).

John Parker, ed., *Merchants and Scholars: Essays in the History of Exploration and Trade* (Minneapolis: University of Minnesota Press, 1965).

Frances Porter and Charlotte MacDonald, eds., *My Hand Will Write What My Heart Dictates: The Unsettled Lives of Women in Nineteenth-Century New Zealand as Revealed to Sisters, Family, and Friends* (Auckland: Auckland University Press, 1996).

Louise Purbrick, ed., *The Great Exhibition of 1851: New Interdisciplinary Essays* (Manchester: Manchester University Press, 2001).

A. L. Rice, *Voyages of Discovery: Three Centuries of Natural History Exploration* (New York: C. Potter, 1999).

Howard Robinson, *The British Post Office: A History* (Westport, Conn.: Greenwood Press, 1970).

Andrew Ross, *David Livingstone: Mission and Empire* (London: Hambledon & London, 2002).

K. T. Rowland, *Steam at Sea: A History of Steam Navigation* (New York: Praeger, 1970).

Robert W. Rydell, *World of Fairs: The Century-of-Progress Expositions* (Chicago: University of Chicago Press, 1993).

Rydell, John E. Findling, and Kimberly D. Pelle, *Fair America: World's Fairs in the United States* (Washington, D.C.: Smithsonian Institution Press, 2000).

Marshall Sahlins, *Islands of History* (Chicago: University of Chicago Press, 1985).

Wolfgang Schivelbusch, *The Railway Journey: Trains and Travel in the 19th Century* (New York: Urizen, 1979).

Hugh J. Schonfield, *The Suez Canal in Peace and War, 1869–1969* (London: Vallentine & Mitchell, 1969).

Donald Simpson, *Dark Companions: The African Contribution to the European Exploration of East Africa* (New York: Barnes & Noble, 1975).

David Norman Smith, *The Railway and Its Passengers: A Social History* (North Pomfret, Vt.: David & Charles, 1988).

Dorothy Stanley, ed., *The Autobiography of Sir Henry Morton Stanley* (Boston: Houghton Mifflin, 1909).

John Tallis, *Tallis's History and Description of the Crystal Palace, and the Exhibition of the World's Industry in 1851*, 3 volumes (London & New York: J. Tallis, 1852).

Alan Villiers, *Captain Cook, the Seaman's Seaman: A Study of the Great Discoverer* (London: Hodder & Stoughton, 1967).

Charles Walker, *Thomas Brassey: Railway Builder* (London: Muller, 1969).

Peter Whitfield, *New Found Lands: Maps in the History of Exploration* (New York: Routledge, 1998).

Brian Winston, *Media, Technology and Society: A History from the Telegraph to the Internet* (London & New York: Routledge, 1998).

Lynne Withey, *Voyages of Discovery: Captain Cook and the Exploration of the Pacific* (New York: Morrow, 1987).

Richard Worth, *Stanley and Livingstone and the Exploration of Africa in World History* (Berkeley Heights, N.J.: Enslow, 2000).

SOCIAL CLASS SYSTEM AND THE ECONOMY

Richard Abraham, *Rosa Luxemburg: A Life for the International* (Oxford & New York: Berg, 1989).

Peter Baldwin, *The Politics of Social Solidarity: Class Bases of the European Welfare State, 1875–1975* (Cambridge & New York: Cambridge University Press, 1990).

Betty Balfour, ed., *Selected Letters of Constance Lytton* (London: Heinemann, 1925).

Doris Beik and Paul Beik, eds. and trans., *Flora Tristan, Utopian Feminist: Her Travel Diaries and Personal Crusade* (Bloomington: Indiana University Press, 1993).

Maxine Berg, ed., *Markets and Manufacture in Early Industrial Europe* (London & New York: Routledge, 1991).

Jerome Blum, *The End of the Old Order in Rural Europe* (Princeton: Princeton University Press, 1978).

Blum, *Lord and Peasant in Russia from the Ninth to the Nineteenth Century* (Princeton: Princeton University Press, 1961).

Duncan Blythell, *The Sweated Trades: Outwork in Nineteenth-Century Britain* (New York: St. Martin's Press, 1978).

M. L. Bush, *Rich Noble, Poor Noble* (Manchester & New York: Manchester University Press, 1988).

Craig Calhoun, *The Question of Class Struggle: Social Foundations of Popular Radicalism during the Industrial Revolution* (Chicago: University of Chicago Press, 1982).

J. D. Chambers and G. E. Mingay, *The Agricultural Revolution 1750–1880* (London: Batsford, 1966).

Mary Ann Clawson, *Constructing Brotherhood: Class, Gender, and Fraternalism* (Princeton: Princeton University Press, 1989).

Judith Coffin, *The Politics of Women's Work: The Paris Garment Trades, 1750–1915* (Princeton: Princeton University Press, 1996).

Elizabeth Crawford, *The Women's Suffrage Movement: A Reference Guide, 1866–1928* (London: UCL Press, 1999).

James E. Cronin and Carmen Siranni, *Work, Community, and Power: The Experience of Labor in Europe and America, 1900–1925* (Philadelphia: Temple University Press, 1983).

Gary Cross, *A Quest for Time: The Reduction of Work in Britain and France, 1840–1940* (Berkeley: University of California Press, 1989).

Maire Cross and Tim Gray, *The Feminism of Flora Tristan* (Oxford & Providence: Berg, 1992).

Geoffrey Crossick, ed., *The Lower Middle Class in Britain, 1870–1914* (New York: St. Martin's Press, 1977).

Hugh Cunningham, *Children and Childhood in Western Society since 1500* (London & New York: Longman, 1995).

Leonore Davidoff and Catherine Hall, *Family Fortunes: Men and Women of the English Middle Class, 1780–1850* (Chicago: Chicago University Press, 1987).

Dominique Desanti, *A Woman in Revolt: A Biography of Flora Tristan,* translated by Elizabeth Zelvin (New York: Crown, 1976).

Jonathan Dewald, *The European Nobility: 1400–1800* (New York: Cambridge University Press, 1996).

W. English, *The Textile Industry: An Account of the Early Inventions of Spinning, Weaving, and Knitting Machines* (London: Longman, 1969).

James R. Farr, *Artisans in Europe, 1350–1914* (Cambridge & New York: Cambridge University Press, 2000).

Karen Fisk, "Richard Arkwright: Cotton King or Spin Doctor?" *History Today,* 48 (March 1998): 25–30.

Robert Forster, *The Nobility of Toulouse in the Eighteenth Century: A Social and Economic Study* (Baltimore: Johns Hopkins University Press, 1960).

Laura L. Frader and Sonya O. Rose, eds., *Gender and Class in Modern Europe* (Ithaca, N.Y.: Cornell University Press, 1996).

Dick Geary, *European Labour Protest, 1848–1939* (New York: St. Martin's Press, 1981).

Gay L. Gullickson, *Spinners and Weavers of Auffay: Rural Industry and the Sexual Division of Labor in a French Village, 1750–1850* (Cambridge & New York: Cambridge University Press, 1986).

Colin Heywood, *Childhood in Nineteenth-Century France: Work, Health, and Education among the "Classes Populaires"* (Cambridge & New York: Cambridge University Press, 1988).

E. J. Hobsbawm, *Labouring Men: Studies in the History of Labour* (London: Weidenfeld & Nicolson, 1964).

Eric Hopkins, *Childhood Transformed: Working-Class Children in Nineteenth-Century England* (Manchester & New York: Manchester University Press, 1994).

Pat Hudson and W. R. Lee, eds., *Women's Work and the Family Economy in Historical Perspective* (Manchester & New York: Manchester University Press, 1990).

Olwen Hufton, "Women and the Family Economy of Eighteenth-Century France," *French Historical Studies,* 9 (Spring 1975): 1–22.

B. L. Hutchins and A. Harrison, *A History of Factory Legislation* (Westminster, U.K.: P. S. King, 1907).

Mathilde Jacob, *Rosa Luxemburg: An Intimate Portrait,* translated by Hans Fernbach (London: Lawrence & Wishart, 2000).

Gareth Stedman Jones, *Languages of Class: Studies in English Working Class History, 1832–1982* (Cambridge & New York: Cambridge University Press, 1983).

Eric Kerridge, *Textile Manufactures in Early Modern England* (Manchester, U.K. & Dover, N.H.: Manchester University Press, 1985).

Jurgen Kocka and Allen Mitchell, eds., *Bourgeois Society in Nineteenth-Century Europe* (Oxford & Providence: Berg, 1993).

Peter Kolchin, *Unfree Labor: American Slavery and Russian Serfdom* (Cambridge, Mass.: Belknap Press of Harvard University, 1987).

David S. Landes, *The Unbound Prometheus: Technological Change and Industrial Development in Western Europe from 1750 to the Present* (London: Cambridge University Press, 1969).

Constance Lytton, *Prisons and Prisoners: Some Personal Experiences by Constance Lytton and Jane Warton, Spinster* (London: Heinemann, 1914).

John M. Merriman, *The Agony of the Republic: The Repression of the Left in Revolutionary France, 1848–1851* (New Haven: Yale University Press, 1978).

R. J. Morris, *Class and Class Consciousness in the Industrial Revolution, 1780–1850* (London: Macmillan, 1979).

Ivy Pinchbeck, *Women Workers and the Industrial Revolution, 1750–1850* (London: Routledge, 1930).

June Purvis and Sandra Stanley Holton, eds., *Votes for Women* (London & New York: Routledge, 2000).

William M. Reddy, *The Rise of Market Culture: The Textile Trade and French Society, 1750–1900* (Cambridge & New York: Cambridge University Press, 1984).

Richard L. Rudolph, ed., *The European Peasant Family and Society: Historical Studies* (Liverpool: Liverpool University Press, 1995).

Kirkpatrick Sale, *Rebels against the Future: The Luddites and Their War on the Industrial Revolution: Lessons for the Computer Age* (Reading, Mass.: Addison-Wesley, 1995).

Wolfgang Schivelbusch, *Geschichte der Eisenbahnreise* (New York: Urizen Books, 1979), translated by Angela Davies as *The Railway Journey: The Industrialization of Time and Space in the Nineteenth Century* (Berkeley: University of California Press, 1986).

James A. Schmiechen, *Sweated Industries and Sweated Labor: The London Clothing Trades, 1860–1914* (Urbana: University of Illinois Press, 1984).

Donald E. Shepardson, *Rosa Luxemburg and the Noble Dream* (New York: Peter Lang, 1996).

Samuel Smiles, *Self-Help: With Illustrations of Character and Conduct* (London: Murray, 1860).

Bonnie G. Smith, *Ladies of the Leisure Class: The Bourgeoisies of Northern France in the Nineteenth Century* (Princeton: Princeton University Press, 1981).

K. D. M. Snell, *Annals of the Labouring Poor: Social Change and Agrarian England, 1660–1900* (Cambridge & New York: Cambridge University Press, 1985).

Peter N. Stearns, *Lives of Labor: Work in a Maturing Industrial Society* (New York: Holmes & Meier, 1975).

Mary Lynn Stewart, *Women, Work and the French State: Labor Protection & Social Patriarchy, 1879–1919* (Montreal: McGill-Queen's University Press, 1989).

Lawrence Stone and Jeanne C. Fawtier Stone, *An Open Elite?: England, 1540–1880* (Oxford: Clarendon Press / New York: Oxford University Press, 1984).

Michael Sullivan, *The Development of the British Welfare State* (New York: Prentice Hall, 1996).

Barbara Taylor, *Eve and the New Jerusalem: Socialism and Feminism in the Nineteenth Century* (London: Virago, 1983).

Pat Thane, *Foundations of the Welfare State* (London & New York: Longman, 1982).

Malcolm I. Thomis, *The Luddites: Machine-Breaking in Regency England* (Newton Abbot, U.K.: David & Charles / Hamden, Conn.: Archon, 1970).

E. P. Thompson, *The Making of the English Working Class* (London: Gollancz, 1963).

Thompson, "Time, Work-Discipline, and Industrial Capitalism," *Past and Present*, 38 (1967): 56–97.

Thompson and Eileen Yeo, eds., *The Unknown Mayhew: Selections from the Morning Chronicle, 1849–1850* (London: Merlin, 1971).

Charles Tilly, Louise A. Tilly, and Richard Tilly, *The Rebellious Century, 1830–1930* (Cambridge, Mass.: Harvard, 1975).

Louise A. Tilly and Joan W. Scott, *Women, Work and Family* (New York: Holt, Rinehart & Winston, 1978).

Lee Shai Weissbach, *Child Labor Reform in Nineteenth-Century France: Assuring the Future Harvest* (Baton Rouge: Louisiana State University Press, 1989).

POLITICS, LAW, AND THE MILITARY

John Alexander, *Emperor of the Cossacks; Pugachev and the Frontier Jacquerie of 1773–1775* (Lawrence, Kans.: Coronado Press, 1973).

Fred Anderson, *The Crucible of War: The Seven Years' War and the Fate of Empire in British North America* (New York: Knopf, 2000).

Daniel Balmuth, *Censorship in Russia, 1865–1905* (Washington, D.C.: University Press of America, 1979).

Derek Beales, *From Castlereagh to Gladstone, 1815–1885* (London: Thomas Nelson, 1969).

Edward Berenson, *The Trial of Madame Caillaux* (Berkeley: University of California Press, 1992).

Robert Billinger, *Metternich and the German Question: States' Rights and Federal Duties, 1820–1834* (Newark: University of Delaware Press, 1991).

Jeremy Black, *Pitt the Elder* (Cambridge & New York: Cambridge University Press, 1992).

T. C. W. Blanning, *The Origins of the French Revolutionary Wars* (New York: Longman, 1986).

James F. Brennan, *The Reflection of the Dreyfus Affair in the European Press, 1897–1899* (New York: Peter Lang, 1998).

John Brewer, *The Sinews of Power: War, Money, and the English State, 1688–1783* (New York: Knopf, 1991).

Peter D. Brown, *William Pitt, Earl of Chatham, the Great Commoner* (London: Allen & Unwin, 1978).

Charles S. Buckland, *Metternich and the British Government from 1809 to 1813* (London: Macmillan, 1932).

Peter Buckman, *Lafayette: A Biography* (New York: Paddington, 1977).

Michael Burns, *Dreyfus: A Family Affair, 1789–1945* (New York: HarperCollins, 1991).

Clive Church, *1830 in Europe: Revolution and Political Change* (New York: Oxford University Press, 1983).

Vincent Cronin, *Catherine, Empress of All Russias* (New York: Morrow, 1978).

John Davis, *Conflict and Control: Law and Order in Nineteenth-Century Italy* (Atlantic Highlands, N.J.: Humanities Press International, 1988).

William Doyle, *Origins of the French Revolution* (Oxford: Oxford University Press, 1988).

Georges Duveau, *1848: The Making of a Revolution*, translated by Anne Carter (New York: Pantheon, 1967).

Alan Forrest, *Conscripts and Deserters: The Army and French Society during the Revolution and Empire* (New York: Oxford University Press, 1989).

Lothar Gall, *Bismarck: The White Revolutionary*, 2 volumes, translated by J. A. Underwood (Boston: Allen & Unwin, 1986).

Giuseppe Garibaldi, *Autobiography of Giuseppe Garibaldi* (London: W. Smith & Innes, 1889).

Norman Gash, *Aristocracy and People: Britain, 1815–1865* (Cambridge, Mass.: Harvard University Press, 1979).

James George, *History of Warships: From Ancient Times to the Twenty-first Century* (Annapolis: Naval Institute Press, 1998).

D. A. Hamer, *Liberal Politics in the Age of Gladstone and Rosebery: A Study in Leadership and Policy* (Oxford: Clarendon Press, 1972).

Theodore Hamerow, *Restoration, Revolution, and Reaction: Economics and Politics in Germany, 1815–1871* (Princeton: Princeton University Press, 1958).

Brayton Harris, *The Age of the Battleship, 1890–1922* (New York: Watts, 1965).

Joan Haslip, *Catherine the Great* (London: Weidenfeld & Nicolson, 1977).

Bascom B. Hayes, *Bismarck and Mitteleuropa* (Rutherford, N.J.: Fairleigh Dickinson University Press, 1994).

Christopher Hibbert, *Garibaldi and His Enemies: The Clash of Arms and Personalities in the Making of Italy* (London: Longmans, 1965).

J. Hittle, *The Military Staff* (Harrisburg: University of Pennsylvania Press, 1961).

Eric J. Hobsbawm and George Rudé, *Captain Swing* (New York: Norton, 1975).

Hajo Holborn, *History of Modern Germany*, 3 volumes (New York: Knopf, 1968).

Kate Hotblack, *Chatham's Colonial Policy; A Study in the Fiscal and Economic Implications of the Colonial Policy of the Elder Pitt* (London: Routledge, 1917).

Roy Jenkins, *Gladstone, a Biography* (New York: Random House, 1997).

James Joll, *The Origins of the First World War* (New York: Longman, 1984).

John Keegan, *The Mask of Command* (New York: Viking, 1987).

George F. Kennan, *The Fateful Alliance: France, Russia, and the Coming of the First War* (New York: Pantheon, 1984).

Cecil King, *H.M.S.; His Majesty's Ships and Their Forbears* (London: Studio Publications, 1940).

Lloyd Kramer, *Lafayette in Two Worlds: Public Cultures and Personal Identities in an Age of Revolutions* (Chapel Hill: University of North Carolina Press, 1996).

Lawrence Lafore, *The Long Fuse* (New York: Praeger, 1965).

Marie-Christine Leps, *Apprehending the Criminal: The Production of Deviance in Nineteenth-Century Discourse* (Durham, N.C.: Duke University Press, 1992).

Colin Lucas, ed., *The Political Culture of the French Revolution* (New York: Oxford University Press, 1989).

Isabel de Madariaga, *Russia in the Age of Catherine the Great* (New Haven: Yale University Press, 1981).

René Maine, *Trafalgar: Napoleon's Naval Waterloo*, translated by R. Eldon and B. W. Robinson (New York: Scribners, 1975).

Robert Massie, *Dreadnought: Britain, Germany, and the Coming of the Great War* (New York: Random House, 1991).

H. C. Matthew, *Gladstone, 1809–1874* (Oxford: Clarendon Press, 1986).

Arthur J. May, *The Age of Metternich, 1814–1848* (New York: Holt, Rinehart & Winston, 1962).

James F. McMillan, *Napoleon III* (New York: Longman, 1991).

Sylvia Neely, *Lafayette and the Liberal Ideal, 1814–1824: Politics and Conspiracy in an Age of Reaction* (Carbondale: Southern Illinois University Press, 1991).

Florence Nightingale, *Letters from the Crimea, 1854–1856,* edited by Sue Goldie (New York: St. Martin's Press, 1997).

Augustus Oakes, *The Great European Treaties of the Nineteenth Century* (Oxford: Clarendon Press, 1918).

Derek Offord, *Nineteenth-Century Russia: Opposition to Autocracy* (London: Longman, 1999).

R. R. Palmer, *The Age of Democratic Revolution: A Political History of Europe and America, 1760–1800,* 2 volumes (Princeton: Princeton University Press, 1959–1964).

Palmer, *The Twelve Who Ruled: The Year of Terror in the French Revolution* (Princeton: Princeton University Press, 1989).

Marie Peters, *The Elder Pitt* (London & New York: Longman, 1998).

Otto Pflanze, *Bismarck and the Development of Germany: The Period of Unification* (Princeton: Princeton University Press, 1963).

Peter de Polnay, *Garibaldi: The Legend and the Man* (London: Hollis & Carter, 1960).

J. L. Richardson, *Crisis Diplomacy: The Great Powers since the Mid-Nineteenth Century* (Cambridge: Cambridge University Press, 1994).

Gunther Rothenberg, *The Art of Warfare in the Age of Napoleon* (Bloomington: Indiana University Press, 1978).

Trevor Royle, *Crimea: The Great Crimean War, 1854–1856* (New York: St. Martin's Press, 2000).

George Rude, *Criminal and Victim: Crime and Society in Early Nineteenth-Century England* (Oxford: Oxford University Press, 1985).

George H. Rupp, *A Wavering Friendship: Russia and Austria, 1876–1878* (Cambridge: Harvard University Press, 1941).

Petr A. Saburov, *The Saburov Memoirs, or Bismarck and Russia: Being Fresh Light on the League of the Three Emperors, 1881* (Cambridge: Cambridge University Press, 1929).

Bernard Schwartz, *The Code Napoleon and the Common-Law World* (New York: New York University Press, 1956).

Robert M. Schwarz, *Policing the Poor in Eighteenth-Century France* (Chapel Hill: University of North Carolina, 1988).

Matthew Seligmann, *Germany from Reich to Republic, 1871–1918: Politics, Hierarchy and Elites* (New York: St. Martin's Press, 2000).

William H. Sewell, *A Rhetoric of Bourgeois Revolution: The Abbé Sieyes and What Is the Third Estate?* (Durham, N.C.: Duke University Press, 1994).

Richard Shannon, *Gladstone* (Chapel Hill: University of North Carolina Press, 1984).

Alan Sked, *The Decline and Fall of the Habsburg Empire* (New York: Longman, 1989).

Adam Smith, *Inquiry into the Nature and Causes of the Wealth of Nations,* edited by Robert Reich (New York: Modern Library, 2000).

Denis Mack Smith, *Cavour and Garibaldi, 1860: A Study of Political Conflict* (New York: Oxford University Press, 1985).

A. J. P. Taylor, *Bismarck, the Man and Statesman* (London: Hamilton, 1955).

E. P. Thompson, *Whigs and Hunters: The Origin of the Black Act* (New York: Pantheon, 1975).

Andrea Viotti, *Garibaldi: The Revolutionary and His Men* (Poole, U.K.: Blandford, 1979).

David Wetzel, *A Duel of Giants: Bismarck, Napoleon III, and the Origins of the Franco-Prussian War* (Madison: University of Wisconsin Press, 2001).

Isser Woloch, *The New Regime: Transformations of the French Civic Order, 1789–1820s* (Princeton: Princeton University Press, 1994).

E. L. Woodward, *The Age of Reform, 1815–1870* (Oxford: Oxford University Press, 1962).

Theodore Zeldin, *The Political System of Napoleon III* (New York: St. Martin's Press, 1971).

LEISURE, RECREATION, AND DAILY LIFE

William J. Baker, *Sports in the Western World,* revised edition (Urbana: University of Illinois Press, 1988).

Denis Brailsford, *Sport and Society: Elizabeth to Anne* (London: Routledge & Kegan Paul, 1969).

Piero Camporesi, *Exotic Brew: The Art of Living in the Age of Enlightenment* (Oxford: Polity Press, 1994).

Edwin Chadwick, *Report on the Sanitary Condition of the Labouring Population of Great Britain,* edited by M. W. Flinn (Edinburgh: Edinburgh University Press, 1965).

Alain Corbin, *The Foul and the Fragrant: Odor and the Social Imagination* (Cambridge, Mass.: Harvard University Press, 1986).

Dorothy Davis, *Fairs, Shops, and Supermarkets: A History of English Shopping* (Toronto: University of Toronto Press, 1966).

Victoria De Grazia and Ellen Furlough, eds., *The Sex of Things: Gender and Consumption in Historical Perspective* (Berkeley: University of California Press, 1996).

John Ford, *Cricket: A Social History, 1700–1835* (Newton Abbot, U.K.: David & Charles, 1972).

Robert Forster and Orest Ranum, eds., *Food and Drink in History: Selections from the Annales: economies, sociétés, civilizations,* volume 5 (Baltimore: Johns Hopkins University Press, 1979).

Jack Goody, *Cooking, Cuisine, and Class: A Study in Comparative Sociology* (Cambridge: Cambridge University Press, 1982).

Elliott J. Gorn, *The Manly Art: Bare-Knuckle Prize Fighting in America* (Ithaca, N.Y.: Cornell University Press, 1986).

Katherine Grier, *Culture and Comfort: Parlor Making and Middle-Class Identity* (Washington, D.C.: Smithsonian Institution Press, 1988).

Alan Guttman, *Games and Empires: Modern Sports and Cultural Imperialism* (New York: Columbia University Press, 1994).

Erna Olafson Hellerstein, Leslie Parker Hume, and Karen M. Offen, eds., *Victorian Women: A Documentary Account of Women's Lives in Nineteenth-Century England, France, and the United States* (Stanford, Cal.: Stanford University Press, 1981).

Eric J. Hobsbawm and Terence Ranger, eds., *The Invention of Tradition* (Cambridge: Cambridge University Press, 1983).

Richard Holt, *Sport and the British: A Modern History* (Oxford: Oxford University Press, 1990).

Holt, "Women, Men and Sport in France, c. 1870–1914: An Introductory Survey," *Journal of Sport History,* 18, no. 1 (1991): 121–134.

Julie L. Horan, *The Porcelain God: A Social History of the Toilet* (Secaucus, N.J.: Birch Lane Press, 1996).

Dominique Laporte, *History of Shit* (Cambridge, Mass.: MIT Press, 2000).

Harvey A. Levenstein, *Revolution at the Table: The Transformation of the American Diet* (New York: Oxford University Press, 1988).

Kathleen E. McCrone, "Class, Gender, and English Women's Sport, c. 1890–1914," *Journal of Sport History,* 18, no. 1 (1991): 159–181.

Neil McKendrick, John Brewer, and J. H. Plumb, *The Birth of a Consumer Society: The Commercialization of Eighteenth-Century England* (Bloomington: Indiana University Press, 1982).

Michael B. Miller, *The Bon Marché: Bourgeois Culture and the Department Store, 1869–1920* (Princeton: Princeton University Press, 1981).

George L. Mosse, *The Nationalization of the Masses: Political Symbolism and Mass Movements in Germany from the Napoleonic Wars through the Third Reich* (New York: Fertig, 1975).

Stephen Nissenbaum, *The Battle for Christmas: A Cultural History of America's Most Cherished Holiday* (New York: Knopf, 1997).

Michelle Perrot, ed., *From the Fires of Revolution to the Great War,* translated by Arthur Goldhammer, volume 4 of *A History of Private Life,* general eds. Philippe Ariès and Georges Duby (Cambridge, Mass.: Harvard University Press, 1990).

Philippe Perrot, *Fashioning the Bourgeoisie: A History of Clothing in the Nineteenth Century,* translated by Richard Bienvenu (Princeton: Princeton University Press, 1994).

R. M. Pritchard, *Housing and the Spatial Structure of the City: Residential Mobility and the Housing Market in an English City since the Industrial Revolution* (Cambridge: Cambridge University Press, 1976).

Donald Reid, *Paris Sewers and Sewermen: Realities and Representations* (Cambridge, Mass.: Harvard University Press, 1991).

Aileen Ribeiro, *Dress and Morality* (New York: Holmes & Meier, 1986).

Daniel Roche, *The Culture of Clothing* (Cambridge: Cambridge University Press, 1994).

Keith A. P. Sandiford, "English Cricket Crowds During the Victorian Age," *Journal of Sport History,* 9, no. 3 (1982): 5–20.

Wolfgang Schivelbusch, *Disenchanted Night: The Industrialization of Light in the Nineteenth Century,* translated by Angela Davies (Berkeley: University of California Press, 1995).

Debra L. Silverman, *Art Nouveau in Fin-de-Siècle France: Politics, Psychology, and Style* (Berkeley: University of California Press, 1989).

Bonnie G. Smith, *Ladies of the Leisure Class: The Bourgeoises of Northern France in the Nineteenth Century* (Princeton: Princeton University Press, 1981).

Rebecca L. Spang, *The Invention of the Restaurant: Paris and Modern Gastronomic Culture* (Cambridge, Mass.: Harvard University Press, 2000).

Valerie Steele, *Fashion and Eroticism: Ideals of Feminine Beauty from the Victorian Era to the Jazz Age* (New York: Oxford University Press, 1985).

John Nelson Tarn, *Five Per Cent Philanthropy: An Account of Housing in Urban Areas between 1840 and 1914* (Cambridge: Cambridge University Press, 1973).

Maguelonne Toussaint-Samat, *A History of Food,* translated by Anthea Bell (Oxford: Blackwell, 1992).

Georges Vigarello, *Concepts of Cleanliness* (Cambridge: Cambridge University Press, 1988).

Margaret Visser, *Much Depends on Dinner: The Extraordinary History and Mythology, Allure and Obsessions, Perils and Taboos, of an Ordinary Meal* (New York: Grove, 1986).

Visser, *The Rituals of Dinner: The Origins, Evolution, Eccentricities, and Meaning of Table Manners* (New York: Grove/Weidenfeld, 1991).

Whitney Walton, *France at the Crystal Palace: Bourgeois Taste and Artisan Manufacture in the Nineteenth Century* (Berkeley: University of California Press, 1992).

FAMILY AND SOCIAL TRENDS

James Albisetti, *Schooling German Girls and Women: Secondary and Higher Education in the Nineteenth Century* (Princeton: Princeton University Press, 1988).

Ann Taylor Allen, *Feminism and Motherhood in Germany, 1800–1914* (New Brunswick, N.J.: Rutgers University Press, 1991).

George Alter, *The Family and the Female Life Course: The Women of Verviers, Belgium, 1849–1880* (Madison: University of Wisconsin Press, 1988).

Massimo Livi Bacci, *The Population of Europe,* translated by Cynthia De Nardi Ipsen and Carl Ipsen (Malden, Mass.: Blackwell, 2000).

Renate Bridenthal, Susan Mosher Stuard, and Merry E. Wiesner, eds., *Becoming Visible: Women in European History,* third edition, revised (Boston: Houghton Mifflin, 1998).

André Burguière, Christiane Klapisch-Zuber, Martine Segalen, and Françoise Zonabend, eds., *The Impact of Modernity,* volume 2 of *A History of the Family,* translated by Sarah Hanbury Tenison, Rosemary Morris, and Andrew Wilson (Cambridge, Mass.: Belknap Press of Harvard University Press, 1996).

Linda Clark, *Schooling the Daughters of Marianne: Textbooks and the Socialization of Girls in Modern French Primary Schools* (Albany: State University of New York Press, 1984).

Hugh Cunningham, *Children and Childhood in Western Society since 1500* (New York: Longman, 1995).

Leonore Davidoff and Catherine Hall, *Family Fortunes: Men and Women of the English Middle Class, 1780–1850* (Chicago: University of Chicago Press, 1987).

Lisa DiCaprio and Merry E. Wiesner, eds., *Lives and Voices: Sources in European Women's History* (Boston: Houghton Mifflin, 2001).

Carol Dyhouse, *Girls Growing Up in Late Victorian and Edwardian England* (Boston: Broadway House, 1981).

Barbara Alpern Engel, *Mothers and Daughters: Women of the Intelligentsia of Nineteenth-Century Russia* (Cambridge: Cambridge University Press, 1985).

Laura Engelstein, *The Keys to Happiness: Sex and the Search for Modernity in Fin-de-Siècle Russia* (Ithaca, N.Y.: Cornell University Press, 1992).

Valerie A. Fildes, *Breasts, Bottles, and Babies: A History of Infant Feeding* (Edinburgh: Edinburgh University Press, 1986).

Genevieve Fraisse and Michelle Perrot, eds., *Emerging Feminism from Revolution to World War,* volume 4 of *A History of Women in the West* (Cambridge, Mass.: Belknap Press of Harvard University Press, 1993).

Rachel Fuchs, *Poor and Pregnant in Paris* (New Brunswick: Rutgers University Press, 1996).

John Gillis, *For Better, For Worse: British Marriages, 1600 to the Present* (New York: Oxford University Press, 1985).

Gillis, *Youth and History: Tradition and Change in European Age Relations, 1770-Present,* expanded edition (New York: Academic Press, 1981).

D. V. Glass and D. E. C. Eversley, *Population and History: Essays in Historical Demography* (London: Arnold, 1965).

Deborah Gorham, *The Victorian Girl and the Feminine Ideal* (Bloomington: Indiana University Press, 1982).

Raymond Grew and Patrick Harrigan, *School, State, and Society: The Growth of Elementary Schooling in Nineteenth-Century France* (Ann Arbor: University of Michigan Press, 1991).

Tamara K. Hareven and Robert Wheaton, eds., *Family and Sexuality in French History* (Philadelphia: University of Pennsylvania Press, 1980).

Colin Heywood, *A History of Childhood* (Cambridge: Polity Press / Malden, Mass.: Blackwell, 2001).

Peter Laslett, Jean Robin, and Richard Wall, eds., *Family Forms in Historic Europe* (Cambridge: Cambridge University Press, 1983).

John Neubauer, *The Fin-de-Siècle Culture of Adolescence* (New Haven: Yale University Press, 1992).

Robert Nye, *Masculinity and Male Codes of Honor in Modern France* (Berkeley: University of California Press, 1998).

Karen Offen, *European Feminisms, 1700–1950* (Stanford, Cal.: Stanford University Press, 1999).

Roderick Philips, *Putting Asunder: A History of Divorce in Western Society* (Cambridge: Cambridge University Press, 1988).

Edgar Royston Pike, ed., *Hard Times: Human Documents of the Industrial Revolution* (New York: Praeger, 1966).

Jill Quadagno, *Aging in Early Industrial Society: Work, Family, and Social Policy in Nineteenth-Century England* (New York: Academic Press, 1982).

Ellen Ross, *Love and Toil: Motherhood in Outcast London, 1870–1918* (New York: Oxford University Press, 1993).

Bonnie G. Smith, *Changing Lives: Women in European History since 1700* (Lexington, Mass.: D. C. Heath, 1989).

Smith, *Ladies of the Leisure Class: The Bourgeoises of Northern France in the Nineteenth Century* (Princeton: Princeton University Press, 1981).

Peter Stearns, *Old Age in European Society: The Case of France* (New York: Holmes & Meier, 1976).

George E. Sussman, *Selling Mother's Milk: The Wetnursing Business in France, 1715–1914* (Urbana: University of Illinois Press, 1982).

David Thomson, *France: Empire and Republic, 1850–1940* (New York: Harper & Row, 1968).

David Troyansky, *Old Age in the Old Regime: Image and Experience in Eighteenth-Century France* (Ithaca, N.Y.: Cornell University Press, 1989).

J. R. Wegs, *Growing Up Working Class: Continuity and Change among Viennese Youth, 1890–1938* (University Park: Pennsylvania State University Press, 1989).

Jennifer Wolfe, *Learning from the Past: Historical Voices in Early Childhood Education* (Mayerthorpe, Alberta: Piney Branch Press, 2000).

Marilyn Yalom, *A History of the Wife* (New York: Perennial, 2002).

RELIGION AND PHILOSOPHY

Karl Barth, *Protestant Thought from Rousseau to Ritschl*, translated by Brian Cozens (New York: Harper, 1959).

Monroe C. Beardsley, ed., *The European Philosophers from Descartes to Nietzsche* (New York: Modern Library, 1960).

Ermanno Bencivenga, *Hegel's Dialectical Logic* (New York: Oxford University Press, 2000).

M. M. Bober, *Karl Marx's Interpretation of History* (New York: Norton, 1965).

T. B. Bottomore, ed. and trans., *Karl Marx: Selected Writings in Sociology and Social Philosophy* (London: Watts, 1956).

Dale W. Brown, *Understanding Pietism* (Grand Rapids: Eerdmans, 1978).

James M. Byrne, *Religion and the Enlightenment: From Descartes to Kant* (Louisville, Ky.: Westminister John Knox Press, 1997).

Owen Chadwick, *The Mind of the Oxford Movement* (Stanford, Cal.: Stanford University Press, 1960).

Demetrious J. Constantelos, *Understanding the Greek Orthodox Church* (Boston: Hellenic College Press, 1990).

James E. Crimmins, ed., *Utilitarians and Religion* (Bristol, U.K.: Thoemmes Press, 1998).

Patrick Gardiner, ed., *Theories of History* (Glencoe, Ill.: Free Press, 1959).

Richard L. Gawthrop, *Pietism and the Making of Eighteenth Century Prussia* (New York: Cambridge University Press, 1993).

A. D. Gilbert, *Religion and Society in Industrial England: Church, Chapel and Social Change, 1740–1914* (New York: Longman, 1976).

Calvin Goldscheider and Jacob Neusner, eds., *Social Foundations of Judaism* (Englewood Cliffs, N.J.: Prentice Hall, 1990).

Justo L. Gonzalez, *The Story of Christianity*, volume 2 (San Francisco: Harper & Row, 1984).

Solomon Grayzel, *A History of the Jews* (New York: Penguin, 1968).

Warren F. Groff and Donald E. Miller, *The Shaping of Modern Christian Thought* (Cleveland: World, 1968).

George Bernard Hamilton, *The Religion of Russia: A Study of the Orthodox Church in Russia from the Point of View of the Church in England* (London: Society of Saints Peter and Paul, 1915).

James J. Hennesey, *The First Council of the Vatican* (New York: Herder & Herder, 1963).

Otfried Hoffe, *Immanuel Kant*, translated by Marshall Farrier (Albany: State University of New York Press, 1994).

Paul Johnson, *Intellectuals* (London: Weidenfeld & Nicolson, 1988).

Kenneth Scott Latourette, *A History of Christianity*, revised edition, volume 2 (New York: Harper & Row, 1975).

Fred Mayer, *The Orthodox Church in Russia* (New York: Vendome Press, 1982).

Francis J. McConnell, *John Wesley: A Biography* (New York: Abingdon Press, 1939).

Ronald H. Nash, ed., *Ideas of History* (New York: Dutton, 1969).

Stephen Neill, *Colonialism and Christian Missions* (New York: McGraw-Hill, 1966).

Neill, *A History of Christian Missions*, second edition, revised by Owen Chadwick (Harmondsworth, U.K.: Penguin, 1986).

Peter Benedict Nockles, *The Oxford Movement in Context: Anglican High Churchmanship, 1760–1857* (New York: Cambridge University Press, 1994).

Ronald L. Numbers and John Stenhouse, eds., *Disseminating Darwinism: The Role of Place, Race, Religion and Gender* (New York: Cambridge University Press, 1999).

Margaret O'Gara, *Triumph in Defeat: Infallibility, Vatican I, and the French Minority Bishops* (Washington, D.C.: Catholic University of America Press, 1988).

Richard E. Olsen, *Karl Marx* (Boston: Twayne, 1978).

Bernard M. G. Reardon, *Religious Thought in the Victorian Age* (New York: Longman, 1980).

Bernard Semmel, *The Methodist Revolution* (New York: Basic Books, 1973).

Jonathan D. Spence, *The Taiping Vision of a Christian China, 1836–1864* (Waco, Tex.: Baylor University Press, 1998).

F. Ernest Stoeffler, *German Pietism during the Eighteenth Century* (Leiden: Brill, 1973).

Roger J. Sullivan, *Immanuel Kant's Moral Theory* (New York: Cambridge University Press, 1989).

E. P. Thompson, *The Making of the English Working Class* (New York: Pantheon, 1964).

Allen W. Wood, *Karl Marx* (London: Routledge & Kegan Paul, 1981).

Charles Yrigoyen Jr., *John Wesley: Holiness of Heart and Life* (New York: General Board of Global Ministries, 1996).

SCIENCE, TECHNOLOGY, AND HEALTH

George Basalla, *The Evolution of Technology* (Cambridge & New York: Cambridge University Press, 1988).

J. D. Bernal, *The Scientific and Industrial Revolutions,* volume 2 of *Science in History,* third edition (Cambridge, Mass.: MIT Press, 1971).

Eric Dorn Brose, *Technology and Science in the Industrializing Nations, 1500–1914* (Atlantic Highlands, N.J.: Humanities Press, 1998).

William Clark, Jan Golinski, and Simon Schaffer, eds., *The Sciences in Enlightened Europe* (Chicago: University of Chicago Press, 1999).

N. F. R. Crafts, *British Economic Growth during the Industrial Revolution* (Oxford: Clarendon Press / New York: Oxford University Press, 1985).

John Ellis, *The Social History of the Machine Gun* (London: Croom Helm, 1975).

Charles Coulston Gillispie, *Science and Polity in France at the End of the Old Regime* (Princeton: Princeton University Press, 1980).

Theodore S. Hamerow, *The Birth of a New Europe: State and Society in the Nineteenth Century* (Chapel Hill: University of North Carolina Press, 1983).

J. R. Harris, *Industrial Espionage and Technology Transfer: Britain and France in the Eighteenth Century* (Aldershot, U.K. & Brookfield, Vt.: Ashgate, 1998).

Daniel R. Headrick, *The Tools of Empire: Technology and European Imperialism* (New York: Oxford University Press, 1981).

Colin Heywood, *Childhood in Nineteenth-Century France: Work, Health and Education among the 'classes populaires'* (Cambridge & New York: Cambridge University Press, 1988).

David A. Hounshell, *From the American System to Mass Production, 1800–1932: The Development of Manufacturing Technology in the United States* (Baltimore: Johns Hopkins University Press, 1984).

Ian Inkster, *Science and Technology in History: An Approach to Industrial Development* (New Brunswick, N.J.: Rutgers University Press, 1991).

Margaret C. Jacob, *Scientific Culture and the Making of the Industrial West* (New York: Oxford University Press, 1997).

Joan Lane, *A Social History of Medicine: Health, Healing and Disease in England, 1750–1950* (London & New York: Routledge, 2001).

Christine MacLeod, *Inventing the Industrial Revolution: The English Patent System, 1660–1880* (Cambridge & New York: Cambridge University Press, 1988).

Peter Mathias, *The First Industrial Nation: An Economic History of Britain 1700–1914,* second edition (London & New York: Methuen, 1983).

James E. McClellan III, *Science Reorganized: Scientific Societies in the Eighteenth Century* (New York: Columbia University Press, 1985).

McClellan and Harold Dorn, *Science and Technology in World History: An Introduction* (Baltimore: Johns Hopkins University Press, 1999).

Joel Mokyr, *The Lever of Riches: Technological Creativity and Economic Progress* (New York: Oxford University Press, 1990).

Mokyr, ed., *The British Industrial Revolution: An Economic Perspective,* second edition (Boulder, Colo.: Westview Press, 1999).

Mary Jo Nye, *Before Big Science: The Pursuit of Modern Chemistry and Physics, 1800–1940* (Cambridge, Mass.: Harvard University Press, 1996).

Sidney Pollard, *Peaceful Conquest: The Industrialization of Europe 1760–1970* (Oxford & New York: Oxford University Press, 1981).

Roy Porter, *The Greatest Benefit to Mankind: A Medical History of Humanity from Antiquity to the Present* (London: HarperCollins, 1997).

W. D. Rubinstein, *Capitalism, Culture, and Decline in Britain, 1750–1990* (London & New York: Routledge, 1993).

CONTRIBUTORS

Michael S. Aradas holds a postdoctoral position at the University of Indianapolis, where he currently teaches courses in world history. He received his Ph.D. from Purdue University in 2001 and has offered courses at six universities across the United States, including Northeastern University in Boston. During the summer of 2002 he served as an editor on the Tsinghua Translation Project at Purdue University, undertaken in conjunction with history professors in the People's Republic of China to translate a contemporary Chinese undergraduate history textbook into English, which will be available in early 2003. He is presently revising for publication his dissertation on hunting in Europe from the fifteenth century to the eighteenth century.

Tony Ballantyne currently teaches at the University of Otago in Dunedin, New Zealand. He earned his Ph.D. at Cambridge University. His research focuses on the culture of British imperialism, intellectual networks in nineteenth-century South Asia and the Pacific, and cross-cultural communication in the Pacific. He is the author of *Orientalism and Race: Aryanism in the British Empire* (2001), and he recently edited a special issue of the *Journal of Colonialism and Colonial History* titled *From Orientalism to Ornamentalism: Empire and Difference in History.*

Bruce Bigelow is associate professor of geography at Butler University. He received his B.A. in history from Syracuse University (1965), his M.S. in geography from Pennsylvania State University (1970), and his Ph.D. in geography from Syracuse University (1978). He teaches "The New Europe" in a World Cultures program. His research interests involve the political and ethno-religious geography of Indiana in the Civil War era. He has written several articles and is currently writing a book on this subject.

Terry D. Bilhartz is professor of history at Sam Houston State University. He holds graduate degrees from Emory University (M.A., 1974) and George Washington University (Ph.D., 1979), and has completed postdoctoral studies in religion and philosophy at Vanderbilt University, Stanford University, and the East-West Center at the University of Hawaii. He has written many books and articles in the fields of history, religion, and psychology, including *Urban Religion and the Second Great Awakening: Church and Society in Early National Baltimore* (1986), and co-edited, with Randy Roberts and Elliot J. Gorn, *Constructing the American Past: A Sourcebook of a People's History,* fourth edition (2001).

Christopher R. Corley is assistant professor of history and affiliate faculty of Women's Studies at Minnesota State University, Moorhead. He received his Ph.D. from Purdue University in 2001. He has presented papers and published articles on the law, adolescence, and parenting in France and is currently working on book-length studies of the legal relationships between parents and children in early modern Burgundy and on the changing conceptions of children's culpability in the West.

James R. Farr is professor of history at Purdue University. He was editor of *French Historical Studies* (1991 to 2000) and is the author of *Artisans in Europe, 1300–1914* (2000); *Authority and Sexuality in Early Modern Burgundy* (1995); and *Hands of Honor: Artisans and Their World in Dijon, 1550–1650* (1988). He has published several articles in French history, most recently "The Death of a Judge: Performance, Honor, and Legitimacy in Seventeenth-Century France," *Journal of Modern History* (Spring 2003). A recipient of a Guggenheim Fellowship in 1998–1999, he received his Ph.D. from Northwestern University in 1983.

Dean Ferguson is an associate professor of history at Texas A&M University, Kingsville. He holds a Ph.D. from Purdue University (1997), where, supported by a Fulbright scholarship, he conducted research in Lyons, France on the unincorporated (nonguild) workers of the seventeenth and eighteenth centuries. His publications include an article in *French Historical Studies* on the regulation of nonguild labor in early modern Lyons, as well as published studies of the work lives of both ferry-boat pilots in Lyons and the informal sector in nineteenth-century Louisville, Kentucky.

Gay L. Gullickson is professor of history at the University of Maryland, College Park. She is the author of *Unruly Women of Paris: Images of the Commune* (1996), *Spinners and Weavers of Auffay: Rural Industry and the Sexual*

Division of Labor in a French Village, 1750–1850 (1986), and several articles on nineteenth-century European history. She received her Ph.D. from the University of North Carolina, Chapel Hill (1978) and her B.A. from Pomona College (1965). She is currently working on two book-length projects, "Secular Martyrdom in France and Britain" and "The British Suffragettes."

Jeff Horn is assistant professor of history at Manhattan College. He received his Ph.D. from the University of Pennsylvania (1993). He has taught at Stetson University and George Mason University. His book *"Qui parle pour la nation?" Les élections et les élus de la Champagne méridionale, 1765–1830* was published by the Editions du Comité des travaux historiques et scientifiques in 2002. Horn was also associate editor of *Liberty, Equality, Fraternity: Exploring the French Revolution* (2001), a CD-ROM and web-based project edited by Jack Censer and Lynn Hunt. He has also published many articles in journals such as *French Historical Studies, French History, Technology and Culture,* and *Annales Historiques de la Révolution française.* His current research has been funded by his institutions and by the National Science Foundation. In 2002–2003 Horn is a Senior Fellow at the Dibner Institute for the History of Science and Technology at the Massachusetts Institute of Technology, where he plans to complete his manuscript titled *The Path Not Taken: French Industrial Policy in the Age of Revolution.*

INDEX OF PHOTOGRAPHS

INDEX

This index is sorted word by word.
Page numbers in bold type indicate the primary article on a topic.
Page numbers in italics indicate illustrations.

Bampfylde, Coplestone Warre, *60*
Baptist Missionary Society, 311
The Bar of the Folies Bergère (Manet), 73, *74*
Barry, James, 57
BASF (Badenese Aniline & Soda Factory), 343
Bastille Day, 220
Bathrooms, 231–232
The Battle of Borodino (Lejeune), *190*
Battle of Omdurman, 189
Battle of Sedan, 220
Battle of Trafalgar, 174, 187, 188, 189
Battleships, 174, 189–190, 342
Bayeu, Francisco, 83
Bazille, Frédéric, 84
Beagle (ship), 351
Beaumarchais, Pierre-Augustin, 60
Beccaria, Cesare Bonesana, 193, 196
Becquerel, Antoine-Henri, 345
Bedrooms, 230
Beds, 230–231
Beethoven, Ludwig van, 57, 61, *81*, **81–82**, 84
Beeton, Isabella, 140, 257, 268
Belinda (Edgeworth), 80
Bell, Alexander Graham, 334
Belle Epoque, 260
Belloc, Hilaire, 343
The Belly of Paris (Zola), 87
Benedict XIV (pope), 83
Benkert, Karoly, 271
Bennett, James Gordon, 121
Benso, Camillo, 202
Bentham, Jeremy, 244, 305
Benz, Karl Friedrich, 344, **349**, *349*, 350
Benz automobiles, *344*
Bergmann-Österberg, Martina, 241
Berlin
    food, *234*
    music, 55
Berlin Conference, 35
Berlioz, Hector, 50, 61
Berthollet, Claude-Louis, 331, 336
Bessemer, Henry, 343
Betts, E. L., 118
Bignami, Amico, 346
Bildungsroman, 59
Bill of Rights (Britain, 1689), 194
Binet, Alfred, 348
Biology, 330
Birth control, 272, *272*
Birth strikes, 274
Births, illegitimate, 272–273, *274*
Births and deaths, 252, *254*, **254–256**
Bismarck, *199*, **199–200**
    Berlin Conference, 35
    neutrality treaties, 185, 186
    Prussia, 180
    railroads and the military, 188
    religion, 294–295
    state pensions and insurance, 274
Black Act (Britain, 1723), 174, 192, 194
Black Paintings (Goya), 83
The Blacksmith (Daumier), 64
Blake, William, 50, 57, 60, 66
Blanc, Louis, 156, 159
Blaxland, Gregory, 103
Bleaching, fabric, 336
Blériot, Louis, 191
Bloch, Marc, 40
Bloomer, Amelia, 224

Bloomers, 224
Bodichon, Barbara Smith, 270
Bohr, Nils, 345
Boileau, L. A., 243
Boileau, Louis-Charles, 68
Bonpland, Aimé, 39
The Book of Household Management (Beeton), 140,
    257, 268
Bordeaux Society for Maternal Charity, 267
Botany, 352
Boucicaut, Aristide, 223, **243**, *243*
Boudin, Eugène, 84
Boulton, Matthew, 340, 355
Bourbon regime, 173, 196
Bourbon Restoration, 176
Bourgeoisie. *See* Middle class
Boxer Rebellion, 311–312
Boxing, 238–239
Boy Scouts, 261
Boys' Brigade, 261
Brahms, Johannes, 61
Braque, Georges, 73, *79*
Brassey, Thomas, *117*, **117–118**
Braudel, Fernand, 40, 41
Breast-feeding, 256, 257
Breechloading weapons, *188*, 188–189, 342
Brentano, Antonie von Birkenstock, 82
Brentano, Franz, 82
Brewing, 354
Britain
    aristocracy, 133, 134
    Army, 189
    bourgeoisie, 139
    censorship, 196
    Chartism, 154–155
    child abuse, 259
    child labor, 258
    constitutional monarchy, 173, 180
    cotton industry, 336
    court system, 194
    crime and punishment, 174
    domestic servants, *139*
    education, 339–340
    exile, 196
    government administration, 182–183
    heat, 232
    housing, 229, 231
    hygiene, public, 244
    imperialism, 173, 203–204
    industrial concentration and railroads, 33
    industry, 341
    iron production, 336
    labor unions, 152–153
    learned societies, 340–341
    Methodism, 297–299
    naval warfare, 187–188
    parenthood, 267
    police, 196
    postal system, 106, 107, *107*
    poverty, 244
    prime ministers, *203*, 203–204, *207*,
        207–209
    prostitution, 273–274
    protective legislation, 157, 258
    public water works, 232
    railroads, 337
    railways, 117, *146*, 147, 148
    religion, 203
    rotten boroughs, 180, 183

Royal Navy, 174, 188, 189, 190, 342
    socialist political parties, 159
    standardized time, 111
    state pensions and insurance, 274
    steam power, 336–337
    steamships, 337
    street sweepers, *142*
    Suez Canal, 113, 114
    technology, 336–337, 338–339
    telegraph, 115, 116–117
    voting rights, 162, 183, 203, *271*
    welfare legislation, 158
Britain and the British Seas (Mackinder), 40
British and Foreign Bible Society, 295, 311
British East India Company. *See* East India
    Company
British Ladies Football Club, 242
Brook Farm, 159, 277
Broughton, Jack, 238–239
"Broughton's Rules" (Broughton), 239
Brown Bess muskets, 186
Brunel, Isambard Kingdom, 337, 350
Brunel, Sir Marc Isambard, **349–350**
Buddhism, 312
Buffon, Georges-Louis Leclerc de, 352
Bulgaria, *182*
Bullets, 342–343
Burghers of Calais (Rodin), 54
Burke, Edmund, 280
Burke, Robert, 103
Burney, Fanny, 80
Burrows, Mrs., 150
Burton, Sir Richard Francis, 105
Business
    big, 152
    family, 141–142
Butler, Josephine, 273–274
Byron, George Gordon, 59–60

C

Cabet, Etienne, 158, 159
Caillaux, Henrietta, 196
Caillaux, Joseph, 196
Caillois, R., 219
Calas, Jean, 193
Calculus, 329
Calcutta International Exhibition (1883–1884),
    101
"Cambridge Rules," 239
Cambridge University, 264
Camilla (Burney), 80
Canada railways, 109, 110
Canadian Pacific Railway, 110
Candide (Voltaire), 193
Canova, Antonio, 54
Capital punishment, 196, 198
Capitalism, 67, 69
Los Caprichos (Caprices) (Goya), 83
Capuchin Friar by the Sea (Friedrich), *56*, 57
Carding machines, 146–147, 336
Carey, William, 311
Caritat, Marie-Jean-Antoine-Nicolas de, 272
Carnival, 220, 238
Carpeaux, Jean-Baptiste, 54
Carré, Ferdinand, 234
Cartels, 152

middle-class men's clothing, 224–225
military dictatorships, 177
military reforms, 186–187
motherhood, 267
National Assembly, 176, 182, 205, 251, 294
National Convention, 182
nationalism, 63
naval warfare, 188
parlements, 174, 192, 193–194
patriotic festivals, 220, *220*
police, 196
postal system, 106
property laws, 265, 266
public water works, 232
railways, 118
religion, 294
republican assemblies, 182
Second Republic, 177, 182
socialist political parties, 159
sports, *238*, 240, 241
state pensions and insurance, 274
Suez Canal, 113
system of justice, 259
system of law, 197
telegraphs, 114–115
welfare system, 158
Francis I (emperor of France), 205, 206
Francke, August Hermann, 302
Franco-Prussian War, 185, 188, 200, 203, 220
Franco-Spanish Navy, 189
Franklin, Benjamin, 332
Franz Ferdinand, 184
Frederick II (king of Prussia), 55, 173, 180, 193, 208, 293
Frederick William III (king of Prussia), 180
Frederick William IV (king of Prussia), 180, 199
Freedom
    of dress, 216
    French Revolution, 56
    Romanticism, 59–60
Freeman, Michael, 147
Frémy, Arnould, 225
French Association of Child Rescue, 258
French Revolution
    arts, 50
    clothing, 227
    family and social trends, 251
    freedom, 56
    government administration, 174, 176
    impact on daily life, 216
    Lafayette, Marie-Joseph-Paul-Yves-Roch-Gilbert du Motier de, 205
    marriage reforms, 276
    nationalism, 51
    nineteenth century, 176–177
    and other European countries, 195–196
    religion, 294
    Romanticism, 59
    sculpture, 54
    social class system and the economy, 156
    and Spain, 179
    technology, 330
    welfare legislation, 158
Freud, Sigmund, 77, 78, 348, 349
Friedrich, Caspar David, 50, *56*, 57, 63
Fripperers, 222, 224
Froebel, Friedrich Wilhelm, *277*, **277–278**
Froebel Society, 278

Frygt og baeven (Fear and Trembling) (Kierkegaard), 315

G

Galvani, Luigi, 332, *333*
Gandhi, Mahatma, 97, 108, 109
Garden design, 57–58, *60*
The Gardens at Stourhead (Bampfylde), *60*
Garibaldi, Giuseppe, *181, 201,* **201–203**
Gas lighting, 151–152
Gauguin, Paul, 73, 75, *76*
Gender differences, 280–281
Gender roles, 268, 269, 270–271, 279
General staff system (military), 190–191
Geographers, *40,* 40–41
"The Geographical Pivot of History" (Mackinder), 40
Geography, **23–42**
    chronology, **24–28**
    climate, 30
    cultural geography, 29, **37–38**
    as a discipline, 29, **38**
    documentary sources, **41**
    economic geography, 29, **31–35,** *36*
    French imperialism, 35
    landforms, 30–31, *31*
    language, 37
    overview, **29**
    physical geography, 29, **30–31**
    political geography, 29, **35–37**
    religion, 37
    significant people, *39,* **39–41,** *40*
    See also Maps
Geological Society (Britain), 340
Geopoliticians, 40, *40*
George II (king of England), 207–208
George III (king of England), 173, 182, 209
Géricault, Théodore, 57
Germ theory, 347–348, 354
German Gymnastics Club, 241
German Workers' Society, *153*
Germanic languages, 37
Germany
    abortion, 272
    bourgeoisie, 139
    cartels, 152
    divorce, 266
    education, 263, 341
    fatherhood, *267*
    government administration, 183–184
    housing, *229,* 230
    industrial concentration and railroads, 33
    industry, 342
    international relations, 185–186
    juvenile delinquency, 261
    labor unions, 152–153, *153*
    nationalism, 51, 63
    neutrality pacts, 185
    patriotic festivals, 220
    property laws, 266
    revolutions, 156
    socialist political parties, 159, *159*
    sports, 241
    state pensions and insurance, 274
    steel production, 343
    technical colleges, 341

technology, 332, 333–334
    weaving, *151*
Gervex, Henri, *282*
Geschichte der Kunst des Altertums (The History of Ancient Art) (Winckelmann), 52
Ghettos, Jewish, 299
Gilbert, William, 80
Gilchrist, Percy, 343
Girton College, 264
Gisborne, Thomas, 269
Giverny, France, 84
Gladstone, William Ewart, 182–183, 184, *203,* **203–204**
Gladwin, Francis, 105
Glasgow Missionary Society, 311
God Worshipers, 311
Godwin, William, 280, 281
Goethe, Johann Wolfgang von, 59, 220, 303
Goody Two-Shoes (Newbery), 264
Gordon, Charles, 204
Gore, John, 119
Gothic revival (architecture), 58
Gouges, Olympe de, 251, 270
Government administration, 173
    Austria-Hungary, 184
    forms of government, *175,* **175–182,** *177, 179, 181*
    France, 174, 175–177
    Germany, 183–184
    Great Britain, 173, 174, 182–183
    offices and institutions, 173–174, *182,* **182–184,** *183*
    professionalism, 182
    Prussia, 174, 184
    Russia, 174
    science, technology, and health, **339–341,** *340*
    Spain, 178–180
    See also Politics, law, and the military
Goya, Francisco, 57, *57, 62,* 83, *83,* **83–84**
Grace, William Gilbert, *245,* **245**
Grand Junction Railway, 117
Grand Trunk Railway, 118
Grassi, Giovanni Batista, 346
Gray, Elisha, 334
Great Britain. *See* Britain
Great Britain (ship), 337
Great Eastern (ship), *116,* 337
Great European Plain, 30–31
Great Exhibition (1851)
    artillery, 189
    Crystal Palace, 65–66, 97, 98, 101, 338–339
    photographs, *66, 98*
    public museums, 100
Great Exhibition (1859), 234
Great Northern Railway, 118
Great Western Railway, 111
Great Western (ship), 111, *112,* 337
Greece
    clothing, 227
    religion, 295
Greeks, ancient
    and Classicism, 52, 53
    universal natural laws and art, 52
Greenwich Mean Time, 111
Gregory XVI (pope), 317, 318
Grenville, George, 209
Grey, George, 103
Grocery stores, 235

"Jerusalem" (Blake), 60
Jessop, William, 108
Jesuits, 293, 295, 310
Jogiches, Leo, 161
Johnson, Samuel, 56, 215
Joseph II (emperor of Austria), 55, 61, 293
Journal of the Resolution's *Voyage, in 1772, 1773,
    1774, and 1775* (Cook), 119
Journalists, *121,* 121–122, *162,* 162–163
Journeymen, 141
Judaism, 37, **299–300,** *300*
Judicial system, 192, 259
Julie (Rousseau), 279
Juvenile delinquency, 261

K

Kant, Immanuel, 277, 303, 312–313, *313,*
    313–315, 319
Das Kapital (Marx), 306, 316
Kay, John, 146
Keble, John, 301, *301,* 316–317
Keith, Sir Robert Murray, 215
Kelly, William, 343
Kenney, Annie, 162
Kergomard, Pauline, 258
Key, Ellen, 259
Khomyakov, Aleksey Stepanovich, 296–297
Kierkegaard, Søren, 313, **315,** *315*
Kilts, 227
Kindergarten movement, 277–278
The King is Dead, *175*
Kipling, Rudyard, 77
Kitchens, 230
Kladderadatsch, 144
Koch, Robert, 347
Kolowrat-Liebsteinsky, Franz Anton von,
    206–207
Korvin-Krukovskaia, Anna, 267
Kosmos (Humboldt), 39
Krapf, Johann Ludwig, 105
Kristin Lavransdatter (Undset), 280–281
*Kritik der praktischen Vernunft (Critique of
    Practical Reason)* (Kant), 314
*Kritik der reinen Vernunft (Critique of Pure
    Reason)* (Kant), 313–314
Krupp, Alfred, 189, 230
Krupp family, 139
Krupp Works, 139
Kulturkampf, 199

L

La Planche, Alexandre, 67, *68*
Labor, division of, 135, 139–140, 141–142
Labor and laboring conditions, **148–152,** *149,
    151*
Labor unions, 152–153, *153*
Labour Party (Britain), 159
Lafayette, Marie-Joseph-Paul-Yves-Roch-
    Gilbert du Motier de, 176, *204,* **204–205**
Laissez-faire capitalism, 67, 69
Lake Victoria (Africa), 105, 121
Lancaster & Carlisle Railway, 118
Land Act (Britain, 1881), 204
Land mines, 189

Lander, Richard, 104
Landforms, 30–31, *31*
Lane near a Small Town (Sisley), *71, 72*
Language, 37
Laugier, Marc-Antoine, 51, 53
Laveran, Alphonse, 346
Lavoisier, Antoine-Laurent, 331, *331,* 332, 354
Law, crime, and punishment, **192–198,** *193, 195,
    198*
    Enlightenment, 192–193
    France, 195, 197
    law codes, 194
    marriage laws, 195
    Napoleon I (emperor of France), 194–195
    Parliament (Great Britain), 193
    property laws, 265–266
    Prussia, 195
    Russia, 192, 200–201
    See also Politics, law, and the military
Law of the Dialectic, 313, 316
Law of Three Stages, 305
Lawn tennis, 240–241
Laws of nature, 53
Lawson, William, 103
Le Play, Frédéric, 251
Learned societies, 340–341
Das Leben Jesu (The Life of Jesus)
    (Schleiermacher), 319
Lecture on the Increase of the Habitable Earth
    (Linnaeus), 352
Lectures on the Present Position of Roman Catholics
    (Newman), 317
Lederhosen, 227
Legislation, protective, 151, 157–158, 258
Leibniz, Gottfried Wilhelm, 329
*Die Leiden des jungen Werthers (The Sorrows of
    Young Werther)* (Goethe), 59
Leisure, recreation, and daily life, **211–246**
    advice to the young ladies, 221
    chronology, **212–214**
    clothing and appearance, *222,* **222–228,**
        226
    dining out, 237
    documentary sources, **246**
    food, *234,* **234–237,** *236*
    fripperers, 222, 224
    housing, *228,* **228–233,** *229, 233*
    leisure and sport, *214,* **237–242,** *238, 242*
    living conditions of British laborers, 231
    Nana, 227
    open-air markets, 235
    overview, **215–217**
    rules of the game, 240
    Saint Monday, 219
    significant people, *243,* **243–246,** *244, 245*
    time, **217–221,** *218, 220*
Leisure and sport, *214,* **237–242,** *238, 242*
Lejeune, Louis-François, *190*
Lenin, Vladimir, 161
Lenoir, Etienne, 343
Leo XIII (pope), 317
Leopold II (Holy Roman emperor), 55, 193
Leopold II (king of Belgium), 122, *183*
Lesseps, Ferdinand de, 113
Letter Addressed to His Grace the Duke of Norfolk
    (Newman), 317
Letter to d'Alembert (Rousseau), 279
Letter writing, **105–106**

Lettre à d'Alembert (Letter to d'Alembert)
    (Rousseau), 279
Levée en masse, 174, 186–187
Liberal Progressives, 199, 200
Liberalism, religious, 294
Liberty Leading the People (Delacroix), 54, 57
*The Library of the Fathers of the Holy Catholic
    Church,* 302
Liebig, Justus von, 332, 341
Liebknecht, Karl, 161
The Life and Labours of Mr. Brassey (Helps), 118
The Life of Jesus (Schleiermacher), 319
Lighting
    domestic, 232–233
    electric, 152, 333–334
    gas, 151–152
    public, *218,* 219
    workplace, 151–152
Lincoln, Abraham, 202
Linear warfare, 186
Linnaean Society, 340
Linnaeus, Carolus, *352,* **352–353**
Lister, Joseph, 346, 348
Liszt, Franz, 61, 85
Literacy, 262
Literature
    Classicism, 56
    Enlightenment, 56
    Modernism, 76–78
    Naturalism, 67, 86–87
    Realism, 67, 69–70, 72, 86–87
    Romanticism, 58–60
Lithography, 64–65
A Little Pretty Pocket-Book (Newbery), 263, 264
Living conditions
    British laborers, 231
    of the poor, 244
    working class, 144–145
Livingstone, David, *104,* 104–105, *120,* **120–121**
Livingstone, Mary, 120
Locke, John, 279, 303, 329
Lodge, Oliver Joseph, 333
Löfving, Concordia, 241
Lombroso, Cesare, 348
London
    elderly, *275*
    housing, 229
    public water works, 232
    Romantic artists, 56
    sports, 241
London Labour & the London Poor (Mayhew), 163
London Missionary Society, 120, 311
London Prize-Ring Rules, 239
Lono, 119
Looms, power, 335–336, *336*
Loues, Spiridon, 241
Louis Napoleon. *See* Napoleon III (emperor of
    France)
Louis XIV (king of France), 175, 178, 179
Louis XV (king of France), 175–176, 194, 196,
    198
Louis XVI (king of France)
    absolutism, 50, 173
    beheading, *175*
    delegation, 175, 176
    and Lafayette, Marie-Joseph-Paul-Yves-
        Roch-Gilbert du Motier de, 204
    laws, 194
    religion, 294